Second Edition

AMERICAN

Mass Media

Industries
and Issues

Second Edition

AMERICAN Mass Media

Industries and Issues

Robert Atwan   Barry Orton   William Vesterman
University of Wisconsin   Rutgers University

Random House
New York

Second Edition
9876543
Copyright © 1978, 1982 by Random House, Inc.

Library of Congress Cataloging in Publication Data
Atwan, Robert.
    American mass media.

    Bibliography: p.
    Includes index.
    1. Mass media—United States—Addresses, essays, lectures. 2. Communication and traffic—United States—Addresses, essays, lectures. 3. Advertising—United States—Addresses, essays, lectures. 4. Mass society—Addresses, essays, lectures. I. Orton, Barry. II. Vesterman, William, 1942–   . III. Title.
HN90.M3A85   1981   302.2′3 81-8834   ISBN 0-394-32668-7   AACR2

Manufactured in the United States of America

Photo Credits:

p. 2: Courtesy Satellite Television Corporation
p. 102: Barry Orton
p. 226: Barry Orton
p. 290: Barry Orton
p. 380: UPI
p. 177: Stanley J. Forman/Boston Herald American

Cover design: Teresa Harmon/Edward Vartanian
Text design: Teresa Harmon/Gina Davis

PREFACE

to the Second Edition

This second edition of *American Mass Media: Industries and Issues* has been designed to serve either as the basic text for introductory-level, college courses in mass communications or as a reader to supplement standard mass media textbooks. *American Mass Media* could be incorporated into courses offered by departments of journalism, broadcasting, English, sociology, social science, political science, and business, as well as communications. When supplemented by lectures and other readings, *American Mass Media* can be used for courses with such titles as "Mass Communications and Society," "Introduction to Broadcasting," "Television, Radio, and Film in America," and "Introduction to Mass Media and Popular Culture." The variety of readings included in this second edition reflects the editors' desires both to select material that would have relevance to students in all these courses and to show the latest developments in the rapidly changing media environment. The use of the first edition of *American Mass Media,* at over 150 colleges and universities, indicated that these goals were met for students and faculty alike. We hope that this substantially revised edition will prove equally beneficial, both to those who have used the book before and to those who are working with it for the first time.

As its title indicates, this collection of articles addresses itself to two dominant features of American mass media: (1) the industries that design and sustain each of the major channels of mass communications, and (2) the significant issues—social, political, and cultural—that shape, and in turn have been shaped by, these industries. In the following essays, students will observe the complex and often changing interrelations among corporate media, individual and collaborative imaginations, and the needs and desires of mass audiences—the relations, in other words, among big business, creative talent, and mass society.

American Mass Media: Industries and Issues provides a range of classical and contemporary readings that will furnish solid background and provoke specific discussion for an introductory course. The collection focuses neither so exclusively on advanced research and specialized technical articles as to intimidate needlessly the potential major still exploring the field, nor so broadly on social controversies as to lose sight of each medium as a unique industry with dynamics, difficulties, and potentialities all its own. In meeting this goal of balanced selection, material has been drawn from a spectrum of scholarly, trade, and popular periodicals, as well as from respected books in the field. Moreover, these particular readings were chosen in an attempt to combine an engaging survey with an informative one.

The book divides into clearly defined, easily manageable sections. The first section offers a set of readings on the "environments" within which all media industries exist—audience behavior, advertising support, and government regulation. The sections that follow contain articles on each of the major forms of mass media —newspapers, books, magazines, radio, recordings, film, and television. The final section, "Personal Media," covers such phenomena as the telephone, computer communications, home video recordings, and cable television. These means of expression and communication seem to us to qualify as mass media in that they are used abundantly by enormous numbers of people and are either massively distributed or highly visible. Moreover, they include the most recent developments in mass communications, many of which students have experienced firsthand.

Within sections, introductions link the various readings and highlight their major points, while headnotes detail the contexts of the individual articles. The selections illustrate a variety of professional approaches by offering not only technological, economic, and political perspectives on the operations of mass media but sociological, cultural, and vocational ones as well. Each section contains a sufficient amount of developmental material (either in the introduction or in a selection) to orient the student historically. For each industry, contemporary articles, with a more than merely topical appeal, describe recent developments and probable future directions.

Arranging the articles according to specific industries has the advantages of lucidity and convenience. Yet, to emphasize cross-media relationships and their social effects, we have also supplied an alternate table of contents that may be used to illustrate some of the relevant topics and issues pervading all forms of contemporary media. To enhance further the volume's practicality, an appended matrix collates the readings with appropriate sections of many leading textbooks in the field. Any of these texts may, therefore, be easily used in conjunction with the materials collected here. A bibliography of selected further readings and an index complete the book's apparatus.

Any collection of readings on mass communications must come to terms with the fact that the field resembles the physical sciences with respect to the rate at which the professional literature tends to become obsolete. Many articles that once were timely soon are outdated as new technologies, organizational remodelings, fresh legislation, and shifts in public concern occur. To assemble a book of readings is to be acutely sensitive to this atmosphere of rapid change. Our principle of selection has been to resist the merely topical while striving for completeness and contemporaneity. First, we have tried to retain some of the classical articles while maintaining an up-to-date, overall level of information. We have also tried to reflect the growing trend in media toward specialized audiences. Moreover, the vocational interests of an increasing number of students have been recognized. We have included essays with historical viewpoints, for background, as well as those that give some feel for what it is actually like to work in a particular industry. Finally, since some of the best writing on developmental topics exists within standard textbooks, we have tried to do justice to that excellence, although no more than one of the sixty selections offered here would ever overlap with any textbook employing it as a supplement. For those courses that do not use a textbook, we have tried to make the collection complete enough to stand alone in all its areas. Yet, however the collection is used, we trust readers will discover enough durable information, topicality, and skillful writing to satisfy a serious and wide-ranging inquiry into a diversified and exciting subject.

The changes in this edition—forty-four articles are new—reflect the rapidly changing field of mass communications. While retaining the organization and apparatus that have proved successful to users of the first edition, we have tried to represent current trends and issues in the mass media industries. All sections of the book have been considerably revised and updated. For completeness and balance, four articles have been expressly written for this volume. The Personal Media section, in particular, has been expanded in response to both readers' interests and new technological developments.

We wish to thank the following people for their help with both editions: Helene Atwan, Blake Kellogg, Donald McQuade, Richard Mikita, J. K. Miller, Marilyn Orton, Harold Schecter, Mark Sherman, Susan Vesterman, John W. Wright, and Daniel Zweig. We appreciate the suggestions and guidance of Jeanne Allen, Robert K. Avery, Stanley Baran, Jennings Bryant, Frederick Burns, Norman Felsenthal, Richard Garretson, James L. Hoyt, Charles E. Sherman, June Smith, Phillip Metcalf, Roth Wilkofsky, Barbara Zimmerman, and, especially, Christopher H. Sterling.

R. A.
B. O.
W. V.
September 1981

CONTENTS

1

The Environments of Media Industries

2

The Print Media

3

The Sound Media

4

The Visual Media

5

Personal Media

ALTERNATE CONTENTS

Technology

Practitioners, Performers, and Personnel

Government: Regulation, Fairness, and Censorship

Audiences: Effects and Responses

Futures

Media Interrelations

Economics: Ownership, Sales, and Marketing

Exploitation

News and Politics

Mass Media and Mass Culture

Second Edition

AMERICAN

mass media

Industries and Issues

PART ONE

The Environments
of Media Industries

Audiences

American media could first be called "mass" media when the popular daily newspaper came into being in the 1880s, in the age of William Randolph Hearst and Joseph Pulitzer. Their formula—combining entertainment features (especially the comics) with a sensational treatment of the news and aiming the mix at the large, newly literate immigrant population (then swelling the large urban centers of America)—created the first mass medium, where circulation could be measured in terms of millions of readers.

The creation of popular and cheap magazines soon followed. With film, radio, recordings, trade paperback books, and then television all developing into major, national industrial institutions, the American mass audience was provided with an information environment of entertainment, product advertising, and news. The mass media audience has become the marketplace for American mass production of consumer goods, the cornerstone of our economic structure. The readings in this section outline the development, social functions, and recent activism of the mass media audience and point toward its increasing fractionalization into specialized subaudiences served by increasingly specialized media forms.

The first selection, from William L. Rivers and Wilbur Schramm's *Responsibility in Mass Communication,* provides us with a major theoretical treatment of the social effects of mass communications, emphasizing the ways that the audience uses mass media messages. Indeed, the mass audience is shown to consume mass communications as a staple of daily life, much as it consumes food, clothing, and shelter. More American homes now have television sets than have indoor plumbing.

In the second article, taken from *Public Opinion Quarterly,* sociologist Richard Maisel examines mass media growth trends in this century. He concludes that "specialized" communications media such as the telephone, college textbooks, and tape recorders, each serving an increasingly fragmented audience, are growing at a much faster rate than are the mass media. In this book's last major section, which we call "Personal Media," we provide a sampler of these nonmass media, with articles on such topics as two-way cable television, personal publishing, home satellite antennas, and public-access cable programming, as well as an analysis of the significance and future of the telephone.

An audience can also respond to the media through organized political action. In the selection from *Telecommunications Policy and the Citizen,* public-interest advocate Howard Symons first examines the historic role of citizen action in broadcasting and telephone regulation. He then proposes some mechanisms to increase the audience's legal power.

Inquiry into the characteristics and behavior of the mass media audience is a primary task of both industry and academic research specialists. In addition to describing the size and characteristics of audiences, prediction of audience preferences is especially important to segments of media industries, particularly advertisers, film and television producers, and the commercial networks. There are many methods used to help predict audience reaction. One of the most fascinating and immediate is the preview testing conducted by Audience Studies, Incorporated (ASI). The final reading in this section, from the *New York Times,* describes the ASI system and the precision with which it can monitor an audience's reactions to a film, TV pilot, or commercial. In the "Recordings" section of this book, Michael Gross's article, "The Hits Keep on Coming," profiles an audience testing method that goes one step further than does ASI; it literally wires test subjects to gauge reactions to potential hit records.

1

The Impact of Mass Communication

William L. Rivers & Wilbur Schramm

The chief functions of the mass media include entertainment, persuasion, and the transfer of essential information. In this opening selection, two pioneers of communications scholarship, William L. Rivers and Wilbur Schramm, provide an overview of the development of media technology and its impact on how we all use media messages in our daily lives. Rivers and Schramm outline the principal theoretical functions of the mass media in this selection from their classic *Responsibility in Mass Communications* (3rd ed., 1980). Moreover, they accurately predict the growth of home computer systems that tie together many functions of television, newspapers, and libraries.

The press has become the greatest power within Western countries, more powerful than the legislature, the executive, and the judiciary. One would then like to ask: By what law has it been elected and to whom is it responsible?
—Aleksandr Solzhenitsyn

The story begins about 1450 in Mainz, Germany, with one of those conjunctions of materials, skills, and idea that turns the course of history. The materials were the wine press, which had been used for centuries in western Europe; cast metal type, which had

Source: From *Responsibility in Mass Communication,* Third Edition, by William L. Rivers, Wilbur Schramm, and Clifford G. Christian. Reprinted by permission of Harper & Row, Publishers, Inc.

been invented fifty years earlier in Korea and again, independently, at Mainz; and paper and ink, both of which had been developed many centuries earlier in China and brought to Europe. The skills were calligraphy and block printing, which had been elegantly developed by Asians and Europeans, especially in the medieval monasteries. The new idea was to print from movable type, so that one piece of type might be used interchangeably in many jobs. The result was a machine for rapidly duplicating writing—the writing being standardized into type faces.

That was the beginning of modern communication. The story of the five hundred years of development in communication since that time is a story of man's changing relationship to machines in the communication process. The difference between communication before and after 1450 was simply that man had finally made an efficient machine to duplicate interpersonal communication. It was, of course, a monumental change. Unfortunately, we do not know the first words that were printed from movable metal type. The earliest dated piece of printing that remains is a papal indulgence, struck by Johann Fust and Peter Schoeffer in 1454. The first book was apparently the forty-two-line Bible, which was printed not later than 1456, probably by Johann Gutenberg.

It is significant that at its very birth the new art served the chief power center of the time: the Church. Had the printing press been a different kind of machine, it could have been restricted—as certain other communication devices, like heraldry, or the semaphore, have been—to one master, or one class, or a certain kind of task, or a certain topic. But the peculiar characteristic of machine-duplicated print communication was that it could be applied to and became involved with all the public affairs of man—and swiftly. William Caxton was printing in England by 1476, Aldus Manutius in Italy by 1494; Juan Pablos was printing in Mexico City less than fifty years after Columbus first saw the new continent. Everywhere it went, the printing press was involved in the matters that exalted or stimulated or troubled man. It served the parties in power, but it also served all the revolutions of the spirit and the body politic.

It was used by the Church, but it also carried the great debate on the Reformation. It circulated the precious books of Aristotle, which had been chained to the library desks of the Middle Ages. It disseminated the extraordinary intellectual output of the Renaissance. It carried commercial news to the merchants of England and northern Germany, and also revolutionary pamphlets—so effectively that anonymous pamphlets are even today the symbol of revolution in some European countries. Without the press there might have been an Enlightenment, but it is doubtful if there could have been a French or an American revolution.

In the vast ground swell of democracy toward the end of the eighteenth century, the press led the people toward their new importance. And just then, shortly after 1800, came the first major improvement in the remodeled wine press. It was a new source of power, a gift of the Industrial Revolution. First steam, then electricity, replaced man's muscles and enabled him to produce more of the same product much faster. The exciting thing about the power press was that it came precisely when it was needed to reach masses of new voters. It offered those who could not read a strong incentive to learn, and thus it was meshed into the growth of public education. Then smart merchandisers discovered that they could sell newspapers for a penny and still make a profit if they sold enough, and if they sold enough they could also lure advertisers, and so we had ''mass communication'': prices the common man could pay, enormous circulations, profitable advertising, large publishing organizations, the attractive concept of the new machine as the voice and servant of democracy, and the misleading concept of a ''mass audience.''

By the middle of the nineteenth century, the telegraph and the cable were speeding communication, and the camera and photoengraving were adding a vivid quality. But none of this was fundamentally new, for the Washington hand presses that rode west in the American covered wagons were essentially only a hardier version of the press that Gutenberg had at Mainz in the middle of the fifteenth century. The presses that printed the Gettysburg Address were essentially the same machines, powered by steam. All this was still a part of the great wave of communication that began to break at Mainz about 1450. The accomplishment of that first wave rested entirely on an ability to make swift duplicates of writing on paper.

The first fundamentally new development came late in the nineteenth century. As the first wave of modern communication can be dated back to 1450, the second can be dated, if not to Samuel F. B. Morse and the telegraph, at least to Alexander Graham Bell and the telephone in 1876. The difference between communication before and after 1876 was that man had finally begun to make efficient machines that could be interposed in the communication chain and be trusted to listen and see for him. In a sense, of course, the printing machine had been interposed in the communication chain, but it merely duplicated; it did not communicate directly. It made a product that could be read at leisure, the reader taking the initiative, setting his own pace, selecting from the material as he wished. The second wave of modern communication made a profound change in shifting the initiative, at least in part, from receiver to sender. That is, once the receiver had made his basic choice, the sender was in charge. The machine, or the force behind it, controlled the pace, the repetitions, the emphasis, the timing.

These attributes of the second wave can be seen clearly in the machines which were developed in a quickening stream after Bell's. A few years after the telephone was invented, Thomas A. Edison's phonograph and his movie camera and projector made it possible to store both sounds and moving sights. De Forest's triode vacuum tube, in 1907, opened the world of radio and television.

Most of the new telecommunication machines which have ushered in the second wave are much faster than the press. They bring tidings more swiftly, answer an argument more quickly. They have about them a sense of reality, a sense of immediacy, that print has never had. They have in their essence an emotional quality that is difficult to achieve in print. These newer media came into being when Western countries were being urbanized, when the work week was being greatly shortened and people began to have more lei-

sure. They came into being at a time when America was on the verge of a striking change from what David Riesman called "inner-direction" to "other-direction"—from an individualistic work-success ethic and a future-time orientation to a hedonistic present-centered ethic concerned mainly with group relationships and opinions.[1] These new sociable little machines were exactly what people needed to keep them informed about the people around them. They brought personalities into one's living room, and they transported one into countless other living rooms, not to mention chambers of state. Much more strikingly than print, the new electronic forms of communication extended man's environment and dominated his leisure.

These are the aspects of modern communication which will concern us in this book [*Responsibility in Mass Communication*]. But it is important to note that there has been another wave, so recent that we are not yet fully aware of its vast dimensions. It can be pretty well dated to an article by Claude E. Shannon in the *Bell System Technical Journal* in 1948.[2] Shannon began modestly: "The recent development of various methods of modulation . . . has intensified the interest in a general theory of communication." That is exactly what Shannon provided. The effect of his paper, and of the formulas in it, was to stimulate a great outpouring of developments in storing and transmitting information.

As machines in the nineteenth century came to do the work of man's muscles, so the new machines now are able to do some of his thinking. The great computers that have come into being in the last few decades and the concept of feedback of information have become so sophisticated that it is now possible to put a machine in charge of other machines and to program a factory to nearly run itself. We have built machines with qualities previously thought to be man's unique prerogative. Under the name of automation this third wave of modern communication has already reshaped industry by processing almost singlehandedly the 75 billion new documents which are generated every year to keep American government and business functioning. Xerox and IBM are only the best-known names in a host of computer-based technology companies which not only store information but use electronic typing systems to create and edit it, telecopier receivers to transmit it, and electronic printers or readout display screens which take their data directly from computer storage banks.

With advances in semiconductor technology and the miniaturization of electronic components, the vast networks of data-processing operations among computers increasingly define what we mean by communication; and most experts predict a doubling of the volume of such electronically transmitted information every five years. The computer-communications marriage, dubbed "compunications," already has profoundly affected man's concept of himself, his cities, his aesthetic and intellectual horizons, and ways of dealing with the world. And with the laser providing new capabilities, the number of breakthroughs in media industries appears endless. Late in the 1970s, for example, the world's first lightwave communication system was installed by Bell Telephone in Chicago, replacing electric currents through copper wires by beams of light traveling through a glass fiber. With sand more abundant than copper, the potential of man's signaling enabled by machine should continue to grow exponentially.

As the 1980s begin, it is increasingly artificial to separate these three waves of technology built essentially around print, then telecommunication media, and now computers. The important point is that these three major forms and all their subforms are being integrated into creative mass communications of giant proportions. Their final configurations —a cross between a video screen, light pipes, and computers—are not always obvious, though many possibilities are already technologically feasible and hundreds of future scenarios are currently being written. Nearly all accounts, however, put homeowners in charge; they order what they want, or more accurately, perhaps, create the environment they desire:

> Architecturally, future homes may be built especially to accommodate the sounds and visual images created by the new electronic

technology—domes, acoustically perfect chambers, hidden speakers, laser projectors in each room, and a "composing room" where the homeowner can sit at a panel and synthesize a variety of sounds and images into an entertainment design for his family. . . . The greatest hazard to the individual could be his isolation from society when he begins to create surrogate friends and conversationalists. As Andy Warhol has phrased it: "Someday you'll be able to go to a party and be the only one there."[3]

Kevin Phillips summarized this emerging and distinctive era as "mediacracy"—rule by the media rather than by the demos, the people. He described with impressive detail how the United States since World War II increasingly shifted to services and information away from manufactured products and physical labor. Very early in the 1980s, 40 per cent of the gross national product will involve the creation and distribution of knowledge; and concentrated knowledge industries will replace the United States steels as our dominant business enterprises. The old economic equations are already undergoing a quantum shift, and one day soon America's elite will not sell industrial goods but control an economy of ideas and information. The linchpin of the post-industrial era will be some form of computer-based electronic communication.[4]

The great voice of print was caught up in the ground swell of democracy and the sharply breaking waves of revolution in the seventeenth and eighteenth centuries; and the impressive new technology (the power press, photoengraving, stereotyping, sound and sight recording on film, and transmission by air waves) was caught up in the steep curve of economic growth in the nineteenth and twentieth centuries. As a result, the tiny hand press, the squeaking earphones, the flickering film, have in our time become huge business enterprises: daily newspapers, publishing houses, radio and television stations and networks, and film studios and theater chains. We call these developments "mass communication" because of their enormous product and the enormous audiences they have come to serve. In fact, with futuristic instruments

Mass Communication Media in the United States

Medium	Number of Units	Circulation and Audiences	Financial Support
Books	1,205 publishers; top 50 firms publish 77% of all	35,469 titles; 1.24 billion copies sold annually	By sales of $4.4 billion annually
Daily newspapers	1,760 dailies	61.5 million copies a day	Approximately 70% from advertising; 30% from circulation; total ad income over $11 billion annually
Magazines	2,394 publishing houses	50 magazines have over 1 million circulation each	Total ad income over $2.1 billion annually
Television	728 commercial stations; 256 public; 3 commercial networks; 1 public	121 million sets; 97.6% households with 1 or more sets	Total ad income over $7.6 billion annually
Radio	4,497 AM stations; 2,837 FM; 839 public stations; 4 commercial networks; 1 public	425 million receivers	By advertising time sales over $2.5 billion annually
Film	6 large corps.; numerous independent distributors/producers; 15,969 theaters	Yearly total attendance about 1.1 billion	Attendance and small local advertising income; total revenue $1.8 billion
Cable	3,832 systems. Top 8 had 37% of all subscribers	12 million subscribers	By monthly fees; total revenue approximately $900 million annually

emerging strongly in all sorts of combinations, this book [*Responsibility in Mass Communication*] projects an urgency about the present. As the new media technologies swell to full extravagance, controlling them responsibly in the future appears infinitely more complex than guiding the media today. Our experience and accomplishments in the present era can strengthen our hand for the next. Meanwhile, as the table here demonstrates, the media arising primarily from the first two waves, products of the Industrial Revolution, are themselves of tidal proportions, demanding all of our moral resolve and ingenuity.[5]

Dramatic as these figures are, their stark form does not sufficiently emphasize that in the lifetime of many of us a new system of public communication has developed. The social bulk of these new enterprises can be gauged only in these terms: One hundred years ago, there was no radio, no television, no movies; newspapers were little more than political organs, and magazines and books were the products of limited industries. Only sixty years ago, there was no public radio, no television; motion pictures were barely advancing out of the nickelodeon stage; newspapers almost everywhere were a combination of political organ and yellow press.

What would people have thought a century ago if someone had predicted that it would soon be possible to buy for twenty-five cents a newspaper connected by leased wires and reporters to all the principal cities of the world, no more than minutes removed from a news event anywhere? What would people have thought fifty years ago if someone had told them that soon most homes would contain a relatively inexpensive little box through which one could see and hear the Metropolitan Opera, the Olympic Games, the meetings of the United Nations, war in Africa and

Asia, and candidates for national political office? What would people have thought if someone had predicted that books bound in paper would soon be purchased in supermarkets along with the weekly groceries?

These developments have made a profound difference in the way we receive information, and in the kind and amount of information we receive. For communicators, they have made an incredible difference in the opportunities they offer and the responsibilities they impose.

Perhaps the most striking aspect of this communication complex is its pervasiveness. If we were describing our culture to a visitor from another planet, we should have to report the set of mass communication experiences which come to us throughout all except perhaps the first year or so of our lives. In imaginative language, we might call these the *teach-please* experiences (after Horace) or the *inform-entertain* experiences, because each of them is intended, in some proportion, to teach and please, inform and entertain. Traditionally a newspaper is mostly designed to inform, most radio and television programs and most films to entertain. A magazine of large general circulation is usually a fairly even combination. Textbooks are mostly to inform; novels mostly to entertain. Each of these teach-please experiences comes from mass communication, and we should be hard put to name any man-made products except food, clothing, and shelter which are more widely pervasive.

Most of us depend upon mass communication products for a large majority of all the information and entertainment we receive during life. It is especially obvious that what we know about public figures and public affairs is largely dependent upon what the mass media tell us. We are always subject to journalism and incapable of doing much about it. We can see too little for ourselves. Days are too short and the world is too big and complex for anyone to be sure of much about the web of government. What most of us think we know is not known at all in the sense of experience and observation.

We get only occasional firsthand glimpses of government by catching sight for a moment of a presidential candidate in the flesh, by shaking hands with a Senator (or talking with one while he absently shakes hands with someone else), by doing business with the field offices of federal agencies, dickering with the Internal Revenue Service—all the little bits and pieces of contact with officialdom that are described, too grandly, as "citizen participation in government."

We learn more at second hand—from friends, acquaintances, and lecturers on hurried tours, especially those who have just come from Washington or the state capital and are eager to impart what they consider, perhaps erroneously, to be the real story of what is going on there.

Yet this is sketchy stuff, and it adds only patches of color to the mosaic. The expanse of our knowledge of public affairs must come from the mass media. There simply are no practical alternatives. The specialists are, for the most part, in the same condition as the lay citizen. The professor of political science who devotes six months to studying municipal government in France will develop from the experience a more precise knowledge which he can pass on to his students when he returns to the classroom, and to his colleagues through scholarly articles. But in the context of the vast sweep of happenings over the world, his study is narrow—and by the time he returns to deliver his lectures and write his articles, the contemporary study he made is part of yesterday. Like the layman, he must learn of today through the mass media. Clearly, all of us live in a synthetic world, and the synthesis is fashioned largely from information supplied through mass communication.

This is one of the chief functions of mass communication, then: It *helps us to watch the horizon,* much as the ancient messenger once did. No longer depending on the running messenger or the distant drum, we watch the horizon through news bulletins or on-the-scene broadcasts or advertisements of opportunities.

Mass communication *helps us to correlate our response* to the challenges and opportunities which appear on the horizon and to *reach consensus* on social actions. In a real sense, tribal actions and town meetings have given way to mass communication, which enables us to read the rival arguments, see the rival candidates, and judge the issues.

Mass communication *helps us to transmit the culture* of our society to new members. We have always had teaching from parents—and we still have. For thousands of years we have had schools of some kind. But mass communication has entered into this function by supplying textbooks, teaching films and programs, and a constant picturing of the roles and accepted mores of our society for both native Americans and immigrants.

Mass communication *helps entertain us.* The ballad singer, the dancer, the storyteller, and the traveling theater—even the pitchman —have gone on television, radio, and film.

Finally, mass communication *helps sell goods and services.* Without it the economic system could not survive. We once listened for the town crier's advertisements, the word-of-mouth tidings of bargains, the bells of the traveling store-wagon—none very different from the practices of tribal times. Now we read the ads in newspapers and magazines, see them on television, and hear them on radio.

Does it make a difference that we presently see so much of the world through the mass media? Harold Innis, Marshall McLuhan, and Donald Theall, the Canadian philosophers of communication, have established a line of argument that suggests it certainly does. Oral cultures, they say, were time-bound; the people with power were those who could remember the past, its laws and lessons. When man invented printing, he moved into a space-bound culture. There was no longer any need to worry about being time-oriented, for records could now be stored conveniently on paper; the men with power in a media culture are those who know the most about space and have the facilities to manipulate it. Before the age of printing, man saw the world with all his senses, three-dimensionally, realistically. Through printing, he saw it only with his eyes, and in an abstracted, linear, sequential form. Printed language very probably acts as a filter for reality. It gives some of its own form to life. Television, on the other hand, is a step back toward the oral culture. It merely extends man's eyes and ears, and lets him see

reality in an immediate sense, much as he used to before Gutenberg.

With machines that bring us incomparably more information, from farther away, than ever before, we are again becoming accustomed to looking at the distant environment without the interpretive filters of print. For some years now we have become accustomed to seeing our candidates on television rather than merely reading about them. We participated as a nation, by means of television, in the tragic assassinations of the 1960s; Vietnam was the first war we witnessed directly on television; and many armed clashes, coups, and rebellions have followed on the screen in its wake. For four centuries, until recently, the West followed reality from left to right across a printed page. Most of our codes and professional standards have been formed from our experiences with print. They must be carefully examined to see whether they still apply to the audio-visual reporting on which we increasingly depend.

The media themselves have an impact; and the way we use them, the structures we give to them, and the messages we put through them also have an impact. Following an Evel Knievel jump on television, for example, several children ended up in hospitals after trying to duplicate Knievel's exploits in their own way. The widespread influence of *Roots* and *Roots II* is even more incredible. Black parents began naming their children Kunta Kinte or Kizzy after characters in the show. New interest sprang up among blacks in travel to Africa. Programs were instituted in public high schools for students to take oral histories of their parents and relatives. Great new interest in genealogies was spawned. Media impact also became the core issue in the criminal trial of Ronald Zamora (fifteen years old), who murdered an eighty-two-year-old woman. His defense was based on a plea of insanity stemming from watching too much television, particularly violent shows such as *Kojak*. Six months later, Mrs. Valeria Niemi initiated a civil suit for $11 million damages against NBC and a local affiliate for showing a program that included a scene of a young girl being sexually abused. A few days after the airing of this program, Mrs. Niemi's daughter, Olivia, was sexually assaulted by four teenagers, who told police that they had imitated an NBC television show. In both cases, TV violence was not successfully ruled a defense, but the issue will surely continue to surface because of our intuitions that television is enormously powerful.

These examples in themselves do not answer all the questions about the media's impact on our society. In fact, if they imply that media are omnipotent, they mislead. Unfortunately researchers have not resolved many of the issues here; we do not fully understand at present what the media system is doing to individual behavior, much less to American culture. These illustrations suggest that mass communication is a mighty weapon, but there are other subtleties which must be brought into focus before we can properly assess mass communication's responsibility.

The media cannot simply be seen as stenciling images on a blank mind. That is too superficial a view of the communication process. We do have one newspaper reaching 500,000 readers, one book selling 2 million copies, a movie gathering an audience of 5 million, and TV shows seen by 30 million. But the one-way model is only a partial truth. We prefer an interactionist view of communication. People are not just receivers and the media senders, but both participate in a complex interaction. A few of these nuances need review in order to appraise accurately what it means to have a world filled with the mass media.

All of us go through life surrounded by messages, so many more than our senses can attend to or our nervous systems handle that we must defend ourselves by paying attention—or perceiving—selectively. One way to determine how individuals select information is to think of a "fraction of selection," which might be represented as

$$\frac{\text{expectation of reward}}{\text{effort thought to be required}} = \text{likelihood of selection}$$

The likelihood that audiences will attend to a message is enhanced when the reward is greater and the effort smaller. This helps to explain why television has made such a dent in movie attendance (less effort is required to enjoy programs at home), why jamming does not entirely stop the listening to foreign shortwave broadcasts (some listeners want very badly to hear them), and why the use of public libraries falls off so sharply after the teen years (the effort becomes much greater). The limitation of this approach is that it implies a rationality that does not always bulk large in the process of selection. Surely much selection is accidental: Persons quite often "just happen" to be where they can attend to a given message. Some selection is impulsive. Much is the result of role patterns or habits learned from obscure experience. It is important to remember, however, that over the years persons tend to seek the kinds of communication that have rewarded them in the past—their favorite television programs, favorite columnists, the advisers they trust. Television's weekly serials are built on this notion. People, therefore, have a built-in expectation of reward developed from looking in certain places. Beyond that, they tend, other things being equal, to select the cues to information which are close at hand and easy to find in the glut of communication.

Advertisers and other professional communicators try to make their messages appear more rewarding by appealing to the needs and interests of their intended audience. Some of the appeals, like the beauties who advertise soft drinks, are quite remote from the rewards their users are actually likely to enjoy from accepting the product. They try to lure acceptance by making their messages stand out with large headlines or color or pictures or cleverness or repetition, and by saturating the channels. They also try to present their messages so as to eliminate interference. One technique is to build in redundancy where it is necessary. When points are obscure, repetitions and examples are used to make them clear. In international news cables, important words are often repeated to negate the possibility that they will be garbled in transmission: "WILL NOT—REPEAT NOT—ACCEPT TERMS," the cable reads, and no editor ever upbraids a correspondent for that kind of redundancy.

Those attending to the message must decide whether to accept it. That acceptance will depend largely on the apparent validity of the message and on a judgment of the sender's credibility or prestige. Many readers would accept a rather shocking news item in a distinguished newspaper like the New York *Times* because of the *Times*'s reputation for accuracy. Persons who accept a message will interpret it as their stored-up experience and built-in values dictate, for they can interpret only in terms of the responses they have learned. We tend to interpret new experience, if possible, in ways that fit with old experience and accepted values. This, of course, sometimes leads to distortion—often to selecting the parts of a message that fit comfortably and discarding the rest.

How this works is suggested by a well-intended communication which went awry when a certain educational administrator was subjected to very serious charges by a local newspaper. A distinguished academic committee investigated and reported that the charges were without foundation. There had merely been, the committee members reported, "a failure of communication" in the administrator's department. They saw this as a vindication of the administrator (after all, what department has not sometimes suffered communication failures?). But the newspaper paid little attention to the acquittal, and trumpeted for weeks the fact that the committee had found a "failure of communication" involving the administrator. Ultimately, the administrator resigned. The chagrined committee members realized that they and the newspaper had approached that communication with different purposes. They had thought to explain the trouble and to indicate that it was not serious. The newspaper, however, was out to get the administrator, and simply seized upon the part of the message that would further its purpose. The process of informing, then, is not at all simple. In fact, it involves so many problems and pitfalls that the constant flow of relatively accurate information in human society may seem almost miraculous.

Different ground rules operate when the goal of the communication process is entertaining rather than informing. True, entertaining communication must get over the same hurdles. The message must be presented so as to be interpretable within the experience of the audience; it must appeal to audience needs and interests; and it must, so far as possible, be designed to avoid the hazards of noise and interference. That is, it must gain attention, be accepted, and be interpreted. Feedback is at least as important in entertainment as in informing; in live entertainment it is the crucial element—the artist fits his act to his audience, or he fails—and in media entertainment it is so important that broadcasters spend millions of dollars every year to learn about their audiences. The chief difference lies in the unwritten contract between speakers and listeners. In informational communication, the sender is to be a good reporter, and the audience is to bring to the experience a reality-seeking and reality-testing mood. Entertainment, however, requires of the audience a certain willing suspension of disbelief. Instead of reacting skeptically to anything that checks poorly with their picture of reality, members of the entertainment audience must be willing to go along with a story or a spoof or a joke, or to agonize and rejoice with a character who never lived or never could live. Instead of expecting simple, clear, unambiguous writing, they may be pleased with a certain level of artistic ambiguity and a host of latent meanings.

Entertainers may be expected to be more concerned with form than informational communicators. *How* they write or speak or move is expected to give pleasure. They are usually imaginative rather than utilitarian, prize rich writing over clear writing, and must expertly turn a phrase or build a scene. In short, although informational communication may be artistic, and although entertainment communication may present a picture of reality, the thrust of informing asks for the skill of the reporter, and the thrust of entertaining asks for the skill of the artist.

The receiver of entertainment communication is expected to be willing to identify with one or more of the characters, put himself in their places, feel with them. In poetry and modern painting, he is expected to enjoy ambiguity rather than be frustrated by it. Indeed, there is reason to believe that resolving ambiguities is one of our most pleasurable experiences, perhaps because so much pride is involved. One who understands J. R. R. Tolkien's trilogy, *Lord of the Rings,* certainly develops a measure of pride. One who understands a joke is almost surely pleased, at least in part, because he "got it."

Like information communication, persuasive communication must get the message through, but that is rarely enough. To accomplish any substantial change, persuasion must set in motion some psychological dynamics by which listeners will, in effect, change themselves. It is not necessarily difficult to implant new attitudes or encourage new behavior in a new area, of course. If our astronauts had returned from the moon with an account of dangerous and hostile little green men, we would have been easily persuaded to view this new threat with alarm. After all, we do not have much in our mental files on the subject of moon men. However, if we had long known of the moon men and had long held attitudes toward them, changing the attitudes would be difficult. For when a strong area is attacked directly, the message is likely to be rejected or distorted.

Consider the situation in which persuasion occurs. Persuasion involves no contract between communicator and audience. Senders are on their own. They must choose the information and package it to fit their goals. They may attract attention by entertainment (the programs accompanying the commercials), by saturating the perceptual field (big type, loud commercials, parades, rallies), by big names and big events. They can advance arguments, make threats, offer rewards. *Caveat emptor!*

Audiences come with their defenses up, prepared to be skeptical. They have experienced persuasion before. They ask, "What is there for *us* in this message?" They come with needs they want satisfied. They already have a set of beliefs and attitudes; some are relatively flexible, but many they are prepared to defend stubbornly. They come with a set of personal relationships and loyalties, and they feel deeply dependent on many of them. They come with a set of perceptions of opportunity and threat in the environment and are not prepared to change them without persuasive evidence. On balance, the persuasion situation is a buyer's, not a seller's, market.

The process of persuasion, so far as it is primarily a *communication process* (as distinguished, for example, from the use of force), consists of introducing information which leads the receiver to reappraise his environment, and through that to reappraise his needs and his ways of meeting them, or his social relationships, or his beliefs and attitudes. Perhaps the closest we have come to the kind of change that might be brought about by discovery of dangerous little moon people is the notorious panic caused by Orson Welles's radio broadcast in 1938 of a dramatization of "The War of the Worlds." The more susceptible listeners believed that invaders were actually sweeping all before them. Suddenly their environmental support seemed to be crumbling, and with it their confidence in law and order and national power. Their need for self-preservation took control, and they fled to the hills.

Although the conscious use of threats to arouse the need for self-preservation can initiate a process of change, this has been shown to be a two-edged sword. In a famous experiment, researchers were somewhat surprised to find that lesser threats concerning tooth decay accomplished more than strong threats of sending their experimental subjects to the toothbrush and the dentist. Later experiments showed that when the threat was too unpleasant, and especially when the cure was remote or difficult or uncertain, the whole topic was often repressed—swept under the rug. This may be one of the reasons why the campaign against cigarette smoking has been relatively ineffective. The prospect of lung cancer is so frightening, the cure so uncertain, the entire relation of smoking to cancer so befogged by counterclaims, that it is easier to change an old habit slightly (switching to a filter) and repress the picture of cancer than to make greater changes. Apparently, threats must be made in a low key unless one can offer a clear and certain remedy. Advertisers are usually careful to offer a carrot even as they brandish the stick: They suggest the horrors of bad breath, but they emphasize that it can be purged with Little Miracle Mouthwash, and that social joys are then available.

A change process can be triggered by altering the audience's perception of their social relationships. Every salesman tries to establish himself or herself as a friend of the prospective buyer. Many of the most successful evangelists place new converts in a group of believers at once so that their decisions will be socially reinforced. Many advertisements hold out the implied hope of being able to join an admired group—"men of distinction" or the sponsors of a particular cause or the effervescent "Pepsi Generation."

One of the most powerful processes available to persuasive communication is what some researchers have called the strain toward consistency. Human beings seem to strive for balance between what they know and believe and what they do. Suppose now that a persuasive message can push its way into cognitive areas that are relatively lightly defended. And suppose that this new information is out of balance with the present position, but not so far out of balance as to be rejected. For example, suppose it says that some admired individual or group holds a position that is inconsistent with the person's present position; or that a new position is not really inconsistent with his own, but rather a development of it. Then there is some reason to hope that the individual may reorganize and change some of his or her more strongly held positions in order to attain consistency.

This may help to explain the success of role playing in attitude change. When young persons are encouraged to prepare a prize-contest oration or essay that takes a specified point of view toward some controversial topic, they are likely to be under some strain to bring their attitudes into agreement with those they have publicly expressed. There are strong defenses against change in any attitudes and beliefs that really matter to the holder. Before persuasion occurs, those defenses must be breached and the process of reappraisal and reorganization of attitudes initiated.

The things we have been talking about are true both of mass communication and of interpersonal communication. Mass communication is certainly different in that it is more complicated. Moreover, social demands and social controls on the mass media are usually louder and stronger than those on the individual. Any society usually has rather definite ideas of what it wants its mass media to be

and do. It may exercise control through law, through executive control, through economic support, or through many informal channels.

On the whole, however, the similarities between the processes of mass communication and interpersonal communication are far greater than the differences. Mass communication faces the same defenses and must leap the same hurdles: attention, acceptance, interpretation, and storing. It requires the same kinds of contracts between sender and receiver for entertainment and instruction. It must depend upon activating the same kinds of psychological dynamics if it is to persuade.

It was fashionable for a number of years to worry about the great and awful power of mass communication because of the enormous number of hours people gave to media entertainment and the size of the media audiences for political information. But the more that scholars investigated the effects of the media, the more they found that the same resistances to change applied there as in person-to-person communication—in fact, rather more strongly. People come to the media, as to other messages, seeking what they want, not what the media intend them to have. Because there are so many media and media units, they have considerable choice. They still have their defenses up; they still defend their strongly held positions. Because of their distance from the media, and the relatively isolated way of reading, viewing, or listening, they tend to put great reliance on their own social groups and their own advisers. Interpersonal channels of information are functioning side by side with mass media channels and these interpersonal channels are exerting much of the influence on society.

The mass media become especially powerful when those who use them are able to build close and influential relationships with their audience. In the 1930s, Father Coughlin used the radio for emotional preaching and melodramatic religious programs to build a following that can only be described as personal. Much of the continuing success of religious broadcasting demonstrates this principle also. Many dictators in our own time feel that control of the media is essential to their power and continuing influence. The birthday and "get well" cards that some people send to entertainers they do not know, and even to cartoon and fictional characters, are evidences that personal attachment can build up through the media.

These few pages reviewing the communication process certainly prompt us always to favor interaction, to search for ways to improve it technologically. Cable television has exciting possibilities because it offers two-way capability, in contrast to our largely one-way structure now. But even until that future day of the new-generation two-way cable, mass communication must still be viewed as interactionist. There is no point in being simplistic. In assessing media responsibility, our interactionist mode cuts like a two-edged sword. We consider it unenlightening to lay all the blame either on the networks or with parents for not controlling the set more closely. We do not favor either extreme. Media professionals cannot simply tell the reader or listener to beware, to drop his subscription or turn off the program. Nor is "giving the public what they want" sufficient. Media reformers cannot merely argue the other side either, blaming broadcasters and writers for all our contemporary difficulties. Even though this book treats *media* responsibility, it does not fixate exclusively there but views the sending of messages as one phase in an oscillating process.

Mass communication media can and do effect change in many cases when they are all in agreement. If one can imagine all those with pivotal roles in all the media agreeing to present the information and develop the psychological dynamics that would persuade the American people to adopt one point of view —toward nuclear weapons, toward sexism in the United States—then there would be a possibility of dramatic change.

In the absence of such an unlikely agreement, we must consider the power of the mass media not as a tidal wave but as a great river. It feeds the ground it touches, following the lines of existing contours but preparing the way for change over a long period. Sometimes it finds a spot where the ground is soft and ready, and there it cuts a new channel. Sometimes it carries material which helps to alter its banks. And occasionally, in time of flood, it washes away a piece of ground and gives the channel a new look.

Undoubtedly the most important role of the media is to feed the ground—to deposit layers of information, day by day, hour by hour, so that a base is laid for the knowledge on which we walk. Compared with the occasional great and dramatic changes we can attribute to the media, this slow, continuing, never-ending effect is immensely more powerful and significant.

This book attempts to clarify how a system of such potential for improving or harming our society can build that information base responsibly.

Notes

1. David Riesman *et al., The Lonely Crowd* (New Haven: Yale University Press, rev. ed., 1961), especially Chap. 1.
2. Claude E. Shannon, "The Mathematical Theory of Communication," *Bell System Technical Journal,* July and October 1948. Reprinted as a book: Shannon and Weaver, *The Mathematical Theory of Communication* (Urbana: University of Illinois Press, 1949).
3. Richard E. Barnes and Thomas Reagon, "The Future of Electronic Entertainment," *The Futurist,* February 1976, pp. 41–43.
4. Kevin P. Phillips, *Mediacracy: American Parties and Politics in the Communications Age* (Garden City, N.Y.: Doubleday, 1975).
5. Standard sources of these figures are *Broadcasting Yearbook, Motion Picture Almanac, Editor and Publisher Yearbook, Ayer's Directory of Newspapers and Periodicals, United States Statistical Abstract.*

2
*The Decline of Mass Media**

Richard Maisel

In this seminal article from *Public Opinion Quarterly,* sociologist Richard Maisel discusses the increasing specialization of the media and a corresponding fractionalization of the mass audience. Maisel believes that these developments are tied to our "post-industrial society," where service and information-related industries replace manufacturing as the driving force in the economy. Maisel points to patterns of rapid growth for telephone usage, specialized publications, tape recorders, and computerized data systems as support for his hypotheses. Subsequent developments in individually programmed media tools, such as videocassette recorders (VCRs), personal computers, and citizen's band radios (CBs), serve as further evidence of the importance of Maisel's propositions.

A new, three-stage theory of social change and media growth, formulated in recent years, challenges many of the ideas long accepted in the study of modern communication systems. According to this theory, the third stage, now evident in the United States, is characterized by a declining growth rate for mass media and an increasing growth rate for specialized communication directed to smaller, more homogeneous audiences.[1] If this theory is correct, the mass media will—contrary to past expectations—play a less important role in the future, and the focus of scientific attention should be shifted to specialized media.

This article reviews media growth trends in the United States during the period 1950–70[2] to determine whether the claims of the three-stage theory are warranted.

The Two-Stage Theory[3]

Most studies of modern communication systems are based on a two-stage theory of social change and media growth, which may be summarized as follows:

1. The history of Western civilization may meaningfully be divided into two periods: a stable earlier period, in which society was small in scale, local in orientation, and organized around a primitive, pre-industrial economy; and a later period of industrialization, extending to the present, in which society has grown in size, scope, and technological prowess.

2. Each of these two periods is characterized by a communication system that is consistent with its needs and resources. In the pre-industrial period, the communication system was restricted to direct face-to-face communication between individuals. In the later period, beginning in the mid-

*An earlier version of this paper, "Mass Media: Fact and Fantasy," was presented at the 1966 annual meeting of the American Association for Public Opinion Research. The author wishes to express his thanks to Alan Bell for editorial assistance.

Source: From *Public Opinion Quarterly,* Vol. 37, No. 2 (Summer 1973). Reprinted by permission of the author and publisher.

fifteenth century with the invention of printing from movable type, a powerful system of mass communication evolved.

3. There is a close, functional relationship between the process of industrialization and the growth of mass communication. The former stimulates and provides the resources necessary for the latter; the latter facilitates the growth of the former. Thus each stage in the growth of the mass media helps provide the conditions necessary for its further growth.

4. Both the mass media and the processes of industrialization that support it have been growing at a rapid rate and will continue to do so in the future.

5. Mass communication develops a powerful "hold" over its audience, thereby closing off potentially competitive forms of cultural experience. This gives the mass media an ever more secure position and an ever more paramount role in determining the cultural content of our society.

The Three-Stage Theory[4]

The newer, three-stage theory of social change and media growth incorporates the older theory through step 3, supplanting the later steps with a third stage of development, as follows:

4. When industrialization and the institutional changes that accompany it reach an advanced level, new forces are released, which channel subsequent social and economic development down a new path, culminating in the third stage—"post-industrial society."

5. Among the forces released at an advanced level of industrialization are increased specialization and the growth of the so-called service industries.

6. The point at which the third stage begins is usually marked by a rapid shift of the work force away from the manufacturing sector toward the ser-

vice sector. In the United States, this shift occurred in the period following the second World War.

7. The service industries are great consumers of specialized media. The needs and tastes of specialized groups can only be satisfied by a form of specialized communication designed for homogeneous audiences.

Thus, the development of the third stage, or "post-industrial society," does not support the rapid growth of mass communication; rather, it stimulates the growth of specialized media. Moreover, technological development and increase in wealth provide the means necessary for the development of these specialized media.

On the basis of these propositions, we would not predict an acceleration in the growth of the mass media; rather, we would expect a rapid growth in specialized media.

Test of Hypothesis

According to the three-stage theory, the United States entered the third stage following the second World War. Therefore, we may test the theory by examining the rates of media growth in the United States during the period 1950–1970, expecting to find an increase in growth rates for the specialized media relative to growth rates for the mass media. We shall measure the growth of media in two ways. First, we shall measure economic support, in current dollars,[5] including advertising revenue, consumer expenditures, and, in some cases, government expenditures. Second, we shall measure growth in the volume of communications using the best measures available throughout the period.[6]

Mass Media, Education, and Personal Message System

The education system is the most important of all specialized media systems. At its core is the school system, a mammoth medium for the communication of specialized information. The school system also supports the use of other specialized media, such as textbooks, technical treatises, and audio-visual materials. Equally important, the product of the education system, particularly of *higher* education, is a stratum of individuals who, both in their work and private life, are consumers of specialized communication. Thus, a crucial test of the three-stage theory is provided by growth in the education system.

In this section, we will compare the growth rates for the education system with those of the mass media. To complete the analysis, we will include the growth rates of the much-neglected personal message system, which includes those specialized media, other than face-to-face interaction, that permit communication between individuals. These include the telephone, telegraph, and correspondence by mail. If the three-stage theory is correct, we should expect to find that the growth rates for both the education and personal message systems are greater than those for the mass media. Analysis of education growth rates, however, remains the more crucial test.

Table 1, depicting economic growth for the mass media, education, and personal message systems, reveals the highest growth rate in the education system, and the lowest growth rate in the mass media system. Table 1 also shows growth rates for the economy as a whole measured as the gross national product (GNP). The growth rates for both the education and personal message systems are well above those for the GNP, indicating that both of these systems—but particularly education—expanded relative to the total economy. The growth rate for the mass media was approximately equal to that of the GNP in the 1950–60 period, but fell behind during the 1960–70 period. Thus, we must conclude that the mass media system is contracting relative to the economy as a whole.

Every media system is composed of new and expanding segments, as well as those that are stable or in decline. The critical element in the development of media systems is found in the growth segments. Table 2 shows the growth rates, measured in terms of dollar-value and facility use, for television, the telephone, and higher education—the most active components of, respectively, the mass media, personal message, and education systems. As we would expect, Table 2 reveals explosive growth for television during the 1950–55 period, but a steady decline in its expansion thereafter. In contrast, the growth rate for higher education was low in the 1950–55 period, but rose sharply in subsequent

Table 1. Volume and Growth Rate of GNP, Education, Personal Message, and Mass Media Systems, 1950–70

GNP and Media	Dollar Volume (GNP in Billions, Media Systems in Millions)			Growth Rate	
	1950	1960	1970	1950–60	1960–70
GNP[a]	284.8	503.7	974.1	1.78	1.93
Media Systems					
Education[b]	8,796	24,722	70,600	2.81	2.85
Personal Message[c]	4,544	10,001	20,636	2.20	2.06
Mass Media[d]	9,254	16,413	28,525	1.77	1.73

[a]Abstract 1971, Table 150.
[b]Consists of educational expenditure at all levels of instruction, public and private (Abstract 1972, Table 155).
[c]Consists of telephone and telegraph operating revenue, domestic and overseas (Abstract 1972, Table 793) and ordinary postal revenue (Abstract 1971, Table 752).
[d]Consists of advertising revenue (Abstract 1972, Table 1260), consumer expenditure on books, maps, newspapers, magazines, sheet music, and motion pictures (Abstract 1972, Table 330), and the number of subscribers to CATV (Abstract 1972, Table 802) times an assumed annual subscription rate of $50.

Table 2. Growth Rate of Higher Education, Telephone, and Television, 1950–70

Media	Growth Rate			
	1950–55	1955–60	1960–65	1965–70
Dollar Volume				
Higher Education[a]	1.52	2.05	1.94	1.93
Telephone[b]	1.70	1.43	1.41	1.52
Television[c]	6.04	1.57	1.59	1.44
Communication Volume				
Higher Education[d]	1.07	1.50	1.58	1.30
Telephone[e]	1.22	1.33	1.29	1.33
Television[f]	4.38	1.46	1.30	1.19

[a]Current expenditure and interest, capital outlay, or plant expansion (Abstract 1971, Table 150, except 1955 data, which were estimated by assuming 1955 expenditure to be equal to 1950 expenditure plus five-sixths of the growth to 1956 [Abstract 1972, Table 139]).
[b]Operating revenue, domestic and overseas (Abstract 1971, Table 759, except 1955 data [Abstract 1960, Table 663]).
[c]Advertising revenue (Abstract 1972, Table 1216) and the number of subscribers to CATV (Abstract 1972, Table 802) times an assumed annual subscription rate of $50.
[d]College enrollment (Abstract 1971, Table 153).
[e]Average telephone conversations daily, Bell and independent companies, local and long distance (Abstract 1971, Table 757, except 1955 data [Abstract 1960, Table 665]).
[f]Average total hours sets in use daily, obtained by the number of television households (A. C. Nielsen Company, Television 1971, p. 5) times the average hours per day of television sets in use per household (National Association of Broadcasters, Dimensions of Television 1968–69, p. 12 and A. C. Nielsen Company, private communication).

periods. By the 1955–60 period, the growth rate for higher education had surpassed that of television, and continued to do so throughout the sixties. The growth rate for the telephone was moderately high compared with the other two media under consideration, and stable throughout the postwar period. In the 1965–70 period, it surpassed the sagging growth rate for television. Thus, in the 1950–70 period, growth rates for the fastest growing segments of the education and personal message systems have increased relative to the analogous component of the mass media system. Moreover, television dollar volume grew by 1.44 during the 1965–70 period, insignificantly more than the 1.43 by which the GNP grew in the same interval. Therefore, by 1970, television, which is usually considered the most successful of the mass media, did not have an expanding position in the economy.

Each medium may also be divided into more or less specialized segments. Higher edu-

cation, for example, tends to be a more specialized medium, while elementary school tends to be a mass medium. Thus we can test the three-stage theory by examining the growth rates for each medium divided into segments along degree-of-specialization lines. In the case of the school system, expenditures in the 1960–70 period grew by 1.14 for elementary schools, 1.43 for secondary schools, and 2.07 for institutions of higher education.[7] Thus growth rates vary directly with the degree of specialization of the individual segment. The same general tendencies are seen in Table 3, which shows that the growth rates for education and special service broadcasting have been increasing relative to those of commercial broadcasting. Table 4 shows that in the 1960–70 period, the quantity of air and first-class mail delivered increased faster than second-, third-, and fourth-class mail (excluding publications), and the purchase rate of tape recorders exceeded that of phonographs.

Therefore, every comparison among the

Table 3. Growth Rate of Commercial, Educational, and Special Service Broadcasting, 1950–70

	Growth Rate			
	1950–55	1955–60	1960–65	1965–70
Number of Authorized Radio Stations				
Educational[a]	1.58	1.42	1.50	1.69
Safety and Special Service[b]	1.24	2.17	2.23	1.26
Commercial[c]	1.10	1.31	1.27	1.17
Number of TV Stations on Air[d]				
Educational	—	4.27	1.95	2.06
Commercial	4.40	1.25	1.01	1.15
Average Weekly Hours of Broadcasting per TV Station				
Educational[e]	—	—	—	1.42
Commercial[f]	—	—	—	1.02

[a]FM only (Abstract 1966, Table 737, except 1970 data [Abstract 1971, Table 765]).
[b]Consists of amateur, disaster, citizens, aviation, industrial, marine, land transportation, and public safety services (Abstract 1966, Table 737, except 1970 data [Abstract 1971, Table 765]).
[c]AM and FM (Abstract 1966, Table 737, except 1970 data [Abstract 1971, Table 765]).
[d]Federal Communications Commission, Annual Report, Fiscal Year 1970, p. 144.
[e]Abstract 1972, Table 803. Data for 1965 were estimated as the average of 1964 and 1966 data.
[f]Abstract 1972, Table 809.

Table 4. Volume and Growth Rate of Mail and Consumer Audio Equipment, 1950–70

	Unit Volume			Growth Rate	
	1950	1960	1970	1950–60	1960–70
Mail Received,[a] Pieces per Capita					
Air and First-class	168	193	246	1.14	1.27
Second-, Third-, and Fourth-class	119	148	149	1.24	1.01
Consumer Audio Equipment,[b] in Thousands of Units Purchased					
Tape Recorders	—	295	8,452	—	28.65
Phonographs	1,260	4,523	5,620	3.58	1.24

[a]Abstract 1971, Table 752.
[b]Electronic Industry Association, Consumer Electronics 1972.

education, personal message, and mass media systems shows that the first two media are growing at increasingly more rapid rates than the third.

Specialization of the Mass Media

Several authors[8] have suggested that the mass media themselves are becoming more special- ized, a proposition deduced from the three-stage theory. We can test this proposition by examining the growth rates of the more specialized and less specialized components of each mass medium. We can, for example, distinguish between the national broadcasting networks and local radio and television stations; the former have larger and more heterogeneous audiences and thereby constitute the less specialized segment of the broadcasting

Table 5. Growth Rate of GNP and Advertising Expenditure by Medium, 1950–69

GNP and Media	Growth Rate			
	1950–55	1955–60	1960–65	1965–69
GNP[a]	1.40	1.26	1.36	1.35
Television[b]				
Network	6.35	1.45	1.57	1.35
Local	4.09	1.24	1.46	1.58
Radio[c]				
Network	.43	.51	1.39	.98
Local	1.19	1.31	1.37	1.42
Magazine				
Regional[d]	—	—	2.06	1.35
Other than Regional[e]	1.41	1.29	1.20	1.11
Newspaper[f]				
National	1.39	1.13	1.03	1.20
Retail	1.48	1.18	1.14	1.28
Classified	1.61	1.31	1.51	1.30
All Media[g]				
National	1.66	1.35	1.28	1.22
Local	1.54	1.22	1.27	1.35
Total	1.61	1.29	1.27	1.28

[a]Abstract 1971, Table 484.
[b]Abstract 1971, Table 1216.
[c]Ibid.
[d]Publishers' Information Bureau/Leading National Advertisers.
[e]Total magazine advertising expenditure (Abstract 1971, Table 1216) minus regional advertising expenditure, ut supra [as above].
[f] American Newspaper Publishers Association, Research Department, Bureau of Advertising, March 1970.
[g]Abstract 1971, Table 1216.

media. Table 5 shows that within all three of the major media—radio, newspapers, and magazines—throughout the years 1950 to 1970 there has been greater growth in advertising revenue directed to more specialized audiences. This finding strongly supports the three-stage theory in two ways: (1) by showing differential growth in the media carrying the advertising, and (2) by *directly* showing differential growth in the medium of advertising, itself a means of communication. The source of support also suggests the direction to which the media must orient themselves in order to obtain further support: the growth of a more specialized type of advertising means the medium must attract the type of audience to which a more specialized advertising is directed. Thus, specialized advertising becomes a factor in the medium's continued specializa-

tion. An outstanding example of this can be seen in the case of radio, where network-originated broadcasts have diminished in favor of locally based fare directed to very special segments within the community. Thus, one station will play "heavy" rock music, while another station operates in the older "top 40" rock 'n' roll format, and a third broadcasts news exclusively. The trend has gone so far that the networks, themselves, have become specialized. The same trend can be found in the area of magazines, in which mass magazines such as *Life, Look,* and the *Saturday Evening Post* have ceased publication, while special interest magazines have been thriving. Many magazines with large national circulations, such as *Time,* have set up regional advertising areas.

The trend toward specialization in magazines and radio has often been noted before,[9] and is usually explained as a consequence of television. But this is only a partial explanation. It does not, for example, explain the fact that the growth rate of local television advertising has been increasing relative to the growth rate for network television advertising (Table 5). The three-stage theory accounts not only for shifts among media, but for shifts within a particular medium as well.

In Table 6, data for the 1950–70 period reveal that the growth rate of consumer economic support for various media is directly related to the degree to which each medium is specialized. Within the print medium, the growth rate for books has been higher than for magazines and newspapers, which are less specialized, and the rate of increase in expenditures for legitimate theater has been greater than the rate of increase in expenditures for motion pictures, which again are less specialized. Table 6 also shows that the rate of increase in consumer expenditures for radio, television, magazines, newspapers, and motion pictures has been far less than the rate of increase in consumer expenditure as a whole, which in turn has been less than the rate of increase in books and legitimate theater. This further confirms that,

relative to the total economy, specialized media are expanding and mass media are contracting.

Table 7, providing 1947–70 growth rates for various segments within the print medium, reveals that in every case, growth of the more specialized segment of the medium exceeds that of the less specialized: the growth rate in the circulation of suburban newspapers is greater than the growth rate in the circulation of central city newspapers; the growth rate in the number of technical books sold and the number of new technical books published is greater than the growth rate in the number of fiction books sold and the number of new fiction books published; the growth rate in the number of bimonthly and quarterly magazines is greater than the growth rate in the number of weekly and monthly magazines.

The same trend toward specialization can be seen in the theater medium, where the number of off-Broadway performances increased by 1.29 from 1960 to 1970, while in the same period the growth rate for the less specialized Broadway performance was .75.[10] An identical trend can be seen in motion pictures, where the size of newly built theaters and their audiences have decreased.

Table 6. Growth Rate of Consumer Recreation Expenditure by Medium, 1950–70

| Medium | Growth Rate | | | |
	1950–55	1955–60	1960–65	1965–70
Radio and Television[a]	1.25	1.25	1.67	1.40
Magazines and Newspapers[b]	1.25	1.17	1.30	1.42
Books[c]	1.29	1.50	1.54	1.66
Legitimate Theater[d]	1.34	1.48	1.35	1.48
Motion Pictures[e]	1.01	.89	1.12	1.33
Total[f]	1.26	1.29	1.43	1.48

[a]Consists of expenditure for purchase and repair of radio and television receivers, phonograph records and musical instruments (Abstract 1972, Table 330), and the number of subscribers to CATV (Abstract 1972, Table 802) times an assumed annual subscription rate of $50.
[b]Abstract 1972, Table 330. Includes sheet music.
[c]Abstract 1972, Table 330. Includes maps.
[d]Abstract 1972, Table 330.
[e]Ibid.
[f]Ibid.

Table 7. Volume and Growth Rate of Print Media, 1947–70

Print Media	Unit Volume			Growth Rate	
	1947	1957	1967	1947–57	1957–67
Newspaper Circulation, 25 Largest Metropolitan Areas,[a] in Millions of Papers Sold					
Central City Papers[b]	22.7	24.7	23.0	1.09	.93
Papers Outside Central City	1.4	2.4	3.5	1.71	1.45
Books,[c] in Millions of Copies Sold					
Fiction[d]	—	480.0	759.2	—	1.58
Technical[e]	—	238.6	602.4	—	1.77
	1950	1960	1970	1950–60	1960–70
New Books and Editions Published[f]					
Fiction	1,907	2,440	3,137	1.28	1.28
Technical[g]	3,200	4,415	13,834	1.37	3.13
Periodicals Published[h]					
Weekly to Monthly	5,553	6,220	6,759	1.12	1.08
Bimonthly and Quarterly	1,040	1,638	2,065	1.56	1.26

[a]M. Lehr and J. Wallis, interoffice correspondence, American Newspaper Publishers Association, Bureau of Advertising, May 3, 1967.
[b]Includes circulation that these papers have outside central city.
[c]Abstract 1972, Table 818. Data for 1957 were estimated from 1958 and 1967 data assuming a constant growth rate between 1957 and 1967.
[d]Includes general book, trade, etc.
[e]Includes textbooks, subscription reference books, technical, scientific, and professional books.
[f]Abstract 1972, Table 816.
[g]Includes agriculture, business, law, medicine, philosophy, psychology, science, sociology, economics, and technologies.
[h]Abstract 1972, Table 810.

Conclusion

Our review of trends in media growth in the United States during the 1950–70 period supports the three-stage theory of social change and media growth. In every case, the growth rate of the more specialized media increased relative to the growth rate of the mass media. The mass media are actually shrinking in size relative to the total economy.

Given these findings, it is clear that the focus of attention in the study of modern communication systems should broaden from its present preoccupation with the mass media to a full examination of all major media and communication systems. This would include studies of important media systems that have been almost completely neglected, such as the telephone system; studies of new media that are growing rapidly, such as the office communication system; and studies that provide perspectives on the total communication system of our society, such as those of Fritz Machlup.[11]

We must also abandon the outmoded view of the individual as simply the recipient of standardized messages emanating from the mass media, whose only recourse in self-expression is the primitive sound of his own voice in direct face-to-face interaction. Rather, we must begin to think of, and study, the individual in our society as a communicator having access to a very powerful set of media tools and as a recipient of a wide range of equally enriched communications directed to him by others. This would lead us to study how he learns about and uses the available media systems, and the effect that this ability to communicate has on him.

Comparing the two- and three-stage theories shows that it is dangerous simply to project trends into the future. Each development seems to bring with it the conditions by which it changes. Thus the development of the standardized industrial culture brought about the conditions that now seem to be causing the development of a more differentiated culture. We should, therefore, not make the same error of simply projecting the third stage into the future. At least two other possibilities exist. First, the explosive increase in the volume of communication directed to the individual creates the problem of dealing with it. Thus we might expect the coming period to be characterized by the growth of receptors,

media for receiving communications; such developments are already apparent in the use of speed reading, computers for data retrieval, tape recorders, and copying equipment.

The second possibility is less auspicious. The growth of a differentiated communication system is part of the larger process by which our society has been producing a differentiated culture. In both economic and psychological terms, the cost of this differentiated culture has been increasing, and it is not clear whether our society will pay the price of supporting it in the future. In recent years, for example, both economic and moral support has been withdrawn from educational institutions, which in the past played a leading role in the development of the differentiated culture.

Notes

1. Conversely, we shall assume that larger audiences are more heterogeneous. Here, "audience" means that *average* audience to which messages sent by a particular medium are directed. We acknowledge, but consider it the exception, that larger audiences are sometimes *less* heterogeneous.

2. Unless otherwise stated, all sources of data given in this article are: U.S. Department of Commerce, Bureau of the Census, *Statistical Abstract of the United States,* Washington, D.C., Government Printing Office, 1960–72. This work will hereafter be referred to as *Abstract,* followed by the year of publication and table number.

3. The two-stage theory was implicitly assumed by both sides several years ago in the then prevalent controversy over mass culture. It is also assumed by several authors as a grounding rationale. See, e.g., Charles S. Steinberg, Ed., *Mass Media and Communication,* New York, Hastings House, 1966, pp. ix–xiii; and Lewis Anthony Dexter and David Manning White, eds., *People and Mass Communications,* New York, Free Press, 1964, pp. 3–10. Explicit statements of the two-stage theory may be found in Joseph Bensman and Bernard Rosenberg, "Mass Media and Mass Culture," in Phillip Olsen, ed., *America as a Mass Society,* New York, Free Press, 1963; and Melvin DeFleur, *Theories of Mass Communication,* 2d ed., New York, David McKay, 1970, chs. 1–4 and 6.

4. The three-stage theory is part of a more general shift from two- to three-stage theories of social change. Colin Clark (*Conditions of Economic Progress,* London, Macmillan, 1957) has formulated a widely used

three-stage theory of economic growth that has been extended to other areas of society by Daniel Bell ("The Measurement of Knowledge and Technology," in Eleanor Bernert Sheldon and Wilbert E. Moore, eds., Indicators of Social Change, New York, Russell Sage, 1968) and others as the "post-industrial society." The clearest statement of the three-stage theory as it applies to media growth, and the one used as the basis for this paper, is given by John Merrill and Ralph L. Lowenstein, *Media, Messages, and Man,* New York, David McKay, 1971, pp. 33–44.

5. Since we are interested in relative growth, there is no need to correct for inflation using constant dollars.

6. In most cases, measures for volume are far from ideal. For example, our measure for the volume of communication by books, the number of books sold, does not take into account the degree to which the books were actually read.

7. *Abstract 1971,* Table 153.

8. Merrill and Lowenstein, *op cit.,* pp. 33–44; and Denis McQuail, *Toward the Socioogy of Mass Communication,* London, Collier-Macmillan Ltd., 1969.

9. See, e.g., Rolf B. Meyersohn, "Social Research in Television," in Bernard Rosenberg and David Manning White, eds., *Mass Culture,* New York, Free Press, 1957, pp. 348–49; and Sydney W. Head, "Some Intermedia Relationships," in Steinberg, *op cit.*

10. *Abstract 1971,* Table 319.

11. Fritz Machlup, *The Production and Distribution of Knowledge,* Princeton, N.J., Princeton University Press, 1962.

3

Making Yourself Heard (and Seen): The Citizen's Role in Communications

Howard J. Symons

The mass audience rarely has a structural impact on media industries except through responses in the marketplace. Broadcasting and other electronic communications, however, are unique in their vulnerability to organized audience pressure because they are licensed to use the public airwaves by the Federal Communications Commission (FCC). The last two decades of FCC regulation have seen significant citizen activism and legal pressure, first on commercial broadcasters and, later, on American Telephone and Telegraph (AT&T).

Recently, various attempts have been made in Congress to rewrite the Communications Act of 1934, which empowered the FCC to regulate telecommunications in "... the public interest, convenience, or necessity." If passed into law, most of these efforts would have dramatically altered this precept by "deregulating" most of FCC's powers and severely limiting citizen input in the broadcast licensing process.

Howard J. Symons, who is chief counsel of the House Telecommunications subcommittee, examines these recent attempts to restructure telecommunications regulation in the United States. Symons feels that we need more, rather than less, government control of broadcasting and of AT&T, and more avenues for citizen action as well. In an article from *Telecommunications Policy and the Citizen,* Symons looks at the impact of these deregulatory proposals on citizen access, broadcast diversity, and telephone rates. Concluding that controls of new technologies, like cable television, should also be strengthened, he proposes the creation of lobbying groups to represent broadcast audiences and telephone customers.

. . . (I)n the darkness behind him the television gaped like a black place where once a front tooth had hung. He'd taken the twelve gauge shotgun to it, three weeks ago. . . .
—John Gardner, *October Light*

We don't care; we don't have to. We're the phone company.
—Lily Tomlin

Source: From *Telecommunications Policy and the Citizen,* edited by Timothy R. Haight. Copyright © 1979 by Praeger Publishers. Reprinted by permission of Praeger Publishers.

I

A little more than a hundred years ago, Alexander Graham Bell was teaching speech to the deaf in Boston, and radio waves were only a theoretical glint in physicist James Clerk Maxwell's eye. People separated from each other by great distances relied on letters, or occasional telegrams, to communicate—if they communicated at all. America around 1870 was a loosely-knit nation: instantaneous communication and the electronic mass media were unknown to all but the most imaginative science fiction writers.

In the succeeding century, we as a nation have come to rely heavily on telecommunications. Most members of the public consider the telephone a necessity. Congress concluded as much in 1934, when it passed the Communications Act. That Act directed the newly established Federal Communications Commission to regulate communications "so as to make available, so far as possible, to all the people of the United States, a rapid, efficient, Nation-wide, and world-wide wire . . . communications service with adequate facilities at reasonable charges. . . ."[1]

Universal service was a goal to strive for in the mid-1930s. So few Americans had phones in 1936 that a *Literary Digest* poll conducted exclusively by telephone predicted that Alf Landon would oust Franklin Roosevelt from the White House that year—while the election returns gave FDR the most lopsided margin of victory in Presidential politics up to that time. Ten elections later, 95% of all American households were wired into a telephone system.[2] Long distance calls are commonplace, no longer the cause for wonderment that they were in 1915, when Bell himself placed the first transcontinental call from New York to San Francisco. Today, wires and microwaves bind the disparate sections of the nation into a unified whole.

Even more dramatic is the growth and penetration of the electronic media, radio and television. Only a few hundred people got the news over station KDKA that Harding had defeated Cox in November 1920—compared with the 98% of all American households that own at least one radio today.[3] And, of course,

in the last 30 years, television has captured the popular imagination. Almost every home has a TV set; nearly half have two; three-quarters have at least one color set—and the set (or sets) are on for more than six hours each day.[4]

Television has come to dominate American life like nothing before it. More people get their news from TV than from any other source. More people buy *TV Guide* than buy any other magazine.[5] The national culture has immediately absorbed the distinguishing features and mannerisms of television characters and personalities—from Davy Crockett's coonskin cap to Maxwell Smart's "Sorry about that, Chief" to the Fonz. By aiming for the mass audience, television is homogenizing the nation—giving us all the same bland programs, selling us all the same deodorant and dishwashing detergent. Through TV, everyone has "seen" the Capitol and the White House, the Grand Canyon and Old Faithful, the wild West and the Mysterious East.

But it is essential for us to realize that television is much more than our "window to the world," and that radio has a greater function than presenting the top 40 each week. Radio and television, in the words of former FCC Commissioner Nicholas Johnson, "constitute our society's cerebral cortex." It is via the electronic mass media that we identify and think through our public policy issues, evaluate our candidates, formulate public opinion, and govern ourselves.[6]

The success of the democratic form of government depends upon an adequately educated and informed electorate; television and radio inform and educate most of America's electorate today. We premise our democracy on the notion that the wisest public policy will emerge from an uncensored dialogue—the clash of opinions in the marketplace of ideas. "Today," observes Johnson, "democracy's dialogue is going to take place on radio and television or it's not going to take place at all. Conversations after Sunday services, debates in the town hall, and occasional handbill campaigns just don't have the impact on society that they did 200 years ago."[7]

Given the immense importance of our

telecommunications network to contemporary America, we must understand who controls neurons and synapses of the societal cerebral cortex. (I would include within that concept not only radio and television, but also the telephone system.) In Europe, citizens, through their governments, own the telephone lines and some of the broadcasting facilities. Americans, by contrast, have left the development of telecommunications to the private sector, under the watchful (in theory, at least) eye of the Federal Communications Commission. The result has been a hugely profitable communications industry, regulated by an FCC that only occasionally safeguards the "public interest, convenience, and necessity."

The Telephone Industry

Since Mr. Watson harkened to Alexander Graham Bell's distress call in 1876, "Ma Bell" has been synonymous with "telephone" in this country. Six out of every seven phones in the United States are hooked into the Bell System.[8] The American Telephone & Telegraph Company (AT&T), the Bell System's parent, is now the biggest corporation on earth. Its assets total $93.9 billion, more than the combined assets of General Motors, Ford, General Electric, Chrysler, and IBM—and larger than the GNPs of most of the world's nations. It employs almost one million people. Its yearly income exceeds $4 billion—$11 million daily, in other words, or $7,500 per minute.[9]

Western Electric, the manufacturing unit of AT&T, produces 95% of all terminal equipment (such as home phones and business exchanges) in use today. Bell Labs (developer of the transistor), Long Lines (which manages all interstate and foreign calls), and 23 operating companies (like New York Telephone and Southwestern Bell, which provide local and intrastate service) are also part of AT&T's gargantuan family. Recently, independent companies have challenged AT&T's vise-like grip on the terminal equipment market, and on the market for private line services that can link distant branch offices of a single business. But AT&T's revenues continue to grow.

Beginning in the early part of this century, AT&T became a regulated monopoly, much like gas and electric companies. State public service commissions set the rates that phone companies may charge for local and intrastate service; the rates must be "reasonable," under the typical state statute, and each phone company must receive a "fair rate of return" on its capital investment. But these are mushy standards, and phone companies' rate requests are often controversial. New York Telephone, for example, requested a $240 million rate hike in December 1978—despite the fact that the New York Public Service Commission has granted the phone company almost $1.5 billion in rate increases since 1970. The Consumer Affairs Commissioner for New York City termed the request "hard to believe," and advised the public to "demand cost-cutting and productivity increases" from the phone company.[10]

Broadcasting

The owners of most commercial radio and television stations—particularly television station owners—have also reaped handsome profits from their investments (though, of course, their profits do not approach the scale of AT&T's). Commercial AM radio stations reported pre-tax earnings of more than $157 million in 1976; in that same year, FM stations earned a total of over $21 million.

As we might expect, however, the big money is in television. The 680 commercial TV stations operating in 1976 netted over $1.25 billion. But the 680 stations did not share in the profit pie equally. For one thing, VHF stations do much better than station broadcasting on the UHF band. For another, power in the television industry is concentrated in the three national networks, and a closer look at the profit figures reflects that dominance.[11]

Each network owns and operates five television stations (the so-called "O & O" stations). Each network has stations in the three largest markets (New York City, Los Angeles, and Chicago) and two others in other major markets (such as Philadelphia (fourth largest), Washington, D.C. (ninth), and Detroit (seventh)). Through their control of the O & Os, each network completely dictates the programming that reaches about one-quarter of the population of the United States. And O & Os do quite well financially, thank you. In 1976, they earned their owners a combined $159 million—well over 10% of the earnings of all the stations in the nation combined. On top of those profits, the networks earned almost $300 million in the same year from their services through their affiliates. The aggregate earnings of the networks and their stations represent more than one-third of the total profits of the television industry.[12]

All of which is not to say, however, that independent businessmen, with close ties to their communities, control the remaining 665 or so television stations. On the contrary, concentration of ownership in the broadcast media is a growing trend. More than 68% of all stations are owned by companies that hold two or more television licenses in the top 50 markets. In the top 25 markets, more than 75% of all television stations are owned by companies that hold two or more licenses. Metromedia, for instance, owns seven stations in the top 25 markets; it controls the programming that reaches 30% of all households in the top 50 markets—markets that account for two-thirds of all the television households in the country. Storer Broadcasting's six stations reach one-quarter of the top 50 market's households.[13]

Newspaper ownership of about 27% of all commercial television stations further illustrates the concentration within the industry. Newspapers and publishers have also bought into cable television: as of 1976, they owned over one-quarter of the systems operating in the U.S. (Not wanting to be left out, broadcasters accounted for the ownership of another 32% of all cable systems.)[14] Recently, the FCC adopted rules barring future newspaper-broadcasting combinations. The rules are a start toward promoting diverse ownership of the electronic media.

II

I have tried to sketch a picture of the extraordinary concentration of economic power (not to mention its twin, political power) that confronts the citizen who wants to make America's telecommunications industries more responsive to the public they are supposed to serve. Not surprisingly, the Goliaths of those industries do not rely solely on sheer size to discourage citizen activism. AT&T, for example, is fond of telling us that "The system is the solution." Never mind accountability and responsibility; a totally integrated, unassailable corporate structure makes America's wires hum most efficiently. Of course, Bell is not so fond of telling us that the U.S. Department of Justice is trying to break up that corporate structure because it allegedly violates antitrust laws. Similarly, AT&T never tires of proclaiming that users of business telephones subsidize residential customers. But in more candid moments, Bell admits that it is not really sure how to allocate the costs of the services it provides, or which way subsidies flow.[15] A Massachusetts study has shown that residential customers are subsidizing everyone else.[16] And one consumer advocate has estimated that the Bell System overcharges residential customers by more than $3 billion yearly, and that residential customers subsidize business customers by as much as $2.25 billion annually.[17] Sadly, Lily Tomlin's reference to the uncaring, arrogant phone company is right on target.

The television industry is not a whole lot better. No doubt more than one disgruntled viewer has considered following the lead of John Gardner's fictional James Page by picking up a shotgun and blowing "that TV screen to hell, right back where it came from." If you are under 18, over 49, not white, or not interested in a steady diet of Westerns, police shows, sitcoms, or jiggle shows (depending upon what's most profitable this season), the industry leaves you little choice. Of course, television executives claim that they merely give the public what it wants; if you don't like it, they say, turn off your set and read a book. But that would not reverse the trend toward concentration of ownership, or replace the triopoly of network domination with "the widest possible dissemination of information from diverse and antagonistic sources (that is) essential to the welfare of the public."[18] Reform demands active citizen involvement, not passive acceptance of the status quo.

Besides, the industry's claim that it simply serves the public taste is self-serving nonsense. Police shows, for example, may be "what the public wants" only because that is all the public gets from the networks. If the public had direct control over network programming departments, it might opt for more well-produced public affairs shows—witness the success of CBS News's *60 Minutes.*

But what about the FCC? Don't the Commissioners protect the public's rights—at least in the broadcasting field? (And many would argue that the FCC decisions permitting competition in the terminal equipment and private line areas will ultimately benefit the public, too.) Well, yes, to some extent they do. The Communications Act of 1934 charges the Commission with the duty of parceling out a scarce public resource—the electromagnetic spectrum—to competing would-be broadcasters. The Commission may grant a license only "if the public convenience, interest, or necessity will be served thereby."[19] Each broadcaster's piece of the public's airwaves costs him nothing (except for a very minimal license processing fee); you more readily understand a broadcaster's ample profits when you consider that he obtains his single most important asset practically *gratis.*

The broadcaster is not totally without obligation to the public, however. The FCC requires that he present some local programming, and some non-entertainment shows. He also has an affirmative responsibility to devote a reasonable percentage of time to controversial issues of public importance, and to present both sides of such issues; this is the so-called "Fairness Doctrine." In compliance with the "Equal Time Rule," a broadcaster who offers time to one candidate for public office must offer equal time to all other candidates for the same office. He must offer reply time to those who are attacked on the air, and to those who disagree with editorial stands that the licensee takes. The FCC also encourages each broadcaster to set aside time for free announcements, known as "public service announcements," that promote programs, activities, or services of Federal, state, or local governments—or the programs of nonprofit organizations.

Each of these requirements is phrased in the most general terms. The FCC has never quantified minimum standards for, say, the number and frequency of public service announcements that a licensee should broadcast in order to serve the public interest adequately. The same is true for programming to meet local and community needs, and for nonentertainment programming. And although each broadcaster must apply to the Commission every three years to have his license renewed—when he must in theory demonstrate his commitment to the "public interest, convenience, and necessity"—the Commissioners routinely approve thousands of renewal applications submitted by broadcasters who present only the most infinitesimal amounts of local, non-entertainment, and public service programming. Some broadcasters present no such programming at all.[20]

The Fairness Doctrine, local programming requirements, encouragement of public service announcements, and the rest of the guidelines mentioned above were designed to enhance the value of radio and television for the listening and viewing public that regards the broadcast media as its prime source of information and entertainment. Indeed, in its first enunciation of the Fairness Doctrine, the FCC recognized "the basic policy of the Congress that radio be maintained as a medium of free speech for the general public as a whole rather than as an outlet for the purely personal or private interests of the licensee."[21] Yet despite this emphasis on the rights of the public, the FCC prevented citizen groups from taking an active role in communications policy until recently.

For many years, the Commission was considered "the guardian of the public interest in broadcasting."[22] Meanwhile, the FCC placed pirmary responsibility for the improvement of programming service upon the broadcasters themselves. The public's role was minimal: "(it) was expected to advise and support stations in their efforts to achieve better quality programming."[23] Members of the general public had no power to intervene directly in the license renewal process. That right was reserved to those who could show that the grant or renewal of a license would cause them economic injury, or would result in electrical interference with their operations. And until 1960, the Commission did not even have procedures for receiving and processing complaints from the public about programming. (In that year, it established the Complaints and Compliance Bureau.)

But one persistent group of citizens was able to change Commission policy, and to gain for members of the public the ability to participate actively in the FCC's decision-making process. The change resulted from a challenge to the license renewal application of WLBT-TV in Jackson, Mississippi.

During the 1950s and 1960s, white-owned WLBT violated the Fairness Doctrine by presenting only one side of the racial integration issue to a broadcast audience that was almost 45% black. In 1955, for instance, the station deliberately cut off a network program about race relations on which the General Counsel of the NAACP was appearing, and flashed on viewers' screens a "Sorry, Cable Trouble" sign. On other occasions, WLBT presented programs urging the maintenance of racial segregation, without airing the opposite viewpoint. When the station sought license renewal in 1964, the United Church of Christ, which had a substantial membership in the Jackson area, filed a petition to block renewal, and to intervene on its own behalf and as "representative of all other television viewers in the State of Mississippi." The FCC denied the petition to intervene, and granted a one-year renewal of WLBT's license.

The Church of Christ appealed to the U.S. Court of Appeals for the District of Columbia Circuit. That court granted the Church standing to intervene in the Commission proceeding. Circuit Judge Warren Burger, now Chief Justice of the U.S. Supreme Court, dismissed the theory that the Commission can always effectively represent listener interests in a renewal proceeding without the aid and participation of listener representatives. That theory, wrote Burger, "is one of those assumptions we collectively try to work with so long as they are reasonably adequate. When it becomes clear, as it does to us now, that it is no longer a valid assumption which stands up under the realities of actual experience," he concluded, "neither we nor the Commission can continue to rely on it."[24] A citizen group that intervenes in an FCC proceeding is "performing a public service" by giving the Commission the fullest possible picture of the licensee's performance: it is the FCC's ally.[25]

Since the Court of Appeals opened the door in the WLBT case, more and more citizen groups have taken advantage of their right to intervene at license renewal time. In 1969, only two petitions to deny renewal were filed against two stations; between July 1, 1972, and May 15, 1977, various groups filed 237 petitions to deny the license renewals of 618 stations.[26] That's the good news. The bad news is that the FCC has dismissed all but 20 of those petitions without even granting the petitioners a hearing. Only one licensee designated for a hearing because of a citizen group's petition to deny has been refused renewal. The Commission has never, on its own motion, failed to renew a broadcast license on the ground that the licensee had failed to serve the needs and interests of its community.

But judicial recognition of the right of ordinary citizens to participate in broadcast regulation has spurred the development of a few tiny, underfunded public interest law firms that work exclusively in the communications field, such as the Media Access Project and the Citizens Communications Center, both in Washington, D.C. One of them argued successfully in court that the public has an interest in a diversity of entertainment formats ("top 40," "all news," etc.) and therefore that format changes can be detrimental to the public interest. Consequently, the FCC has been ordered to "consider format changes and their effect on desired diversity" when it reviews proposed station sales.[27] Citizens Communications Center has also participated in FCC rulemaking proceedings regarding the Prime Time Access Rule (which limits the amount of network programming a station can air during an evening); the limitations on newspaper-television cross-ownership; the availability of program logs and public file material; and the development and enforcement of equal employment opportunity guidelines.[28]

What's more, according to *Broadcasting* magazine, the petitions to deny license renewals filed over the years "have helped sensitize broadcasters to the needs and demands of groups in their communities, even if few stations have actually lost licenses."[29] Granting citizen groups the right to appear before the FCC has given those groups a strong bargaining position: rather than spend money in an administrative battle, a number of station owners have made agreements guaranteeing the kind of employment and programming practices that local citizens regard as being in the public interest. Negotiations between citizen groups and a Texarkana, Texas, television station, for instance, produced promises from the station to hire more black reporters, to air more shows dealing with controversial issues, and to increase local programming.[30]

Far fewer citizen groups have attempted to call the telephone company to account, perhaps because the prospect of grappling with Ma Bell before a state regulatory commission requires more resources than most citizen groups can command. A locally based consumer organization, for example, does not ordinarily have the money or the staff to undertake a study of Bell's rate structure—yet no group could challenge a rate hike request without thoroughly understanding the concepts upon which Bell bases its charges. Effective citizen monitoring—of the phone company or of the broadcasting industry—requires broad based organization and a steady, independent source of adequate funding.

III

Congressional efforts to rewrite the Communications Act began in 1977 with oversight hearings conducted by the House Subcommittee on Communications, under the direction of subcommittee Chairman Lionel Van Deerlin (D-Calif.). Following the hearings, the subcommittee published a volume of "Options Papers" that described a range of policy choices in broadcasting, cable, and common carrier.[31] Van Deerlin's own preferences in communications policy became clear with his

introduction of the "Communications Act of 1978" in June 1978. Underlying his proposal was a desire to "deregulate" communications. "Government," the chairman wrote shortly after he introduced the bill, "should regulate only when marketplace forces are deficient."[32]

Van Deerlin's deregulation of broadcasting was breathtaking: the Communications Act of 1978 eliminated the requirement that broadcasters serve "the public interest, convenience, and necessity"; it immediately granted radio stations licenses with indefinite terms, good unless the Communications Regulatory Commission (successor agency to the FCC) granted a "petition to revoke"; it did the same for television licenses beginning in 1988; it assessed a "spectrum use fee" on all broadcasters; it weakened the Fairness Doctrine, scaled down the Equal Time Rule (making it valid only for local elections), and restricted the applicability of both to television —totally absolving radio from committing any resources to public affairs programming.

Under this first Van Deerlin proposal, a deregulated phone industry would have seen increased competition in the private line and terminal equipment markets (which the FCC has already sanctioned). But, in exchange for divesting itself of Western Electric, a still-gargantuan AT&T would have been allowed to enter the data processing field (which a 1956 agreement with the Justice Department closed to Bell), and presumably the cable TV field.

While Van Deerlin's bill was never enacted, subsequent debate over communications policy has centered around the merits of deregulation. House and Senate bills introduced since 1978 have differed on details (one bill would simply extend licenses for radio and television from three years to ten years, rather than grant permanent licenses, for example; the most recently-proposed legislation would permit AT&T to keep Western Electric, but require Bell to establish a "fully separate subsidiary" to manufacture and market unregulated products and services), but the belief that "marketplace forces" will serve the public better than any regulatory scheme still animates many Capitol Hill policymakers. As they see it, unfettered competition in telecommunications will promote the development of new technology. In the telephone field, competition and new technology will lower the price we pay to communicate with each other—while simultaneously expanding our notion of what it means to communicate. As the line between telephone and data processing blurs, for example, homes may be equipped with computers that can tap into our libraries, news wire services, banks, and stores. Letters could be sent electronically. In broadcasting, two-way cable, fiber optics, and direct satellite-to-home transmission would offer wider program choices than the three networks and syndication companies offer now. Diversity brought into the home over a 60-channel cable system would eliminate the need for the Fairness Doctrine and the Equal Time Rule: if you have something to say, simply lease a channel (with 60, one won't cost much) and put your views forward.[33]

The deregulators' vision is tempting—especially to a nation that has always been fascinated by gadgets and would probably relish the prospect of new sophisticated communication technology. "Deregulation" is their way of ensuring that the dead hand of the FCC cannot block that vision as it has blocked innovations in the past. Van Deerlin himself illustrated the point several years ago:

> FM radio, with its superior tone and spectrum space for hundreds of new stations, waited more than two decades for licensing. Pay TV —the option of watching programs without commercial interruption, for a fee—was long denied American householders under FCC rules that the courts recently adjudged arbitrary and capricious.[34]

But while deregulation is appropriate for airlines and trucks, it may not be proper for broadcasting and telephones. Freed from the Civil Aeronautics Board's price and route restrictions, numerous air carriers will compete to offer passengers more and cheaper service. Reason? The airline industry is workably competitive right now, and deregulation will allow market forces to operate. Contrast this with the concentration of power that characterizes telecommunications: three billion-

dollar conglomerates control our television; the largest company in the world provides our phone service. Deregulating telecommunications would replace government direction with an anti-competitive private cartel.

Under those circumstances, leaving the development and dissemination of new technologies to "the marketplace" is at best naive. It's a little like trusting the wolves to make sure that the sheep population increases. With their reservoirs of capital and their stranglehold on the industry, AT&T and the networks' parent companies could assume a dominant role in developing new technologies. And by dominating new technologies, those companies would continue to control telecommunications.

At the very least, the established giants' control over information means that they will to a large extent determine how much the public learns about new communications technology. And if the recent past is any indication, the answer to "how much" is "not much." In the . . . years that the House Communications Subcommittee has been considering the rewrite, no commercial network has produced a program to publicize this unprecedented effort. No network has produced a program introducing advances in communications technology to the public. We have had to rely on commercial messages and the print media for information on video cassette recorders, satellites, cable, alternatives to Bell terminal equipment, and the rest. The networks and AT&T understand well that the uninformed consumer will out of habit desire nothing more than the three detective shows, and the same overpriced telephone equipment, that he already has.

In 15 or 20 years, technological advances could loosen the grip that the giants now have on American telecommunications. But that will not happen in ten years simply because someone sets a date for deregulation of television ten years hence. And it will not happen simply because Bell is forced to divest Western Electric. Decentralization of our telecommunications system will come only as a workably competitive market develops and matures. Until then, deregulation will serve merely to give some of the largest conglomerates in the world the power to determine the shape of communications for the next 50 years.

Ultimately, total deregulation is an inappropriate policy for telecommunications. Even in the most perfect of markets, it would reduce the citizen's role to that of a consumer voting with his dollars. That role is proper when the subject is ordinary consumer goods. But when we are dealing with communications —society's "cerebral cortex"—we cannot rely solely on marketplace forces to determine what is in the "public interest." A broadcaster who is concerned only with his balance sheet would probably not choose to air news and public affairs shows, which are generally less popular than light entertainment (at least as measured by the ratings services). Yet we as a society may decide that such programs are essential if we are to remain informed about the issues of the day. There are other social goals—such as the dissemination of minority views to the majority—that competition alone will not fulfill because fulfilling those goals is unprofitable.

Given this critical flaw in the marketplace model, any reformulation of communications law must guarantee citizens an *active* role in shaping the nation's telecommunications system. At the very least, that means retaining a legal mechanism that will allow citizens to challenge the actions of the telecommunications industries—the rate-setting practices of AT&T, for example, or the programming or minority hiring decisions of broadcasters and cablecasters. New legislation would serve a valuable purpose if it fleshed out the citizen rights inherent in the public interest standard. Once citizen rights are in place, Congress and the state legislatures could take specific steps to ensure that industry and government can hear the public's voices. I propose a few steps below; they are not mutually exclusive.

Public participation funding. Prior to the WLBT decision in 1966, the FCC heard almost exclusively from representatives of the telecommunications industries. Those industries possessed (and continue to possess) the high degree of involvement, economic strength, and organizational cohesion to present their views to the FCC consistently and coherently.

Since 1966, the participation of citizen groups has provided the Commissioners with a greater range of ideas and information than the communications industries alone have offered. The addition of alternative viewpoints has made it more likely that some Commission decisions will serve the interests of the general public.

But it's not as though the FCC now simply referees a fair fight between citizen groups and industry representatives. A Senate study on public participation in regulatory agency proceedings found that "participation by public or nonregulated interests before Federal regulatory agencies is consistently exceeded by the participation of regulated industries . . . In agency after agency, participation by the regulated industry predominates—often overwhelmingly."[35] When the FCC, for instance, was considering the need for adequate television service for New Jersey (which has no VHF station of its own), 64 industry groups submitted comments; only 14 public interest groups did so.[36]

Remember also that citizen groups appearing before the FCC must take on some of the wealthiest corporations in the nation— and sometimes the wealthiest in the world. In a single proceeding, AT&T spent over $1 million to submit studies to the Commission in support of its position. For the year ending December 31, 1975, the communications behemoth reported almost $2¼ million in FCC expenses. Eighty percent of that amount was incurred in just three dockets.[37] The Senate study's conclusion that "comparing public interest costs to industry costs is like comparing David to Goliath" is especially true for FCC proceedings.[38]

In light of the importance courts have placed on citizen participation, particularly before the FCC, Congress and the State Legislatures should enact some means of funding citizen groups that can substantially contribute to a fair determination of Commission proceedings, but that lack the wherewithal to participate effectively. On the Federal level, funded citizen groups could intervene in license renewals, as well as help determine communications policy by initiating and participating in Commission rulemaking. On the state level, a funding mechanism would facilitate consumer participation before the utility commissions that set rates for phone service.

Congress has already authorized several agencies and departments—including the Federal Trade Commission, the Civil Aeronautics Board, and the Department of Agriculture—to fund public participation in their proceedings. According to Senator Edward M. Kennedy, the citizen funding program at the F.T.C. has "exceeded all expectations." Public participation, Kennedy has said, "greatly assisted the F.T.C. in issuing trade regulations."[39]

Citizen access to the airwaves and the cable. Scarcity of spectrum space, and the understanding that the broadcasters were trustees of public property, have over the years meant that the broadcast media has enjoyed less than the full First Amendment rights accorded to the print media. The Supreme Court put its finger on this distinction when it upheld the constitutionality of the Fairness Doctrine:

> Where there are substantially more individuals who want to broadcast than there are frequencies to allocate, it is idle to posit an unabridgeable First Amendment right to broadcast comparable to the right of every individual to speak, write, or publish.[40]

In short, not everyone can have a frequency; thus, those fortunate enough to get one must present both sides of controversial issues, afford candidates for public office equal time, and generally serve the "public interest, convenience, and necessity." The government does not encroach on day-to-day programming decisions as long as broadcasters follow those general rules. The public, for its part, presumably benefits from exposure to a wide variety of opinion on the issues of the day.

But under this regime, broadcasting has evolved into a multi-billion dollar business, and the public has had to make do with superficial newscasts and inadequate public affairs programming. Broadcast executives talk knowingly of "what the public wants," but whenever someone suggests giving the public air time to say what it wants, those same executives raise the First Amendment banner

high.[41] Providing citizens with airtime violates the broadcaster's constitutional rights, we are told; the broadcaster can present all the important views on all the important issues.

Yet is is hard to believe that CBS News, a division of a billion-dollar conglomerate, has First Amendment rights that protect it from "encroachments" by American citizens. And, fortunately, that is not the case. "It is the rights of the viewers and listeners, not the right of the broadcasters, which is paramount," a unanimous Supreme Court declared in the Fairness Doctrine case. "It is the purpose of the First Amendment," continued the Justices, "to preserve an uninhibited marketplace of ideas in which truth will ultimately prevail, rather than to countenance monopolization of that market, whether it be by the Government itself or a private licensee."[42]

The First Amendment rests on the assumption that "the widest possible dissemination of information from diverse and antagonistic sources is essential to the welfare of the public."[43] Editors have a right to be free from government interference; members of the public have a right to communicate ideas and information to one another. And the public's right is hollow in this day and age unless citizens have access to the nation's most powerful medium.

Ultimately, citizen access validates the notion of the marketplace of ideas. We do not tolerate economic concentration in the commercial marketplace, and Congress has passed antitrust laws to prevent it. By the same token, competition in the marketplace of ideas requires many spokespersons putting forward many opinions. Concentrated control of the outlets for expression discourages competition.[44] A citizen (or a citizen group) must have the freedom to present his views in whatever form he chooses. As Supreme Court Justice William J. Brennan has stated:

> It is clear that the effectiveness of an individual's expression of his views is as dependent on the style and format of presentation as it is on the content itself. And the relegation of an individual's views to such tightly controlled formats as the news, documentaries, edited interviews, or panel discussions may tend to

minimize, rather than maximize the effectiveness of speech.[45]

The Federal government could effectuate the citizen's right of access by conditioning broadcasting licenses on the licensee's promise to set aside a certain amount of time (a few hours each week, say) for presentations by members of the public. Airtime could be granted either on a first-come, first-served basis, or on the basis of demonstrated community support for a particular citizen group, or some mixture of the two. Nowhere is it written that a commercial broadcaster must have use of his portion of the spectrum all the time. (In England, two separate companies share a single frequency. In Holland, citizen groups of 15,000 or more are entitled to some airtime each week.) We must bear in mind that the spectrum remains a public resource, and the public may reserve time on its property for its own uses.

Lionel Van Deerlin argues that the scarcity rationale for treating electronic mass media differently than print media disappears when one considers the abundance of channels that cable and fiber optics will make available. But Van Deerlin overlooks two things. In the first place, a local cable TV operation, like a local telephone system, is a natural monopoly: it will only pay one firm to run a coaxial cable (or an optical fiber) through a city. Unless the Fairness Doctrine, the Equal Time Rule, and provisions for citizen access are applied to a cable operator, that operator would have complete control over the information that electronically entered the homes connected to the cable system. The opportunity for diverse groups to express their views would be left solely in the hands of the businessmen who owned the cable.

Alternatively, we could regulate the cable system as a "common carrier," just as we regulate the phone system. As a common carrier, the cable company would not originate any programming. It would instead act simply as a conduit for whoever wanted to send a program through the wires; the sender might reach a viewer connected with the cable system, but he might not.

The very real possibility that someone using one of 60 or so cable channels to communicate with others will reach almost nobody raises the second problem with Van Deerlin's conclusion that cable abundance will end the need to regulate the electronic media. Cablecasting, as one writer has observed, "does not promise a solution to the problem of access to the mass media for minority views and expression."[46] If as a society we truly desire to expose the majority to minority opinions, then it is insufficient merely to give the minority a cable channel that few citizens will ever watch. The First Amendment goal of producing an informed public capable of conducting its own affairs is more effectively served by positive regulations that encourage the exposure of minority views on the mass medium that will doubtlessly remain. A "separate-but-equal" policy that relegates minority positions to channels that only serve audience fragments runs the risk of further isolating the majority from minority opinion.[47]

Citizen action groups. The citizen groups that have appeared before the FCC tend to be loosely structured organizations that have taken an interest in a particular proceeding—such as the license renewal application of a local station owner, an application for the transfer of a license, or a challenge to a specific licensee's programming or employment practices. Only a few organizations have participated in FCC rulemaking proceedings. No citizen group has had the resources to operate on a systematic and continuing basis with a full-time staff of lawyers, economists, and media experts—all with adequate funding; no group has had the political clout to urge revisions in communications law that would benefit members of the public. The establishment of "citizen action groups"— with the requisite resources and clout—would guarantee effective public participation in all phases of telecommunications policy.

I suggest the formation of two such groups: one would concentrate on broadcast and cable issues—call this group Audience, Inc.: the other would give residential telephone customers a voice in rate making proceedings—call it the Telephone Citizen Action Group (TeleCAG).[48]

How would a citizen action group work? As a first step, Congress or a state legislature would establish a nonprofit corporation, say

Audience, Inc., to represent the interests of its members before relevant regulatory bodies (the FCC, state cable commissions), the courts, and the legislature itself. Anyone over the age of 16 who watches television or listens to the radio could become a member of Audience by contributing a small amount, perhaps two dollars annually, to the organization. Members' contributions would constitute Audience's sole source of revenue; the group would require no expenditure of tax dollars. If there were insufficient interest in the Audience concept, the group would fail for lack of funds. A member of the group who disagreed with the course the group took could simply stop contributing, or become more involved in Audience's activities.

Audience would be governed democratically. Members would elect a board of directors to decide what sort of projects the group would pursue. Projects might include lobbying for passage of a broadcast reform measure; litigating a case of racial discrimination by a station manager; conducting economic studies into the effect of cable on off-the-air transmissions; and monitoring children's programming on local stations. Of course, the directors would remain accountable to their constituency, and a director who advocated unpopular policies would risk defeat when he or she stood for re-election to the board.

So that Audience could reach members of the public, the FCC would grant the group a sublicense on each broadcast and cable station. Under the terms of the sublicense, Audience would have one minute each night during prime time television to present a message. During that time slot, Audience could solicit members, explain its activities, or inform viewers about current media reform issues. The sublicense would also guarantee Audience an aggregate of four hours of prime time during the year for longer program presentations. While air time would be free to Audience, the organization would pay all production costs of its messages and programs. The Audience group, in short, would serve as a self-funded, independent, ongoing communications link among members of the listening and viewing public.

TeleCAG would serve the same function for residential telephone customers as Audience would for viewers and listeners. Before state public utility commissions, the FCC, the courts, the state legislatures, and Congress, TeleCAG—a governmentally-chartered non-profit corporation—would represent the interests of the consumers who contributed a small monthly amount to the group. Like Audience, TeleCAG would be organized democratically, governed by an elected board of directors who would decide what projects to undertake. TeleCAG's functions would not be restricted to litigation or lobbying. The group might, for instance, hire economists to conduct studies of the telephone rate structure.

To solicit funds and members, TeleCAG would enclose information about itself in each residential phone bill. Customers would be invited to check a box on the phone bill if they wished to join the group, and then add a minimal sum, perhaps 25¢, to the amount that they sent to the phone company. The phone company would then calculate the amount of contributions to TeleCAG, segregate that sum from total monies received, deduct any processing costs, and forward the remaining amount to TeleCAG. Alternatively, customers could send contributions directly to TeleCAG.

By no means would Audience and TeleCAG purport to represent all viewers or all telephone customers. Many groups, with varied views, should be encouraged to participate in communications issues. The citizen action group model is simply an attempt to institutionalize consumer representation through a citizen-run, citizen-funded organization that can engage in sustained, wide-ranging activity on behalf of its members. That sort of institution is missing from the American scene, though it has long been needed. And besides, participating in Audience would get you infinitely more than blasting a hole in your TV screen.

Notes

1. Communications Act of 1934, 47 U.S.C. §151 (1970).
2. STAFF OF HOUSE SUBCOMM. ON COMMUNI- CATIONS, 95TH CONG., 1ST SESS., OPTIONS PAPERS 354 (Subcomm. Print 1977).

3. C. STERLING & T. HAIGHT, THE MASS MEDIA (1978), 368. Hereinafter cited as MASS MEDIA.

4. MASS MEDIA, 372, 374.

5. MASS MEDIA, 273, 346.

6. The New York Times, November 19, 1978, §2, at 1.

7. The Nation, September 30, 1978, at 299.

8. OPTIONS PAPERS, 356.

9. The New York Times, January 9, 1978, D1; Business Week, November 6, 1978, 118.

10. The New York Times, December 12, 1978, A1.

11. Network dominance is also illustrated by the fact that the three webs provide 80% of each day's total programming to about 600 affiliated stations.

12. MASS MEDIA, 203, 211; 42 Fed. Reg. 4993 (1977).

13. Comments of NAACP, submitted to the Federal Communications Commission in the matter of Amendment of Section 73.636(a) of the Commission's Rules, August 7, 1978, at 2; Appendix I at 10, 2.

14. MASS MEDIA, 96, 105.

15. Business Week, November 6, 1978, 125.

16. Report of the Massachusetts Department of Public Utilities, cited in J. Oppenheim, Wrong Number—Consumer Frauds, Inflated Costs and Predatory Prices (speech delivered at the Consumer Telephone Workshop, Washington, DC, December 11, 1978), at 9.

17. Oppenheim, note 16 *supra*, at 1.

18. Associated Press v. U.S., 326 U.S. 1, 20 (1945).

19. Communications Act of 1934, 47 U.S.C. §307(a) (1970).

20. B. COLE & M. OETTINGER, RELUCTANT REGULATORS (1978), 146–187. Hereinafter cited as RELUCTANT REGULATORS.

21. 13 F.C.C. 1257 (1949).

22. Volner, Broadcast Regulation: Is There Too Much "Public" in the "Public Interest," 43 CINN. L. REV. 267.

23. Volner, note 22 *supra,* at 270–271.

24. United Church of Christ v. F.C.C., 359 F.2d 994, 1003–1004 (D.C. Cir. 1966).

25. United Church of Christ v. F.C.C., 425 F2d 543, 548–549 (D.C. Cir. 1969).

26. RELUCTANT REGULATORS, 205.

27. Citizens Committee to Save WEFM v. F.C.C., 506 F.2d 246, 261 (D.C. Circ. 1974).

28. Public Participation in Federal Agency Proceedings, S. 2715: Hearings Before the Subcommittee on Ad-

min. Practice & Proced. of the Senate Judiciary Comm., 94th Cong., 2d Sess., 196–209 (statement of Frank Lloyd).

29. Broadcasting, July 2, 1973, quoted in Hearings, note 28 *supra,* 182 (statement of Frank Lloyd).

30. RELUCTANT REGULATORS, 232–233; see generally, 228–241.

31. OPTIONS PAPERS, note 2 *supra.*

32. Newsday, July 31, 1978, 37.

33. For descriptions of the new broadcast technology, see Newsweek, July 3, 1978; The New York Times, July 31, 1978, C12; Saturday Review, September 16, 1978, 24.

34. Newsday, note 32 *supra.*

35. SENATE COMM. ON GOVERNMENTAL AFFAIRS, STUDY ON FEDERAL REGULATION, VOL. III, S. DOC. NO. 95–71, 95TH CONG. 1ST SESS. 12, 16 (1977). Hereinafter cited as SENATE STUDY.

36. SENATE STUDY, 14.

37. SENATE STUDY, 18, 21.

38. SENATE STUDY, 22.

39. Edward Kennedy, Citizen Involvement: Present Realities and Future Prospects (September 29, 1978) (Speech delivered at Tufts University)

40. Red Lion Broadcasting Co. v. F.C.C., 395 U.S. 367, 388 (1969).

41. See, e.g., The New York Times, Dec. 11, 1978, A24.

42. 395 U.S. 390.

43. Associated Press v. U.S., 326 U.S. 1, 20 (1945).

44. For a discussion of the pluralist interpretation of the First Amendment, see D. Simon, Who Governs After Buckley (May 1, 1978) (unpublished paper submitted in satisfaction of the written work requirement, Harvard Law School), 59–64.

45. CBS v. DNC, 412 U.S. 94, 190 (1973) (Brennan, J., dissenting).

46. D. LaPierre, Cable Television and the Promise of Programming Diversity, 42 FORD. L. REV. 25, 120 (1973).

47. LaPierre, note 43 *supra,* 123–124.

48. For detailed discussions of citizen action groups, including model statutes, see R. Leflar & M. Rogol, Consumer Participation in the Regulation of Public Utilities: A Model Act, 13 HARV. J. LEGIS. 235 (1976); A. Best & B. Brown, Governmental Facilitation of Consumerism: A Proposal for Consumer Action Groups, 50 TEMP. L. Q. 253 (1977).

4

How Networks Test for Audience Impact

Miles Beller

Predicting audience response to television programs, movies, and commercials is important to networks, studios, producers, and advertisers. While these groups use many research methods to gauge audience reaction in advance, one of the most prominent is the testing technique used at Preview House by Audience Studies, Incorporated (ASI).

In this selection, Miles Beller explains how the ASI method pinpoints particular elements in a program and measures the audience's precise reactions. Despite arguments that the system promotes mediocrity, television and movie executives rely heavily upon such research in making critical programming or promotion decisions.

Modern audience testing practices go far beyond Beller's account of Preview House, particularly for advertising and popular recordings. Peter Bernstein's article on psychographics in advertising research (selection 6 in this book) and Michael Gross's look at "skin testing" for hit records (selection 39) provide additional insight into current methods of predicting audience response.

The coming season's war between the networks promises to be more fierce than ever. Will ABC, accustomed to the top spot, be able to maintain its position over second-place CBS? Will Fred Silverman, the commander of beleaguered NBC, be able to deliver on his recent prediction that by Christmas his network will overtake at least CBS? While the results will only begin to come into focus this fall, what is clear now is that all three of the networks have enlisted an arsenal of "weapons" to help gain the upper hand in the fray. Of those weapons, one that is becoming increasingly relied upon is ASI (Audience Studies Incorporated), an influential entertainment testing organization headquartered in Preview House on Sunset Boulevard.

While A. C. Nielsen and Arbitron rate programs after they have been broadcast, ASI measures the likelihood of a show's success before it reaches home screens. During the past 12 months, ASI conducted some 500 testing sessions on "entertainment packages," ranging from feature films to paperback book covers, grossing an estimated $13 million in the process. So, when ASI speaks, networks and studios listen. But ASI speaks only to networks and studios, zealously guarding its operations from all others.

ABC benefited from ASI's ministrations last season when the network brought the pilot of its situation-comedy "Angie" for a diagnostic checkup. ABC executives had felt that the actor playing the husband in the pilot lacked appeal, and that the story was weak in spots, failing to show why a rich blue-blooded Philadelphia pediatrician would marry a hash-slinging waitress. Uncorrected, such lapses could be fatal.

"As a direct result of ASI tests," says

Source: From *The New York Times* (June 3, 1979). © 1979 by The New York Times Company. Reprinted by permission of the publisher.

Marvin Mord, ABC's vice president of research, "we discovered that audiences were indeed skeptical about the actor playing Angie's husband, Brad, and that people were confused about why these two [Angie and Brad] would ever marry." The network tested three actors for the role of Brad, finally choosing Robert Hayes, and completely rewrote the pilot/first-episode to show the couple's relationship before marriage.

"Now viewers can understand why an old-line Philadelphia doctor would be attracted to this girl and why she'd . . . be attracted to him," says Mr. Mord.

ASI and its Preview House have proven invaluable, Mr. Mord adds, not only by revealing a show's strengths and weaknesses but by also helping to discover "hidden characters in the background—like a Rhoda or a Fonzie—who have real charisma" early in a series' development. "I guess the best testimonial to ASI's work is the fact that we've been going to them for over 15 years."

Founded by Pierre Marquis, currently chairman and chief executive officer of ASI, and Ralph Wells, a vice president and chief engineer, as an internal research department for Columbia-Screen Gems in 1960, this division began taking on "outside" clients a year later. Advertising agencies and companies like Bristol-Myers soon hired the young firm to evaluate product packaging and commercials, as did ABC and M-G-M to test their pilots and feature films.

In 1965, ASI moved to its present Sunset Boulevard location, a three-story building containing offices and a 400-seat theater equipped with projection facilities for 16-mm., 35-mm., and 70-mm. film. In 1972, ASI was bought by Planning Research Corporation, a California service conglomerate, and became a privately owned company five years later, with ownership passing to a group of ASI's executives, including Messrs. Marquis and Wells, and several vice presidents. Today, ASI has a staff of 500 and has offices in Los Angeles, Chicago, New York, Frankfurt, Tokyo and Hong Kong.

But ASI's major selling point is not its size but rather its sophisticated hardware. The firm employs up to eight full-time engineers

to design and refine equipment in its continuing search to better track audience responses. A voice-activated TV camera that automatically "follows" discussions in a Preview House first-floor conference room makes it possible for a client in New York to experience West Coast consumers' reactions to his product via videotape. Another ASI innovation is a modified lie detector that is used primarily in record evaluating sessions, a service begun two years ago. Velcro strips covering sensors wrapped around a listener's fingers transmit basal skin responses to a computer in the control room that produces a "subconscious involuntary response graph."

The heart of ASI hardware, however, is an innocuous hand-held black plastic oval case with a dial on its face that registers "Very Dull," "Dull," "Fair," "Good," and "Very Good." As the viewer moves the dial to the setting of his choice while watching a presentation, corresponding impulses feed into an analogue computer that instantly registers his responses on a scale of 1 to 1,000. The resulting "flow chart," together with information gleaned from questionnaires filled out during a testing session, plays a key role in the shaping of a new TV series or feature film.

At one such ASI testing session, the first episode of NBC's now defunct "Brothers & Sisters" situation-comedy, which centered around a college fraternity and sorority, was evaluated by 400 dial-clutching guests. As with all ASI screening sessions, the viewers were culled from reverse directories, that is, telephone books listing addresses rather than names, and selected from lists compiled by canvassers interviewing potential candidates from such areas as Fox Hills Mall and Westwood Village in Los Angeles. Age, sex, income and TV-viewing habits are salient factors in determining who gets invited to these "Network Television Program Previews" (as worded on the invitations), since ASI wants test audiences to conform to national demography.

As audience members enter Preview House, they are handed numbered clipboards (corresponding to seat numbers), questionnaires and pencils, and are guided by ASI ushers to assigned seats. Once the audience is seated, more questionnaires are distributed and a master of ceremonies explains how the dials work. He cautions against using the devices as "cheer and jeer" meters. "Don't register a positive or negative position just because you think a character is good or evil. The dials should reflect your feelings about the story and characters—do they hold your interest?—and not whether someone is a villain or hero." He finishes by explaining that a short cartoon will precede the main screening and that the dials should be used to register reactions to the cartoon.

For 15 years ASI has used this cartoon, "Mr. Magoo Goes Skiiing," as a "thermometer" to gauge if an audience is "warm or cold" and to adjust data accordingly. Having been "tested" hundreds of times, the Magoo cartoon has provided voluminous statistics, and a typical audience response profile has been developed. Any given audience can then be measured against this standard.

The cartoon ends and "Brothers & Sisters" begins.

Ushers cruise the aisles making sure dials are turned. If a viewer appears derelict in his dial-turning duties, the control booth is notified and the culprit "electronically removed" from the audience.

At the conclusion of the NBC show, house lights come up and another questionnaire is handed out, seeking answers to such questions as:

If the following pairs of programs were on television at the same time, which would you watch? (Mark ONE answer for each group.)

> The Waltons
> Brothers & Sisters
> or Mork & Mindy
> Neither
> Can't Decide

Questionnaires are then collected and a clipboard number is drawn for a doorprize of $100 worth of groceries at a local supermarket. The audience leaves, allowing another group of previewers, already lined up outside, to judge a different show. From start to finish, ASI's testing session has taken 85 minutes.

"We've been using ASI for better than 10 years," notes William Rubens, NBC's vice president of research, "and find it cost efficient to hire them [ASI] to test our concepts [TV pilots in outline form], special episodes of existing series, and pilots." ASI's $5,000 price tag for screening and testing is minimal, he believes, considering the millions a hit show can earn during a four- or five-year run.

"ASI is convenient, too," adds Mr. Rubens. "Since most product comes out of Los Angeles, it makes sense to use someone who's there." In addition to testing by dial, NBC uses ASI cable hookup services to screen pilots, telephoning viewers at home for their comments. The network executive stresses, however, that in both Preview House and cable testing NBC analyzes the data, not ASI.

Estimating NBC's research budget at "well over $100,000 a year," Mr. Rubens puts the number of shows the network tests each season at "20 to 30," and says the "big testing push" comes in late March, early April, during a three- to four-week period when most new TV series are screened for the upcoming fall season.

"ASI's testing system is basically sound," he concludes. "I can't remember even one show testing poorly and then doing well on the air. And I've been with NBC for nine years." For strategical reasons, Mr. Rubens was reticent to discuss specific NBC projects currently being tested by ASI.

While ASI has its supporters, there are those who are critical of ASI's machines and testing methods. "To me, 400 people sitting in a room spinning dials around while watching TV is just not normal," says Garry Marshall, "Angie's" producer and the creator of "Happy Days," "Laverne and Shirley" and "Mork and Mindy," and a self-professed veteran of some 100 ASI testing sessions. For Mr. Marshall, a critical shortcoming of ASI's system is in getting "the feel" of the audience. "I sit in the theater while a screening goes on to get the mood of the people. If I hear someone laughing, chances are pretty good he thinks what's happening on the screen is funny. A 'ha-ha' isn't something you need a dial to hear."

In this simple way, without dials or graphs, Mr. Marshall has gathered valuable, and at times even startling, information. He recalls "sitting in" on ASI's testing session for the "Happy Days" pilot. "The network had already done some preliminary research on the show," he explains, "and told me that the opening segment where the credits come up wasn't getting any laughs. They told me it was 'too arty,' had too many dissolves, stuff like that." But Mr. Marshall felt something else was wrong, unrelated to the camera work: "So when the show went to ASI for testing, I sat in with the audience. The beginning scene comes on, shots of Richie's room with pennants and pictures on the walls, and I hear from this lady in front of me, 'Oh, poor boy —he's blind.' So, I look back up at the screen and right above his bed is a sign that says 'Blind.'" After changing this segment, dial scores in a follow-up test jumped dramatically. "It was just a matter of listening and looking, something those dials would never have caught."

A bit bolder with criticism of ASI is Michael Eisner, president of Paramount Pictures. "I know ASI very well," he says. "When I was with ABC, we used them extensively." Today, however, Mr. Eisner shies away from ASI, believing its testing apparatus and general approach not well suited for feature films. "We believe in sneak previewing a movie in regular theaters without dials or gadgets, in cities like Denver and Atlanta." Mr. Eisner contends that ASI's free invitations attract blase viewers. "We're not interested in recruiting people from Farmers' Market. We're interested in a paying audience."

The harshest judgment of ASI comes from creative people like director Hal Ashby [acclaimed for] his film version of Jerzy Kosinski's novel "Being There." Mr. Ashby finds ASI's rating system, with its scales and scores, inherently inaccurate.

"Once you put electronic gizmos in an audience's hands, you're altering the way that audience perceives what's on the screen," says Mr. Ashby. For him, the most sensible way to test a movie is to ask 10 or 15 friends over to view the film and get their opinions before final edit. "That's what I did with my last film, 'Coming Home,'" he says, "and it seems to have worked out just fine."

In the past, ASI has helped decide whether viewers were to see more or less of Peter Falk's raincoat on "Columbo," and whether the private lives of "Adam-12's" police officers were to be revealed. Trivial matters perhaps. But on such trifles an "entertainment package" often either thrives or dies, a fact that will keep ASI's dials twirling and its computers humming no matter what critics say.

Advertising

Advertising in America goes back to the earliest days of colonial life. In fact, advertising circulars played a significant role throughout the seventeenth and eighteenth centuries in luring colonists to the New World. American scholar Richard Hofstadter has called this steady outpouring of promotional brochures, circulars, and broadsides "one of the first concerted and sustained advertising campaigns in the history of the modern world."

At first a staple of the colonial printing trade, advertising gradually worked its way into the back pages of books, pamphlets, and almanacs, and by 1704 into America's first successful newspaper, *The Boston News-Letter.* By the middle of the century, printer-publishers like Ben Franklin had discovered that the young newspaper business depended as much upon advertising patronage as upon news coverage. As a media support system, the power of advertising was noted as early as 1803 by Alexander Hamilton in his New York *Evening Post:* "It is the advertiser who provides the paper for the subscriber. It is not to be disputed, that the publisher of a newspaper in this country, without a very exhaustive advertising support, receives less reward for his labor than the humblest mechanic."

The first advertising agents were enterprising newspaper canvassers, who discovered in the 1840s that, instead of procuring advertisements from a number of local merchants for a single newspaper, they could more profitably work for themselves by taking single advertisements from the same local merchants and placing them in a number of different newspapers. A decade before the Civil War a handful of agents were operating, if not exactly thriving, in a few large cities by building up "lists" of newspapers they represented and in which they would guarantee to place and monitor advertisements. Copywriting and design were occasionally done in-house, but usually the advertiser would submit his own compositions and the agent would supply professional advice. Not until the 1870s did agents begin to consider magazines as a possibly effective medium. And not until the 1890s did agencies employ full-time copywriters and commercial artists.

With the birth of the cheap mass magazine, the growing demand for graphic journalism, and the dramatically increased output of mass-produced, brand-named, and nationally distributed consumer goods—all in the 1890s—advertising itself became big business and its artifacts grew more and more indistinguishable from the products of mass culture and mass entertainment. A major stage in the cultural evolution of advertising was reached in 1896 when the editor of one of the most successful mass magazines, *The Ladies Home Journal,* allowed feature articles and fiction to overflow and intermingle with the advertising section. Until then, most magazines had staunchly maintained a separate place for advertisements in the back pages. By the twentieth century, advertising had assimilated so much of American popular culture and so enmeshed itself in existing networks of mass media that, as historian Daniel Boorstin observes in the opening essay of this section, it had become "the characteristic folk culture of our society."

Although magazines have accounted for a substantial part of total advertising expenditures since the 1890s, magazine copy had pretty much attained its contemporary form and style by the mid-1920s, just as a new medium, radio, began to make its presence felt in American cultural and business life. As agencies adjusted to radio (see "Radio and the Foundation of American Broadcasting," p. 230), and then to television, they had to find new ways, through commercials and sponsorship of shows, to structure advertising messages.

Radio and television produced new methods and new marketing strategies. By the late 1950s and 1960s, marketing research developed into a sophisticated and indispensable tool as advertisers began worrying more about such on-the-money matters as cost per thousand, audience recall, test markets, gross impressions, accumulated audience, and media buying than about getting a catchy commercial on the air. "It's not creative unless it sells" became a leading slogan of the industry in the 1970s. One of the newest marketing techniques devised by agencies to make sure that creativity sells is the subject of Peter W. Bernstein's article, "Psychographics Is Still an Issue on Madison Avenue."

Back in the earliest days of national advertising, the owner of *The Ladies Home Journal,* Cyrus Curtis, remarked to an audience of advertisers that it was only an illusion to think his magazine was published for the benefit of American women: "the real reason, the publisher's reason, is to give you who manufacture things that American women want and buy a chance to tell them about your products." Curtis would be astonished today by networks of mass communications he could have imagined only in the wildest moments of profiteering prophecy. But he would have undoubtedly endorsed the principles behind television programming outlined by producer Bob Shanks in "Advertising Agencies and Sponsors." Shanks acknowledges that "commercial television is paid for by advertisements and programmed by networks and stations which are usually publicly owned corporations and always meant to be profit-making organizations." However, Shanks does not go so far in his account of agency-network relations to suggest, as do some media critics, that the networks do not sell programs but rather *audiences* for those programs.

Advertising, however, is not only an economic support system for the various media. Rather, it should also be thought of as a highly developed media operation in itself, one whose styles and strategies are continually shaped by complex requirements of business and art. In "Now a Few Words About Commercials . . . ," theater critic and video artist Jonathan Price describes how producers of spectacular thirty-second spots defy time, reality, and budgets to create an astonishing fantasy world that may be "the best thing on TV."

In the final article of this section, Carol Caldwell, a former copywriter, examines one of the leading issues of contemporary advertising (and of American mass media in general): the persistent use of offensive sexist stereotypes at a time when even advertising research is beginning to show they no longer have any social or demographic basis in real life.

The literature on advertising continues to grow at a phenomenal rate, as more and more academic disciplines and private studies examine the subject from a variety of social, cultural, psychological, ethical, and economic perspectives. The following set of readings provides a brief theoretical and practical introduction to the intricate role advertising plays in contemporary mass communications.

5
The Rhetoric of Democracy

Daniel J. Boorstin

Daniel J. Boorstin's historical overview of advertising's complex role in American culture first appeared in *Democracy and Its Discontents* and was later featured in the bicentennial issue of the marketing industry's magazine, *Advertising Age.*

One of the nation's most prominent historians and author of a three-volume study of our civilization *(The Americans),* Boorstin has served as senior historian of the Smithsonian Institution, director of the National Museum of History and Technology, and is currently Librarian of Congress.

In addition to his work in American history, Boorstin has written extensively on mass media; *The Image: A Guide to Pseudo Events in America* (1961) remains one of the most influential studies of contemporary language and culture. In the following essay, Boorstin argues that "we are perhaps the first people in history to have a centrally organized mass-produced folk culture" and that "advertising has become the heart of the folk culture and even its very prototype."

Advertising, of course, has been part of the mainstream of American civilization, although you might not know it if you read the most respectable surveys of American history. It has been one of the enticements to the settlement of this New World, it has been a producer of the peopling of the United States, and in its modern form, in its world-wide reach, it has been one of our most characteristic products.

Never was there a more outrageous or more unscrupulous or more ill-informed advertising campaign than that by which the promoters for the American colonies brought settlers here. Brochures published in England in the seventeenth century, some even earlier, were full of hopeful overstatements, half-truths, and downright lies, along with some facts which nowadays surely would be the basis for a restraining order from the Federal Trade Commission. Gold and silver, fountains of youth, plenty of fish, venison without limit, all these were promised, and of course some of them were found. It would be interesting to speculate on how long it might have taken to settle this continent if there had not been such promotion by enterprising advertisers. How has American civilization been shaped by the fact that there was a kind of natural selection here of those people who were willing to believe advertising?

Advertising has taken the lead in promising and exploiting the new. This was a new world, and one of the advertisements for it appears on the dollar bill on the Great Seal of the United States, which reads *novus ordo seclorum,* one of the most effective advertising slogans to come out of this country. "A new order of the centuries"—belief in novelty and in the desirability of opening novelty to everybody has been important in our lives throughout our history and especially in this century. Again and again advertising has been an agency for inducing Americans to try anything and everything—from the continent itself to a new brand of soap. As one of the more literate and poetic of the advertising copywriters, James Kenneth Frazier, a Cornell graduate, wrote in 1900 in "The Doctor's Lament":

> This lean M.D. is Dr. Brown
> Who fares but ill in Spotless Town.
> The town is so confounded clean,
> It is no wonder he is lean,
> He's lost all patients now, you know,
> Because they use *Sapolio.*

The same literary talent that once was used to retail Sapolio was later used to induce people to try the Edsel or the Mustang, to experiment with Lifebuoy or Body-All, to drink Pepsi-Cola or Royal Crown Cola, or to shave with a Trac II razor.

And as expansion and novelty have become essential to our economy, advertising has played an ever-larger role: in the settling of the continent, in the expansion of the economy, and in the building of an American standard of living. Advertising has expressed the optimism, the hyperbole, and the sense of community, the sense of reaching which has been so important a feature of our civilization.

Here I wish to explore the significance of advertising, not as a force in the economy or in shaping an American standard of living, but rather as a touchstone of the ways in which we Americans have learned about all sorts of things.

The problems of advertising are of course not peculiar to advertising, for they are just one aspect of the problems of democracy. They reflect the rise of what I have called Consumption Communities and Statistical Communities, and many of the special problems of advertising have arisen from our continuously energetic effort to give everybody everything.

If we consider democracy not just as a political system, but as a set of institutions which do aim to make everything available to everybody, it would not be an overstatement to describe advertising as the characteristic rhetoric of democracy. One of the tendencies of democracy, which Plato and other antidemocrats warned against a long time ago, was the danger that rhetoric would displace or at least overshadow epistemology; that is, *the temptation to allow the problem of persuasion to overshadow the problem of knowledge.* Democratic societies tend to become more concerned with what people believe than with what is true, to become more concerned with credibility than with truth. All these problems become accentuated in a large-scale democracy like ours, which possesses all the apparatus of modern industry. And the problems are accentuated still further by universal literacy, by instantaneous communication, and by the daily plague of words and images.

In the early days it was common for advertising men to define advertisements as a kind of news. The best admen, like the best journalists, were supposed to be those who were able to make their news the most interesting and readable. This was natural enough, since the verb to "advertise" originally meant, intransitively, to take note or to consider. For a person to "advertise" meant originally, in the fourteenth and fifteenth centuries, to reflect on something, to think about something. Then it came to mean, transitively, to call the attention of another to something, to give him notice, to notify, admonish, warn or inform in a formal or impressive manner. And then, by the sixteenth century, it came to mean: to give notice of anything, to make generally known. It was not until the late eighteenth century that the word "advertising" in English came to have a specifically "advertising" connotation as we might say today, and not until the late nineteenth century that it began to have a specifically commercial connotation. By 1879 someone was saying, "Don't advertise unless you have something worth advertising." But even into the present century, newspapers continue to call themselves by the title "Advertiser"—for example, the Boston *Daily Advertiser,* which was a newspaper of long tradition and one of the most dignified papers in Boston until William Randolph Hearst took it over in 1917. Newspapers carried "Advertiser" on their mastheads, not because they sold advertisements but because they brought news.

Now, the main role of advertising in American civilization came increasingly to be that of persuading and appealing rather than that of educating and informing. By 1921, for instance, one of the more popular textbooks, Blanchard's *Essentials of Advertising,* began: "Anything employed to influence people favorably is advertising. The mission of advertising is to persuade men and women to act in a way that will be of advantage to the advertiser." This development—in a country where a shared, a rising, and a democratized standard of living was the national pride and the national hallmark—meant that advertising had become the rhetoric of democracy.

What, then, were some of the main features of modern American advertising—if we consider it as a form of rhetoric? First, and perhaps most obvious, is *repetition.* It is hard for us to realize that the use of repetition in advertising is not an ancient device but a modern one, which actually did not come into common use in American journalism until just past the middle of the nineteenth century.

The development of what came to be called "iteration copy" was a result of a struggle by a courageous man of letters and advertising pioneer, Robert Bonner, who bought the old New York *Merchant's Ledger* in 1851 and turned it into a popular journal.

He then had the temerity to try to change the ways of James Gordon Bennett, who of course was one of the most successful of the American newspaper pioneers, and who was both a sensationalist and at the same time an extremely stuffy man when it came to things that he did not consider to be news. Bonner was determined to use advertisements in Bennett's wide-circulating New York *Herald* to sell his own literary product, but he found it difficult to persuade Bennett to allow him to use any but agate type in his advertising. (Agate was the smallest type used by newspapers in that day, only barely legible to the naked eye.) Bennett would not allow advertisers to use larger type, nor would he allow them to use illustrations except stock cuts, because he thought it was undignified. He said, too, that to allow a variation in the format of ads would be undemocratic. He insisted that all advertisers use the same size type so that no one would be allowed to prevail over another simply by presenting his message in a larger, more clever, or more attention-getting form.

Finally Bonner managed to overcome Bennett's rigidity by leasing whole pages of the paper and using the tiny agate type to form larger letters across the top of the page. In this way he produced a message such as "Bring home the New York Ledger tonight." His were unimaginative messages, and when repeated all across the page they technically did not violate Bennett's agate rule. But they opened a new era and presaged a new freedom for advertisers in their use of the newspaper page. Iteration copy—the practice of presenting prosaic content in ingenious, repetitive form—became common, and nowadays of course is commonplace.

A second characteristic of American advertising which is not unrelated to this is the development of *an advertising style.* We have histories of most other kinds of style—including the style of many unread writers who are remembered today only because they have been forgotten—but we have very few accounts of the history of advertising style, which of course is one of the most important forms of our language and one of the most widely influential.

The development of advertising style was

the convergence of several very respectable American traditions. One of these was the tradition of the "plain style," which the Puritans made so much of and which accounts for so much of the strength of the Puritan literature. The "plain style" was of course much influenced by the Bible and found its way into the rhetoric of American writers and speakers of great power like Abraham Lincoln. When advertising began to be self-conscious in the early years of this century, the pioneers urged copywriters not to be too clever, and especially not to be fancy. One of the pioneers of the advertising copywriters, John Powers, said, for example, "The commonplace is the proper level for writing in business; where the first virtue is plainness, 'fine writing' is not only intellectual, it is offensive." George P. Rowell, another advertising pioneer, said, "You must write your advertisement to catch damned fools—not college professors." He was a very tactful person. And he added, "And you'll catch just as many college professors as you will of any other sort." In the 1920's, when advertising was beginning to come into its own, Claude Hopkins, whose name is known to all in the trade, said, "Brilliant writing has no place in advertising. A unique style takes attention from the subject. Any apparent effort to sell creates corresponding resistance. . . . One should be natural and simple. His language should not be conspicuous. In fishing for buyers, as in fishing for bass, one should not reveal the hook." So there developed a characteristic advertising style in which plainness, the phrase that anyone could understand, was a distinguishing mark.

At the same time, the American advertising style drew on another, and what might seem an antithetic, tradition—the tradition of hyperbole and tall talk, the language of Davy Crockett and Mike Fink. While advertising could think of itself as 99.44 percent pure, it used the language of "Toronado" and "Cutlass." As I listen to the radio in Washington, I hear a celebration of heroic qualities which would make the characteristics of Mike Fink and Davy Crockett pale, only to discover at the end of the paean that what I have been hearing is a description of the Ford dealers in the District of Columbia neighborhood. And

along with the folk tradition of hyperbole and tall talk comes the rhythm of folk music. We hear that Pepsi-Cola hits the spot, that it's for the young generation—and we hear other products celebrated in music which we cannot forget and sometimes don't want to remember.

There grew somehow out of all these contradictory tendencies—combining the commonsense language of the "plain style," and the fantasy language of "tall talk"—an advertising style. This characteristic way of talking about things was especially designed to reach and catch the millions. It created a whole new world of myth. A myth, the dictionary tells us, is a notion based more on tradition or convenience than on facts; it is a received idea. Myth is not just fantasy and not just fact but exists in a limbo, in the world of the "Will to Believe," which William James has written about so eloquently and so perceptively. This is the world of the neither true nor false—of the statement that 60 percent of the physicians who expressed a choice said that our brand of aspirin would be more effective in curing a simple headache than any other leading brand.

That kind of statement exists in a penumbra. I would call this the "advertising penumbra." It is not untrue, and yet, in its connotation it is not exactly true.

Now, there is still another characteristic of advertising so obvious that we are inclined perhaps to overlook it. I call that *ubiquity*. Advertising abhors a vacuum and we discover new vacuums every day. The parable, of course, is the story of the man who thought of putting the advertisement on the other side of the cigarette package. Until then, that was wasted space and a society which aims at a democratic standard of living, at extending the benefits of consumption and all sorts of things and services to everybody, must miss no chances to reach people. The highway billboard and other outdoor advertising, bus and streetcar and subway advertising, and skywriting, radio and TV commercials—all these are of course obvious evidence that advertising abhors a vacuum.

We might reverse the old mousetrap slogan and say that anyone who can devise another place to put another mousetrap to catch a consumer will find people beating a path to his door. "Avoiding advertising will become a little harder next January," the *Wall Street Journal* reported on May 17, 1973, "when a Studio City, California, company launches a venture called StoreVision. Its product is a system of billboards that move on a track across supermarket ceilings. Some 650 supermarkets so far are set to have the system." All of which helps us to understand the observation attributed to a French man of letters during his recent visit to Times Square. "What a beautiful place, if only one could not read!" Everywhere is a place to be filled, as we discover in a recent *Publishers Weekly* description of one advertising program: "The $1.95 paperback edition of Dr. Thomas A. Harris' million-copy best seller 'I'm O.K., You're O.K.' is in for full-scale promotion in July by its publisher, Avon Books. Plans range from bumper stickers to airplane streamers, from planes flying above Fire Island, the Hamptons and Malibu. In addition, the $100,000 promotion budget calls for 200,000 bookmarks, plus brochures, buttons, lipcards, floor and counter displays, and advertising in magazines and TV."

The ubiquity of advertising is of course just another effect of our uninhibited efforts to use all the media to get all sorts of information to everybody everywhere. Since the places to be filled are everywhere, the amount of advertising is not determined by the *needs* of advertising, but by the *opportunities* for advertising which become unlimited.

But the most effective advertising, in an energetic, novelty-ridden society like ours, tends to be "self-liquidating." To create a cliché you must offer something which everybody accepts. The most successful advertising therefore self-destructs because it becomes cliché. Examples of this are found in the tendency for copyrighted names of trademarks to enter the vernacular—for the proper names of products which have been made familiar by costly advertising to become common nouns, and so to apply to anybody's products. Kodak becomes a synonym for camera, Kleenex a synonym for facial tissue, when

both begin with a small *k,* and Xerox (now, too, with a small *x*) is used to describe all processes of copying, and so on. These are prototypes of the problem. If you are successful enough, then you will defeat your purpose in the long run—by making the name and the message so familiar that people won't notice them, and then people will cease to distinguish your product from everybody else's.

In a sense, of course, as we will see, the whole of American civilization is an example. When this was a "new" world, if people succeeded in building a civilization here, the New World would survive and would reach the time —in our age—when it would cease to be new. And now we have the oldest written Constitution in use in the world. This is only a parable of which there are many more examples.

The advertising man who is successful in marketing any particular product, then—in our high-technology, well-to-do democratic society, which aims to get everything to everybody—is apt to be diluting the demand for his particular product in the very act of satisfying it. But luckily for him, he is at the very same time creating a fresh demand for his services as advertiser.

And as a consequence, there is yet another role which is assigned to American advertising. This is what I call "erasure." Insofar as advertising is competitive or innovation is widespread, erasure is required in order to persuade consumers that this year's model is superior to last year's. In fact, we consumers learn that we might be risking our lives if we go out on the highway with those very devices that were last year's lifesavers but without whatever special kind of brakes or wipers or seat belt is on this year's model. This is what I mean by "erasure"—and we see it on our advertising pages or our television screen every day. We read in the *New York Times* (May 20, 1973), for example, that "For the price of something small and ugly, you can drive something small and beautiful"—an advertisement for the Fiat 250 Spider. Or another, perhaps more subtle example is the advertisement for shirts under a picture of Oliver Drab: "Oliver Drab. A name to remember in fine designer shirts? No kidding. . . . Because you pay extra money for Oliver Drab. And for all the other superstars of the fashion world. Golden Vee [the name of the brand that is advertised] does not have a designer's label. But we do have designers. . . . By keeping their names *off* our label and simply saying Golden Vee, we can afford to sell our $7 to $12 shirts for just $7 to $12, which should make Golden Vee a name to remember. Golden Vee, you only pay for the shirt.''

Having mentioned two special characteristics—the self-liquidating tendency and the need for erasure—which arise from the dynamism of the American economy, I would like to try to place advertising in a larger perspective. The special role of advertising in our life gives a clue to a pervasive oddity in American civilization. A leading feature of past cultures, as anthropologists have explained, is the tendency to distinguish between "high" culture and "low" culture—between the culture of the literate and the learned on the one hand and that of the populace on the other. In other words, between the language of literature and the language of the vernacular. Some of the most useful statements of this distinction have been made by social scientists at the University of Chicago—first by the late Robert Redfield in his several pioneering books on peasant society, and then by Milton Singer in his remarkable study of Indian civilization, *When a Great Tradition Modernizes* (1972). This distinction between the great tradition and the little tradition, between the high culture and the folk culture, has begun to become a commonplace of modern anthropology.

Some of the obvious features of advertising in modern America offer us an opportunity to note the significance or insignificance of that distinction for us. Elsewhere I have tried to point out some of the peculiarities of the American attitude toward the *high* culture. There is something distinctive about the place of thought in American life, which I think is not quite what it has been in certain Old World cultures.

But what about distinctive American attitudes to *popular* culture? What is our analogue to the folk culture of other peoples? Advertising gives us some clues—to a charac-

teristically American democratic folk culture. Folk culture is a name for the culture which ordinary people everywhere lean on. It is not the writings of Dante and Chaucer and Shakespeare and Milton, the teachings of Machiavelli and Descartes, Locke or Marx. It is, rather, the pattern of slogans, local traditions, tales, songs, dances, and ditties. And of course holiday observances. Popular culture in other civilizations has been for the most part both an area of continuity wtih the past, a way in which people reach back into the past and out to their community, and at the same time an area of local variations. An area of individual and amateur expression in which a person has his own way of saying, or notes his mother's way of saying or singing, or his own way of dancing, his own view of folk wisdom and the cliché.

And here is an interesting point of contrast. In other societies outside the United States, it is the *high* culture that has generally been an area of centralized, organized control. In Western Europe, for example, universities and churches have tended to be closely allied to the government. The institutions of higher learning have had a relatively limited access to the people as a whole. This was inevitable, of course, in most parts of the world, because there were so few universities. In England, for example, there were only two universities until the early nineteenth century. And there was central control over the printed matter that was used in universities or in the liturgy. The government tended to be close to the high culture, and that was easy because the high culture itself was so centralized and because literacy was relatively limited.

In our society, however, we seem to have turned all of this around. Our high culture is one of the least centralized areas of our culture. And our universities express the atomistic, diffused, chaotic, and individualistic aspect of our life. We have in this country more than twenty-five hundred colleges and universities, institutions of so-called higher learning. We have a vast population in these institutions, somewhere over seven million students.

But when we turn to our popular culture, what do we find? We find that in our nation of Consumption Communities and emphasis on Gross National Product (GNP) and growth rates, advertising has become the heart of the folk culture and even its very prototype. And as we have seen, American advertising shows many characteristics of the folk culture of other societies: repetition, a plain style, hyperbole and tall talk, folk verse, and folk music. Folk culture, wherever it has flourished, has tended to thrive in a limbo between fact and fantasy, and of course, depending on the spoken word and the oral tradition, it spreads easily and tends to be ubiquitous. These are all familiar characteristics of folk culture and they are ways of describing our folk culture, but how do the expressions of our peculiar folk culture come to *us*?

They no longer sprout from the earth, from the village, from the farm, or even from the neighborhood or the city. They come to us primarily from enormous centralized self-consciously *creative* (an overused word, for the overuse of which advertising agencies are in no small part responsible) organizations. They come from advertising agencies, from networks of newspapers, radio, and television, from outdoor-advertising agencies, from the copywriters for ads in the largest-circulation magazines, and so on. These "creators" of folk culture—or pseudo-folk culture —aim at the widest intelligibility and charm and appeal.

But in the United States, we must recall, the advertising folk culture (like all advertising) is also confronted with the problems of self-liquidation and erasure. These are by-products of the expansive, energetic character of our economy. And they, too, distinguish American folk culture from folk cultures elsewhere.

Our folk culture is distinguished from others by being discontinuous, ephemeral, and self-destructive. Where does this leave the common citizen? All of us are qualified to answer.

In our society, then, those who cannot lean on the world of learning, on the high culture of the classics, on the elaborated wisdom of the books, have a new problem. The Uni-versity of Chicago, for example, in the 1930's and 1940's was the center of a quest for a "common discourse." The champions of that quest, which became a kind of crusade, believed that such a discourse could be found through familiarity with the classics of great literature—and especially of Western European literature. I think they were misled; such works were not, nor are they apt to become, the common discourse of our society. Most people, even in a democracy, and a rich democracy like ours, live in a world of popular culture, our special kind of popular culture.

The characteristic folk culture of our society is a creature of advertising, and in a sense it *is* advertising. But advertising, our own popular culture, is harder to make into a source of continuity than the received wisdom and commonsense slogans and catchy songs of the vivid vernacular. The popular culture of advertising attenuates and is always dissolving before our very eyes. Among the charms, challenges, and tribulations of modern life, we must count this peculiar fluidity, this ephemeral character of that very kind of culture on which other peoples have been able to lean, the kind of culture to which they have looked for the continuity of their traditions, for their ties with the past and with the future.

We are perhaps the first people in history to have a centrally organized mass-produced folk culture. Our kind of popular culture is here today and gone tomorrow—or the day after tomorrow. Or whenever the next semi-annual model appears. And insofar as folk culture becomes advertising, and advertising becomes centralized, it becomes a way of depriving people of their opportunities for individual and small-community expression. Our technology and our economy and our democratic ideals have all helped make that possible. Here we have a new test of the problem that is at least as old as Heraclitus—an everyday test of man's ability to find continuity in his experience. And here democratic man has a new opportunity to accommodate himself, if he can, to the unknown.

Psychographics Is Still an Issue on Madison Avenue

Peter W. Bernstein

Fred, the Frustrated Factory Worker—unhappy, cynical, and dissatisfied with his marriage—flips through a pornographic magazine and fantasizes escapes from his humdrum world. According to the advertising agency that constructed Fred out of reams of statistical data, Fred represents 19 percent of the male consumer population. Marketing researchers refer to him as a "life-style type." Many agencies find such consumer profiles helpful in targeting products to the specific groups of people most likely to be interested in those products. Fred, for instance, would not be interested in yogurt ads designed for Candice, the Chic Suburbanite type.

In the following essay, veteran business writer Peter W. Bernstein examines how advertising's latest marketing tool, "psychographics," plots out relationships between people's attitudes and spending habits. To accomplish this kind of market segmentation, American consumers were divided into ten different "life-style types" (five female and five male).

Although virtually nothing has been written about it in the business press, a technique called "psychographics" has been playing a role in some critical decisions at advertising agencies. At least, the technique gets to play a large role at some agencies; advertising people are sharply divided on the merits of psychographics. Its boosters point to some expensive, and apparently successful, campaigns on behalf of Ford Motor, General Foods, Colgate-Palmolive, and other blue-chip advertisers, and say the technique was at least partly responsible for those successes. Its detractors deny that it's helpful and argue that psychographics is just another fad on Madison Avenue.

The boosters begin with the proposition that much conventional market research is inadequate. Based on demographic data, it may tell us a lot about the age, income, education, and family size of prospective customers—but it doesn't tell us anything about their attitudes and living styles. It can't clearly differentiate between swingers and stand-patters, between militant feminists and women with traditional values, between those who admire Ralph Nader and those who identify with Archie Bunker. Psychographics is aimed at making these kinds of distinctions and, so its advocates claim, adds a new dimension to the marketing effort.

Among the leading boosters are two Chicago-based agencies, Leo Burnett and Needham, Harper & Steers. Psychographics has also been touted as "a very powerful marketing tool," and frequently used, by New York-based Grey Advertising. Other agencies that use it occasionally include J. Walter Thompson, Young & Rubicam, Doyle Dane Bernbach, and Benton & Bowles. Market-research people at B.B.D.O. and Ogilvy & Mather believe that psychographics is not helpful.

A Question About Wigs

Practitioners of the art, or science, or whatever it is, measure attitudes in rather exhaustive surveys. The most ambitious of these are called general life-style studies. One such study, prepared two years ago by Needham, Harper & Steers, began by asking the respondents to indicate, on a scale of one to six, agreement or disagreement with each of 199 statements. Some of the statements referred to personal preferences and habits. ("I try to avoid foods that have additives in them.") Others examined social and political views ("Communism is the greatest peril in the world today") and basic attitudes toward life ("I dread the future"). The study also asked each respondent what he was doing with his life. How often did he take a nap, buy common stock, jog, wear a wig, attend an X-rated movie? And there were hundreds of questions about the different kinds of products, from detergents to dog food, that each one used. All told, the study called for more than seven hundred responses.

The data obtained from 3,288 consumers were then fed into a computer that had been programmed to perform a "Q-factor analysis," which involves sorting the answers into groups. People who answered certain questions alike were clustered together. The results of this exercise are contained in two thick volumes called *Market Segmentation by Psychographics*.

One major result was the breaking down of the U.S. consumer population into ten different life-style types—five female and five male. The ten were given names, like Thelma, the Old-Fashioned Traditionalist, and Needham indicated the proportion of the male or female population represented by each one. (Thelma is said to represent twenty-five percent of the women.)

Each of these composite characters is described in detail in the two volumes. To give clients a taste of the data, the agency has prepared a videotape and slide presentation, for which actors were hired to play the characters. Take Candice, the Chic Suburbanite (who represents twenty percent of the women). An urban woman, well educated, probably married to a professional man, she is a prime mover in her community and is active in club affairs. Her life is hectic; when the film's announcer asks Candice if she likes watching soap operas on television, Candice snaps back, "Soap operas are a complete waste of time."

Thelma is a different proposition. A devoted wife, doting mother, and conscientious housekeeper, Thelma has fewer interests outside her own family. She does not condone sexual permissiveness or political liberalism, nor can she sympathize with women's libbers. "Thelma," the announcer calls, "what do you think of using sex appeal to sell toothpaste?" "How can *that* possibly sell toothpaste?" asks Thelma. "The good Lord gave us teeth to chew with, not to have sex with."

Among the men there is Fred, the Frustrated Factory Worker (representing nineteen percent of the men), flipping through a girlie magazine. He married young and is now unhappy and cynical. He likes to think that he is a bit of a swinger, and he fantasizes and goes to the movies to escape from his everyday world. Scott, the Successful Professional (twenty-one percent), is much smoother. His speech is confident, his manner sure. He carries three major credit cards and uses them primarily to pay for business travel. The announcer asks: "Do you agree that men should not be fashion conscious?" "No, by no means," says Scott assuredly. "Men should have the ability and willingness to exercise their judgment in this area as well as others."

General life-style studies like the one prepared by Needham have several applications for marketing. One is simply to help determine who buys what. The Needham study shows that liquor, for example, is primarily bought by four types: Eleanor, the Elegant Socialite; Candice, the Chic Suburbanite; Ben, the Self-Made Businessman; and Scott, the Successful Professional. For yogurt and cottage cheese, Candice would be the prime target.

The Appeal of Dog Food

Not all psychographic research involves these general life-style studies. There are also "product specific" studies, which do not aspire to segment the whole consumer population, only to identify the attitudes and living styles of those who use, and don't use, particular products. In 1970, for example, General Foods did a psychographic study to determine which types of consumers were likely to buy dog food and what kind of product would be most appealing to them. At the time, the company's Gaines and Gainesburger products had strong positions in the dry and semimoist dog-food categories, but the company did not have a canned dog food. This meant that G.F. was unrepresented in a significant area. (Canned dog food now accounts for about thirty percent of the $2 billion dog-food market.)

The study concluded that there were six basic types of dog owners, and that each type had somewhat different preferences in dog food. Two of the six were most likely to buy a canned product—the most expensive kind of dog food. G.F. had these two groups in mind when it decided to market a canned dog food.

One of the groups tended to regard dogs as "baby substitutes." These consumers, who typically own very small dogs, are apt to be women who do not have any children and who live in small apartments in the city. The woman is willing to spend a lot on dog food, allows her dog to be a finicky eater, and tends to switch brands often. The other group was identified as "the nutritionalists." A researcher describes them as the intelligent dog owners, well educated and with high incomes. Many people in this group are willing to spend a lot to keep their dogs healthy.

General Foods did a lot of other research on dog food, and it would be forcing the facts to suggest that the products it finally developed originated in psychographics alone. Still, the company was plainly influenced by the finding that both of those groups thought a lot about their dogs' needs and were careful in their choice of foods.

Cycle, which G.F. introduced nationally in February 1976, is the first dog food to come in four different types. Cycle 1 is for puppies up to eighteen months. Cycle 2 is for young adult dogs aged one to seven. Cycle 3 is for overweight dogs. Cycle 4 is for dogs over

seven years old. There is already some evidence that General Foods has reached the market segments it was aiming at.

An End to Friskiness

Ford Motor Co. experimented with psychographics in 1971 after it had brought out the Pinto. The first television commercials presented the Pinto as a frisky, carefree little car. The car was identified with a pinto pony. When a Pinto car was seen whisking down a country road on your television screen, there, superimposed over it, was a galloping pony. But initial sales were disappointing, and Ford decided to change the commercials.

The new commercials were based in part on a psychographic study done by Grey Advertising. The study, which examined the attitudes of people identified as potential Pinto buyers, made it clear that they were not looking for friskiness; they wanted a practical and dependable little car. Grey came up with an ad campaign that portrayed Pinto as just that. Instead of comparing its performance to that of a pony, Grey chose to show Pinto on a split screen with the old Ford Model A, a car of legendary reliability and value. Shirley Young, Grey's executive vice-president and research director, notes pointedly that Pinto went on to become the largest-selling subcompact in the U.S.

Psychographics may be thought of as a descendant of motivation research (M.R.), a technique, much ballyhooed in the 1950s, that often employed Freudian psychoanalytic concepts to seek out the real and sometimes unconscious reasons people buy. Pioneered by a psychologist named Ernest Dichter, M.R. brought to Madison Avenue's research departments such new tools as depth interviews and sentence-completion and word-association tests. But there was always great skepticism about the validity of the results. For one thing, M.R. necessarily relied on small samples of people to produce its data.

Disillusioned with what M.R. was accomplishing, a number of researchers came to believe that much larger samples were needed; they also developed the idea that researchers should look for direct correlations (e.g., between attitudes and product preferences) rather than strive for insights about the unconscious. One of these researchers, Emanuel Demby, a social psychologist who had worked with Dichter, believes today that psychographics is the "fulfillment of the promise of motivation research."

One research firm that has done a great deal to make psychographics intellectually respectable is New York-based Yankelovich, Skelly & White. Founded by Daniel Yankelovich, who is also well known for political polling, the firm has undertaken a general life-style study every year since 1970. Last year, eighty of the country's largest corporations paid ten thousand to fifteen thousand dollars each for these data. The Yankelovich analysts break the market into six life-style segments, versus Needham's ten (and versus nineteen in a Leo Burnett study).

Does Eleanor Exist?

Critics of psychographics have aimed most of their volleys at the general life-style studies. Even some practitioners of psychographics have attacked these studies. "I almost totally reject the concept of grouping people into life-style clusters," says Douglas Tigert, who is a practitioner and is also a professor of marketing at the University of Toronto. "There is just no such thing as an Eleanor or a Candice. They are just not out there." However, the Toronto-based market-research firm with which Tigert is associated is a heavy user of product-specific studies.

His central point about the life-style studies is that those "types," who seem to have been so neatly segmented by their attitudinal differences, actually overlap one another to an enormous degree. Other researchers agree. "Anyone who has done a cluster analysis is disturbed about how diffuse the clusters are," says one researcher. Others note that responses to survey questions about particular subjects (e.g., communism) cannot be used to predict responses about different subjects (e.g., fashion)—at least, the confidence levels assigned to any such predictions will be low.

Those who rely on the general life-style studies to differentiate between consumer types will generally allow that the overlaps are large. But they insist that even marginal differences can be significant to the marketer. A Yankelovich senior vice-president, Sender Hoffman, acknowledges that the data do not show large attitudinal differences between the types. But, Hoffman maintains, the differences between clusters are still large enough to be the basis for marketing decisions. William Wells, who is Needham's research director, and who was one of the pioneers of psychographics, concurs in this judgment. Says Wells: "Differences of a couple of percentage points are routinely used in making marketing decisions."

But even if all the studies are statistically impeccable, there remain some other questions about the usefulness of psychographics. One question is whether those elaborate studies, based on responses by thousands of people, really tell a shrewd marketing executive anything that he couldn't have figured out for himself. Another question is whether the insights into attitudes and living styles really help to create good advertising.

Some difficulties have, in fact, been encountered in applying psychographic findings to specific advertising and marketing campaigns. Leo Burnett once had some psychographic data indicating that women who bought TV dinners tended to lead hectic lives and had trouble coping with everyday problems. Burnett thereupon came up with an ad for Swanson showing a rundown woman flopping into a chair just before her family is to arrive home and demand dinner. Suddenly realizing that she has a problem, she gets the bright idea of cooking a TV dinner. "We couldn't have made a worse mistake," confesses Joseph Plummer, Burnett's senior vice-president and director of research. "The last thing those ladies wanted to be reminded of was how tired they were."

There isn't much doubt that psychographics will be around for a while. Several high-powered agencies believe that it helps them to create better advertising; in addition they suspect that it helps them to attract clients. "It impresses the client," says Pat

Cafferata, associate research director at Needham. "A psychographic study is a terrific selling tool."

As to whether it really does help create better advertising, the jury would appear to be still out. Possibly, it never will come in. And, possibly, the lingering uncertainty about the value of psychographics shouldn't be thought remarkable. It has always been one of the charms of the advertising business that, while everybody knows advertising "works," nobody ever knows for sure what makes it work.

7
Advertising Agencies and Sponsors

Bob Shanks

The average television viewer usually objects to advertising when a commercial is particularly irritating, interferes with the flow of a program, or runs over into performance time. But for media critics a more serious objection to advertising is that, since it pays production costs, it consequently dominates all aspects of programming.

In the following selection from his recent account of the television industry, *The Cool Fire: How to Make It in Television,* producer Bob Shanks argues that advertisers, though undoubtedly powerful, "are only components in a complex system." According to Shanks, a number of factors (such as network control of production and fierce competition among agencies) contribute to an advertiser-network relation that is more interdependent than domineering.

"Nothing is for nothing," it has been truthfully if inelegantly said, and certainly this pungent expression applies to "free" television, which, of course, is not free at all. While there is no direct payment by viewers in the United States for the programs they watch on television, they are expected to pay for the programs, ultimately, by purchasing the products and services which are advertised in the commercial messages. Program makers are supposed to devise and produce shows that will attract mass audiences without unduly offending these audiences or too deeply moving them emotionally. Such ruffling, it is thought, will interfere with their ability to receive, recall, and respond to the commercial messages. This programming reality is the unwritten, unspoken *gemeinschaft* among all professional members of the television fraternity.

Even those who should know better have a tendency to respond to this reality with indignation and swollen self-righteousness. They begin to cast stones—at the sponsor and the advertising agencies. Ridiculous. Com-

Source: Selection is reprinted from *The Cool Fire: How to Make It in Television,* by Bob Shanks, with the permission of W. W. Norton & Company, Inc.

mercial television is paid for by advertisements and programmed by networks and stations which are usually publicly owned corporations and always meant to be profit-making organizations. These networks and stations must seek the widest possible mass audiences whose levels of taste vary and whose intellectual appetites are frequently base. Television will not get better until all or most of the foregoing changes. The *Daily News* outsells the *Times;* there are more McDonalds than Luteces; and, in our architecture, there is more that is wrong than Frank Lloyd Wright.

I think we should have an elitist national service as a companion to the three commercial networks. Until one is established in this country—where tastes and decisions are dictated as they are with our museums, symphonies, and our opera and ballet companies—any changes in programming will be more apparent than real. Ripples, not tides.

So, if you mean to work in commercial television, do not blame the advertising agencies or the sponsors. They are only components in a complex system. Concentrate rather on their roles as they may affect you as a program maker, and how you should function in relationship to them. Consider also the very real possibility that you may one day work for an advertising agency.

Advertising agencies are not so much in television programming or such "really closh frens wish Carol Burndette un Walsher Conkrite," as a drunken account executive, whom I have not been able to avoid in a mid-Manhattan bar and who has missed his train to Connecticut, is likely to try to tell me; but they are in it—as representatives of the corporate Sforzas and Medicis.

As advisors and decision makers about where and how to spend their clients' monies, advertising agencies exert forceful influence on television programming, though today this influence is circumscribed and not commensurate with the over $2 billion they spend annually for advertising on the three commercial networks. (This amount is spent for time and programs; it does not include costs of production for the commercials themselves.)

Radio started airing commercials in 1925. In those early days and in the beginning of television, advertising agencies, and sometimes the sponsors, directly controlled much of the time and produced many of the programs carried in the schedules. To wit, the "Colgate Comedy Hour," the "Kraft Music Hall," "Armstrong Circle Theatre," the "U.S. Steel Hour," "Lux Presents Hollywood," the "Dinah Shore Chevy Show." They exercised veto power over all programs, other than news and sports which were autonomous or at least more distantly influenced. Since the mid-1960s, however, the networks themselves have insisted on or have had thrust upon them dominance in the control, production, and scheduling of programs.

Currently, no regularly scheduled prime-time programs or time periods are owned or produced by one advertising agency or single sponsor. Seldom are these programs even fully sponsored or supported by one advertiser. Procter & Gamble, Bristol-Myers, General Foods, and other major purchasers do come down with considerable weight in certain daytime situations and Coca-Cola, in the 1974–75 season, for instance, did have full sponsorship of "Kojak" and "Barnaby Jones" in prime-time. Even so, Coke neither produced nor controlled these programs. Persuasion with regard to program content was the only force available to them.

An advertiser's power to control or affect programming is reaction rather than action. When presented with a program idea or schedule not to his liking, the advertiser can refuse to buy in. An advertiser, already committed to a program, can and frequently does, pull out his message if he does not like the script, or if the star should make page one of the *News* for moral turpitude. (On this point, it is difficult to imagine what situation might not make the star more salable than repellent, however.) Pulling out or pulling your commercial usually means that an advertiser will be entitled to a make good. The network makes good the commercial by running it in another comparable minute. Or, *in extremis,* sometimes a network will rebate in full or in part if a commercial does not run, runs without video or audio, is cut in too late, is up cut (cut before it finished), or if one or more affiliated stations does any of these things.

No network likes to rebate; when there is acknowledged trouble, each would prefer to make good. But a big advertiser can threaten to take his big dollar across the street, i.e., to another network, if he is not listened to. But finally, advertisers are to regularly scheduled television what the Queen of England is to the British Commonwealth.

Why do agencies and sponsors accept this modest role when they have such money to muscle around—the money that makes the whole system work? It began, I suppose, in the early sixties (Remember Newton Minow's "The Vast Wasteland"?*) when strong pressures from government and citizens' groups attacked the low quality of advertiser-dominated television and reckoned that the networks should bear full responsibility for the kinds of programs they transmitted. This coincided roughly with rocketing program costs, which few individual advertisers could sustain.

The networks also played a part. With increasing sophistication they realized that individual shows, though fully sponsored, could pull down the shows on either side of them or be incompatible with these shows, not only in gross numbers but in audience differences. Thus were born program flow, block booking, and counterprogramming.

Program flow means that the audience that watches one program will flow into the program that follows. CBS Monday night is designed as a female-appeal, full-comedy menu to achieve flow from its super lead-off hit, "Rhoda." A network attempts to achieve this flow in all parts of the broadcast day. Flow strategy is most effective when a programmer is working around a clear hit. A network can attempt program flow from another network's hit. A strategy of CBS for instance might be to put two situation comedies in the Friday night hour following NBC's hit comedies, "Sanford and Son" and "Chico and the Man," in the hope that the large NBC audience would flow to still more comedy on CBS.

Block booking is an extension of program flow. You schedule, or book, a block of compatible programs.

Counterprogramming means designing a schedule to offer programs that are different from (counter to) the programs available in the same time periods on the other networks. A clear example of counterprogramming is Tuesday night at 9:00 P.M. (autumn 1976): ABC with "Rich Man, Poor Man," a continuing family drama; CBS with situation comedies, "M.A.S.H." and "One Day at a Time"; and NBC with action-adventure, "Police Woman."

Frequently, program flow and counterprogramming turn out to be as scientifically precise as a tout on a race horse from your mailman. Nevertheless, these notions of programming are viewed as golden tablets of faith by the industry and are, in fact, more valid than not.

Where were we? Oh yes, the advertisers got out of programming and the networks got in—"Kinda like us taking over for the French in Vietnam," one jaundiced TV hand has said. In any case, there are additional reasons that make the moneybound agencies submit to network programming dominance while continuing to spend their $2 billion.

Advertisers must use television on whatever terms they can get it, for television is the most potent merchandising vehicle ever devised. Despite your battered senses, there are only a fixed and preciously small number of desirable commercial minutes—six network commercial minutes in a single network prime-time hour, or eighteen minutes in that same hour for all three networks (per half hour in other parts of the day). If it seems at least twice as many, it is because, since 1970, the networks have been selling thirty-second commercials instead of sixties. Most advertisers simply could no longer afford to buy sixty seconds; at the time, this upped the Gelusil intake, but the resourceful advertisers adapted and learned to sell as effectively in thirty seconds as in sixty. Since there are usually more than enough sponsors competing to fill these limited number of "availabilities," as the commercial minutes are called, the advertisers are caught between a rock and

---

*Newton Minow, a Chicago attorney, served as chairman of the Federal Communications Commission and depicted American television in a stinging address as "a vast wasteland."

hard place. Their decision is not so much whether to buy the time or not, because they like the program or not, but rather at what bearable price and delivery efficiency—before they are shut out completely. As one agency man said once, "Bad television is better than no television."

Moreover, the advertising agencies and sponsors know that everyone plays it safe. The networks and program makers are not going to come up with shows that are too esoteric or far-out; that is, no shows that are very different from those the agencies or sponsors themselves would produce, in pursuit of mass audience.

Everyone understands. Even with specials —good drama, for instance—you will more likely get marbleized Tennessee Williams and Arthur Miller than Bertolt Brecht, George Bernard Shaw, or, God forbid, a serious new playwright. A truly noteworthy exception to this rule is the "ABC Theatre" which has presented new works such as "Pueblo," the "Missiles of October," and work from Joseph Papp and the Negro Ensemble Company.

In fact, if a particular program fails or is embarrassing or controversial, the agencies or sponsors can always blame the network or producing company or team or star, which they could not so readily do with more direct involvement. (In turn, of course, a great many programmers sit sunning themselves next to their swimming pools and blame the agencies and sponsors for "what we have to put on.")

Finally, it is not the function of an advertising agency or sponsor to produce programs. To do so would place them in potential conflict-of-interest situations, since they might put their clients or products in such a television program to sustain its success, or simply on a whim, rather than objectively determining if such a show is truly the most efficient outlet for selling.

Nowadays, most network advertising dollars for regularly scheduled programs go toward the purchase of isolated network minutes; that is, as we now see most often, thirty-second commercial messages which are inserted into the programming. These messages are called participating spots, and they are not particularly identifiable with the shows. Usually they must run cheek-by-jowl with the messages of other sponsors' advertisements. (To keep your soap from washing up against your competitor's soap, however, there is a provision called product protection. Product protection means that you are promised a minimum time separation between your brand and their brand of a same product.) Participations are usually part of what is called a scatter plan. This means that an advertiser will scatter the same message in many shows and times and different networks. The scatter plan strategy looks to accomplish with volume what might be missed with intensity. It is Machine Gun Kelly as opposed to William Tell or, more simply, not putting all your eggs in one basket. Given the economics and vagaries of present-day television, scattering is a sound way to reach the maximum audience at the most efficient cost; moreover, for the fainthearted, it is a hell of a lot smaller risk than betting on one show that might be a disaster.

Spot sales are those commercial times bought by national advertisers in local stations (not network), usually in many markets and frequently at the same time, but not necessarily. By the same time I mean 8:00 P.M. in New York, 8:00 P.M. in Seattle, and so on. Local spots are commercials bought by advertisers, mostly in a single or in their local market.

Of course, a big advertiser can still sponsor, say, "Streets of San Francisco" for a whole season (even with participating minutes) and, yes, the sponsor's salesmen can still go on the road talking about our show. There are additional promotional advantages, too. But, even though he may get larger numbers, the advertiser nowadays gets very little identification with the show or the star, Karl Malden, and he certainly will not be allowed to dictate content, time, or day of the series in the schedule.

The mention of Karl Malden brings to mind a new advertising strategy. Malden, as the very visible star portraying a clearly defined detective in a hit series, was hired as a spokesman by American Express Traveller's Cheques to play virtually the same character in a series of "law-and-order" commercials. This way, American Express gets the identification, or rub off, as it is called, with a hit program without having to buy into that program.

Sponsors who make sizable buys are often given star lead-ins—the star of a show, usually holding the product, leads-in to the commercials by saying something like, "And now here's a word from Big Mouth the new antiperspirant toothpaste." Or they get opening and closing billboards. (A billboard is a visual and/or voice-over identification of a product or sponsor tied to the show's title and/or star billing.) For instance, an opening billboard might be, " 'On the Give,' starring Nelson Rockefeller, is brought to you by Virtue Is Not Necessarily Its Own Reward, Inc." A closing billboard alters this to say ". . . *has* been brought to you by . . ." I think these star lead-ins and billboards are meaningless in terms of audience recall or response; they are most valuable as face-saving sweeteners from the networks to the agencies.

But I can recall Mobil bringing us "Masterpiece Theatre," now that I think about it, and I have purposely sought out Mobil filling stations because of it. Billboards are most effective on public television, I think, since they are rarer, though a growing menace.

Thus, the networks decide everything—which programs will be made, where these will go into the schedules, who will be in them, and who will produce and direct and write them. The programs are generally made by the major and independent outside suppliers or by the networks themselves. The advertising agencies and sponsors acquiesce.

But are they so docile that they can only call up networks' Sales Departments and say, "Sell me a minute between 8:00 and 11:00," or "I need daytime the week before Christmas"? Not really. Yes, the smaller agencies and sponsors are not too far removed from such subservience to the networks, but the major agencies and sponsors exert considerably more clout in trying to get exactly the space they want. The networks, for their part, expend millions of dollars and manhours to court and satisfy the important agencies and sponsors.

Here, roughly, is how it works for the prime-time schedule. When the networks have chosen the programs, contracted with suppliers to make them, and have announced their fall schedules (usually around April 15) the major agencies and clients are invited to presentations of those schedules and for screenings of the pilots. From these encounters they will decide about or recommend which shows they think they should buy into.

These days, of course, most of the pilots of programs being seriously considered for a new season can be seen on the air in early spring, before the schedules are set. Here is why: In former times a television season ran for thirty-nine weeks (episodes) from mid-September until late May. More recently, with costs ascending, it has become imperative that networks cut back the number of original episodes and increase the number of reruns, thus amortizing the costs over two plays. This shorter season leaves open time periods in the spring. Furthermore, pilot program costs have also multiplied—each network spends roughly $20 million a year to develop new programs—so it is a further economy to recoup some of these staggering expenditures by playing these sample shows on the air, with commercials. And, what better means of testing audience appeal of a new series than to play the pilot of the series for the general audience which will ultimately judge it in any case?

Even so, the pilots continue to be shown in private screening rooms to important advertisers. In the case of variety shows, where there is seldom a pilot, the star of the show or the producer or both are introduced to potential buyers via conference meetings, luncheons, dinners, or cocktail parties, at which the star or producer will talk through the show.

These are the Rites of the Television Spring, "the Selling Season," the "Mating Season," when advertising agency buyers are avidly sought by the network salesmen. In its four to eight weeks, the voices of advertisers may be heard rising in the land of Manhattan: "Wow, that's gonna be a hot show," or "What a bummer—who dreamed that one up?" "It's a winner; a breakthrough; the guy's a genius; it's perfect for my client." "It's stale; a loser; they must have something on him; I hope the producer's sleeping with the broad playing the lead so it shouldn't be a total loss; that show's a Dunkirk for my client —the *Andrea Doria,* the Edsel, the Havana Hilton, Watergate!''

Agency people pay studious heed to these programs and schedules and consider that their human involvement in the ceremony is essential. The more conscientious ones read all the available scripts and outlines for appeal (and client biases) and go watch the production or meet stars or creators in California. Some do not sleep as they sincerely ponder how to make the shows better or more creative. But all of this is really just so much making love with your clothes on. The truth is, if these people did not like the programs, believe in them, read the scripts, worry about casting, or go to California—nothing much would be different. Finally, they must buy, and they buy mostly on bloodless data, or, as

one agency man told me, ''Our computer calls your computer.'' Do I need that night or time of night or season? (Research, computer, decision.) What preceded and follows the show? What will the other networks be playing against it? What is the station line-up? Live clearance? What has been the track record of the production team? The leads? Will the star do the commercials? The lead-ins? The sales convention? Not just how many people are likely to watch, but what audience composition in terms of my product—young, old, children, women, men, educated, disposable income? How short a commitment can I make? How much will it cost? Does the network really believe in it and will they promote and advertise it? Then, finally, more practically, and a lot more humanly—what choice do I have anyway? And, maybe—maybe—I'll get a couple of tickets to the Super Bowl out of it or meet Mary Tyler Moore.

8
"Now a Few Words About Commercials..."

Jonathan Price

The earliest television commercials were usually broadcast live: a fast-talking pitchman demonstrated twenty ways his jiffy slicer could work miracles in your kitchen. But before long, advertisers turned to film. By the mid-1960s, commercials began to rival programs in their cinematic effects, extravagance, and audience impact. In "Now a Few Words About Commercials . . . ," Jonathan Price argues that TV commercials—far from being program interruptions—"are also part of the entertainment—the best part if we define entertainment as the fantasy satisfaction of more or less unconscious impulses."

The author of *The Best Thing on TV,* from which the following essay is excerpted, Jonathan Price has also written *Life Show: How to See Theater in Life and Life in Theater.* He is the director of the Shakespeare Institute, a video artist, and a critic.

Source: From *The Best Thing on TV,* by Jonathan Price. Copyright © 1978 by Jonathan Price. Reprinted by permission of Viking Penguin Inc.

Somebody was shooting an airline commercial, and they were going to use a condor to simulate flight,'' says Brian Olesky, associate creative director at the ad agency Bozell & Jacobs. "Everyone was ready—they were below a plateau where they were going to let the bird go, and the director gave the signal, and they yelled, 'Release the condor!' Well, they threw the bird up, and somehow they had gotten a bird that didn't fly. Film crews from New York don't know much about birds. These guys couldn't have told a condor from a Mercury Montego. So this bird went up in the air and plummeted about two hundred feet straight down. The crew was filming, and the actors were acting, and the bird went straight down and splattered. And from then on, 'Release the condor' has been a standing joke in the business.''

One measure of the energy admen put into making dreams look real is the money spent on production. Simply staging and filming a thirty-second spot in which an announcer just stands there holding a product can cost over $20,000—when you include labor, editing, and duplicating the final commercial to send around to TV stations. But people tend to tune out mere talking heads, so writers search for the exotic location, the wild break-apart car, the overdone dramatic scene, the coloratura graphics. These can drive costs up to $60,000 at 1978 prices, and if you add a kick line, as in the Busby Berkeley dance-hall routine done for Heinz's "great American soups," you may find production costs these days running over a quarter of a million dollars. If you were to make a feature film at the same rate per minute, you would have to pay thirty million.

It is a strange fantasy world that is reflected in these seconds-long extravaganzas. We see ourselves dancing in a pinball machine, chopping down trees in forests we have never visited; the impossible seems as likely in this world as a car driving down a canal. A paranoid's worst fears are acted out by tanks running over his foot or by a plane landing on his rug; we can follow our unconscious impulses even if it means leaving the football parade to run home for another bite of Kellogg's raisin bran. We see miraculous transformations—people whose bodies suddenly bloat up or turn into bright outlines. We can imagine we have the power to hurl a car into space. We can fantasize about impressing a billionaire. More than any show on adult TV, commercials put their money on the unconscious, reshooting, tinkering, editing, perfecting the unreal until it almost seems real, making one image turn into another at the sound of some disembodied voice, as in our interior life. Admen, sponsors, and audiences participate in these expensive fantasies. Perhaps such productions work for us because they approach the clarity, force, and speed of dreams.

But this dreamworld costs money, at least if we want to see it with Kodak detail on TV. The producer, in fact, has to act like a foreman for God, bossing around forty or fifty people, building the sets, soothing the director, terrifying the talent. He must create—and destroy—a small universe in less than a week. In the Fifties, a producer really did run the whole show, but gradually his role has been reduced from that of a lofty archangel to that of an officious angel with the spirit of an accountant. In the Fifties and early Sixties, a producer working for J. Walter Thompson or some other advertising agency would call up three or four production houses and say, "I've finally got a script here; we'd like you to bid on it." The production house would look at the outline of the commercial, figure on yellow paper, and call back with a total dollar figure; for that money, the agency would get 4,500 feet of clear, professionally shot film, ready to be edited. But big spenders like Lever Brothers or Procter & Gamble wanted to know exactly where their pennies were going, so they made up forms that the production houses had to fill out, showing the budget breakdown. In the late Sixties, after years of dickering, the Association of Independent Commercial Producers—the production houses—made up their own forms so that their people could fill out the same slots, no matter what agency or sponsor they were dealing with.

Here is a list of some of the costs a producer has to figure:

Preproduction and Wrap Costs
Shooting-Crew Labor

Studio Costs: Build/Shoot/Strike
Travel to, Expenses at, Location
Equipment Costs
Film Stock, Develop and Print
Props, Wardrobe, Animals
Payroll Taxes
Director/Creative Fees
Insurance
Markup for Producer
Editorial/Videotape
Extra Days if Bad Weather Strikes
Camera Operator
Prop Crew
Electricians
Grips
Recordist
Boom Man
Makeup
Hair Stylist
Wardrobe Attendant
Home Economist
Video Engineer
Nurse
Generator Man
Actors
Stuntman
Still Photographer
Location Scout
Teamsters

Five pages break these items down even further, and one page summarizes the costs. Most commercials in 1978 run from $20,000 to $40,000 to make, but fancy ones regularly go up to $60,000 and $100,000, and exceptional ones can run past $250,000, plus deposits of as much as $1,000,000 as insurance against damage.

The cash register starts ringing as soon as you decide:

■ to use animals or kids (they are unpredictable, hard to work with, slow, and fussy, so they add days to the shooting time);
■ to go on location in lousy weather (rain postpones shooting a day, but everyone has to sit there in the tent getting paid);
■ to do it in a rush (you may have to use videotape—with a lot of generators, ticklish gear, and temperamental color cameras—just because with videotape you can edit as soon as you have gotten a

shot you like and you can then go on the air that night instead of waiting for film developing and editing, which takes days and sometimes weeks);
■ to try for special effects (you may have to take a few weeks to build a giant tomato, or you may have to buy time in a computer animation studio).

Most producers pad these bids so that if something goes wrong, they can absorb the cost overrun. If you have written about a herd of bulls galloping along the Mississippi next to a steamboat, as in one Merrill Lynch commercial, you will find that no one knows how much it costs to pay for run-amuck bulls, frightened passersby, dung left on the pier, and drowned cattle. So most production houses add a hundred thousand dollars to the estimate just to cover possibilities. Many big advertisers agree to pay all direct costs, giving the production house a certain percentage of those costs as its profit; and to make sure the production house does not simply run up the costs on the sly, the advertiser often has its own overseers, who make sure that every penny spent is necessary. Poor folk, who only spend a few million a year on TV, cannot hire pros to go over the details, so they have to settle for a guaranteed bid: The production house says, in effect, "For $40,000 you get your commercial filmed; if we can keep costs down, we get the profit, but if costs run over that, we'll absorb the loss."

Most scriptwriters, of course, have no sense of costs. One who does is George Lois. "The production of my commercials is a piece of theatrics—but it's done very simply, with great strength. I'll shoot all six of these commercials in one day. It'll come out to maybe four thousand dollars on each one. Young & Rubicam, BBDO, these cinematographers, these film makers, they run sixty, seventy, eighty, maybe a hundred thou a spot."

As Lois suggests, he is an exception. Many writers and ad directors tend to think big. Even if the commercial could be shot in a studio in New York or Los Angeles, as most are, writers tend to ignore how long it takes to capture just the right angle, the right smile, the exact exit. Time—with the entire crew waiting and getting paid to wait—costs the most. If you had a month to shoot and if you could hire electricians and actors for an hour here and an hour there, you could spend much less. But admen are always late, and no one works for less than a full day, so a producer picks two days next month, hires everyone to come then, and the waiting begins.

Jerry Della Femina likes to write but hates to go on shoots. How come? He rolls his eyes to heaven. "Shooting? Shooting? Everybody be there at seven o'clock. You wonder why you must be there at seven o'clock. But you show up at seven o'clock. And you're there at seven o'clock watching guys move a camera. And we've improved everything in the world except the equipment you use to make a commercial. I mean, you pull and you push. There are two guys carrying things on their back, like over the Burma Road, guys stripped to the waist moving giant equipment over the floor, guys hurting themselves, breaking their backs. We shoot a commercial the way we used to build pyramids.

"Then there's the guy who stands there to spray food and make it look pretty. There's the guy who's assigned to read the *Daily News.* He weighs two hundred and seventy-five pounds. You don't even want to ask him what else he does because you know he's going to punch you. So he sits there. He never gets up. He never takes his eyes off that one column. And he's not sleeping. There's another guy who's sleeping. There are maybe thirty-five or forty guys running around doing things. There's the script girl timer lady. Her main job is to look as though she can be made. She works hard. She's like the Red Cross lady, giving people doughnuts filled with garbage and bad coffee. Everyone's staring at the girl; at the beginning of the spot, the actors are playing to her. She's about thirty-one years old, attractive. She always has a stopwatch in her hand. I always suspect that if she really went to bed with anyone, she'd be timing it. 'I'm sorry, that was twenty-seven seconds, you've got to try again.'

"And the first take is always at eleven thirty-five. Guy says, 'What do you think?' The director says, 'I think we should set that

up a little differently.' They set it up till about twelve-fifteen. Guy says, 'We got to break for lunch.' They always go to a very bad restaurant, somewhere downtown. They come back at two. They get their first shot.

"Now the time passes.

"The guy is still reading his *Daily News.* You look up, and it's eleven-thirty at night, and the director is getting very mad at everybody. The script girl will not go home with anybody. The actors are blowing their lines now; it's two in the morning, and everyone feels like they're in movies, they're Frank Capra or Harry Warner.

"If we were really in advertising, the shoot would be over at two o'clock in the afternoon. We'd get set up, shoot, get it done, pack, and get out. It would be fine. But everyone's getting ready for that great script, so we stay up until five in the morning."

Sometimes a rush drives costs up. Brian Olesky, a rising star, says, "I have spent fortunes on commercials. When I was at Wells, Rich, Greene, I did a thirty-second commercial that cost the client over one hundred and thirty thousand dollars. It was such a simple commercial—one man in the first-class lounge of a 747. It could have been shot very inexpensively, but the client—TWA—needed it very quickly. The expenses involved—oh, my God—casting on both coasts, flying people back and forth, the logistics of putting together a commercial in two weeks. One hundred and thirty thousand is a lot of money, but not when you think of the profits in the airline business, when somebody is paying three or four hundred dollars a ticket and you have three or four hundred people on the plane and you're talking about three or four flights a day. Maybe that's why the commercials are the best thing on TV."

And sometimes you have to rent a hangar to build your sets.

Olesky says, "I remember a job that caused a producer to leave the business. We were shooting some TWA commercials in a big sound studio in California. It was a very big-budget job—we were shooting a whole packet of commercials. We had built, well, almost an entire city. We had mock-ups of the

747 on one side, mock-ups of the 707 on the other, mock-ups of an older plane on another —we had sets built in different parts of the studio. We were in there a couple of days shooting, and the thing had been built during the week before we came. The producer had been there to supervise the building. We shot our four commercials, two sixties and two thirties. We wrapped. We did all this to produce three minutes.

"I remember this producer and I were sitting on this piece of wood in the middle of this huge vast studio, with the workers like ants all over the place, tearing down what he had just built for over two hundred thousand dollars. They were ripping it apart. He looked at me, and he said, 'I think this is gonna be my last job. I can't take the unreality of it. I'm living in a fantasy world. I come out here, I spend a fortune, two hundred and fifty thousand dollars more than the average working man makes in twenty years—to build this, we shoot some film, and I tear it down, and I'm off to do something else for Alka-Seltzer! The unreality of it, the money of it. I can't face it.'"

Such men are rare in this business, where most writers and directors dream of going on location. One writer came up with the idea of putting a five-story box of detergent out on an open plain, to be worshiped by hundreds of people. They went to Yugoslavia to build the thing, and as soon as it was built, rain came. For three weeks. The box fell over. So they went to Israel. They built another box. Protesters showed up: The film crew was desecrating an ancient shrine.

Another writer decided to show a Chevy floating down the Grand Canal in Venice. They put the car on a raft that sank under the surface of the water but still floated; by putting the towboat far enough in front, the director made it look as if the Chevrolet was really driving down the canal. They showed Italians saying things that the subtitles translate as, "Look at the beautiful car." That commercial made a brief splash.

When Daniel & Charles agency sent people from the Lee Lacy studio to England to shoot a commercial demonstrating the "crushed look" of Wohl Shoes, they borrowed the Duke of Bedford's front lawn, sprayed it with green paint, added two thousand daisies, built a bunker for the cameraman, rented a Sherman tank, and had the tank run over the shoes several times. Said the duke afterward, "If it was a crushed look they were after, they should have seen my face when I saw my lawn."

One scriptwriter found out that in Soviet Georgia, where some people live to be over 100 years old (one is 140), they eat a lot of yogurt. In a few weeks, an ad team looked up a town, booked flights, moved in, and interviewed some friendly old folks who could claim a century or so working outdoors as beekeepers, shepherds, or gardeners. Most did eat yogurt—and vegetables—but not much meat. They drank homemade wine. The film crew gave out Dannon yogurt and filmed the centenarians eating it and dancing in their native outfits. They made several commercials from these cute scenes. One ends: "Eighty-nine-year-old Bagrat Topagua liked Dannon so much he ate two cups. That pleased his mother very much." She smiles and pats him. Soviet scientists were annoyed at the popularity of this commercial and—flat-footedly taking it seriously argued that yogurt was not the only thing that keeps people alive for a century. Hard work outdoors and the respect of an extended family are at least as important as yogurt, stated a doctor from the Kiev Institute of Gerontology: "The person made things, and he was happy."

Some commercials don't need to be shot on location to get astonishing effects, though. Some, shot from airplanes, often involve hours of ticklish preparation and testing, but they let us see things as if we were birds—or golf balls. Leber-Katz Partners decided that we might want to see what a golf course looks like from on top of the ball as it spins down the first hole. And so we do. *Whack!* We go up fast, just behind a Maxfli ball spinning backward as we look down at the Braemar Country Club, in Tarzana, California. The Maxfli is really a specially made "golf ball" the size of a basketball, painted white and mounted on a rotisserie slung under a helicopter. The cameraman was strapped underneath the helicopter; below him was a net in case he fell. Even more extravagant, Mohasco once made up a giant Mohawk carpet, unrolled it the length of the local airport, and had a plane land on it.

Such spots encourage us to imagine life the way kids do: Planes can land on the rug, we can fly, and cars can too—until we drop them. Jack Keil, at Dancer Fitzgerald Sample agency, wanted the new Toyota to float in space, but he didn't want any trick photography, and he needed the finished commercial in a month. He hired "one of the best riggers in the business," who took a big truck and built a stanchion on it with a strong steel arm that went out like a question mark. "Now this arm did a dogleg to hold the car. And inside the car we put gears. When we activated this electronically, it would turn. We could shoot underneath, back to front; it could tilt and turn and twist; and we could go underneath it.

"But when we first rigged this out in the field and he yelled, 'Okay, let her go,' as soon as he said that, whoop, the truck went up in the air, and the car dropped. 'Oh, well,' he said. So then he put eight tons on the front of his truck to hold it down. Then we worried about the bar holding the car. We went into the studio and cut through the floor and put chains around the axles of the truck and chained it to bedrock. So then the car starts doing that turning and bucking some twenty feet up in the air, and we start filming.

"We had dummies up in the car—we couldn't get real people up there with all the gears, and besides, no person would get in that thing—and every once in a while the car would tilt and a dummy's arm would fly out." The commercial's "look" was finished off by adding Christmas tree lights on black drapes to look like stars.

Extravagant fantasies like this are simply bigger, realer, more expensive versions of a child's knocking a toy off a table or skimming it over the water in the bath. In a minor extravaganza of its own, Volkswagen once drove a car off a pier and onto the water: *onto* the water because it floated. Floated? It skipped! In fact, it shot so far out to sea they

had to use a motorboat to bring it back. Ford figured their car was just as airtight and rented a pool. They lowered the car into the water. It sank.

More expensive are the operations in which the producer plays doctor on a car, taking it apart. Of course when a child takes something apart, it stops. But why can't it go on moving, in pieces? Several productions have spent hours of mechanics' time recreating this fantasy. Chevrolet once cut an Impala in half lengthwise and drove both halves down the street. Extra wheels and tiny gas tanks were added on the inside, and the ad agency hired a midget as the driver.

Such effects may look like trick photography, but they aren't. They appeal to our unconscious, which is always a child, because they make "real" what we previously only imagined. Sometimes this "reality" is impossible to achieve; then the Alice in Wonderland effect must be put across with the cameraman's magic: When the tiny woman walks among West Bend slow cookers twice as tall as she is or leans against the buttons of Sanyo radios as big as a house, one camera shoots the product, another shoots the spokeswoman, very far off; and by pressing a button labeled "key," the producer "keys" the woman into the pot. But whether they do it in reality or in video gear, most producers insist on making the unreal as real as possible—for themselves and their lawyers, not just for us.

Some inner experiences, though, cannot be shown photographically—the feeling of an attack of indigestion, for instance. So the producer may turn to a computer-animation studio like Dolphin Productions in New York for help. With Pepto-Bismol, for example, we see a sorry-looking executive worrying his eyebrows, his pencil, his manila folder, his mouth. Behind him a guy is washing the windows. The executive looks up with white-eyed horror. He turns green, literally, and says, "Indi-i-i . . ."—as his ghostly form bubbles like a fun-house mirror—"gestion." The window washer stares at him. And the announcer says, "Pepto-Bismol" as the label runs across the screen and erases the scene. Now a woman is sitting on a white sofa with her terrier. "Indi . . ."—she turns purple, and her swollen belly wiggles toward the dog—"gestion." The dog gets up; he backs off, fearful. Now a construction worker gets hit: His belly fills out in orange. Then the logo's words get coated with pink liquid: It pours down inside the white letters that spell out COATS, SOOTHES, RELIEVES. How's it done? First the Dolphin crew records the image of a real environment for the background. Then they place the actor who is about to suffer in front of a blue curtain. His image is fed into an analogue computer that allows Dolphin to manipulate his shape to express a particular form of digestive distress—rubbery bones, billowing belly. Appropriate colors, such as purple, green, and orange, are washed over the actor at the same time. Then, showing the background throughout, the Dolphin team assembles the pieces so that we can watch the real picture dissolve into the "unreal" one while the surroundings remain unchanged. The entire scene is then wiped away by a huge bottle of Pepto-Bismol while the announcer reverently repeats the product's name.

Even more spectacular electronic effects mimic the rush of information, stored images, and linked ideas brought up to consciousness by psychedelic drugs. For Pepsi, a bicyclist rides across the screen in outline. He leaves behind about twenty afterimages, white lines that trail him, moving behind him. In this wake of electrons, a blue tumbler—partly real, partly abstract—flips into place from the right. From the left, about fifty orange basketball players rush in and become one; from the right, twenty hockey players lift strangely glowing blue sticks; now the basketball players shoot. All dissolve as a bottle top tips toward us, with the Pepsi label. We open that and see real pictures through it: a golfer, tennis doubles, scuba divers; then the fast-cut disco scenes reduce into the bottle again. We hear a loud sound of pouring. As we hear the gurgle, a line forming waves rises through the picture; what shows below is a picture of Pepsi bottles on ice, revolving. The circular motion gets mimicked by a blue mist that ebbs in from all sides, narrowing down so we can only see the bottles through an oval in the middle of a solid-blue field. Then from the lower right, blurred letters rush up, tossing off loose electrons, to form the logo: Pepsi.

The producer of such commercials presides over a fairy world in which he uses dozens of people, tons of time and talent, and hundreds of feet of film to create the illusion that with a certain product we can fly like a golf ball or drive on water. If asked why he does this, a production chief might answer, "To make money and to sell the product."

But for most of these grown-ups, working all these hours, eating so many bad doughnuts, the real product is the commercial. Yes, it may move paper towels—later. But for the production crew, such results seem transcendental. And what kind of product have they made? Forty-five feet of film, or nine hundred frames of videotape, when edited. An artificial universe in which we can indulge in dreams of having magical powers to change our size, shape, location, car, even our visual perceptions by swallowing something, saying a rhyme, or buying a shiny object.

When we watch these spots, we're not spending time on comparative shopping or intellectual testing of rival claims. So what are we doing? Radical critics of television point out that television executives tend to view television as a device to collect thousands of viewers, a "product" to be sold to the advertisers. But in fact, the commercials are also part of the entertainment—the best part if we define *entertainment* as the fantasy satisfaction of more or less unconscious impulses.

From this point of view, the writers, actors, director, and producer of a commercial may all be seen as unwitting partners with the audience in a vast dance of culture as we perform and applaud our own inner life writ large and bright in thirty-second fragments. As emblems for our collective unconscious and as the ironic end result of our constant financial interaction, commercials may be America's most significant product.

9

You Haven't Come a Long Way, Baby: Women in Television Commercials

Carol Caldwell

The resistance of women's groups to advertising has been a mass media issue since the end of the nineteenth century, when a midwestern women's association protested the depiction of women in posters and advertisements. The association felt that advertisers had finally gone too far: advertisements were irresponsibly endangering American family life by portraying women in roles *outside* the hearth and home.

In the following article, Carol Caldwell, a former copywriter, examines the current resistance of women to advertising and summarizes the contemporary social issues involved in the media's perpetuation of unflattering stereotypes. Her central question is fundamental to an understanding of how advertising works to shape personal values and funnel social change: "Why have advertisers, who make their living keeping up with trends, been so slow to get on board with the women's revolution?"

It's the beginning of the age of television, and all around it's black and white. Millions of minuscule scan dots collide in electronic explosion to create Woman in her Immaculate Kitchen. She is Alpha, Omega, eternal and everlasting Mother Video, toasting and frying, cleansing and purifying, perfectly formed of fire and ice. Permanent-waved, magenta-lipped, demurely collared and cuffed, cone-shaped from her tightly cinched waist down through yards and yards of material that brush coquettishly midcalf, she is Betty Furness for Westinghouse; and you can be *sure* if it's Westinghouse.

The year is 1951. On the set of CBS-TV's *Studio One,* Furness has just captured the part to become America's first full-time product spokeswoman on television. Advertising execs at Westinghouse are taking a stab at having someone other than the host sell their product; they reason (and quite correctly) that Furness, with her Brearley School cool and her Broadway glamor, is a figure thousands of women will admire and listen to. During the audition Betty alters the script supplied by the casting director. Later, she tells *Time* magazine that she ad-libbed the refrigerator routine because "it was written like men think women talk!"

1952. While John Daly, Bill Henry, and Walter Cronkite monitor Ike and Adlai at the conventions, Betty Furness opens and shuts forty-nine refrigerators, demonstrates the finer points of forty-two television sets, twenty-three dishwashers and twelve ovens for a total of four-and-a-half hours of air time. General Eisenhower is on the air approximately an hour and twenty minutes; Mr. Stevenson, fifty minutes.

Source: From *New Times* (June 10, 1977). Reprinted by permission of the author.

1956. Bright and blondeened, twenty-eight-year-old Julia Meade is the commercial spokeswoman for Lincoln on the *Ed Sullivan Show,* for Richard Hudnut hair products on *Your Hit Parade,* for *Life* magazine on John Daly's news show. She is pulling down a hundred thousand dollars a year, which moves *Time* to comment, "Julia (34–20–34) is one of a dozen or so young women on TV who find self-effacement enormously profitable." Howard Wilson, a vice-president of Kenyon & Eckhardt, Lincoln's ad agency, hired Julia for the spots with trepidation: a woman just couldn't be convincing about such things as high torque, turbo drive, and ball-joint suspensions. His fears, it turns out, were unfounded, and Meade becomes the perky prototype for a whole slew of carefully coiffed women selling cars—selling *anything*—by means other than their technical knowledge. And so Julia Meade begat Bess Myerson, who begat Anita Bryant, who begat Carmelita Pope, who begat Florence Henderson, each wholesome, flawless, clear of eye and enunci ation, in short, sixty-second reminders of everything the American woman ought to be.

Times change, however, and eventually infant TV's ideal, untouchable dozen spokeswomen were replaced by hundreds of nameless actresses who portray "the little woman" in scenarios believed, by the agencies who create them, to be honest-to-God, middle-American, slice-of-life situations. As early as 1955, this new wave of commercial realism got a pat on the back by the industry's weekly trade paper, *Advertising Age.* Procter & Gamble had just come out with a revolutionary new way to sell soap on TV: "It is very difficult for a soap commercial to emerge from the mass of suds, with every known variant on the familiar theme of the woman holding up a box of 'X' soap powder with a grisly smile pointing to a pile of clothes she has just washed. Cheer has come up with the unique approach of dramatizing an everyday washing problem from the poor woman's point of view with a sound-over technique of stream of consciousness."

That stream of consciousness flowed unchecked until Bill Free's famous National Air-

lines "Fly Me" faux pas in 1971. Women activists carried signs, stormed Free's and National's offices, read proclamations, and permeated the media with protest. Free talks of this trying and critical time with a humor and stoicism that comes from a six-year perspective, and from no longer handling the account. "The women's movement was identifying itself—and our 'Fly me' campaign was an opportunity for a public platform. We were deluged with letters and calls. I even got an absurd letter from one of the leaders of the movement (who must go unnamed) demanding that I surely planned the sexual innuendo in the word 'fly'—she meant as in men's trouser pants." He paused. "The ad community continues to demean women, far more subtly than in our campaign."

There are some easy hints at why this is so: Of the seventy-five thousand people currently employed in advertising, only 16.7 percent are women in other than clerical positions—not exactly an overwhelming voice. And, while advertising executives often live in the suburbs of large cities, they just as often tend to have a low regard for anyone who isn't an urbanite. As one New York agency executive quipped, "All I really know about the Middle America I sell to everyday is that it's the place I fly over to get to L.A."

But these notations still don't answer the question: Why have advertisers, who make their living keeping up with trends, been so slow to get on board with the women's revolution? Where was everybody the recent night David Brinkley closed the book on America's traditional homelife structure, citing the fact that a mere seven percent of our nation's homes still maintained the time-honored tradition of the everyday housewife. Mom has officially flown the coop just about everywhere, except on TV in the commercials.

At a roundtable on women's advertising sponsored by the agency trade publication *Madison Avenue,* Harriet Rex, a vice-president at J. Walter Thompson, had this comment to make: "There's always been a lag between what is and what the ad business has codified as what 'is.'" And Rena Bartos, a senior VP at the same agency, said, "Advertising may be a mirror of society but somehow the image in that mirror is a little out of focus. It plays back a 1950s reflection in a 1970s world.''

Madison Avenue's ''little woman'' is hardly new, and only partially improved. When feminists cite advertising that is ''acceptable,'' it's invariably print ads. This isn't surprising, since magazine ads are prepared for specific subscribers whose personal backgrounds and attitudes have been carefully documented by the publication and noted by the agency. Television, on the other hand, commands a much larger and subsequently less definable audience.

So it is left to the advertisers and their agencies to define who television's consuming woman might be and what type of commercial she might like. The reward is compelling: Americans heap a total $9.2 billion every year into the coffers of the nation's top three TV advertisers—Procter & Gamble, Bristol-Myers, and General Foods. Still, the women portrayed aren't always to the customers' liking, and last year agitated viewers marched en masse outside P&G headquarters in Cincinnati, suggesting in rather unladylike terms what to do with Mr. Whipple and his grocery store groupies. Inside, P&G stockholders took little heed, voting down a suggestion that their commercial portrayal of women be reconsidered.

Others in the business did listen. When the National Organization for Women sent all major advertising agencies a position paper on the role of women in commercials, no one was surprised that most of the commercials on the air didn't jibe with the NOW requirements. Several agencies, fearing intervention by the Federal Trade Commission, prodded their own regulatory outfit to consider the matter. The National Advertising Review Board formed a panel, including Patricia Carbine, publisher of *Ms.*; Joyce Snyder, coordinator of the task force on the image of women for NOW; the vice-presidents of broadcast standards for ABC and NBC; and a number of officers of sponsoring companies. A twenty-one page directive came out in 1975, in which the panel made a number of suggestions concerning ways in which advertisers could improve their portrayal of women. Here's what came out in the wash: ''Advertis-

ing must be regarded as one of the forces molding society,'' the study asserted. ''Those who protest that advertising merely reflects society must reckon with the criticism that much of the current reflection of women in advertising is out of date.'' Before airing a commercial, the panel urged advertisers to run down the NARB checklist, which included the following points:

- Are sexual stereotypes perpetuated in my ads? Do they portray women as weak, silly and over-emotional?
- Are the women portrayed in my ads stupid?
- Do my ads portray women as ecstatically happy over household cleanliness or deeply depressed because of their failure to achieve near-perfection in household tasks?
- Do my ads show women as fearful of not being attractive, of not being able to keep their husbands or lovers, fearful of in-law disapproval?
- Does my copy promise unrealistic psychological rewards for using the product?

Well now, does it? With these self-regulatory commandments in mind, I spent four weeks in front of daytime TV, logging current household product commercials and trying to determine just where women stand in the advertising scheme of things. During that time, Iris dickered with Rachel and Mac's teetering marriage, Beth died, Stacy miscarried, and Jennifer killed John's wife so they could finally be together.

Now a word from our sponsors.

Ring around the collar lives. After eight long years, the little woman is still exposing hubby and the kids to this awful embarrassment. It can strike virtually anywhere—in taxis, at ballgames, even on vacation doing the limbo. Our lady of the laundry is always guilty, always lucky to have a next-door neighbor who knows about Wisk, the washday miracle, and always back in hubby's good, but wary, graces by the happy ending. The Wisk woman faces the same unspoken commercial threat that the Geritol woman faces: ''My wife, I think I'll keep her . . .'' *if* she keeps in line.

Jim Jordan is president of Batten, Barton, Durstine and Osborn Advertising. Eight years ago, in a fit of cosmic inspiration, he came up with "ring around the collar" for his agency's client, Lever Bros. Since then, Jordan has run check-out-counter surveys on his commercials, asking shoppers who were purchasing Wisk, "You must be buying this product because you like the commercials." The reply he got was always the same. "Why no! I hate those commercials; but why should I hold that against the product?"

Jim Jordan echoes advertising's premier axiom: "The purpose of the commercial is not the aesthetic pleasure of the viewer—it's to sell the product." And Wisk is selling like gangbusters. He doesn't believe "ring around the collar" commercials show women in an embarrassing light; and to assume that, he says, "would be giving commercials more credit than they deserve."

Perhaps. And perhaps his "ring around the collar" campaign is getting more credit than it deserves for selling Wisk. Take any commercial with a simple message, repeat it again and again, and the product, if it's good, will sell, even if the spot is mindless and annoying. It's fixing the name of the product in the consumer's mind with a quick, catchy phrase that's important.

The household slice-of-life commercial is one of the classic offenders of the NARB checklist. (Are sexual stereotypes perpetuated? You'd best believe it. Are the women portrayed stupid? And how.) Crisco's current campaign is a flawless example of this much-imitated genre, which has been developed and designed by Procter & Gamble. In it various long-suffering husbands and condescending neighbors are put through the heartache of greasy, gobby chicken and fries, all because some unthinking corner cutter spent "a few pennies less" on that mainstay of American cookery, lard. These pound-foolish little women cause their loved ones to live through "disasters" and "catastrophes." At the cue word "catastrophe," our video crumples into wavy electronic spasms and thrusts us back to the scene of the crime: to that excruciating point in the Bicentennial picnic or the backyard cookout when Dad has to wrinkle his upper lip and take Mom aside for a little set-to about her greasy chicken. The moral, delivered by some unseen pedantic male announcer, is plain: "Ladies who've learned—buy Crisco."

These examples are, sad to say, still very much the rule for women's portrayals in thirty- and sixty-second spots. They occur with alarming regularity during the daytime hours, when stations may sell up to sixteen commercial minutes an hour. (The nighttime rate is a mere eight minutes, forty seconds per hour.) Now, you are probably not the average American who spends some six hours a day in front of the old boob tube (which, when the maximum number of commercials per hour is computed, means over an hour and a half of product propaganda). And you probably are quite sure that commercials have absolutely no effect on you. Maybe they don't. But a shaken agency copywriter told me the first word his child spoke was "McDonald's," and I've stood in a grocery line and watched while a mother, tired of her child's tears, lets him wander off and return—not with a candy bar, but with a roll of Charmin. Make no mistake about it: the cumulative effects of commercials are awesome. As the NARB study argues: "An endless procession of commercials on the same theme, all showing women using household products in the home, raises very strong implications that women have no other interests except laundry, dishes, waxing floors, and fighting dirt in any form. . . . Seeing a great many such advertisements in succession reinforces the traditional stereotype that a 'woman's place is *only* in the home.' "

There have, in the past few years, been commercials that break the homebody mold. The Fantastik spray commercial, "I'm married to a man, not a house" (which, incidentally was written and produced by men), has reaped much praise, as has L'Orcal's "I'm worth it" campaign. "Ten years ago, it would have been, 'John thinks I'm worth it,' " says Lenore Hershey, editor of *Ladies' Home Journal. Ms'* Pat Carbine thinks United Airlines is flying right when they address women executives, "You're the boss." She also likes the Campbell's soup "working wife" commercial, in which a man scurries around the kitchen, preparing soup for his woman, but adds, "I'm afraid they took the easy route and resorted to total role reversal—making her look good at the expense of the man."

Indeed, Lois Wyse of Wyse Advertising fears that advertisers are not only failing to talk to today's women, but they're missing men as well. The reason for this, as she sees it, is research—the extensive demographic studies done on who buys what product. Last winter Wyse told *Madison Avenue,* "About twenty years ago we were all little Ozzies and Harriets to all the people who do research, and now their idea of contemporizing is to make the Ozzies into Harriets and the Harriets into Ozzies."

Marketing research, with its charts and graphs and scientific jargon, has increased in importance over the last ten years or so, while creativity, the keystone to the Alka-Seltzer, Volkswagen, and Benson & Hedges campaigns of the sixties, has taken the backseat. Ask anybody in advertising why commercials still show the little woman bumbling around in a fearful daze, and you'll find the answer is always the same: "Because our research tells us it is so." Agencies devote hundreds of thousands of dollars to find out who's buying their client's stuff and why. And it's not just Mom up there on the charts and graphs. Marketing researchers dissect and analyze the buying habits, educational and income levels of every member of the family. They even know what we do with our leisure time, and how much God we've got.

This subjective form of research is amorphously titled life-style research, explained by the respected *Journal of Marketing* in the following brave-new-world lingo: "Life-style data—activities, interests, opinions—have proved their importance as a means of *duplicating* the consumer for the marketing researcher. . . ." And more: "Life-style attempts to answer questions like: What do women think about the job of housekeeping? Do they see themselves as homebodies or swingers? Life-style provides definitions like 'housewife role haters,' 'old fashioned homebodies' and 'active affluent urbanites.'"

But life-style research is still in its infancy

and very, very expensive. The trendiest and most attainable form of research going is called focus-group research, the grassroots movement of advertising research. From lairs of hidden cameras and tape-recording devices, agency and client-types, despite the experts' warnings that focus-group samples are far too small to be projected on a national scale, eke out a vision of their consumer that almost invariably fits just the stereotype they had in mind in the first place, and proceed to advertise accordingly.

The theory, quite simply, is to get inside women's heads in order to get inside their pocketbooks. From Satellite Beach to Spokane, fact-finding specialists are retained at grand sums to commune with the natives and document their particular buying habits. For instance:

The canned-meat industry's advertising wasn't paying off in the Southeast. Focus-group researchers were called in and groups of eight women were randomly selected from Memphis neighborhoods. The women fit the product's buyer profile—in this case, all came from families with middle to lower-middle incomes. Each woman was paid ten dollars. On an assigned day each focus group would meet for a two-hour session at the suburban home of the researcher's field representative—a woman who was a veteran of several similar exercises. As the women took their seats around the dining room table, loosening up with coffee and homemade cake, the client and agency folk sat, out of sight, in the rumpus room, carefully scanning the meeting on closed-circuit monitors. This is what they heard.

MODERATOR: Do any of you ever buy canned meats?
VOICES: Oh yes. Yeah. Uh, huh.
MODERATOR: When do you buy them?
ANN: Well, my husband went to New Orleans, so I bought a lot of canned goods. The children enjoy them.
LOU: Well, I bought Vienna sausage the other day 'cause the Giant had a special on it—seventy-nine cents a can—it's usually a dollar nine, a dollar nineteen. You could only get four at a time, so I went back twice that week.

MODERATOR: Do you buy these for particular members of the family?

NORMA: If they didn't like it, I wouldn't buy it.

DELORES: Melvin loves the hot dog chili. And the baby—you can just stick a Vienna sausage in her hand and she'll go 'round happy all day.

MODERATOR: Do you read the labels on canned meats?

VOICES: Oh sure. Yes.

NORMA: The children read the labels first and called my attention to it. When I saw it had things like intestines and things like that, I didn't want to buy potted meat any more.

LOU: Fats, tissues, organs. If you read the labels on this stuff—when they say hearts . . . I don't know. I don't like hearts.

VIRGINIA: Well, psychologically you're not geared to it.

ALMA: They could lie on the label a little bit. Just don't tell us so much. (Laugh.) It would taste pretty good, but . . . yeah. I'd rather not know.

MODERATOR: What do you think ought to be on the labels?

ANNE: I think you ought to know about the chemicals.

NORMA: I love to read calories on the side of a can.

DELORES: I wonder what all's in those preservatives?

IDA: The side of this Hormel can here says that this meat is made by the same company that makes Dial soap. Says Armour-Dial.

NORMA: At least you think it's clean.

DELORES: Some preservatives do taste like soap. . . .

IDA: I wouldn't be eating that stuff with them chemicals.

ANN: Well, if you worry about that, you're going to starve to death.

VIRGINIA: You'd never eat in a restaurant if you ever got back in the kitchen.

MODERATOR: Would you buy a product because of the advertising?

VOICES: No. No. Maybe.

IDA: My children love that Libby's—the one, "Libby's, Libby's, Libby's. . . ."

NORMA: Now, if there's young kids that go to the grocery store with you, everytime they'll pick up something. . . "Libby's, Libby's, Libby's."

DELORES: Every time I see Hormel chili . . . I think about them people out at a fireside by the beach eating that chili. One of them is playing a guitar and they start singing.

VIRGINIA: Armour has a cute hot dog commercial, that's where they're all marching around, weenies, ketchup and mustard. . . .

IDA: Yeah. That's cute.

MODERATOR: Do any of you ever buy Spam?

IDA: What's Spam?

ANNE: It's chopped something. Or pressed.

LOU: It's beaver board.

MODERATOR: Beaver what?

Most researchers claim that their studies are only as good as the people who interpret them. The interpreters are usually the agency and clients who—many advertising executives will admit, but only off the record—read their own product concerns into the comments of the panelists. Quite often, complaints about daytime commercials ("They're awful!" "Ridiculous!" "Laughable!") are brushed aside. "You can formulate breakthrough approaches in order to reach this new woman," Joan Rothberg, a senior VP at Ted Bates, told *Madison Avenue,* "and yet the traditional 'Ring Around the Collar' approach wins out in terms of creating awareness and motivating people to buy the product."

One of the final research tests a commercial can go through after it's been created and storyboarded is the Burke test. One day up at my old agency, the creative director, a writer, and an art director came blazing through the halls with hats and horns, announcing at 120 decibels, "We Burked twenty-nine! We Burked twenty-nine!" Now this may sound to you as it did to me that day, as if these people were talking in tongues. What having "Burked twenty-nine" actually means is the percentage the commercial scored in recall after one viewing by a large audience. The average number on the Burke scale for the particular product my friends were testing was twenty-five—so you can understand the celebration.

Because the agencies and their clients accept Burke scores as valid, the scores become a powerful factor in what types of commercials will run. It's no accident that the Burke company is located in Cincinnati, since Cincinnati is the birthplace of Crest, Crisco, Comet, Charmin, Cheer, Bonus, Bounce,

Bounty, Bold, Lava, Lilt, Pampers, Prell, Downy, Dash, and Duz—in other words, Cincinnati is the home of the King Kong of Household Cleanliness, Procter & Gamble. From high atop magnificent offices, P&G executives control daytime television and a goodly portion of prime time, too. They are the top-dollar spender on TV, having put out $260 million last year alone in commercial time bought. They produce and have editorial control over five of the biggest soap operas on TV: *As the World Turns, Another World, Edge of Night, Guiding Light,* and *Search for Tomorrow,* which reach some forty million women every day.

Procter & Gamble is the most blatant offender in perpetuating "the little woman" commercial stereotype. Because of its monopoly on both media and marketplace (it pulls in $3.6 billion every year) and because its research is the most expensive and extensive, P&G is the recognized leader and arbiter of format and content in household product commercials—where P&G goes, others will follow.

This does not spur innovation. In one P&G agency, the creative people have two formulae they use for "concepting" a commercial: regular slice-of-life (problem in the home, solution with the wonderful product) or what the agency guys call "two C's in a K." The "K" stands for kitchen; the "C" is a four-letter word.

Once a commercial is written, tested, and approved by the client, it's got to be cast and shot. I asked Barbara Claman to talk about what agency people and their clients ask for when they're casting housewife roles. She should know: Barbara's built up one of the largest commercial casting agencies in the country. The day we talked all hell was breaking loose outside her office door. Scores of women and children had come to try out for a McDonald's commercial.

I wondered if agencies ever called for a P&G-type housewife for their commercials.

"Absolutely. She should be blond—or, if brunette, not too brunette. Pretty, but not too pretty. Midwestern in speech, middle-class looking, gentile. If they want to use blacks, they want *waspy* blacks."

"What about P&G-type husbands?"

"Same thing," Claman said. "But you'll find that the husband is getting to play the asshole more and more in American commercials."

"But do you see a change occurring? A trend in women's portrayals away from the traditional P&G type?"

"A little. I think they'd like to be a little more real. They're realizing, very slowly, that the working woman has a lot of money."

"What if they want a Rosie, a Madge or a Cora—one of the Eric Hoffer working-class philosopher-queens?"

Barbara laughed. "They'll say, 'Let's cast a ballsy one.'"

"Are you offended by the roles they want to put women in? Do you try to change their thinking on this?"

"I'm totally offended. I'm tired of seeing women hysterical over dirt spots on their glasses. I get lady producers in here all the time. We've tried to change their minds about the roles. You see how successful we've been."

Jane Green is another casting director in New York. She tells of a friend who was auditioning for a P&G spot in which the agency's creative people were trying to break out of the housewife mold. They'd called interesting faces—real people who wore real clothes. A couple of hours passed and the P&G client was obviously agitated. He turned to the agency producer: "What are you people trying to pull over on me? The woman in this commercial needs to be *my* wife, in *my* bathroom in Cincinnati—not some hip little chickie. Whom do you think we're selling to?"

One wonders. Recently an agency producer asked me and my cat Rayette to be in a kitty litter commercial. I arrived wearing blue jeans and a shirt, my usual at-home ensemble. The art director, who was wearing jeans himself, wasn't pleased: "Where is your shirtwaist? I told the producer I wanted a *housewife* look in this commercial." I tried to explain that most women—housewives and otherwise—had left those McMullans and Villagers back at the Tri Delt house in '66. The shoot was postponed until we found something that looked more housewifey.

Some commercial trends have passed:

The damsel in distress has, for the time being, retreated to her tower. (Remember the thundering White Knight? The mystical, spotless Man from Glad? Virile, barrel-chested Mr. Clean?) But others remain, the most blatantly offensive, perhaps, being those commercials using women as sex objects to entice the consumer into buying the product. Most agency people aren't allowed to comment on the scheme of things in such commercials (one slip of the tongue and that multimillion-dollar account might choose another, more circumspect agency). But Dwight Davis, VP and creative director on the Ford dealers' account with J. Walter Thompson in Detroit, says it's no secret Detroit is still the national stronghold of selling with sex. Why? The male is still the decision maker in car buying ("Our research tells us it is so"); and the auto is still an extension of the American male libido. So we've got Catherine Deneuve hawking Lincoln-Mercurys. She circles the car in her long, slinky gown and slips inside to fondle the plush interior. Catherine signs off, sprawled across the hood of the car, with a seductive grrrrr. She is, as Davis describes the phenomenon, the car advertisers' "garnish on the salad."

Commercials like this, and the little woman slice-of-life, are caricatures of themselves. That's precisely why Carol Burnett and the people at *Saturday Night Live* have so much fun with them. Even the new wave of women's commercials isn't spared. In a spoof Anne Beatts wrote for *Saturday Night,* a middle-class Mom, dressed not in a shirtwaist but a polyester pantsuit, rushes into the kitchen, crashing through a café-curtained dutch door. She starts to have a heart-to-heart with the camera: "I'm a nuclear physicist and Commissioner of Consumer Affairs." She starts to put her groceries away.

"In my spare time, I do needlepoint, read, sculpt, take riding lessons, and brush up on my knowledge of current events. Thursday's my day at the day-care center, and then there's my work with the deaf; but I still have time left over to do all my own baking and practice my backhand, even though I'm on call twenty-four hours a day as a legal aid lawyer in Family Court. . . ." Our New-Wave Mom is still running on, all the time very carefully folding the grocery bags and stuffing them into a cabinet where literally hundreds of other carefully folded bags are stacked incredibly neatly, when the omniscient announcer comes in:

"How does Ellen Sherman, Cleveland housewife, do it all? She's smart! She takes Speed. Yes, Speed—the tiny blue diet pill you don't have to be overweight to need."

If the "average" woman is true to her portrayal in commercials, we've got a pretty bitter pill to swallow. But you know, we all know, commercials don't portray real life. Nice Movies' Dick Clark, who's done spots for Coca-Cola, Toyota, and Glade, points out, most commercials are "formula answers to advertising questions—bad rip-offs of someone else's bad commercials." They are bad rip-offs of their viewers too. But, someday, some bright young advertising prodigy will begin a whole new trend of commercials that don't talk down, don't demean or debase, and still sell soap or toothpaste or cars like crazy. And then everyone will be doing it. Double your money back, guaranteed.

Why am I so sure? Because, as Brinkley so neatly points out, only seven percent of our homes have the traditional resident Mom. Because there are more women doctors, engineers, copywriters, jockeys, linesmen, you name it, than ever before. Because women are becoming more selective in their buying habits. Because, quite simply, research tells me it is so.

Government Regulation: Freedom and Controls

At the heart of the government's relationship to the mass media in the United States is the First Amendment to the Constitution: "Congress shall make no law respecting an establishment of religion, or prohibiting the free exercise thereof; or abridging the freedom of speech, or of the press; or the right of the people peaceably to assemble, and to petition the Government for a redress of grievances." While the language of the First Amendment seems, on the surface, rather absolute, the only communications media its authors knew were those of the printed and spoken word. Recordings, radio, films, and television each presented new legal and regulatory difficulties that could not possibly have been envisioned by the framers of the Constitution.

For example, to bring order to a chaotic electromagnetic spectrum, Congress had to pass the landmark legislation that set up the Federal Communications Commission, the Communications Act of 1934. This act, still in effect today, created the regulatory body that allocates broadcast frequencies and licenses individuals to use them "in the public interest, convenience, and necessity." The problems involved in the subsequent regulation of broadcast media otherwise protected by the First Amendment remain a major concern of communications practitioners and scholars.

The basic legal differences in modern media regulation are compared in this section's first selection. In an excerpt from *The Mass Media and Modern Society,* William L. Rivers, Theodore Peterson, and Jay W. Jensen outline the history of government regulation, involving the Congress, the courts, and the Federal Communications Commission.

One specific regulatory issue, the growing power and profits of large media conglomerates, merits closer attention. In the second selection, Ben Bagdikian, of the University of California at Berkeley, holds that the nation's largest communications corporations represent an alarming degree of control over the public's sources of information. Strong antitrust remedies are necessary, according to Bagdikian, especially in cases of "cross-media" ownership (ownership of more than one type of media outlet in a single market).

Supreme Court Justice Potter Stewart provides a strong warning against those who would take Bagdikian's prescription one step further and have the media regulated as "common carriers," or neutral conduits for the messages of others. Justice Stewart, in excerpts from a post-Watergate speech, sees grave dangers in any regulation that might restrict the independence and aggressiveness of the press—a protected and fundamentally necessary institution under the Constitution.

The next selection, by Supreme Court Justice William J. Brennan, Jr., addresses the extent of legal protection afforded the press by the Constitution. Justice Brennan defends his votes in favor of the news media's right to shield reporters' notes, newsroom files, and confidential sources from government subpoena and discovery. Together, the opinions of Justices Stewart and Brennan provide eloquent testimony in support of the critical legal rights and social responsibilities of the press as defined in the First Amendment.

The closing essay in this section explains the technical and political rationale for the regulation of the airwaves and the licensing of those who use the electromagnetic spectrum. Consulting communications engineer Charles Lee Jackson surveys the legal procedures of the International Telecommunications Union of the United Nations, which governs spectrum use internationally, and of the Federal Communications Commission, which regulates electronic communications in the United States.

10
Differences in Media Regulation

William L. Rivers, Theodore Peterson, & Jay W. Jensen

In this selection from their book *The Mass Media and Modern Society,* William L. Rivers, Theodore Peterson, and Jay W. Jensen compare the parameters of government regulation as it applies to the print media, films, and the broadcasting industry. The authors explain the paramount role of the Supreme Court in press freedom cases, where the broad protections of free expression in the First Amendment to the Constitution are tested and redefined.

The more substantial history of censorship in the motion picture industry is analyzed as the interplay of industry self-regulation, audience reaction, and government intervention. In broadcast regulation, the focus is on the administrative and judicial power of the Federal Communications Commission, with particular emphasis on that agency's allocation of scarce frequency space.

William L. Rivers is Paul C. Edwards Professor of Communication at Stanford University. Professors Theodore Peterson and Jay W. Jensen are on the faculty of the College of Journalism and Communications, University of Illinois at Champaign-Urbana.

Source: From *The Mass Media and Modern Society,* Second Edition, by William L. Rivers, Theodore Peterson, and Jay W. Jensen. Copyright © 1971 by Rinehart Press, a division of Holt, Rinehart and Winston, Inc. Copyright © 1965 by Holt, Rinehart and Winston, Inc. Reprinted by permission of the publisher.

If the media stand equally before the law in some cases, they stand at different levels in others. While our theories of freedom were evolving, the major media were the printed ones. The electronic media of the twentieth century—movies, radio, and television—brought new problems. How much freedom should be granted to media that appeal less to man's critical faculties than to his suggestibility? How much freedom should be given media that have entertainment, not information and discussion, as their chief objective? And how much freedom is it possible to grant to media, like radio and television, which are limited in number by the availability of channels?

To consider these questions, let us look first at the print media . . . then in greater detail at the electronic media.

The Print Media

As long as a publisher shows a decent respect for a few laws, he may do what he likes with his newspaper. If he opposes the Democratic candidate for President, the candidate's name can be stricken from the paper. If he hates golf, he can instruct his sports editor to forget that the game exists. If he visualizes thousands of little circles of family readers being offended by photos revealing the sex of naked animals, he can have his art department use an airbrush appropriately. The Democrats, the golfers, and the artists on his staff may rebel, readers may protest, a rival paper may thrive as a result, but the publisher's power in such cases is unmistakable.

This kind of freedom is available, too, of course, to publishers of magazines and books. As some of the observations above make clear, the print media are not entirely free of legal restrictions. Every society restricts free expression to some degree—usually with at least four basic controls: a law designed to protect individuals or groups against defamation, a copyright law to protect authors and publishers, a statute to preserve the community standard of decency and morality, and a statute to protect the state against treasonable utterances. It should be noted that two Justices of the United States Supreme Court,

Black and Douglas, argue that the First Amendment means *literally* what it says. Black held in *Ginzburg v. United States,* "I believe that the Federal Government is without power whatever under the Constitution to put any type of burden on speech and expression of ideas of any kind." Justice Douglas wrote in *The Right of the People:*

> The First Amendment does not say there is freedom of expression provided the talk is not dangerous. It does not say there is freedom of expression provided the utterance has no tendency to subvert. . . . All notions of regulation or restraint by government are absent from the First Amendment. For it says in words that are unambiguous, "Congress shall make no law. . . ."

Government encroachment protested by many leaders of the print media is that directed at commercial practices. A successful suit was brought under antitrust laws against monopolistic advertising practices of the Kansas City *Star.* In other cases government has sought to require newspapers to pay newsboys a minimum hourly wage. The papers resisted successfully, arguing that the newsboys were "independent merchants" who actually bought papers from the publisher and sold them to subscribers.

Perhaps the most important commercial case was brought under antitrust laws against the Associated Press. The AP, which is cooperatively owned, had long protected its members by refusing to sell its service to their competitors. The new Chicago *Sun,* competing in the morning field with the Chicago *Tribune,* was unable to obtain AP service, and its suit became pivotal. That the *Sun* supported Franklin D. Roosevelt against the Roosevelt-hating *Tribune* added emotional overtones. Robert Lasch described the struggle:

> Almost to a man, the publishers of America interpreted the filing of this action as a foul assault against the First Amendment, and with frightening unanimity exerted all their power to impress upon the public that point of view.
>
> "We see in this, not the end perhaps, but

surely the greatest peril, to a free press in America," said the Detroit *News*. From the citadel of its monopoly position in a city of 600,000, the Kansas City *Star* cried: "This is the sort of thing that belongs in the totalitarian states, not in a free democracy." "In the event of a government victory," said the New York *Daily News,* "the press services of the United States will be under the thumb of the White House."

These were not extremist positions. They represented a fair sample of the opinion handed down by the press. . . .

In retrospect the press outcry seems a bit silly. The government won the case, the *Sun* got AP service, the White House did *not* put its thumb on the wire services, no newspaper was restrained or censored. The question was commercial: whether a news service could be withheld from some newspapers for competitive reasons.

In 1970 a similar question was resolved by the Congress of the United States in favor of newspapers. The "Newspaper Preservation Act" exempts from the antitrust laws any joint newspaper operation in which one paper can show it was failing at the time the joint agreement was adopted.

Now the press is fighting another battle with government decisions that come much closer to infringing concepts of freedom. Again the antitrust laws are pivotal. The question is whether, as the numbers of large metropolitan newspapers diminish, the remaining giants should acquire suburban papers in the same area. The Department of Justice has stepped into several such acquisitions, objecting that competition is diminished. It is not yet certain that the government will be able to establish guidelines for ownership to which the press must adhere, but magazine and book publishers are watching the developing battle between newspapers and government with keen interest, and some fear that a formula that will prevent wholesale acquisitions and mergers may be established. Obviously this is a question related not so much to historical concepts of freedom as it is to the press as a business institution.

Like the other instruments of mass communication, the newspaper is a business enterprise as well as an informative public service. As Zechariah Chafee observed, it is like a combination, in one organization, of a college and a large private business, the one devoted to educating the public, the other to making money for a few owners. This is an awkward combination, and yet it must be maintained. Newspapers must be economically strong so that they can remain independent of the government and report on it; yet we must expect an unusual kind of responsibility from newspaper owners. For the free expression of ideas they have been granted is broad. In *Winters v. New York,* a case involving the right to public accounts of crime and violence, the Supreme Court made it clear that entertainment is also protected:

> We do not accede to appellee's suggestion that the constitutional protection for a free press applies only to the exposition of ideas. The line between the informing and the entertaining is too elusive for the protection of the basic right. Everyone is familiar with instances of propaganda through fiction. What is one man's amusement, teaches another man's doctrine.

Clearly government regulation is sharply limited when the highest court construes freedom so broadly.

Films

Motion pictures in the United States have never enjoyed the breadth of freedom granted the printed media. For more than a half a century, a number of states and municipalities have had official movie censorship boards.

Chicago was among the first in 1907. Then came New York in 1909, Pennsylvania in 1911, and Kansas in 1913. The Pennsylvania law set the pattern from which most subsequent censorship laws were designed. No movie film could be shown in Pennsylvania without the approval of the state board of censors. The United States Supreme Court in 1915 upheld the Pennsylvania law—and similar laws in Kansas and Ohio—as a reasonable exercise of state police power.

Censorship of the movies seems to have been tolerated for a number of reasons. From their beginnings the movies were looked on primarily as an entertainment medium. In their infancy they were linked with vaudeville houses, where they sometimes rounded out the bills; as they matured, they became associated with the legitimate stage. In England, where much of libertarian traditions developed, the theater was regarded as an institution quite properly coming under government control on political and religious as well as moral grounds. The excesses of the film industry in the United States immediately after World War I created a climate of opinion favorable to restrictions. Producers tried to outdo one another in luring the public with risqué titles, lurid advertisements, and passionate love scenes. The stars themselves became involved in a succession of highly publicized off-screen scandals. Public pressure for governmental regulation was strong, and the movies had no tradition of freedom to prevent it.

Except for a few isolated instances, the young motion-picture industry itself did little fighting to enlarge its freedom. Aiming at a mass market, the major producers were much more interested in giving the public what it wanted than in championing the right to dissent. They cooperated with both official and unofficial censors, and they tried to keep screen fare antiseptic by a voluntary production code.

In *Treasury for the Free World* Darryl F. Zanuck stated:

> The fear of political reprisal and persecution . . . has prevented free expression on the screen and retarded its development. The loss has not been merely our own. It has been the nation's and the world's. Few of us insiders can forget that shortly before Pearl Harbor the entire motion picture industry was called on the carpet in Washington by a Senate committee dominated by isolationists and asked to render an account of its activities. We were pilloried with the accusation that we were allegedly making anti-Nazi films which might be offensive to Germany.

Similar pressures have been exerted in every time of tension during the lifetime of the motion-picture industry, especially during the early 1950s, when McCarthyism was rampant. Blacklists of suspected Communists among actors, writers, and directors were circulated through studios. The listed actors and directors could not work; some of the writers prepared scripts under other names. When an Academy Award was announced for a script written by one Robert Rich, no one came forward. "Rich" was actually Dalton Trumbo, a blacklisted writer. The power of the blacklist lasted for almost two decades.

But censorship by states and municipalities has influenced film content more strongly than any federal action. Film-makers have had a long history of conflict with states. For example, a film was banned in Ohio in 1937 because "the picture encourages social and racial equality, thereby stirring up racial hatred . . . the above doctrines are contrary to the accepted codes of American life." A documentary film on the Spanish Civil War was banned by the Pennsylvania Censor Board, with the suggestion that the film would be acceptable if the words "Fascist," "Nazi," "Italian," "Rome," "German," "Berlin," and others were deleted. Such experiences lead to anticipatory censorship, with film-makers themselves judging the political winds in each period of American stress and often producing their films accordingly. It is not so much that they fear the results of court action; taken to the highest level, films usually win legal tests. But until they win, the result of banning may be financial failure.

In 1952 the Supreme Court, in *The Miracle* case, moved motion pictures a step closer to freedom by ruling that a state may not ban a film on the censor's conclusion that it is sacrilegious, that motion pictures come under the protection the Constitution gives the press, and that their importance as an organ of public opinion is not lessened by their preoccupation with entertainment. But the court interpreted the Constitution as not authorizing absolute freedom to show every kind of movie at all times and places. Since sacrilege was the sole standard involved in *The Miracle* case, the court did not pass on other standards whereby states could ban films.

The 1952 decision established that the movies are entitled to the protection of the

First Amendment, an important victory, which was consolidated and extended in later cases. Two years later the court held that New York could not ban *La Ronde* and in 1955 that Kansas could not ban *The Moon Is Blue.* In 1959 it rejected a ban that New York had imposed on a movie version of *Lady Chatterley's Lover,* which the censors said seemed to advocate immoral ideas. Justice Potter Stewart remarked that the Constitutional guarantee is not confined to majority opinions: "It protects advocacy of the opinion that adultery may sometimes be proper, no less than advocacy of socialism or the single tax."

In recent years the film industry has been bolder in testing the limits of indecency. Two feature films, which began playing in theaters across the United States in 1966, illustrate this point strikingly. *Who's Afraid of Virginia Woolf?* was a pioneer in its use of realistic dialogue: "Jesus" or "Christ" is used (irreverently) seventeen times; "God," "God damn," or "Lord" is used forty-four times; "damn," seven times; "hell," three times; "bitch," twice; "bastard," eight times; and "son of a bitch" or "S.O.B.," seven times. In comparison all other risqué films shown in first-run theaters in the United States prior to *Who's Afraid of Virginia Woolf?* were hesitant and tentative. The other film, *Blow-Up,* was similarly a pioneer. By comparison with it, nudity and sex scenes in other pictures seemed hesitant and tentative; nothing so unabashed had been shown in first-run theaters. A new spirit of tolerance was developing. Americans soon found a growing number of erotically candid quality films, by American as well as foreign producers, being made available to them.

As the 1970s began, it looked as though nearly all the taboos were dead. Only the few "family movies" failed to carry earthy dialogue or nude scenes or both. Explicit scenes of sexual intercourse were playing in neighborhood movie houses.

Broadcasting

In the early 1920s, when commercial broadcasting was in its infancy, one new radio station after another began sending its signals into the airwaves. The only laws regulating broadcasting then were those designed for radio telegraphy, and they were powerless to prevent chaos. Cacaphony filled listeners' earphones and speakers as amateurs cut in on the programs of professional broadcasters, as ships' radios punctuated musical programs with the dots and dashes of Morse code, as commercial stations tried to crowd competitors from their wavelengths.

The broadcasting industry turned to government for help in bringing some order from all the confusion. The eventual result was the Communications Act of 1934, which created the Federal Communications Commission to regulate broadcasting in the "public interest, convenience, and necessity."

The FCC is made up of seven members, each of whom is appointed for seven years by the President of the United States. Their terms expire at different times, so that no President is likely to appoint all the commissioners. Only four of the seven may be members of the same political party. These provisions of the Communications Act were designed to protect the Commission against partisan politics. They have succeeded, but not completely. Dean Burch, who was appointed Commission Chairman by President Nixon in 1970, remarked, after an FCC decision that was not to his liking, that the expiring terms of two FCC members would soon enable the President to appoint commissioners with more favorable attitudes.

Although the FCC has other duties—regulating military and police communication, transcontinental telephone and teletype, and, increasingly, CATV and communication satellites are among its many responsibilities—the chief public focus falls on commercial broadcasting. Congress gave the FCC the authority to license stations, to assign wavelengths, to decide hours of broadcasting for various stations, and to suspend or revoke the licenses of stations not serving the public interest. These are the kinds of decisions that make the FCC controversial.

On the one hand, the Commission is a regulatory agency. Its authority to regulate broadcasting stems from the assumption that the airwaves belong to all the people. A broadcaster may use the airwaves only under license after showing his qualifications for serving the public interest. The FCC decides to award a license partly on the basis of a proposed program schedule submitted by the applicant. And although a license may be renewed at the end of its three-year term, it may also be suspended or revoked if the FCC decides that the broadcaster has failed to serve the public interest—or if he has failed to live up to the promises in his original proposal. Rarely, however, has the FCC revoked a license.

On the other hand, the FCC is also a judicial agency, for it has been given the power to decide what constitutes the public interest. The scope of its judicial powers, however, is yet to be determined. The law specifically forbids the FCC to censor broadcast content, apart from such items as profanity, [and] obscenity. . . . Yet, since it is charged with making sure that stations operate in the public interest, the FCC has taken the position that it must necessarily concern itself with over-all program content. Broadcasters have argued that any interference with content runs counter to libertarian principles and that the FCC should do no more than regulate frequencies.

To what extent the FCC may concern itself with the over-all performance of stations has never been settled conclusively by either Congress or the Supreme Court. The Supreme Court has indicated that broadcasting is protected by the Constitutional guarantees of free expression. But it also has upheld the government's right to regulate the use of airwaves and to decide the composition of the traffic on them. . . . The FCC does have the power to require broadcasters to adhere to the "Fairness Doctrine," which opens the airwaves to dissident voices.

In 1970 the FCC began to tighten the obligations of the "Fairness Doctrine" by requiring that broadcasters who present a series on controversial issues, or who editorialize, invite specific spokesmen to state contrasting views. Except for the first program in a series, the licensee would no longer be permitted to rely solely on an announcement offering time to anyone with a contrasting view. The spirit of the requirement, Commission spokesmen said, is that a broadcaster "who should be as

outspoken and hard-hitting as he wishes in presenting his view of an issue should be equally vigorous in getting the other side before the public."

Not long after that decision was announced, however, the FCC considered several complaints that armed forces recruitment broadcasts present only one side of an important public issue. A typical complaint was that "when such a large segment of our population is vehemently opposed to our military involvement in Vietnam and the foreign policy that it represents, the advocacy of the benefits and advisability of volunteering or enlisting in the military as opposed to seeking a deferment or exemption definitely constitutes a controversial issue of public importance." All those who complained stated that their local stations had refused their requests for free air time to present opposing views. The Commission majority decided that the complaints were not justified. But Commissioner Nicholas Johnson said:

> Today one branch of the Federal Government ignores the orderly complaints of its citizens and rules that another branch of that same government, the U.S. Army, can propagandize without preserving for the young their First Amendment right of self-defense. The Army and Marine Corps will be permitted to harness all the seductive merchandising talents of Madison Avenue to persuade draft-age young men to enlist in the armed forces. . . . To put it bluntly, the majority has held that the young people of this nation must find their path to the Fairness Doctrine in the streets. I dissent.

The Commission's vacillating on the Fairness Doctrine is fairly typical. Like all regulatory agencies, the FCC is often friendly with the institutions it regulates. Commissioner Johnson has rounded up this record of FCC actions:

> —The FCC once decided that a radio station proposing thirty-three minutes of commercials per hour would be serving the public interest.
>
> —It permitted the wholesale transfer of

construction permits from one licensee to another, prompting the Special Investigations Subcommittee of the House Interstate and Foreign Commerce Committee to conclude in 1969: "The Commission apparently confused its role as guardian of the public interest with that of guardian of the private interest."

—The FCC approved a license transfer application for a station that quite candidly conceded it proposed to program no news and no public affairs at all.

—When presented with charges that a Southern station was engaged in racist programming, the FCC first refused to let the complainants participate in the case, then found that the station's performance entitled it to a license renewal. Even technical violations get little attention. Recently the Commission refused to consider revoking the license of a station whose owner, it was charged, had ordered his engineer to make fraudulent entries in the station's log book, operated with an improperly licensed engineer, and whose three stations had amassed eighty-seven other technical violations over a three-year period.

Violations of the most elementary principles of good business practice don't arouse the Commission to action. Recently the FCC examined the record of a station guilty of bilking advertisers out of $6,000 in fraudulent transactions. The local Better Business Bureau had complained. The station was already on a one-year "probationary" license status for similar offenses earlier. The result? The majority had no difficulty finding the station had "minimally met the public interest standards," and it therefore renewed the license.

As this record suggests, it is nearly always true that when broadcast licenses come up for renewal every three years, licensees can count on favorable Commission action. Thus it was a shock to WHDH-TV (Channel 5 in Boston) when the FCC denied it a renewal in 1969 and awarded the license to another group of Boston businessmen. That brought challenges in large cities across the United States, as group after group sought to demonstrate that licensees had not been operating in the "public interest, convenience, and necessity." Then broadcast lobbyists went to work

on Capitol Hill. Soon more than one hundred bills had been introduced in the House and Senate to protect licensees. The most important, the bill introduced by Senator John Pastore of Rhode Island, would have virtually eliminated the possibility of a successful challenge. It would not allow the FCC to entertain an application for an existing channel until the Commission itself had first found that the licensee had not lived up to his responsibilities (which, considering the small FCC staff, is highly unlikely). Moreover the bill required that the FCC rely almost wholly on the licensee's report of his own performance. It may not matter whether this bill or one like it becomes law. It is clear that the FCC will deny license renewals only in the most extreme cases—usually to break up a concentration when a single proprietor or a group owns a newspaper and broadcasting facilities in one market.

And yet it is sometimes true that vacillation rather than weakness is characteristic of the FCC. Even as it was granting license renewals almost automatically in 1970, the Commission was announcing a rule that would limit network domination of prime-time programming. Designed to promote diversity in programs, the rule prohibits network affiliates in the fifty largest markets from accepting more than three hours of network programming from 7 P.M. to 11 P.M. (6 and 10 P.M., Central Time) after September 1, 1971. "Our objective," the commissioners reported, "is to provide opportunity—now lacking in television—for the competitive development of alternative sources of television programs so that television licensees can exercise something more than a nominal choice. . . ."

At about the same time the FCC announced such revolutionary plans to restructure patterns of ownership that *Broadcasting* magazine headlined its report "Major Moves to Rip Up Broadcasting." One decision barred the owner of any full-time station—AM, FM, or TV—from acquiring another station in the same market. Moreover the Commission announced that it was proposing a rule to break up existing combinations of radio, television, and newspapers in the same market. Only AM-FM radio combinations would be allowed.

Owners would be given five years to reduce their holdings in a single market to an AM-FM combination, a television station, or a newspaper. A Commission staff member explained that this rule was designed to "promote diversity of programming and viewpoints that might have an influence on public opinion, and to promote competition among the media." All this was a response to the increasing criticisms of heavily concentrated media ownership. Tabulating cross-ownership figures in 1969, the Commission found that 256 newspapers were jointly owned by broadcast licensees in the same city. It was also found that 68 communities had only one commercial radio station owned by the only daily newspaper and that of 666 commercial television stations 160 were affiliated with daily newspapers.

Such actions lead broadcasters to speak of the FCC in tones that are fretful when they are not fearful. The trade journals of radio and television—especially *Broadcasting*—are heavy with denunciations of what the FCC has done or what it may do. All this is evidence that, however essential commission regulation of broadcasting may be, regulating communication in a society that grew from libertarian roots can never be wholly acceptable.

11

The Media Monopolies

Ben H. Bagdikian

Concentration of ownership and its potential for control of the news is a major area of concern to mass media critics. Although the Federal Communications Commission strictly controls broadcast licensing, government control is less stringent for other types of mass communications.

In the following essay from *The Progressive*, Ben H. Bagdikian, of the University of California at Berkeley's Graduate School of Journalism, argues for regulating the nation's large newspaper chains under antitrust legislation. Bagdikian also fears the increasing trend of cross-media ownership, where one company owns and controls several types of media either in one location or nationally.

If the trend toward concentration of control in the news media is alarming, as I think it is, and if doing something about it is locking the barn door before the horse is stolen, I'm afraid I am writing about an empty barn. All media with routine access to mass markets are already controlled by too few people. If we are serious about preserving maximum practical access to the marketplace of ideas and information, we ought to be deeply concerned.

The fifty largest broadcast chains already have three-quarters of the audience. The fifty largest cable television companies have two-thirds of all subscribers. The fifty largest newspaper chains have more than two-thirds of all daily newspaper sales—and this is particularly troubling because concentration of control of daily newspapers has unique effects on all information media.

Our daily newspapers are still the dominant source for all news in the United States. I wish it were otherwise. I wish NBC, CBS, and ABC each had bureaus in all medium-sized and large cities, that all local radio and television stations spent 10 per cent of their revenues on origination of news, and that the daily harvest was not limited to a dozen items. We would all benefit if we had a number of truly independent and comprehensive sources of daily news. But we do not.

Most news in all media comes overwhelmingly from two wire services, United Press International and the Associated Press. But UPI and AP do not originate most of their news; they pick it up from their local clients and members, the daily newspapers around the country. When there is a newspaper strike in New York City, not only the individual subscribers suffer: The national media—radio, television, *Time,* and *Newsweek*—originate a small amount of their own news but depend mainly on sitting down each morning and fearlessly reading *The New York Times.*

So when we talk about concentration of ownership of daily newspapers, we are talking about control of the only comprehensive and self-sufficient news system we have. There are more than 1,500 cities in the United States with daily papers, but only forty with competing newspaper managements. Of all cities with newspapers, 97.5 per cent have newspaper monopolies.

The business trend among newspapers runs parallel to the trend in other industries. For example, there used to be more than 200 makers of automobiles in this country, and now there are only four. But even with this drastic concentration in the automobile industry, General Motors still competes with Ford, which competes with Chrysler, which competes with American Motors, and they all compete with Datsun, Toyota, Volkswagen, and other imports. But in concentration of ownership in daily newspapers, there is no competition even among the consolidated giants.

The Gannett chain, which had seventy-six papers the last time I looked, does not compete with Lord Thomson's fifty-six papers or with Knight Ridder's thirty-two papers or with Samuel Newhouse's thirty papers. They are secure systems of local monopolies, effectively insulated from competition with each other. They are less like Ford and General Motors and more like AT&T, with its local operating subsidiaries, each an established monopoly in its own region.

This consolidation of monopolies is not something over the horizon; it is an accomplished fact. There are 1,760 daily papers in the country—a number that has remained stable since World War II. Of these, 73 per cent are owned by 170 corporations. And now these 170 corporations are consuming each other, with large chains buying small chains, so that control is gathering with disproportionate speed among the few at the top.

In 1950, 20 per cent of all individual daily papers were owned by chains; by 1960, it was 31 per cent; by 1970, 47 per cent. Today it is 62 per cent.

The same alarming concentration applies to total daily circulation. From 1950 to 1960, chain control of daily newspaper circulation remained at about 45 per cent. But from 1960 to 1970, the percentage of papers sold each day owned by an absentee corporation rose from 46 per cent to 61 per cent. From 1970 to 1977, it went from 61 per cent to its present 73 per cent. So almost three-quarters of all newspapers sold every day in this country are owned by a chain.

Some daily papers are so small—less than 5,000 daily circulation—that their annual cash flow does not interest chains. For all practical purposes, there are 400 remaining independent daily papers with enough cash flow to interest outside corporations, and there are only twenty-five large chains that can effectively bid for them. Like beach-front property, independent daily papers are a disappearing commodity. So now big chains are buying small chains, multiplying the rate of concentration. Since 1960, the twenty-five largest newspaper corporations have increased their control of daily national circulation from 38 per cent to 53 per cent. Ten corporations now publish 37 per cent of all newspapers sold daily in the United States.

Newspapers have followed other industries in another form of concentration—the conglomerate. But as with chains, there is a qualitative difference in the social impact of media conglomerates as against companies that make plastics or musical instruments. If an ordinary conglomerate uses one of its companies to further the interests of another of its companies, it may be unfair competition but it is largely an economic matter. If a conglomerate uses its newspaper company to further the interests of another of its subsidiaries, that is dishonest news.

This subversion has happened in the past. William Randolph Hearst used his newspapers, magazines, and movie companies to urge us to declare war on Mexico to protect his mines in that country. The DuPonts owned, until recently, the major papers in Delaware, and used those papers to promote the financial and political interests of the parent company. The heirs of Jesse Jones in Houston used to do the same thing with their wholly owned subsidiary, the *Houston Chronicle,* ordering it not to run news that would discomfort its other properties, such as banks and real estate. The Florida East Coast Railroad owns papers in Jacksonville and has a history of using the news to promote or suppress information to suit the owners' other interests.

The growth of non-news investment in newspapers is not troublesome in itself; most original investment money in newspapers came from some other source. What is bothersome is that these are no longer single units in which the owner is locally based and recognized. And with chains, when contamination of the news occurs it can be on a massive scale. Atlantic Richfield recently bought *The London Observer.* Mobil Oil says it is in the market to buy a daily newspaper. We might judge Mobil's dedication to independent journalism from its recent withdrawal of support from the Bagehot Fellowship for training business writers at Columbia University because the director of the program once wrote a book about the oil industry that Mobil disliked.

Blue Chip stamps now owns the *Buffalo Evening News* and 10 per cent of *The Washington Post.* The biggest newspaper conglomerate, the Times-Mirror Corp., owner of the *Los Angeles Times,* also owns companies that publish most of the telephone directories in the West, produce maps for oil companies,

and operate large agricultural and timber lands—all industries that are continuing issues in the news.

Some conglomerates seem to be focused on domination of national news. The Washington Post Company, in addition to its stable of newspapers, television and radio stations, owns *Newsweek* magazine. Time, Inc., another large publishing conglomerate, recently moved to match *The Post*'s position astride news out of the Government by purchasing the only other Washington paper, *The Star.*

Finally, there is growing vertical control of information and cross-media ownership, not just between newspapers and broadcast stations, but among magazine and book publishers. RCA, for example, owns NBC and therefore has a lively interest in promoting books or magazine pieces that might make good television programming. A magazine article that leads to a book that leads to a TV series is considered ideal. So RCA also owns Random House book publishers and such subsidiaries as Ballantine Books, Alfred Knopf, Pantheon, Vintage, and Modern Library. CBS owns Holt, Rinehart, and Winston, *Field & Stream* magazine, *Road & Track, World Tennis,* and *Cycle World,* plus the former Fawcett magazines. ABC has a big stake in the religious movement, since it owns Word, Inc., a major producer of religious literature. And, of course, it owns Howard Cosell.

Music Corporation of America, in addition to large-scale control of entertainment, owns the G.P. Putnam book publishing firm, Paramount Pictures, and *New Times* magazine.

Concentration of ownership and acquisition by conglomerates sometimes happen in the business world when independent units begin to lose money and are, therefore, tempted to consolidate for survival. The opposite applies to newspapers: Chains are growing because individual newspapers and newspaper chains are making so much money that it is profitable to pay even exorbitant prices to buy up the few remaining independent entities.

Newspaper economics has always been a

---

*Random House, Inc., has subsequently been sold to the Newhouse Newspaper chain [Eds.].

trade secret, but since 1963 major newspaper companies have begun to sell their stock to the public, and therefore must disclose their finances in accordance with requirements of the Securities and Exchange Commission. We know from brokers and others in the trade that the profits of publicly traded papers are comparable to those of privately held papers. Available data indicate that the newspaper industry is one of the most profitable: In 1976 —not a banner year for the economy—the publicly traded newspaper companies, which collectively control 25 per cent of all daily circulation, had pre-tax profit margins of 19.4 per cent, after-tax profits of 10 per cent, average return on stockholders' equity of 16 per cent, and return on invested capital of 14 per cent.

A journalist might rejoice at such fat figures. A logical assumption would be that the more money a newspaper makes and the better its chances of survival, the more it will invest in the paper and the community that provides its earnings. But the tendency is the opposite: The more money a paper makes, the more likely it is to attract a takeover or, if it is already in a chain, to use the profits to purchase other properties.

My own impression is that most papers were mediocre before they were bought by chains and remain mediocre after they are bought. With few exceptions, chain operators like to buy medium-sized monopoly newspapers which require them to spend a minimum on the news. Newspapers are a multiple-appeal product—sports, stock reports, comics, news, fashions, supermarket prices, television listings—so it is usually not clear why people buy papers. Many publishers who issue daily junk as news find it easy to believe they are geniuses—but genius in publishing a daily paper consists of having a monopoly in a growing market.

No distinguished newspaper was ever created by a chain. I doubt that *The New York Times* would have been created by Adolph Ochs if the *Times* had been a wholly owned subsidiary of a Texas cement company. Or *The Washington Post* if Eugene Meyer had worked for Rupert Murdoch. Or the *Los Angeles Times* if Otis Chandler was a hired publisher sent from Rochester to keep the paper out of controversy and collect an annual bonus based on increased earnings.

But let us assume, for the sake of argument, that chain ownership actually makes newspapers better—that every property bought by a chain quickly becomes a first-rate paper. I don't think that eases the problems of narrow control.

At the present rate of concentration, we can expect that in less than twenty years almost every daily paper in the country will be owned by about ten corporations. There is no assurance that the present trend will continue, but neither is there any reliable evidence that consolidation will stop.

One reason concentration in the media is dangerous is that media power is political power. There is no reason why newspaper publishers and broadcast operators should not promote their corporate welfare the way other industries do. But it would be naive not to recognize that for politicians there is a difference between being asked to support a corporate bill for the computer industry and being asked to support something wanted by the newspaper publishers and broadcast managers in the politician's home district. Remarkably many members of Congress believe that when a publisher or station manager comes to Washington to lobby a bill or fight some regulation, these are the people who will decide how to treat the politician in their media at the next election. And most of them preface their acknowledgment of this belief by saying it is strictly off the record.

I see no constitutional problem in establishing some limit on how many papers or how much circulation one corporation may control. At the same time, I believe that no one should be prevented from printing or saying anything, any time, anywhere. If there were a legal limit to the existing media any one corporation could control, and Gannett, for example, wished to buy an existing paper in Peoria, it could do it by selling its paper in Pensacola. If it insisted, as it ought to, that it has a First Amendment right to print in both Peoria *and* Pensacola, then I would defend that right and insist that it could retain its paper in Pensacola and express its First

Amendment right in Peoria by starting a *new* paper in Peoria.

I doubt that even the most energetic chain-builder in the business would insist that it is socially healthy to have one corporation control every daily paper in the country. We now have twenty-five chains that control a majority of all papers sold daily. If one corporation in control is bad and twenty-five is good, what is the proper number? At what point should someone—presumably the Department of Justice or Congress—step in and say No?

But I don't believe that the Department of Justice or Congress *will* step in. They have not so far, and the pace of concentration has increased in the last decade. And I believe the Department of Justice and Congress do not step in precisely because concentrated control of the media also represents concentrated political and economic power. But I can suggest more modest remedies:

One small gesture would be to end the meaningless ownership statement issued annually to the post office and printed as obscurely as possible each October. Instead, each paper using the second-class mailing privilege should be required to have available for public scrutiny at the local post office the names of all officers, directors, and major stockholders, the precise percentage of their ownership, and all their significant financial holdings. This is the same requirement of disclosure the SEC makes of officers, directors, and major stockholders of publicly traded companies. Local people should at least know who owns and controls their monopoly media and what other financial interests are held by those who make ultimate decisions about the news.

Another measure that would afford some insulation from potential subversion of news would be the election of editors by professional journalists on the staff of the paper. Obviously, this would require the consent of the owner, but one always dreams of owners

with vision. Election of editors would also mean office politics, but office politics in the present methods are not unknown, and staffs as a whole could not make worse choices than managements as a whole. For those who insist this would make for mediocre papers, I suggest taking a look at *Le Monde,* one of the world's great newspapers, whose staff elects its editor.

An irrational decision of the tax courts that for years has fueled the growth of chains ought to be reversed. The Internal Revenue Code permits a newspaper to retain without normal taxation any undistributed earnings as a necessary cost of doing business if the purpose of this accumulation is to buy another newspaper. That makes neither social nor business sense.

Newspaper and broadcast editorials regularly warn against the potential danger of Big Government. They rightly fear uninhibited power, even in the hands of a wise and benevolent leader. But that fear should apply to corporate as well as to political power. We have 1,700 daily papers, 8,000 weeklies, 8,000 radio stations, 900 television stations, and 10,000 periodicals. But we can no longer assume that these large numbers represent comparable diversity in control. We now must fear these numbers; most of our 215 million citizens are reached not by thousands of corporations in the media business but by the relative few that control consolidated organizations.

If we believe in the indispensability of a pluralistic marketplace of ideas and information, we can not be complacent about a narrowly controlled management of that marketplace, whether it is governmental or corporate, benign or malicious. The greatest danger in control of the mass media is not, I think, the likelihood that Government will take control, but that the public, seeing little difference between narrow corporate control and narrow governmental control, will be indifferent to which dominates the media.

12
The Press:
Not Merely a "Neutral Conduit"

Potter Stewart

The aggressive role of the news media in exposing the Watergate scandal has brought about a reexamination of the legal and political functions of the press. Should the media merely provide a "neutral conduit" for ideas and information, or should the press serve to scrutinize and critically examine public affairs at all levels? Supreme Court Justice Potter Stewart leans toward the latter view and feels that an independent and strong press plays a major role in insuring constitutional balance. The following remarks are excerpted from a speech Justice Stewart delivered at the Yale Law School in 1974.

Justice Potter Stewart was appointed to the Supreme Court in 1958 by President Eisenhower.

The public-opinion polls that I have seen indicate that some Americans firmly believe that the former vice president and former president of the United States were hounded out of office by an arrogant and irresponsible press that had outrageously usurped dictatorial power. And it seems clear that many more Americans, while appreciating and even applauding the service performed by the press in exposing official wrongdoing at the highest levels of our national government, are nonetheless deeply disturbed by what they consider to be the illegitimate power of the organized press in the political structure of our society. It is my thesis that, on the contrary, the established American press in the past ten years, and particularly in the past two years, has performed precisely the function it was intended to perform by those who wrote the First Amendment of our Constitution. I further submit that this thesis is supported by the relevant decisions of the Supreme Court. . . .

In very recent years cases involving the established press finally have begun to reach the Supreme Court, and they have presented a variety of problems, sometimes arising in complicated factual settings. . . .

It seems to me that the Court's approach to all these cases has uniformly reflected its understanding that the free-press guarantee is, in essence, a *structural* provision of the Constitution. Most of the other provisions in the Bill of Rights protect specific liberties or specific rights of individuals: freedom of speech, freedom of worship, the right to counsel, the privilege against compulsory self-incrimination, to name a few. In contrast, the free-press clause extends protection to an institution. The publishing business is, in short, the only organized private business that is given explicit constitutional protection.

This basic understanding is essential, I think, to avoid an elementary error of constitutional law. It is tempting to suggest that freedom of the press means only that newspaper publishers are guaranteed freedom of

Source: From *Columbia Journalism Review* (January/February 1975). Reprinted by permission of the author and publisher.

expression. They *are* guaranteed that freedom, to be sure, but so are we all, because of the free-speech clause. If the free-press guarantee meant no more than freedom of expression, it would be a constitutional redundancy. Between 1776 and the drafting of our Constitution, many of the state constitutions contained clauses protecting freedom of the press while at the same time recognizing no general freedom of speech. By including both guarantees in the First Amendment, the Founders quite clearly recognized the distinction between the two.

It is also a mistake to suppose that the only purpose of the constitutional guarantee of a free press is to insure that a newspaper will serve as a neutral forum for debate, a "market place for ideas," a kind of Hyde Park corner for the community. A related theory sees the press as a neutral conduit of information between the people and their elected leaders. These theories, in my view, again give insufficient weight to the institutional autonomy of the press that it was the purpose of the Constitution to guarantee. . . .

The British Crown knew that a free press was not just a neutral vehicle for the balanced discussion of diverse ideas. Instead, the free press meant organized, expert scrutiny of government. The press was a conspiracy of the intellect, with the courage of numbers. This formidable check on official power was what the British Crown had feared—and what the American Founders decided to risk.

It is this constitutional understanding, I think, that provides the unifying principle underlying the Supreme Court's recent decisions dealing with the organized press.

Consider first the libel cases. Officials within the three governmental branches are, for all practical purposes, immune from libel and slander suits for statements that they make in the line of duty. This immunity, which has both constitutional and common-law origins, aims to insure bold and vigorous prosecution of the public's business. The same basic reasoning applies to the press. By contrast, the Court has never suggested that the constitutional right of free *speech* gives an *individual* any immunity from liability for either libel or slander.

In the cases involving the newspaper reporters' claims that they had a constitutional privilege not to disclose their confidential news sources to a grand jury, the Court rejected the claims by a vote of five to four, or, considering Mr. Justice Powell's concurring opinion, perhaps by a vote of four and a half to four and a half. But if freedom of the press means simply freedom of speech for reporters, this question of a reporter's asserted right to withhold information would have answered itself. None of us—as individuals—has a "free speech" right to refuse to tell a grand jury the identity of someone who has given us information relevant to the grand jury's legitimate inquiry. Only if a reporter is a representative of a protected *institution* does the question become a different one. The members of the Court disagreed in answering the question, but the question did not answer itself.

The cases involving the so-called "right of access" to the press raised the issue whether the First Amendment allows government, or indeed *requires* government, to regulate the press so as to make it a genuinely fair and open "market place for ideas." The Court's answer was "no" to both questions. If a newspaper wants to serve as a neutral market place for debate, that is an objective which it is free to choose. And, within limits, that choice is probably necessary to commercially successful journalism. But it is a choice that government cannot constitutionally impose.

Finally the Pentagon Papers case involved the line between secrecy and openness in the affairs of government. The question, or at least one question, was whether that line is drawn by the Constitution itself. The Justice Department asked the Court to find in the Constitution a basis for prohibiting the publication of allegedly stolen government documents. The Court could find no such prohibition. So far as the Constitution goes, the autonomous press may publish what it knows, and may seek to learn what it can.

But this autonomy cuts both ways. The press is free to do battle against secrecy and deception in government. But the press cannot expect from the Constitution any guarantee that it will succeed. There is no constitutional right to have access to particular government information, or to require openness from the bureaucracy. The public's interest in knowing about its government is protected by the guarantee of a free press, but the protection is indirect. The Constitution itself is neither a Freedom of Information Act nor an Official Secrets Act. . . . Newspapers, television networks, and magazines have sometimes been outrageously abusive, untruthful, arrogant, and hypocritical. But it hardly follows that elimination of a strong and independent press is the way to eliminate abusiveness, untruth, arrogance, or hypocrisy from government itself.

It is quite possible to conceive of the survival of our Republic without an autonomous press. . . .

The press could be relegated to the status of a public utility. The guarantee of free speech would presumably put some limitation on the regulation to which the press could be subjected. But if there were no guarantee of a free press, government could convert the communications media into a neutral "market place of ideas." Newspapers and television networks could then be required to promote contemporary government policy or current notions of social justice.

Such a constitution is possible; it might work reasonably well. But it is not the Constitution the Founders wrote. It is not the Constitution that has carried us through nearly two centuries of national life. Perhaps our liberties might survive without an independent established press. But the Founders doubted it, and, in the year 1974, I think we can all be thankful for their doubts.

13
Why Protect the Press?

_____

William J. Brennan, Jr.

In the previous article, Supreme Court Justice Potter Stewart argued that the Constitution includes special protection for the press as an institution. In the following selection, Justice William J. Brennan, Jr., takes Stewart's argument even further: Brennan says that the First Amendment provides qualified protection for the press' internal communications. Justice Brennan's opinion is relevant for several recent cases: the government's right to search newsroom files *(Zurcher* v. *Stanford Daily)*; subpoenaing a reporter's notes to discover confidential sources *(Branzburg* v. *Hayes)*; and asking a journalist about editorial state of mind to establish malice *(Herbert* v. *Lando)*. While Justice Brennan's position calls on the press to take a more moderate position on these issues, he remains a strong voice on the Court in favor of the media's First Amendment freedoms.

Justice Brennan was named to the Supreme Court in 1956 by President Eisenhower.

I begin with the premise that there exists a fundamental and necessary interdependence of the Court and the press. The press needs the Court, if only for the simple reason that the Court is the ultimate guardian of the constitutional rights that support the press. And

Source: From *Columbia Journalism Review* (January/February 1980). Reprinted by permission of the author and publisher.

the Court has a concomitant need for the press, because through the press the Court receives the tacit and accumulated experience of the nation, and—because the judgments of the Court ought also to instruct and to inspire —the Court needs the medium of the press to fulfill this task.

This partnership of the Court and the press is not unique; it is merely exemplary of the function that the press serves in our society. As money is to the economy, so the press is to our political culture: it is the medium of circulation. It is the currency through which the knowledge of recent events is exchanged; the coin by which *public* discussion may be purchased.

In recent years the press has taken vigorous exception to decisions of the Court circumscribing the protections the First Amendment extends to the press in the exercise of this function. I have dissented from many of these opinions as hampering, if not shackling, the press's performance of its crucial role in helping maintain our open society, and have no intention of now defending them. I am concerned, however, that in the heat of the controversy the press may be misapprehending the fundamental issues at stake, and may consequently fail in its important task of illuminating these issues for the Court and the public.

The violence of the controversy cannot be explained merely by the fact that the Court has ruled adversely to the press's interests. While the argument that the ability of the press to function has suffered grievous and unjustified damage may have merit in some cases, in others the vehemence of the press's reaction has been out of all proportion to the injury suffered. The source of the press's particular bitterness can, I believe, be identified. It stems from the confusion of two distinct models of the role of the press in our society that claim the protection of the First Amendment.

Under one model—which I call the "speech" model—the press requires and is accorded the absolute protection of the First Amendment. In the other model—I call it the "structural" model—the press's interests may conflict with other societal interests and adjustment of the conflict on occasion favors the competing claim.

The "speech" model is familiar. It is as comfortable as a pair of old shoes, and the press, in its present conflict with the Court, most often slips into the language and rhetorical stance with which this model is associated even when only the "structural" model is at issue. According to this traditional "speech" model, the primary purpose of the First Amendment is more or less absolutely to prohibit any interference with freedom of expression. The press is seen as the public spokesman *par excellence.* Indeed, this model sometimes depicts the press as simply a collection of individuals who wish to speak out and broadly disseminate their views.

This model draws its considerable power —I emphasize—from the abiding commitment we all feel to the right of self-expression, and, so far as it goes, this model commands the widest consensus. In the past two years, for example, the Court has twice unanimously struck down state statutes which prohibited the press from speaking out on certain subjects and the Court has firmly rejected judicial attempts to muzzle press publication through prior restraints. The "speech" model thus readily lends itself to the heady rhetoric of absolutism.

The "speech" model, however, has its limitations. It is a mistake to suppose that the First Amendment protects *only* self-expression, only the right to speak out. I believe that the First Amendment in addition fosters the values of democratic self-government. In the words of Professor Zechariah Chafee, "the First Amendment protects . . . a social interest in the attainment of truth, so that the country may not only adopt the wisest course of action but carry it out in the wisest way." The Amendment therefore also forbids the government from interfering with the communicative process through which we citizens exercise and prepare to exercise our rights of self-government. The individual right to speak out, even millions of such rights aggregated together, will not sufficiently protect these social interests. It is in recognition of this fact that [in *Grosjean* v. *American Press Co.*] the Court has referred to "the circulation of information to which *the public is entitled* in virtue of the constitutional guarantees." (The emphasis is mine.)

Another way of saying this is that the First Amendment protects the structure of communications necessary for the existence of our democracy. This insight suggests the second model to describe the role of the press in our society. This second model is structural in nature. It focuses on the relationship of the press to the communicative functions required by our democratic beliefs. To the extent the press makes these functions possible, this model requires that it receive the protection of the First Amendment. A good example is the press's role in providing and circulating the information necessary for informed public discussion. To the extent the press, or, for that matter, to the extent that any institution uniquely performs this role, it should receive unique First Amendment protection.

This "structural" model of the press has several important implications. It significantly extends the umbrella of the press's constitutional protections. The press is shielded not only when it speaks out, but when it performs all the myriad tasks necessary for it to gather and disseminate the news. As you can easily see, the stretch of this protection is theoretically endless. Any imposition of any kind on the press will in some measure affect its ability to perform protected functions. Therefore this model requires a Court to weigh the effects of the imposition against the social interests which are served by the imposition. This inquiry is impersonal, almost sociological in nature. But it does not fit comfortably with the absolutist rhetoric associated with the first model of the press I have discussed.

The decisions that have aroused the sharpest controversy between the Court and the press have been those decisions in which the Court has tried to wrestle with the constitutional implications of this structural model of the press. For example, the reporters in *Branzburg* v. *Hayes* argued that if they were compelled to reveal confidential sources or notes before a grand jury, their ability to gather the news would be impaired. In its decision, the Court acknowledged that First Amendment interests were involved in the process of news gathering, but concluded that these interests were outweighed by society's interest in the enforcement of the criminal law.

Similarly, in *Zurcher* v. *Stanford Daily* a student newspaper contended that its offices could not be searched, as is usually the case, upon the issuance of a valid search warrant, but that a subpoena which would give the newspaper the opportunity to contest the search in advance was necessary. Again, the issue was not any restriction on what the newspaper could actually say, but rather whether special procedures were necessary to protect the press's ability to gather and publish the news. Once again, the Court held that whatever First Amendment interests were implicated were outweighed by society's interest in law enforcement.

Both these cases struck vehement, if not violent, reactions from the press. About *Zurcher,* for example, the president of the American Newspaper Publishers Association [Allen H. Neuharth] stated that the opinion "puts a sledgehammer in the hands of those who would batter the American people's First Amendment rights." Unfortunately, the resulting controversy generated more heat than light, and the reason, I think, is that the press, in order to strengthen its rhetorical position, insisted on treating these cases exactly as if they involved only the traditional model of the press as public spokesman. *The Washington Star,* for example, argued that "it matters all too little whether abridgment takes the obvious forms of suppression and censorship, or the casual rummaging of a newspaper office on a search warrant."

Of course, as I have been trying to make clear, it matters a great deal whether the press is abridged because restrictions are imposed on what it may say, or whether the press is abridged because its ability to gather the news or otherwise perform communicative functions necessary for a democracy is impaired. The two different situations stem from two distinct constitutional models of the press in our society, and require two distinct forms of analysis. The strong, absolutist rhetoric appropriate to the first model is only obfuscatory with respect to the second. The tendency of the press to confuse these two models has, in my opinion, been at the root of much of the recent acrimony in press-Court relations.

The press has reacted as if its role as a public spokesman were being restricted, and, as a consequence, it has on occasion overreacted.

Perhaps the clearset example is the case of *Herbert* v. *Lando*. The case raised the question whether a public-figure plaintiff could in discovery ask a defendant journalist about his state of mind when publishing the alleged defamatory falsehood. Now it is clear that a journalist's state of mind is relevant to his "subjective awareness of probable falsity," and thus to the issue of actual malice. And traditionally a plaintiff is entitled to discovery on all relevant issues. Privileges are rare and strictly construed. Nevertheless, the press argued that it could not perform its functions under the First Amendment unless a special "editorial" privilege were created to shield it from such inquiries.

The Court rejected this argument, and the result was a virtually unprecedented outpouring of scathing criticism. But in its outrage against the *Herbert* decision, the press unfortunately misapprehended the role model of the press involved. The true role model involved can be ignored, however, only on the assumption that a journalist's state of mind is somehow special, and cannot be impinged for any purpose. It is important to note that this assumption gathers its rhetorical basis from the model of the press as public spokesman. For when a citizen speaks publicly he *is* special, and, with only rare and stringent exceptions, what he says cannot be restricted for any purpose. But this is not the model of the press at issue in *Herbert*. The decision does not affect the actual malice standard set out in *Sullivan*. Instead the question raised by *Herbert* is whether the press's ability to perform the communicative functions required by our democratic society would be significantly impaired if an editorial privilege were not created.

Note that this is a difficult and factual question, and one that cannot be illuminated by sharp or sensational rhetoric. In my view reporters will not cease to publish because they are later asked about their state of mind. On the other hand, predecisional communications among editors may well be curtailed if they may later be used as evidence in libel suits. Since a democracy requires an informed and accurate press, and since predecisional editorial communications contribute to informed and accurate editorial judgments, I would have held that such communications should receive a qualified privilege. I say a *qualified* privilege because even the executive privilege bestowed upon the President of the United States so that he may receive the informed and unimpeded advice of his aides is, as the case of *United States* v. *Nixon* makes clear, a qualified privilege.

A majority of my colleagues rejected my position because it believed that the accuracy of resulting publications would not be impaired if predecisional editorial communications were revealed. This is a matter of judgment, about which reasonable men may differ. It is also, at least in form, an empirical question, upon which the lessons of later experience may be persuasively brought to bear. If the press wishes to play a part in this process, it must carefully distinguish the basis on which its constitutional claim is based, and it must tailor its arguments and its rhetoric accordingly. This may involve a certain loss of innocence, a certain recognition that the press, like other institutions, must accommodate a variety of important social interests. But the sad complexity of our society makes this inevitable, and there is no alternative but a shrill and impotent isolation.

14
The Allocation of the Radio Spectrum

Charles Lee Jackson

The Federal Communications Commission was originally created, in 1934, to allocate scarce space in the electromagnetic spectrum. That task is still difficult, technically and politically. Both broadcasters and governments compete for use of the airwaves, and new technologies, such as satellites, make the conflict even more laborious. While the FCC is charged with management of the spectrum in the United States, international allocation is determined through treaty agreements between nations, which are administered by the International Telecommunications Union of the United Nations.

In the following article, from *Scientific American,* Charles Lee Jackson outlines the technical, political, and economic considerations involved in dividing up the airwaves. Jackson was formerly on the technical staff of the Federal Communications Commission and is now a Washington, D.C., consulting engineer.

It is clear that both national and international wireless communication would dissolve in chaos without some system for allocating the finite number of places on the radio spectrum among the many claimants. It is not so clear that the systems now in force are the best ones possible or that they work as efficiently as they could. My purpose in this article is to describe how the spectrum is currently managed (with the system in the U.S. serving as the principal example) and to outline the major reforms that are under consideration.

The part of the electromagnetic spectrum that is regarded as the radio spectrum (the term radio encompassing all forms of wireless communication, including television, all radio broadcasting, telephone calls sent by microwave radio and so on) can be described in terms of both frequency and wavelength. It ranges from very low frequencies of a few kilohertz (thousands of cycles per second) and wavelengths of several kilometers up to 300 gigahertz (billions of cycles per second), where radio microwaves shade into the far infra-red. The officially allocated part of the spectrum extends from 10 kilohertz (wavelength 30 kilometers) to 300 gigahertz (wavelength one millimeter) and is densely populated by communication services of all kinds.

Frequency is not the only component of the spectrum resource. Geographical location also makes a difference. A given frequency can be assigned to several locations if they are far enough apart. For example, in the U.S. Channel 4 serves television stations in Boston, New York, Washington and about 50 other communities. The necessary separation is determined by the propagation characteristics of radio waves at the particular frequency and by the design of the communication system.

The primary international institution established to allocate places on the spectrum and to promulgate technical rules is the International Telecommunications Union, usually referred to as the ITU; it is a specialized agency of the United Nations. In the U.S. the responsibility for managing the spectrum is divided between the President, in whose name the part of the spectrum assigned to agencies of the Federal Government is controlled by the National Telecommunications and Information Agency in the Department of Commerce, and the Federal Communications Commission (FCC), which oversees all other users. The FCC's jurisdiction extends not only to commercial television and radio stations but also to state and municipal mobile-radio activities, the wireless part of the telephone system, citizens-band radio and even the small radio units that open and close garage doors.

Although the focus of this article is on the allocation of the spectrum, the reader should bear in mind that national and international policy on the management of the spectrum deals with other issues. It has a bearing on the structure of a nation's system of mass communications. In many countries it involves the question of how to manage the design of large communication systems with multiple owners. It also addresses the questions of how to distribute the benefits of a public resource and how to compromise such conflicting alternatives as expanded broadcasting service and improved communications for power-company repair crews. I shall treat such issues as special subproblems of allocation, but actually the subject of spectrum policy could be discussed with any of them as the focus.

To understand spectrum-allocation policies one must understand how the spectrum is utilized. Its use is governed by the physics of radio-wave propagation and by the practical limitations of communications engineering. The operation of a typical amplitude-modulation (AM) radio station, WNBC in New York, illustrates a simple radio-communication link.

When an announcer speaks in the studio, the microphone transforms the sounds into electrical signals. They are carried by cable from the studio to the transmitter, which is on High Island, 20 kilometers east of New York. There the signals modulate an electromagnetic wave oscillating at a carrier frequency of 660 kilohertz. The modulated wave is fed to an antenna, from which it spreads out in all directions as electromagnetic radiation.

Now picture a listener with a portable transistor radio on Jones Beach, about 30 kilometers from the transmitter. A small fraction of the radiated signal is captured by the antenna of the radio. The radio selects the WNBC signal from among all the radio signals reaching the antenna because the radio is tuned to 660 kilohertz. The radio amplifies the signal and demodulates it, thereby recovering the electrical signal that represents the announcer's voice. The signal then goes to a speaker that transforms it into sound.

The radio captures only a tiny fraction of the 50 kilowatts transmitted by WNBC. If the transmitted power were spread out evenly in all directions from the transmitter, the density of the energy at a distance of 30 kilometers would be down to .000004 watt per square meter. Actually, the power does not spread out evenly, since the transmitter directs most of it toward the horizon. Nevertheless, the signal the transistor radio must work with is about a millionth of a watt.

Noise, meaning various kinds of interfering radio waves, ultimately limits a receiver in picking up a signal at a certain level of weakness. Noise can be generated both within a receiver and by external processes. External noise comes from many sources but can be classified in three broad categories: natural radiation, incidental man-made radiation and radiation from other communication systems. Natural phenomena, notably lightning, generate radio signals that can interfere with communication. Electrical equipment such as sewing machines and power tools can generate radio waves capable of interfering with communication, as when horizontal streaks appear on a television screen during the operation of a power tool nearby. Finally, each radio transmitter generates signals that constitute noise to anyone who is not trying to receive that particular signal. An example is the common experience of not being able to tune in a particular AM radio station at night without picking up another station in the background or hearing an objectionable whistle caused by interference.

The control of interference lies at the heart of spectrum allocation, which entails the development of systematic plans for the use of frequencies in radio communication. The process usually involves three steps: allocation, assignment and licensing. In the allocation step regions of the spectrum are set aside for specific purposes. For example, the band from 535 to 1,605 kilohertz is reserved internationally for AM radio broadcasting.

Setting aside regions of the spectrum for clearly defined, compatible uses simplifies the control of interference. Television broadcasting stations interfere with one another symmetrically: if station *A* interferes with station *B*, *B* interferes equally with *A*. A mobile radio and a broadcasting station, however, may interfere quite asymmetrically. For example, a mobile radio may interfere with television reception whereas the signals from the television station do not affect the mobile station. Hence the incentives for cooperation and coordination are much greater if a single class of radio users is assigned to each region of the spectrum.

The methods of assignment vary. For citizens-band radio there is no method; anarchy prevails. For the AM broadcasting band and the land mobile-radio bands the method is first come, first served. A prospective user searches for a place in the band where a new assignment is possible. If he finds one, he registers his intent to use it, and assignments must not conflict with his choice.

Sometimes the regulators put more structure into the assignment process. The FCC worked out a table of assignments for television broadcasting before it opened the band for licensing. The commission's objectives were to simplify the process of licensing and to ensure balance in assigning frequencies to communities. Licensing is a specific authorization to a broadcaster to use a frequency. The steps of assignment and licensing are often combined.

The allocation of the spectrum can be viewed as the allocation of a resource. The problems of spectrum allocation and management can also be viewed in other ways. In the most fundamental one the spectrum-management process is seen as providing the crucial coordination needed to avoid interference. Even if twice as many channels were available as could ever be used, it would still be necessary to register and coordinate the uses in order to avoid interference.

Another view sees spectrum management primarily as the structuring of communications, in particular mass communications. Broadcasting policy consists of many elements: technical standards, the choice of the number of outlets in each community, rules on ownership and the definition of the kinds of service to be provided by broadcasters. In many countries only the government owns broadcasting stations. In the U.S. the FCC puts on broadcasters certain requirements that are not applied to the owners of other media. For example, broadcasting stations are required to cover controversial issues of public importance "fairly." No such rule applies to newspapers, magazines or book publishers. The Supreme Court has upheld the policy, stating: "In view of the scarcity of broadcast frequencies, the Government's role in allocating those frequencies, and the legitimate claims of those unable without governmental assistance to gain access to those frequencies for expression of their views, we hold the regulations and ruling at issue here are both authorized by statute and constitutional."

The point to be emphasized is that (at least in the U.S.) broadcasting policy flows from spectrum-management policy. The practical result is that since the Government allows some people to broadcast and excludes others, it must have a mechanism for choosing among applicants. Nothing in the laws of physics or politics requires this mechanism of choice to focus exclusively on technical standards. Indeed, social and political forces push toward the consideration of nontechnical criteria in deciding who should operate broadcasting stations. Spectrum-allocation policy becomes linked with fundamental social and political activities.

The allocation of the spectrum can also be viewed in terms of economics. Economists writing about spectrum-allocation policy usually treat the spectrum as an example of a resource (like land and water) that requires economic management. It is an unusual kind of resource, however, in that the people who are authorized to use it do not pay for their part of it and cannot sell or share the allocation without the approval of the granting agency. Moreover, large bands of the spectrum are allocated to various users—commercial television and radio, mobile radio, local governments and so on—that may underuse their part of it, but it cannot be transferred from one type of user to another.

Another aspect of spectrum allocation is the creation and distribution of wealth. The close link between the two is illustrated by an idealized television market based on three assumptions: (1) total advertising revenue is fixed at $20 million per year regardless of the number of stations in the market; (2) the operating cost for each station is $3 million per year, and (3) the revenue is shared equally by all the stations. If the regulating agency assigned three stations to the market, each station would make $3.6 million in profit per year. The assignment of a fourth station would lower the profit of each station to $2 million; with a fifth station the profit would be $1 million. One can see how sensitive the economics of broadcasting is to slight changes of policy on allocating television stations and what incentives broadcasters have to oppose the addition of new stations to a market.

Historically the allocation of the spectrum has followed a simple pattern. The regulatory authority would set aside a region of the spectrum for a service and would establish technical rules. Prospective users would then apply for licenses on a first-come, first-served basis. Latecomers had to engineer their systems around the earlier ones. This pattern has been followed consistently both internationally and within nations, with few exceptions. The system had (and to a large degree still has) several major advantages, among them its simplicity, low cost and the fact that only a minimal transfer of information is needed to make it work.

The system has been able to meet the expanding demand for space on the radio spectrum by the fortunate circumstance that as demand grew, technology advanced, so that more of the spectrum could be exploited and all of it could be utilized more efficiently. The system does give rise to certain problems, however, a major one of which can be illustrated with a comparison of the broadcasting and telephone systems in the U.S. In 1960 the U.S. had 474 television stations on the very-high-frequency (VHF) band, encompassing channels 2 through 13. Today there are 617. In 1945 the country had 900 full-time AM radio stations; now the band set aside for them supports 2,000 full-time stations. As for telephones, in the early 1950's the Bell System began sending some of its telephone calls by microwave radio. At that time the common-carrier equipment could fit only 2,100 telephone circuits into the microwave band. Today's equipment can fit 36,000 telephone circuits into the same band.

To put it another way, the technical efficiency of the broadcasting system has not really improved at all during a time when the efficiency of the common-carrier microwave system improved by 2,000 percent. This disparity grows out of the incentives offered by the system of spectrum management. The telephone industry and its customers share in the benefits of improved efficiency, so that a telephone company has an incentive to develop and install equipment that makes more efficient use of the spectrum. A broadcasting station cannot share in such benefits, all of which flow to others (such as the buyers of radios and television sets). Indeed, more efficient technology would make it possible for more stations to operate in each market. The advertising revenues and profits of the existing stations would go down.

It should also be recognized that the adoption of new technology is harder in broadcasting than in the telephone system. The ownership of a broadcasting system is divided between the broadcaster, who owns the transmitter, and the listeners, who own the receivers. The larger part of the investment is in the receivers. Most technical changes require changes in both the transmitter and the receiver, and coordinating any change in the millions of receivers would be difficult.

Another kind of difficulty with the present system appeared at the general meeting of the World Administrative Radio Conference in Geneva last fall. (The general meetings, which are held about every 20 years, provide the means whereby the member nations of the International Telecommunications Union allocate regions of the spectrum. The group also holds more frequent meetings on specific subjects, such as satellite communications. All the meetings entail complicated multilat eral negotiations, whose substantive results are embodied in treaties.) Many of the newer nations, which were colonies at the time of the last general conference, are now moving to establish their own satellite-communications and short-wave radio systems. They are therefore competing fiercely to obtain places on the spectrum, many of which are already occupied or assigned to developed nations. The issues were largely unresolved by the conference and therefore remain pending.

Many people have put forward detailed suggestions for making the process of spectrum allocation work better. The suggestions fall into three groups: (1) Improve the current system. (2) Find ways to design radio systems that require less human management. (3) Change the economic incentives so that all users are encouraged to adopt the most appropriate technology.

The current system can be improved in at least two ways. One is to apply more resources (people, money and computers) to the problem. Another is to computerize the traditional process to a greater degree. Both approaches are being taken to some extent already. Data on the uses of the spectrum were once kept in manual files; now they are increasingly being put into a form that can be read out by machine. Searches of the files are being done by computer rather than by hand. Expenditures on the management of the spectrum are increasing.

Another possible improvement in the U.S. is to do away with the present two-headed system of managing the spectrum. Although the division of authority between the FCC and the President has worked reasonably well in the past, a single authority for the allocation of the spectrum would probably do better at shifting allocations between Federal and civil users when such shifts are possible and appropriate.

Improvements that come under the heading of designing radio systems that require less human management introduce a concept that could be called the "anarchy band." (Other names that have been suggested are freedom band, bedlam band and frontier band. They all reflect the relative lack of formal management embodied in the concept.) To make an anarchy band work the regulators would have to arrive at two initial decisions. The subsequent tasks of enforcement and collecting data would then be minimal.

First the regulators must designate a band where anarchy would be the operating principle. Then they must define the technical standards for the equipment that would serve the band. The standards must be chosen to make the overall system work well. The remaining task for the regulators is to ascertain that only the proper equipment is put in service. They can accomplish the task by controlling the sale of equipment.

A good example of an ideal anarchy-band technology would be a radio with a range limited to 10 meters. Such a radio would be particularly suitable for communications within a household or between adjacent households for such purposes as burglar alarms, garage-door openers and the remote control of appliances. The limited range of the transmitters would preclude interference.

To some extent the anarchy-band concept has already been adopted. The Advanced Research Projects Agency (ARPA) of the Department of Defense has developed a system called packet radio that provides voice and data communication over ranges of up to several kilometers. The essence of the system is that each packet, or short sequence, of data is sent over whichever one of a designated group of channels is available. A receiving radio can detect an error in the transmission of a packet due to interference or noise; when such an error is detected, the packet is automatically retransmitted. In terms of the utilization of the spectrum the system can be described as dynamic allocation; it contrasts with the preallocation that characterizes commercial television and radio.

Citizens-band radio is another example of a working anarchy band, although it is far from the ideal because the technical rules applying to the band are so loose. As a result a user of the band often encounters excessive interference. Nevertheless, the band provides a communication service with a minimum of regulatory activity.

The application of economic techniques to the management of the radio spectrum is both promising and possible. The techniques include charging users a fee, auctioning places on the spectrum and even assigning property rights so that a user could buy or trade an allocation. The methods would give the user an incentive to make the most of an allocation and would help to guide the use of the spectrum into more valuable areas. They would also enable the regulators and the users to treat the spectrum as another economic resource like land or electricity. Legislation authorizing the utilization of economic techniques in the management of the radio spectrum has been introduced in each house of Congress by the chairman of the respective subcommittees on communications. Moreover, last September, President Carter sent Congress a message supporting the use of economic techniques in managing the nonbroadcasting portion of the spectrum. Even with such high-level support, however, the concept will be difficult to enact because it is opposed by many of the spectrum's present users.

Both the anarchy-band concept and the application of economic techniques can be characterized as moves away from the present system of centralized regulation toward a decentralized system dominated by the users. Actually all three systems can coexist. They are complementary. Different uses of the spectrum require different techniques of management. No single approach is ideal in all cases.

Looking to the future, one can predict that the already valuable radio spectrum will become more valuable as the cost of complementary resources, particularly electronic equipment, goes down. Hence one can foresee increasing demands for access to the spectrum and an increasing need for its better management. The most easily adopted of the new management techniques, and therefore the most promising one, is the anarchy-band concept. It can be applied within the constraints of the current regulatory framework. The essence of it is the replacement of high-cost human administrators with low-cost electronic equipment.

Controversy over the allocation of the spectrum is likely to be focused on two areas: the ultrahigh-frequency (UHF) television band and the satellite bands. UHF will draw attention because of its convenience and availability. Designers of communications systems find the UHF region of the spectrum well suited to their purposes. The equipment is inexpensive and the propagation of the signal is good. Moreover, much of the UHF spectrum is unused even though it has been nominally allocated to broadcasting.

That situation arises from decisions made by the FCC when it originally assigned UHF channels. The commission carefully assigned the channels to cities by taking into account technical constraints that would minimize the cost of UHF sets to the public. Because of improvements in electronics the constraints no longer need to be applied. All existing UHF stations could be accommodated in less than half of the present UHF band, thereby freeing a significant portion of the spectrum for expanded broadcasting or for other services.

The problem with communication satellites arises chiefly from the fact that they must be "stationary," that is, the period of their orbit must coincide with the period of rotation of the earth. They are positioned above the Equator at an altitude of about 22,300 miles. As one might expect, satellite systems at that altitude become an international concern. The U.S. must coordinate its use of the orbital arc with the other nations in the Americas. If markets for satellite communication develop rapidly but the technology advances slowly, contention over the utilization of the satellite portion of the spectrum is certain to arise.

PART TWO

The Print Media

Books

When the technology of printing was developed in Europe during the fifteenth century, it was first used to produce books by small tradesmen who combined the functions of printer, publisher, bookseller, and, not infrequently, author or translator as well. As all these activities became more specialized and more separate, publishing companies (or "houses") were formed to coordinate them. The publishing houses of today, owned largely by media conglomerates, continue to perform the same basic function for a growing number of books.

Despite early fears that film, radio, and television would lead to a decline in book publishing, more people buy and read more books of more kinds than ever before in this country. Keeping pace with this demand, hundreds of publishers produce anywhere from a few titles every year to several every day. Since the seventeenth century, book publishing has referred to itself as "the trade," and the term "trade books," used often in the selections that follow, describes what one finds in a general-audience, commercial bookstore. Taken together with millions of students buying millions of textbooks each year, one can see that the publishing business continues to grow.

Book publishing is really several businesses (and not a few arts) working together. This section, therefore, begins with an overview of the various interrelated phases of publishing and then continues with representative readings describing a few of those phases in some detail.

In a selection from *Book Publishing: What It Is, What It does,* John P. Dessauer outlines the history of publishing and goes on to explore its diverse operations at the present time. To bring a writer's manuscript to a reader's hand requires close coordination between operations as different as jacket design and warehouse management, literary agencies and local bookstores.

The second selection is a case study in publishing a book from the viewpoints of manuscript acquisition and promotion. Ted Morgan shows how the bestseller *Jaws* grew from a conversation between writer and editor into one of the best publicized and most profitable novels of recent years.

A less dramatic but certainly more typical aspect of publishing is described by N. R. Kleinfield in "On the Road With a Book Salesman." To bring the 30,000 titles published each year to the attention of the reading public requires both business sense and artistic sensitivity. These skills are frequently found in publishers' representatives or "reps." A day in the life of a "trade" rep reveals how (until quite recently) books came to be stocked in bookstores.

Bruce Porter explores the expansion of large bookstore chains in the next article, "B. Dalton: The Leader of the Chain Gang." Through their power to order and display books by the thousands, large chains exercise enormous influence in publishing. Opinion as to the desirability of this effect is divided. In the words of one book salesman, the chains are "doing for reading what the fast-food operations have done for eating." The chains respond, as Porter points out, by calling such views "elitist." They claim that by taking the "awesomeness" out of buying books, they expand the size of the reading public.

A significant part of that reading public does not read fiction, or poetry, or textbooks; they buy religious and "self-help" literature. T. S. Carpenter describes that side of publishing in "The Gospel According to Revell." The article not only reveals how many religious and self-help books are published, but how, on occasion, specialty books become bestsellers.

15
Book Publishing:
What It Is, What It Does

John P. Dessauer

Long-time publisher John P. Dessauer explores the history and organization of publishing in the following selection from his *Book Publishing: What It Is, What It Does.* Most people visualize this industry through the image of an editor (pipe in hand) giving advice and contracts to young writers (themselves). How much more there is to the process called publishing Dessauer shows in a quotation from a later part of his book: "The basic functions of the publisher involve the selection of manuscripts or the planning of projects; the preparation of manuscripts for the typesetter; the supervision of the book manufacturing process; marketing and publicizing; the processing of orders; the warehousing and shipping of inventory; and the necessary financing, accounting, and housekeeping tasks attendant upon the preceding obligations."

Books in History

Books in one form or another are as old as civilization. We encounter them in ancient Mesopotamia as clay tablets and in ancient Egypt as papyrus rolls. Rolls were also the form they took in Greece and Rome, where bookselling already flourished and the "scriptoria" or copying establishments plied a vigorous trade. Cities like Pergamum and Alexandria boasted of great libraries; the latter is said to have housed at one time as many as 700,000 rolls.

The format of books as we know them

dates from the first century A.D. when the codex, a volume of parchment pages bound on one side, was introduced. A massive and often beautiful object, the codex remained the characteristic book of the Middle Ages. The religious and secular works then produced, mostly in monasteries, were often duplicated assembly-line style with copyists, proof-readers, and illustrators each fulfilling separate, coordinated functions.

As early as the twelfth century the stationers make their appearance as commercial duplicators and purveyors of books. Many were attached to the universities then being founded and which were taking over the publishing function from the monasteries. Later the stationers organized themselves into corporations and guilds and, like other craftsmen of the period, assumed monopolistic control over their own profession.

The fifteenth century witnessed two vital developments: the introduction of paper and the invention of movable type. Some bibliographers doubt that Johannes Gutenberg should be credited with the invention of type; they claim that Johann Fust and Peter Schöffer actually printed the Bible which bears Gutenberg's name, and that in any case the Constance Missal antedates that Bible as the first printed book. Be that as it may, the practice of printing books by the new method spread with great rapidity throughout Europe and a wealth of "incunabula," as fifteenth-century books are known, survives. By 1500 books were paginated and title pages listed publishers' imprints and dates of publication much as they do today. In 1501 Aldo Manuzio designed the first small book which thereafter replaced the large and awkward codex.

The Reformation and Counter-Reformation proved to be potent stimuli to reading and the publication of books. Not only were the Scriptures made available in the vernacular and widely distributed, but religious controversy found in the newly established printing presses ready means for spreading argument and counterargument far and wide. If the distribution of a great many books was thus encouraged, so was a good deal of suppression, confiscation, and burning. Censorship became a way of life. Even John Milton, who in 1644 wrote the *Areopagitica,* a ringing defense of freedom to publish, later turned censor for the Commonwealth. But literacy gained ground embracing by one estimate 60 percent of the population of sixteenth-century England.

In 1638 the Puritans set up a press in Cambridge, Massachusetts, on which in 1640 the *Bay Psalm Book* was printed. It was among the first of nearly 90,000 titles which were produced in the American Colonies, mostly in English but also in German, Dutch, French, and in Indian languages. Colonial production was of course heavily supplemented by books brought to the new continent from all parts of Europe by immigrants, travelers, and merchants.

Modern Publishing Begins

During the eighteenth century the common people in the Western world shared a growing belief that they could acquire learning through reading. Women had attended the common schools and helped enlarge the audience for books. The farmer or artisan who was a man of letters was no longer a rarity. This was the era of the founding of the great encyclopedias, such as the *Britannica* in England, and the establishment of circulating libraries in many countries. The cause of authors, who had been restricted by monopolistic printers, was aided by such legislation as the British Copyright Act of 1710 which enabled them to negotiate for favorable compensation and terms.

But if book production was substantial in the eighteenth century, with two million titles issued worldwide, the nineteenth century was a period of even more significant development. Some eight million titles were published. By 1900 a best-selling novel would sell 600,000 copies in the English-speaking world. Urbanization, industrialization, and the impetus given to universal education by the growth of democratic influences were among the principal factors in this growth.

Many publishing houses still active today were founded during this period. Among imprints surviving in the United States who can trace their ancestry to the late eighteenth or the nineteenth century are Lea & Febiger (1785), Abingdon Press (1789), J. B. Lippincott (1792), John Wiley & Sons (1807), Harper & Row (1817), G. & C. Merriam (1831), Houghton, Mifflin (1832), Little, Brown (1837), G. P. Putnam's Sons (1838), Charles E. Merrill (1842), E. P. Dutton (1852), Rand McNally (1856), Ginn & Co. (1867), Allyn & Bacon (1868), Johns Hopkins University Press (1878), and Doubleday (1897). It is noteworthy that many of these publishers specialized from the beginning in educational, professional, and religious books while others addressed themselves to the general public.

During the nineteenth century also paperbound books made their appearance, notably in Germany and France where they became firmly and permanently established. In the United States they managed to flourish briefly during the 1830s, but an adverse postal ruling ended the experiment abruptly in 1843. They were resurrected by 1870 and had quite a vogue, particularly in the celebrated dime novel form. But so large a portion of these books was pirated from foreign editions that the copyright act of 1891 once again effectively put an end to that brief paperback era.

The Early Twentieth Century

Most of the houses active in the United States today, including some the largest and most influential, were founded in this century. Some like McGraw-Hill (1909), Prentice-Hall (1913), Simon & Schuster (1924), and Random House (1925) during early decades, others like Atheneum (1959) more recently. The advent of the modern paperback was responsible for the creation of some, such as Pocket Books (1939), Bantam Books (1946), New American Library (1948), and Fawcett World Library (1950); the development of book publishing for direct mail distribution, particularly by magazine publishers, was responsible for the founding of others such as Time-Life Books (1961) and American Heritage Press (1968). New York became the center where most houses operated, but Boston, Philadelphia,

and Chicago were also points of concentration. Only recently has the Western region also begun to play a role as a locale for book publishing.

The contemporary era for the book industry dates from the post–World War II period. Not that some of the trends, phenomena, and practices shaping the present scene had not been initiated before. But the educational boom and the general prosperity in the postwar period were among the principal factors contributing to the shape and character of today's publishing world.

It would be fair to say that prior to World War II the industry had, in economic terms, been a minor one in the United States. Its healthiest segments, the educational, professional, and reference book areas, were able on the whole to attract sufficient capital to meet their obligations and opportunities but were not generally regarded as prime prospects for investment. Publishers serving the general consumer were often struggling to keep alive; it is no secret that in some diversified houses the educational department's income would keep the trade department in existence and only the fascination of owners and managers with general consumer books allowed those divisions to function at all.

Salaries in the field during this period, particularly in the trade area, were low. Few authors could support themselves by their writing. A book could rise to the national best-seller list, particularly in nonfiction, by selling less than 50,000 copies. College enrollments, confined to a cultural-economic elite, were modest as were the textbook sales catering to them. The great depression intensified what was then, even more than now, a minority interest in books.

Book distribution reflected these conditions. Booksellers were struggling to survive, caught in an economic squeeze that on the one hand required them to operate in expensive locations in order to maintain traffic and attract customers, while on the other hand did not allow them to sell their wares expensively enough and in sufficient volume to earn an adequate margin. Many communities were consequently not adequately served or not served at all by book outlets. Some of the great bookstores of the nation could not have kept their doors open had it not been for their used book departments, where markups were more adequate, or their rare book sections that catered to wealthy collectors.

As today, booksellers looked with concern on the activities of book clubs. The Book-of-the-Month Club had been founded in 1926, the Literary Guild in 1927. Undoubtedly book clubs stole some sales away from retailers, but they also reached readers who had no access to or no opportunity to visit bookstores and they succeeded by their membership arrangements in making book buying a habit for some consumers who might otherwise have been very sporadic in their purchasing. By their promotion they created wider interest in titles they selected and in fact created new readers who subsequently proved a boon to booksellers and publishers alike. The same could be said of paperbacks when they made their appearance under the Pocket Books imprint in 1939. Though seen initially by many booksellers as a threat, they have on the whole benefited the industry beyond measure.

But these and other marketing innovations, while helpful and important in laying foundations for the future, did not then succeed in bringing prosperity to the industry. Book people, like teachers, scholars, artists, and musicians, in those days before affluence was widespread, were resigned to an existence of genteel poverty. They found other compensations. To be near books, to share if only indirectly in the literary process, to be midwife to an author's blessed event, these were exciting and rewarding. A deep commitment and dedication grew from the love of books that sustained many a publisher and bookseller despite the lack of significant financial reward.

At the same time, however, the industry —in particular its trade publishing segment— suffered from a paucity of business acumen. While there were publishers who, like Alfred Knopf, combined editorial genius with sound business sense they were unfortunately the exception rather than the rule. When an endeavor, by its very nature, attracts people who find their rewards in its nonmaterial aspects, it is not normally going to find the best talent in American business management flocking to its doors. Nor is it likely that the people

whom it does attract will arrive with the persuasion that sound management ability is one of the prime requisites expected of them.

Thus many publishing houses became victims of a vicious circle: because they were not successful businesses they did not enlist the interest of good business people—with the result that they remained largely unsound from a business standpoint. Only recently has this trend begun to be reversed.

War and Postwar

World War II itself played a role in changing conditions in the industry. In a patriotic and enlightened move publishers made available thousands of "Armed Forces Editions" of their books to the military in the field. Books thus became companions and solace, entertainment, and relaxation to countless individuals many of whom might otherwise never have acquired the habit of reading. As these volumes were paperbound they also helped pave the way for the incipient paperback revolution.

The war, furthermore, resulted in the beginnings of the college explosion: the era in which higher education was to become the perceived birthright of the masses rather than of a mere elite. The veterans who flocked into college classrooms under the G.I. Bill established a precedent which, partly successful and partly a failure, has nevertheless become an article of national faith and commitment. The veterans purchased a great many books with government funds, thus giving college publishing its first big postwar shot in the arm.

Shortly after the war's end the new era in paperbound books was born. The titles which Bantam Books, New American Library, Pocket Books, and others who soon joined them were disseminating were not only different in format, size, and price—they used new channels of distribution which books had never before found open to them. By making use of the facilities of national magazine and independent local distributors, books were displayed on newsstands and cigar counters, in drugstores, railroad terminals, etc. The market they created was in large measure new and previously untapped.

Quite a different paperbound development occurred soon after during the early 1950s in the traditional book field when so-called "quality" paperbacks made their appearance. These titles of serious nonfiction and literary classics, while enjoying a certain vogue with the general consumer, found their prime markets in education. Most were used in college courses. During the late fifties, when secondary school programs were upgraded, high schools also contributed to their consumption. In fact, as time went on, both quality and "mass market" paperbacks enjoyed increased educational uses.

Simultaneously with these developments several educational book publishers, noting a trend toward the use of audiovisual materials in the classroom, began to diversify their production by introducing such materials separately or in multimedia combinations. McGraw-Hill had entered the field as a lone pioneer in 1946; other textbook houses did not follow suit until several years later. While the extensive displacement of books predicted by enthusiasts for audiovisual education never materialized, multimedia publishing became a significant factor in the decades that followed.

In fact the growth and upgrading of education on all levels that followed the 1957 shock of Sputnik had profound effects on the entire book industry. Publishers benefited from the massive infusion of federal funds that characterized the late fifties and sixties. School classrooms, library resource centers, and college and public libraries became the beneficiaries of programs that enabled them to enlarge their holdings of books and of audiovisual and related materials which had rarely before been supported by such funding and certainly never on such a scale.

These events coincided with a consistently growing wave of affluence and also with substantial increases in enrollments on elementary, high school, and college levels (the postwar baby boom was having its effect).

The Merger Period

By the early 1960s journalists, economic forecasters, Wall Street analysts, and other custodians of the national crystal ball began to make ecstatic predictions for the future of education, for the use of leisure time, and, by implication, for book publishing. Unfortunately their analyses were often superficial and they badly overstated their case. Nevertheless many of the factors to which they pointed were real and, for a while at least, their forecasts appeared plausible.

They succeeded in whetting the appetite of investors and corporations searching for ways to diversify their holdings. Wall Street was at that time not particularly renowned for its restraint and detached judgment; even so all the earmarks pointed to book publishing as a sound investment with future growth. Thus publishing stocks, particularly those of educational companies, became glamour holdings. And conglomerates began to woo every independent publisher whose future promised to throw off even a modest share of the forecast earnings.

The publishers being wooed were often very happy at the prospect of a merger. Few had the resources to make the growth the new markets promised a profitable reality. Some privately held companies solved the problem by offering shares to the public, though such moves often proved mere stopovers on their way to being absorbed by larger companies. Some, determined to preserve their independence, succeeded in maintaining their status quo. But a major segment of the industry found itself involved in merging, acquiring, or, more frequently, being acquired.

Thus, Random House was purchased by RCA after previously absorbing Alfred Knopf and Pantheon Books. Holt, Rinehart & Winston, itself the product of two mergers, became a subsidiary of CBS, as did W. B. Saunders. The Times Mirror Company of Los Angeles made subsidiaries of New American Library, World Publishing Co., Popular Science, Harry N. Abrams, Matthew Bender, C. V. Mosby, and Year Book Medical Publishers, among others. Litton Industries acquired Van Nostrand, Reinhold, American Book Company, and McCormick-Mathers. Xerox took over Ginn & Co. and R. R. Bowker. Meredith Corporation bought Appleton-Century-Crofts and Lyons & Carnahan. Time, Inc. acquired Little, Brown and New York Graphic Society. ITT purchased Bobbs-

Merrill and Howard Sams. Harcourt Brace Jovanovich absorbed Academic Press and Grune & Stratton. Encyclopaedia Britannica purchased G. & C. Merriam and Praeger. Raytheon captured D. C. Heath, and so on and so forth.

These mergers and acquisitions have had a profound effect upon the book field. They made resources available without which the industry could probably not have capitalized on its opportunities and fulfilled its obligations to educational and consumer audiences alike. They brought new management and business acumen to the field which had been seriously lacking and which, in many instances, resulted for the first time in orderly budgeting, forecasting, planning, and fiscal arrangements. But in many cases they also placed the power of ultimate decision and policy making in the hands of people unfamiliar with books, their peculiarities, and their markets.

Boom and Aftermath

What liabilities were being engendered by these changes were not readily apparent during the prosperous sixties. From 1963 to 1969 publishing industry sales, including those of book clubs, increased by 59 percent, from $1.7 billion to $2.7 billion. These were times when books seemed to sell despite the inadequacies of their publishers, when even inferior materials were readily absorbed by a well-funded, gluttonous market. So many factors worked together to benefit the various segments of the industry that almost everyone enjoyed a slice of the pie. Research projects supported by government and foundation grants encouraged acquisition of professional books; generous federal and state budgets, bringing unaccustomed affluence to colleges, universities, and their faculties, augmented sales of scholarly materials; newly founded colleges were stocking libraries; parents eager to strengthen their children's educational resources avidly bought encyclopedias for the home; general and specialized book clubs were flourishing.

There was, in addition, the factor of growing export and foreign sales. The postwar scholarly and scientific community had embraced English as the international language and American publishers were reaping some large benefits. Translations and the leasing of publishing rights to foreign publishers were also growing phenomena. Soon American publishers of professional and reference materials saw the advantages of founding their own subsidiary companies abroad, thus enjoying the best of both worlds.

It could not last. The 1970s ushered in some substantial reverses. General economic conditions initially declined, then recovered only sporadically. Enrollments in elementary schools, reflecting the population patterns of the preceding years, went on a downward trend. Taxpayers' revolts in many areas curtailed school budgets. College enrollments, too, began to decline even as state legislatures cut appropriations for higher education. Federal support for schools, libraries, and research were threatened and embroiled in political controversy. Home sales of encyclopedias were falling off substantially.

The pace of book industry growth was expectably slowed. From 1969 to 1972 sales increased by only 11 percent, from $2.7 billion to slightly over $3.0 billion, hardly more in some segments than could be accounted for by inflationary factors. Understandably textbook and other educationally related sales suffered above-average reverses.

But if the boom era had apparently come to an end, the industry had matured and advanced significantly during this period and many of the gains appeared to be permanent. Large numbers of new readers had come into the fold. Lower education had been upgraded and higher education expanded to a larger segment of the population with related advances in book consumption. Even if readers and book buyers still represented only a minority, or more accurately a group of cultural minorities, these minorities had grown substantially.

New financial and management resources had come into the industry during the merger period. Many of the new owners and stockholders, sold initially on excessive expectations, had of course suffered disappointments.

Many had become affiliated with the industry without an adequate understanding of books, their cultural role, or their commercial possibilities. But as excessive optimism gave way to a more realistic view, the genuine opportunities confronting book publishers in the last quarter of this century were becoming more apparent. Such realism supported by adequate fiscal means and genuine management capability is in a position to capitalize on these opportunities and to overcome the serious obstacles standing in their path such as antiquated, inadequate methods of distribution.

Already signs of continued growth for the book industry are apparent. In the United States, since the beginning of the seventies, more new bookstores have been opened than in any comparable period in history. Several new book clubs, catering to specialized consumer tastes, have come into being. In 1972 mass market paperback sales increased by 10.5 percent over the prior year.

It is against this background, a generally reassuring history despite its share of reverses, that we must take the measure of the industry in its present state.

A Cultural Industry

Book publishing, as we have noted, is both a cultural activity and a business. Books are vehicles of ideas, instruments of education, and vessels of literature. But the task of bringing them into existence and of purveying them to their readers is a commercial one requiring all the resources and skill of the manager and entrepreneur.

It is appropriate, therefore, to describe book publishing as a cultural industry. The theater, film, and record businesses which share these characteristics can be similarly defined. It is important to recognize the dual character and demands of book publishing and of similar enterprises because their success depends on it. Both the environment in which they function and the qualifications of their practitioners reflect this duality; in both instances we must consider cultural *and* business requirements if our enterprise is to flourish.

A Mass Industry?

What environmental factors have an impact on book publishing? Well—certainly it is influenced by the general cultural climate to which we have already referred. Book buying though a growing phenomenon in America is not a habit with a majority of the population. Sales figures of individual books are most revealing. When a national best seller after going through hard-cover and paperbound editions sells two million copies the industry rejoices and points to it with pride. Yet such a sale represents a purchase by less than 1 percent of the population. An ordinary, mediocre television show on a national network will have exposure to many times that number. The same is true of the major magazines.

The average hard-cover trade book published may sell up to 10,000 copies, the average "mass market" paperback perhaps 100,000. The designation "mass market" for that paperback may be justified when comparing it with the hard-cover volume—but in relation to the total potential market it is something of a fiction. In America books do not really reach the masses—at any rate not yet.

Unfortunately many editorial and marketing concepts the industry has formulated in recent years are based on the assumption that books are a mass commodity. Thus the best seller, which supposedly will reach a mass audience, receives major emphasis; the more specialized book, appealing to a more limited market, is given less attention. yet all the evidence suggests that in aggregate the industry receives the bulk of its income and support from book buyers who indulge specialized interests and tastes. To the extent that the emphasis on imagined "mass" interests neglects these buyers, the industry is cutting its nose to spite its face.

It would be fair to say, in fact, that the single greatest challenge facing American book publishing today—the goal that would most enable it to reach its potential—is simply to reach effectively the people willing and anxious to buy books. This would entail emphasizing editorial choices aimed at satisfying the real interests of consumers as well as the development of adequate means of placing books into their hands. In both ways American book publishing in the seventies leaves much to be desired. Editorial emphasis is far too much on potential "mass" titles—most of which do not perform as expected. As for obtaining specialized books, such titles are rarely available in retail outlets, are difficult to obtain even by mail, and take interminable time to arrive when ordered. Uncounted book sales are lost in this country every day because willing buyers cannot find what they want on display nor can they order books with reasonable ease.

Publishing and Education

Closely related to the general cultural climate as an environmental factor for book publishing is the state of education. Many stresses currently trouble this field: broad public disillusionment with what are perceived to be its failures; demands for greater accountability by educators; rising costs coupled with public reluctance to meet them. Educators themselves are anxious to introduce methods that will improve performance, centering mostly around great individuation in approach to students.

Recently two trends in the choice of educational materials have been challenging the traditional textbook: the use of general books, particularly paperbacks, and employment of audiovisual and other nonprint media. Many educational publishers have diversified their products and are in a position to respond effectively to these trends. But industry sales figures suggest that although textbooks have lost some ground, the attrition is far smaller than the lively rhetoric would lead one to believe. If a significant trend is emerging it seems to be that in the majority of schools and colleges the textbook will remain the principal tool of instruction. Other books and other media will play their roles, of course, but they seem destined to remain secondary ones.

This is not to suggest that the textbook is not going to change as conditions change. Certainly new emphases in instruction—including, one must own, new fads—will influ-ence the content and appearance of text materials. We may see more softbound texts, more consumables (materials on which the students work directly and which they, therefore, use up), more modular packages (kits consisting of small units). What is of the essence, however, is that from all appearances printed materials especially designed for the classroom—or for individualized instruction within formal educational settings—remain the favored choice of educators and students alike.

Another factor, touching upon education in a broader sense, deserves the attention of book publishers. The knowledge explosion, TV, and heightened career demands, among other factors, have greatly increased the thirst for continuing education which has always motivated a sizable segment of the book-buying public. (Even thirty years ago I discovered to my amazement that the best-selling books in a somewhat seedy store in New York's Times Square area were not sex manuals but College Outlines. And they were selling not to college students but to truck drivers, subway guards, accountants, and office girls.) This interest does not appear at the present time to be effectively served through normal book outlets, yet holds great potential for publishers who will have the imagination to exploit it.

Copying and Copyright

Two other rather specific phenomena affecting the environment for book publishing need to be considered here because of their timeliness and significance: unauthorized copying and censorship.

Unauthorized copying of copyrighted materials is a problem that has become widespread since the invention of the Xerox and other copying machines which have made it easy and relatively inexpensive to duplicate not only pages but whole chapters and sections of books. As today no self-respecting public or academic library is without a copying machine and as schools and colleges make them available to their teaching staffs, the opportunities for disregarding the legally protected rights of authors and publishers in this regard are numberless.

The present U.S. copyright law dates back essentially to 1909, long before the invention of the automatic copier. Because of this and other modern developments, notably in such areas as films, television, and recordings, a proposed new law intending to deal effectively with present conditions has been before Congress for several years. Unfortunately considerable controversy has embroiled several areas of the bill, including that of copying permissible for research and educational purposes. On this issue traditional allies in education, the library world, authors, and publishers have become sharply divided.

Authors and publishers have stood on the principle that the right to literary property is a natural right recognized in common law, forbidding, for instance, the unauthorized copying or publication of unpublished writings and correspondence. When a work is published it must enjoy statutory protection from unauthorized duplication for a specific period (the present law provides for 28 years with the possibility of renewal for a like period; the new law proposes 50 years following the author's death without renewal). Without such protection the economic interests of authors and publishers will be seriously threatened and the incentive lost to invest time or money in the production of literary property. On the other hand, the time limitation exists so that after the investors in such property have had an opportunity to gain justifiable earnings, the public—including other authors and publishers—may have free use of the material.

Although the present statute does not specifically provide for it, the courts have ruled on many occasions that limited use of copyrighted matter—such as the quotation of a passage or paragraph in another published work—is permissible and does not infringe on the rights of the original owner. Authors and publishers have indicated that such "fair use," as the courts have termed it, is acceptable as is, on the same principle, the limited copying of books such as a single page for research purposes. But they have insisted that extensive copying—of whole chapters or parts of books—is not acceptable without authorization and that libraries and educational institutions that make copying machines available to educators or the public have a responsibility to control their use.

Libraries have protested that the responsibility is the patron's, not theirs; libraries are service institutions and should not be used to enforce the law. Educators think that publishers are too restrictive; some can see no wrong in duplicating a chapter or two from a book even for the use of (and sale to) several hundred students. Researchers express alarm over the complexities of a process that requires them to write to a publisher and pay a fee each time they want to copy a dozen pages from a book or journal.

Efforts have been made to resolve these questions and to devise convenient permissions methods for users while safeguarding the interests of copyright owners. A system would have to be created—perhaps for licensing or collecting copying fees—that would be effective yet simple and inexpensive to administer. Certainly if such a system cannot be successfully developed the interests particularly of educational and scientific publishers will continue to be seriously jeopardized. Since investments in their publications are customarily large—and growing in cost—these publishers are highly vulnerable and understandably anxious for an effective solution.

Publisher vs. Censor

If the issue of unauthorized copying is volatile and controversial, that of censorship is infinitely more so. It is also far more complex.

Most authors and publishers have traditionally opposed attempts to curtail freedom of expression. Basing their position on the First Amendment, which they contend makes any restraint on publication illegal, they have fought—often courageously and at great personal sacrifice—against efforts at suppression and censorship inspired by political, philosophical, religious, and moral persuasions. Had it not been for the battles and unceasing vigilance of many authors and publishers some great works of philosophy, religion, political theory, and literature would not now be available in libraries and bookstores.

What was in the minds of the fathers who passed the First Amendment may be more difficult to establish but judicial interpretation has never regarded it as an absolute guarantee of unfettered expression. Libel and obscenity are among the forms of speech and writing which the courts have consistently held are not protected by the First Amendment. Nor, to recall the ever popular statement of Justice Holmes, does freedom of speech entitle one to shout "Fire!" in a crowded theater.

Some commentators point out, furthermore, that a publisher has a responsibility beyond the law when he makes his decision to publish. He may not have the right to injure another human being without reason whether or not the libel law is sufficiently vague or vaguely interpreted to permit his publication of a work filled with destructive innuendo. The public may have a right to know what is in the public interest but its hunger for sensation may perhaps not be justifiably satiated if in the process a man's right to a fair trial is hopelessly jeopardized.

Publisher's Weekly, in a July 2, 1973 editorial, critical of the Supreme Court decision which effectively places the power to determine what is obscene in the hands of local communities, states:

> . . . it may not be amiss to point out that some publishers, by their own actions in recent years, have helped to create a climate in which such a ruling can be regarded as an acceptable one by large numbers of the American people. . . . This is not to say that the publishing industry deserves the new and more stringent approach the Supreme Court has taken; merely that it becomes much harder to say where a stand should be taken when segments of the industry have already gravely undercut normal publishing standards.

Novelist Anthony Burgess, in an article in the *New York Times Magazine* of July 1, 1973 entitled "For Permissiveness, with Misgivings," speaks to the literary issue when he says:

> When novels about sodomy, bestiality, multiple coition and murderous-rape-with-willing-victim cram the bookstalls, what hope has the serious and well-written novel that takes sex as merely one aspect of life? Can the present-day cinema audience watch without restiveness a film in which a couple fall deeply in love without taking off their clothes? Appetites are growing coarser and ears deafer. And there are more pseudo writers about than there should be capitalizing merely on the freedom to be brutal or erotic or both.

The industry's well-founded case against censorship might be more persuasive therefore, and likely to gain greater public acceptance, if publishers were to exercise more consistently the responsibility that is the inevitable concomitant of freedom.

What Makes a Publisher?

If the environmental conditions to which we have referred have an influence on the publishing process, the determining factor remains the publisher's decision. It is he who by his judgment, taste, vision, integrity, and business acumen shapes in the end not only the industry but to a significant degree the literary and general culture which harbors him.

What qualifications must he bring to this important role? Granting that dispositions and aptitudes vary greatly from individual to individual, there appear to be certain general traits of personality and mind that are observable not only in the giants who have left their indelible mark upon the profession, but also in those more numerous women and men who in each age have contributed solidly to its progress.

The true publisher moves with equal comfort in the world of mind and art and in the world of commerce. This may not be a common personality combination; in fact it is probably rather rare. But it appears to be an indispensable prerequisite for achievement in book publishing. A publisher who consistently disrespects the demands for quality and worth in the manuscripts he publishes will, despite temporary successes, find his enterprise dying of spiritual starvation in the end; just as a publisher who consistently ignores the commercial needs of his establishment will find before long that his cultural opportunities are negated by bankruptcy.

Curiously in this age of often extreme ideological moralities these compatible, indeed complementary, traits have been thought to be irreconcilable. Some purists express shock at any attentiveness to solvency. The moneymen, at the other extreme, often have no patience with any concern for literary or scientific excellence. "Will it sell?" is their only question. "Will it help build and maintain the imprint so that ten years from now our books will still be received with interest and confidence, and books we published ten years ago will still be selling because of their lasting significance?" may be the question both sides should be asking.

Obviously no publisher of vision can afford to be indifferent to the total atmosphere for writers, particularly for new writers. It is a wise and honorable tradition in publishing that one should give opportunities to new talent so that such talent may eventually produce salable manuscripts. Many an author's first book is published at a loss in anticipation of substantial gains on his second or third book. At times publishers will even knowingly publish an author whose work they suspect will never be successful commercially simply because they assess it to be of such quality and stature that its value to civilization far outbalances any financial loss it may incur. Such publishers display enlightened self-interest for they persuade readers and writers that publishers honestly love books.

But such commitment to the future of writing must be made with sound judgment and with a shrewd eye upon the general fiscal health of the publishing venture. The truly distinguished manuscript deserving the publisher's unselfish support is rare indeed; totally aside from the fact that not-for-profit publishers (like university presses) exist precisely for the purpose of allowing material to be published that may not succeed in the commercial market. That market itself is for most literary and informative writing a simple and true test of merit: if a book cannot be published viably perhaps it is simply not good enough and should not be published at all. Vox populi—vox Dei.

This leads to a second major qualification for the publisher: the ability to empathize with public tastes. Obviously, given the lively cultural pluralism of his audience, a publisher cannot personally share its every enthusiasm, every persuasion, every perspective. But his should be a sufficiently sympathetic imagination to enable him to make judgments on behalf of the tastes and interests he hopes to serve. Whether it be the world of students and teachers or the complex universe of consumers, he should, in evaluating a manuscript, be able to bring their needs, attitudes, and predilections to his decision and act, as it were, as their advocate in making his choice.

A publisher is a specialist in his own profession—but when it comes to learning and literature the publisher must be a generalist. In fact publishing and its sister cultural industries may be the last bastions of generalism in a world in which the vastness of information and the variety of available diversions are pushing most of us into narrower and narrower areas of competence.

Finally a publisher needs courage. It takes courage to place one's faith in an untried author and use one's resources on his behalf, to adhere to quality and standards in a world often addicted to mediocrity, to shoot ahead of the cultural target, and to open new paths in the hope that they may become highways for literature and knowledge.

Divisions of the Industry

The products publishers develop, the markets to which they are addressed, and the methods used to reach those markets are the principal criteria by which the industry has divided itself into certain categories. Such divisions as trade, text, professional, or mass market paperback publishing have come about naturally because houses engaging in these activities share common editorial objectives and economic concerns.

I say houses but should clarify that this may often mean a department or internal division of a house, particularly since the days of diversification and merger when many formerly independent enterprises became parts of empires.

In defining and describing the industry's divisions and, later, the various publishing functions, it becomes necessary to adopt a standard terminology. Words such as "trade books," "editorial," or "production" are generally in use throughout the industry but they do not always have the same meaning in every establishment that employs them. Local conditions have in fact introduced considerable variation into the industry's vocabulary. Since this makes communication between publishers difficult and precise comparisons of their activities impossible, standard terms and definitions have had to be developed and are employed in the statistical surveys conducted for the Association of American Publishers (AAP). I have generally utilized these terms and definitions throughout this book.

In keeping with this approach I have also adhered to the AAP definition of books themselves. This definition includes all nonperiodical hard-cover volumes regardless of length; all juveniles, hardbound or softbound regardless of length, except coloring books; and all nonperiodical softbound volumes of more than 48 pages. Normally a softbound nonperiodical publication of between 5 and 48 pages is considered a pamphlet although it may be classified as a book if generally accepted as such (as for example a short text-related workbook or a volume published as part of his regular program by a mass market paperback publisher).

The following are the industry's major divisions:

Trade books are designed for the general consumer and are sold, for the most part, through bookstores and to libraries. They may be hardbound or paperbound and include works for both adults and children.

Typical trade books are hard-cover fiction, current nonfiction, biography, literary classics, cookbooks, hobby books, popular science books, travel books, and art books. Also books for self-education, such as those in foreign languages, books on sports, music, poetry, and drama. The main distinction between trade books and textbooks is that the latter are designed for classroom use rather than for general consumption and contain pedagogical apparatus such as summaries and test questions. It does not follow, however, that trade books are not used in classrooms or for educational purposes. In fact, in recent years, increasing numbers of trade titles have been bought for use in colleges and schools. This is particularly true of trade paperbacks—often referred to as "quality" paperbacks—which are widely used in college courses.

It should be noted that juvenile trade books range anywhere from picture books for the prereading age to works for "young adults" in their latter teens.

Religious books include Bibles, testaments, hymnals, and prayer books (but traditionally exclude Sunday school materials). This category also embraces other works of specifically religious content, such as theology and popular devotional literature.

In recent years religious publishers have increasingly engaged in the production of titles which, though of interest to a religious readership, are nevertheless not specifically religious in character, as for example material on social work, racial problems, and world peace. Such books are classified as trade books or as textbooks, depending on their content and intended market, rather than as religious materials.

Professional books are, as the designation implies, books directed to professional people and specifically related to their work. AAP surveys distinguish among three major areas of professional publishing: *Technical and Scientific Books* which treat of subjects in the physical, biological, earth, and social sciences as well as technology, engineering, and the trades and are addressed to practicing and research scientists, engineers, architects, technicians, mechanics, and teachers in these and allied fields; *Medical Books* designed for physicians, nurses, dentists, hospital administrators, veterinarians, pharmacists, *et al.*; and *Business and Other Professional Books* addressed to businessmen, managers, accountants, lawyers, librarians, or other professional individuals not covered under the technical, scientific, and medical categories.

As with trade books, the use of professional books in educational programs is widespread. However, if the editorial character of a volume and its predominant intended audience is professional and its educational use represents a secondary market, the book is classified in the professional category. When professional publishers publish textbooks—for example, medical publishers' nursing texts—the textbook classification applies.

Book clubs could be regarded as a retail market channel rather than as publishers, particularly as for the most part they do not originate the materials they distribute to their members but acquire the rights from other publishers. However, traditionally book clubs have been considered to be part of the publishing industry, and as a few clubs do originate books and as all clubs prepare separate editions for their specific distribution, the classification has some rationale.

AAP surveys provide for distinctions between *consumer* and *professional* book clubs. Consumer clubs in turn involve those who cater to *general interests,* such as the Book-of-the-Month Club and the Literary Guild who offer a great variety of titles without attempt at a subject specialization, and *special interest* clubs whose members have particular subject enthusiasms, such as cooking, the outdoors, or the military, or who represent a special population group such as do students served by clubs which distribute paperbacks in the schools. Professional book clubs partake of the characteristics of professional book publishers so far as their offerings and audience are concerned.

Mail order publications are books created for the general consumer and are marketed to him by direct mail. The principal differences between book club and mail order publications programs are that the latter are originated by the publisher who does the marketing and the publications are distributed without the specific commitments by the purchaser which characterize book club memberships. Although mail order publishers often market series or multivolume sets on a so-called continuity basis (i.e., after placing his order the purchaser receives volumes automatically unless he instructs the publisher to stop), the buyer incurs no obligation nor enters into a membership arrangement of any kind.

Mail order publications, too, have secondary markets consisting of trade sales through bookstores and to libraries, as well as of educational sales similar to those enjoyed by trade books.

Mass market paperbacks are softbound books on all subjects whose predominant distribution is through "mass" channels: newsstands, chain stores, drugstores, supermarkets, and the like. Many are reprints of hard-cover trade books; others are originally published in this format.

It is often very difficult to discover the differences between trade and mass market paperbacks. (Sometimes the originating publisher's imprint provides the only clue.) Generally mass market paperbacks use less costly paper and employ covers more likely to attract the "mass" audience than do their "quality" counterparts. Yet they, too, enjoy large secondary markets in trade outlets (book and department stores) and in educational settings.

University press books provide an instance where the content of titles and the methods used in their distribution are disregarded in their classification and the sole criterion employed is the originating source. University presses which are, for the most part, not-for-profit departments of universities, colleges, museums, or research institutions, publish mostly scholarly materials or titles of regional interest. However, occasionally they produce trade books and textbooks as well, which are then categorized here rather than in the area which content and market would dictate.

University presses publish hard-cover and soft-cover books. Their principal customers are scholars and libraries but many titles, particularly paperbacks, are used in classrooms. Bookstores absorb some sales, notably of trade-oriented materials.

Elementary and secondary textbooks are hard-cover and soft-cover textbooks, workbooks, textbook-related tests, manuals, maps, and similar items all intended for classroom use and equipped with specific pedagogical features which distinguish them from consumer-oriented materials such as trade juveniles. The industry refers to producers of these materials as "elhi" publishers.

Many publishers in this field also produce audiovisual and manipulative items such as films, filmstrips, slides, recordings, transparencies, duplicating masters, games, magnetic boards, etc. Sometimes these are combined with books or at least with printed components (cards, pamphlets, etc.) in so-called multimedia packages or kits.

Schools are the primary market. (AAP surveys consider kindergarten to the eighth grade the elementary grades and grades 9 through 12 high school.) Lately some junior colleges have begun using elhi materials. Government and libraries (other than school libraries) also constitute secondary markets.

College textbooks include hard-cover and soft-cover textbooks, pamphlets, reprints, course-related tests, and other materials, and certain audiovisual items such as films, slides, and cassettes. "College" here embraces all higher education (grades 13 and up), from junior college to postgraduate level. The upgrading of secondary school programs has created an interesting additional market in high schools for college publishers. Government, industry, and libraries also account for some of their sales.

It is probably more difficult to distinguish between college textbooks and trade books than it is between their counterparts on the elhi level. Some publishers have even produced trade and textbook "editions" of the same title with differences so slight (such as that the trade edition is equipped with a dust cover while the text edition is not), as to make the task of classification almost impossible.

(AAP survey practice utilizes the criterion of predominance in making some distinctions: if a book finds its principal market in the textbook area, it should be classified there, if in the trade-book area then in that category. Where distribution is evenly divided and two quite separate editions are actually marketed, each edition is considered to be a distinct title and classifiable in its own area.)

Standardized tests are a small industry segment closely related to textbook publishing. Standardized tests, as distinguished from "objective" tests which accompany specific textbooks and materials, measure intelligence, ability, aptitude, achievement, and other personality traits. Schools and colleges employ such tests and the evaluation services provided by their publishers, but significant markets exist also in industry and other areas outside formal education.

Subscription reference books are principally sets of encyclopedias marketed by their publishers to consumers on a door-to-door or direct mail basis. Since this marketing pattern often involves package arrangements, other reference or self-educational materials such as dictionaries, atlases, sets of the classics and similar publications originated by these publishers also fall under this heading. Sizable secondary markets include public and educational libraries and schools.

It is noteworthy that nearly every division of the industry enjoys substantial markets outside its primary sales focus. This growing phenomenon is of relatively recent origin. Prior to World War II, product and market distinctions were nearly synonymous: trade books sold almost exclusively through bookstores and to libraries, elhi textbooks to schools, college textbooks to students in higher education. The advent of the mass market and the growing practice, in education, of supplementing texts with other books have served to blur what were once fairly precise market lines.

The industry has sometimes found it difficult to adjust its organizational structure to these changes. Most publishing houses have retained the product-oriented divisional and departmental arrangements of the prewar era while attempting to meet new marketing opportunities by making interdivisional sales arrangements or creating sales departments independent of their editorial counterparts. On an industry-wide basis the divisions we have enumerated continue to prevail mainly because they still provide opportunities to publishers in similar economic circumstances to compare experiences and address common problems.

The complexity of the field is such that no reliable figures are available citing the number of publishers active in each division. The R. R. Bowker Co. maintains a list of more than 6,000 book publishers in the United States of which approximately 1,000 produced five or more titles during 1972. *Literary Market Place,* an annual Bowker publication, lists the latter individually, enumerating some of their specialties and areas of interest.

The Association of American Publishers does, however, provide annual estimated sales figures for these divisions. The figures for 1979–80 are shown in Table 1.

The figures in Table 1 include domestic as well as export sales (not, however, sales of subsidiary companies of American publishers operating in foreign countries). The last category, "Other," embraces nonbook sales such as sales of audiovisual products, as well as sales of book overstock at sacrifice prices ("remainders") and sales of unbound pages ("sheets") to foreign publishers [. . .]

Publishers' receipts are not identical to consumer expenditures. Many books are sold by publishers at a discount to bookstores or to wholesalers—who in turn market to bookstores and other retail outlets—and bookstores and wholesalers must have their markup on the merchandise before it is sold to the consumer. Only in cases where the publisher sells directly to individuals or to libraries and institutions (which then makes the library or institution the consumer), is the publisher's sales income identical to the consumer expenditure.

Eliminating nonbook sales, and confining the estimate to the domestic market (ex-

Table 1. Estimated Book Publishing Industry Sales, 1979–1980

	1979 (millions)	1980 (millions)	Increase for 1980
Trade (Total)	$1086.2	$1271.3	17.0%
Adult Hardbound	608.3	695.9	14.4
Adult Paperbound[1]	292.9	364.6	24.5
Juvenile Hardbound	151.5	168.5	11.2
Juvenile Paperbound	33.5	42.3	26.4
Religious (Total)	295.4	351.4	19.0
Bibles, etc.	138.9	168.3	21.2
Other	156.5	183.1	17.0
Professional (Total)[2]	885.1	999.1	12.9
Technical	301.1	334.8	11.2
Business	370.0	424.4	14.7
Medical	214.0	239.9	12.1
Book Clubs	501.7	538.3	7.3
Mail Order	485.8	566.9	16.7
Mass Market—Rack Size	603.2	653.3	8.3
University Press	68.0	80.7	18.7
Elhi Text	930.1	940.3	1.1
College Text[2,3]	825.6	952.7	15.4
Standardized Tests	61.6	67.2	9.1
Subscription	383.5	384.7	.3
Audiovisual	146.3	166.7	13.9
Elhi	129.6	147.9	14.1
College	7.8	8.7	16.1
Other	8.9	10.1	13.4
Other	59.7	66.8	11.9
Total	**6332.2**	**7039.4**	**11.2**

[1] Adult paperbound includes Non-Rack-size sales by Mass Market Publishers of $70.1-million in 1979 and $85.9-million in 1980.
[2] Data in these categories are still under review by the U.S. Census.
[3] The projections used in this report are based, in part, on the statistical projections by the Bureau of Census. The difficulty of clearly defining the college text market for statistical purposes continues. However, the matter is now under careful review and is expected to be resolved shortly.

Table 2. 1979 Estimated Domestic Consumer Expenditures on Books

Category	Millions of Dollars	Percent of Total
Trade	$1,586.3	22
Religious	463.7	6
Professional	868.0	12
Mass market paperback	1,073.5	15
Book club	492.6	7
Mail order publications	498.6	7
University press	71.3	1
School (elhi) text	912.9	12
College text	925.9	13
Subscription reference	356.5	5
	7,249.3	100

Source: Book Industry Trends—1980

cluding, therefore, all export and foreign sales), consumer expenditures on books in 1979 are shown in Table 2.

Industry Markets

As we have seen, publishers' customers include individual consumers and institutions to whom they market directly as well as through intermediaries such as retailers, wholesalers, and jobbers. More specifically the major domestic market areas may be described as follows:

Retail outlets include bookstores; book departments in department stores; shops selling religious, stationery, and gift items; museum stores; chain stores, supermarkets, and drugstores; and newsstands, among others. Professional books are often sold in medical and engineering supply stores, hobby books in hobby stores, art books in art supply stores, etc.

Of the above, book, department, and other stores which have traditionally handled books for the general consumer are thought of as trade outlets. Chain stores, drugstores, supermarkets, and newsstands comprise the so-called "mass market."

College stores are often classified separately since they provide the principal channel for books utilized in higher education. However, they also account for substantial non-educational sales to the students and faculty whom they serve.

Publishers may deal with the above retail outlets directly or through *wholesalers.*

Libraries include public, college, and university, and special (i.e., industrial, research, or special interest) libraries. School library sales are usually classified with sales to schools and institutions. Some library sales are consummated by publishers directly; however, most are supplied through the facilities of *library jobbers,* i.e., specialists in supplying the library trade.

Schools and institutions comprise school systems, districts, depositories, classrooms, resource centers, libraries, and school stores, as well as other educational institutions public or private from kindergarten level through grade 12.

Direct to consumer transactions are those in which the publisher or book club markets directly to the individual by mail or door-to-door.

Other markets for publishers include industry, government, premium users, foundations, research establishments, etc.

Table 3 shows estimated 1979 consumer expenditures for the market categories just described.

Table 3. 1979 Channels of Domestic Book Distribution

	Estimated Consumer Expenditures	
Channel	Millions of Dollars	Millions of Units
General retailers	$2,496.0	691.79
College stores	1,223.4	189.68
Libraries and institutions	601.5	71.87
Schools	1,175.2	319.25
Direct to consumer	1,659.5	320.09
Other	93.6	54.01
	7,249.3	1,640.93

Source: Book Industry Trends—1980

In addition to these domestic markets publishers enjoy *export sales* to foreign bookstores, libraries, and individuals. Sometimes they make arrangements with foreign publishers for the sale of an entire edition of bound books or of unbound sheets which the foreign publisher then markets under his own imprint. A number of American publishers operate subsidiary companies abroad to which they export books and sheets but which also manufacture indigenous editions and originate titles in their own territories.

Finally, publishers gain important income from the marketing of domestic and foreign *rights*. Book clubs and paperback publishers will purchase the right to reprint books, as may magazines for certain portions of a book or for serialization of the whole. Foreign publishers will buy translation or reprint rights. Motion picture and TV rights, though often controlled exclusively by the author, are also occasionally a source of revenue for the publisher. "Subsidiary" rights as the industry terms them are of particular importance in the economics of trade-book publishers.

16
Sharks:
The Making of a Best Seller

Ted Morgan

Jaws, the saga of a twenty-foot "great white" shark that terrorizes a Long Island resort town, was brought out by Doubleday early in 1974 and, within a few months, it became one of the fastest selling books in American publishing history. When the film version appeared the next summer, it set new box office records by grossing over $124 million in the first three months.

In the following article, free-lance writer Ted Morgan takes us through the editorial and business phases of the publishing industry, showing how the efforts of author, agent, editors, sales personnel, artists, reprint houses, and merchandising staff are coordinated to propel a potential best seller from "a one page outline to a million dollar property."

The publishing business is to other businesses as a tightrope walker is to a jogger. Both are moving from one point to another, but while the jogger remains fairly secure on the ground, the tightrope walker teeters in mid-air. With each step he risks a fall. So it is with publishing.

A company that sells food products, for example, may launch one new product every two years, after months of market research and supermarket test runs, and is on firm ground when it comes to projecting sales. But publishers do not know what makes a book sell 100,000 copies; if they did, they would publish more books that do. So their business is filled with risk. The publisher is up there without a net, tentatively placing one foot in front of the other as he tries to keep his balance.

Doubleday, the Flying Wallendas of the publishing business, brings out 700 new titles a year in its trade book department. (Trade books are works of fiction and nonfiction sold commercially, as opposed to academic texts or other specialized works.) This means that its 53 trade salesmen must sell 700 new products a year to bookstore buyers. In marketing these products, Doubleday, like other publishers with smaller lists, labors under four major disadvantages:

■ The publisher's imprint is almost meaningless—the customer who buys tea from Lipton or shoes from Florsheim does not buy a book because it carries the Doubleday imprint.

■ The customer who likes the tea will keep coming back for more, but the reader who likes a book will not buy another copy, unless he happens to work for the company that bought the film rights and has been told to help put it on the best-seller list. A book salesman's axiom is that he cannot count on repeat sales.

■ People usually buy something they know they will like. They know their butcher; they try on clothes. But you cannot know if you will like a book—even if you saw the author on the "Today" show and he reminded you of Cary Grant—until you read it.

■ Publishers do not control their distribution. They are at the mercy of bookstores. A shoe store with a line that is not moving will advertise a sale. But a store can return unsold books for a full refund. Returns are a publisher's nightmare. Not only is he tightrope walking then, he is standing on a frayed rope.

Given these complications, there is something slightly fortuitous about a publishing success. Suddenly a book takes off and no one quite knows why. Besides the obvious reasons—an author's reputation, or the subject, or a stunning jacket—there is an elusive factor. Call it luck, or divine intervention. Or, more prosaically, as I learned when I studied a specific best seller which grew from a one-page outline to a million-dollar property, call it the successful orchestration of many different instruments.

On June 14, 1971, Tom Congdon, a Doubleday senior editor, had lunch with the writer Peter Benchley, son of Nathaniel and grandson of Robert. Congdon at 43 has a silken poise that reminded me of certain Vatican dignitaries I had known. He is like a youthful, defrocked cardinal, the kind who, as an altar boy, sipped sacramental wine in the vestry. His face still has traces of the cherub, but the eyes above the pink cheeks reflect a blend of instant empathy and cunning. He is known in the trade as a skilled manipulator who combines obsessive thoroughness with a Florentine sense of strategy. When he talks about his work, he reverts to the vocabulary of physical love. He will say: "An editor is someone who likes to make love to strangers," or, "In the case of this book there was a year of foreplay," or, "We were stroking each other over drinks."

He came to Doubleday three years ago via Yale (he dropped out part of his sophomore year to work in a gold mine in Fairbanks, Alaska, and has been looking for the mother lode ever since), 12 years at *The Saturday Evening Post,* where he learned to be a meticulous editor, and three years at Harper & Row, where he served his apprenticeship in book publishing. "You can't know anything about publishing until you've seen 500 deals," he says. "My style is 10 or 12 books a year and work the hell out of them."

When I asked about his family background, he sent me a memo, which read in part: "I'm the son of a Yankee businessman and a North Carolina Southern-belle type, and from that combination I apparently got, on the one hand, a big streak of the Protestant work ethic . . . and on the other, the belle's obsession as well, which is to make everything come out gloriously, to make everyone love the things she loves, to get everyone to turn out for the Magnolia Jubilee."

Congdon had admired some magazine articles of Benchley's and had booked a table at the Clos Normand on East 52d Street, which he described as "the kind of place you take someone you don't need to dazzle." Peter Benchley in 1971 was 31, a big, rangy, athletic and perpetually collegiate-looking man who had made a specialty of writing about deep-sea diving and sharks.

Benchley fits a line used to describe a character in the book he would soon begin to write: "Privilege had been bred into him with genetic certainty." He had an East Side brownstone upbringing—sailboats in Central Park ponds and dancing class at age 11 in black tie and a Lester Lanin beanie. Like his father and grandfather, he went to Philips Exeter and Harvard. As a third-generation member of a literary dynasty, with only a first name to make for himself, it had never occurred to Peter Benchley to be anything but a writer. He had started trying to market his work when he was 16, and had sold his first short story to *Vogue* when he was still in his teens. He acquired an agent, Roberta Pryor of International Famous Agency, when he was 21. Another I.F.A. agent represented Peter's father, Nathaniel, the author of numerous novels and juveniles, and Mrs. Pryor took Peter on a "will you do my kid a favor" basis. He worked briefly at the Washington *Post,* pounding out three-paragraph obits like all beginners, and moved to *Newsweek,* where he wrote his first piece on sharks in 1965.

In 1967 and 1968, he worked as a speech-writer for Lyndon Johnson. "I was a low-level aide," he recalled, "but it was a chance to see the inside of the White House. I wrote proclamations, like 'On Your Knees, America' for the National Day of Prayer. We'd meet on Fridays and sometimes he'd be there. He'd pick up something I'd written and say, 'This is the worst thing I ever read—all these chicken——writers giving me names I can't pronounce.' Depending on his mood, he would know your name or he would forget it —but he always knew my wife's name. God, he was a good politician."

Benchley's wife's name is Wendy, and she is tall and slender and attractive, and goes underwater diving with her husband. Benchley met her in Nantucket where she was working as a summer waitress. She was not allowed to smoke, saw him at a table with a cigarette, and went over and asked him for a drag. Pleasant things seem to happen to Peter Benchley almost effortlessly.

Over creamed mussels at the Clos Normand, Congdon asked Benchley about book ideas. Benchley, who had recently spent a month in Bermuda for the *National Geographic* diving for sunken ships, wanted to write a book about pirates as they really were, "without Errol Flynn." The idea appealed to Congdon only mildly, and to fill out the lunch, he asked: "Have you ever thought about fiction?"

"As a matter of fact I have," Benchley said. "I've been thinking about a novel about a great white shark that appears off a Long Island resort and afflicts it." Sharks had fascinated Benchley ever since his father had taken him swordfishing in the waters off Nantucket as a child. "The water was lousy with sharks, and we began to catch them *faute de mieux*," he recalled. "I'd take them home and cut the jaws out and be left with 150 pounds of rotting meat on the lawn. I was struck by their inherent menace—they are prehistoric eating machines that have not evolved in 30 million years."

Congdon liked the idea. "O.K., that sounds good," he said. "What you must do is go to the typewriter and write me a page, and if it's all right I can get you enough money to go to the next step."

Now it happened that several days before, Benchley had lunched with another editor, Richard Kluger of Atheneum, who had made him an identical offer for his shark idea. Benchley and his agent decided to take it to Doubleday, the big commercial house.

On June 15, Congdon followed up with a note to Roberta Pryor in which he was, despite the wording, expressing no more than his personal interest: "Doubleday is very interested indeed in Peter Benchley's shark novel, which sounds like something our 53 trade salesmen could flog with gusto . . . if Peter provides me one page of description, I'll get a good deal for you."

Congdon was not as sanguine as he sounded. Doubleday is run by committee, and he knew it would not be easy to get money for a first novelist. "In fiction," he said, "track record means everything. Bookstores are very conservative; they won't even stock a novel until they've heard of the author. Of course, I didn't realize at the time that Benchley did have a track record—his father and his grandfather."

On June 23, Benchley's one-page description arrived. "The purpose of the novel," he wrote, "would be to explore the reactions of a community that is suddenly struck by a peculiar natural disaster—not an earthquake or a flood . . . but a continuing, mysterious devastation that, as time goes on, loses its natural neutrality and begins to smack of evil. . . . Suppose a Long Island resort community was suddenly visited by a great white shark? A young woman is killed. . . . How does the community cope with this inexplicable menace?"

Benchley had intuitively combined two certified formulas of best-sellerdom. I say intuitively because I do not believe that anyone who begins with the deliberate intent of writing a best seller can succeed. Jacqueline Susann, like William Faulkner, is trying to write the best book she can; she simply has a more highly developed sense of the meretricious. No one really sits down to write "Lincoln's Doctor's Dog," and Peter Benchley's outline had the metaphysical overtones of a serious work of fiction.

But it also combined the two formulas. One was the something-about-which-the-general-public-knows-a-little-but-wants-to-know-more formula: how to run a hotel, inside the Mafia, a movie star's private life. The other was the external menace formula: A group of people are threatened by some outside force, an emergency is created by the threat, and the crisis is resolved. Perhaps there is something in our race memory that makes us want to live out vicariously the cycle of menace and survival. The menace can be a fire trapping a group of people in a skyscraper, an airliner about to crash, a hungry shark or a diphcritic sailor on 48-hour leave in New York who is going to start an epidemic if he is not found and quarantined. The sailor is found, the fire is put out, the plane lands, the monster is destroyed and the reassured reader can turn out the light and go to sleep.

On June 30, Congdon wrote the Doubleday editorial director Betty A. Prashker: "Peter Benchley mentioned an idea he's had for a novel . . . about the marauding of a seacoast resort town by that fearsome creature a great white shark . . . (Peter is something of an expert on sharks) . . . he has written a page of description, attached, which his agent, Roberta Pryor, hopes will be enough to get him a $1,000 option, one half of which would be returnable. . . . I have a persistent feeling that Benchley might have the makings of a good adventure novelist."

Congdon's memo was returned with an appendant signed BAP: "Tom: I think Benchley's idea is a good one. I would go for the option. He is supposed to be an authority on sharks (an in subject at the moment) and his basic idea is intriguing . . . he's a good bet and it would be money well spent."

Congdon began to build in-house support by showing the outline to other editors, one of whom, veteran fiction editor Walter Bradbury, had mixed feelings in a comment dated July 1: "He (Benchley) has been talking about this book for a long time, and never doing anything about it." Bradbury agreed that the idea was worth pursuing, however, and concluded: "In any case I know he has talent, and he would be a good name to publish."

Armed with the positive comments of other editors, Congdon prepared a contract request for the weekly editorial meeting on July 13. The contract request gives a descrip-

tion of the book, the author's previous work and experience, and this all-important business information: The B/E or break-even point, the sales figure at which Doubleday gets back the money it put in; and the A.E.O. or author earn-out, the sales figure at which the author earns back his advance. "What we're shooting for here is a popular novel with best-seller potential," Congdon told the nine other editors at the Wednesday meeting. The contract request next had to be submitted to the publishing board, which includes members of the business and advertising departments, where it was approved on condition that $500 of the $1,000 would be returned to Doubleday if the four trial chapters Benchley came up with were unacceptable and could not be sold elsewhere.

This provision met with the resistance of agent Roberta Pryor, who said: "For me it was the principle of the thing. Are they in the risk business or not? They should pay $1,000 to be in the first position. You want the publisher's vote of confidence, not the money on a yo-yo."

For Doubleday it was a matter of principle, too. There is a traditional reluctance on the part of the publishing board to offer an option against an unspecified total advance. They continued for 10 days arguing over $500 for what would become a million-dollar property. Congdon wrote Roberta Pryor that he had "forced the house to its elastic limit . . . $500 is really an absurdly small amount of money to lose such a nice book over . . . despite all the editorial lust rising within me . . . I share the wistfulness here at the prospect of subsidizing another publisher's book."

Mrs. Pryor, behind whose office desk there is a headline that reads, "Perfect art is Roberta's aim," would not budge. "Of course," she explained, "you're only as strong as your client. If he says I want the deal, don't blow it, that's one thing. If he says, you tell me what's right, that's another." On July 22, Doubleday agreed that Benchley could keep the $1,000 if he wrote four chapters by April 15, 1972. On July 27, Congdon received a note from Roberta Pryor saying: "Here are three signed copies of the option agreement . . . enough yet—send money."

At this point, Congdon, in his letters and memos, had written about 10 times as many words as his author. He sent Benchley little reminders, like the one dated October 11: "I think often of you and your book and hope you are reserving the best portion of your genius for regular sessions of work on it."

The first four chapters arrived on March 20, 1972, well within the deadline, with a covering note from Roberta Pryor: "I hasten to send you the first 174 pages of Peter Benchley's untitled novel. I trust, in accordance with our previous correspondence, that you will find these conscientiously wrought."

Congdon was disappointed. He found the shark far more convincing than the human characters. He wrote Roberta Pryor on March 27: "There is no question but that Peter Benchley's material is conscientiously wrought . . . I'm not entirely sure, however, that it's successfully wrought. . . . I find the opening of the book marvelous, and the shark scenes good almost all the way through. But almost everything else seems pretty mild. . . ." Congdon objected that the main character, the police chief who decides to close the beaches after the shark strikes, was constantly cracking corny jokes. "The author is seeking both chuckles and gasps of horror," he wrote, "and it just doesn't seem to be working. You just can't graft light humor onto a gory five-death tragedy. . . . I find the narrative unfolding pretty limply and uncertainly . . . there are lots of small confusions . . . the shark scenes, though powerful at first, get repetitive."

Congdon did not think the four chapters were good enough to show and asked Benchley to rewrite them. Benchley took that and subsequent criticism with uncommon good grace. He was bombarded with letters and memos from Congdon, and one long memo from editor Kate Medina, and accepted their suggestions without a shiver of petulance. "When they insisted, I gave in," he said. "They've been in business a long time, and I'd never written a novel." Betty Prashker saw the rewrite soon after it had come in on April 24 and wrote Congdon: "I think the story has too many predictable elements at the moment . . . a lot of plot without real

character or drive . . . but if Benchley is willing to work with you, I would certainly go ahead with the contract."

Four days later, and nine gestative months after the initial lunch at the Clos Normand, Congdon could at last write Benchley: "I'm delighted we're going to do your book." The Contracts Department approved a $7,500 advance: $1,000 for the option, already paid, $2,500 on signing, $2,000 on delivery of the first draft, and $2,000 on acceptance of the final manuscript.

Congdon continued to send Benchley a stream of editorial suggestions—don't spell out things too much, less is more, don't be too predictable, keep a tight time frame. Benchley remained patient and pliable. Congdon gratefully wrote Roberta Pryor on June 1: "Peter was gracious enough not to sputter at anything I suggested."

When Benchley wrote a sex scene between the police chief and his wife, Congdon's sense of propriety was offended: "I don't think there's any place for wholesome married sex in this kind of book," he wrote. Benchley obediently turned the wife into an adulteress, who has an affair with a young marine scientist. The sex scene is written as an exchange of fantasies over lunch, avoiding bedroom descriptions, like a chaste 19th-century novel. One editor described it as "the great American cop-out."

After two complete and several more partial rewrites, a weary Peter Benchley turned in a manuscript on December 1, with the comment: "Here is the opus. Following your instructions meant running through three typewriter ribbons and cleaning the keys with a needle every 10 pages." More editorial suggestions arrived for Benchley to work in, until he felt he could do no more, and delivered the final draft on Jan. 2, 1973.

Congdon recognized the possibilities at once. "It was such a good story," he said. "You've got to think of the whole country as a child that climbs up on its daddy's knee and says, 'Tell me a story.'" He began what he calls his "psychological build-up—you talk it up to the editors until it becomes a book you have to like." On Jan. 5, a memo from Walter Bradbury, the editor who had expressed initial misgivings, said: "I think it's a fine job! Irresistible, edge-of-the-chair, fast-breathing, gripping reading."

"That was my first piece of gold," Congdon said. "I could spew that out all over the company. If I get praise here I take it there, back and forth, until everyone is behind the book."

With his final draft, Benchley had included a title suggestion: "A Stillness in the Water." Congdon said that sounded like a Françoise Sagan novel about a young woman who goes to the Riviera to forget an unhappy love affair. Congdon offered "The Summer of the Shark," but Benchley warned that the word "shark" in the title would put the book on the nature shelves. "There was constant noodling for the title," Congdon said. "We tried a total of 237." The word "jaws" made its first appearance in a memo from Congdon to Walter Bradbury: "What do you think of this title for the Benchley novel—The Jaws of the Leviathan?"

"Little, I'm sorry to say," Bradbury replied. "I don't know why, but it seems a little flat to me. Any possibility, if Leviathan is desirable, in: The Terror of Leviathan, or The Terror of the Monster, or The Year They Closed the Beaches?"

At lunch with Benchley some days later, Congdon was scribbling the title "Why Us?" on a pad. "Why not just 'Jaws,'" Benchley said, and Congdon felt a pleasant rush of certainty.

The next step was to get the salesmen's support. "You can have a *summa cum laude* in comparative literature at Harvard and possess exquisite literary taste, but if you don't like salesmen you'll never make an editor," says Congdon. He likes salesmen. A salesman will walk down the hall at Doubleday, and he will say: "Look at his feet—you can see sidewalk under them," or, "You see the way he walks; he always has the bags with him, even when he doesn't." He sent the first five pages to each salesman with the comment: "Friend: If you thought the beginning of SHOOT (another Congdon action novel) was powerful, read these first five pages of our fall novel JAWS." Salesmen's comments began coming in on blue memo sheets: "Truly a 'skip dinner and read through the evening' tale," one said. "Just enough sex and profanity to make the story enjoyable but not offensive." "I knew on the basis of salesmen's reactions that they would load it into the stores," Congdon said.

By then, in March, 1973, the manuscript was in the hands of Bob Banker, Doubleday's head of subsidiary rights, a frosty man with a tight smile and a reputation as "one of the top men in the business." He sent it out to the book clubs and received a call from Bantam, the paperback house, expressing interest. Oscar Dystel, the president of Bantam, was acting on a tip that there was a book Doubleday was very excited about. Here is where the size of the company counted. Dystel knew that if Doubleday was behind a book, they would advertise it, promote it, and get it into the stores.

"I started reading the book as I was riding home in midwinter," Dystel recalled, "and it was dark. After the first three pages, I was horrorstruck, and I asked myself: How can anyone sustain readership at this level of monstrosity? But I was also fascinated. It was like watching a cobra . . . but Peter Benchley —that turned me off. The name stood for humor, a certain lightness of tone; the incongruity might have been negative. Still, the authenticity came through. He seemed to be writing out of his own experience.

"Having gotten a strong visceral feeling, I discussed it with the other editors—we all felt it was going to be a big one, and we wanted to establish our position with a substantial floor." A floor is a first offer; the reprint house that makes it has topping privileges if there are other bids.

Bantam editor Alan Barnard called Bob Banker and offered a floor of $200,000. Banker was surprised. He had not expected such a high floor on a first novel. If Bantam thinks this is worth $200,000, he thought, maybe we've got something really big. On the other hand, there was the temptation to take the money and run. "That's a very interesting offer," he told Barnard. "I'll let you know."

Banker told Congdon: "We have a very good offer. The agent and the author should be contacted to see if they want us to take it out of hand. I don't know how Bantam would respond if we went shopping around."

After some soul-searching, it was decided to shop around, and Banker informed Bantam that "the book is out with other paperback publishers. We feel we must give them a chance. We will give you every opportunity to top other bids if you wish."

The book was submitted to eight other paperback publishers. Two rejected it, and an auction was set up for the other six. All offers had to be in by the close of business on April 23.

In the meantime, Banker had been asked for six copies of the manuscript by the Book of the Month Club. This meant that it was an "A" book, one of the eight or nine books a month that has passed the first screening for appraisal by the club's four judges, Clifton Fadiman, Gilbert Highet, John K. Hutchens and Wilfrid Sheed.

With the sales conference coming up on April 8, Congdon got together with art director Alex Gotfryd about the jacket. Gotfryd, an urbane man with a Polish cavalry mustache who turns out 700 jackets a year, agreed to use the author's idea: to show a peaceful unsuspecting town through the bleached jaws of a shark. When Congdon saw the sketch, he said: "Can we make it a bit more ominous? Can we make the sky red? Also, the shark's bones look too liplike and pendulous." Gotfryd worked with the artist to improve the sketch.

At the sales conference at the Tamiment Country Club in the Poconos, six regional sales managers sat around a table listening to the editors make their presentation, and a slide of the jacket was projected on a screen. The sales managers were given the one-sentence sales "handle," which is practically all the salesmen, who usually have an hour to sell a buyer 60 or 70 titles, will have time to say. The handle for "Jaws" was: "The exciting tale of a resort town fighting for its life against a Great White Shark." The salesmen were also given Title Information sheets, or TI's, which provide capsule information about the book and the author. Each TI has a "keynote," and the keynote for "Jaws" was: "One of the big books of 1974." Another important heading was "School and Library limitations: One sex-fantasy scene; some profanity."

Congdon rose and made his presentation: "Of all the fish in the sea the fiercest is the great white shark," he began. He tried to create a sense of drama. He talked about the excitement generated by the book. He tried to convey a feeling of "you'd better get with it or you'll be sorry." The sales managers loved the book and the title, but there was considerable resistance to the jacket. It made them think of Freud's classic dream of castration, the *vagina dentata*.

That afternoon, the sales managers met without the editors and estimated the advance, the number of copies they could place in book stores by the October publication date. The first printing is based on these commitments and an extrapolation of early orders. They came up with an advance of 25,000. At the same time, advertising manager David Cathers decided on an initial budget of $25,000, or about a dollar a book. The average advance for a first novel is 4,000 copies, with a tiny advertising budget. Only a few of the 75 novels Doubleday publishes annually (aside from mysteries, Westerns and science fiction) sell more than 5,000 copies.

Shortly after the sales conference, "Jaws" was taken by The Book of the Month, *Reader's Digest,* and *Playboy* book clubs. It was not hefty enough for a Book of the Month full selection, and it was teamed up with another book called "Dummy," by Ernest Tidyman, the author of "Shaft," for a combined price to members of $8.95. The advances from the three clubs totaled more than $85,000.

On April 23, Bob Banker, an auctioneer with a telephone instead of a hammer, started taking bids from the paperback houses, using the bid from one house to raise the ante with the next caller. The bids kept spiraling until they passed the half-million mark. But Bantam still had topping rights on the final bid. Dystel was ready to pay for a first novel on the basis of a gut feeling that it would be a "big" book, which for Bantam means more than a million copies. He also thought it would make a "tremendous" movie, and movies spur paperback sales. Another factor was the paperback houses' "loss-leader" approach. Bantam sells 100 million books a year, mostly in 100,000 retail outlets such as variety stores, drug chains and supermarkets. They fight for rack space with the competition, and one big book a month helps them get more space for the rest of their list, like little fish swimming in the wake of a big fish.

These huge prepublication sales to reprint houses are probably the most important development in publishing in the last quarter century. It used to be that paperback houses would pay big money for a book only once it was an established success. "The Naked and the Dead" was sold in 1949 to paper for $35,000, then considered big money, only after it was a runaway best seller. Today, paperback houses are paying million-dollar advances based on an editor's feelings about a book. The highest rollers are not in Vegas. Elaine Geiger, the editor-in-chief of New American Library, which lost out to Bantam, later said: "I never would have bid half a million dollars if it hadn't been called 'Jaws.'"

Congdon was at a regional sales conference in Dallas on April 24 when he got a call from Ted Macri of the Doubleday subrights department.

"Tom," said Macri, "are you sitting down?"

Congdon said he was.

"Would you consider a paperback offer of $575,000 for 'Jaws'?"

Congdon said he would, and called Benchley at his home. Benchley was in the kitchen eating breakfast.

He told Benchley, who said, "Good God, Thomas," and told his wife, Wendy, who burst into tears. She was afraid that they could no longer lead a quiet, pleasant life in a small town, that her husband was being raised to celebrity and remoteness.

The publication date was delayed to early 1974 to give the Book of the Month a chance to come out first, and Congdon began to send early copies around, "to build up the drumroll." He sent copies to 60 agents "because they talk a lot," and to print upon their minds an image of Tom Congdon, the editor with the golden touch. He also sent copies to writers, with a self-addressed postcard for comments. The blurb is a science all its own— an author may not want to ignore a publisher,

but does not really want to be quoted, so he finds a way around it. The essayist Heywood Hale Broun, for instance, wrote Congdon: "Not since Dumas Père et Fils has there been a succession of storytellers like Nathaniel and Peter Benchley. 'Jaws' is in the best tradition of those masters of 'and then.'" The comment was just tongue-in-cheek enough to be unusable. David Halberstam told Congdon over the phone that "Jaws" was "fabulous." Benchley wanted to use the quote, but Halberstam, concerned about his image, pleaded that "I'm absolutely overexposed. My house is stacked up with books. People are going to think I'm a promiscuous overpraiser. I've decided I'm going to help only three books a year. I leave it up to you whether this will be one of them." "I understand," Congdon said. Doubleday author Leon Uris came in with a good quote. His wife later told a friend: "Oh, Leon never even read it. I read it and I didn't like it, but I didn't want to let the team down."

"Jaws" was ready for publication in mid-January 1974, but a small crisis over the jacket caused a two-week delay. When the salesmen had vetoed the first jacket, Congdon had gone back to Alex Gotfryd and said: "We've got a problem. Can we have just a fish on the cover?" "The cover's not big enough," Gotfryd said. "It will look like a sardine." Finally, they decided to go with a typographical jacket, the title and the author in stark lettering against a black background. They printed 30,000 copies and jacketed the books—an operation that is still done by hand —in Doubleday's Berryville, Va., printing plant.

When Oscar Dystel of Bantam saw the jacket, he was unhappy. "Without an image," he said, "no one would know what 'Jaws' meant. It could have been a book about dentistry." He asked Congdon to put a shark on the jacket. Congdon went to see Gotfryd and said: "Dystel wants an illustration. He's advanced a lot of money. I think we should honor his request." Gotfryd stifled his exasperation and called artist Paul Bacon, who made a rough layout of the enormous head of a fish. "Why can't we have a swimmer as well to have a sense of disaster and a sense of scale?'' Gotfryd asked. Bacon came in the next morning with the completed jacket, an open-jawed shark's head rising toward a swimming woman. Dystel was pleased and wrote Congdon on Dec. 20: ''The jacket design for 'Jaws' is much improved. If you sell 100,000 copies we'll follow you to the letter.'' ''We realized that the new version looked like a penis with teeth,'' Congdon said, ''but was that bad? I placated Alex by buying him a $17 necktie at Paul Stuart.''

In the meantime, Congdon's fertile mind was dreaming up promotion ideas. He wanted to send each reviewer a shark's tooth with his copy of ''Jaws,'' and asked his assistant, Susan Schwartz, to buy some. Miss Schwartz called half the taxidermists in the yellow pages, the New York Aquarium, and the American Museum of Natural History, with no luck. She found some at The Collector's Cabinet, but they cost between $5 and $40, depending on size. The idea was dropped.

Julie Coryn, in charge of publicity at Doubleday, usually has trouble promoting fiction. This time, she started early, dropping news about ''Jaws'' over lunch with reviewers, planting the seeds of interest and hoping that her own enthusiasm would be contagious. She played down the money aspect with some critics ''because they think that if a book is making a lot of money it can't be any good. But there was plenty to build on. Here was the third-generation Benchley, from a family of wordsmiths. We've got a best seller before we've even been published. It's a page-turner, the kind of thing E. M. Forster described in 'Aspects of the Novel,' the sense of and then, and then, and then.'' She sent dozens of letters to media people that said: ''Just try to read 'Jaws' and try to put it down. Then let's talk about it.'' As the replies started coming in, one memo had a big HOORAY scrawled over it. It said: ''Peter Benchley, author of 'Jaws,' will appear on N.B.C.'s 'Today' show on February 12, 1974.''

By this time, Roberta Pryor had sold the movie rights to Brown-Zanuck for $150,000 plus $25,000 for the screenplay. ''It conjured up the old Hollywood days,'' she said. ''Instead of going to them with your hat in your hand, they were clamoring for it. Instead of,

'Say, I've got a book you might be interested in,' it was 'I want that book.' ''

Benchley rewrote the screenplay three times. ''A finer hand than mine is at work on it now,'' he said, ''someone who is doing what they call a dialogue polish, which is like referring to gang rape as heavy necking.''

''We're going to Australia for our shark footage,'' Richard Zanuck told Benchley.

''What if the sharks aren't big enough? It won't look right,'' Benchley said.

''Ah, we'll put a midget in the cage,'' Zanuck said, meaning the cage the marine scientist is lowered in at the end of the book to try to kill the shark.

In addition, Disneyland is building a mechanical shark, for use in the film, with a 65-foot hydraulic catapult to launch it out of the waters. Will wonders never cease?

On Jan. 18, an item in *Publishers Weekly* said: Peter Benchley has written a major novel, one that has created virtually unprecedented prepublication excitement . . . Over $1 million in subsidiary rights sold; 35,000 initial printing, major ad-promo.'' On Feb. 11, 10 days after the book's publication, *Publishers Weekly* ran an interview with Benchley. The interviewer, Jean F. Mercier, wrote that ''Benchley has candid praise for Tom Congdon and Kate Medina, his editors.'' Corporate survival is no empty phrase, however, and in a subsequent issue PW printed a correction: ''Doubleday asks us to point out that, while Kate Medina served as consultant on Peter Benchley's 'Jaws,' Tom Congdon was the sole editor.''

As soon as the book was in the stores, it started selling well. A Feb. 13 memo from Congdon said: ''The best of the bulletins I'm getting on 'Jaws' is this: It's Ingraham's fastest-moving book [Ingraham is a big wholesaler].'' By mid-March it had sold 40,000 copies and jumped in one week from number 10 to number 3 on *The New York Times* best-seller list (where it remained at this writing). There were by then 75,000 copies in print.

Advertising manager David Cathers knew that ''Jaws'' had broken out of the hard-core market of people who regularly go into book stores, which he estimates at roughly 60,000, and was reaching an audience that seldom buys hard-cover books. He scheduled some TV spots to supplement newspaper ads. He figured that the total advertising campaign for "Jaws" would cost between $50,000 and $60,000 (once a year, Doubleday will spend as much as $100,000 in advertising a book).

Congdon was still working the book, asking everyone at Doubleday to bone up on shark lore and circulating a memo with a table of shark lengths. But "Jaws" fortunes were now in the hands of a man named Walter Thompson who works in Doubleday's merchandising offices in Garden City, L.I. He is in charge of inventory control, which means that he orders new printings. Like a general who decides the precise moment to throw fresh troops into battle, a mistake on his part can be costly—if he prints too many there will be returns; if he prints too few the book may be out of stock with readers clamoring for it.

"Jaws," starting from a one-page outline and a tiny advance, had grown to proportions as awesome as its subject. The great white shark was the most profitable fish in 20th-century fiction. Doubleday received half the paperback and book club advances, or about $330,000, plus an estimated $65,000 profit on hard-cover sales of 100,000 copies, which would probably go higher, at $6.95 a copy. Bantam, having paid a large advance, planned to price the book at $1.50 or $1.75, and projected a break-even point of 1.6 million copies, after which it would be earning roughly 20 cents a book, or $200,000 on every subsequent million. Oscar Dystel felt it was the kind of book that could sell five million copies. The Book of the Month club, which saves money on large printings and avoids the 44 per cent discount to book stores through direct mail sales, offered the book to its members at about $4.50 as half of a dual selection, and would earn substantially more per book than Doubleday. Benchley, with half the paperback and book club advances, the movie money, the foreign rights totaling about $100,000, and a 15 per cent royalty on hard-cover sales, would easily earn more than $600,000, of which his agent Roberta Pryor received 10 per cent. The only principal who

made no immediate financial gain was Tom Congdon, who said: "Remember, they don't dock my salary when I lose money on a book." But his reward was apparent soon enough: He was named this month to be editor-in-chief of adult trade books at E. P. Dutton & Co.

When Benchley had started the book, his brother-in-law had asked him: "Can you make money off a novel?"

"If everything were to break right," Benchley had replied, "but the odds against it are astronomical." In 1973, he was in debt, and he was about to ask the *National Geographic* for a job, when he was saved from the specter of regular employment by the news that the book clubs were nibbling. Now, with his book selling about 8,000 copies a week, he estimated that he had the freedom to write for another 10 years on the income from "Jaws."

We now come, in a votary offering to those novelists whose works sink without a ripple, to the liabilities of success. In Benchley's case, unkind comparisons were made between Peter and his father, who once wrote a "fish" juvenile entitled "The Several Tricks of Edgar Dolphin." Benchley's family spirit is so fierce that he once blackballed a figure in the publishing world who had had a disagreement with his father from membership in the Coffee House, a midtown, men-only, eating and drinking club frequented by writers and editors. And now, in one scene-stealing appearance, he had permanently upstaged his father. A family friend, however, described Nathaniel as "stuffy, maybe, but not petty. He doesn't envy Peter, and they continue to have the very supportive relationship they have always had."

Benchley was also concerned about his nationwide promotion tour. He is afraid of flying, an eccentricity he shares with other wealthy men, such as J. Paul Getty. "I know all the statistics that you're safer than in your own kitchen," he said, "but tell that to the 345 people who went down outside Paris. My only explanation is that after so much success I'm due for a disaster, that being on the best-seller list increases the possibilities of a plane crash." Benchley is solidly in the grip of the

Puritan ethic, which ordains that a night of pleasant drinking with friends must be punished by a terrible hangover.

Another disappointment, not counting the thinly disguised envy of several writer friends, was the reviews. "I was hoping for good reviews to justify the prepublication hysteria," he said. "Old Carl Cocky here, I said, 'Tom, I want to know the good ones and the bad ones.' He read me a short review in *Playboy,* a savage attack. It bothered me for three days. I called him back and said, 'No more, I don't need this.' He had warned me, 'You put your ass on the line; you've got to be prepared to have it kicked as well as kissed.' But I still don't understand how a book can get raves from one reviewer and be considered garbage by another."

What heart-wrenching problems, and would that we all had them. Benchley's main concern, however, is getting into his second novel. The subject is marine archeology, and the story is based on a true incident—a ship carrying opium and morphine sank off the coast of Bermuda some years ago, over the wrecks of two Spanish galleons. Two young American diving enthusiasts, male and female, find the drug ship by accident . . . and then, and then, and then.

17
On the Road with a Book Salesman

N. R. Kleinfield

Few books sell as well as *Jaws* did and few receive any general publicity. Bringing the many other trade books published each year to the attention of potential readers is usually the function of publishers' representatives or "reps," who try to place new books in bookstores. In the following article, by N. R. Kleinfield of the *New York Times,* some typical days in the life of a trade rep provide an inside account of trade-book distribution.

It is four minutes past nine in Greenfield, Mass., on a muggy summer Wednesday morning. The flow of pedestrians is just beginning down the leafy streets. A leased yellow-and-brown Monarch swings into a parking spot on Federal Street, across from the World Eye Bookshop. Piled high in the back seat are two gaily colored canvas tote bags stuffed with book catalogues, order sheets, galleys, prints and actual books. Oliver Gilliland, a book salesman for William Morrow and Co., gets out of the Monarch and fetches the tote bags, which, fully loaded, seem heavy enough to qualify as training material for the Olympic weightlifting team.

Carrying himself erect as a soldier, Mr. Gilliland strides into the World Eye, where Ann Smith, a quiet woman who buys the

Source: From *The New York Times Book Review* (August 24, 1980). Copyright © 1980 by The New York Times Company. Reprinted by permission of the publisher.

books, gives him a crinkling smile. An unfailingly polite man of 31, friendly as a cocker spaniel, Mr. Gilliland sports a mustache, glasses and dark, curly hair containing more than a few hints of gray. Escorted to a musty elevated space furnished in the Non-Executive Style, he removes a catalogue, then spreads out a black ring binder in which book jackets repose under transparent plastic. This is Morrow's list—a trove of 54 adult hardcovers, 66 juveniles, 13 trade paperbacks. The list is sold with jackets, not books, except for art books and juveniles, where illustrations are paramount. Settled comfortably, Mr. Gilliland begins his spiel, rhetorically garlanded with capsule comments on each of the titles, all of which he has sampled, many of which he has read.

A book said to be authored by Morris the Cat: "This is a terrific nonbook item. There are little asides about how cats manipulate people to get more food and all that."

A memoir by Sammy Davis Jr.: "Very gossipy. You know, the-day-I-told-Frank-Sinatra-to-go-to-hell."

A Victorian novel: "This is for the perm set."

A train thriller: "This is fake Tolstoy with a little Agatha Christie thrown in."

Fiction, except for solid gold, draws a glazed look. As in most small-town shops, the World Eye shuns fiction in favor of nonfiction and paperbacks.

Mr. Gilliland nods knowingly and notes, "You'll be happy to see that Morrow has cut its fiction by about 30 percent, because they finally got the message that fiction is not what is needed."

Many titles are tough ordering choices, but others seem sure winners. A new Ken Follett novel, "The Key to Rebecca," and "Hollywood in a Suitcase" by Sammy Davis Jr. are, in Mr. Gilliland's phrase, the list's "megabooks" and step forth to speak their names. In theory, a sales manager expects his troops to extol every title. In practice, most salesmen refuse to sing songs for books that insult the paper they are printed on. Mr. Gilliland, who used to manage bookstores, recalls fuming at reps who insisted that every book was what the entire galaxy was waiting for. Now that he sits on the other side of the order

form, he adheres to a simple selling credo: Stick close to the truth. "Quite forgettable" is his summation of one book. Another: "I'm sorry, I don't know why this is being published." Still another: "I hope it vanishes from the face of the earth."

A good order in hand, Mr. Gilliland breezes down the block to Canterbury Books, where Beethoven seeps from Sony speakers. Mainly paperbacks and a scattering of hardcover heavies. Mr. Gilliland races through a few cloth titles and the cream of the juveniles, then buzzes off to Northampton, Mass.

Mr. Gilliland is one of seven sales reps employed by Morrow, a medium-sized publishing house strong on best sellers that is eager to accumulate more of a backlist. Mr. Gilliland sells three lists a year: spring, fall and winter, for which he is paid a straight salary (Morrow, like most publishers, also relies on three salesmen who work strictly on commission). His domain consists of Massachusetts, Connecticut, Rhode Island, Vermont, New Hampshire, Maine and part of New York, wherein 37,000 miles are annually put on his Monarch to call on some 180 accounts of vastly discordant types. He skips the slew of Waldenbooks and B. Dalton outlets that have increasingly come to dot the country, since the two mighty book chains buy their wares centrally, and they merit attention from Morrow's senior sales hands. When he was buying books, Mr. Gilliland says, he occasionally squared-off with salesmen who were veritable tigers, some of whom furtively padded orders, while others were lambs. Mr. Gilliland believes that far fewer high-pressure reps ply the highways today. "You can't get away with it anymore. Reps are much more sympathetic with the bookseller's plight. For a long time, hyping was really profitable. But the public won't be fooled anymore." By and large, then, all publishers hawk their books pretty much the same way, and, in most respects, Mr. Gilliland is representative of the modern-day book salesman.

Barrelling down the road, Mr. Gilliland talks about the independent bookstore. "Right now, being an independent bookseller is an absolute heartbreak. It's unbelievable work and the return on your work is very small. I sense that many of my accounts are barely getting by, and some are certainly losing money. I think many independents will go under that can't withstand this onslaught of economic trouble and this expansion that the two major chains are doing.''

He goes on, ''I think the key to the independent bookseller's survival is personal service, knowledgeable service and an efficiently run business. I see a lot of independents forced to carry a smaller selection. It makes it difficult for a new author to break in. You'll see that many of my booksellers will say, 'Just give me your big titles.''' Though fall orders have been encouraging and Morrow has been prospering on the strength of such books as Sidney Sheldon's ''Rage of Angels,'' which tops fiction best-seller lists, this has been a sluggish year for book sales. In March and April, Mr. Gilliland says, ''all I saw was suicide on everyone's face.''

In Northampton, Mr. Gilliland digests a speedy lunch at a quaint health food eaterie, then zips over to Bookland, a combination book, card and gift store that is heavily slanted toward paperbacks and fast-moving hardbacks. The buyer tells Mr. Gilliland, ''You know, when I see reps I tell them we're just going to order the top of the line and they're not even surprised anymore.'' Still, Mr. Gilliland extracts a decent order and hurries off.

The Odyssey Book Shop in South Hadley, Mass. is teeming with activity. A white clapboard shop, it carries an extensive range of titles regularly plucked from the shelves by scholarly sorts at nearby Mount Holyoke College. There are academic titles to be found here that would draw puzzled looks from the other booksellers on Mr. Gilliland's route. Romeo Grenier, the owner, is a peppery character who is never in the mood for malarkey. It is possible that a Univac computer is housed in his head that, upon seeing a title, automatically intuits the potential South Hadley audience.

Mr. Grenier and Mr. Gilliland huddle behind a desk on which books are scattered like oversized confetti. Mr. Gilliland begins a spiel, and before the spiel is halfway to its conclusion, Mr. Grenier interrupts to say, ''Why don't you send us five and we'll see what happens and you can save your propaganda.''

Mr. Gilliland speeds on: ''This is a major book. . . .''

Mr. Grenier: ''Well, that's all you've got here.''

Mr. Gilliland: ''Oh, we've got a few turkeys.''

Mr. Grenier: ''Two.''

A pair of cookbooks enters the discussion. ''How much are these?''

''$14.95 and $19.95.''

''One of each without the propaganda.''

At all of the stops, most orders are for two or three copies, until a Ken Follett appears, when the quantities mount to 10 or more. Stores are afforded between a 43 and 46 percent discount on Morrow's new titles, depending on the quantity. Returns, however, are permitted as long as books stay in print. Mr. Gilliland rarely challenges a buyer's judgment because overselling is punished by a blizzard of returns. But, when Mr. Gilliland feels someone has ordered light, he will take another stab. ''If the answer's the same, I shut up, but I tell him I think he's making a mistake. I just want him to know that *he* blew it, not *me*.''

A lashing thunderstorm begins as Mr. Gilliland swoops into the Howard Johnson's in Springfield, Mass. ''Initially, I stayed at country inns, which are a thousand times more charming,'' Mr. Gilliland remarks. ''But their mattresses are generally lousy, and you wake up with a backache. I usually have work to do at night, and Howard Johnson's are perfect because they are so tacky that there are no distractions.''

Over dinner at a bustling seafood house, Mr. Gilliland recaps his winding path to bookselling. He grew up in Topeka, Kan., and early on was smitten by books. He recalls dragging his mother to the library at a point when he could barely reach her hand. In college, he contemplated becoming a minister, but vetoed the notion and quit school. He laid bricks, milked cows, worked in a Topeka bookstore, went to California, then returned to college and picked up a degree in humanistic psychology. Eventually, he became the manager of a children's bookstore in San Francisco. A large chain store settled in nearby, and Mr. Gilliland's employer bit the dust in 1978. Mr. Gilliland heard that Morrow had a sales rep opening, applied and, like many erstwhile bookstore managers, hit the highways.

Home is now a rented house in Newton, Mass. Mr. Gilliland is single and is not optimistic about wedlock. "I've known a lot of reps in the years I've been in the book business," he says, "and I've seen a lot of marriages and relationships break up."

Nursing his coffee, Mr. Gilliland says, "I think in the future you are going to see some fairly abrupt changes in the rep's function. The costs of putting a man on the road are astronomical. Morrow says that it costs it $60 to $80 for me to step into a store. It's about to test telephone solicitation for smaller accounts. Eventually, there may only be regional reps who call on the biggest accounts. Electronic ordering and video selling may become commonplace at some point, and reps may serve more of a public relations function than anything else."

After dinner, Mr. Gilliland retires to his Howard Johnson warren, where he immerses himself in copious paperwork. Orders have to be checked and mailed in for processing. "I haven't had it happen," Mr. Gilliland says, "but I know of reps who were supposed to be ordering somebody a new Michener, and instead they ordered 25 copies of 'My Life in Outer Trenton' or something."

The next morning, the sun is already frying the pavement as Mr. Gilliland arrives at the Transworld Book Company, a library jobber. It orders copies of every title. This is one stop where Mr. Gilliland could use a relief throat that could come in after seven innings and go the rest of the distance. Two-and-a-half hours of yakking. A Guinness World's Record for the fastest clocked lunch, then on to Longmeadow.

En route, Mr. Gilliland says: "There are three books on this list that I will not sell to any of my retail accounts. That's because they have no redeeming value. They're not good pieces of trash. They're not good pieces of literature. I could sell some of them if I wanted to, but they would just come back and it would ruin my credibility. I think that it's psychologically important to have a few skips on a list. It builds trust. It's something you can giggle over with the buyer. 'Hey, look at this dud!'"

Sidewalk Days are in progress at the Longmeadow Shops, the small mall that contains Gilbert's Book and Stationery Store. People are pawing through stuffed bunnies, picture frames, needlework. Longmeadow is populated by New England ultra-conservatives, reasonably well-fixed, who like good books, and hence Gilbert's is a classic example of the small-town bookseller, where it is axiomatic that the proprietor know every customer's reading tastes. Lynne Josephson, a former teacher who runs the shop, says, "It's a joke in this town that you have to get a bill from Gilbert's the same as from the telephone company and the electric company. Someone will come in here and I'll say, 'Oh, Mrs. Brown, we got a book in today that's written for you,' and she'll buy it based entirely on our recommendation."

Miss Josephson is an expeditious buyer, slightly slower than Romeo Grenier, possibly because the computer in her head is a previous generation model.

"The Mature Man's Guide to Style."

"Two."

"Morris."

"Four."

"Digging Up the Bible."

"One."

Speed is the operative word in bookselling. The essence of the profession is to come up with a "handle" for each title—a succinct phrase or two that will capture the flavor of the book. Mr. Gilliland is helped in this quest at Morrow sales conferences, where the editors present their books to the sales force. However, as Mr. Gilliland observes, "Every book is a best seller to its editor. So you have to separate the grain from the chaff. Sometimes it's a struggle getting a handle. I had trouble with a book I'm selling now called 'The Landscape in Art.' I was saying to myself, What is this book and why is it being published? I spoke to the sales manager, and I finally came to an understanding that it's not so much a history of landscape art but a history of man's relationship with nature as revealed in landscape art."

Mr. Gilliland has scant seconds—at best

a minute—to present a work that may have consumed grueling years of an author's life. "Authors seeing this would probably go through the wall, they would buy guns," Mr. Gilliland says, and he is at times reproofed ad nauseam by authors who fail to comprehend why their books are occupying de facto Worst-Seller Lists. "But it's simply impossible to present the whole list at every account. If I went into some of these stores and tried to present everything I would be told to get out and not ever come back." If Mr. Gilliland spent any more time—or if booksellers had the chance, which they rarely do, to read books before they bought them—he doubts that sales would differ markedly. Any adroit bookseller, after he's been in the business for some time, knows what to buy and what not to buy almost instinctively, or he is in the wrong calling.

Mr. Gilliland does not believe that good books are lost in the rapid-fire presentations, though it is clear that, at most of the stores he visits, his will alone could get the spine of virtually any title onto the shelves. In any event, books have never been sold any differently, and although publishers and booksellers perpetually grouse about the manner in which books are gotten to the public, no one has yet come up with a better way of doing it.

Now it is Chicopee, Mass. and the Paperback Booksmith. Mr. Gilliland learns that the big Uniroyal plant in town recently closed, escalating unemployment. The store expects to take it on the chin. The clientele here is mainly blue collar, which is reflected in the heavy paperback stock. The order is fairly slim.

On to Stamford, Conn., for dinner and sleep. Lush landscape glides by. There is much solitary driving involved in selling books. To pass the time, Mr. Gilliland keeps a cassette tape recorder on the seat beside him and he dictates letters to friends as he tools along.

In Stamford, Mr. Gilliland always lodges with Michael Coates, a friend who is a sales rep for Avon Books, a paperback house. Almost invariably, they dine first at a Mexican restaurant called Mama Vicky's.

Mr. Coates and Mr. Gilliland leisurely chat about the changing ways of the book business. At one point, Mr. Coates says, "Bookselling is not as personalized as it used to be. It's more of a supermarket type of business. There's more emphasis on the bottom line."

Mr. Gilliland says, "When I got into the business 12 years ago, three turns of stock per year was considered the norm. Now five turns is used as the measuring stick."

On Friday morning, Mr. Gilliland learns from Morrow that Shelley Winters's autobiography has just soared to No. 1 on The New York Times Best Seller List, giving Morrow both the No. 1 nonfiction and fiction slots. "I am high as a kite," Mr. Gilliland says. "That's one of the rewards of being a rep—seeing your work pay off."

David Rose, the benign-looking proprietor of the Barrett Bookstore, has just finished with another rep when Mr. Gilliland strolls in. Mr. Rose is a true bookman, and his store reflects quality. Yet its days may be numbered. Across the street stands a Caldor's, boasting discounted best sellers. Down the block is a Waldenbooks. A new shopping mall is rising from rubble around the corner that will house a second Waldenbooks and doubtlessly another chain store. Rose confesses that the mall's opening may force him elsewhere. He has already lost much of the suburban housewife patronage to malls, and attracts chiefly business people.

Between ordering books and puffing Chesterfields, he says, "You can only cut a pie into so many slices. The chains have moved into all of the choice book locations and hurt the independents. I don't think the chains are healthy for the book business in the long run. They're after a big profit; they're not personal. I think they create a mass-market culture. All they care about are big prints and the tried-and-tested back stock. They're not going to be concerned about a little old English lady who likes a book about cathedrals."

Mr. Gilliland lunches in Westport with Livia Ryan, the buyer for Klein's. The Klein's cash register seems to play a continuous melody. A full-line bookstore, Klein's has been around for 44 years, and not even the recent arrival of a Waldenbooks has muted its prosperity. Westporters are people who like to read, and they are not bashful with a dollar. There is more fiction on the shelves than at any of the previous stops; a Gilliland rule of thumb is that the closer you get to New York, the more ravenous the fiction appetite. "Mr. Klein says do anything customers want, because we want them back," Miss Ryan says. "One woman called and said she couldn't find a nutcracker, could I add that to the order. Now, I thought maybe this was stretching things, but Mr. Klein said get the nutcracker, so I went across the street to the hardware store, got the thing and added it to the bill."

The week's final stop is at Atticus, a small East Coast chain based in New Haven across from the Yale campus. Expanding too rapidly, Atticus was recently forced to seek asylum under the Federal Bankruptcy Act while it reorganizes. Due to its tenuous state, Mr. Gilliland cannot sell it any books. But, as a courtesy, he still shows up to present the list, which the buyer can then order from jobbers. The weariness shows in Mr. Gilliland's face as the session winds up. He stands up, attempts some bending exercises, retreats.

Bidding goodbye, Mr. Gilliland snatches up his tote bags and files out to the car. He is greeted with a parking ticket. He deposits his bags in the back seat, buckles his seat belt. "I'm going to finish the paperwork tonight," he says. "Sometimes I do it Sunday, but I want to forget publishing this weekend. I'm pooped."

18

B. Dalton: The Leader of the Chain Gang

Bruce Porter

The Mercury Monarch in the first paragraph of the preceding article, and the Porsche in the first paragraph of the following one, provide convenient symbolic contrast between traditional methods of trade distribution and the changes being created by new, nationwide book chains. By profiling one such chain, Bruce Porter raises issues that impinge not only on the marketing side of publishing but on its editorial traditions as well.

I hold with Charles Lamb, a wise bookseller does more for the community than all the lecturers, journalists and schoolmasters put together.
—John Cooper Powys

Dick Fontaine, merchandising director of the B. Dalton bookstore chain, downshifted his burnt-umber Porsche 924 into the parking lot of the company's one-story office building south of Minneapolis and finished off a long lament on the dim commercial aspirations of book editors in New York. Wind whipped off the former prairie land, converted to office parks and housing developments.

"Everything you try to do to popularize books is going to be sneered at," said Fontaine, a 37-year-old former schoolteacher from South Dakota. "Most editors still have the elitist carriage-trade mentality. They don't want to be associated with the likes of Harold Robbins and Jacqueline Susann. . . . But I don't give a damn what starts people reading. If it's a sexual high, voyeurism, I say 'Fine.' No one starts off by reading Proust."

Until recently, such philistinism would get about as much attention along Publishers Row in Manhattan as an unsolicited manuscript. But these days when B. Dalton says something book publishers and their editors pause to listen. A year and a half ago, the company passed Waldenbooks of Stamford, Connecticut, as the largest chain owner of bookstores in the country. As such, Dalton not only sells an awful lot of books, some 47 million, in its 364 shops, but together with the other chains, it is beginning to exert tremendous influence over what the country is reading. While the approximately 2,300 stores controlled by the different chains amount to only a fraction of the 20,000 bookshops listed in the American Book Trade Directory, they account for more than 50 percent of the stores doing at least $100,000 worth of business a year. Dalton, which grossed $174 million in 1978, sells about one out of every 10 hardcover books published. It is growing so fast—adding 60 to 70 new stores a year—that corporate executives back in Bloomington, Minnesota, never know exactly how many shops they have.

Last fall, the company made a bid to capture the pearl of the book trade when it opened its mammoth, 100,000-title dual-level store at 666 Fifth Avenue in New York City. "It's going to be a real dogfight," says Floyd Hall, the boyish-looking president of Dalton whose classmates in a recent Harvard executives' course had never even heard of his company. "We've been trying to get into New York for three years. This means we're finally going to be recognized by the best book market in the country."

It is too early to tell just who will survive in New York's already overcrowded book district. The new Dalton's has taken some business away from the Doubleday's across the street, but with 25,000 square feet located in the richest retail district in Manhattan, the Dalton outlet has a whopping rent bill. And despite its barrage of publicity, said Hall, the new store so far "is not a shooting star." The company hopes that other bookshops it plans to open in the city, including one in Greenwich Village, will generate more business for the main branch.

While bookstore owners are understandably nervous about the growth of the Daltons and the Waldens, it is in the publishing industry—and, more importantly, in the literary community itself—that the chains are having the largest impact. Corporate executives in the trade houses, many of which have also fallen under control of large conglomerates, tend to see the chains in a positive light. Their large number of stores and modern merchandising techniques generate more profits for the whole book business. "It used to be that commercialism was a bad word," says Roger Straus III, marketing director of Harper & Row. "You'd put all your energy into creating a book, and when it came time to sell the product, everyone ran out of gas."

Those concerned with the literary quality of books, however, fear a more Faustian consequence. Using the selling methods made famous by supermarkets, such as self-service, limited selection of big brand names, and rapid turnover of goods, the Daltons and Waldens make their money selling books with strictly mass appeal.

As the chains put pressure on independent bookshops and gain more control over the retail end of publishing, the shelf space reserved for that *other* kind of book—serious literature, poetry, and works of scholarship—gets smaller. Correspondingly, the pressure grows on editors to begin passing up manuscripts they know won't fit the formula.

"What the chains are doing is like the farmer who takes things out of the soil; but doesn't put anything back in," says a top editor at Little, Brown. "If the booksellers no longer take risks trying to sell American letters, then the pantry starts to get bare. As an editor, you spend less and less time on the things you feel are of real cultural value and more on the stuff that will sell.''

Historically, the great personal bookshops, whether bohemian salons or caterers to the carriage trade, have always seen themselves more as literary institutions than as outlets for pushing goods. While the chains buy only 20 to 70 percent of a publisher's seasonal offering, Scribner's on New York's Fifth Avenue buys every single title issued by the major houses and stocks authors to considerable depth.

In Chicago, the Stuart Brent Bookshop on North Michigan Avenue has done almost as much to influence reading habits in that city as its book critics have. A loud, raspy-voiced son of a Kiev immigrant, Brent, 58, holds court around an oaken table in the back of his shop. As a bookseller, he sees himself somewhere between a literary messiah and the high-school English teacher he once was. He refuses to carry mass-market paperbacks and regularly goes around ripping Harold Robbinses and Sidney Sheldons out of the customers' grasps. When Saul Bellow's *Humboldt's Gift* came out, he sold 2,400 copies, mostly by going out and stopping passers-by in the street. ''I can't tell you what a burden it is being the guardian of the human spirit in Chicago,'' he once shouted during a lunch in the ornate Drake Hotel.

In the Dalton stores, which are run by the Dayton Hudson department store chain of Minneapolis, it is, of course, advertising and promotion, rather than zealous managers, that are supposed to sell books. ''There's nothing in the chains that has to do with tears or suffering or the human spirit,'' says Brent, who is currently fighting off competition from a new Dalton's one block away. ''The pain and the agony the authors put into books —the feelings! How do you equate that with turning a profit?''

No titles are tolerated that don't earn their shelf space, and stores are stacked on a demographic formula that reduces reading habits to simple mathematics. Its outlet in a working-class neighborhood of Troy, Michigan, for instance, is stocked with almost triple the number of home-improvement books and auto-repair manuals found in its middle-class store five miles away. Dalton also knows working-class readers buy more dictionaries than middle-class people who purchased theirs long ago, and they seek more comfort from religion: Bibles sell four times better in the working-class store, as do books containing ''inspirational sayings.''

While the stocks may be different, all Dalton stores, big and small, look pretty much alike. On entering, customers are assaulted by a cacophony of cheeriness, the insistent message that books can be *fun*. Throughout the store, colored pieces of cardboard dangle from the ceiling depicting smiley green worms chomping on books or little red engines carting around books in their tenders. Here and there, a large display hawking a TV tie-in leaps out at customers.

''Traditionally, bookstores have been stuffy places with parquet floors, heavy fixtures, and a little old lady who's been there 30 years,'' says John Pope, Dalton's advertising director who formerly promoted Wheaties and Toro lawnmowers. ''You felt you had to *know* books before you could go in. What we've done is take the awesomeness out of the book-buying experience.''

The real commercial success of Dalton, however, can be attributed to its IBM 158 computer, which stocks the books and dictates how they are displayed. Keyed into the cash registers of all Dalton stores, the computer knows how many books have sold in 100 categories, from Philosophy to Rocks and Gems. With that information, headquarters can detect an early blip of interest in a book and begin shoving it under customers' noses simultaneously in all 364 stores. The object is to see if a better-than-average seller can be hyped into a bonanza. ''Given a lot of display, any book will sell,'' says Jeffrey Hohman, a senior buyer for the chain. ''The trick is to find out what book will sell best and put it where people can see it.''

To do this, the computer is cued to lift out of the gaggle of new titles those books that sell more than 80 copies a week and place them on what the store calls its ''hot list.'' The hot-list books get placed on special racks near the front of the store to attract attention. Then, once the buying gets even hotter than hot, the books move to Dalton's best-seller list, a special honor that thrusts them into the front window and into displays that confront people directly when they enter the store.

At the bottom line of such strict economic determinism lies a very thin selection of books. A large Dalton store, such as the first one opened in Edina, Minnesota, carries as many different titles as Scribner's in New York City—about 40,000—but serious readers would look in vain for anything of real interest. Most of those 40,000 Dalton books fall in such categories as pop-psychology, how-to, cookery, and gothic romances; the store has the best selection of "me-first" books in Christendom *(Looking Out for No. 1, See You at the Top).* A recent visitor found nothing in the hardcover history section, for example, about Napoleon, Mao Tse-tung, Benjamin Franklin, the French and Russian revolutions, or any of the British kings or queens. The only general American history book was the *Reader's Digest Story of America.* But there were 19 books about the Nazis. "Hitler," said the Edina store manager, "is very big this year." In paperback, the Current Affairs/ Political Science section was so sparsely stocked that *Das Kapital* and *On Revolution* by Hannah Arendt were lumped together with *Dog Days at the White House: Memories of the Presidential Kennel Keeper.* The store's Movie/TV section contained more books than the section for the History of Civilization.

"I think of the chains as doing for reading what the fast-food operations have done for eating," says John Dessauer, author of the yearly *Book Industry Trends,* and the unofficial statistician of the book trade. "You can preach to them about cultural obligations, but with their economics, they really can't afford to mess with paté de foie gras."

Dalton rarely considers buying a book with a printing of fewer than 10,000 copies, and the ones it buys heavily have almost always generated plenty of interest inside the publishing industry.

"When they buy books, they don't want to hear about plot outlines, they want to know your advertising plans," says Roger Straus III of Harper & Row, whose *Thorn Birds* drew $1.9 million in a paperback sale before Dalton bought it. "If I walked into Dalton's and told them what a great cry the book was, they'd laugh me out of the place."

If a book has not been built up by its publisher before publication Dalton will stock the title heavily only if it has a strong regional appeal or receives rave reviews after its release. In 1977, when Knopf sent around *Dispatches,* Michael Herr's compilation of his grim *Esquire* pieces on the Vietnam War, Dalton agreed to buy only 700 copies, hardly enough to put it in all its outlets. "It was a depressing book," says John Shulz, merchandising director for the chain. "And it was coming out at Christmas, when no one wants to read depressing books." Depressing or not, the book was praised across the country as one of the most important works on the war. By mid-February it had moved to the front of Dalton's best-seller racks.

Hardest hit by the chain formula are books of poetry. Of all the titles carried by Dalton's Edina store, there was only one by John Ashbery, and that a paperback. Other victims are first novels, whose printings rarely run to more than 8,000 copies. Some editors think the dampening effect on new novels is all to the good. "What's in trouble because of the chains," says Herman Gollob, editor-in-chief of Atheneum, "is that gentle, sincere, highly introspective work with no narrative power and no psychological insights." And as far as he's concerned, it's good riddance. "I'm always amused by the people who call themselves avant-garde or experimental writers. They have nothing but contempt for the reader, and then they complain that no one buys their books."

Others, though, are worried that chain pressure is seriously eroding the commitment some publishers still have to encouraging good new writing, even if it is not immediately profitable. "There are lots of writers who are not terrific now but who will be terrific in five years," says Gene Young, a former editor at Lippincott and Harper & Row who is now with Little, Brown. "If you don't do something to encourage them, they tend to go off and do something else with their lives." One of her favorite exhibits is John McPhee, whose writing habit, until his recent book, was supported by *New Yorker* magazine rather than by his 12 previous books which, while highly praised, sold only marginally.

Whether the Daltons and Waldens are driving the independents out of business is a sorely debated point in the trade. Dalton likes to say that the hoopla it creates for books spills over to other shops as well. But because of the bigger discounts Dalton can command from publishers, its massive outlays for advertising, and the sheer size of its stores, few independent bookshops celebrate when the chain moves down the block. Shortly after Dalton arrived in Portland, Oregon, for instance, the three dominant independents went out of business, as did one on Long Island, two Doubledays in St. Louis, and another in San Francisco after the chain opened up in those places.

In 1977, when Dalton unveiled a gigantic $1 million-a-year bookstore on Chestnut Street in Philadelphia, the owner of a small bookshop a half block away got cold comfort when he complained the new store would hurt him badly. Said Dalton's East Coast man Brad Johnson: "I told him he had to specialize. I said we had 12,000 square feet and he had only 1,600 and he couldn't compete." But he said, 'I've been here 15 years as a general bookstore and I can't change.' I could tell by talking to him that he didn't want to hear it."

19

The Gospel According to Revell: Blessed Are Bestsellers, for They Shall Reap the Profits

T. S. Carpenter

The preceding articles show how many categories of books are published each year in addition to fiction and textbooks. Many specialty houses continue to serve their markets for years without any title ever coming to the attention of the general public. In the following account, T. S. Carpenter, who won a Pulitzer Prize in Journalism in 1981, describes how one house has begun to bring its titles out of small religious bookstores and onto the bestseller lists.

Source: From *New Jersey Monthly* (November 1978). © 1978, NJM Associates, Inc. Reprinted by permission of the publisher.

Hugh Barbour and his brother William publish religious books, Christian bestsellers that drop like little M&Ms off the Fleming H. Revell press in Old Tappan to melt in the mouths of evangelical Christians everywhere. The Barbours have, in the prose of their own public relations kit, "hit upon the key to success, a way to package religion to make it painlessly palatable." That is, to make the Father, the Son, and the Holy Ghost as familiar and lovable as the cast of "Three's Company." They have done for religious publishing basically what Fred Silverman did for prime-time television—studding it with stars, adding sitcom sex and violence, and packaging it for popular consumption.

In the world of evangelical publishing, which exists on the far fringe of mainstream publishing, the Barbours are the impresarios of pop piety, and they hustle talent better than any other evangelical competitor. Revell's fold of Christian name writers includes Anita Bryant, Marabel Morgan, Charles Colson, Dodger pitcher Tommy John, and Manson cult killer Tex Watson. In the past five years three of Revell's little Christian M&Ms have made it onto the *New York Times* bestseller list. That is rather remarkable and—fumbling for a Biblical precedent—a little like the rout of Jericho, since the *Times* doesn't normally monitor sales in Christian bookstores. It relies instead on secular metropolitan bookstores, where evangelical books have traditionally triggered the gag reflex.

Hugh Barbour is a grinning, eager man in his late forties whose aspect is dominated by a head of wavy, prematurely silver hair. His is not the close-cropped coiffure of a pious prig; rather that of a guy who has perceived the benefit of hanging loose when all around him are uptight. He cannot be insulted, for he is insulated by the knowledge that the more controversy stirs around him and his writers, the better sales are going to be. Whereas his evangelical forebears at Revell might have bristled over a gibe at Anita Bryant, Barbour basks in abuse. In the end it means that the public, evangelical and secular, will have to reckon with Revell. Barbour's conscience, to all appearances at least, is unfettered by such theological musings as,

would Christ chase the moneychangers out of the bookstore? "We've got to operate in a businesslike way here," he says. "And any business that does that has got to depend upon profits. We go about our ministry in a very businesslike way." Profits, promotions, and marketing are the means to the message. He could make you believe this is the purest form of evangelism.

"There was a big market out there we hadn't touched," he says. "And we started in the late sixties to really zeeeeerrrro in on that market. It meant we were going to get more and more into general bookstores. And that meant automatically that we would be selling much larger quantities of books."

The books Barbour is interested in selling more and more of are the "crossovers," evangelical books with enough general appeal to get them into Walden Books and B. Dalton stores. These are books about Christian athletes who overcame their trials with a combination of prayer and wheat germ, or the testimonies of born-again scoundrels like Colson and Watson, whose religion is a denouement to their bizarre careers. The largest potential secular market for Barbour's evangelical books, however, is not among the hard-core godless, but rather among casual Christians who would not go out of their way to seek out a Christian bookstore but might, while browsing B. Dalton's, pick up *The Tommy John Story*.

Nobody keeps very good statistics on the amorphous world of evangelical publishing; most of the companies are small and privately held. But the Christian Booksellers Association estimates that over 80 percent of all Christian books are now purchased from secular outlets, which compels an evangelical publisher to cross over or perish. Doubleday and Harper & Row are enlarging their own religious lines to appeal to the browsing casual Christian. They have aggressive designs on the Christian market, and some would even like to market paperbacks in evangelical bookstores, the sacred ancestral preserves of Revell and its competitors, Zondervan and Word Books. Everybody wants the best of both worlds. So who can blame Hugh Barbour for appealing to the primordial prime-time instincts in all of us? In recent seasons, for example, Revell has featured:

Sports, including the Stan Smith and Tommy John stories, and the Christian testimony of Tom Landry and the Dallas Cowboys. (Barbour was pursuing both Steve Garvey and Don Sutton, but the two Dodgers had a fight in the dugout, which placed them off limits for the time being.)

Fast money. The capitalist success story was big this year. In April 1977 Revell published *The Possible Dream.* Billed as a "candid look at Amway," it is actually a fawning authorized profile of the enormous direct sales company whose grass roots sales people sell tons of toothpaste and household products each year, and whose founders are evangelical Christians. Incredibly, this offensive piece of puffery made its way onto the *New York Times* bestseller list. The book found an avid and undiscriminating audience among Amway's 500,000 "legs," or sales reps. Revell will soon follow up this bestseller with a sequel, *The Winner's Circle,* rags to riches stories of Amway representatives.

Comics. Revell's Spire Christian Comics, appealing chiefly to teens and prisoners with low reading skills, present the religious adventures of entertainers like Johnny Cash and Andare Crouch, and real-life Christian conversions such as that of "Hansi, the Girl Who Loved the Swastika" and Chuck Colson. Revell also bought Christian rights to Archie and His Friends, all born again for the benefit of an evangelical audience.

Sex. The sexiest, most adorable crossover in evangelical publishing history was Marabel Morgan's *Total Woman.* Its airy recipes for restoring Christ and carnal relations to marriage made it the Christian's own *Sensuous Woman.*

"With that one, we knew we had something . . ." says Barbour. "We knew there would be controversy. The gist is that you cater to your husband. That you are—uh, I hate to use the word 'subservient,' it sounds pretty awful. But that you Accept him, you Adapt to him, you Admire him. And that you . . . something else. There is another 'A'."

You Appreciate him. That is Marabel Morgan's fourth "A." Her alliterative prescriptions made the nonfiction hardcover bestseller list, outselling *All the President's Men* and *Centennial* combined.

"We knew the secular market would make a lot of noise about it," Barbour says. "At that time women's lib was coming on pretty strong, and women's lib doesn't buy that. There was a lot of controversy, and it was wonderful because the more controversy there was, the better sales were. The more lib groups pooh-poohed it, the more middle-American housewives bought it. And we knew our evangelical Christian market would really buy this approach."

Revell readers are quintessential middle Americans. They are generally white and Protestant, and they live in the suburbs of the Midwest, Southwest, and Southeast. They most likely subscribe to *Good Housekeeping.* Revell knows its market and appeals to it by bleaching the stains off a whole spectrum of subjects that might otherwise be considered quite unsanitary. A quick scan of Revell's back list turns up prostitution, drug addiction, murder, and rape. And all of it is in incredibly good taste. Sex is never gratuitous and invariably didactic. An encounter with depravity in Revell may leave you feeling idly titillated but, more generally, instructed.

Lust, the Other Side of Love is a pretty good example. Author Mel White is not a big-name Christian writer. He's a pastor from California who is less interested in royalties than in ministering to a global flock. His message in this case is that having sexual fantasies is perfectly normal Christian behavior. But you must never, never touch. Pastor White tells of a lust attack he had once on a business trip to New York City. Cold showers and long-distance phone calls to his wife do not help. "Why shouldn't I take advantage of New York's many ways to relieve my sexual pressure?" Pastor White asks himself. "No one knows me here. It could be my little secret." He quickly snaps to his senses, however, and calls a married Christian couple he knows in New Jersey. In half an hour they are all "laughing hilariously at how quickly I became a dirty old man."

Revell tackles a seamier side of life in its fictional paperback series about teenage prostitutes. The novelist John Benton, a New York City social worker, takes the experiences of dozens of girls and distills them into *Cindy, Carmen, Dirty Mary,* and *Patti,* who all turn to Christ and go cold turkey. The books look for simplistic solutions. Occasionally they will make you wince. But Barbour, who cannot be insulted, defends them.

"There *is* a very simple answer to the problem. Let me be honest with you. I haven't read *Cindy.* I haven't read any of those books. But I'm sure that the answer is very concisely stated."

And it is, of course. No matter how avant-garde Revell becomes, Christ is still the answer. The formula is still the same.

It would be difficult for Barbour to ignore his roots even if he were so inclined. His evangelical pedigree is impeccable. Barbour's father, William Sr., was a nephew of Fleming H. Revell, who in 1870 started a small publishing house in Chicago with the most prominent evangelist of the era, D. L. Moody. The company was burned out in the great Chicago Fire and moved shortly thereafter to New York. During the first half of the twentieth century, Revell published an occasional Christian adventure story, but for the most part produced dry religious texts and later the poetry of women with quivering Christian sensibilities, such as Helen Steiner Rice. Paper shortages plagued the company during both World Wars and the Depression, and in 1948 crime and taxes drove it out of Manhattan to Westwood and later to Old Tappan.

The year 1953 was a turning point for Revell. A senior editor scouting around for a potential Easter gift book heard through the grapevine about a manuscript written by Dale Evans. The book, a gut wrencher about the actress's mongoloid child who died at the age of two years, had been rejected by Prentice-Hall. Dale Evans was in New York doing a show with husband Roy Rogers at Madison Square Garden when the Revell editor contacted her and asked to see the manuscript.

"It's hard to believe it now," says Barbour, "but there was actually objection to it around the editorial table. One guy just couldn't understand why we were publishing Roy Rogers's wife. Who was she, anyway?"

Revell published the book with a first printing of only 5,000 copies. But the one-dollar hardcover began disappearing from Christian bookstores as fast as it could be stocked. Revell quickly printed another 15,000. That little Easter book, *Angel Unaware,* eventually sold a million copies. More important, it piqued secular interest. Pyramid Books bought paperback rights for $25,000. Today the same book would probably go for $300,000.

"Pyramid started selling it like crazy," says Barbour. "So we went back to Pyramid and said, 'Look, you don't sell in our market. We'll buy it from you, an imprint edition with our name on it, and we'll sell it in Christian bookstores.' And that was the start of a major mass market line of paperback books we call Spire. And that's what opened it all up for us in the sixties."

Other things were happening in the sixties that foreshadowed an evangelical renaissance. For one thing, Tyndale Press published *The Living Bible.* Revell had been offered the manuscript, but did not as a rule publish Bibles and turned it down. *The Living Bible* was a huge success. Protestant middle America liked the conversational style and began turning to a kind of religion where the Holy Spirit gave practical advice on daily living. The trend toward demystifying the Trinity led to a spate of Christian self-improvement books. One of the big bestsellers of that genre was Prentice-Hall's *'Twixt Twelve and Twenty* by singer Pat Boone. *TT&T* was the Christian teen's guide to acne, alcohol, and sex. Boone's secular appeal caused the book to sell nearly a million copies.

Revell at that time was developing some bestsellers of its own. Nothing in the league of Pat Boone, but sturdy perennials like Corrie ten Boom, an aging Dutch woman who during World War II hid Jews from the Nazis above her father's watch shop. Corrie ten Boom's *The Hiding Place,* published in 1971, sold three million copies. Revell retained Christian paperback rights and sold secular rights to Bantam for $50,000. Had Revell been wiser in the ways of the secular publishing world, it could probably have gotten $75,000 or $80,000. In today's market, rights to a seller like *The Hiding Place* might go for $500,000.

Anita Bryant signed on in the early seventies and produced a string of innocuous personal testimonies. It was Bryant, however, who put Revell on to her friend Marabel Morgan. Morgan, a Florida housewife who had rejuvenated her own marriage with trial-and-error tactics, was teaching a course in marriage enrichment to other wives. She was thinking about turning her course outline into a book. The Barbours flew to Florida to check out Marabel and her manuscript.

"We went out to dinner together," Marabel now recalls, "and Hugh and William seemed almost like family. I operate on intuition a lot, and I felt they were honest people. I'd heard a lot about writers getting rooked. Five different publishers were bidding on the book, but I knew Revell was *my* publisher."

Hugh Barbour remembers it a little differently. "She wasn't very enthusiastic about it. One of the problems we have with her is that she wants to write everything herself. She doesn't like to have outside editorial help, and she is never satisfied. We were waiting two years before we got that book."

Revell got that book in 1973, and *Total Woman* turned out to be just as controversial as Barbour had hoped. Feminists were ready to break Marabel's knees. Revell's own public relations woman left because she could not conscientiously promote it. But Marabel and her disciples made the talk-show circuit unruffled by insults and blithering euphorically.

"I thought the controversy was marvelous," Marabel recalls. "I couldn't believe people could get stirred up over something as innocent as looking cute for your husband. I mean that's really naive compared to *Hustler*. We got wonderful publicity."

Total Woman sold 600,000 in hardback and nearly 2.5 million in paperback. Secular paperback rights were auctioned to Pocket Books for $675,000, a record bid for a religious book. Revell grossed around $2,200,000, and the author received about $710,000 in royalties. She had, however, received a rather meagre advance of $1,500. Three years later, when Revell published Morgan's *Total Joy,* she drove a harder bargain. (Or at least her husband Charlie drove a harder bargain. Marabel says she doesn't remember what she got for either book.) Hugh Barbour will say only that he paid the Morgans "high in the five figures for *Total Joy*." The second book, a virtual rehash of the first, sold only 130,000 hardcover copies.

Total Woman gave Revell a rush. Sales increased 10 to 20 percent a year. "If any publisher has one good success," says Barbour, "it sucks everything along with it. We have a back list of about six hundred titles. If you have a super bestseller—and understand that I'm saying *Total Woman* was not just a Christian blockbuster, but a blockbuster, period—it's going to pull everything along with it. When your salesmen go into a store, they are going to get more attention. And most important, it's given us power to bid on other books, really socko ones that we want bad."

Money has not always been the biggest factor in bidding for evangelical writers. At least the fat advance has never had as much prominence among evangelicals as it has in secular publishing. The average advance offered by religious publishers is $3,000 to $5,000. At secular houses $10,000 is a pittance. Revell pays no advance at all on 75 percent of its published manuscripts. Christian writers who are not particularly sophisticated in the ways of the publishing world are often more concerned about control of their material than making money. Most have little heart for cutthroat negotiations and are willing to settle for a smaller return in exchange for the assurance that they won't get rooked. Above all, they are interested in distribution and promotion. Being extremely, well, evangelical, they want to be sure their books reach as wide a Christian audience as possible. Revell offers these intangible benefits. Nearly every major bookstore in America stocks Revell books. And it is becoming increasingly apparent to Christian writers that Revell is becoming more acceptable to the secular market. Because Hugh Barbour has sloughed off fusty notions of evangelical publishing decorum—he promoted Anita Bryant with banana cream pie on her face—and was the first of his breed to buy ads in the *New York Times,* Revell's evangelical writers know they are likely to be read. A rather heady notion. Still, as competition for big-name Christian writers steps up among evangelical publishers, money does make a difference. With annual sales in excess of $13 million, Revell leads the field in bidding power, but its nearest competitor, Zondervan of Grand Rapids, Michigan (annual sales of $11 million), has been coming on strong. Zondervan recently signed up Kathleen Cleaver, wife of Eldridge Cleaver, black former radical and author of *Soul on Ice.* Husband and wife were both hot properties in evangelical publishing. Word Books of Waco, Texas, beat out Revell for Eldridge two years ago. (Revell ostensibly dropped out of the recent round of bidding because it felt Cleaver's Christian rebirth was spurious. Eldridge was recently featured in *Time* magazine promoting trousers with codpieces to highlight male genitalia.) Zondervan's celebrity list includes Johnny Cash and Debby Boone; Word's stable includes Ruth Carter Stapleton and Billy Graham. But Revell got the big one, Chuck Colson. Colson's story, Barbour felt, would be the socko successor to *The Total Woman.* And it was Revell's new affluence that in the end helped to snag him.

Colson was still in prison when he was contacted by a representative of Chosen Books, a Virginia company that works exclusively in developing Christian manuscripts. While evangelical publishers had hung back, a little skeptical of Colson's conversion, Doubleday and MacMillan were already talking money with him. He was, however, leery of secular publishing and receptive to Chosen Books because of the control he would retain over his manuscript.

Chosen Books, however, didn't have the front money and so drew Revell into an ad hoc partnership that paid Colson $25,000. "He could have gotten $200,000 or $300,000 for that book," says Barbour. "But he just didn't want to work with a secular house." Chosen Books edited the manuscript—discreetly deleting Nixon's obscenities—and Revell printed and distributed it. Paperback rights went to Bantam for a figure rumored at half a million dollars.

Born Again also made the *New York Times*'s bestseller list, selling 450,000 hardcover copies (still shy of *Total Woman*'s record by about 150,000 copies). In both Christian and secular paperback, however, the book sold less than a million copies. Secular sales were clearly disappointing, but reasons weren't easy to come by. The public objected to old Nixon cronies profiteering on Watergate. There was also resistance from Brentano's, which traditionally refused to stock Revell books, and which only ordered *Born Again* for its Washington stores at customers' requests. (Colson's second book, with a working title of *The Cost of Being Born Again,* will be published around June 1979. He is working with Chosen Books, but they will not be working with Revell. The book will be published instead by Word Books, which offered Chosen a better royalty.)

Revell drastically miscalculated the appeal of Charles "Tex" Watson, who was born again while serving life in prison for the Tate-LaBianca murders. *Will You Die for Me* refutes the account of prosecutor Vincent Bugliosi, author of *Helter Skelter,* that defendant Susan Atkins actually brought the knife down on Sharon Tate. Watson tells how, after mechanically stabbing Polish producer Voytek Frykowski to death, he returned to the Tate house where Susan Atkins sat on a couch next to Sharon Tate. The sobbing actress begged him to let her have her baby before he killed her: "It was my hand that struck out, over and over, until the cries of 'mother . . . mother . . .' stopped. Suddenly it seemed very quiet. It was over."

Barbour was certain that *Will You Die for Me,* released this spring, would sell at least 200,000 copies. Revell promoted it hard. ABC's "Good Morning America" did an interview with Watson from inside California Men's Colony, and West Germany's *Stern* magazine sent an editorial team to cover him. But book sales have been disappointing. To date it has sold only 38,000 copies in hardcover, and paperback rights have not yet been sold.

Barbour suspects the memoir was a little too gruesome for his audience. There are limits. Generally speaking, Revell has its best success with audacious, adorable Christian women. Marabel Morgan, Dale Evans, and Anita Bryant have at least one thing in common: a simplistic militancy. Yet as standard-bearers against insidious liberal vices, they soothe the fears of the *Good Housekeeping* class. Dale Evans's newest book, *Hear the Children Crying,* calls for an end to child abuse in America and is certain to be a big seller.

But the sleeper of the season may be a book that was released a full year ago, the chronicle of Anita Bryant's battle with the gays in Dade County. In the heat of battle, she suggested the story to her publisher, Revell. "It was the only means to tell the real side of the issue because of the vicious press reports," Bryant explains. "They [Revell] were excited about it, perhaps a little scared of it at the beginning." Today, almost two years later, you cannot find anyone who is neutral about Bryant. A recent *Good Housekeeping* poll named her America's most admired woman. A recent poll of teenagers named her America's most hated woman. Around Revell the controversy was at first reminiscent of the love-hate relationship America had with Marabel Morgan. But while Morgan and feminists for the most part parried and poked at one another, Bryant and gays were engaged in a blood battle. Bryant was apparently blacklisted by the recording industry—a practice that resurrected the quiet dread of McCarthyism in many readers who loathed Anita Bryant's politics. Religious bookstores that ordered the Bryant book had shipments destroyed, and no paperback house, including Bantam, which has published all her earlier testimonies, will touch the book.

"One publisher told me 'I can't even bid on that book because if I got it, I'd lose half of my editorial staff,'" Barbour says. "Isn't it strange I haven't gotten one bid on that book? Defenders of the First Amendment really kill me."

As a result, Revell will begin in February to distribute *The Anita Bryant Story* as a Spire paperback to secular booksellers, a rather ambitious move for an evangelical publisher. But the Anita Bryant affair actually only triggered an expansion that was imminent, since Revell has a new parent to bankroll its excursions into the secular world. Over the past five years, Revell has been one of the most desirable little pieces of property in publishing and has been approached by Simon & Schuster among other major publishers looking to buy. Last June Scott, Foresman, and Company of Glenview, Illinois, the nation's largest publisher of textbooks, purchased about 95 percent of Revell's privately held stock from Hugh and William Barbour for an undisclosed amount of cash. Each brother received a ten-year management contract and assurances that Scott, Foresman would leave hands off editorial matters.

Revell is now the only old-line evangelical press to be a wholly owned subsidiary of a major American publisher. That gives it even better prospects for secular distribution just at a time when secular publishers such as Bantam are getting ready to make a push into Christian bookstores. "We are no longer really interested in split market rights," says Don Hayes, Bantam's national sales manager for religious markets. "We would now like to negotiate with Revell for its own market." Revell is, at least, in a position to launch a counteroffensive.

Scott, Foresman also underwrote the Barbours's recent entry into magazine publishing. In July Revell produced the first issue of *Today's Christian Woman,* sort of an evangelical supplement to *Ladies' Home Journal.* The cover story? "America's Love-Hate Relationship with Anita Bryant." Barbour continues to tinker with Revell's editorial alchemy, trying to isolate the elusive elements of a blockbuster. He needs that one socko manuscript that will prove that Marabel Morgan wasn't a fluke. His adrenalin started flowing just the other day when he came across something titillating. A woman in Washington State who had been corresponding for some time with .44 caliber killer David Berkowitz sent in an unsolicited manuscript documented with letters and telephone calls that she said proved Berkowitz was possessed by demons.

"It was a great book," says Barbour. "It's the darndest thing you ever saw. From a theological position it makes very good sense. We wouldn't have any trouble with our people. Let's face it, what could be any better example of demon possession? But . . ." It's hurting him to say it. "It looked very much like we were exploiting the whole Son of Sam thing. So we turned it down. I think we turned down something that will have tremendous appeal."

Berkowitz might, at any rate, have proved as repugnant to Christian sensibilities as Tex Watson. More promising is the adorable evangelical that Barbour is now seeking to recruit. This one is a Christian ingenue so exquisitely cast in the *Good Housekeeping* mold that if she did not exist, Hugh Barbour would have had to invent her: Julie Nixon Eisenhower.

"She reeeaaaallly appeals to our market." Barbour lusts in his heart after Julie's signature. "We haven't had too much success with her in the past, but we're still working on it. We won't get Julie Nixon for less than six figures."

Newspapers

Newspapers were, as mentioned previously, the first truly mass medium in America. The entertaining, scandalous "yellow journalism" of the late nineteenth century and the tabloid-form sensational "jazz journalism" of the early twentieth century created the habit of regular daily newspaper reading in most metropolitan areas, a custom that still sells over 60 million city, suburban, and metropolitan issues each day. Smaller, local, weekly newspapers account for about another 35 million copies sold regularly.

While the social, entertainment, and advertising content in most newspapers takes up more space and generates a much larger readership than does the hard news and editorial material, the newspaper remains the sole daily source of detailed information about those events we call the "news." Regular broadcast news programs, while heard, seen, and believed by more people than read newspapers, contain relatively little in-depth information and are, in fact, no more than a "headline service" of the air.

The national information gathering and processing system that shapes the news on a daily basis is dominated by newspapers and two major newspaper-owned news agencies: the Associated Press (AP) and United Press International (UPI). The complex matrix of news agency wire copy and locally generated staff material that becomes the news in each daily paper depends heavily on a process of editing, composing, and printing that has changed very little since the turn of the century.

Recently, however, computer-related technology has begun to revolutionize the process by which the daily newspaper is produced and distributed. In this section's first selection, from *Antioch Review,* Arnold Rosenfeld, news editor of the *Dayton* (Ohio) *Daily News,* provides an overview of how the new technology works and its impact on the process of publishing and selling newspapers.

An inside look at newspaper ownership and management is provided in N. R. Kleinfield's profile of the prosperous Gannett chain and its aggressive chairman, Allen H. Neuharth. The key to Gannett's success is the fact that most of its papers are local monopolies, each supplied by the parent chain with cut-rate feature material and the latest in cost-saving newspaper technology. While Gannett enjoys the business advantages of many economies of scale from its large size, Gannett also publishes the only daily newspaper in town in many of the local areas it serves.

The next selection, by Mitchell and Blair Charnley, focuses on the craft of newspapering: gathering and reporting the news. Excerpted from the Charnleys' textbook *Reporting,* the reading concentrates on a typical, medium-size daily newspaper and the hundreds of small tasks that make up the journalist's working day.

The importance of the photographer's contribution to the daily newspaper is provided in Nora Ephron's "The Boston Photographs." Ephron's article points out that Stanley Forman's dramatic shots from the *Boston Herald American* add an emotional dimension to the news, and, in some cases, become news on their own.

The final selection examines the phenomenon of the "alternative" press. Originally called "underground" newspapers in the 1960s, these publications have changed with their readers. They have become less politically active and are more concerned with local entertainment and culture. *New Yorker* writer Calvin Trillin analyzes this transformation and the papers' attempt to gain respectability and profits in the process.

20
A Complete Electronic Newspaper?

Arnold Rosenfeld

Since colonial days, newspapers have taken many forms. In this century, however, methods of producing newspapers have remained almost the same, with printing technology and distribution systems being the limiting factors. During the last decade, computer-related innovations in composition and printing have increased production efficiency while holding down labor costs. Now, newspapers can compete with the electronic media for advertising revenues.

Government agencies and private companies have recently begun to experiment with "teletext" systems, which program a home television to "print out" information delivered via cable or broadcast. The newspaper then becomes an instant electronic service, rather than a package of paper that has to be physically delivered to the home. In an article from *Antioch Review,* Arnold Rosenfeld, an editor of the *Dayton* (Ohio) *Daily News,* examines the possibilities for the newspaper of the future. Versions of the service Rosenfeld describes are already in operation at selected test sites in the United States, Canada, England, France, and Japan.

I am writing this on a television screen. The first sentence was typed perfectly, and I did nothing to it. I had some trouble typing the word "typed" in the second sentence. I manipulated a small flashing rectangle about the size of a matchhead into position on the screen over the word "typed," and corrected it. When I am finished working, I will push a button on the keyboard marked "END," and the article I have written will enter a computer as a series of electronic impulses. It will rest there until it is "called up" by an editor. He

Source: From *The Antioch Review,* Vol. 35, No. 2–3 (Spring–Summer 1977). Copyright © 1977 by The Antioch Review, Inc. Reprinted by permission of the Editors.

will edit what I have written by moving the small rectangle of light across the face of the television screen, inserting words, sentences, paragraphs, letters, erasing others, transposing some. If this were a newspaper story, the editor would reach into the upper left corner of the keyboard and simultaneously depress two red keys etched "CONTROL" and "COMP ROOM." The story, in a few minutes, would be "set" in type on a strip of photographically sensitive paper. The result is called "cold type." "Hot type," which was created during the Linotype revolution, as distinguished from the Gutenberg, was formed when molten lead cooled into letters. It was the standard industry production technique until only a few years ago. Few papers now use it. Those that do are trying to decide how to stop. The costs, compounded by newsprint price increases, of forming letters from molten lead had become prohibitive. The newspaper plant, a tribute to the best of late nineteenth-century industrial revolution technology, had become obsolete. Something had to be done. I will now instruct the screen to create this paragraph entirely in italics. It is done.

This is an off time for newspapers. The winds of change whip across the industry, it sometimes seems, in conflicting directions.

There is, first, a technological revolution. The industry—why not, it was the nation's fifth largest employer in 1970—has just engaged in what by any industrial standards has been a Gargantuan conversion, virtually closing the print cycle begun by the late Johann Gutenberg, who only wanted to speed up the monk thing. The incarnate idea that broke Sam Clemens's purse and heart, the production of cheap, fast print, is now done. But what has been done is, relentlessly, only the beginning. The next step, a small matter, is developing the hardware.

Then there is the content problem. The great mandarin barons of print, who had previously never lacked for certitude concerning their grasp of the public taste, are now somewhat disoriented. They have been reading numbers, and the numbers are troubling.

Two will suffice.

National newspaper readership, over the past several years, has been down slightly, while subscription prices are unhappily up. The decline is small—down 2.4 million annually since 1973 to 60.7 million—but it is beginning to look a bit like a trend. A trend is something to do something about.

The other is the parallel frustration of newspapers to attract a vital new audience of young readers. That is a little more frightening, conjuring up images of a readership more significantly reflected by funerals than by births. Beyond that, the young readers they are getting appear to be less skilled, demonstrating a decline in college board verbals of thirty-five points since 1967. Print journalists regard this as a national scandal.

None of this accounts, strangely, for the current popularity of special-interest publications and books of all kinds—presumably, costly vehicles for print, but crafted to appeal to audiences already predisposed to buy particular intellectual wares, whatever they may be, from self-help books on the care and maintenance of recreational vehicles to Zen meditation. One possible explanation is that a reader comes to them as a willing participant with an expectation, a hope, a *desire* to be pleased, already filled with cheerful good wishes for the success of writer and editor. One suspects the same reader opens the more generalized newspaper package with a foreboding of displeasure, never knowing what horror will leap from its pages, its most predictable element being its annoying unpredictability.

Times change, certainly. In more bucolic times, trauma was a quite marketable item. This was replaced by an era of journalism nostalgically akin to porch swings and rigid daily habit and the time each day to savor the prejudices of one's favorite columnist. If the newspaper experience is not only communications but the opportunity to enjoy a pleasant interlude in the day, editors are now attempting to build into their products areas of special interest—television, rock music, entertainment, homes, participation sports—to provide substantive islands of seductive content allied with reader, rather than editor, interest. Newspapers prospered best when they seemed, for whatever frequently cynical reason, to be allied with their readers. Today's audience is so splintered, demographically and psycho-

logically, that it is immensely difficult to identify broad themes of agreement that cut
across huge swatches of general readership. In
other words, a few of the chips which were
once left to fall where they may are now being
placed thoughtfully and with great care.

The search for mass readership, upon
which advertising rates are generally based,
has gone in a number of different directions,
ranging from repeated and profoundly sophisticated surveying of the audience, to a newly
discovered interest on the part of both editors
and publishers in marketing techniques, of fit-
ting the product to the market. Editors who
never searched beyond their own thought
processes, now try to fix, like a colorful and
fantastic insect on the point of a pin, the elusive and shifting nature of their audience.

Editing and publishing people sit raptly
listening to Harvard Business School professors, demographic experts, futurists, educators, and behaviorists looking for a clue to
how they can move a mass audience back into
the benign business of spending a few minutes
a day reading a newspaper. The beleaguered
audience, when it is not being surveyed, re-
sentfully snaps back that it wants something it
calls "positive news." The newspaper types
retreat before the phrase like a mythological
hero confronting a hydra, bemused, uncom-
prehending, retreating to their caves simultaneously to rely upon and question the conventional wisdoms of journalism.

But these vanguard wisdoms also change,
refusing to be fixed upon a single point. As in
the physical sciences, observation seems to
change the nature of the thing that is being
observed. In the beginning, there were politics
and personal gain. Then, in the wake of embittered public reaction, there was objectivity.
That lasted, albeit imperfectly, for a long
time. New Journalism, fashionable, it seems,
only a few weeks ago, can no longer seem as
sturdy an instrument as it once appeared to
be. The journalism schools were recently in-
undated with post-Watergate students, each
eager to bring down the government, the university administration, the dog pound, or
whatever other institution might submit to the
attentions of journalistic morality.

None of which has solved the essential

problem, readership. The name of this journalistic hydra is, to use the word, legion, and
need not be dealt with here, unless you suffer
from either an incipient masochism or a desire to spend the rest of the night reading
about newspapers and their difficulties, both
real and imagined.

It is at this point we pick up the story of an
industry that has begun to reckon with the implications of print technology and the communications technology of the culture in general.

There is, at first, a limited view of the
technology, and that is what is going on
within the newspaper plant itself. This involves extending what is currently being done
electronically in both news and composing
rooms at least as far as the press room, probably into the distribution system, the end of
which remains, in most cases, a small child on
a bicycle.

If a newspaper, for instance, can be written and edited on a television screen, and type
produced from these efforts, is it not logical
to assume that whole pages can be assembled
and composed, complete with stories, advertisements, pictures and all typographical im-
pedimenta, on a huge television screen? In a
limited way, it is already being done.

And would it not be possible, eventually,
to place these pages electronically on the
press, bypassing platemaking altogether?

Not an entirely wild dream. The Mead
Corporation of Dayton, Ohio, has been experimenting and has put into relatively limited
use a computer-driven press that could, eventually, do exactly that. Tiny spray nozzles in
the press would form the letters, the photographs, the advertisements, giving editors the
capacity, if not always the wisdom, to change
pages on demand, paper by paper, serving up
news on demand from a kind of editorial
menu. All that would be required would be
for the reader to select the kind of newspaper
in which he or she were interested. Heavy on
sports, for instance, light on market news.
Heavy on market news, light on local, with a
soupçon of theater and culture. Only national
and international news. Since newspapers already discard possibly ninety percent of the
perfectly valid, highly priced material they
receive, the raw matter is already there.

And, if all of this were possible, why stop with the presses? Why not place these words, these electronic impulses, directly into the home on yet another television screen? (A BBC experimental program in Great Britain has already given it a try, somewhat more interestingly than the rather static, primitive images occasionally served up by American cable television carriers.)

All of this, admittedly, careens along a little too logically. The culture responds haphazardly to technology, in unpredictable ways. Things begun, as with Gutenberg, to save a bit of energy, capture the culture for other reasons. The logical, on the other hand, finds no market.

The technology, nevertheless, awaits.

For the time being, most of the technology and the changes will be applied on an in-house basis, somewhat fitfully working at the improvement of the conventional newspaper and the techniques for its production. Electronic composition—called "pagination"—awaits the development of less cumbersome gear than that provided by early, more experimental models. Most newspapers, by way of explanation, are produced by pasting columns of news (cold type) and advertising on large, page-sized boards. These boards are photographically etched on thin plates that are placed directly on the presses.

Refinement of long-established press and distribution techniques will allow newspaper publishers and editors to more narrowly refine and segment their approaches to the audience through what is called "zoning."

Zoning is not particularly new. Readers are very often "zoned" without realizing it. Few readership riots, based on zoning, have been noted, assuming there has been no massive coverup. Basically, what this means is that newspapers have been able to look at gross, rather obvious segments of their market, and devote sections of interest to them. Ordinarily, these segments are divided geographically into, for instance, north, south, east, and west suburban zones. News of special interest to these zones accompany advertisements that allow smaller businesses to buy into the paper without purchasing a larger circulation that is relatively useless for their purposes. Ad rates for these zoned sections are scaled down in relationship to the reduced circulation.

Should computerized ink jet printing become a reality, each reader could become a "zone." News and feature content could be crafted to a reader's demands and interests. Advertising could also be more intensively individualized through a close reading of the colossal libraries of audience demographics that have been developed over the years.

In the meantime, the same demographics already provide a valuable key as to how to approach varied audiences as they naturally divide themselves by age, income, education, leisure-time activities, psychological and sociological outlook, or any one of a hundred sensitive indices to readership composition. To say the only major problems are financial and the refinement of delivery techniques is to overly simplify. One might as easily say that the only problems involved in the geographical movement of the state of Texas fifty feet to the east are financial and the development of an adequate system of pulleys.

The most immutable law of journalism is that money buys coverage. That which is not profitable cannot be done. Or at least not professionally, or for damned long. Sorry. Slicing a readership into infinitely thin layers is a potentially expensive editorial proposition. How thinly the cuts can be made and remain profitable is a question not yet answered.

So much for the first set of fairly logical steps.

The next, already referred to here, but somewhat blue sky, is the electronic solution, delivery of print from one television screen to another. The problems here are sticky, but the prospects are interesting, and for the time being, imponderable.

Let's suppose for a moment that the thing is technologically possible. What, then, are the advantages? Well, for one thing, the elimination of that awfully expensive item, newsprint. Aside from its obvious expense—one newspaper executive commented wryly recently that he was considering cutting costs by printing on thin gold sheets—the stuff is not entirely popular in the culture. It is bulky, presents a handling problem for both publisher and reader; the publisher before, the reader after. It is, briefly, something of a mess. Resentment of the stuff may grow. Publishers aren't all that fond of it themselves.

If, as has been proven in newsrooms, people can grow entirely comfortable with writing on television screens, it is logical to assume that readers likewise would find it also an entirely comfortable experience to read off a screen, particularly if a screen were developed that was paper thin, handheld, and entirely portable. Space-consuming and expensive paper storage, except for selective printouts of particular items, would be eliminated.

The screen option also has another seductive potential, a reactive function that would allow the reader to order from an almost unlimited menu of news and service.

Conceivably, the reader could ask for a standardized news format that would be regularly provided. Beyond that, he could select from a vast set of facts and interests. Since computerized news archives are *currently* being developed, it does not seem unlikely that the reader would have access not only to "live" news but the entire factual base of monumental news libraries.

The BBC system, called Ceefax, is already semi-reactive, containing a small printed circuit that permits a reader to select from a currently limited index of news and features available for viewing, and to call up the selected items, at will, on the screen of an ordinary television receiver. Other systems, including one developed by the Reuters Agency for satellite transmission, are currently being tested. (The question now is the economic potential of such systems, and, if they are advantageous, whether newspapers will see them as a logical extension of themselves and move naturally into the field. The decision, if it has to be made, is likely to be complex, since newspaper technology, by the standards of the electronics industry, is not considered terribly sophisticated. Lacking interest from major suppliers and developers of technological gear, newspapers might be bypassed, except for hardware developed for straight print technology in the grand tradition.)

Special services might also be offered. Current driving conditions between home and, say, Buffalo, N.Y.. Manuals on how to take scholarship tests. Recipes, complete with color pictures of the food itself at any given stage of preparation. Always changing, always new.

The possibilities are fascinating. Whether or not this would actually be a news*paper,* it would certainly be *print* in another form. Newspaper or print news *service*?

There are several difficulties involved in achieving this brave new world of graphics. The first is money. If the principle expressed earlier that money buys coverage has any validity, where does this money come from? Advertising? How? Subscription fees? Who would pay? How much? Who, in any case, would pay for the expensive hardware?

The second is government regulation. Print, as long as it is on paper, has been traditionally free of pre-publication governmental regulation. The electronics communication industry has not been so lucky. Will the submission of print to the airwaves—or, at least, the cablewaves—subject publishers to the attentions of a government bureaucracy already eager to have its say about what may or may not be permitted?

The third, perhaps the most important, is time. Readers—or, to put it less parochially, *people*—are already being subjected to a devastating assault on their senses. Television, the multiple possibilities of cable, radio, citizens band, recording equipment, computers, newspapers, still photography, motion pictures, mass-circulation magazines, special-interest journals, trade publications, hand calculators, television games, instructional devices, and all their combinations and permutations, scream that attention must be paid.

The implosion in the individual mind is unremitting. The twenty-four-hour day remains, nevertheless, rigidly intact despite all efforts to the contrary; twenty-four hours to live real lives, to work, play, learn, converse, rest and sleep; twenty-four hours, also, to engage in the terrible responsibility of being informed, well or ill.

How much time people will be willing to give to the process of embracing infinitely accessible print is, obviously, imponderable.

In this case, what is possible may not be probable.

On the other hand—there is always *another hand,* life's like that—never underestimate the seductions of an attractive and possible technology.

21
The Great Press Chain

N. R. Kleinfield

The publisher of a city's daily newspaper is usually a powerful figure in the community; the publisher of a large chain of newspapers has national importance. The largest newspaper chain in the United States is the Gannett Company, which owns papers that reach over three million readers from New Jersey to Guam. Gannett is an extremely profitable operation, primarily because most of its papers are local monopolies. Unlike many other newspaper chains, Gannett does not dictate editorial policy to its papers. Rather, it gives them great autonomy in local coverage, but they must be successful in making money.

In the following selection from the *New York Times,* N. R. Kleinfield analyzes the performance of Gannett both as a business enterprise and as a collection of individual newspapers. Gannett's president, Allen H. Neuharth, is profiled by Kleinfield, who specializes in reporting on the world of publishing for the *New York Times*

In Tarentum, Pa., the newspaper office is a small building of Colonial design in the middle of town. "Valley News Dispatch" is written on its facade. On a recent afternoon, a pair of hounds was snoozing in front of the ramshackle V.F.W. headquarters next door. Except for the hounds, there wasn't a sign of life. Inside the cramped newsroom, though, the very air crackled and smoked with an undercurrent of aliveness. Copy paper was in motion, reporters were hugging telephones, and there were sporadic bursts of typing.

The afternoon's paper had just rolled off the presses. The front page was given over to, among other things, a story about a gubernatorial candidate demanding Federal dollars to finish the Allegheny Valley Expressway, and a dispatch on a wildcat strike at a nearby auto plant. There was a three-paragraph item on radioactive waste being discovered on Interstate 80. Inside the paper, things were happening all over. The "Hospitals" column noted that 42 people had been admitted yesterday to area hospitals; 49 were discharged. The lead editorial railed against legalized dog racing in Pennsylvania.

Inside his snug office, Paul Hess, the laconic managing editor, leaned back in his chair and plonked down some papers he was scanning. "There has been a load of improvements since Gannett bought this paper several years ago," he said. "Our circulation hasn't moved much; it's still around 45,000. But the newsroom has been totally reorganized. We used to have two managing editors, and nobody knew whom to report to. The paper is packaged better. And did we increase our local coverage! I don't want to pass on the image that The Valley News Dispatch was the worst paper on earth and now it's the toast of the profession. Gannett didn't come rolling in here and pull off a modern-day miracle. This was a good paper before. Now it's a better one.''

Out in the newsroom, John O'Donnell, a rumpled feature writer, shared similar feelings. ''It's a more professional paper. Some of these small-town papers are real rags. We did lose some of the family atmosphere around here when the big guy moved in. I had my fears about casting my lot with him. But we've been given local autonomy. I think all Gannett does is look at the bottom line. Each of us is like a little gold mine. As long as the golden stuff keeps pouring out, they leave us be.''

Now approaching the age of 74, the Gannett Company has gone from its position as a one-paper operation to its status as the biggest newspaper chain in the United States. There are 1,764 daily papers in the country. Gannett owns 78 of them. Its short-term objective is to publish an even 100. Several other newspaper groups—Knight-Ridder, Newhouse, Scripps-Howard—own a slew of papers, but it would take an Everest climb for them to catch up. Spaced out from Guam to New Jersey, Gannett's papers thud on the doorsteps of three million readers a day, more than the combined daily audience of The New York Times, The Los Angeles Times and The Washington Post. The chain has doubtlessly done more to change the nature of how America's newspapers are owned than any other company. Not that long ago, most papers were independently owned; today, all but around 500 belong to one or another of 167 newspaper groups. Independents are being bought out by chains rapidly, at a clip of 50 to 60 papers a year.

The trend is well established. With few exceptions, newspapers in this country are more desirable investments than ever. There are bidders enough for them, and the gavel is being brought down for some pretty sums. As with the auto industry, as with the supermar-

ket industry, the likelihood is that there will be fewer and larger newspaper empires in the future. Already, the bigger chains are turning their attention from individual newspapers to entire groups. The building of newspaper chains is not a phenomenon that everybody is happy with. It raises sticky issues of monopoly ownership, the concentration of power, and whether newspaper excellence suffers when competition dwindles. Deeper than all this, it brings up the matter of how, in fact, people get the news that informs their decisions.

Many of the country's daily newspapers fall short of the standards that most journalists aspire to. And other papers, sadly, do not even try to reach those standards at all. Throughout the United States, too many readers are given a smattering of canned local stories crammed in among a flurry of wire-service dispatches and a mass of advertisements. Ben Bagdikian, a longtime press critic, sees little evidence that these papers are going to get any better; indeed, they may get worse. With mounting pressure to show high profit margins, some newspapers seem to have discovered that it is cheaper not to gather, edit and print the news than to perform these functions. ''I'm convinced that we're not going to see any more great papers, at least not any coming out of chains,'' Mr. Bagdikian told me. ''It takes five or six years or more of pouring money into a paper to make it really distinguished. No modern corporation is going to wait that long for good dividends. There's real danger that the number of distinguished papers will decline, because they're part of chains now, too, and the pressure is great on them to produce the dollars.''

Gannett's magnitude and its role as a management trendsetter make it the very model of a modern American chain. Gannett has become a publishing empire that grossed $690.1 million in 1978, and routinely has added 10 or more papers every year. In addition, the Gannett Company interests have spread to include radio and TV stations, a scattering of 19 weeklies and the Louis Harris pollster organization. Gannett is also in the midst of wrapping up one of the biggest media deals of all time, the acquisition of the huge Combined

Communications Corporation, owner of seven television and 12 radio stations, an outdoor advertising group and two good-sized newspapers, The (Oakland) Tribune and The Cincinnati Enquirer.

This deal has not escaped the notice of the Justice Department's Antitrust Division, nor of some members of Congress who are perturbed by the trend toward concentration of news media power. Also, the sheer size of Gannett, and some of the other newspaper chains, has stirred fears among those who feel that, in becoming vulnerable to government interference through possible antitrust action, the chains also make the nation's press itself susceptible to government encroachment and possible control.

Curiously, though, despite Gannett's ranking as the mammoth in the press industry, with seemingly immense power to inform or misinform or omit to inform, the chain commands practically no national influence, as influence is usually measured. The reason for this obscurity is that it owns no big-name papers. It has got to the top by purchasing papers situated in towns like Battle Creek, Mamaroneck, Freemont, Ossining, Port Chester, Bridgewater, Elmira, Tarrytown, Santa Fe, Boise, Pensacola, Lansing, Honolulu and Saratoga Springs. The papers are a mixed bag of editorial voices (from arch conservative to obstinately liberal), and Gannett makes no effort to bring them into chorus. "It's like a choir where everyone sings something different, and so the effect is that nobody pays any attention," an observer of the industry suggests. At least from the point of view of the profit-and-loss column, this policy seems to have paid off. Since going public a decade ago, Gannett has never had to report a down quarter.

Few people expected such big doings when Frank E. Gannett founded the company in 1906. He was a bulldog-faced, garrulous man, born on Gannett Hill, N.Y., to a father who flopped both at farming and as a hotel keeper, and to a mother who set maxims before him like stepping stones ("Little strokes fell big oaks," "You don't get nowhere by making enemies"). After working his way through Cornell, Mr. Gannett climbed to the editorship of The Ithaca Daily News, before he bought a half-share of the floundering Elmira Gazette in 1906 for $20,000. He later merged it with the competing Evening Star and had the slender makings of a newspaper company. He at once started shopping for other money-losing propositions to buy and merge.

From Rochester, where he merged The Union and Advertiser with The Times, he proceeded to combine Utica's Herald-Dispatch and Observer, Elmira's Telegram and Advertiser, Ithaca's News and Journal. He bought with an auditor's eye. Before he was done (after 51 years of buying dailies), he would acquire 30 papers, plus a string of radio and television stations. He took over more papers than any other United States publisher ever acquired without the aid of inheritance.

Instead of taking on a deadening conformity, papers in the Gannett "group," as the publisher liked to call it, were urged to vary their typography, select their own features and shape their editorial policies to suit their own communities. It is a hands-off policy that continues to this day. Mr. Gannett always sent his political pronouncements to his editors with the notation scrawled on them: "For your information and use, if desired" and editors were free to ignore them, as many of them did. As a result, the papers taken together came to be known as the chain that isn't. It has been officially called the "World of Different Newspapers."

The papers were not altogether dissimilar. Most of them were (and still are) staid organs with a Rotary-Kiwanis conservative bent. Exposés or stories of sex and crime rarely turned up in their pages. "A newspaper to suit me," Mr. Gannett once declared, "must be clean, one that I would be willing to have my mother, my own sister or my daughter read, and one for which I myself need never apologize." Disaffected readers, however, groused that modern mothers would not object all that much to more spirited coverage and sharper writing.

In 1940, Mr. Gannett interrupted the shepherding of his papers to run as the highly unsuccessful "businessman's candidate" for the Republican Presidential nomination. Shrugging off the loss, he continued to direct his empire until 1955, when he fractured his spine in a fall. He died in 1957, at age 81.

On Oct. 24, 1967, the Gannett Company went public. Then, it consisted of just 28 papers in five states, with a total circulation of 1.3 million. Soon afterward, the company initiated a shopping spree that continues with gusto. The man doing all the buying was Paul Miller, once Washington Bureau chief of the Associated Press and later its chairman, who took over as Gannett's president in 1957. He subsequently became chairman, before stepping down at the end of last year at the age of 71; he remains active as a director and chairman of the executive committee. Gannett's earnings have routinely improved 15 to 20 percent a year, up to $83.1 million last year, and the price of its stock has spiraled from $6.87 a share in 1967 to over $43 today.* Wall Street newspaper watchers have long gushed at Gannett. "The company is one honey of an investment," one securities analyst told me. "It's got to be the premier newspaper stock," said another analyst.

The main man at Gannett today is 55-year-old chairman and president Allen Neuharth. He has silver, wavy hair combed back, a movie-star smile and the confident air of a man who is good and who knows it. He has a reputation as a merciless prankster. Once he hustled his first wife (he has remarried) off in his rental car, then reported the car stolen. His wife wound up being stopped by the police. Before joining Gannett in 1963, Mr. Neuharth was a crackerjack editor with the Knight-Ridder chain's Miami Herald. He was then asked to take over as assistant executive editor of the beleaguered Detroit Free Press and quickly got caught in one of the last of the great journalistic street fights with Hearst's Detroit News. There were three stoppages during Mr. Neuharth's three years there, including one by the Teamsters, when Jimmy Hoffa spearheaded the local. Mr. Neuharth says he learned there were easier ways to make a living. Newspaper industry

critics maintain that the experience left Mr. Neuharth a cautious businessman. "There are people in the business who say I'm 'No-Guts Neuharth.' I don't care what they say. You can say I don't think big, but three million readers isn't exactly small." Since becoming Gannett's president in 1970, Mr. Neuharth has carefully avoided the big cities, shrugging aside big circulations, big advertising markets and journalistic glory. Mr. Neuharth is said to have spurned offers to go with The Washington Post and The (New York) Daily News, preferring to remain with Gannett and its string of obscure newspapers. "He's like the oboe player who has performed to ovations all over the country, but shies away from Carnegie Hall," says one Gannett watcher.

"I don't think I have influence, and I don't want it," Mr. Neuharth said recently. "I get my kicks working with journalists. I personally don't care about power or influence."

I spoke with Mr. Neuharth in his starkly modern Manhattan office, situated high in the Pan Am Building. Sipping a Coke, he casually laid out the elements of the Gannett philosophy: Basically, the company goes after papers with circulations of between 25,000 and 100,000 that are located in cities free of competition—meaning that there are no other papers and no dominant television or radio stations. The average circulation among the 78 dailies is no more than 38,400. Only four circulate above 100,000 copies a day, and those lie in less than big-time cities—Rochester (two of them), Honolulu and Camden, N.J. What accounts for the company's huge success is that it is, in effect, a chain of small monopolies. Since they are the only papers in town, the papers do not feel inhibited by competitors' ad rates and newsstand prices. The papers are therefore less reliant on help-wanted classified and national advertising than their big-city counterparts. Gannett has found that the smaller the town, the faster the paper tends to grow. And the faster the paper grows, the faster its profits grow, since in the newspaper business editorial and makeup costs increase much less sharply than the rate of circulation. As one observer sums it up, "Gannett has basically built a cathedral out of pebbles."

---

*Gannett stock was selling for $52 a share as this book went to press [Eds.].

Mr. Neuharth doesn't like just to sit around. He spends much of his time traversing the country in the corporate jet, wooing newspaper magnates. He is paid a salary of $390,000. He glows like an ember when he describes the deals he has brought off. To acquire a paper, he has bargained for as little a time as a few weeks and for as long as 12 years. Some critics contend that Gannett is given to absurd speculation, sometimes laying out a stiff 40 or 50 times earnings for a newspaper. Mr. Neuharth scoffs that balance sheets are not always what they appear to be, and that family owners rarely are crafty businessmen, and that all that matters is how much black ink Gannett figures it can get out of a paper. Mr. Neuharth's greatest disappointment, he says, was one of the few papers that failed. It stands as a perfect illustration of why Gannett doesn't buy into two-paper markets. Gannett had long owned The Hartford Times, but it steadily began to lose ground to The Hartford Courant in a classic case of an afternoon paper succumbing to a morning paper. Gannett sank a lot of money into the operation, including enough dollars to start a Sunday edition. Nothing worked. The newspaper was sold in 1973 to The Register Publishing Company. It had no more success, and folded the paper three years later.

As energetic as Gannett is, it has stiff competition. Knight-Ridder, the owner of 32 dailies, reaches the biggest combined circulation of any chain (3.5 million), and, in stark contrast to Gannett, it operates in some of the large cities, with papers like The Miami Herald, The Philadelphia Inquirer and The Detroit Free Press. Prosperous and well-managed, the chain posted revenues of $879 million last year. Many in the business maintain that Knight-Ridder's commitment to editorial excellence qualifies it as the best chain of all. Like the other giants, it grants its papers local autonomy.

The Newhouse combine . . . is known as the money factory. It publishes for the most part small papers—29 of them (3,281,000 circulation)—in addition to the Condé Nast publications (Vogue, Mademoiselle, House & Garden, Glamour, Bride's). Knowledgeable

analysts put revenues at about $1 billion and profits somewhere near $100 million.

A mighty fortress and bulwark of conservatism is The Tribune Company, owner of The Chicago Tribune, The (New York) Daily News and seven additional dailies (3.1 million circulation). Revenues last year amounted to $967 million. Recently, the group has emerged as an aggressive acquirer of small monopolistic papers. Another chain interested in acquisition is Scripps-Howard; its collection of 17 dailies is read by 1.8 million people in sizable cities like Cincinnati, Cleveland and Denver. Sources of income include United Press International and The World Almanac. Financial statements aren't made public, but an informed source puts revenues at about $425 million. Of late, it has been purchasing weeklies.

No longer the cynosure it once was, the Hearst Corporation is still an important owner of newspapers and has been reviving its empire with mixed success. Its interests include 10 dailies (1.4 million circulation) and a batch of magazines (Harper's Bazaar, Good Housekeeping and Cosmopolitan, among others). Knowledgeable sources put Hearst's revenues at $400 million. Notorious in earlier days for forging its papers into political weapons, Hearst has lately been more magnanimous in letting its editors take charge.

Other powers include the well-fixed Dow Jones & Company, which, fueled by the wealthy Wall Street Journal, has been expanding fast; Times Mirror, the mighty parent of The Los Angeles Times; The Washington Post Company; and, of course, The New York Times Company, which has five weeklies and nine dailies in Florida and North Carolina in addition to The Times. (The total circulation for all 10 daily newspapers is 1,055,400.) The newspapers and the company's other interests (magazines, broadcasting, books) took in $491,558,000 last year.

As the big chains continue to increase in size, where does this leave the readers of newspapers? What about "the people's right to know"? To some extent, this has to do with the editor's right to edit, which brings up the matter of centralized control. Yes, most large groups claim they grant local autonomy.

However, some of them hold editorial confer- ences annually, or more frequently, to ex- change ideas—and, some say, to exercise con- trol over policy. Some smaller chains are more overt about telling editors what to do. Consider the Panax empire, which publishes six dailies and 40 weeklies. Two years ago, the command came from president John McGoff's office that all papers were to give prominent display to a pair of articles sharply critical of President Carter (one alleged that the Presi- dent condoned promiscuity among his staff). Two editors refused (one said that if he had printed the articles he "wouldn't be able to shave in the morning"), and found them- selves looking for new jobs. Even though the large combines don't exert editorial control, many newspapermen wonder whether chain- paper editors might not edit more with an eye on the home office than on local needs. "I tend to think that a chain paper would be less likely to go with something that might cause advertisers to start foaming at the mouth," one newspaper editor said to me. The leaders of chains, for their part, reply that the chain paper, with a deeper money well to draw from, doesn't have to concern itself as much with what flusters advertisers or those in the local community. It can be more of a gadfly.

Anyway, as the chains start to increase in size, the specter of monopoly looms larger and larger, to some observers. Representative Morris Udall, a Democrat from Arizona, worries a lot about all of this. "I really shud- der to see the day down the road when you have four or five organizations that have a hammerlock on what Americans read," he told me late one afternoon. Mr. Udall doesn't quibble with the contentions of many chains that they've improved a good many papers. "But you strike a bargain with the devil," he went on. "I know the folks who run these chains and they're nice people and they love their kids and all, but the day may come when you have some leaders who hunger for politi- cal power. The power is there. It's not com- forting to know that it isn't being used." Is there a way out? Mr. Udall hopes so, and in 1977 he introduced two pieces of legislation to discourage these trends. One—the family- newspaper bill—would allow a much longer period of time for estate taxes to be paid, since he found that many family papers went on the block because the owners couldn't scrape together the tax dollars. His competi- tion-review bill would establish a Federal commission to look into industrial concentra- tion. Neither bill made it . . . and both were in fact met with a good deal of yawning. Mr. Udall is nothing if not tenacious. "I'm going to introduce them again and again," he said, "and I'll make speeches and shout and whine and run around the country waving lanterns, until people see this threat."

Virtually every week, a paper comes up for auction. Bid. Bought. Sold. As the papers get assigned to their various chains, what about individual differences between news- papers? John Morton, a veteran student of the newspaper business for John Muir & Company, the investment firm, suspects that papers will become more homogenized. They will look alike, and read alike, and may differ no more than a Big Mac bought in Keokuk does from a Big Mac bought in Brooklyn. Mr. Morton says, "There'll be fewer papers that print and raise hell. You'll see fewer gad- flies. Newspapers, I think, are going to have less distinctive personalities. All papers are becoming more service oriented, and the chain-owned papers, with their sophisticated market-research techniques, are most aggres- sive in this area."

What of the nature of the Gannett news- papers themselves? John Morton, for one, says that Gannett publishes no papers of great distinction, but holds that Gannett improves what it buys. "I don't think they are a fire- eating dragon," he said. "In recent years, with the emergence of weeklies and shoppers and cable TV in many Gannett markets, the company has had no choice but to better its product."

Others disagree. When Gannett kicked off a new Sunday paper in Westchester, one dis- gruntled reader wrote in: "Six days every week is just about all I can take of your tid- ings. I simply do not savor the thought of having to cope with The Herald Statesman every single day for the rest of my life."

To figure out where the Gannett newspapers fit into the spectrum of American journalism, you have to look at the diet that average daily newspapers feed their readers. A recent study conducted by Arthur D. Little, the consulting outfit, carved up the average paper this way: Local news, 4.5 percent of the total column space; foreign and national news, 7.5 percent; leisure time, 5 percent; people, entertainment and opinion, 6.5 percent; sports, 4.5 percent; data and listings, 8 percent; retail advertising, 36 percent; national advertising, 8 percent, and classified advertising, 20 percent.

Gannett itself has never tried to cook up a comparable profile of its chain. To get some notion of how it stacked up, I combed through more than a hundred copies of several dozen Gannett papers, and chatted with a number of Gannett editors and publishers. Some of the papers were pretty much in line with the composite. A number differed in providing somewhat greater percentages of local coverage, noticeably more service material and a more generous dose of sports news, which are things Gannett readership studies indicate are in demand. Most papers I looked at carried more local material than the total of national and foreign news combined. However, the local news columns tended to be plump with docile town-and county-government stories, some feathery features and generous graphics and photos. There was a lot of syndicated material—Ann Landers, Erma Bombeck, horoscopes, puzzles. Business news often amounted to a couple of wire pieces and some stock tables. Some Gannett papers have produced notable investigative work, though my readings showed that many seem uninterested in raising any storms. The papers were fleshed out with wire copy for national and international coverage. My own reckonings (confirmed by several Gannett editors) indicated that many Gannett papers were composed of at least 60 percent wire copy. As one editor told me: "What you do with a small-town paper like ours is to run every last shred of local stuff that hits the desk, then fill up the rest of the paper with the wires." (Papers like The New York Times and The Los Angeles Times are about 90 percent staff-written.)

More often than not, changes are made in a paper after Gannett buys it, though they are often slow in coming, and are not always as galvanic or profound as readers would like. John Quinn, Gannett's low-keyed senior vice president for news, is the master blacksmith who takes new purchases and attempts to remake them, if not into brilliant journals, at least into respectable ones. Most papers, he finds, are horridly organized. He suggests that they split things into several sections and create departments. Modern makeup is introduced. Mr. Quinn keeps tabs on 30 papers a day, and by now nothing astonishes him. "Even I was a little amazed when we bought the Rockford, Ill., papers and found they had no Monday morning edition. They skipped from Sunday to Monday afternoon. The reason was that nobody wanted to work Sunday afternoon."

The "before and after" reviews of Gannett papers more often reveal cosmetic refinements—the papers look nicer—than changes in substance. Though news budgets are frequently beefed up, it is true that most papers were tightfisted to begin with. The additional money might be used to hire a few more staffers or to provide a slightly larger "news hole" (the space devoted to editorial matter). The daily Gannett news holes go from about 70 columns to 150 columns; the bulk are around 90 columns, the same as at similar-sized papers. At papers like The Los Angeles Times, The Miami Herald and The Chicago Tribune, the news hole hovers at around 200 to 300 columns, but these papers are, of course, much larger.

Some editors theorize that it's impossible to tell the news suitably without a minimum of 40 columns of "hard news." Some Gannett papers offer no more than 20. The overwhelming majority of American newspapers do not station a reporter abroad, and the Gannett papers are no exceptions. Fielding foreign correspondents is costly, and few readers, Gannett officials say, are all that keen for news of distant lands.

"We operate community newspapers," Al Neuharth explained to me. "We stress local- and regional-interest news. We get from other sources the amount of foreign news we feel our readers want. Basically, we respond to reader studies. Whatever diet the readers want, we custom-tailor the paper for that diet.''

What, then, ought the reader to get in the way of vital news?

''We give readers what they want, because we are in the business of selling news,'' Mr. Neuharth said. ''If we meet the wants of the audience in a community—as we try to—successfully, then we can also give readers a percentage of what they need. But that isn't what sells. And if we tried to give people more of what they need, we wouldn't be successful. If the readers in Ithaca want to know the school menus for all the schools in the area, we'll give them that. That's no great practice of journalism, but it's what the readers want. You can't ram an unwanted object down an unwilling throat, no matter what business you're in.''

Does a newspaper have an obligation to educate its readers? What if Gannett readers asked for nothing but puzzles and comics and cooking tips?

''If readers said they wanted zero international coverage, we wouldn't give them zero,'' Neuharth said. ''But they get predominantly what they want.''

Since Gannett newspapers consist mainly of wire copy—the same wire copy fed to hundreds of other papers—and since these papers are more precisely distributors of news than they are news-gathering organizations, what then is Gannett's contribution to journalism?

''We do not depend on anybody but ourselves for coverage of state capitals and local news,'' is Mr. Neuharth's answer. ''That's our contribution. We provide an additional resource on the state and national level for the Gannett papers.''

That resource is the Gannett News Service (G.N.S.). At present, the operation consists of a Washington bureau made up of 19 reporters, along with 17 additional reporters scattered in 10 state capitals and in New York City. All told, figuring in the filings from staffers at member papers, G.N.S. sends about 70 stories a day clacking over the wire. However, the philosophy of G.N.S. is to leave all the major breaking stories to the Associated Press and United Press International and to deploy its people to file analyses, background pieces, stories with a regional angle that might perk the interest of, at most, a couple of Gannett papers, and occasional enterprise stories. G.N.S. doesn't write the major news flowing from a Presidential news conference or report a big Supreme Court ruling, nor, in state capitals, does it cover most legislative action. Although the service will ship somebody overseas when there's a strong local angle somewhere, it disdains permanently stationing anybody abroad. As it happens, Gannett newspapers typically run only two to seven G.N.S. stories a day. Several editors I spoke with freely admitted that these stories rarely are the stuff of the front page. The G.N.S. budget in 1978 was $2.9 million. That works out to less than half of 1 percent of Gannett's revenues spent on G.N.S.'s staff of 36 reporters covering a fifth of the nation's capitals for a market of 78 papers.

To know a newspaper chain, you need to know its newspapers. One of the biggest and most flourishing, and possibly the best, in the Gannett stable is The (Camden) Courier-Post. The paper is housed in a low-slung building with a well-barbered front lawn in Cherry Hill, N.J., a community of some 75,000 with one of the heaviest concentrations of warehouses on the East Coast. Gannett bought The Courier-Post in 1959 for $5.5 million. It was fairly lackluster then and had a circulation of 76,000. Its readership has since increased to 124,000, while other papers in the area, notably The Philadelphia Inquirer and The Philadelphia Bulletin, have suffered dwindling circulations.

One of the blessings the Gannett chain brings to its newspapers is technology. I dropped in on Sal DeVivo, the affable, 42-year-old publisher of The Courier-Post (who, as one of the chain's mobile publishers, was recently reassigned to the Gannett paper in Binghamton). As he escorted me on a tour of the plant, it was plain that the newspaper has benefited enormously from Gannett munificence (munificence that showered $31.8 million in capital expenditures on the chain last year). The composing room was free of molten lead, since the paper, like all Gannett papers, uses cold-type production. Mr. DeVivo pointed out a new garage that had been built, and another addition for storage of newsprint. "There's not much standing still here," he said.

Some newspapers, particularly big-city dailies that have sought to modernize, have found their path blocked by organized labor. Not Gannett. A mere 3,400 of the chain's 17,000 employees belong to unions. Among them, the 78 papers have been hobbled by only four strikes since World War II. Gannett, though, has cut its work force strictly through attrition.

The Courier-Post has billed itself as "New Jersey's Really Great Newspaper." Nobody can really say whether it is or isn't, though some of the credentials are impressive. It rakes a lot of muck. It has a three-member investigative team that pursues scandal with the exhilaration of a pack of beagles on the trail of a fox. Recent unearthings have included a seven-month study of the municipal court system that triggered closer monitoring of the courts and that provoked bills to be introduced into the State Legislature.

However, The Courier-Post tries to be the town billboard as well as the town scold. "Lorelei's List" runs down upcoming yard sales and fashion parties. Until recently, a "Trouble Shooter" column solved problems and tried to "make dreams come true."

The news hole of The Courier-Post averages around 110 to 120 columns. But of that, about 15 columns are typically devoted to local news, 12 columns to national coverage, five to state news and about four to international coverage. Entertainment, self-help and social news eat up roughly 20 columns, and sports account for about 25 columns. Comics are spread across six columns, two more than are used for business news (not including stock tables). Space is devoted to editorials, columnists and obituaries. A good hunk of the news hole, moreover, is taken up by giant headlines, lots of white space and a liberal dose of graphics and photos.

John Quinn, Gannett's senior vice president for news, says that any paper ought to "chase a story wherever the hell it is" within a 60-mile range of the office. Yet even though the Gannett News Service has a full-time reporter in Trenton, and although Trenton is a mere 35 miles from The Courier-Post, many Trenton stories I found in the paper were the work of the Associated Press. Three editions I browsed through turned up 10 A.P. stories to a single staff piece. Philadelphia, which is a few miles away, is also predominantly covered by the wires.

Gannett never dickers with the editing of the paper, it was agreed by everyone. "I've been with Gannett for 13 years and not once —I mean not once—have I had a directive from headquarters telling me how to do something," managing editor Phil Bookman said. "They don't hold a gun and say, 'Run this, don't run that.'"

Later, I was told by N. S. (Buddy) Hayden, who is now publisher of The Courier-Post: "I used to own my own paper, so I think I'm pretty well qualified to compare independent ownership to Gannet ownership. The Gannett management is just like the board of directors at the bank I used to go to for loans. I don't have any less freedom, and there is the beauty that Gannett people understand the newspaper business."

Like other chain members, The Courier-Post picks up almost all of its office supplies from Gannett's wholly owned subsidiary, the Empire Newspaper Supply Company. Everything from newsprint (325,000 tons of it a year) and ink to typewriters and pencils are bought by Empire, all at hefty discounts. A national advertising headquarters is situated in New York, with regional offices spotted around the country. Package deals among papers bunched close together can be arranged.

Nevertheless, there are clouds shadowing the World of Different Newspapers. For most of four years, Gannett had been negotiating to buy The Springfield (Mo.) Daily News and The Springfield Leader and Press, morning and evening papers jointly published out of the same squat building on Booneville Avenue, across from City Hall. Together, they circulate among 80,000 readers. The deal finally came to fruition in 1977. This seemed cause for jubilation. Reporters had been paid among the worst salaries and suffered among the worst benefits in journalism. Gannett promised to sweeten things up.

Six months later, salaries had risen some, but not enough, apparently, to satisfy many members of the staff. Some staffers sought union representation. Gannett strenuously opposed the idea. Last September, in a close vote (30 to 26) the union—the International Typographers Union—was beaten back. Conditions, according to some reporters, have taken a turn for the better since the union battle, though dissatisfaction among a lot of the staff still lingers.

I asked Dale Freeman, the executive editor, who began his career on the paper as a cub reporter at age 16, if he thought Gannett had done enough for the paper. "Let me say this," he answered. "Some people thought the newsroom would be paved with gold the day Gannett took over. Others thought the sky would fall. I tried to tell them that neither would happen. I didn't think things would move fast. I must admit that I probably hoped things would move a little faster."

Meanwhile, Gannett has vigorously pursued its program of expansion. It is eagerly awaiting the completion of the $420 million annexation of Combined Communications. The deal will nudge Gannett to more than $1 billion in revenues, a plateau attained by precious few communications companies. More important, it will give it muscle that it can flex in every portion of the business except magazines. That, Gannett people suggest, will probably be next. By any financial yardstick, the company's giant leap into broadcasting is interpreted as an idyllic arrangement, what

Gannett itself calls a "merger made in heaven."

On the other hand, the linking of various combinations of communications properties —like Gannett and Combined Communications—prompt those with antitrust leanings to stir in their lairs, and such mergers are starting to be considered as possible antitrust targets. The Gannett deal looks as if it will clear Justice Department scrutiny, though it will make no friends among the people who deplore the conglomeration of America. Morris Udall says, "The merger is legal, I suppose, and it will probably make some money for the shareholders, but it's just one more threat down this road of concentration of media power. I don't like it." The day the proposed merger was announced, Mr. Udall colorfully characterized it as a case of "a whale swallowing a whale."

. . .

Despite all its profits, though, one wonders whether the exponent of the small-town daily can ever rest easily without the benefit of prestige. I asked Mr. Neuharth if there were ever days when he wished he owned just one big-name newspaper, one Detroit Free Press, one St. Louis Dispatch, one Chicago Tribune.

Mr. Neuharth smiled. "I don't miss the prestige and influence of a big-city paper," he answered. "I've been there and a lot of the allure is myth. I think I have as exciting a job as exists in the newspaper business."

Did he dislike fighting, I asked.

The smile widened.

"I don't dislike fighting," Mr. Neuharth said. "I just like to win."

22
Reporting

Mitchell V. Charnley & Blair Charnley

The related crafts of editing and reporting are crucial to even the most technologically modern newspaper. The handling of local news stories becomes a routine of tasks for both editor and reporter: assigning the story; gathering, assembling, and checking the facts; writing the story, editing the copy for publication—all under deadline pressure. In this selection from their textbook *Reporting*, Mitchell Charnley, of the University of Minnesota, and Blair Charnley, of the *Minneapolis Star*, profile a typical editor and reporter at work on a medium-sized daily newspaper. The operations of the newspaper portrayed here are similar to those found at smaller papers, where most reporters start their careers.

The Newsroom

. . .

News reporting relies on imagination, fact gathering and competent writing. But it starts with organization. Some reporters work in an unorganized vacuum; featured columnists, for example, may write their own assignments. So do free-lance writers if they have ready markets—or wealthy grandmothers.

But reporters live with editors who direct their work, in greater or less detail. Newspapers, radio, television, newsmagazines—in each field an organizer tells reporters what to cover.

In newspaper organization, local news-gathering starts with the city desk, specifically with the city editor. (In electronic media the title is usually news manager or director, but the responsibilities are the same.) Here is a view of the city room operation of a daily in a middle-size city—an actual case that is typical of many.

This afternoon paper, the *Sun,* has a circulation of about 40,000; its presses start at 1:45 p.m. It serves a county seat of 44,000 population, the center of a farming region. A principal activity of the city is an expansive medical facility. The city's power plant serves its area and sends power to the metropolis 100 miles away; the area has a small college, two high schools, some agricultural service agencies, and some light manufacturing. The *Sun* has no local newspaper competition, but there are two TV and two radio stations.

Make the city editor a man of 40, a college journalism graduate who has worked for the *Sun* ever since college. He reported for 12 years and has been city editor for five. Moonlighting for a TV station got him through college. Give him a name: Miller.

Miller gets to work at 7:15 each morning. He has listened to a radio newscast on the way to work and combed rapidly through the metropolitan morning paper. At 7:30, with his first cup of coffee, he tunes into a local newscast (one local station has a news staff; the "rip-and-read" station Miller ignores). Already he has an overview of the day's news.

The metropolitan paper has just opened a bureau in his city, and a good young bureau reporter has burned the *Sun* a couple of times. Today, thanks to advance planning, the *Sun* is what Miller would call well set on news from its area. He picks up two "local angle" ideas from the national news, however.

Source: From *Reporting,* Fourth Edition, by Mitchell V. Charnley and Blair Charnley. Copyright © 1979, 1975, 1966, and 1959 by Holt, Rinehart and Winston. Reprinted by permission of the publisher.

One is so routine for an editor in a farm area that he doesn't really need the reminder: the national crop forecasts from Washington. The other may not be so obvious, and Miller hopes his competitors will miss the "short" in the metro daily about the unknown actor picked as a surprise lead in a forthcoming movie. He pegs those for the day's work.

The City Desk

Miller's first task is to glance through the "slop" or overset—proofs or computer-stored copies of stories that didn't make yesterday's paper. Some get a bold black **X** through the middle; in others Miller changes "today" and "tomorrow" to "yesterday" and "tonight." One short story is marked "AAA": it *must* run today. The slop proofs go along to the news desk so the wire editor can go through the same process with wire news, then send the proofs to the composing room.

Next comes the day's news budget. The copy and news desks have to know just what Miller is offering for today's paper, how much space it will take, where he wants to "play" it (city desk doesn't always win, but its average is pretty good), and when it will be ready. Miller works with a "city staff" of 11 reporters. In addition, the "lifestyle" section has three and sports five, including the editor. Miller's sharpest competition for space comes from the wire editor, with whom he carries on a more-or-less friendly war. Miller's budget looks like this:

POWER. Third in a series on new plant. P-1, 35 inches. In type. Ostman

GOVERNOR. Finally got the interview with him on the new ag commissioner. P-1, 17″. Moved last night. King

HEATERS. Three local stores sold those water heaters the FTC says will blow up if a gizmo isn't replaced. P-1, 2 pages. Moving soon. Mueller

RAPE. Mailman in Sunrise arraigned for having sexual relations with 12-year-old. 4″. In type. Inside. Howell

SCHOOL. School board meeting. Small stuff. 8″. Inside. Handberg

ACTOR. Robertson working on feature on Lance Elkins, who got that movie role. Turns out he's Bobby Ingebretsen (local boy who makes good). Moving late. P-1

The budget goes on through a score of items. One of the area reporters has a good piece on a jewel robbery two counties away; the city hall reporter has information on the cost of the new sewer line. Miller probably is being too hopeful in offering four stories for page one, but it never hurts to try; and he knows the ones that don't make it will get good play inside. He also lists three local pictures.

By 8 a.m. he's done with the budget. As he works, he deals with reporters and answers phone calls. One of the first tasks is to phone the entertainment reporter—who grumbles sleepily that he was up late the night before on a story—and ask him to come in to work on the movie star story. The reporter is new to the area, so Miller spends a couple of minutes explaining who the Ingebretsen family is and where to go for information on the next Robert Redford.

The budget completed, Miller turns to the copy on hand. He works swiftly at his VDT, deleting a sentence here, polishing a phrase there; and occasionally mumbling an indictment of reporters' command of English or the politicians at the school board. The eight-inch school story gets a complete rewrite because, though the veteran education reporter knows everything that's happening in the school district, she never has learned to pick the right lead in a board meeting story. At least, Miller tells himself, I've got her cured of writing 10-page narratives of everything routine everybody said.

With finished copy on its way to the copy desk, Miller turns to planning the day's activities—many of them directed toward tomorrow's paper. He starts with the "tickle file"— a daily file of upcoming activities. Everybody on the staff files notes on things that might be of future interest, and the city desk secretary sees to it that everything for today winds up in Miller's "in" bucket. Miller also has a large desk calendar covered with scrawled notes.

The "tickles" range from a note that it's time to start working on previews of state legislature elections to stories clipped out of yesterday's paper with a noted "folo?" The oldest tickle in today's file is 10 years old—somebody's suggestion that local cemeteries might be running out of space. "Maybe in 10 years," the memo says. Today Miller refiles it in the wastebasket.

Readers are a bonus news source. Tips on local events that escape the news net come into most newsrooms—if not in a flood, at least in useful quantity. Most of them are trivial: "there's an albino squirrel nesting in our oak" or "we have a sunflower that's 14 feet high." The albino squirrel might warrant a photo in an area that didn't have lots of them, but Miller gets the same call about once a month, and once he had a reporter follow it up unprofitably. Others are more useful: "There's a buffalo running down Maple Street!" two years ago yielded a feature about the chase and killing of an escaped "beefalo," a hybrid from a nearby farm.

Some media make pitches for audience help. The Kokomo (Ind.) *Tribune* wasn't unique when it established a "red alert" phone number for readers to report crimes in progress; in Indianapolis a similar program contributed to the capture of nearly a hundred lawbreakers. Such efforts draw favorable attention, and this may be more important than their value in news tips.

The 11 reporters Miller directs cover beats like those on most papers: environment-outdoors, medical-police, county government, city government, agriculture, politics, entertainment, schools, business, "area" beats. Area reporters cover just about everything in the six counties of the *Sun* circulation area outside the "home" county. The *Sun's* one beat unusual for a paper of its size is that of the part-time medical reporter.

Outside Miller's direct control are three reporters in the "lifestyle" section and five sports reporters. The *Sun* also has three photographers and a lab technician, and a full complement of copy editors.

By 9 a.m. Miller has things rolling. All the reporters are at work, covering beats or working on features. The stories called for by the budget have been written, and most of the day's copy has been given its quick city desk editing (the copy-desk does close editing and, sometimes, rewrites). It's time to go to the "huddle" to decide on news play for the day. The huddle is the daily conference of the paper's principal news executives. Often its

---

"The System," VDT, and the Reporter
The scene: an up-to-date newsroom. The news editor and the copy desk chief, a deadline near, are talking urgently about a story—not what it says, but where they can find it in "the system." The acronyms and computer jargon they use, to outsiders, sound like gibberish.

"Some idiot put the wrong format on the Carter story," an angry copy editor snarls.

"The computer just ate my story," a reporter wails.

Typewriter out, tube in Reporters of a few years back would be struck dumb. The newspaper business, a backwater of obsolete mechanical procedures for the first two-thirds of the 20th century, has plunged into new technology. A breakthrough this morning may be passé this afternoon.

Newsrooms don't sound the same. The clack of typewriters has been replaced by the muted click of electric keyboards as reporters and editors work not on paper, but at what look like small TV screens—video display terminals, VDTs.

Copy pencils are hard to find in modern newsrooms. Reporters "type" their stories on the VDT, edit and alter them with correction keys, send them electronically to the city desk. A computer "stores" them until they're ready for editing (also by VDT). Most newsworkers adjust readily to "the system," though some copy editors find it a mixed blessing.

Newspapers today—many small ones as well as the giants—make the investment in "the system" because it's faster and a money-saver. It even sets type with a punch of the button.

But the new methodology does not change what a reporter does as reporter—gather the news and put it into words. Reporting is reporting.

decisions are obvious; there are usually both local and wire stories that merit page-one space. But today Miller and the wire editor each have four stories for page one; somebody's got to give. Today it's Miller. The decision is made that if the movie-star story arrives in time, the water heaters will go inside; otherwise, the movie star will hold for tomorrow.

Miller and the wire editor get in their usual good-natured debate: "how many of our readers care about a revolt in Afghanistan?" and "When is Ostman going to quit blathering about that silly power plant?" The "Old Man," the *Sun*'s 68-year-old owner-publisher, plays peacemaker; this time, along with the managing editor and news editor, he sides with the wire editor. Today's decisions made, the huddle turns to less immediate matters. The sports editor tells of a proposed series on high school football injuries. Miller reports that the county reporter is spending a lot of time looking at deeds because she smells a rat in a county land sale. (The Old Man harumphs; he has a hard time understanding why a mother of two would want to work. And he can't get used to women covering anything but "society" news. But mostly he keeps his views to himself, and women hold three of the top seven beats on the *Sun*.) The huddle breaks up.

The rest of the day, Miller says, is devoted to "playing city editor." He answers phones, arbitrates between reporters and the copy desk, edits copy and works on advance schedules. And he puts final touches on today's paper—the *Sun* goes to press at 1:45—and starts work on tomorrow's. The key job is the assignment sheet. Each reporter gets a daily memo about stories to cover, when they are due, probable length, special future assignments. A typical assignment sheet:

OSTMAN—Fourth in power plant series runs tomorrow, fifth Friday. You're late with the fifth. I need it today.

The governor told King that the environmental group over on the river is happy with him now. (He refused to meet with them last summer.) You might check and see if they really like him now.

Remind me to talk with you about the wild-river canoeing feature. You've been do-

ing so much environment there hasn't been much outdoors stuff.

MUELLER—The old man gave the go-ahead on the land deal. We've got to be really careful with this one; among other things, the county board chairman is the old man's hunting buddy. He won't spill it, but he's going to be looking over your stuff like a hawk.

Tickle file shows they should make a decision on fixing up the Hwy. 14 bridge soon. Anything on that?

Is Goldsmith going to resign from the county board to run for the state senate? I keep hearing rumors.

ROBERTSON—We're probably going to hold the Ingebretsen piece for Thursday. Sorry I had to roust you out of bed. Anyway, this'll let you do a more thorough job. Keep an eye out for art, pictures of him from the family scrapbook, or something we can shoot of the family. What do his folks think of his changing his name?

Lemme know what else you're working on. I don't like surprises.

HOWELL—Sunrise city council tonight. Anything from over there? When's the trial for that mailman? How are people taking it? It's not often you get sex crimes against kids in a town that small.

(The copy desk points out that you just about convicted that guy in your story today. Forget the word "allegedly." It doesn't protect you a bit when they come with the libel suit. We've got to play cases like this straighter than we used to. Take another look at the "free press-fair trial" guidelines I sent out last month.)

Have you got time to work up any features from your school districts?

JOHNSON—Localizer on the federal crop forecasts.

The process goes on. Beginners get detailed instructions. Veterans like the agriculture reporter need little direction.

Though the city editor on a paper the size of the *Sun* doesn't write straight news, Miller cranks out a couple of columns a week on local politics, social events or other topics that interest him. Today he uses his half-hour of lunch to interview a local high school teacher who is the center of a controversy on sex education. The education reporter has covered the issue in detail; Miller wants to try to capture the man's personality.

Back at the office, Miller edits the late copy. There's nothing major: the police reporter has a couple of shorts; the education reporter has a small story about hot school lunches served cold in one school because of an equipment breakdown; the two area reporters have routine government stories from the six counties they cover. The budget Miller wrote in the morning is his major working paper. Additions are penciled in at the end; stories that fell through are crossed out. As the city desk deadline nears, he photocopies the revised budget for the news and copy desks. He edits the final stories on his VDT and lets the news desk know, "You've got it."

Miller has had a fairly routine day. Some are more strenuous—the days of blizzards, elections, a major fire, a teachers strike. On those days the relaxed atmosphere of the newsroom vanishes. Reporters are yanked off their beats to help out, the city desk hums. But the daily schedule usually resembles this one, with its rhythm of covering focal news points, identifying salient events that must be covered, and seeing to it that staffers are where they ought to be.

Deadline and After

Most of the day's work is finished by 1 p.m. Today's local copy has been written; the beats have been covered; the wire and local news for the day has been selected, edited and prepared for the press. The newsroom turns its attention to tomorrow. Robertson is at the Ingebretsen farm interviewing the actor's mother. Mueller is sitting through an interminable county board meeting, wishing she could be in the records room three doors down, finding out which commissioner owned what land. Johnson is sipping coffee in the county agent's office, learning how the crops are doing.

Back at the office, Miller updates the tickle file and gives reporters additional assignments. He gets started on his column about the sex-education problem and talks by phone with King, the political reporter in the state capital. He jots some story ideas for the paper's annual "Harvest Edition," which is coming up again (all too soon, reporters mumble darkly). He answers the ever-present telephone, and toward the end of the day he drops over to the mayor's office to defend the city hall reporter against His Honor's ire. He's likely to be at it after most of the reporters have gone home.

. . .

What's in a Name? On small staffs, titles may not mean much. On a paper not much smaller than the one described in this chapter, for example, the "city editor" might also cover city hall. The managing editor might be the wire editor and part-time sports reporter as well. Among larger newspapers, the duties of city editors, news editors and managing editors vary widely; each news system, with the people in it, molds its own pattern. The sum of all functions, however, is about the same on comparable papers, no matter how the jobs are described or the work divided.

. . .

Reporters

. . .

News beats are organized in two ways: by subject and by geography.

The first, which zeroes a reporter in on one field or a group of related fields, is common to big newspapers, network news operations and news magazines. Most familiar beats follow the subject-matter pattern: police, city hall, education, sports, business, religion, courts, politics. Reporter-specialists concentrate on science and health, environmental concerns and other fields, some of them defined by local circumstances (Seattle has waterfront reporters, but Butte doesn't). A sportswriter is as much a specialist (or ought to be) as is an agribusiness reporter. A newspaper that can afford a corps of specialists can do its job most effectively.

A geographical beat—the second kind—groups news centers that can be conveniently covered by a single pair of legs or a single automobile. It's the common beat on smaller newspapers and in most radio stations with genuine news operations. For example, a reporter may be assigned to cover a city's largest industry. This could be a full-time assignment by itself, with union problems, demands for better housing for workers, pollution questions, plant expansions or labor layoffs, management's response to a city plan to broaden the tax base. But, says the city editor, "The plant is way out there between Wilshire and Brighton. You might as well cover those suburbs too. And the veterans' hospital is on the way back to town."

Covering a Beat

Follow the medical-police reporter who works for the paper . . . as she goes on her daily rounds. Diane Slovut is 40, married, mother of two and a thorough pro. She earned her B.A. after six years of raising children and started on the *Sun* covering three outlying counties—police, city and county government, social events, disasters, whatever the areas had to offer. She had a long-standing interest in medicine, and when the police beat opened up, she talked Miller into juggling other reporters' responsibilities so she could take on medicine as a sideline. The importance of the town's big medical center economically and in many other ways, she pointed out, made it sensible to devote more attention to medicine than most comparable papers would.

Though her heart is in the medical beat, Slovut knows police news is bread and butter. Accordingly, when she gets to the office at 7:30 a.m., her first attention goes to police news. She raps out a short story on a burglary she picked up the day before, then begins the day's rounds. The first "rounds" are by telephone: the county coroner's office, the hospital emergency ward, the fire department, the state highway patrol office. She chats easily with the people in all four spots, because she spends enough time there that they all know and trust her. She reminds herself to get over to the emergency room sometime this week— she hasn't been there recently, and there's a new nurse she ought to know.

This morning's calls yield little, but the coroner's assistant has heard a rumor that a coroner in a neighboring county is working on an "odd" case. "It may be nothing," the assistant tells her, "but they've been taking a long time on it, with a couple of calls to the pathology department at State University." She passes a note along to the reporter who covers that county, asking for a check on it; if it's a criminal matter, the reporter will cover it. If it's a medical oddity, she'll do it.

It's 8:15, and after conferring briefly with Miller, she takes off. Her first stop is at the city police station, where she chats with the desk sergeant, an old acquaintance. It's routine for both of them. The sergeant has already shuffled through the night's thin stack of reports and picked out the four he knows will interest her. One is on a minor traffic accident that produced no injuries but did heavy damage to a car and a streetlight. She takes quick notes, for a short: readers will be curious about the bent lamppost downtown.

The second is also minor—a fight in a bar that's been the scene of a number of brawls. She takes careful notes because she's building a file on the place. The repeated "incidents" may make it, eventually, a story of some importance. She's aware that similar incidents in other bars don't get more than one-paragraph attention; but the police would like nothing better than public notice that would move the city council to revoke the bar's license. She makes a comment about that, and the sergeant grins.

She ignores the report on another traffic accident.

The fourth catches her eye. Her city isn't large enough that rapes are common, but this is the fourth in six months, and there have been no arrests. Once again she wishes the police didn't forbid her to photocopy the offense reports; they're public records and she can hand-copy everything, but the police won't let her duplicate them. She suspects she could win if she made an issue of it, but victory might not be worth the ill will it would arouse.

As she goes over the reports, she chats with the desk sergeant. He makes his routine jibe that "dainty young women" aren't suited to police reporting, and she makes her customary offer to take him on in karate any time, any place. It's a tired routine, but it saves Slovut from more of his endless fishing stories.

Her next stop is the police chief's office. In the two years she's had the beat, morning coffee with the chief has become a habit (she has her own coffee mug by the coffee machine). Today she wants to find out more about the rape—whether the police see a pattern, what they're doing to identify the rapist, whether they think one man is responsible for more than one incident, what precautions women should be taking. She also knows the chief will try to jolly her out of doing more than a brief report of the latest incident.

That's exactly what he does; but when he realizes she isn't buying, he switches tactics. "Look, Diane—if you give this a lot of ink, you're going to panic everyone in town. We're making some progress on it, and when we catch the guy, you'll be the first to know." "Then you think it's one man, chief?" "Dammit, that's not what I . . ." Finally he gives up and decides to level with her. There is a clear pattern, and there are some clues. There are no sex offenders with criminal records living in the area, as far as the police know, but there are suspects. Gradually Slovut convinces the chief that careful reporting won't create a panic, and they work out a story pattern that satisfies both. The chief obviously is relieved when she turns to questions about precautions women should take, and talks at length. As she leaves, she realizes that the chief is exasperated with her, and it's going to be a while before their relationship is entirely mended.

Her next stop is the county sheriff's office, where the process is similar to that in the police station. Today's finding is petty: a burglary of a grocery store. The sheriff's on vacation, and his replacement is reluctant to talk. Slovut next checks the booking sheet in the city-county jail. Normally she picks all the major stories from the offense reports, but sometimes there's a surprise. Once she found that a prominent local doctor had been booked on drunk-and-disorderly charges, but the arresting officer hadn't completed his offense report. She might not have known about it without the extra check.

Her final check on the police round is at the two courts in town, county and district. Here, as at the other spots, her technique is to combine chatting with people she knows on the beat with close looks at official records. At the county court the clerk of court is helpful and interesting; the records and court docket get a cursory check in case the clerk forgot something or didn't recognize a news story. At the district court she has a different problem. The clerk is a fussy man who regards anyone meddling with his records as an intruder. Slovut once had to get the judge to remind the clerk that the records, by law, are open to the public, and she studies them closely. She gets no help from the clerk, though. She's not without sources, however; the office secretary has formed an alliance with the reporter.

There's nothing in the court records today—the day's trials will be dull. Knowing she has two medical stories coming up in the afternoon, Slovut heads back to the *Sun* office to write the morning's stories. All but the rape story get routine handling, but that one is written with great care, after a conference with Miller; they agree that the story should be played down. It goes on page one, at the bottom, under a small head. Sensational play, they know, might panic the community. Under the news policy common to most news media, the name of the woman will not appear, but other facts will be spelled out straightforwardly. Similarities to previous rapes are reported, along with the police chief's belief that only one man is involved, and that the police have some leads. No detail on the evidence—using it might help a suspect to cover up. Slovut decides to give space to the chief's suggestions on ways women can protect themselves.

It's 10:30, and time for Slovut to put on her medical reporter hat. The principal story is the regional medical association's annual meeting. Slovut had asked Miller for a substitute on the police beat today, but he couldn't accommodate her: "Two reporters on vacation this week," he explained. So she has missed some seminars that would have provided grist for her weekly medical column. She will, however, cover the important talk about a new approach to treating certain kinds of cancer.

At the hotel where the meeting is being held, Slovut passes a protest group passing out pamphlets and locates the Chamber of Commerce secretary who is acting as receptionist. From her the reporter gets a copy of the cancer speech, information about where to find the speaker, and a tip: "Dr. Osborn is furious about the people who are handing out a Laetrile pamphlet, and I think he'll bring it into his talk."

Slovut finds Dr. Osborn and reduces his initial reticence with questions that indicate she knows something about him and his topic. He assures her that he won't deviate from his text, "except that I'll probably have something to say about the Laetrile bunch." It's going to be a tight squeeze to cover the story by 1:30 deadline, so she heads back to the office. She stops to get a Laetrile pamphlet, and finds that the pamphleteers like Osborn as little as he likes them. They believe their drug is a cure for cancer, suppressed by the medical profession because it would hurt business; Osborn says Laetrile is a quack drug that keeps people away from appropriate treatment.

Back at the office, Slovut scans the speech and prepares "A matter" on it. A matter, ("advance matter") is used by reporters who have part of a story, but won't get the rest until just before deadline. Slovut's 10 paragraphs of A matter summarize the Osborn talk. She gives a copy to Miller (or stores it in the computer), warning him that Osborn might change it, and takes a copy (or a printout) back to the hotel.

Osborn is true to his word; he doesn't change his text. But he adds a stinging attack on "Laetrile quacks." Before the applause has died down, Slovut goes to a telephone and starts dictating her story. The lead paragraph is conventional: Osborn describes a new approach to cancer treatment at the medical convention. The second brings in the Laetrile matter. The third and fourth return to the cancer approach, with major details; two paragraphs then report the attack on Laetrile and quote the pamphlet. "Now," she tells the rewrite man on the phone, "pick up the A matter." Rewrite asks for a few clarifications; then Miller comes on the line: What about the hospital addition story for tomorrow? "After lunch, slavedriver. I'm starved."

She goes to a working lunch—an interview with a visiting physician about a flu epidemic warning and what people should do to protect themselves. Then she sits in on a medical seminar, which will produce a four-paragraph item for her Friday column. Her day is rounded out with another check of the police and fire departments, the emergency room, the sheriff's office and the courts—and writing the hospital addition story.

Developing a Beat

When reporters have covered a beat for six months, they think they're "beginning to know it." As they tagged along with their predecessors for two or three days before taking over, they probably thought it was going to be a killer. How could they ever get to know everybody in the county building? After six months they may say cautiously that they have it pretty well under control. In another six months or so—if they're good, and if they work hard—they will have mastered not only the idiosyncracies of their own beats, but also many of the techniques of successful reporting.

Few reporters verbalize all the things they have learned. They know about their craft by experience and by repetition, but they rarely reduce their knowledge to formula or analysis. It's unfortunate, because there are few ways to improve one's own knowledge as effective as explaining it, precisely and in detail, to someone else. The organization process reveals gaps and faulty emphasis, flaws and strengths. It's as true for halfbacks, bricklayers and pastry cooks as it is for artists (reporting is a craft, and it is an art), all of whom are likely to do their work by impulse, instinct and reflex.

The memo from a beat reporter to a beginner that follows is a compendium of precepts and suggestions from a hundred sources, but principally from men and women on the job. This memo concentrates on a government beat, but it applies to most beats.

KNOW YOUR BEAT—The cardinal rule, underlying all others, is: *know your beat.*

That's easy to say and tough to accomplish because there are hundreds of things to learn about any beat. You've barely started when you've mastered the obvious indicators—the names on doors, the principal activities of the offices, the telephone numbers. You can absorb these in a few days. But the kinds of knowledge that make you a subsurface reporter instead of a skimmer take time and thought and a lot of pure hard work.

Your beat covers a certain amount of routine activities and responsibilities, and you might say that any kid in a high-school social-studies class could name them. But that's all he could do. *You* have to go much deeper. You should get the official government manuals, statutes and ordinances and learn the county organizations in your state, especially if you crossed a state line to get into this job. No two states (and not many pairs of counties) have identical practices or laws. Official records and proceedings have different names from one state to another, and different areas allow public access to different records, either as a matter of law or of local practice.

You should also read up on public administration to see whether the offices you cover depart from standard practice, and find out why. You'll need time in the library, in your paper's morgue and in other sources of information.

In addition, you'll have to be thoroughly familiar with the issues on your beat. You can't cover the county recorder this year without knowing what news his office yielded last year. *Spend some time going through back issues.* If your predecessor was doing the job properly, last year's stories should give you material without which stories this year might be incomplete.

KNOW YOUR SOURCES—In major offices in the county building you'll find a principal officer —a county clerk, an auditor, an assessor, a sheriff— and a lot of second- and third-level employees. Beat reporters have to *know "their" people.* Sometimes they have to know the county recorder's staff better than they know the recorder. Most offices have an employee who keeps an eye on everything and who loves to gab. The office motormouth can be an invaluable source of tips, though most such tips have to be corroborated by the top man, by official records or by other sources.

Not everything a source—even a reliable one— tells you is fact. It may be opinion, or it may be just plain wrong. Your gabby receptionist may tell you that "a woman died in the courtroom today—I saw them carrying her body out." A check shows that she fainted and is at home cooking dinner.

Along with knowing your beat, *be sure that your beat knows you.* Reporters on their first visit to a news source introduce themselves so that they'll be remembered. Frequently they write down name and phone numbers (office and home) for each contact—a good way of making a firm initial impression. They get on informal terms with the staff; this is frequently easier than becoming friendly with the boss.

Nevertheless, you have to rely heavily on the men and women at the top. They have the last word, can hold back or release information. They usually know more than you do about the topic, and you have to depend a lot on their judgment. Beat reporters don't necessarily have to see the boss every time they step into the office, but they should touch base on a regular schedule, perhaps every other day. If you can get minor information without bothering the bosses, they'll probably appreciate it.

Word from the chief, however, is only one way of finding out what's going on in an office—and not always the best way—in a world where concealing news, for good reason or bad, is common. You chat with people who are knowledgeable—or who think they are. Bulletin boards can be a source of tips; so can the janitor or the girl at the candy stand. They may notice things "insiders" think too routine to mention. You can't be too curious. Get the head man to tell you what the most important work of his office is; then find out what the staff thinks. They may not agree. And, further, you may have your own ideas; when yours are different, remember that the employees know more than you do about the office. But also remember that your main interest is news; theirs is something else.

A beat reporter must be constantly aware of the politics of his beat. County Commissioner Smith, a Democrat, may loathe Commissioner Jones, a Republican. Auditor Johnson may be furious at Recorder Peterson. You can use that, but use it gingerly; if Smith tells you something Jones says ain't so, remember that Smith has an axe to grind. Use the information as a starting point for checks and double checks.

READ THE SIGNPOSTS—You quickly learn to watch for signposts that help you *establish rapport with your sources.* If you see a mounted northern pike on an office wall or a rod and reel in a corner, chances are that fishing talk will please the man behind the desk. If a secretary has a stack of travel folders about the Virgin Islands on her table, you've got an opening. You may be surprised to find how many questions you can ask about the Caribbean and how much they'll yield in goodwill, in news tips and in access to information.

This leads to a warning: *Don't be phony.* If you think fishing is for the birds, don't try to pretend. You'll be caught for sure, and you'll lose credibility. Confession of ignorance in such a case may be a door-opener. People respond to interest in their interests. Sometimes a reporter finds the role reversed—interviewer becomes interviewee.

GET UNDER THE SURFACE.—Much significant news is under cover, either because someone's hiding it or because of its nature. Getting it requires imaginative questions and the drive to dig out answers. Digging pays dividends in readership; many surveys indicate people are more likely to read backgrounders than they are surface or "event" stories.

It's routine to report the motions passed at city council meetings. But suppose you note that every vote for six weeks showed the same eight councilmen on one side and the same five on the other. If it's not a party-line split, is it mere coincidence? Probably not. If instead of the usual two bailiffs stationed in a courtroom there are six, you need to find out why. If a local industry starts buying up all the property in an area south of town, there has to be a reason, and it's probably newsworthy. Suppose the county clerk tells you that twice as many marriage licenses—or dog licenses—were issued last month as in any previous month. If you can find a reason, it's probably a story. If you can't find out why, it still may be worth a couple of paragraphs.

DON'T BLOW SMOKE—Above all don't blow it in an office or living room where you can't spot ashtrays. Good manners—and that doesn't necessarily mean formality—are an important tool in any reportorial kit. The play called "The Front Page"—like most plays, movies and television shows about newspapers that have followed it— gives the impression that reporters are drunks and/or boors. "The Front Page" may give a reasonably accurate portrayal of one kind of Chicago newspaper life in another era and generation; it doesn't have much to do with today's journalists.

A New York *Times* staff memo insisted on a reasonably short haircut and "clean, business-style shirts with neckties where appropriate." Even the good, gray *Times* admitted that situations differ. Heavy boots, jeans and a sweat shirt may be appropriate for a story on farm life, but they could be resented at a governor's press conference. And that could interfere with getting the news.

BUT BUILD SMALL FIRES—Being courteous doesn't preclude being aggressive. Sources often don't want to talk for reasons good or bad. It could be that some sources simply don't know the answers; but they may be covering up private gain at public cost or hiding misbehavior. Sometimes it can take weeks of asking the same question, in different places and in different ways, to break the facts you need into the open. If you *keep digging* long enough and hard enough, chances are you'll find answers.

Sometimes publishing evasive, doubletalk answers dries up news sources. Reporters face a dilemma when they uncover information that damages or offends a productive source. A beat reporter who's only peaches and cream with his sources may be no reporter at all. But there is usually a middle ground. Every reporter has to define no-man's-land for himself.

If you're stuck, there's no virtue in not looking for help. Maybe the seasoned business reporter who has known the reluctant banker for years can get him to talk when you can't.

It's important to remember that *you, rather than a source, are the expert on news.* Everyone thinks he can run a newspaper better than its editor, and everybody tells reporters how to do their jobs. A news source may say that you "can't" run such-and-such a story—"that's not news, and it would wreck our negotiations"—or that you'd better run it or else. You don't have to get rough, but you may have to be tough. If it's important to the public, and if you've come by the story legitimately, you'll have to stick to your guns. In such cases it's a good idea to go over the conflict with your city editor.

Reporters increase their efficiency if they have cooperation from news sources. You'll probably be asked to hold off publishing some stories, and sometimes you can't honor the request. In other cases, however, the request is legitimate and you serve your readers just as well—or better—by going along with it.

One final word: if you are going to "burn"

any sources, prepare them for it. You'll have a better chance of salvaging your relationship if they get the bad word before they pick up the paper.

REPORTERS KEEP PROMISES—A prime responsibility of reporters is to keep their word to sources. They don't loosely break release dates; they don't print information given to them in confidence; they don't reveal the identity of sources they have agreed to protect.

This, however, can be used against them. A news source can gag you by putting you "off the record." If you find you've been had by this kind of ruse, you may decide you have to break the promise (with due warning to the source). You can avoid this trap. A Boston editor once said, "I make it a practice to refuse to let people tell me news facts 'off the record.' In almost every case I can get the facts through other channels. Some news sources have said to me, 'Well, I'm going to tell you anyway. Use your own judgment as to whether to print it.'" Once in a long, long while it works to accept material off the record; but do it cautiously.

RELIABILITY—Responsibility means other things, too. It means that you *keep appointments and keep them punctually*. It means you return the stenographer's carbon copies as promised—in good shape and on time.

You don't have to see every source on your beat every day; some produce news only once or twice a month. And some executives and government officials are much too busy to *waste* time with a reporter. They'll resent wasted time, but rarely will they resent legitimate, well-thought-out questions. You usually can check things with their secretaries or others in their offices. And once they trust you to be respectful of their time—and to get the facts straight when you do talk to them—they frequently will call *you*.

Be specific. One of the most practical pieces of advice experienced reporters give is "don't ask general questions." "Why is the county spending $28,000 for new staff cars?" is likely to elicit a detailed, specific answer. "What's going on?" is likely to elicit a response appropriate to the question: "Not much." People think more clearly and respond more fluently to concrete questions than to vague or abstract.

Keep your own calendar or futures book. If you rely on memory, chances are you'll forget, especially if you have a large, complicated beat. In addition to noting upcoming meetings, report releases and other facts, the futures book is a good place to *jot down feature ideas* or hunches for pieces you can develop. Though beat reporters have the primary assignment of covering the regular news, they are doing no more than 51 percent of the job if they cover only events and neglect features, stories that may take extra time and digging. If you keep your eyes open, you'll soon have far more work than you can handle. Feel free to let the city desk know about story ideas you don't have time for; perhaps another reporter will have some spare time.

Always keep the desk informed of what you're doing. City editors rage about surprise stories that don't need to be surprises. Among other things, such a surprise can make the difference between good display for your copy and display on page 11Z, back with the truss ads. In addition, the city editor will know whether someone else is working on the same yarn you are.

. . .

23
The Boston Photographs

Nora Ephron

In journalism, the difference between "sensational" and "sensationalism" can mean the difference between a truly professional scoop and crass exploitation. This issue is particularly troublesome in the field of photo-journalism. In the following essay, noted reporter and media critic Nora Ephron examines the controversy behind the famous "Boston Photographs" of Pulitzer Prize winner Stanley Forman and attempts to show "why photojournalism is often more powerful than written journalism."

"I made all kinds of pictures because I thought it would be a good rescue shot over the ladder . . . never dreamed it would be anything else. . . . I kept having to move around because of the light set. The sky was bright and they were in deep shadow. I was making pictures with a motor drive and he, the fire fighter, was reaching up and, I don't know, everything started falling. I followed the girl down taking pictures . . . I made three or four frames. I realized what was going on and I completely turned around, because I didn't want to see her hit."

You probably saw the photographs. In most newspapers, there were three of them. The first showed some people on a fire escape —a fireman, a woman and a child. The fireman had a nice strong jaw and looked very brave. The woman was holding the child. Smoke was pouring from the building behind them. A rescue ladder was approaching, just a few feet away, and the fireman had one arm around the woman and one arm reaching out toward the ladder. The second picture showed the fire escape slipping off the building. The child had fallen on the escape and seemed about to slide off the edge. The woman was grasping desperately at the legs of the fireman, who had managed to grab the ladder. The third picture showed the woman and child in midair, falling to the ground. Their arms and legs were outstretched, horribly distended. A potted plant was falling too. The caption said that the woman, Diana Bryant, nineteen, died in the fall. The child landed on the woman's body and lived.

The pictures were taken by Stanley Forman, thirty, of the *Boston Herald American.* He used a motor-driven Nikon F set at 1/250, f 5.6–S. Because of the motor, the camera can click off three frames a second. More than four hundred newspapers in the United States alone carried the photographs: the tear sheets from overseas are still coming in. The *New York Times* ran them on the first page of its second section; a paper in south Georgia gave them nineteen columns; the *Chicago Tribune,* the *Washington Post* and the *Washington Star* filled almost half their front pages, the *Star* under a somewhat redundant headline that read: SENSATIONAL PHOTOS OF RESCUE ATTEMPT THAT FAILED.

The photographs are indeed sensational. They are pictures of death in action, of that split second when luck runs out, and it is impossible to look at them without feeling their extraordinary impact and remembering, in an almost subconscious way, the morbid fantasy of falling, falling off a building, falling to one's death. Beyond that, the pictures are classics, old-fashioned but perfect examples of photojournalism at its most spectacular.

They're throwbacks, really, fire pictures, 1930s tabloid shots; at the same time they're technically superb and thoroughly modern— the sequence could not have been taken at all until the development of the motor-driven camera some sixteen years ago.

Most newspaper editors anticipate some reader reaction to photographs like Forman's; even so, the response around the country was enormous, and almost all of it was negative. I have read hundreds of the letters that were printed in letters-to-the-editor sections, and they repeat the same points. "Invading the privacy of death." "Cheap sensationalism." "I thought I was reading the *National Enquirer*." "Assigning the agony of a human being in terror of imminent death to the status of a side-show act." "A tawdry way to sell newspapers." The *Seattle Times* received sixty letters and calls; its managing editor even got a couple of them at home. A reader wrote the *Philadelphia Inquirer:* "*Jaws* and *Towering Inferno* are playing downtown; don't take business away from people who pay good money to advertise in your own paper." Another reader wrote the *Chicago Sun-Times:* "I shall try to hide my disappointment that Miss Bryant wasn't wearing a skirt when she fell to her death. You could have had some award-winning photographs of her underpants as her skirt billowed over her head, you voyeurs." Several newspaper editors wrote columns defending the pictures: Thomas Keevil of the *Costa Mesa* (California) *Daily Pilot* printed a ballot for readers to vote on whether they would have printed the pictures; Marshall L. Stone of Maine's *Bangor Daily News,* which refused to print the famous assassination picture of the Vietcong prisoner in Saigon, claimed that the Boston pictures showed the dangers of fire escapes and raised questions about slumlords. (The burning building was a five-story brick apartment house on Marlborough Street in the Back Bay section of Boston.)

For the last five years, the *Washington Post* has employed various journalists as ombudsmen, whose job is to monitor the paper on behalf of the public. The *Post*'s current ombudsman is Charles Seib, former managing editor of the *Washington Star*; the day the Boston photographs appeared, the paper received over seventy calls in protest. As Seib later wrote in a column about the pictures, it was "the largest reaction to a published item that I have experienced in eight months as the *Post*'s ombudsman. . . .

"In the *Post*'s newsroom, on the other hand, I found no doubts, no second thoughts . . . the question was not whether they should be printed but how they should be displayed. When I talked to editors . . . they used words like 'interesting' and 'riveting' and 'gripping' to describe them. The pictures told something about life in the ghetto, they said (although the neighborhood where the tragedy occurred is not a ghetto, I am told). They dramatized the need to check on the safety of fire escapes. They dramatically conveyed something that had happened, and that is the business we're in. They were news. . . .

"Was publication of that [third] picture a bow to the same taste for the morbidly sensational that makes gold mines of disaster movies? Most papers will not print the picture of a dead body except in the most unusual circumstances. Does the fact that the final picture was taken a millisecond before the young woman died make a difference? Most papers will not print a picture of a bare female breast. Is that a more inappropriate subject for display than the picture of a human being's last agonized instant of life?" Seib offered no answers to the questions he raised, but he went on to say that although as an editor he would probably have run the pictures, as a reader he was revolted by them.

In conclusion, Seib wrote: "Any editor who decided to print those pictures without giving at least a moment's thought to what purpose they served and what their effect was likely to be on the reader should ask another question: Have I become so preoccupied with manufacturing a product according to professional traditions and standards that I have forgotten about the consumer, the reader?"

It should be clear that the phone calls and letters and Seib's own reaction were occasioned by one factor alone: the death of the woman. Obviously, had she survived the fall, no one would have protested; the pictures would have had a completely different impact. Equally obviously, had the child died as well—or instead—Seib would undoubtedly have received ten times the phone calls he did. In each case, the pictures would have been exactly the same—only the captions, and thus the responses, would have been different.

But the questions Seib raises are worth discussing—though not exactly for the reasons he mentions. For it may be that the real lesson of the Boston photographs is not the danger that editors will be forgetful of reader reaction, but that they will continue to censor pictures of death precisely because of that reaction. The protests Seib fielded were really a variation on an old theme—and we saw plenty of it during the Nixon-Agnew years—the "Why doesn't the press print the good news?" argument. In this case, of course, the objections were all dressed up and cleverly disguised as righteous indignation about the privacy of death. This is a form of puritanism that is often justifiable; just as often it is merely puritanical.

Seib takes it for granted that the widespread though fairly recent newspaper policy against printing pictures of dead bodies is a sound one; I don't know that it makes any sense at all. I recognize that printing pictures of corpses raises all sorts of problems about taste and titillation and sensationalism; the fact is, however, that people die. Death happens to be one of life's main events. And it is irresponsible—and more than that, inaccurate—for newspapers to fail to show it, or to show it only when an astonishing set of photos comes in over the Associated Press wire. Most papers covering fatal automobile accidents will print pictures of mangled cars. But the significance of fatal automobile accidents is not that a great deal of steel is twisted but that people die. Why not show it? That's what accidents are about. Throughout the Vietnam war, editors were reluctant to print atrocity pictures. Why *not* print them? That's what that war was about. Murder victims are almost never photographed; they are granted their privacy. But their relatives are relentlessly pictured on their way in and out of hospitals and morgues and funerals.

I'm not advocating that newspapers print these things in order to teach their readers a lesson. The *Post* editors justified their printing of the Boston pictures with several arguments in that direction; every one of them is irrelevant. The pictures don't show anything about slum life; the incident could have happened anywhere, and it did. It is extremely unlikely that anyone who saw them rushed out and had his fire escape strengthened. And the pictures were not news—at least they were not national news. It is not news in Washington, or New York, or Los Angeles that a woman was killed in a Boston fire. The only newsworthy thing about the pictures is that they were taken. They deserve to be printed because they are great pictures, breathtaking pictures of something that happened. That they disturb readers is exactly as it should be: that's why photojournalism is often more powerful than written journalism.

24
"Alternative" Newspapers: Up from the Underground

Calvin Trillin

In the 1960s, counterculture-oriented newspapers sprung up in almost every major city and college town in America. Originally called the "underground" press, the papers, usually weeklies, thrived on a mix of radical politics, drugs, rock music, and sex—all topics largely ignored by traditional local journalism. There were even alternatives to the major wire services for these newspapers: the Underground Press Syndicate (UPS) and the Liberation News Service (LNS) at one time distributed stories to a total readership of over thirteen million.

In the 1970s, however, the surviving papers changed their editorial focus as their readers' interests matured. Known now as the "alternative" press, the papers have developed into very profitable vehicles for consumer advertising. Moreover, they have begun to provide their communities with in-depth feature coverage of the arts, entertainment, and local politics.

New Yorker writer Calvin Trillin recently attended a national alternative newspaper conference. He discovered that their identity is changing again—they now want to be called "metropolitan weeklies" or "newsweeklies." In the following article, Trillin examines the demographic and economic trends behind the growth of these papers and provides a glimpse of the motives of their proprietors. Calvin Trillin, novelist, reporter, and humorist, is also well-known for his appreciative writing about indigenous American food.

The alternative press is now respectable enough to be edgy about being called alternative. Apparently, the word was actually an attempt at respectability in the first place—a way for proprietors of certain weeklies to distinguish their papers from the underground press—but when it is uttered out loud inside of a bank or an advertising agency it still seems to give off little puffs of incense and marijuana smoke. Representatives of about thirty alternative weeklies met recently in Seattle to discuss, among other matters, the possibility of forming a sort of trade association—a notably respectable goal in itself—and, almost without discussion, they decided against describing their papers as "alternative." That left them temporarily at a loss for word. When an alternative weekly is mentioned in the national press—usually as the source for a story that the local daily, through ignorance or exceedingly good manners, failed to print—it is customarily described as "lively" or "sprightly," but I can't imagine a trade association's calling itself the National Association of Sprightly Weeklies. Although the Seattle conference was announced as a gathering of "metropolitan weeklies," a couple of statewide papers were represented, and one that was not, *Maine Times,* is considered a prototype for the entire field. The *Pacific*

Sun, whose editor played a prominent role in the conference, serves neither a city nor a state but the kinky exurbia of Marin County, California. The gathering in Seattle provided an exception to any single definition. Almost all alternative weeklies are tabloids that use their front page as a sort of two-color magazine cover; *Willamette Week,* of Portland, Oregon, is about the shape, if not the thickness, of the *New York Times.* Although almost all are small independent businesses, the three *Advocate* papers in Connecticut and Massachusetts constitute a small chain, and two alternative weeklies, like two of almost everything else, were purchased recently by Larry Flynt. Just about all alternative weeklies are directed at readers who were born after the Second World War, but the Seattle paper that organized the conference, the *Weekly,* has a readership with a median age of thirty-six. Some alternative weeklies and some of their staffs did evolve from the underground press; names like *Steppin' Out* or *Creative Loafing* remain, like vestigial plumage, from the sixties. But some of them, like the San Francisco *Bay Guardian* and *Maine Times* and the *Pacific Sun,* were founded ten or fifteen years ago by people who spent the early sixties as daily newspapermen rather than as graduate students—people who actually took the fling newspaper reporters have always spoken of in boozy fantasies on days when the assignment seemed particularly boring or the deskmen particularly thickheaded. The working title that the Seattle conferees finally decided on was the National Association of Newsweeklies, which sounds to me like the managing editor of *Time* meeting the managing editor of *Newsweek* for lunch to talk about why their covers so often turn out to have the same person on them. It also fails to describe one of the most successful papers at the conference—the *Reader,* of Chicago, which considers itself more of a features weekly and is particularly proud of having run a nineteen-thousand-word piece on beekeeping in the Chicago area.

As reluctant as I am to give up the word "alternative," I can sympathize with the efforts of any journalistic enterprise to put as much distance as possible between itself and the underground press. With one or two exceptions, I found the underground weeklies I once read to be sloppy collections of rock glop and drug fantasies and political-conspiracy theories—all of which had the appearance of being both undependable and likely to come off on your hands. Five years ago, when a number of weekly-newspaper proprietors attended a meeting in Boulder, Colorado, it was already customary to say that what remained of the underground press was evolving into newspapers run by people who thought of themselves as journalists rather than revolutionaries or harbingers of the New Zonked-Out Millennium. But the survivors of the Boulder meeting who made it to Seattle, editors of *Straight Creek Journal,* of Denver, and *New Times Weekly,* of Phoenix, remember it as being so dominated by the rhetoric of the period—angry speeches by women about to form their own caucus, philosophical arguments pitting people committed to keeping their bodies free of all chemicals against people who had too many chemicals in their bodies to put up much of an argument, long discussions about whether the true goal of journalism was overthrow of the government or getting one's head together—that those few conferees who wanted to exchange information on how to put out a newspaper had to sneak off to the coffee shop for informal discussions. In the past five years, though, an increasing number of American cities have found themselves with a weekly paper that is not so much the source for news of an alternative way of life as the alternative source for news of subjects the daily papers are or should be dealing with. It is the paper that is likely to treat, say, a neighborhood dispute over the opening of an X-rated movie theatre with what amounts to a magazine piece—without a daily paper's restrictions on space or a daily paper's version of objectivity. It is the paper that is likely to carry the sort of unsparing analysis of the new stadium's financial implications which the daily paper might not carry even if its publisher were not one of the stadium's most active boosters.

In Seattle, everybody wanted to exchange information about putting out a newspaper. Just about everyone wanted to talk about taking market surveys and collecting accounts receivable and figuring out the hideous problems of distribution. ("Is there anyone here who has a wholesale distributor who isn't a rotten, monopolistic son of a bitch?") Most alternative newspapers are still small, financially precarious operations, but there are alternative weeklies well enough established to have their own public-relations man or even their own labor strife. On the rare occasion when someone at the Seattle meeting raised the sort of moral question that would have presumably set off a two-hour discussion and several caucuses in Boulder—when, for instance, someone from the *Alaska Advocate* asked whether alternative papers really differed corporatively from the monopolistic daily press they all abhorred—the answer was a quick return to the business at hand. One of the prominent participants in the Boulder conference—the proprietor of an underground press service—showed up with a friend at the Seattle conference for an appearance that was considered significantly brief. Looking more or less like a retired punk rocker and his manager, they made their entrance into a room where forty or fifty respectable-looking people, some of them in tweed sports coats, were discussing such subjects as circulation acquisition. The news-service proprietor and his companion sat down for a few minutes and then quietly took their leave—like a couple of massage-parlor operators who had rushed over to work the largest convention in town without having first bothered to find out that it was a conference of Lutheran liturgists. For the remainder of the conference, they were referred to as "the two gentlemen in costume."

Among the demographic analyses offered in Seattle to explain who reads alternative weeklies, the one I was particularly taken with was what is sometimes called the Rat Through a Python Theory. It is based on the belief that people who were born in the baby boom that started in the late forties and were educated in the late sixties are moving in a self-contained lump through American society, like a rat moving through the body of a python. According to a strict Rat Through Python analysis, underground papers have tended to fade away and the sort of papers represented in Seattle have tended to prolifer-

ate simply because people in what is sometimes called "the demographic bulge" have outgrown rock glop and are now ready for analytical news features—meaning, presumably, that in a few years they will want to read even less about Elton John and much more about how to put hanging plants to the best decorating use. The publisher of an alternative weekly that took a readership survey two years ago which showed an average age of twenty-six is likely to assume that the average age of his readers is now twenty-eight. The Rat Through Python explanation of why the staff of *Straight Creek Journal* has felt a growing acceptance from the respectable citizens of Denver in the past year is not that people in Denver are beginning to become aware of the sort of reporting *Straight Creek* has been doing—a series of investigations into the financing of the Denver Center for the Performing Arts, for instance—but merely that many of its core readers have reached the age of being respectable citizens.

According to the theory, the boom babies provide a strong core readership within what is sometimes called "the upper half of the eighteen-to-thirty-five market" not just because of their numbers but also because of their habits. A lot of them remain in the city —or, at least, in certain cities—instead of settling down in the suburbs, which are considered more the territory of the slick city magazines. (The ability of Boston to support two of the strongest alternative weeklies, the *Real Paper* and the *Phoenix,* is normally explained by the fact that Boston has several hundred thousand residents under the age of thirty-five.) A lot of them remain single, or at least childless. The readers of the *Real Paper* have an average age of twenty-eight, and only fourteen per cent of them are married people with children. (The readership survey of an alternative paper is likely to come close to describing its staff: Of the seventy-five people working in one way or another for the *Real Paper,* only one is both married and living with children.) Having resisted the temptation to toss away their disposable income on mortgages and baby carriages, readers of alternative weeklies have a lot of it to spend on films and restaurants and stereo sets. The results are visible not just in advertisements but in the amount of space alternative weeklies devote to arts and entertainment. The skimpier weeklies represented at the Seattle meeting have not gone much beyond being an entertainment listing; even those that have can tell from surveys that their principal appeal for a lot of readers remains entertainment listings or even entertainment advertisements. The customary way for an established daily to strike back at an alternative weekly that seems to have reached the point of costing it some business is not to begin running longer and livelier features but to publish a weekly entertainment calendar.

These days, most editors of alternative weeklies—even editors who may have once had visions of energizing the proletariat—have accepted the fact that they are putting out what one editor in Seattle described as a special-interest publication for a minority audience. ("Each of us is the FM newspaper in our community.") "The upper half of the eighteen-to-thirty-five market" includes people still in college, of course, but proprietors of alternative weeklies tend to talk more about reaching "urban sophisticates." It is not unusual to hear an editor of an alternative weekly describe the age and education and purchasing power of his readership by saying that his paper has "upscale demographics."

Around the college daily I worked on, the editorial department was always referred to as Upstairs; the people who handled advertising and business matters were Downstairs. The separation was strict, reinforced Upstairs by that weirdly contradictory system of values common to liberal-arts colleges in a capitalist society—the notion that a business career is acceptable for people not quite bright enough for writing and scholarship. Although observers of American press lords may have been puzzled as to why Henry Luce, who was, in effect, the chief executive of a huge corporation, bore only the title of editor-in-chief, the reason was never in doubt to anyone who shared with Luce the experience of working on that college daily: He obviously couldn't bear to think of himself as Downstairs. Magazines are sometimes started by Downstairs types—a number of the city monthlies, in fact, were started by the local Chambers of Commerce—but Upstairs people start weekly newspapers.

The place to start them used to be a small town. The motivation usually had something to do with liberation from the constraints of a big-city daily. But a lot of irritations connected with a big-city daily are also present on a small-town weekly. City dailies are weighed down with the baggage of being the newspaper of record—the water-board-meeting reports and the United Fund-drive results and the routine economic statistics from Washington—but, for its own territory, a weekly in a small town is just as much a newspaper of record as the New York *Times*. A small-town weekly is likely to be thought of by its readers as a receptacle for more or less official notices rather than as an independent news-gathering organization—so that people in small towns, whether discussing a visit by out-of-town grandchildren or a potentially controversial real-estate transaction, may ask one another, "Are you going to put it in the paper?" The problem of a big-city daily's being a loyal member of the community it is supposedly examining—the problem represented by the publisher's having been among those civic leaders who decided over lunch at a downtown club that a new stadium would be a great boon for the citizenry—is not much different in a small town, except that the civic leaders, not having a downtown club, make their decisions over morning coffee in a Main Street café. For a reporter who thrives on issues and controversies, the significant difference may be that the small-town decisions have to do with matters of less interest. There are a few small-town weeklies whose editors manage, in the tradition of Hollywood films, to battle the entrenched interests and print the social notes from outlying hamlets at the same time—the *Mountain Eagle,* of Letcher County, Kentucky, is probably the best known —but most of the small-town weeklies I have seen across the country turn out to be routine appendages to a small printing business.

John Cole, the co-founder of *Maine Times,* once told me that one of the greatest freedoms he felt running a statewide weekly was freedom from the stories he did not have to print. The metropolitan weeklies that have developed in the past five years or so have found the same sort of freedom: They are not the newspaper of record or a stalwart of the Chamber of Commerce, but, like a statewide weekly, they exist in a place large enough to provide plenty to write about. They can exist in a large city partly because offset printing has made it easier to start a newspaper from scratch—only one of the thirty newspapers represented in Seattle owns a printing press—and partly because "the upper half of the eighteen-to-thirty-five market" provides definable readership with special interests. It may be that the baby boom, among its other cultural effects, has made the traditional fantasy of disaffected reporters a practical possibility—without, of course, changing the traditional long hours and the traditional threat of bankruptcy.

The reporter involved, people at the Seattle meeting seemed to agree, has to be willing to spend a lot of time running what one of them summed up as "a small business with a limited access to capital." When a few of the conference participants were interviewed on public television in Seattle, Bruce Brugmann, the editor of the San Francisco *Bay Guardian,* was asked how he accounted for the success of his newspaper—a weekly that recently forced the withdrawal of a Presidential appointment and has over the years persuaded a significant number of San Franciscans that what was happening to their business district was not economically stimulating redevelopment but destructive "Manhattanization." Brugmann's explanation of the *Bay Guardian'*s success was direct: He had a view of commerce inherited from a father and grandfather who ran a small-town pharmacy in Iowa, he said, and his wife happens to be a first-rate businesswoman. In three days of discussions by editors whose newspapers have published some remarkable prose, the only passage I can remember hearing quoted was from a lawyer's letter that *Gris Gris,* a weekly in Baton Rouge, sends to advertisers who have not paid for their ads. (The lawyer threatens the deadbeats with legal actions "that will amaze and astound you.") The editorial workshop at the conference seemed to turn rather quickly in the direction of editorial payrolls. The participants seemed untroubled about paying their writers less than their advertising salesmen, on the theory that a lot of people will write articles for fun or glory but nobody will sell advertisements for any reason other than money. In a small business, how much of the budget to spend for freelance articles is a decision more or less the same as how much to spend for office rental. The person who makes it, even if he is also the person who writes the editorials, is Downstairs.

Magazines

In the history of American communications, magazines took longer than any other media to reach mass proportions. Postal rates, distribution problems, inadequate printing operations, lack of advertising revenue, high subscription cost, and a predominately genteel, literary tone kept most American magazines from attaining impressive national circulation figures until the late nineteenth century. In 1885, for example, nearly 145 years after the publication of the first American magazine, only four general interest monthlies could claim circulations of 100,000 or more. But within ten years the magazine business was booming. An inexpensive, combination mail-order catalogue and home magazine, *Comfort,* was selling well over a million copies per issue and a number of other, more legitimate, general-interest magazines enjoyed circulations that would have amazed editors a generation before. The total number of American magazines was also increasing at an exhilarating pace: from 575 in 1860 to 5,100 in 1895.

What accounted for the sudden growth of this new, mass media industry? One important factor, of course, was that along with a sharp rise in national literacy went a corresponding cultural propensity among the general public to read more of everything. It was a period in which three-volume and sometimes even four-volume novels could turn into best sellers. But other, more specific, factors played a crucial role in generating the preconditions for the mass magazine industry: more lenient postal regulations and eventually rural free delivery; more stringent copyright laws; radical improvements in printing technology, especially in the linotype and photo-engraving processes; the manufacture of cheaper paper; and the enormous impact of national, brand-name, glossy, full-page advertising.

But probably the single most important factor was the sudden reduction in cost per issue. Most of the older, traditional magazines cost between twenty-five and thirty-five cents, a price that, at the time, limited their market to the fairly affluent. In the depression year 1893, one of the new popular magazines, *Munsey's*, with a solid circulation of 40,000, cut its cover price to ten cents. Other magazines soon followed suit and many began to increase circulation at unprecedented rates; by 1895, *Munsey's* circulation jumped astoundingly to 500,000, and a younger rival, *McClure's,* surged from 8,000 to 250,000 in the same two years.

Impressed by such gigantic strides in circulation, advertisers began to invest more heavily, which in turn resulted in even greater circulation. In 1903, *Ladies Home Journal* became the first general magazine to exceed a circulation of one million; six years later, the *Saturday Evening Post* reached the same magic mark. It was no coincidence that both of these magazines contained an exceptionally high number of advertisements.

Around the same time that circulation records were being set and broken on a monthly basis, magazines also started to take on a more active journalistic role. Aggressive editors and a new breed of magazine reporters began to coordinate talent and efforts to produce a series of investigative articles on corruption in American corporate and political life—a "new journalism" that Theodore Roosevelt in 1906 labeled "muckraking." By World War I, heavily illustrated, oversized, advertisement-packed mass magazines, with a heavy contemporary emphasis—both progressive and moderate—had become an inseparable part of American cultural and business life.

Throughout the twenties, thirties, and forties, general magazines survived the competition from radio largely by keying their issues to photo-journalism and focusing editorial matter on entertainment and celebrities. As movies grew increasingly popular in the late twenties and thirties, magazines discovered a profitable form of media tie-in: close-ups and pictorial "interviews" of movie stars. By the time *Life* and *Look* magazines got started in the late thirties, the photo-essay of a current screen star, or, better yet, a promising starlet, had become a fixture of the magazine world. Although the total number of general magazines rose from 57 in 1920 to 104 in 1946, by the late forties, the number of "big books" (as they were known in the industry) began to drop gradually as the "moving" photo-journalism of television began to compete with magazine "stills" for public attention. By the mid-fifties, advertisers had begun to pull out of magazines, concentrating instead on electronic commercials.

In this section's opening essay, "Magazines and the Fragmenting Audience," media scholar Don R. Pember outlines the reasons behind the collapse of the mass magazine and analyzes the current trend to specialty periodicals. As Pember points out, one of the crucial factors behind the demise of the mass magazine has been the advertiser "who pays the bulk of the cost" and who has begun to turn to magazines that promise to deliver more selective audiences of consumers.

In all media decisions, advertisers and agencies have come increasingly to rely on statistical research for information on audience composition, demographic data, newsstand and subscription sales, and—a key statistic in the industry—the average readers-per-copy (r. p. c.) of a magazine. This information is primarily the domain of the W. R. Simmons Market Research Bureau, Inc., which audits the magazine industry in much the same way that A. C. Nielsen monitors television. Since magazines require advertising for their economic survival, and since advertisers depend heavily upon market research figures, magazines, too, must concern themselves with the numbers. Specialty magazines, which appeal to homogeneous readerships (such as joggers, antique collectors, golfers, gardeners), are more likely to succeed in today's market because they can deliver what advertisers are looking for—the most accurately targeted audience for a particular product. That means that a jogging magazine, for example, does not come into existence simply because large numbers of people are jogging; rather, because large numbers of people are jogging, a clearly definable market for sportswear and equipment can be delivered to advertisers through the magazine. In "The Magazine Industry: Developing the Special Interest Audience," Benjamin M. Compaine argues that certain types of magazines succeed when "the editorial matter centers around the activities of the readers themselves and the advertising usually is an extension of the editorial content."

To be sure, the limited audience magazines have not put mass audience magazines entirely out of business. In part, the mass magazine can assimilate different types of advertising, whereas the special interest magazine, given its restricted editorial stance, will necessarily eliminate many major advertisers: cigarette companies will avoid health and fitness magazines; certain household products will shun the pages of *Ms.*; few reputable consumer goods manufacturers want to be associated with magazines like *Violent World.* Moreover, mass magazines can specialize, to some extent, by putting out separate geographic or demographic editions so that advertisers can feel more secure about the type of reader they are getting for their money. To stay competitive in the marketplace, for example, both *Time* and *Newsweek* now publish special editions with advertising targeted to specific income groups, though the overall demographic audience for these magazines is essentially the same. In "Fierce Rivals: *Newsweek* versus *Time*," David Shaw takes a close look at how an intense and longstanding competition—for advertising dollars, for readers, for news—has shaped two of America's most influential and durable mass audience magazines.

Besides acquiring the demographic numbers that attract advertisers, magazines are also dependent upon retail distribution and display. Publishers know that future subscriptions are often sold at the newsstand, and high display visibility is crucial. Cover image, therefore, can be a critical sales feature. In fact, in the hyped-up world of mass market magazines, "coverage" has increasingly become synonymous with "cover," as Peter S. Greenberg's article, "Star Wars," makes clear. Greenberg points out that even *Time* and *Newsweek* "now compete for personality covers the way they once competed for news." He believes that many serious magazines have bartered away editorial control in the interests of expanding their celebrity coverage. The result has been to blur the distinction between journalism and publicity.

If *Newsweek* and *Time* represent the magazine industry's most sophisticated product, then, by critical consensus, its trashiest, bottom-of-the-line product has long been the comic book. Since their evolution from newspaper comic strips ("funnies") in the 1930s, comic books have, for the most part, been viewed as a social and cultural nuisance: at their worst, trashy, violent, and morally dangerous to young people; at best, extremely low-level, harmless entertainment. Either way, comic books represent the magazine industry and the mass media's degree zero, where all prejudices, pieties, traditions, and character-types are frozen into their most rudimentary level of expression.

Yet, as our concluding selection, "The Mad Generation" by Tony Hiss and Jeff Lewis, clearly demonstrates, students of mass communication and culture should give comics serious thought. For one thing, they frequently display a sophisticated artistry with a complex media history of their own. For another, comics often serve the same function that Daniel Boorstin claims for advertising; that is, they are an important substitute for folklore in a highly industrialized society. And the myths comics trade on, the gratifications they supply, are as tightly bound up with other forms of mass media as is Superman's strength with the mysterious planet Krypton.

25
Magazines and
the Fragmenting Audience

Don R. Pember

The most dramatic trend in contemporary magazine publishing has been away from general mass magazines toward special interest publications. In 1971, *Look,* a family magazine with a circulation over seven million, folded. It could no longer compete with television as a medium for mass entertainment. Moreover, advertisers began to invest in smaller magazines (such as *Psychology Today* and *Money*) that would deliver more selective audiences. In the following chapter from *Mass Media in America,* Don R. Pember, of the School of Communications at the University of Washington, describes the economic and cultural factors that led to the virtual extinction of the American mass magazine.

What is the most striking and profound change in American mass media today? As we will see [. . .] the media themselves are undergoing important and sometimes radical technological development. But the changes in the *media* are not the most significant changes; it is the change in the *mass,* or at least our perception of the *mass,* that is having the most profound impact upon communications industries in this nation. In simple and understandable terms, the mass audience is beginning to disintegrate, fall apart, crumble.

The readers of our newspapers, books, and magazines, television and movie viewers, and radio listeners exist today in a state of disarray that could not be found just thirty years ago. No more is the audience being perceived as one big lumpenproletariat. The mass is beginning to fragment into hundreds of smaller parts. And this fragmentation is being reflected in media tastes and preferences as well as in consumer goods and services.

In the 1930s, as far as American media merchants were concerned, the audience for newspapers, radio, movies, magazines, and other media was perceived as a single mass. Oh, yes, it was recognized there were tiny groups at either end of this mass that displayed some extreme characteristics. The poor and uneducated were at one end; the very wealthy, highly educated elite were at the other. But the primary audience was in the middle. And we created a media culture or milieu to suit the needs of these folks. Advertisers aimed their messages at these consumers, the average Americans. There was evidence to suggest that it was the correct perception of the audience. Mass attendance at the movies was very high. Giant urban daily newspapers maintained circulations above or approaching the millions. Network radio reached tens of millions of listeners each night. Brand-name products attained sales never before dreamed of. Truly, these were *mass* media, reaching a mass society with a mass culture.

Now whether this kind of society actually existed or not is fairly unimportant. Adver-

Source: From *Mass Media in Media,* by Don R. Pember. © 1981, 1977, 1974 Science Research Associates, Inc. Reprinted by permission of the publisher.

tisers believed it, so publishers and broadcasters acted as though it were the case. This philosophy became the operational basis for the mass media. Reaching as many people as possible became equated with success and made possible the premium advertising rates the media charged. This was the period when the ratings first began. How many are listening or reading or watching? The number—not who they were—was the key.

Sometime between the end of World War II and now things began to change, slowly at first, more drastically later. And today the inherent goodness of the mass is no longer taken for granted. Today there are those who question whether the mass audience really exists—or ever existed. Today the key to success is not the number of people who are listening or watching or reading—but in getting the right people to listen or read or watch. The mass has begun to fall apart.

Why?

In a 1973 article [see "Audiences," p. 17] in the *Public Opinion Quarterly,* sociologist Richard Maisel suggests that the United States has moved from an industrial society to a post-industrial society, which is characterized by increased specialization and the growth of service industries. In such a society, he asserts, the populace tends to fragment into segments with various interests and various concerns—a differentiated culture, according to Maisel. In *The Power to Inform,* Jean–Louis Servan–Schreiber makes the same argument: "Americans today find that, as a result of an era of progress from which their country benefited before any of the other industrialized nations, their immense, reputedly homogeneous society of 200 million individuals is fragmenting." He tries to explain this phenomenon by suggesting that it is caused by increased job specialization that requires publications for fields of interest, the assertion of new freedoms and tastes, an increase in liberal education with its concurrent multiplied and varied curricula, and fussy consumers who are more specific in their tastes and desires. But we really don't need social scientists to explain this phenome-

non. Just look around you. America in the eighties is a nation in which a majority of the population has more money to spend than ever before and a great deal more leisure time in which to spend it. Gone are the ten- or twelve-hour, six-day work weeks. Seven hours a day, five days a week is more common today. And three-day weekends abound. To do those jobs around the house we have assembled an arsenal of gadgets and tools to make the work simple and less time-consuming. We are better educated today; our horizons on life and its many diversions have been significantly broadened.

Americans like to do things with other people today; in a sense we have become a nation of "joiners." Many of us are no longer satisfied to identify ourselves either as individuals (which was a common American trait for the better part of our history) or as part of the entire society. We seek to be something more than a single person but clearly less than the common mass. We are young, middle-aged, or old. Many of us find an attachment to a racial or ethnic minority more important than a status as an American. We are Easterners or Southerners or Westerners or Texans or Californians—and proud of it. We are environmentalists, runners, women's liberationists, part of the counter culture, Jesus freaks, skiers, sports car enthusiasts, concerned parents, swinging singles; we collect stamps and coins and beer cans and model trains and antique cars and nostalgia items; we ski, surf, hike, climb mountains, scuba dive, sail, camp, fish, hunt, bowl, golf, ice skate, and swim.

American industry—including the mass media—has responded to these changes in our society. Leisure activities have grown rapidly in the past decade with hundreds of new golf courses, par courses, bowling alleys, pool parlors, racquetball clubs, tennis clubs, and boating and yachting clubs sprouting up in all parts of the nation. Scores of what were once strictly luxury items have become required hardware in most middle-class homes. From the vast array of electric grooming gimmicks and kitchen gadgets to more expensive power tools, stereos, cameras, and creative playthings, Americans are buying and buying and buying.

The leisure time and consumer interests of the American people have provided a fertile field for the mass media in this country. There are a great many more things for the media to talk about today and a great many more personal interests to appeal to. And there are a great many more products to advertise. But the significant fact in all this is that while these new interests and new products appeal to a great many people, they are not appealing to the mass. Lots of people are interested in running, but not everybody or even the majority. So a large-scale proliferation of the media has occurred to take advantage of these minority interests.

All this happened at about the same time advertisers were beginning to grouse about the high cost of advertising—especially since many of their product messages were being seen by people who weren't likely to buy these products. Many advertisers tried to isolate these minority groups through specialized media and reduce their costs at the same time. For example, an airline that sought to sell the advantages of flying to Hawaii for the holidays could put an ad in *Reader's Digest* and reach many potential customers among the twenty million or so readers of the magazine. But for less than one-quarter of the cost the same ad could appear in *Holiday* magazine and reach nearly four million people, most of whom by virtue of their purchase of the magazine have a strong interest in traveling. An advertisement for an expensive aftershave lotion might reach twenty million men if it were carried in *TV Guide*. But for far less money, the advertiser could place an ad in *Playboy,* and while the ad might not reach as many men, the millions of readers of that expensive and pseudosophisticated magazine for men would be far better prospects for the purchase of costly toiletry items than the general audience of *TV Guide.*

With some products it makes little difference who is in the audience; everybody buys aspirin and toothpaste. But it is foolish to advertise sailing equipment to a general audience when you are after sailors or at least people who live near the water. Why attempt to sell hearing aids to a mass audience? Your real target is the elderly. How many members of the general audience are in the market for a Jaguar or Lincoln Continental—both $30,000 automobiles? You want to aim at an affluent market.

The trend in marketing toward smaller, "better" audiences for many advertising messages has made the proliferation in the media possible. Alternatively, the proliferation of media has made the narrow, specialized advertising messages possible.

But this change in philosophy has not only spawned new media, it has forced older established media to specialize and develop a new image—or else. The seven million or so readers of *Look* magazine appeared quite happy with the product being published by the Cowles Communication Company. It was the advertisers who no longer wanted to shell out the big bucks necessary to get a message in the mass circulation magazine. When the advertising support died so did the magazine. The same was true with *Colliers',* the *Post,* and *Life.* The demise of many large urban daily newspapers can also be tied at least partially to the advertisers' desire for smaller suburban papers to carry their message at lower costs to the new affluents in the suburbs.

The magnates of network television, the editors of the few remaining metropolitan daily papers, and the publishers of a dwindling handful of general interest magazines are the only people in recent years who have operated their media as if a mass audience existed. Everyone else has become more and more content with getting to fewer people with something they know will interest them.

The ultimate expression of satisfying the diverse interests of the fragmented audience lies in the near future with the development of "a la carte" information channels. While these media changes will be discussed more fully in the final chapter of the book, let us note at this point that it will soon be technically possible for you or I to select the content of our news or information media like we now select dinner items from a restaurant menu. The press will send out its information menu on one channel of a multi-channel information system to a television-like device in the home. The menu or index will represent all the material that is stored in the newspaper or magazine's computer. The medium-user will select which items he or she would like to read. If all the user wants is sports, that is all that would be taken; or perhaps just local news, or specific local stories; or maybe only the comics, the stock market returns, fashion news, or whatever. The user or reader will be able to create what we would now call a newspaper or magazine to satisfy his or her specific tastes or interests. This is the ultimate in serving the fragmented audience. As this [. . .] was being written the first generation of this equipment became a reality to the people of Columbus, Ohio. Subscribers to the *Columbus Dispatch* who own a home computer terminal can have the paper beamed into their homes via telephone lines. Reader-selected stories are flashed on a television screen upon request. Advertising messages were to follow in coming months.

Some view this system quite positively. They see it as a kind of technological Valhalla which will satisfy the wants and needs of a self-oriented people. But others view this prospect—and indeed most attempts to satisfy the fragmented audience—more ominously. Dominique Wolton, a European journalist who investigated the technological developments in American media, found the potential changes frightening. Selecting and providing information to an audience is the essential journalistic task, Wolton wrote in the *Columbia Journalism Review.* The "a la carte" periodicals of the future that allow the audience to do the selection preempt this task —and this is a serious break with an important tradition. "Since the eighteenth century, the press has struggled to offer the most general information possible to as wide a public as possible," he noted. "The availability of universal information is one of the gains of the democratic era." Wolton adds:

> We all know that we learn things by coming across them unexpectedly. Read "by chance" is one of the high roads to culture. It is also a way to communicate. This is especially so in the United States, where the newspaper has linked different ethnic and racial groups by providing them with a shared experience and a shared knowledge of their environment. What

will remain of this democratic function when each person reads—or punches up on the console—only what his or her information needs require?

Wolton argues that the proliferation of diverse kinds of information is not synonymous with democracy. And he expressed a fear that the "a la carte" press of the future may only serve to reinforce existing social divisions.

Wolton and other thoughtful observers raise the specter of social isolation through reliance upon only specialized information. The current phenomenon of single-issue politics—where groups and organizations oppose or support political candidates or political parties because of their stand on but a single issue —might be an early manifestation of the problems cited by Wolton. The social and political isolation generated by exposure to only narrow and specialized information is bound to make both communication and governance more difficult. The lack of shared interests, values, goals, and basic assumptions can make compromise, understanding, and ultimately political agreement impossible to reach. The result could be a system of national governance similar to the United Nations today, where it is all but impossible to reach consensus on anything but the most mundane issues. In the past the mass media have provided the people of the nation with a common body of information, ideas, and even values, out of which we have woven a kind of national fabric. This could change radically in the future; we see the beginnings of these changes now.

In order to understand the magazine industry today we need to look back to the 1950s when the giant, general interest magazines like *Life, Post,* and *Look* were at their peak. Interestingly the tremendous growth of the special-interest magazines during the past three decades resulted from the same forces that spelled the ultimate doom of the mass circulation magazines. But few people realized this in the post-World War II era; least of all some of the publishers of the mass magazines.

> The power of *Look* is that it spans the whole universe of interests. It is a platform of all

Americans to turn to, to learn about the basic issues, the real gut issues of the day . . . It is information and entertainment for the whole family.

Those words were uttered in 1970 by Thomas R. Shepard, Jr., the publisher of *Look* magazine in a speech to magazine editors and publishers. In little more than a year the magazine was dead, gone, defunct. It was all over. Despite predictions of impending death of the publication, its sudden demise still took many by surprise. What happened? Were readers no longer interested in a platform they could turn to for the real issues of the day? Or didn't the magazine provide this platform? Didn't the audience seek an informative and entertaining magazine for the entire family? There is no evidence to suggest that any of these factors had much to do with the death of *Look*. It appears, at least, that most of its millions of readers (circulation rested at about seven million when it died) were pleased with the magazine.

Why did it die then? Basically because advertisers weren't too happy with the product. And of course this is the primary constituency for magazines today. It's the advertiser who pays the bulk of the cost of the magazine.

Look was not the first magazine to die during this century. The dirge of the doomed that came before the sprightly picture magazine included *Colliers'*, the *Saturday Evening Post, Coronet, American, Woman's Home Companion,* and others. And, of course, since the demise of *Look, Life* has faded away as well—a victim of the same advertising-oriented illness. *Post, Life,* and even *Look* have reappeared since their demise in the sixties and seventies. *Look* died a second time in 1979, and *Life* and *Post,* issued monthly, command a small audience compared to their earlier circulation. Neither has an audience that places it in the top 50 circulation leaders (which includes such titles as *Boy's Life, Today's Education* and *Scouting*). In managing editor Ralph Graves's final editorial, he wrote that *Life* was a magazine that had attempted to talk to readers across special interests. "We don't want to reach you as skiers, or teenagers, or car owners, or TV-watchers, or

single women, or suburbanites, or inhabitants of New York City, or blacks or whites. Instead," he wrote, "we wanted to talk to you as people, who share a common experience of humanity." But it was not to be. Today we are left with but two truly general audience national publications—*Reader's Digest* and *TV Guide.*

Two Sunday supplement magazines aimed at the general audience have died in the past fifteen years as well—*This Week* and the *American Weekly.* Two mass audience supplements remain—*Parade* and *The Family Weekly*—in a once crowded market. In addition, the black-oriented supplement *Tuesday* is being distributed with many Sunday papers.

The demise of the mass magazines is not a simple thing to explain. It involves at the very least the content of the magazine, the audience, and perceptions of advertisers. At one time the mass mags had a good thing going for them. Forty years ago if a person wanted a graphic and visual depiction of an important happening or event, he went to a magazine to find it. For example, in the forties, the nation saw the first pictures of its war dead when *Life* magazine published a full page black and white photo of American G.I.'s lying crumpled on the beach of some far-off Pacific island. And if you wanted in-depth and personal reportage, again it was the mass magazine you looked toward.

Short stories and the serialization of novels were another staple of the mass mags in their heyday. Much of the nation's important literature first saw the light of day in publications like the *Post* or *Colliers.*

But today television has taken over the role of presenting the nation with a visual report of what is happening here and abroad. And to most people moving pictures that talk as well have more impact than still photos. In-depth reporting is also no longer found exclusively in the magazines. Both newspapers and television have begun to use this technique as well. And first radio, and then television, usurped the magazine's role as the primary source of fiction for the masses. What happened to the mass magazines, then, was that they lost a good deal of their reason for being. Many editors denied this. As late as 1970

Look's Shepard argued: "The entire demographic thrust of our nation is in the direction of a merger of interest, of the elimination of extremes at both ends and a massive gathering together toward the middle . . . I see an especially bright future for the publications that bring various groups of Americans together in a climate of mutual interests and shared concerns."

At the same time the *Look* publisher was saying this, advertising men were arguing that the better educated people become, and the more leisure time and money people have, the more discriminating they become in their media usage habits. A shot-gun editorial approach just isn't worth that much to them.

The financial data seemed to support the adman. In the *Columbia Journalism Review* (August 1971), former *Life* editor Chris Welles noted: "The most financially successful magazines of the past ten years have been designed to appeal to highly particularized intellectual, vocational, and avocational interests and are run by editors who know exactly what they are saying, and to whom they are saying it." The examples cited by Welles were numerous, but included the *Cosmopolitan* girl, *New York*'s urban dwellers, the popular science fans of *Psychology Today, Playboy*'s so-called sophisticated males, and so forth. Madison Avenue believes rightly or wrongly that a magazine lacking a specific, well-defined purpose is not really "needed" by its readers. And a publication that is not needed is a poor advertising vehicle. Media specialists pointed out, for example, that the newsstand sales of *Life* dropped from 2.5 million copies in 1947 to little more than 200,000 in 1971. This was an important statistic to the adman, who interpreted newsstand sales as a deliberate and conscious effort by the reader to buy the magazine at the premium newsstand price. Other important factors were these: In the last years one-third to one-half of all *Life* advertising was for cigarettes and liquor—two commodities that could not be sold on television. In 1972 *Life* advertising revenues were only $91 million, just a little more than half of the $170 million in 1966. Author Welles wrote in 1973: "It *(Life)* had become a kind of weekly Edsel, and it was simply rejected by the marketplace."

But the "need" factor was not the only problem that faced the magazine. Another thing mass magazines had been able to do well for many years was to present a graphic and colorful advertisement to a great many people at one time. While many advertisers were interested in the special audience, some were still concerned with selling to the masses —something magazines could do. But television began chipping away at this stronghold as well. It could reach more people and present a more graphic advertisement for many products. Magazines responded by trying to increase their circulation to compete in the numbers game with TV. When the *Post* died, *Life* bought its subscribers, pushing its circulation to 8.5 million, which is a readership of more than 25 million since it was established that three persons read each copy. But to sell the magazine to this many people the price of a full-page ad went up to more than $64,000, which was more costly than a minute on prime-time television. The result: *Life* sold 13 percent fewer pages of advertising in the year after the circulation hike. In addition to a higher cost per advertising message, magazines lost in the cost per thousand race as well. It cost an advertiser about $7.75 to reach 1000 advertisers via *Life*. A seller could reach a thousand television viewers for only $3.60, about half as much.

To boost their advertising, *Life, Look,* and *Reader's Digest* went to General Foods in 1969 and suggested that the giant brand-name manufacturer conduct a study of the value of magazine advertising. The three mass circulation magazines even agreed to help finance the project. The results of the study showed that magazines could be effective advertising and selling vehicles and stimulated some advertising money. But in 1970 when Procter and Gamble, General Foods, Bristol-Myers, and Colgate-Palmolive—the big four brand names—spent $434 million in TV advertising, they spent only about one-tenth that much in all magazines.

The mass mags tried other ploys in an effort to salvage part of the market. If bigger circulation wasn't the answer because it sent costs up, why not intentionally cut circulation, which would in turn cut costs? This would permit a reduction in per page advertising rates. Many magazines did this, aiming to trim those subscribers on the bottom end of the economic scale. This was not a particularly easy task, and precision was often lacking. Before its death, the *Post* cut none other than Winthrop Rockefeller, former governor of Arkansas, from its list of subscribers.

Another device used by some magazines to trim costs was to cut the size of the magazine —not the number of pages, but their size. *Esquire* did this successfully in the early part of this decade, trimming many thousands of dollars from its production and mailing costs while maintaining the same subscription and advertising rates.

But with all the devices, the evidence had been clear for some time that the future of mass magazines was not too bright. Even the magazines themselves had admitted it in a backhanded way by allowing advertisers to buy space in less than the entire circulation of the magazine. This is done in several ways. Most mass circulation magazines, both the general interest and the specialized ones, publish regional editions. The editorial content is generally the same but there are pages devoted to regional advertisers at rates far below the price of an ad that is carried in all editions. For example, before it died, *Life* charged $64,200 for a four-color full-page ad. But a Minnesota company interested in reaching only people in that state could have run a four-page ad in the 150,000 copies circulated in Minnesota for only about $2500. In 1969 *Life* was publishing 133 regional editions and *Look* 75. This device vastly increases the number of advertisers who can use the magazine. Many companies don't want to advertise nationally because they don't distribute nationally. The cost reduction also makes it possible for those national firms that seek to advertise in several but not all regions to be selective and place their ads at a much lower rate.

Another means the mass mags have of using audience fragmentation to their advantage is through what are called "demographic breakouts"; that is, allowing an advertiser to aim an ad at a specific subgroup or fragment in the mass audience. For example, before it died *Look* had one breakout called Top Spot—

1.2 million readers with an average annual income approaching $24,000. An advertiser who was selling a luxury item—expensive cars or stereo equipment, for example—could have run an ad only in this breakout where it would be seen by consumers most able to buy the product. The cost was significantly reduced and the advertiser got more for the money. Again, the lower costs allowed smaller advertisers who couldn't pay the $60,000 per page price to use the magazine. However, the breakouts are not 100 percent accurate. They are based on Zip codes and census data. In a given town, for example, certain areas house people with higher incomes than other areas. These can be identified by the Zip codes. The Top Spot edition went to these areas. The breakouts are also used to pick out younger or older consumers or suburbanites as opposed to urban dwellers.

A more effective means of accomplishing the same thing, and one that is used with increasing frequency today by some smaller trade magazines, is to give free copies of the magazine to all members of the target audience. For example, assume for a moment that you publish a magazine for physicians. One of the mainstays of your publication is advertising by the pharmaceutical companies. These companies, however, are very concerned that a large number of doctors see their ads. Getting a list of the names of all the doctors in America is a simple task. It would be possible to ask each physician to subscribe to your publication, and if you have a good magazine you might end up with subscriptions from 25 percent of the physicians. Or you could send each doctor a free copy of the magazine each month. This way you could guarantee to your advertisers that 100 percent of the doctors receive the magazine and therefore you could charge much higher advertising rates.

The Magazine Revolution of the Sixties

Despite the emphasis on the negative impact the fragmentation of society has made on the magazine industry, its positive effects have been really far more important. For although we did lose a few familiar faces in the industry, many new ones have popped up. Magazines of all shapes and sizes have been founded in the last two decades in an effort to cope with the expanding interests of the reading public. It is difficult even to enumerate the categories of these new magazines. Think of something that might be interesting to several thousand Americans and you can be fairly certain of finding one or more magazines on that topic.

Consumerism, the province of the highly regarded *Consumer Reports* for decades, has fostered the birth of several consumer-oriented publications, the slickest of which is *Money* from Time-Life. Leisure activities have spurred scores of publications on golf, sailing and boating, climbing and hiking. *Psychology Today,* using a kind of "social sciences for the masses" approach, was successful enough to spawn a handful of imitators as well as to give its publishers the capital to buy *Saturday Review.* Even such esoteric subjects as the occult, which has gained a new prominence, have created a market for magazines about witchcraft and black magic.

Perhaps some of the most spectacular successes in the past ten years have been the regional magazines, more specifically the city magazines. Regional magazines have always existed, many as supplements to Sunday newspapers, a few on their own. *Sunset,* on the West Coast, is a good example of a magazine that has based its appeal on catering to the life styles of the American West. Its monthly sections on food, gardening, and culture are avidly consumed by thousands of readers in California, Oregon, and Washington.

But the city mags are something different. They have been around for a long time, since the late part of the last century. It has been only recently that they have begun to take on any kind of lifelike posture. *The New Yorker,* a sophisticated literary-style magazine for Gotham residents, was really the only successful city magazine for decades. And although it sparked many imitators, none shared its success. Most of the city magazines lacked quality; they had no clearly defined editorial format. Many tried to copy *The New Yorker* with its sophisticated style and content, despite the fact they were circulating in

smaller, less worldly cities in the East and Midwest. They ignored the milieu of their own towns in an attempt to be a New York magazine. None was large enough or had the prestige to attract national advertisers. So most were impoverished from the beginning. Finally, too many of them acted more like publicity releases for the local chamber of commerce than anything else.

Around 1967 a kind of turn-around took place. New magazines began, and many that already existed took on the posture of "civic gadflies." They provided an outlet for tough and perceptive in-depth reports about their towns and cities. A kind of sophisticated muckraking became their standard fare. As one editor put it, "Our job is to plug the city —and to attack the city and its problems." By 1968 there were at least sixty such magazines in the country. Some, like *Detroit* and *West,* were part of large metropolitan newspapers like the *Detroit Free Press* and the *Los Angeles Times.* Others like *Atlanta, Texas Monthly,* and *Philadelphia* were not associated with newspapers but were successfully published on their own.

Because they are well done (for the most part) and well read, such magazines get more support than they have in the past. Some, like *Seattle,* still can't hack it, and fail. But most hold on, giving readers a kind of journalism on the local level that they have come to expect only from national media. They are able to give the kind of depth reports to problems that too many newspapers are reluctant to spend time on. Since style is traditionally important to magazines, their stories are brighter and better written than those in newspapers. And they offer readers colorful artwork and photography about their own home towns— something appealing to many people. Writing in the *Christian Science Monitor,* Kemmis Hendrick has noted: "Handsomely put together, they keep talking about local concerns. In this day of vastly increased regionalism and great world concerns . . . this may prove tremendously important." "The motto of this new type of local magazine journalism is know thyself, and forget other people's cities," noted Bob Abel in a recent *Columbia Journalism Review.*

Magazines Today

The magazine industry in the eighties is large, generally successful, and seemingly growing. There are three broad categories of magazines; consumer magazines, which account for about 60 percent of all periodicals; business, trade, professional, and organizational magazines, which make up about 38 percent of periodicals; and farm magazines, about 2 percent of the business.

In the last thirty years the total number of magazines has gone up about 40 percent. In 1978 there were almost 10,000 different titles published in this country. The last time the Magazines Publishers Association counted total circulation was 1975, and in that year 5.7 billion copies of magazines were printed. This was a one-third increase since 1960.

The magazine business improved in the seventies, after the rather sluggish sixties. A singularly important development in the industry was the decrease in the importance in advertising dollars in total magazine revenues. As late as 1960 advertisers still paid most of the bills for most periodicals with 60 percent of total revenues coming from advertising. By the seventies less than half of total revenue was from advertising. Magazines were beginning to revert to their past and rely more upon subscription revenues. In 1975 the *Ladies' Home Journal* announced that it was earning a true profit on circulation revenues alone—reader revenue exceeded the cost of producing the magazine. This was the first major magazine to reach such a position. Compare this with *Life* magazine, which in the years just before its death, was getting about 12 cents per copy from readers for a magazine that cost 41 cents a copy to edit and print. Many magazines in the seventies sought to sell most of their copies off the newsstand rather than through subscriptions. Success in this distribution method did two important things. First, it provided evidence to advertisers of reader need and reader interest, as opposed to "ritual readership." (A "ritual reader" is a person who gets a magazine by subscription in the mail and may or may not crack it open.) Second, it helped publishers reduce costs. Magazine postal rates went up 413 percent between 1971 and 1979 with more increases in sight. Magazines sold at a newsstand are not sent through the mail. Some of the magazines which have most successfully used newsstand sales are *Family Circle, Women's Day, Playboy, People,* and *TV Guide.* Those magazines that continue to rely upon subscriptions have raised rates dramatically. Benjamin Compaine, in *Who Owns the Media,* estimates that the average annual subscription fee in 1978 was $17.26, up more than 104 percent over the 1970 average of $8.47. These statistics applied to general interest consumer magazines.

Consumer magazines only get about 6 percent of total national and local advertising revenues, considerably less that they got in the thirties and forties, before television began to compete for these revenues. Advertising revenues did increase as the seventies came to an end. In 1978 $2.7 billion was spent on advertising in consumer magazines—up 20 percent from the preceding year. Advertising revenues went up in other media as well, but only by about 15 percent.

The most popular kinds of magazines in the modern era are women's and home service magazines, which command more than 36 percent of total consumer magazine circulation. These were followed by comic books, news magazines, men's magazines, youth magazines, and hunting and fishing periodicals. What magazines had the largest circulation? Here is a list of the 20 top-selling magazines in 1980.

Magazine	*Circulation*
TV Guide	19,881,726
Reader's Digest	18,193,255
National Geographic	9,960,287
Better Homes and Gardens	8,057,386
Woman's Day	7,574,478
Family Circle	7,366,482
McCall's	6,256,183
National Enquirer	5,719,918
Ladies' Home Journal	5,403,015
Good Housekeeping	5,138,948
Playboy	4,824,789
Penthouse	4,510,824
Time	4,451,816
Redbook	4,234,141

The Star	3,008,948
Newsweek	2,952,515
Cosmopolitan	2,812,507
American Legion	2,597,816
Sports Illustrated	2,343,380
People	2,308,624

There were magazine failures in the seventies. *New Times,* started in 1973 as a kind of counterculture news magazine, died in 1978. Its circulation had been a steady 350,000, its advertising revenues were up slightly, but the magazine was facing sharply increasing costs. With renewals dropping as its old constituency seemed to be breaking up, the publication had to fight for each new subscriber to maintain a circulation level. MCA, the entertainment conglomerate which owned it, let *New Times* die quietly. *Viva* also died in 1979. The magazine had seen a sharp drop in circulation from 700,000 in 1976 to less than 400,000 in 1978. One observer noted that despite a changed format, the magazine could not shake the "beefcake" image it had fostered in the past. Penthouse International stopped the publication of the magazine with the January 1979 issue. There were many other failures as well. But the successes of the late seventies and early eighties are more important.

Perhaps the two most successful magazines of the seventies were *Family Circle,* owned by The New York Times Company and *Woman's Day,* owned by CBS, Inc. Both magazines were born in the Depression and grew steadily with the growth of the suburbs. They are the epitome of the successful magazine of the last quarter of the twentieth century. They are virtually totally newsstand sold —free of the very expensive postal delivery system. The price of the magazine just about pays the cost of the publication. They are heavily oriented toward the basics of life— food, shelter, money, the family. And they specialize in editorial matter that television generally ignores. They are not very pretty. One critic said that the graphics often look as if they have been done with subway car spray paint. But their editorial formula has been tremendously successful. A typical edition of either magazine includes thrift menus, seven new hairdos, decorating and beauty hints, ad-

vice columns, sixteen ways to fix beef stew, dress or clothing patterns, and some home craft ideas. *Woman's Day* claims that almost half of its female readers hold jobs and both magazines offer survival strategies for the staggering inflation of the late seventies and early eighties. One observer called it the "blueing of America"—inflation has made proletarians of a lot of people, and these two magazines meet those needs. Practicality is another hallmark of these magazines. One research study compared the covers of *Woman's Day* and *Family Circle* with those on other women's magazines. Over a two-year period *McCalls* and the *Ladies' Home Journal* carried the faces of personalities or celebrities on 35 of their 48 issues. In the same period *Woman's Day* and *Family Circle* had 14 food covers; most of the remaining covers were devoted to dolls, holiday crafts, flowers, or candles. These two magazines are not only successful themselves—they set a pattern for other magazines. Although focusing upon different topics, Time, Inc.'s *People* has used many of the same marketing strategies as the two successful women's magazines.

People began publication in 1974 and made a profit after only 18 months. It was the first successful national weekly magazine launched in almost 30 years. It has already spawned one competitor—*Us,* established by the New York Times Company, but sold to Macfadden Publications in 1980—and ranked twentieth in circulation in 1978. Media critic Edwin Diamond wrote that "*People* is a weekly celebration of the new entertainers of our post-industrial society. It is a magazine for people who don't want to read too much about the stars. . . . *People* makes few demands; it can be dealt with like television." The profiles in the magazine are short, usually no more than 400 words. And although the cover is always colorful and eyecatching, the inside of the magazine is largely black and white on a low-grade pulp paper. Diamond notes that, "The magazine has surpassed Andy Warhol's prediction that in the future everyone would be famous for fifteen minutes. The personalities of *People* live only until the page is turned."

People was designed as a respectable substitute for the scores of movie magazines and gossip sheets that fill the newsstand, but that most middle Americans were too embarrassed to buy. The content of *People* and a periodical like *Modern Screen* is remarkably similar. Yet those who buy *People* are generally urban, educated, up-scale, high-income consumers who wouldn't be caught dead with a "real" gossip publication. Readers for *People* tend to be younger females, nearly half of whom have attended or graduated from college. Median family household income of *People* readers was more than $20,000 in 1980.

The magazine is sold as scientifically as it was created. Eighty-five percent of the copies are picked up off news racks—generally in check-out lines at supermarkets. Precise positioning of the rack at the counter is the key, according to publisher Richard Durrell. "The strike zone for a sale is between the waist and eyes of the average-height woman and the closer you come to eye level the better chance you have for sales. It is really a matter of inches," he added, noting that the average height of women today is 5 feet 4 inches, or 151 centimeters. In addition to using sophisticated research to help sell the magazine, many of the "new" magazines of the eighties use similar research techniques to aid them in selecting covers and content. *Us,* the competitor to *People,* used the two-way cable television system in Columbus, Ohio, called QUBE to test the audience reaction to five possible cover subjects. The results indicated that people wanted to see John Wayne or The Incredible Hulk on the cover of *Us* rather than Goldie Hawn, Dolly Parton, or Kris Kristoferson.

Considering its relatively short life the success of *People* has been staggering. It reflects the entertainment orientation of much of what is published today, something noted in the previous discussion on newspapers. *People* as well as *Family Circle* and *Woman's Day,* represent the success stories of the past decade. As such these magazines epitomize numerous periodicals that have selected a relatively narrow focus, have developed cost saving distribution methods, that both please advertisers and save the publishers money, and have given readers something they apparently want. They are the new wave of periodicals which filled the void left by the demise of the giant mass magazines. They represent the change in our perception of the audience, the disintegration of the mass into diverse fragments. Chris Welles, a former editor of *Life,* summed it up quite well in 1973 when he attempted to explain the demise of the publication on which he formerly worked:

> Though (the reader) was willing to pay fifty cents or a dollar per issue for magazines he really wanted—magazines that addressed themselves to specific areas of his concern— twenty-five cents was far more than he wanted to lay out for an issue of *Life,* which, in trying to appeal to everybody, ended up, in a sense, appealing to nobody.

26

The Magazine Industry: Developing the Special Interest Audience

Benjamin M. Compaine

By studying magazines according to editorial content and audience profile—the types of information they provide and the kinds of people they reach—Benjamin M. Compaine picks up where the preceding survey of magazine readership left off. "It is the successful development of special interest audiences," Compaine argues, "that has given magazines an expanded major role and enabled them to thrive into the 1980's." Compaine finds the key to the success of the new special interest magazines in their high reader involvement—"subscribers are participants in the subjects being written about."

Benjamin M. Compaine is executive director of Media and Allied Arenas at Harvard University's Program on Information Resources Policy and is the coauthor of *Who Owns the Media? Concentration of Ownership in the Mass Communications Industry.*

Magazines have changed—out of necessity as much as through foresight—into a medium for serving discrete interests within the mass population. The threshold of the 1980s finds the magazine industry having substantially completed a fundamental change. As a modern publishing form, the magazine is barely a hundred years old. For much of their lives, magazines served as the primary mass medium in American society. Now that other media, principally television, have usurped that purpose, magazine publishers are justifying their existence by serving either portions of the entire literate audience, or small groups of readers with intense interest in particular subjects. This change does not mean, as has been reported, that the mass circulation, general interest magazine is dead. It does mean that an increasing proportion of magazines published

—and probably of total magazine circulation —will be accounted for by special interest or limited audience publications.

Magazines evolved because of two unique characteristics that differentiated them from newspapers. First, since they did not have to carry up-to-the minute news, they could rely on more leisurely delivery systems than newspapers, especially to spread-out rural areas. More importantly, in an age before television and radio, they were able to offer advertisers national coverage. As Americans spent increasing amounts of money on raising their material standard of living, magazines benefited from the expanding market for the goods and services advertisers offered.

Throughout the twentieth century, the magazine responded to the dynamics of several factors:

Job specialization. A more complete society creates a need for specialized subgroups of managers, engineers, researchers, and financiers. To meet the needs of these subgroups, many of which do not understand the language of the other, there are special publications tailored to them—the business and professional press.

The assertion of new freedoms and tastes. American society is becoming more permissive, resulting in magazines that have responded to different groups asserting their potential as a new market. This includes the "new" women's magazines like *Ms.,* the city magazines like *Philadelphia,* or the sex magazines, from *Playboy* to the more explicit *Penthouse.* Youth is served as *Rolling Stone* moves beyond rock music to youth culture, while blacks are finding a continually widening range of magazines directed at them.

Spread of education. In the past two decades, higher education has become mass education in the U.S. Half of all high school graduates now go on to college. In the past ten years more than 12 million individuals have received a bachelor's degree (millions more attended college but did not receive a diploma) and the number receiving degrees in the next ten years will be even greater. The result has been the creation of a vast college-educated, literate audience with a multiplicity of personal and intellectual interests.

A consumer haven. With a market as vast and wealthy as that of the U.S., almost any well-presented idea can create a highly lucrative, if limited, submarket for itself.

Increased opportunities to pursue interests. In addition to increased leisure time, Americans have the discretionary income to embrace a wide variety of pursuits, from bowling to camping, furniture building to wine-making. People with similar interests join together, identifying with each other.

The magazine has always faced competition in taking advantage of these changes. In the early years of the century, newspapers and to a lesser extent books were the primary competition. Soon movies became an important form of entertainment. In the twenties, radio swept the nation, unmatched in speed of penetration until television came along be-

ginning in the late 1940s. And inexpensive paperback books, getting under way just before World War II, have become a major form of mass media in the past two decades. *Under this barrage of competition, magazines nonetheless continue to expand, for in many ways each new medium helps the older ones.*

Just as book publishers have learned that a successul movie spurs rather than harms book sales, so magazine publishers have learned to take advantage of television. Popularity of televised spectator sports has stimulated sales of sports magazines, and fast-breaking news on TV has created opportunities for deeper analysis and perspective in the news weeklies (since 1946 the combined circulation of the news weeklies has about quadrupled).

But perhaps the most significant reason for the magazine's survival has been its ability to adopt to a changing role in society. It is no longer needed as a national advertising tool for mass-oriented products; television can simultaneously supply far-flung regions with the same advertisement. Nor is it needed for purely entertainment purposes, as television and the movies satisfy those needs. Whereas most magazines used to be published for a mass readership, today even most of the so-called mass consumer magazines have narrowed their audiences down to smaller proportions.

This trend of specialization applies not only to consumer interests, but also to the diverse information needs of business and the professions, as evidenced by a steadily increasing number of trade magazines with both paid and controlled (sent free to an eligible population) circulations. As with consumer magazines, business magazines serve the need of advertisers who wish to reach a well-defined audience for their product or service.

One indication of this specialization is that the number of magazines has been growing, even though total magazine circulation is fairly level. In 1950 there were 6960 periodicals in the *Ayer Directory of Publications.* By 1978 the number had increased by almost 38 percent, although with deaths and births the actual number of different titles is no doubt much greater. Most of these have been small circulation, specialized publications serving alumni groups, industry associations, clubs, professional societies, and the numerous consumer interests that have emerged. But there has been less growth in total circulation, since it takes many 25,000 and 150,000 circulation magazines to replace the mass circulation versions of *Life, Saturday Evening Post, Look,* and *Collier's.* (Although the first two have reappeared, they are all structured to survive on a smaller circulation than the six or eight million of their predecessors.)

Publishers have always been quick in sensing new interests within the public and then establishing new publications to cater to them. When the movies made Hollywood a center of attention, *Photoplay* appeared and grew into a fat fan magazine. In 1934, with model railroad hobbyists numbering in the hundreds, an entrepreneur put out *Model Railroader,* a magazine whose circulation is now near 175,000. And when, in 1951, the aqualung made underwater adventure available to skilled swimmers, an enthusiast launched *Skin Diver,* now selling 166,000 copies a month.

Whole categories have sprung up to meet new interests, and imitators have joined the successful innovators. By 1980, there were magazines for gamblers, private pilots, brides-to-be, horse breeders, home decorators and fixer-uppers, antique collectors, and followers of politics, sports, news, hair styles, and psychology. Business periodicals exist for food engineers, automotive mechanics, consumer electronics, retailers, and even magazine publishers.

A magazine is one of two things, depending on which side of the newsstand one sits. For the advertiser and publisher, a consumer magazine is little more than the delivery of a market: a market for skiers, smokers, automobile buyers, furniture dusters, *ad infinitum.* A mass circulation magazine must, by its very nature, deliver a generalized market, one that is held together not by any single interest but by some vaguely defined patterns. The readers of these magazines can be identified only by toting up their demographics and trying to come up with some useful groupings. On the other hand, there are magazines that deal with a single product or concept.

Moreover, this product or concept is central not only to the editorial material but also to the bulk of the advertising. Such a magazine is thus able to deliver to an advertiser a specific, highly defined audience.

For the editor and consumer, a magazine is a source of information: what it was like in Atlanta's ballpark when Aaron hit the 715th homerun, why inflation is so high, how to bake chocolate chip cookies, the latest in ski bindings. Notice that the type of information provided, however, is of two types. Much information in magazines is purely for the edification of the reader, included not to be acted on but because it is interesting or entertaining. Contrast this with information that the reader can directly utilize, or even information that exhorts the reader to act. *Tennis* has Ken Rosewall demonstrating "The Way to Improve Your Backhand," and *Apartment Life* offers "Overnight Guests and No Guest Room—What To Do?"

Magazines differ not only in the types of information they provide, but also in the characteristics of the audience they reach. For the purposes of this study, the first criterion—type of information provided—can be divided into two categories: passive and active. Passive information is information intended for the reader's entertainment or general knowledge. Active information, by contrast, is intended for a specific use.

The second difference in magazines, type of audience reached, can be conveniently divided into mass audience and limited audience. Obviously, the subject matter of a magazine might appeal to a vast potential readership or to a very restricted one.

Thus, magazines can be categorized by whether their subject matter is basically active or passive as well as whether the subject is applicable to a relatively mass or limited audience.[1] These divisions are shown in Table 1, which also includes examples of the specific magazines applicable to each block. The term "special interest" is used here to refer particularly to the types of consumer periodicals that fit into the limited audience/active information block in the matrix. General interest magazines are considered to be those that are mass audience/passive interest in content.

Table 1. Sample Magazines by Editorial Content and Type of Audience

	Passive editorial content (median circulation = 668,000)	Active editorial content (median circulation = 406,000)
Mass audience (median circulation = 2.1 million)	Reader's Digest TV Guide People Ladies' Home Journal Sports Illustrated Newsweek Playboy Ebony Esquire National Geographic Psychology Today	Family Circle Better Homes and Gardens Outdoor Life Apartment Life Glamour Popular Mechanics Sports Afield Popular Science
	(median circulation = 3.0 million)	(median circulation = 1.8 million)
Limited audience (median circulation = 339,000)	Saturday Evening Post Harper's New Yorker Ms. New Republic Ellery Queen Mystery Magazine Philadelphia Forbes Rolling Stone Commentary Modern Romance Gourmet	Golf Digest Trains Popular Photography Flying Yachting Ski Modern Bride Camping Journal Antiques Dirt Bike Car & Driver High Fidelity Shooting Times Trailer Life
	(median circulation = 478,000)	(median circulation = 306,000)

Note: Circulation medians derived from 1st six months, 1977 Audit Bureau of Circulation statement.

To grasp the dynamics of special interest magazine publishing, it is necessary to understand the importance of reader involvement, conveyed by the nature of "active" information. Special interest magazines deal primarily with high technology, high performance requirements. A person with a casual or spectator interest in sports may read *Sports Illustrated,* but the serious golfer will likely read *Golf* or *Golf Digest* in addition to, or instead of, *Sports Illustrated.* In fact, the better or more serious an individual is at some particular skill-oriented task, the more likely he or she is to subscribe to a magazine in that field. Special interest magazines are written for the practitioner, general interest magazines for the observer. Of course, there is overlap—the tennis buff who subscribes to *Tennis* has other interests as well and might buy *Time* or *Playboy,* too.

The key is that the special interest publications demand high reader involvement—subscribers are participants in the subjects being written about. In a special interest magazine, the editorial matter centers around the activities of the readers themselves and the advertising usually is an extension of the editorial content. Thus, the special interest magazine is selling a readership of unquestionable homogeneity as related to a specific product or activity, while providing a waiting audience with sought-after information that often results in intense cover-to-cover reading of editorial and advertising content alike. The less a magazine focuses on very specific activities or products, the more it moves into a mass audience category, though it may still be activity-oriented.

Limited audience/passive interest magazines, as noted, share many of the economic and logistical characteristics of the special interest publications. The crucial difference is that the former must rely on demographic data to establish their validity as useful marketing outlets for advertisers. There is no doubt that all magazines can be called special interest to the extent that they involve some concept of varying specificity, and they are limited audience to the extent that not everyone wants to read them. However defined, it is the successful development of special interest audiences that has given magazines an expanded major role and enabled them to thrive into the 1980s.

Note

1. In terms of magazine publishing economics, the major distinction is circulation size, rather than type of audience, in which case *Harper's* has more in common with *Flying* than with *Reader's Digest*.

27
Fierce Rivals:
Newsweek Versus Time

David Shaw

Two mass circulation magazines with general interest coverage that give no signs of becoming extinct are *Time* and *Newsweek.* Read by over forty million Americans every week, they compete intensely with each other (and with *U.S. News and World Report*) for circulation, scoops, and cover stories. The rivalry is made especially fierce, as *Los Angeles Times* staff writer David Shaw points out in the following essay, because both magazines appeal to essentially the same demographic audience. Widely perceived at one time as quite different news magazines, *Time* and *Newsweek* "are probably more alike now than ever before, even as they adapt individually to new societal demands."

Ten years ago, Jonathan Larsen was a reporter in the Los Angeles bureau of Time magazine. Disenchanted with his editors and with his assignments, Larsen threatened to quit.

But Larsen was a talented reporter. He

Source: From *Los Angeles Times* (May 1, 1980). Copyright, 1980, Los Angeles Times. Reprinted by permission of the publisher.

was also the son of the vice-chairman of the Time Inc. board. Instead of quitting, it was suggested, perhaps he might like to come to New York and spend a few months making a formal study of Time. Then he could write a confidential, authoritative report on just what he thought was wrong with the magazine.

Larsen accepted. He went to New York. Three months later, he wrote a 43-page report.

Many Time editors, Larsen wrote, were sycophants; many Time departments were "very erratic and frequently poor"; Time prose was often "mealy-mouthed"; entertainment stories were "identified by one-dimensional shallowness . . . gushy worshipfulness."

The Time editing process, Larsen wrote, encouraged "corporate henpecking"; certain kinds of stories were often published "as much on the basis of internal politics and persuasion as on merit"; the magazine had developed "a tendency to preach, to philosophize and to bore"; staff morale had "slipped into apathy and . . . bitterness."

The result of all this, Larsen concluded, was that Time "is no longer preferred reading among people in their 20s and early 30s. It is not necessarily even preferred reading among its own younger employees. Among the people we know . . . Newsweek is the favored magazine. . . ."

If the trend continued, Larsen warned, "Newsweek will be the number one newsmagazine."

Larsen, now a Nieman fellow at Harvard, admits that he may have been "a little impetuous" in a few of his 1970 judgments. Ten years of maturation and his own experience as a magazine editor (New Times) helped him better understand some of Time's problems, he says.

But Larsen and most other knowledgeable observers still think the alarums he sounded in 1970 were largely justified.

Time had invented the newsmagazine format in 1923, and it had thoroughly dominated the field for 40 years. But in the seven years before Larsen's report, Newsweek's circulation had increased 62%. Its number of pages of advertising had exceeded Time's for two consecutive years and—most important of all—Newsweek had come to be widely per-ceived as the quicker, brighter, better newsmagazine.

Since Larsen's report, Newsweek has continued to have more advertising pages than Time each year—and slowly but steadily increased its share of total Time/Newsweek advertising revenue (from 36.9% in 1968 to 43.7% in 1979). Newsweek also continues to have more readers per copy than Time each week—5.92 people read each copy of Newsweek; 4.67 read each copy of Time.

But Larsen's predictions of Time's decline have not come true. New editors, new departments, new policies and a whole new design have revitalized Time magazine.

Now, a decade after Larsen's grim report, Time still leads Newsweek in circulation (4.25 million to 2.9 million in the United States; 1.5 million to 500,000 abroad), and this has enabled Time to charge higher advertising rates and to earn more advertising revenue (1979 margin: $218 million to $169 million). More significantly, even many past and present Newsweek staff members concede that Time is now—once again—the better newsmagazine.

Interviews with more than 60 past and present staff members at both magazines have produced a surprisingly strong consensus on Time's current narrow superiority—and on what appears to be a nascent comeback at Newsweek.

It is widely agreed, for example, that Time does the better job covering foreign news, science, religion and music, as well as in its overall design, appearance, use of color photography and, generally, in its overall writing and editing.

But Newsweek is thought to be superior in domestic reportage, columns, sports coverage, book reviews and most entertainment cover stories. Despite some lapses, Newsweek has also long been quicker than Time to react to most major news events and social trends.

"Time and Newsweek are a lot like the nightly CBS and NBC news shows," says one man who's worked at both magazines. "They're both damn good at what they do. One week, one is a little better; the next week, the other is a little better. But over the last few years, I think Time, like CBS, has usually been just a little bit better more often."

When this analysis was repeated recently to a high-ranking Newsweek executive, the executive's reluctant response was:

"I don't disagree with your scenario."

Why not? What happened to Jon Larsen's forecast of Newsweek's ascendancy? Why does even Larsen now say Time is better than Newsweek?

Time and Newsweek, now read by 40 million Americans every week, are this country's only general-interest national news publications —read in rural villages and urban metropolises from coast to coast. As such, they are enormously successful—and enormously influential.

President John F. Kennedy used to say the newsmagazines were the single best way to reach large groups of undecided voters on virtually every important issue, and to this day, the White House schedules special weekly briefings for the magazines.

Sometimes, newsmagazines cover stories actually influence government policy. When President Gerald R. Ford reversed his stand on providing federal aid to financially troubled New York City in 1975, it was widely believed in Washington that he had done so largely because both newsmagazines had done cover stories that week on Ronald Reagan, an opponent of the aid bill—and Ford's chief rival for the 1976 Republican presidential nomination.

Although Time and Newsweek both largely disregard the nation's third newsweekly, U.S. News and World Report—which is smaller and different in approach and style—they are fiercely competitive with each other for essentially the same demographic audience. (The median age for Time/Newsweek readers is late 30s; most tend to be married, have some college education and live in a metropolitan area, in a home with an annual income of more than $20,000; about 60% are male.)

Fewer than 10% of the regular readers of either magazine also read the other, but Mel Elfin—chief of the Newsweek bureau in Washington, D.C., for 15 years—reads both newsmagazines side-by-side every week, he says, and he circles "every significant fact, anecdote or quote that they have and we don't" in each Washington story. Then he questions the appropriate Newsweek reporters about the discrepancies.

Competition for advertising at the newsmagazines is as intense as it is for readers. Both Time and Newsweek now have many separate geographic and demographic editions; Time, for example, sells advertising space in copies sent exclusively to students or doctors or businessmen—or to homes with annual incomes exceeding $56,000 (or $77,000).

Competition between Time and Newsweek exists at the corporate level, too: The Washington Post Co. owns Newsweek; in 1978, Time Inc. bought The Washington Star. Time Inc. publishes Sports Illustrated; last month, Newsweek began publishing Inside Sports.

But the real competition is between Time and Newsweek themselves—and few members of the general public seem to know much about how the two magazines are actually assembled each week . . . or about how they differ from each other, what they have in common, how they complement (and compete with) newspapers and television, why Newsweek challenged Time so successfully in the 1960s, how Time subsequently fought back, how Newsweek is now recouping—and why the two are probably more alike now than ever before, even as they adapt individually to new societal demands.

Significantly, the single most oft-asked question about Time and Newsweek demonstrates all too clearly this pervasive ignorance.

The question: "Why do they always have the same covers?"

The answer: "They don't."

Over the last six years, Time and Newsweek have had the same cover stories about once every five weeks on the average—and almost all of these have come when major news stories were breaking.

"When that happens," says Peter Goldman, who's written more than 100 cover stories for Newsweek since 1962, "the people at the two newsmagazines—in the same craft, the same milieu—are often going to do covers on the same subject, just the way the (New York) Times and the Washington Post would have the same lead story."

Thus, in a period dominated by big news events, the percentage of similar covers will be higher. In the first four months of this year, for example, the two newsmagazines had the same cover stories five times—when Reagan won the Republican presidential primary in New Hampshire (and fired his campaign director), when President Carter announced his major anti-inflation program, when the United States unsuccessfully attempted to rescue the hostages in Iran and (twice) when the Soviet Union invaded Afghanistan.

In 1973, during the Watergate scandals, Time and Newsweek had the same covers 23 times—almost every other week.

On occasion, the two newsmagazine covers may actually look alike or sound alike ("Fiasco in Iran;" "Debacle in the Desert,") and since editors at both magazines are working in similar formats, for almost identical audiences, they sometimes produce remarkably similar covers, even when the rhythm of the news suggests non-news covers to editors at both magazines the same week: Newsweek did a cover story on "diet crazes" the same week in 1977 that Time did one on "cooking crazes." Newsweek also did a cover story on "heroes" the same week in 1979 that Time did one on "leadership."

But these coincidences are infrequent, and identical non-news covers are far less common than most people in and out of the media seem to think. Time and Newsweek haven't had the same non-news cover subject in more than three years, and given the renewed emphasis on news-oriented covers at both magazines of late, it isn't likely to happen with any frequency in the forseeable future.

Actually, the predominantly news-oriented cover is a relatively recent development at the newsmagazines. When Henry Luce and Briton Hadden founded Time in 1923, they saw the cover story primarily as an opportunity to publish a profile on a prominent, interesting individual not necessarily involved in the week's news.

But the newsmagazine format has changed considerably since Luce and Hadden sold 20,000 copies of Time a week—and lost $39,454—in 1923. Both magazines are now less polemical that Time once was. Both have much more original reporting—and much longer, more comprehensive stories on a wider variety of subjects. Both are better written, far less stodgy in appearance and somewhat more national in perspective.

Time's original function, Luce said at the time, was "to summarize the week's news in the shortest possible space." For many years, the magazine did that by unabashedly clipping and rewriting the major newspapers—a practice Newsweek often emulated after its founding in 1933.

When early Time editors first suggested that the magazine hire its own correspondents, Luce rejected the idea, saying, "Time *is* a rewrite sheet. Time *does* get most of its news and information from newspapers. . . . It takes *brains and work* to master all the facts dug up by 10,000 journalists and put them together in a little magazine."

Even when they first began developing their own staffs of correspondents around the world, the newsmagazines initiated little reporting themselves—so little that Roy Alexander, managing editor of Time from 1949 to 1960, used to say, "A newsmagazine with an exclusive (story) is like a whore with a baby. You don't know what to do with it."

That problem lingers to this day.

Peter Greenberg, who worked for Newsweek for five years in Houston, Los Angeles and San Francisco, remembers sending his editors a memo in 1975, urging them to do a story on the DC-10 after a DC-10 crash in Paris, a subsequent trial in Los Angeles and Greenberg's own insights as a longtime aviation buff led him to think the plane might be unsafe.

"But the editors hadn't seen that subject dealt with anywhere else," Greenberg says, "so they rejected it. I still have the memo they sent me." The memo said:

"Let's scrub the DC-10 story unless and until developments compel doing it."

Four years later, the crash of a DC-10 in Chicago and the death of almost 300 people triggered widespread investigations . . . and compelled Newsweek to do a cover story on the DC-10.

"Newsmagazines would rather take a story that the world is already hooked on and advance it three inches than do something that no one else is doing," says Anthony Marro, a former Newsweek reporter and now chief of the Newsday bureau in Washington.

"Newsmagazines," Greenberg says, "are essentially reactive in nature. They practice cover-your-ass journalism. They're afraid to be first on something. If some newspaper had done the DC-10 story in 1975, then we probably would've done it, too.''

Greenberg may be right. Newsmagazines traditionally have been almost as afraid of being too early on a story as they have been of being too late. The best way for them to avoid both syndromes is to quickly follow a major newspaper on a given story but to beat the other newsmagazine.

When the Wall Street Journal ran a front-page story on skyrocketing housing prices in Southern California in 1976, Time ran an almost identical story the very next week—in much the same words, with many of the same examples. The most "significant" difference in the two stories: The Journal said real estate speculators were "about as welcome as cockroaches"; Time said they were "about as welcome as dry rot."

But historically, it's the New York Times that the newsmagazines have looked to for ideas—and for legitimization.

Jerry Lubenow, San Francisco bureau chief for Newsweek since 1969, says he once suggested that a high-ranking Newsweek editor read the Chicago Tribune, the Los Angeles Times and other papers occasionally, instead of limiting himself to the New York Times.

The editor, Lubenow says, just laughed and said, "Why would I want to do that?"

The New York Times is "the gospel," says Ed Boyer, who worked for Time in Detroit and Los Angeles from 1974 until early this year. "When the (New York) Times printed something, that gave it credibility. Then we could do it, too."

Newsmagazine correspondents say they have frequently suggested stories to their editors, been rejected, subsequently seen the same stories in the New York Times—and then received queries from their editors, asking them to do the stories after all.

One former Newsweek bureau chief in the South says he used to read the New York Times carefully every Sunday, then start work immediately on his best stories. "I knew I'd get a query on them from New York . . . and I was usually right," he says.

A former Time reporter in the Midwest says he called the New York Times bureau chief in his city every Monday to ask what he expected to be working on the next week, then started working on the same stories himself. "Sure enough, I'd get a query on it from New York, and I'd be ahead of the game," he says.

Some newsmagazine reporters say they've occasionally leaked a story to a friendly New York Times reporter, knowing that might be the best way to ultimately get the story into their own magazines.

"I leaked stories to the Times all over the world for that reason," says Frank McCulloch, a Time correspondent and bureau chief for 16 years and now managing editor of the Sacramento Bee.

It is understandable, of course, that since Time and Newsweek editors work (and, often, live) in New York, "a lot of what you see in those magazines originates with stories they tear out of the Times over breakfast each morning," in the words of Richard Clurman, chief of correspondents for Time from 1960 to 1969.

But in recent years, the newsmagazines have begun trying to shift away from their reliance on the New York Times—or any other newspaper—largely because they increasingly see themselves as competing with these papers.

Newspapers have become more like newsmagazines in their style and content, with more analytical, behind-the-scenes stories, more impressionistic writing and more social trend stories; simultaneously, newsmagazines have become more like daily newspapers in their pursuit of breaking news stories.

"Now," says Steve Shepard, a senior editor at Newsweek, "if the New York Times has a story, that's a good reason for us not to do it. The bias has been reversed."

But what of a similar, longstanding newsmagazine bias—what some call their "New York myopia"?

The owners of both Time and Newsweek once considered moving their main offices out of New York to avoid having the New York perspective dominate their magazines. The magazines didn't move, the New York perspective does often dominate—and the newsmagazines' claims to be truly national publications have suffered accordingly.

Benjamin C. Bradlee, with Newsweek from 1953 to 1965 and now executive editor of the Washington Post, says he can recall the joking in Newsweek's offices every time one editor's commuter train from Connecticut was 10 minutes late.

"We knew there'd be a big story in the magazine the next week on the nation's 'latest massive commuter snarl,'" Bradlee says.

Thus, the New York fiscal crisis made the cover of both Time and Newsweek in 1975, but Cleveland's fiscal crisis made neither cover. ("The magazine's edited in New York," says Time Managing Editor Ray Cave. "It's difficult to get excited here about Cleveland's financial problems.")

Similarly, when "Son of Sam" went on a murderous rampage in New York in 1977, Newsweek put him on the cover, and Time wrote five separate stories on him. But when equally bizarre mass murders erupted in San Francisco, Chicago, Los Angeles and Houston, most were dismissed in a single short story in each magazine. None appeared on the cover. Two were ignored altogether.

Reporters in bureaus for both magazines can provide scores of comparable examples of this phenomenon in virtually every field—politics, sports, education, life style, medicine, the media. . . .

"You can get non-New York stories into the magazine more easily if they conform to the editors' stereotypes," says one Time reporter. "Do an academic story out of Boston, a farm story out of the Midwest or a kook/weirdo story out of L.A. and you can get it in."

Thus, Time had a two-column story last month on Southern Californians who seek tranquility by immersing themselves—naked and alone—in small tanks filled with warm salt water. But William Rademaekers, Time's bureau chief in Los Angeles, says he initially had to "work like a bastard" to persuade his editors to cover the destructive rainstorms that struck Southern California earlier this year.

"Their first perception," he says, "was that all the rain had done was ruin Farrah Fawcett's and Linda Ronstadt's hair and it wasn't worth much in a national magazine."

The New York bias of the newsmagazines is most noticeable in their cultural coverage. During the last six months of 1979, for example, Time reviewed 20 plays—all of them in New York City.

"There's almost no way in hell you can get a Chicago play or concert reviewed," says Barry Hillenbrand of Time's Chicago bureau. "The editors are just provincial, parochial, patronizing and condescending when it comes to the arts anywhere outside New York."

Newsmagazine editors admit they continually have to fight their New York bias, but they insist they are improving.

Time decided not to do a major story when political activist Allard Lowenstein was killed in March, says the managing editor, "because we were afraid he might be too much an Eastern political figure, not well-known elsewhere."

Time's periodic "American Scene" column (set most recently in Hartford, St. Paul and Seattle) and several other stories this year from the South, Midwest and West also suggest a possible broadening of the magazine's geographic scope.

At Newsweek, Executive Editor Maynard Parker—born in Los Angeles, educated in California and Oregon—helps make his fellow editors aware of news outside the New York-Washington axis. Several months ago, Newsweek ran a cover story on television talk show host Phil Donahue "precisely because he's not a New York figure," says Lynn Povich, senior editor at the magazine.

Newsweek is even reviewing more regional theater now. Jack Kroll, the magazine's theater critic, recently won a major award that cited his willingness to venture beyond Broadway.

Some reporters are skeptical of their editors' ability—and commitment—to make the newsmagazines truly national, but recent improvements are encouraging, they say, and—as one longtime Time reporter points out—"I was skeptical when they (Time editors) said they were doing away with 'Timese,' too, and I was wrong then."

For decades, "Timese" was a Time trademark—a linguistic roller coaster of puns, clichés, precious prose, loaded adjectives and a syntax often so convoluted that it was once parodied as "Backward ran the sentences until reeled the mind."

Writing in both newsmagazines is more restrained and less self-conscious today, although both magazines are still prone to occasional cuteness and overwriting when doing stories on Hollywood personalities. (Actress Genvieve Bujold was once described as having "a voice like a kitten purring Beethoven"; just last month, Time said, "The famous lines of Bette Davis are as fixed in the national consciousness as the Pledge of Allegiance.")

A more important stylistic characteristic —one that has remained relatively constant through the years in newsmagazine writing— is that of subjective viewpoint, in many ways the newsmagazines' real raison d'etre.

Except in their longest stories—and often even then—the newsmagazines are compressing a great amount of information into a short space. A typical story might run only 600 words—compared with perhaps 6,000 words (or 16,000 words) that a major newspaper might print on the same subject in several stories over the same week.

To compress so much data effectively, a newsmagazine writer must have a viewpoint— a thesis.

"The basic function of the newsmagazine," says former Newsweek Editor Kermit Lansner, "is to give order and meaning to the flow of the week's events—to leave out the repetition and fits and starts that are part of daily newspaper coverage and provide perspective."

On a complex, evolving issue, that's not easy to do in 100 typed lines—which is why Lansner calls newsmagazine journalism "as much a knack as a skill."

"The strength of the newsmagazine format," says one former Time bureau chief, "is that when it's done right, it enables the reader who's confused after reading three long newspaper stories every day for a week on Tehran to read just one story and say, 'Ah ha, now I know what's going on in Tehran.'

"But the basic problem in the system," he says, "is that to do this well, in so little space, you have to tell a narrative story—with a beginning, a middle and an end. You have to adopt a specific, narrow viewpoint. That can mean throwing all subtlety and contradiction out the window. On a complicated, controversial subject, you can't avoid doing the reader—and the subject—a disservice."

For many years—more than 40 years— Time did its readers an even greater disservice by often throwing something else out the window. Balance. Fairness. Honesty.

Henry Luce was a Calvinist and a conservative, and his view of the world was Time's view of the world—morally, socially, intellectually and, most important of all, politically.

Time was "dishonestly written. . . . Every single story carries the slant of the editor, Henry Luce," former Time writer Merle Miller once wrote.

Or, as Earl Long, then governor of Louisiana, put it:

"Mister Henry Luce is like a shoe salesman, but all the other shoestore owners stock all different sizes of shoes. . . . Mr. Luce, he only sells shoes that fit hisself."

Luce thought he knew what was best for America—and what was best for America, he was convinced, was best for the world.

Luce's blatant favoritism for Republican candidates and causes made him what David Halberstam, in his book "The Powers That Be," calls a "national propagandist . . . the most important and influential conservative-centrist force in the country."

The German weekly *Der Spiegel* went a step further: "No other American without a political office—with the possible exception of Henry Ford—has had a greater influence on American society."

There are many other voices in the land now—most notably, the three television networks—and while the newsmagazines perform a valuable service in helping to sort out and synthesize what all these other voices are saying, they are not quite as influential as they once were. Nor are they as narrowly partisan as Time was for so long.

But despite Newsweek's 1960s promotional claims that it was "the newsweekly that separates fact from opinion," both newsmagazines do promulgate a viewpoint on virtually every story. They regularly blend—and blur— fact and opinion, and the civic impulse and oracular quality provided by Luce is often evident to this day in Time.

"There is here the attitude of 'Now hear this . . . This is in Time, so it's the word,'" says writer Tom Griffith, who has spent more than 30 years at Time.

This attitude—and its inevitably resultant bias—has been most noticeable in recent years in Time's treatment of big business.

Even Time Publisher John Meyers concedes, "We're pro-business, very pro-business. We believe in business and the free enterprise system, and it comes out in the magazine."

Until recently, Time had an economics editor, Marshall Loeb (now managing editor of Money magazine), who wrote a regular series of profiles on business leaders—columns so flattering that in-house critics dubbed Loeb's column "The Lives of Our Saints."

Time has been particularly sympathetic to the nuclear industry. Seven months before the nuclear accident at Three-Mile Island last year, Time published an essay ("The Irrational Fight Against Nuclear Power") that scoffed at those who questioned the safety of nuclear power plants, and accused them of being "obstructionist," "emotional," foolish, insincere and blindly resistant to change.

Time is no longer a house organ for the Republican Party—or for America. In fact, some conservative critics see it (as well as Newsweek) as part of the "Eastern liberal media." But some Time editors still regard the magazine as America's ambassador to the world.

In Luce's day, Time correspondents lived much as ambassadors—big salaries, big expense accounts, chauffered limousines, unrivaled access to the corridors of power. Although Time still spends more money than Newsweek—a 1980 editorial budget of about $37 million to Newsweek's $24 million—inflation and competition long ago ended Time's halcyon days abroad; the major newspapers now pay comparable salaries and have comparable access.

But Time still tends to take a global, Olympian view of its role—and America's role —in the world. That's probably why Time does more (and often better) foreign cover stories than Newsweek—and periodic state-of-the-system cover stories on capitalism

(1975: "Can Capitalism Survive?" 1980: "Is Capitalism Working?").

Time also still permits a "rally 'round the flag, boys" tone to creep into its stories occasionally—as in a March 20 essay on "The Return of Patriotism" and a Feb. 3 cover story ("America Attacked") that some critics saw as irresponsibly jingoistic and inflammatory.

Some Time stories on communism and socialism also smack ever so faintly of the Lucean world view of the "Red menace"— especially when compared with the magazine's more evenhanded stories on democracy and capitalism. A 1978 cover story on world socialism, for example, lacked the historical perspective accorded a 1975 cover story on capitalism.

There are even those critics who see Time's flattering 1979 cover story on former Texas Gov. John B. Connally as evidence of the arrival of a new generation of *realpolitik* at Time Inc.: Arthur Temple, a Texas industrialist who now owns the controlling interest in Time Inc., is a political supporter of Connally's.

Time editors deny rather persuasively that Temple or any of his Texas business associates influenced their coverage of Connally, but they are far less persuasive in denying charges that Time took an early, proprietary interest in Jimmy Carter's fortunes four years ago.

"I thought Time was getting its wind up too much for Carter during the '76 campaign," says Murray Gart, Time's chief of correspondents from 1969 to 1978, and now editor of the Washington Star. "The editors' enthusiasm for him was creeping into their queries (to Time correspondents) and then into the correspondents' files (stories). I finally sent out a memo cautioning against that.

"I think the reporters ultimately welcomed that, but it infuriated the editors."

Time editors insist they make every effort now to guard against political bias—and against insensitivity to their correspondents. That they should. It was precisely those two factors that helped Newsweek first become a serious challenger to Time in the 1960s.

28
Star Wars

Peter S. Greenberg

In the ultra-hype world of celebrity publicity, exposure is the name of the game. And one of the best kinds of media exposure today—as the careers of Farrah Fawcett-Majors or Bruce Springsteen prove—is the magazine cover. An appearance on the cover of *Time,* for example, would certainly make anyone a national sensation overnight. Why? Historian Daniel J. Boorstin puts it best: "The celebrity is a person who is known for his well-knownness."

Recently, as magazines have added "people" sections or turned entirely to celebrity formats, many publishers have discovered that circulation figures can rise or fall depending upon whose face is on the cover or who agrees to an "exclusive" interview. In the following article, Peter S. Greenberg, former west coast editor of *New Times* magazine, observes that even *Time* and *Newsweek* "now compete for personality covers the way they once competed for news." Greenberg believes that celebrity coverage has greatly reduced the boundaries between news and entertainment, journalism and publicity.

There's a new twist to the old game of sweetheart journalism: it's called contract coverage. From Anwar Sadat to the Sex Pistols—with predecessors from Jerry Rubin to Richard Nixon—the name of the game is: understand the media; then try to manipulate it. Unfortunately, many celebs are succeeding beyond their wildest dreams. The growing club of superstars and would-be giants who have successfully maneuvered the press includes Robert Redford, Henry Kissinger, John Denver, Glen Campbell, Helen Reddy, James Taylor and Carly Simon, Daniel Ellsberg, Sylvester Stallone, Robert DeNiro and Barbra Streisand. As a result, a fine and fragile line has been established between news and package entertainment, journalism and press release.

Celebrities, particularly of the show business variety, have found themselves with the upper hand in their old arm wrestle with the media. One simple statistic tells the tale: *Newsweek* ran twice as many show business covers in 1977 as it did in 1976.

"There's a great deal of public apathy towards news," says *Newsweek* cultural affairs editor Charles Michener. "Jimmy Carter is a risky property as a cover for the newsweeklies now. There just isn't that intense public interest. The line is growing very blurred between news and entertainment. The *New York Times,* Time Inc. and *Newsweek* are giving entertainment a legitimacy it never had. Let's face it, it's big business, and agents and PR people are now in the position of playing magazines off against each other in ways they never could before. It obviously has to do with people seeking escape . . ."

"In some strange way," says Shep Gordon, manager of Alice Cooper, Raquel Welch and a host of other stars and one of today's most successful packagers, "we're really dealing with the inevitable here. Whether you're a Dodge salesman, a Good Humor man, an entertainer or a member of the press, you're dealing in a product. We've all come to the terrifying realization that we're all in business

Source: From *New Times* (February 6, 1978). Reprinted by permission of the author.

and business ain't nice. It's just a matter of how deeply involved in business the press care to admit to being."

There is no doubt, of course, that Kate Jackson on the cover of *People* magazine sells more copies than a profile of Secretary of Agriculture Bob Bergland. How *much* more is a frightening demographic statistic. "It's all very well researched," says publicist David Horowitz. "People are reading so much less that sometimes they'd much rather have a star on the cover with hardly any copy than five pages on the inside." A *Playboy* issue which featured Barbra Streisand on the cover, for example, was one of the year's better-selling issues.

The hype stakes have simply gotten higher. "We've reached a point where the public has become accustomed to hype," says Gordon. "And they seem to accept it in all its forms." A recent example was *The Land of Hype and Glory,* an NBC News special hosted by Edwin Newman. It was meant to *report* the hype phenomenon, but was loaded with a menagerie of subtle mini-hypes. The show was sponsored in part by the *National Star,* which was promoting a story on how Tony Orlando was "saved by God." Large portions of the program were devoted to the rock group Kiss, movies *The Deep* and *Close Encounters of the Third Kind,* and singer Donna Summer. The prime-time exposure was priceless. And even as Edwin Newman pontificated on the evils of the current hyperbolic state of America, all three networks were hosting junketing TV "critics" from newspapers around the country at the Century-Plaza Hotel in Los Angeles—to promote their revised "second season" program schedule!

Another recent example that illustrates the point, but didn't work out so well, hypewise, involves Bob Dylan. Mr. Tambourine Man has a new movie, a four-hour effort called *Renaldo and Clara,* into which he has sunk a significant amount of his own money. To retrieve some of it, he has come out of seclusion—and his current divorce case—long enough to launch a blitzkrieg media campaign aimed at getting the film maximum exposure. Last spring, Dylan associates approached writers Lucian Truscott and Jesse Kornbluth

about chronicling Bob's metamorphosis into a serious, adult film artist. Both writers were selected as "serious," not "hippie rockwriters," but the project was dropped.

Paul Wasserman handles publicity chores for Dylan. He's considered one of the best press agents in the business. Wasserman, or "Wasso" as he likes to be called, is as aggressive and pushy as he is mild and softspoken. He is extremely well-liked, and his client list reads like a Malibu Colony Who's Who: Linda Ronstadt, James Taylor, Paul Simon, etc. In the business, Wasso is known for protecting his clients, for being, if you will, a sup-press agent. However, with the Dylan campaign, the tactics are different.

It's a simple carrot and stick approach. Here's the pitch, made to a number of pre-selected magazines including *Rolling Stone, Newsweek, Time, Us, People, Esquire* and *New Times:* big Bob wants to talk, but he'll only do it for the cover. In some cases, Dylan also asked for and received copy approval.

One by one, writers for some of the publications mentioned above have been escorted into Dylan's brave new world—a bleak former furniture factory in Santa Monica he's been renting as a rehearsal hall for his new band. (The hall is close to Santa Monica's Superior Court, where Dylan's divorce from his wife, Sara, is now proceeding.) One of his new girl-friends, a well-known country singer, called him up after *Rolling Stone's* piece appeared: "Why are you doing all these interviews, Bob?"

"Well," he supposedly replied, in his normally subdued manner, "I don't have the money for the advertising I'd like to do for the movie. If I do this I'll get it anyway, but in a more credible way."

Dylan has a point. In return for access, *Rolling Stone* gave him a cover. Also, it reportedly gave him the interview transcript to edit. One source told *New Times* that *Playboy,* too, gave Dylan total copy approval, but executive editor G. Barry Golson vehemently denies it: "We're not about to give Dylan anything we didn't give Carter. Because of our long lead time, we usually give 'em [interview subjects] a chance to check galleys for *accuracy.* And that's all we did with Dylan, except for one thing: we acceded to his request to delete some references to his children, because he's going through divorce proceedings.'' The interview will appear in the March *Playboy,* which goes on sale roughly the time *Renaldo and Clara* opens.

But Dylan is far from being alone in his demands.

When Larry Grobel, an interviewer for *Playboy,* finally arrived at Barbra Streisand's Holmby Hills home after waiting seven months for a firm date, he was greeted by a two-page, single spaced contract giving Streisand total editorial control and ownership of the tapes. Grobel claims Streisand ultimately agreed to the interview without the document being signed. Prior to *Playboy, Rolling Stone* had offered Streisand the cover and both copy and photo approval if she would sit for an interview. When Barbara Walters interviewed Streisand and Jon Peters for an ABC News special, Streisand was given final cut on the unfinished videotape. To soften the blow to its news credibility, ABC ran the edited program under the aegis of its entertainment division.

"You want to know why the stars are getting away with this?" asks Los Angeles PR man Bob Gibson. "It's simple dollars and cents. In the music business we're in the era of platinum consciousness and disposable journalism. Major magazines have allowed themselves to become talk shows for the semiliterate. And the publications are as guilty as the publicists. We're both involved in an aggressive competition to sell an image first."

Selling the image best means the cover. "I don't think there's anything wrong with Dylan demanding the cover," says publicist Ronni Chasen, who represents Kate Jackson and George Burns, among others. "If you're a superstar, you should try to get as much control over the press as you can. It's like everything else in this business. It's just making another deal."

The entertainment cover story had a record year in 1977. "It's all a question of need," says *Newsweek*'s Charles Michener. "When the news was hot during Watergate I could pretty much pick and choose what entertainment stories we wanted to cover. We

could develop ideas and profiles at our own pace. Today if Donna Summer or even Grace Jones twitches her nose in public, PR people are calling you and demanding coverage."

Irving Azoff doesn't demand coverage. Most of the artists he manages need more publicity like America needs more nerve gas. "My people talk only when they have something to say," he says, "but I'm constantly being besieged by magazines who want covers on groups like the Eagles." When he demands it, some magazines—Azoff won't say which—offer both copy and art approval. "I only demanded it because I wanted to set some ground rules for the interviews," Azoff explains. "But I can't believe it when they agree right away. I've always felt it just wasn't ethical to do things that way." Not everyone agrees with Azoff. "We need some control of the press," says agent-manager Jay Bernstein, who is generally credited with publicizing and marketing Farrah Fawcett. "If I can get a story approval, I do," he says. "When a magazine calls and wants Farrah, the only thing she'll do is the cover." Already, the former Charlie's Angel has done 48 (including a *New Times* spoof). "When you've reached our level," says Bernstein, "you're the buyer, not the seller."

And therein lies a major problem. "Sooner or later," says James Willwerth, a West Coast *Time* correspondent, "the big stars become so powerful they believe, rightly or wrongly, that they can manipulate the media. The more powerful they think they are, the more paranoid they become towards the press."

As a result, many publicists are caught in the middle between the coverage demands of their clients and the interests of good journalism. The client usually wins. Reliable sources have informed *New Times* that in 1973, *Rolling Stone* gave Art Garfunkel copy approval for his cover; the magazine reportedly gave the same deal to James Taylor in 1971 and Carly Simon in 1975; Daniel Ellsberg is supposed to have had approval. *Playboy,* according to Sylvester Stallone's manager, Jeff Wald, offered a number of copy and art checks and control in return for an interview with the actor: "Utter bullshit," laughs

Golson. "When Larry Linderman was in the middle of the Stallone interview, Sylvester saw our Streisand cover—a departure, I might add—and thought it would be a good idea if we did the same for him. I told him, 'But Syl, we only put *girls* on the cover of *Playboy.*' We are not going to make the interview conditional." Most music and entertainment-oriented magazines, however, do. They offer copy approval as a regular negotiating tool. *Time* and *Newsweek* insist that they don't, "but it's all a matter of semantics," says one New York studio publicist. "You might call it a demand, and we might label it a polite request. If that request becomes a prerequisite to coverage, we find more often than not that it is eventually honored. The more intense the competition, the faster the major magazines cooperate."

"It's getting so vicious out there," says Ronnie Lippin, former publicist for Elton John and ABC Records, "that we're approaching the level of written contracts between the artist and the press for just about everybody."

Unfortunately, that may already be the case. Just last spring *Us* magazine (which is owned by the *New York Times*) approached Glen Campbell for a story. "You can have Glen if I can have the cover," publicist Bob Levinson told them, "and I want copy and photo approval." *Us* declined. "Then you don't get Glen," he said.

"I was only doing my job as a publicist," says Levinson now. "Glen and Sarah (the former Mrs. Mac Davis) didn't really want to do interviews. He was getting a lot of bad raps, so I asked for controls. I never dreamed we'd get them."

Surprisingly, the magazine capitulated a few days later. It not only agreed to the cover, but both the writer and photographer signed away virtually all the magazines' rights to the interview. On May 13, the reporter affixed her signature to the following: "The undersigned acknowledges and consents that the interview this date with Glen Campbell, Sarah Campbell is exclusively relative to a story assigned by US Magazine, and that the story derived by this and allied interviews will be submitted to Glen and Sarah Campbell for re-

view and approval of accuracy of content prior to publication, with their approval in writing necessary in any and all events to said publication. The undersigned further acknowledges that the agreement is with the full knowledge and understanding of US Magazine, its publishers and involved editors, and that no other editorial use of the story or facts developed during the interview is contemplated or intended."

When the issue date was upon them, however, Levinson realized that neither the promised manuscript nor the photo proofsheet had arrived. He call *Us* in New York. "An editor there told me they never let anyone have any copy approval," Levinson recalls, "but I said you gave it, and I got it in writing, and if you run this piece without showing it to Glen, you're in trouble."

Despite a handful of telegrams and protests, *Us* chose to ignore Levinson's warning. They ran the piece. Levinson was promptly fired by Campbell after ten years of representation (the *Us* cover now hangs in his Hollywood office bathroom directly above the toilet). The magazine was then promptly sued by Campbell's attorney. Not for libel, not for invasion of privacy, but for breach of contract! The suit, which also seeks $1 million in punitive damages for fraud, alleges that the Campbells were a "source" for a story about them in *Us,* and that as sources they were given certain assurances about how their information would be used. The assurances were broken. As a result, the Campbells also claim they deserve all profit made by *Us* on the story.

The *Us* managing editor at the time, Reynolds Dodson, declined to comment. The present managing editor, Ron Martin, told *New Times:* "It's certainly not our policy to make any such deals," but refused further comment.

The *Us* suit follows an action filed by Jeff Wald (he is also manager and husband of Helen Reddy) and others against *New York, New West* and writer Mary Murphy, concerning Murphy's controversial piece on superstars and their husbands. After an initial run in both Murdoch publications, the piece was syndicated in the *National Star* and elsewhere.

Wald promptly sued, claiming breach of contract. In this case there was no written contract, but Wald claimed a copyright infringement of Helen. Wald settled the suit out of court, and the case may have set a precedent on the question of who exactly owns an interview once it is completed.

"You can't really get made at publicists," argues Dick Grant, who represents Ann Margret, Valerie Perrine and Cheryl Ladd, "because you should realize that these magazines are creating problems for themselves by agreeing to these cover demands."

When *Us* wanted to put the rock group Heart on the cover, it negotiated with the group's public-relations firm in Los Angeles. "They were hot for the cover," says Bob Emmer, Heart's PR man, "and after much discussion, we set it up in Seattle where the group lives. But then the magazine called us back and openly solicited us to pay the writer's transportation to Washington. Here was a situation where we had not used the transportation cost as a barter for the story, but at the same time we didn't want to stand in the way of a cover."

Emmer convinced CBS Records, the group's label, to advance the round-trip air fare between Seattle and San Francisco for the writer, and, according to Emmer, picked up the tab for a hotel room as well. But the story never ran, and Emmer dashed off an angry letter to *Us* editors in New York essentially demanding CBS' money back. "We don't like to be in the position of financing their cover story," Emmer says, "*especially* if we're not going to get it."

Time and *Newsweek* now compete for personality covers the way they once competed for news. And they do it exceedingly well. When Lily Tomlin was about to open on Broadway last year, both magazines commenced a game of journalistic "chicken" in which no one blinked. *Time* flew to Chicago for her pre-New York performances, convinced it had an exclusive. Then *Newsweek*'s Jack Kroll arrived in the Windy City after the *Time* cover had been written and a week before it was scheduled to run. Both magazines had approached Tomlin some time earlier,

and, according to one *Time* reporter, Tomlin's PR people had asked *Time* to guarantee a specific cover date. Barring confrontation in the Middle East, they did. "We thought we had an exclusive," says Leo Janos, who reported the cover for *Time,* "and Henry Grunwald (*Time*'s managing editor at the time) couldn't believe we hadn't been double-crossed by the PR people. But I think it was just a matter of Jack Kroll being an assertive, good journalist. The problem," he adds, "is that we both looked rather dumb."

Newsweek rushed its cover, hoping to beat *Time* to the newsstand. When it learned both covers were going to coincide, *Newsweek* ran Kroll's piece—which turned out to be the better of the two—on the inside.

Then came Richard Pryor. *Newsweek* apparently persuaded Pryor not to talk to anyone else in return for a cover, but *Time* wanted him as well. The result? *Newsweek* got its exclusive, but Pryor lost his cover: David Berkowitz, the Son of Sam, preempted him. *Time* ran an inside cover of Pryor the same week without ever having talked to the comedian.

Perhaps the most flagrant example of recent manipulation was United Artists' promotion of the movie *New York, New York*. Leo Janos claims that when he had originally called United Artists to express his interests in a possible cover on the project, "the producers told me they had decided to go with *Newsweek,* claiming they were angry at *Time* for a cover story on *Rocky* they said *Time* promised but didn't deliver." Several weeks later, however, United Artists approached *Time* in New York. "They told the editors *Newsweek* had not decided about whether to go with the cover," says Janos. "Therefore they were going to allow *Time* to do the cover instead." UA even went so far as to suggest *who* at *Time* should write the piece. The screening was arranged in Los Angeles, and some of the magazine's top editors flew out to see the DeNiro/Minelli musical. It was only after they arrived and viewed the film that they learned—by accident—that *Newsweek*'s Kroll had once again beaten them. "You should have seen their faces," says Janos, "when they discovered that Kroll had already interviewed DeNiro for hours.'' (*Newsweek* ran a cover; *Time* waited two months and ran their story inside.)

Then, of course, there was the notorious case of the simultaneous Bruce Springsteen covers. It was considered a major PR coup for Columbia Records at the time, but the truth is that it was one notable case where press agentry was innocent—the media simply manipulated itself. Henry Grunwald at *Time* later confided to a friend that he felt the Springsteen incident was his greatest mistake as managing editor.

"Publicists have been under the gun ever since Springsteen,'' says PR woman Ronnie Lippin. "The minute those covers hit the stands, every two-bit artist in the world ran to us saying, 'If he can do it, how come you can't do it for me?' For some of the big PR firms with large client rosters it was particularly rough. "Everyone wanted press, and a lot of PR people were forced to use the superstars as bait for some of their lesser clients,'' says Lippin. "The way they handled it, if you wanted to speak to God, you had to talk to thirty disciples first; if you wanted Fleetwood Mac, you had to talk to twenty other people on the label first. That is really dirty shit,'' she says, "because that's when people get space who never deserve it.'' The Springsteen incident caused a mini-revolution among mediocre entertainers: they *had* to see their names in print. "And the problem,'' Lippin shrugs, "is that you must do it for them or you lose the account. These artists are making your job impossible, and so you make these ugly deals and hope the editors won't hate you for it later.''

"We want *The Wiz* to penetrate all the markets,'' Motown film producer Rob Cohen tells New York PR wizard Bobby Zarem on the NBC *Hype* program. "And we've come to you because I think you can manipulate the media sufficiently well.'' Indeed he can. Zarem, who has represented everyone from Dustin Hoffman and Cybill Shepherd to Arnold Schwarzenegger, was the recipient of what has to be the orgasmic PR coup of 1977. Last January, both *Newsweek* and *Time*—in the same week, with virtually the same headline—ran pieces on . . . Bobby Zarem. "The public

doesn't understand the difference,'' he says, "between hype and intelligent relating to the press.'' Some media watchers contend that the public is long resigned to the cynical conclusion that the press has always been too cozy with its subjects. "The only practical answer I see,'' says Ben Bagdikian, our best journalism critic and author of *The Effete Conspiracy: And Other Crimes by the Press,* "is to treat these people the same way you would a politician who wants control of the copy or the questions that are to be asked. If they won't give you the information just go somewhere else. Journalists need to bargain from a position of strength. Until *someone* is willing to spoil the deal, we're all going to be trapped in this business of offering up goodies.''

Unfortunately, in recent years one of the major weekly newsmagazines has tended to treat its political subjects the same way it treats the stars. When pressured, it has been known to send prepublication copies of interviews to world leaders and decision-makers, presumably to check "quote accuracy.'' (Kissinger was notorious for demanding this.) Lately, Monachim Begin and Anwar Sadat have had the opportunity to edit their interviews. "We're always under pressure from these people to get the interviews played back well before our closing,'' says one newsweekly editor. "The implication, at the very least, is that they'll have time to change it.''

And the notion that the press can *literally* be bought is growing, as the Sidney Schechtman incident in Los Angeles amply illustrates. For almost three years, beginning in the summer of 1974, Schechtman ran a profitable little operation convincing American and Canadian businessmen that he could buy them an article in one of a number of respectable magazines: for $6,000, they could read about themselves in *Fortune*; for $1,000, in *People*; and for $350, in *Business Week*. In Los Angeles alone 30 victims payed Schechtman a total of $33,000 (only the reported figure; authorities feel the actual figure was higher), many with the idea that their money was going to pay off editors.

When Schechtman was running his con game in New York in 1970, he tapped Robert Veech, a Long Island inventor. When he asked

Schechtman how he could do it for so little money, Schechtman assured him that $350 slipped to the right *Life* magazine editor would take care of it. "I wish I had just picked up the phone and called Time-Life when Schechtman first approached me," Veech told *New West* magazine in an interview last year. "But I wasn't surprised when he told me editors took bribes. I think it's probably a very common attitude among lay people. It exists everywhere else, why should the publishing business be any different?"

Bagdikian says public confidence in responsible reporting is still being buoyed by the recent Woodward/Bernstein Watergate feat, but that with the Schechtman case in point it has begun to erode. "There's a growing dilemma in the press," says Farrah Fawcett's manager, Jay Bernstein, "between writing about someone and selling a product. You realize the hype industry is a definite two-way street."

Journalism has truly become a marketing problem. Defining the lines of privacy and good taste daily becomes more acute. "We've become too obsessed with the private lives of personalities," says Barbara Wilkins, former West Coast bureau chief for *People* magazine. "I wouldn't be interviewed by one of us, would you? It gets to the point where the only entertainers you respect are the ones that turn you down. I mean, how many times can you listen to someone ask you when was the first time you slept with your wife?" *Newsweek*'s Michener agrees. "We're making heroes and heroines of people in the arts because politicians and businessmen are seen as corrupt. Entertainers are more innocent. No matter what they do wrong, it can't be that serious."

The answer, according to Shep Gordon, is somewhere in a mythical flow chart of synthetic news. "In the end it's all manufactured," he says. "Before, the news was managed by the White House with more death and despair. Now we're managing the news, but we're doing it with stars and the kind of hype everyone wants to believe in. And," he adds, "nobody dies."

At hype's end, the official word from Santa Monica is that Dylan has exhausted the "A" list and is now talking—for the cover, of course—to the likes of *Circus* magazine. *Time* saw his movie and was not impressed. Nor did *Newsweek* do a cover. *Esquire* is doing nothing; neither are *Us* and *People*. And *New West,* which had planned coverage, has changed its mind: "I doubt we'll do anything now," says editor Frank Lalli, "we think he's getting too much exposure elsewhere." And that, as they say, is positively, or maybe, main street.

29
The "Mad" Generation

Tony Hiss & Jeff Lewis

If celebrities can make the covers of magazines, the covers of magazines can also make celebrities. Perhaps the most famous personality to be manufactured entirely by a magazine cover was none other than the celebrated Alfred E. Neuman. His flap-eared, grossly freckled, idiotically smiling, "what, me worry?" face, loved by kids and despised by parents, became the trademark of *Mad* Magazine in the 1950s. But, more important, Neuman became, according to comic book aficionados Tony Hiss and Jeff Lewis, "a generation's first emblem of protest—not angry, not nasty, not dogmatic, not self-righteous, nor any other bad, bad thing, but something far worse—he was *yecchy!*"

The following essay, a tribute to *Mad* on its twenty-fifth birthday, traces its evolution from an absurdly funny and self-consciously trashy comic book to a broadly ranging satirical magazine that went after "cant and hypocrisy wherever it found it."

Twenty-five years ago, little Bobby Crumb down in Milford, Del., hid in a corner of his mother's house and started studying a brand-new, 32-page, full-color comic book called Mad. Ostensibly, the little rag was a satirical comic book that made fun of other comic books, but in reality it had different fish to fry. In a broad Bronx fashion, much like the broad Bronx personality of its founding editor, Harvey Kurtzman, Mad made fun of everything, including itself, which made it into a slippery proposition right from the start.

Little Bobby Crumb grew up to be R. Crumb, the world-famous underground cartoonist, but his experience was the experience of a generation of kids all across America, including the authors of this article. We were all kids of the air-raid-shelter generation, the first primary-school group taught to hide under school desks and cover our faces in order to ward off atom bombs and hydrogen bombs. We sensed that this made us somehow different from kids in previous generations, but no one ever told us anything that indicated that things were any different from what they had been.

And then came Mad. Month after month and issue after issue, in a relentlessly good-natured way, Mad told us that everything was askew—that there were lies in advertising, that other comic books lied, that television and movies lied, and that adults, in general, when faced with the unknown, lied.

A lot of us found this information, which confirmed many of our own observations, useful and stimulating in terms of further development. In the south Texas town of Pharr, young Billy Helmer (now a senior editor of Playboy) awaited the appearance of Mad as the only cultural event of the month; he was delighted that all the grown-ups in

town considered the sheet subversive. In New York, 11-year-old Phil Proctor (now one-half of the successful comedy duo of Proctor & Bergman and one-quarter of the equally successful comedy quartet called The Firesign Theater) pored over Mad's jumbled-up use-every-square-inch, madcap profusion of detail for such extended periods that his mother resorted to the old "you'll go blind" plea to get him to lay off. In Albuquerque, N.M., young Gwyn Cravens, the author of a new thriller about a black plague that destroys New York, discovered in Mad a revelation and a colorful new language (Kurtzman used Yiddish words like *furshlugginer*—also spelled *farshloginer* or "beaten up"—in just about every article). "Here," she says today, "was a magazine that came all the way from New York City—so of course it had to be official —and I opened it up and inside it said that teachers were stupid!" Hundreds of thousands of other kids who are now plumbers and lawyers and backwoods hippie farmers were going Mad in similar ways—and part of the experience was absorbing Mad's attitude toward the furshlugginer mess it saw everywhere: "What, me worry?"

Of course, this attitude made some adults worry a lot. Unlike the Hardy Boys or Horatio Alger books, Mad seemed to be attacking capitalism, consumerism and advertising, government, education, the family, and authority in general. Parents argued that Mad was inculcating destructive attitudes, that it taught teenagers cynicism and, ultimately, disengagement. It was unhealthy. Even after 25 years, it is difficult to assess Mad's cultural impact. Mad, by itself, did not shape a generation. Yet it reflected a social fact and gave expression to feelings shared by young people at a great turning point in American life.

The summer of Mad's first appearance in 1952 was the summer Dick Nixon was attacking Adlai Stevenson as soft on Communism, corruption and costs. The big names-in-the-news in Mad's first few years, as it struggled out of the red, were John Foster (Brinkmanship) Dulles, Tailgunner Joe McCarthy, and Engine Charlie (What's Good for General Motors is Good for the Country) Wilson—men for whom the world was grim, dangerous and humorless. Into the middle of that world and loudly giving it a Bronx cheer skidded Mad, a (in its own terms) tiny, trashy, disgusting, demented and probably anti-American publication that just happened to speak to some of the deepest fears and perceptions of a nation's puzzled kids.

Today, Mad's publisher, Bill Gaines, is a happy-go-lucky millionaire; Mad's first editor, Kurtzman, is a living legend; and Mad itself (full original title: "Tales Calculated to Drive You MAD: Humor in a Jugular Vein") is coining money and still speaking directly to millions of kids each month. And the skeptical generation of kids it shaped in the 1950s is the same generation that in the 1960s opposed a war and didn't feel bad when the United States lost for the first time and in the 1970s helped turn out an Administration and didn't feel bad about that either.

Of the thousands of obviously trashy and disgusting, completely furshlugginer and probably anti-American publications that a kid growing up in the U.S.A. in the 50s might have laid his hands on, Mad was the only one that blatantly admitted its trashiness. And not just admitted it, but reveled in it, advertised it, never allowed it to be forgotten, wore it like a badge of honor. Which of course it was, and kids across the country knew it instantly. Kids felt it right from the beginning: Mad told the truth.

Mad got started when a young genius from the Bronx named Harvey Kurtzman contracted jaundice. Kurtzman was then producing two war comic books—"Two-Fisted Tales" and "Front-Line Combat"—for a Manhattan comic-book empire called Entertaining Comics (E.C.). The jaundice came from working too hard to make comic-book combat look realistic. The soldiers Kurtzman saw in other war comics didn't look like real people—they didn't bleed, they weren't scared, they were always right, and they killed only subhumans. "Even in my war comics, I avoided the usual glamour stuff of the big good-looking G.I. beating up the ugly little yellow man," Kurtzman said later. He had been spending hours interviewing real Korean War vets, taking apart and reassembling Army rifles and generaling his E.C. staff. Once he even sent his legman, Jerry De Fuccio, off to New London, Conn., to go down in a submarine in order to devise precise onomatopoeic words for the sounds the sub made during its descent.

Then Kurtzman got jaundice and, during his recuperation, decided to create a comic book that he could write without leaving his room. But what did he know about without leaving his room? "All the junk I'd been accumulating from childhood—I was writing from layers of baby fat," Kurtzman says. "It came right out of my gut." And imagination. Other comic books seemed unrealistic to Kurtzman—repressed and harmful to the minds of children. "Steve Canyon" and "Prince Valiant" in particular grated on his gizzard. "They showed an idealized world with no truth in it," he says. "It made me mad to see what stuff they were handing out to kids."

The result was a brave experiment: Kurtzman and a small staff consisting of E.C.'s three top-rated comic-book artists, Will Elder, Wally Wood and Jack Davis, decided to try to put out the kind of comic book that *they* wanted to put out. E.C. let them and, without a doubt, a large part of Mad's later success came from E.C.'s initial willingness to let four very talented, exuberant young men try out a format that wasn't guaranteed to make money. Kurtzman wrote the stories and sketched them out, frame by frame, assisted by Elder, his old friend from New York City's High School of Music and Art. Then Elder, Wood and Davis drew in the details of the actual pictures.

The first issue was dated Oct./Nov. 1952, but came out in August, postdated as comic books always are. To a parent or other nonaficionado of comic books, this first issue of Mad probably looked no different from a dozen other horror comics on the market. But to any halfway-attentive 11-year-old, it was something radical and amazing. The cover, drawn by Kurtzman (who always signs his work H. Kurtz) was the tip-off. It showed an average American family cowering in a haunted house before a looming shadow. The father says, "That thing! That slithering blob coming toward us!" The mother asks, "What is it?" Their little boy, who is calmly picking his nose, says, "It's Melvin!"

Inside, everything was crazy, mixed-up and Melvinized. Contrary to convention, the comic contained one of everything: one horror story, one science fiction, one western and one detective story. And every story was a blatant, grotesque parody of its genre. In the horror story, called "Hoohah!," a complete schlep with pimples named Galusha is driving at night with his gorgeous, bosomy girl in a low-cut blouse. You see the car driving in the blackness, but it's not a classic, horror-comic, scary car; it's a rickety old heap with bowlegged wheels and two huge rabbity white eyes peeping out of it. The car runs out of gas, so Galusha and his girl have to go to a haunted house for help. The girl at once switches from her colloquial "Getcher hands offa me, creep" style of speech to the neoclassical declamation of the horror-story narrator: "They tell many stories of the Bogg House in the village! Stories of two brothers, Gog and Magog Bobb. . . ." Just as abruptly, she switches again. "But . . . we do need that gasoline bucket, eh, Galusha!" she yells, dragging him by the neck and pounding like crazy on the door of the haunted house. (In Mad, sounds are exaggerated and distorted far beyond even comic-book convention, until they fill up entire panels with stuff like "KAPOKA KAPOKA KAFONK FZZT." Emotions are similarly enormous: Fear is eyes bulging until they are telescopes, anger an instant sock in the puss, and all emotions come and go instantaneously.) It turns out the haunted house is haunted by the ghost of a caretaker named Melvin.

Also in Issue 1 there was a sci-fi story

about blobs of the future, one of whom is named Melvin; a western yarn about a Gary Cooper look-alike who's out to avenge the death of his friend Melvin; and a Melvinless crime story called "Gonifs," in which the slimy little big-nosed crook practices his pocket draw, his shoulder-holster draw and his under-the-hat draw in the mirror while his huge oaf of a henchman impeccably reels off an incredibly complicated robbery plan.

Mad was off and running. Subsequent issues continued the format of parodying a number of different comic book genres in each issue. Soon "big names" were showing up: "Prince Violent," "Superduperman," "Ripup's Believe It or Don't," "Darnold Duck," "Poop-eye," "Flesh Garden," "The Daily Poop" (a parody of The Daily News, with a "Kwestioning Kameraman" who, promising to pay $10 for every intelligent, thoughtful, important question submitted, asks, "You ever get punched inna nose?") and "Little Orphan Melvin." "Melvin" evolved as a running joke, and soon the name Melvin Cowznofski (coined by Ernie Kovacs) was associated with the drawing of a freckled, big-cheeked, cow-licked idiot boy who later became Mad's trademark, the infamous and glorious Alfred E. Neuman.

Actually, the face of Mad's Neuman is copied from a very old photograph of a real child. No one can remember his name or origins, but his genealogy is still hotly debated. According to one theory, he was first seen in a photograph in a 19th-century European medical textbook that discussed his extra-large ears. Then the photograph began turning up in America on postcards selling in penny arcades, with the slogan "What, me worry?" "The kid was depicted as a salesman, a cowboy, a doughboy and was rendered in dozens of slight to grossly altered variations, selling patent medicine, painless dentists, shoes and soft drinks," Kurtzman says. "But the answer I have always liked to believe was that the face came from an old high-school biology text—an example of a person who lacked iodine." In any case, Mad's Alfred E. Neuman was not related to the late Hollywood movie-music man named Alfred *New*man.

Mad was so rich in content that kids

could find all kinds of different things to like in it, but any analysis of Mad's success must begin with this idiot boy Alfred. In a short time, he appeared everywhere in Mad, especially on the cover, often drawn by an artist named Norman Mingo. If there was one thing about Mad that parents could recognize, it was Alfred, and they hated, loathed and despised him, were often nauseated at the very sight of him, and in general lived in complete terror of his entry into their house. It was downright frightening, after all, that such an obviously repulsive, *smiling* degenerate should not only not be locked away deep in a mental asylum but should be foisted on their kids as ideal companion and playmate. Alfred E. Neuman was everything that parents prayed deepdown their kids wouldn't turn into—and feared they would. Kids knew this, and clutched revolting Alfred to their chests. He was a generation's first emblem of protest—not angry, not nasty, not dogmatic, not self-righteous, nor any other bad, bad thing, but something far worse—he was *yecchy!*

What else about Mad made kids love it? Rick Meyerowitz, who in 1953 was one more little cryptodegenerate Melvin Cowznofski lover and who today is one of the top commercial artists in the country (the friendly little Amtrak engines to Florida are one of his more recent creations), put it succinctly: "I couldn't believe it. Somebody was putting down on paper all these things that were in my mind." Mad made public, and lent confirmation to, tens of thousands of thoughts that kids around the country had been afraid they were crazy for having. It was magical, objective proof to kids that they weren't alone, that in New York City on Lafayette Street, if nowhere else, there were people who knew that there was something wrong, phony and funny about a world of bomb shelters, brinkmanship and toothpaste smiles.

Mad's consciousness of itself, as trash, as comic book, as enemy of parents and teachers, even as money-making enterprise, thrilled kids. In 1955, such consciousness was possibly nowhere else to be found. In a Mad parody, comic-strip characters knew they were stuck in a strip. Darnold Duck, for instance, begins wondering why he has only three fin-

gers and has to wear white gloves all the time. He ends up wanting to murder every other Disney character. G.I. Schmoe tries to win the sexy Asiatic Red Army broad by telling her, "O.K., baby! You're all mine! I gave you a chance to hit me witta gun butt. . . . But naturally, you have immediately fallen in love with me, since I am a big hero of this story." Often the reader himself is made starkly self-conscious. In "Ripup's Believe It or Don't," a stone lion head stares out of the panel. The copy underneath reads: "Symbol of death! Sacred South American Indian symbol, when gazed upon, causes death within the year! Too bad if you looked."

A happy, anarchic profusion of life, combined with brilliant attention to detail, also characterized Mad from the beginning. One of the best early parodies was Wally Wood's "Superduperman," which appeared in Issue 4, copies of which now sell for $160 (original price: 10 cents). The plot has Clark Bent, who coughs a lot and has flies circling around his head, destroying Captain Marbles and then revealing to Lois Pain that he is really Superduperman. She says, "Hands off! Big deal! Yer *still* a creep!" The moral of the story is: "Once a creep, always a creep."

The first panel—a typical Mad panel—shows Superduperman crashing out of a tenement building to punch a harmless old cripple in the stomach. The cripple's glasses have jumped six inches off his nose, a set of false teeth is suspended in midair in front of his mouth, and he's lost his crutches. Lois Pain is simpering in one corner, and there are at least 19 other clearly identifiable characters in this one tiny picture. These include a brigade of citizens cheering Superduperman on, a skywriter writing "SUPER" in the sky, four infants who have no idea what's going on, an old codger who has no idea what's going on, and an incredibly tiny dog. Instead of an "S" on Superduperman's chest, there's the Good Housebreaking seal. Bricks and puffs of smoke are also flying around, and there's still room for two more tenements, seven billboards, one ad for the E.C. company and two for Mad, as well as an ad for Wally Wood cartoons with a self-portrait pasted to a tenement wall and surrounded by several "POST NO BILLS" signs.

It was the background detail in Mad that little Bobby Crumb studied hour after hour in his corner, and Phil Proctor, too. Proctor says: "Mad was a puzzle of comedy. You couldn't take it all in in one reading, so you'd delve back in. When Firesign started to make records, we wanted to do the same thing— create something so rich in activity that people would want to return to it again and again. We even sent one of our albums to Harvey Kurtzman and thanked him for his influence." Rick Meyerowitz remembers "Superduperman" particularly. "Wally Wood literally littered every picture, and I loved them because they were telling me, 'There are no rules, you can do anything.'"

Anarchy in art, anarchy in life: No wonder parents were scared. But was it really anarchy Mad preached, or was Mad simply, and merrily, offering to kids a kind of safety valve, a way of letting off steam, without which a generation might really have gone nuts? R. Crumb: "A lot of people know better now, but so many people just went along back then. If you were growing up lonely and isolated in a small town, Mad was a revelation. Nothing I read anywhere else suggested there was any absurdity in the culture. Mad was like a shock, breaking you out." Gloria Steinem, noted feminist and publisher, native of Ohio, former Harvey Kurtzman employee: "There was a spirit of satire and irreverence in Mad that was very important, and it was the only place you could find it in the 50's." Patti Smith, rock star and self-proclaimed "hick from southern New Jersey": "After Mad, drugs were nothing." There are people like Richard Goodwin, the writer, who say, "Mad had no social significance whatsoever," but many more who say things like actor Marty Feldman: "Mad had the courage to do things in very, very bad taste. . . . There is a link between Mad and Voltaire, Swift, Rabelais and S.J. Perelman—they all made bitter criticisms of society and values."

The argument can certainly be made that the cynicism Mad planted in its young readers' minds later flowered into the civil-rights, anti-war and hippie movements of the 60's. Maybe

so. But another way of looking at the effects of MAD's blithe spirit is to see that it saved a lot of kids in the "crazy years" from becoming the victims of their own movements. It doesn't show up in the newsreels of Lincoln Park, or in the tomes of the "serious" historians who have gone after the subject, or maybe in the memories of parents, cops, mayors and presidents of prestigious universities, but inside every one of the "heavy" movements was a great deal of self-deprecation and humor. R. Crumb exemplified it, and so did the Firesign Theatre. The late 60's presented a great opportunity for young people to be consumed by their own anger, but most weren't. Here Mad deserves some credit: Alfred E. Neuman put the lie to society, but he was too dumb and smiley to be entirely serious about destroying it, or himself.

In this connection, Mad's editorial policy in the late 60's is interesting. It seemed to abandon its children. Just as often as it satirized Nixon or L.B.J., it lambasted a protest movement or hippies. In December 1966, it ran a parody called "Protest Magazine," featuring articles like "Police Brutality and 10 Sure Ways to Excite It." In January 1969, it ran "Songs of Crime, Violence, War, Hate, Bigotry, and Lunatic Fringe and All-Around Ecchiness," introducing them as follows: "In the past, we've presented songs that glorified 'Food,' 'Pets,' 'Creeping Materialism' . . . However, there are some people who aren't content with such mundane and tame pursuits as these. And so, for those poor misguided idiots, Mad presents . . ." But was there really an abandonment here? Or was Mad simply, if rather blandly, carrying on its old function of pointing out cant and hypocrisy wherever it found it? Mad's teaching of humility seems fairly constant: A war may be lousy, and a government less than candid, and a society not quite what it seems, and if you see all this you may be able to do something about it— but never forget, no matter what you do, you'll still be in one great big boat with the likes of Melvin Furd and Alf. E. Neuman.

As a comic book, Mad lasted only three years. In 1955, a psychologist named Dr. Fredric Wertham brought on a Senate investigation and national uproar with his claim that horror comics and violence in comics caused juvenile delinquency. Mad, which not only contained a healthy amount of apocalyptic violence in every third frame but which depended on E.C.'s horror-comic business to carry it financially, hurriedly transformed itself into a 25-cent, large-format, slick, black-and-white magazine with "name" humor talent like Ernie Kovacs and Bob & Ray on the cover to give it drawing power and a certain hint of respectability. As a comic book, Mad had focused its satire on other comics. As a magazine, it quickly broadened its range to take in the movies, television shows, ads, products, politicians, celebrities and fads, all of which remain its staple diet today.

From the very first, Mad was arranged in "departments." A typical Mad of any vintage might contain anywhere from 10 to 20 of them, from a "Terror Dept." to a "Scenes We'd Like to See Dept." to a "Davy Crockett Dept." to a "Don Martin Dept.," reserved for a master of squiggly lines who has been a great favorite of Mad readers over the years.

The "department" format and the range of subject matter have remained stable through the years, yet Mad has undoubtedly changed since 1955. Part of the difference lies in the fact that kids get wised up a lot earlier now than they used to, so Mad has found itself playing to an increasingly younger audience, for whom it has felt obliged to be in some ways less sophisticated than it once was: 9-year-olds today pick up immediately on the phoniness of advertising, but do they catch an allusion to James Thurber? Another difference lies in Mad's acquisition of regular, by-lined contributors, each of whom puts a personal stamp on a portion of the magazine. Finally, Mad has spawned such a wide variety of rivals, imitators and offshoots that, no matter what its contents, it simply doesn't look as special as it used to.

In 1955, just after Mad adopted its new format, Harvey Kurtzman got into a dispute with Bill Gaines over control of the magazine. Kurtzman left Mad and went on to found a number of other influential though not very long-lived satire magazines—among them, Help!, where Gloria Steinem worked, and

Terry Gilliam and John (Minister of Funny Walks) Cleese, the cofounders of "Monty Python," first met. These magazines are all expensive collectors' items today. Al Feldstein replaced Kurtzman, and, 22 years later, is still the editor, just as Gaines is still Mad's publisher (though his E.C. Publications Inc. is now part of Warner Communications Inc.). Mad today is alive and healthy. It sells as many as two million copies a month in the summer and at Christmastime but hits a low of 1,650,000 during school months, according to the staff. It still contains no "real" advertising, although its phonies for such products as Canadian Clubbed and Iron-Maiden Fit bras have been favorites of kids over the years. Mad appears monthly in Swedish, Norwegian, Finnish, Dutch, Italian, German and British editions, and later this year plans to inaugurate publication in Japan and Greece.

You can still get an argument from some people if you say that Harvey Kurtzman was the real genius at Mad and that the magazine has never been the same since he left. Even Mel Furd wouldn't be so stupid and furschlugginer as to get into an argument like that one, but a couple of things are certain: (1) In the 22 years since Kurtzman left Mad, the magazine has published a lot of very funny material, and millions of grown men and women who never saw a Kurtzman Mad nevertheless have been strongly influenced by the magazine. (2) Those first 28 issues of Kurtzman's Mad, large portions of which can be found in the first volumes of Mad's extensive paperback reprint series, contain some of the deepest, most probing and hysterical humor in American history.

If Mad isn't as eye-opening as it once was, most of the responsibility lies with the entire new generation of artists, writers and media people who were weaned on it. "Mad sowed a lot of seeds that have sprouted in the unlikeliest places," says Henry Beard, one of the two cofounders of The National Lampoon. "If you read Mad, you had to be influenced by it. And everybody read it." There's a whole school of highly respected cartoonists in France whose style is directly derived from Mad, via René Gozzini, a French cartoonist who studied and shared a Greenwich Village studio with Kurtzman in the 60's. The French cartoonists also copied the idea of a novelistic story line from Kurtzman, who is the father of the modern comic strip in Europe, according to David Pascal, the scholarly foreign-affairs chairman of the National Cartoonists Society and author of "The Art of the Comic Strip."

Here at home, Mad silently left its mark on a generation of writers. "There's no one I know in the media today," says Michael Frith, art director for the outfit that makes the muppets for "The Muppet Show" and "Sesame Street," "who didn't read Mad as a kid. It has been a profound cultural force on the generation which, if not yet in control, is at least in vogue in the media as art directors, writers and editors. Jack Davis himself now draws Time magazine and TV Guide covers, in a style called 'bigfoot drawing'—a kind of satire that shows knobby knuckles in a lovable way—that is now in a great demand everywhere. A whole generation of art directors grew-up wanting to be Jack Davis."

On television, as Gloria Steinem notes, strong echoes of Mad resounded through "That Was The Week That Was" (where she also once worked) and are still to be heard weekly on "Saturday Night Live." "Jack Davis was one of the first artists I used at 'Sesame Street,'" says Christopher Cerf of the Children's Television Workshop, adding, "I loved Mad—I *loved* it. I used to make my father [Bennett Cerf] read it. He was always giving me things to read, and it was very hard for me to find things he hadn't read. Every now and then he would admit there was something funny in it." Andy Warhol also liked it—"Mad made me fall in love with people with big ears. That's a good influence, isn't it?" he says. "I founded The Realist as a Mad for adults," says Paul Krassner. "I now do stand-up comedy at colleges all over the country, and I'm getting good responses, and I know the audiences were made hipper for me by Mad." "Mad shaped my discernment of art," Phil Proctor sums it up, "and that has allowed me to have an effect on other people's discernment of art. We can take in more now because of Mad."

And what of Mad's redeeming social significance? We asked Prof. Melvin Furd Cowznofski, resident lepidopterist at prestigious Haaren High on 10th Avenue in New York City. Surprisingly, Cowznofski had a couple of mildly interesting things to say. "Sex," he said. "Got your interest up now? Yes, the one thing people always forget to say about Mad is that it had the healthiest, most wide-open, sexiest attitude toward sex that a kid was likely to find in the mid-50's. The girls, when they weren't literally horsefaces, were all beautiful, buxom beauties in tight-fitting clothes. Their boyfriends, or suitors, were nearly always on a par with Alfred E. Neuman in nurdiness. The boys were always trying to grab the girls, and the girls were always clobbering them with a pocketbook or a fist. If you see the theme of all Woody Allen movies prefigured here, you are quite right, but never mind. In the 50's, Mad was the truest expression available to many kids of the Complete Hopelessness and Craziness of True Love. Obviously, the sex in Mad was so healthy because it was so sick. Neurotic, sexist, sadomasochistic, idiotic, moronic, glorious furshlugginer trash! Kids from the Bronx telling kids from Des Moines the facts of life! . . . Now do you see what Mad was about?"

What us worry? Twenty-five years since Harvey Kurtzman got jaundice and decided to relax and do something that wouldn't give him jaundice, we may as well take the opportunity to thank Mad. We're all still here and it's still here, and that alone means something. Who would have thought that that trashy, furshlugginer Mad, which once made its cover like a black-and-white-speckled composition book so that kids could slip it past their teachers into class, which another time put out a cover like Foreign Affairs so that you could read it on the subway and "make people think you're reading high-class intellectual stuff instead of miserable junk," which once ran Mona Lisa on its cover clasping Mad to her breast, would one day rate a celebratory feature in this esteemed, prestigious, undeniably high-class and intellectual publication? It's a little like the kid from Brooklyn getting to Carnegie Hall, no? Or the sandlotter from the Bronx who makes the Yanks and, after 20 glorious years, is honored by a day at the Stadium? Well, Alfred E. Neuman would have a word for all of that: Yeccch! Yeccch, but there it is.

Happy birthday, Mad!

PART THREE

The Sound Media

Radio

Conceived at the turn of the century primarily as a combination wireless-telegraph-telephone, radio developed rapidly into a diversified medium with an instantaneous mass appeal. The pace of its organizational growth alone was startling. Within a little more than fifteen years after the first random, private "broadcasts" (originally an agricultural term for scattering seed widely), an entire media industry was created: receivers and equipment were manufactured, broadcasting schedules and stations designated, networks established, licensing regulations decided upon, advertising accepted, a Federal Radio Commission founded, and major patterns of programming instituted. By the late 1920s, "listening to the radio" had become a leading national pastime.

The statistics speak for themselves. In 1928, eight years after the first commercial station went on the air, 10 million radio sets were in operation; by 1935, the total had risen to nearly 31 million. The number of sets grew to 105.3 million in 1952 and, despite severe competition from television, continued to rise, reaching 456.2 million by January 1980. Currently, 99 percent of United States homes have at least one working radio, while the average household contains 5.7 sets. The most recent estimates* show that the average American adult spends 3 hours and 32 minutes per day with radio (compared to 4 hours and 3 minutes with television, 34 minutes with newspapers, and 27 minutes with magazines). College students, incidentally, spend more time daily with radio than with television—2 hours and 45 minutes as opposed to 2 hours. In terms of the advertising dollar, radio accounted for $3.1 billion in 1979.

If competition with television, however, did not prevent radio's growth, it did radically alter the direction of its development. As listeners gradually became viewers, the major shows of radio's "Golden Age," unable to contend with evening television entertainment, signed off the air, one by one. At one time the dominating, national medium for both entertainment and advertising, by the mid-fifties, radio found itself forced into a total redesign of its "product" in order to stay alive as a leading media industry.

The history of radio, as described by John W. Wright in the opening selection of this section, is the success story of a medium continually able to reinvent itself: from a practically oriented telegraph-telephone communications system to a "home music box" for mass entertainment; from a clumsy living room instrument to a slim, portable transistor. Yet, perhaps its greatest transformation was from a major national medium to a predominately local one. (In 1979, for example, local advertising accounted for nearly 75 percent of total radio advertising, compared with 4 percent for network). By changing its program format and concentrating on local

*from Radio Advertising Bureau, Inc.

audiences and local advertising, radio survived its household clash with television and entered the 1970s as a growth industry with a new, flexible personality.

In its evolution, radio has displayed what Richard Maisel, in another essay in this book (see "The Decline of the Mass Media," pp. 17–25), has described as "an increasing growth rate for specialized communication directed to smaller, more homogeneous audiences." This upward trend was spurred on largely by the commercialization of FM stations, which allowed for specialization, especially in music programming. In "FM," Peter Fornatale and Joshua E. Mills discuss how the superior FM signal led to a new, beautiful stereo sound, enabling, in turn, progressive radio stations to attract an appreciable portion of the young adult market.

As radio began to segment and target its audience, in much the same way as did the magazine industry (see pp. 199–203), profits for both AM and FM stations rose enormously. According to the *Business Week* article in this section, "radio is enjoying a prosperity undreamed of just five years ago." Much of this new prosperity is due to the quantity of local advertising radio can readily obtain; radio already has a greater share of the advertising dollar than has the magazine industry. Moreover, since radio is not nearly as labor intensive or capital intensive as are newspapers and television, it may outpace these rivals as advertising budgets tighten in the near future. Specialization in programming formats has contributed significantly to radio's increased advertising revenues. Local advertisers can now tie their commercials into syndicated shows targeted directly to optimum markets—for example, record shops can sponsor weekend-long histories of rock music, hardware stores can underwrite programs on home repair.

Specialization, moreover, requires specialists. As more and more stations want to overhaul formats, improve ratings, or hook up with standardized, prepackaged programming, they find themselves turning to a new professional group—independent programming consultants. In her report, Donna L. Halper labels these influential specialists a "power elite," for they wield enormous authority in determining the kind of radio programs the public hears. Independent consultants, she points out, play an especially powerful role in popular music programming, a high-risk marketing area that affects "millions of people and in turn generates billions of dollars in record sales."

The "elitism" of the consultants, however, has little to do with radio's overall public image and responsibility. Of all the nonpersonal media featured in this book, radio is at present the most receptive to the individual members of its audience. For the ordinary citizen, book publishing, the recording business, and films are considerably remote, formidable enterprises, their authors, stars, and even staffs often glamorized personalities. But even allowing for letters to the editor, advice columns, quiz shows, teenage dance programs, and occasional post-news rebuttals, newspapers, magazines, and television still do not permit as much spontaneous, individual participation as does radio. The sense of personal participation, to be sure, is often accomplished synthetically by a highly polished, colloquial, chatty broadcasting style with frequent allusions to actual listeners tossed in along the way: "Congratulations, Mrs. Riley, you have just won"; or, "To Freddie and Fern in Fernwood who have been going together for two weeks now. . . ." Yet, as Gay Sands Miller observes in "King of the Night," the specialized "talk-jockey" format of call-in radio can thoroughly engross an audience by giving its individual members an opportunity to get their opinions, gripes, and schemes on the air, even if only to a zany, unsympathetic host.

Despite all its diversified features, however, radio still means one thing to most listeners—music. Rock, classical, country, jazz, ballroom, blues, folk, popular, disco, easy listening. One of the most significant aspects of radio programming is its uneasy relationship with the recording companies. These two enormous industries, each highly dependent upon the other, maintain within the silence of studios a continual dissension the average listener never hears. Out of this marriage of convenience most popular music is born.

30
Radio and the Foundation of American Broadcasting

John W. Wright

In April 1912, a radio operator atop Wanamaker's department store in New York received an urgent message: "S.S. *Titanic* Ran Into Iceberg. Sinking Fast." The twenty-one-year-old operator who stayed at his post for seventy-two hours keeping the public informed was future communications magnate David Sarnoff. Sarnoff was to guide radio from its infant "wireless" stage to the complex national network system we now know. In the following account of radio's development, media historian John Wright demonstrates how the interlocking operations of big business, advertising, and programming set the organizational and entertainment patterns for subsequent electronic mass media.

A writer and editor with a major publishing house, John Wright is the author of *The Commercial Connection: Advertising and the American Mass Media* (1979), *The American Almanac of Jobs and Salaries* (1982), and a coauthor of *Edsels, Luckies & Frigidaires: Advertising the American Way.*

Marconi and Sarnoff: Communications and Big Business, 1900–1920

In February of 1896 Guglielmo Marconi arrived in England, bringing with him his Irish mother, his unshakeable confidence, and his little black box. His invention had been treated scornfully by the Italian government, so he decided to approach the pragmatic English, for surely they would understand the importance of what he had done. But the customs guards could not understand what was in the little black box, and mindful of recent assassinations and growing anarchist activities, their duty was clear: they smashed the box to splinters, for they were sure Marconi was a revolutionary. They were, of course, right.

After rebuilding his invention, Marconi's victory was swift and complete. He had little trouble convincing British businessmen and government officials of the possible impact of wireless telegraphy, so they let him run a series of demonstrations which proved that Marconi's waves travelled effortlessly over the countryside and even penetrated the famous English fog. Patents were quickly applied for and business deals completed. In 1901 Marconi started an American corporation with a capitalization of $10 million. Both the telegraph and the telephone had been funded in the same way and, of course, wireless, like the earlier forms of communication, would be expected to turn a profit. As the new century began, the twenty-seven-year-old Marconi had become a wealthy man, his name an international synonym for the Communications Revolution.

Marconi's success with dots and dashes helped to arouse interest in the possibilities of wireless voice transmission. As early as 1906 a Canadian named Reginald Fessenden broadcast a Christmas Eve "program" of music and poetry from the shores of Massachusetts which was heard by many ship's operators. In 1908 Lee DeForest, an American, broadcast from the top of the Eiffel Tower; foreshadowing later practice, the music was played on a phonograph and was heard more than 500 miles away. Two years later he broadcast the voice of Enrico Caruso live from the stage of the Metropolitan Opera. DeForest believed he was creating "a new Aeolian harp" which would bring the great music of the Western world to all of the people. The people, for their part, thought the radio experiments interesting, but frivolous. A disaster of great magnitude helped to change that notion.

On April 14, 1912 a wireless telegrapher sitting at his post high atop the Wanamaker department store in New York received the following message: "S.S. TITANIC RAN INTO ICEBERG. SINKING FAST." The telegrapher quickly notified the press and officials of American Marconi, and then returned to the telegraph key to establish contact with other ships in the area. In a few short hours the news of the sinking of the Titanic came through. Shock waves tore through the city and soon the crowds gathered outside the store for further information. For seventy-two hours the same telegrapher stayed at his post and copied down the names of survivors as they were wired across the Atlantic by the rescuing ship. Almost 1500 people died in this unparalleled disaster of the sea, but were it not for wireless communication the number would have been much greater—and it might have taken weeks for the world to learn of it. The newspapers incorporated this theme into many of their stories, and they also told of the dedication of the twenty-one-year-old telegrapher whose name appeared in print for the first time. The career of David Sarnoff was launched.

Sarnoff's life spans the entire history of broadcasting: from wireless to television, from the transmission of dots and dashes to the projection of visual images of man in space into millions of homes. The raw facts of his life constitute the typical American success story. Born in 1891 of Jewish parents in a peasant village in Russia, he came to the United States when he was ten, quickly learned English, and displayed remarkable mental agility and a love of hard work: he was at various times a delivery boy, a paper boy, a singer in the local synagogue, and, even for a short time, a newsstand operator. At sixteen he took a job as an office boy with American Marconi and soon became a telegrapher. His expertise helped him receive an appointment to the important Wanamaker station and, after the sinking of the Titanic, his skill came to the attention of Marconi himself. Sarnoff's unusual ability to deal with both businessmen and scientists in a fair and even-handed manner enabled him to reach management level within three years. Here he showed himself to be the ideal businessman for a technological age. He was interested in communications for itself but determined to make it useful for society. Moreover, his faith in the large corporation as a vehicle for rapid technological and social change never wavered. And in the years immediately preceding America's entry into World War I it was the established corporations who gained control of radio.

General Electric, Westinghouse, and American Telephone and Telegraph, all spawned by earlier technological breakthroughs, acquired most of the important patents of the radio pioneers and began their own research departments. This is not to say that many people had a clear idea of what broadcasting would be. In fact, as late as 1916, when Sarnoff (an assistant chief engineer at Marconi) wrote a now famous memorandum about the future uses of radio he was completely ignored by his superiors. Although American Marconi owned most of the wireless patents needed to create a broadcasting system, it never actively engaged in researching radio technology, so Sarnoff's prophetic words fell on the wrong ears.

> I have in mind a plan of development which would make radio a "household utility" in the same sense as the piano or phonograph. The idea is to bring music into the house by wireless. . . .
>
> The receiver can be designed in the form of a simple "Radio Music Box" and arranged for several different wave lengths, which could be changeable with the throwing of a single switch or pressing of a single button.
>
> The "Radio Music Box" can be supplied with amplifying tubes and a loudspeaking telephone, all of which can be neatly mounted in one box. The box can be placed on a table in the parlor or living room, the switch set accordingly and the transmitted music received.
>
> The same principle can be extended to numerous other fields as, for example, receiving lectures at home . . . also events of national importance. . . . Baseball scores can be transmitted in the air by the use of one set installed at the Polo Grounds [New York]. The same would be true of other cities. This proposition would be especially interesting to farmers and others living in outlying districts removed from cities. By the purchase of a "Radio Music Box" they could enjoy concerts, lectures, music, recitals, etc. . . .

Music, baseball, national events, lectures —all in the parlor! Even before broadcasting had been born its essential characteristics—entertainment and information—could be delineated, its place in the daily lives of the people clearly foreseen.

America's entrance into the Great War quickly ended any dreams of cosmopolites dancing to "Radio Music Boxes," but like all modern wars this one brought about a tremendous upsurge in technological research, and improvements in wireless multiplied rapidly. Thousands of young men were trained in the use, repair, and construction of wireless and when they returned to America the interest in radio increased considerably.

The war also raised nationalistic sentiment to a new high, and American businessmen were happy to go along for the ride. With the full cooperation of the government authorities, British domination of American Marconi was ended and a new company called the Radio Corporation of America was established in 1919. GE and AT&T both agreed to buy enormous blocks of stock with the predictable result that all three corporations were soon sharing in each other's patented knowledge. The exclusion of Westinghouse, GE's major rival, from this alliance was to provide the impetus for the beginning of broadcasting in the United States.

Stations, Sponsors, Networks, 1920–1930

Frank Conrad worked in the radio department of Westinghouse in Pittsburgh. Although he had never gotten past the seventh grade, he held over 200 patents, many of them as a result of his war-time research into radio. Like thousands of others around the country, he was an avid amateur radio operator who tinkered in his garage every free moment. In 1919 he started playing phonograph records over the air much to the delight of his friends, and soon he had a small but faithful following. By mid-1920 Conrad and his sons had a regular broadcasting schedule, including Saturday evening "concerts" and weekday performances. An important Westinghouse official, eager for his company to stake an early claim in radio, convinced the firm to let Conrad establish a permanent, more powerful station where a daily advertising schedule of broadcasting could be developed. The expected increase in the sale of Westinghouse receiver sets would more than pay for the investment. Station KDKA was set up in October 1920, just in time to broadcast the results of the Harding-Cox election.

The ramifications of this simple election returns broadcast, heard by only 2,000 people, were immediate and far reaching. RCA, General Electric, and AT&T all began to explore ways of entering this new field, since everyone now feared that Westinghouse or someone else might secure a preeminent position in broadcasting. But these large corporations were not the only interested parties: by the end of 1922 more than 450 new stations had sprung up all around the country, many of them owned by newspapers, department stores, or manufacturers of radio equipment. The public, too, was growing increasingly interested in radio so that sales of tubes, batteries, receiver sets, etc., totalled $60 million in 1922 and $136 million the following year. By that time many of the more powerful stations —WWJ (Detroit), KYU (Chicago), WFAA (Dallas), WOR (New York) and WJZ (Newark)—were broadcasting on a fairly regular basis. Although their programs seem odd by our standards, the radio audience, headsets firmly in place, listened in continued astonishment to the crackling sounds of tenors and sopranos singing arias from the most famous operas, or internationally acclaimed orchestras playing Bach or Beethoven gloriously through the static. Most of the time the stations used phonograph records but there was occasionally a live performance. The music was generally of the staid, conservatory variety, or, for a lighter touch, the mellow sounds of a society orchestra such as Vincent Lopez's. Radio was growing in popularity but it was clearly not a mass medium. Gradually, the nature of the programs changed as the size and make-up of the audience began to reflect a broader social base.*

And, of course, the radio audience did continue to grow, spurred on by broadcasts of special events such as college football games, the 1924 World Series, and the National Democratic and Republican conventions of the same year. It wasn't much, but the American people responded to what was there with overwhelming enthusiasm: in 1924 they invested $358 million in radio equipment. Even Sarnoff had underestimated the visceral appeal of the "Radio Music Box"; in four short years it had captured the imagination of a nation and it would soon transform the nature of its leisure time.

During these first formative years of radio's history the growth of the system was so rapid, indeed so chaotic, that no one could give much thought to the future development of the broadcasting structure. How would the system be organized: locally, regionally, or nationally? Who would be the final arbiter of what constituted acceptable content? How would radio be financed? Would there be a tax on receiving sets as there was in England? Or should radio be treated as a museum or library, as Sarnoff once believed, so that the wealthy could provide the necessary funds? Could there be advertising on the air? During this period the federal government under the leadership of Secretary of Commerce Herbert Hoover called several radio conferences, but matters of licenses and attempts to clear up interference had to take precedence. As a result, the burden of establishing a broadcasting structure fell to individual stations, especially to those owned by the giant radio corporations. Of these, none was more important than WEAF, the New York station owned and operated by American Telephone and Telegraph.

For good or ill, WEAF was the station most responsible for bringing advertising to radio and for developing the idea of sponsorship. AT&T began operation of WEAF in the

---

*Early radio did have its share of fascinating characters, such as Iowa's TNT "Cancer is Curable" Baker, and "Tea-leaf Kitty" from Jersey City who promised to answer any three questions which came to her in a sealed envelope "together with one dollar." But the most interesting of all was Dr. John R. Brinkley of Kansas, who first acquired fame by transplanting goat gonads into men who believed themselves sexually impotent. He parlayed this success into a million dollar patent medicine business and a run at the governorship before the federal government and the AMA drove him to Mexico.

summer of 1922 with the express purpose of providing a radio service to all who wished to avail themselves of the station's facilities, and who could afford to pay the fee. AT&T expressed its belief that radio should be financed in the same way as the telephone, i.e., the sender of the message pays the bill. Known at the time as "toll broadcasting," this system, said AT&T, was the best way to insure high quality radio programs because it put broadcasting, like other American businesses, on a profit-making basis.

During the first six months the station and its clients struggled to find a method of using the new medium in a way that would not only be profitable for both, but which would also be entertaining to the listening audience. At first most of the paid announcements took the form of fifteen minute lectures on some aspect of the speaker's business enterprise. The station's first commercial message, aired on August 28, 1922 for a fee of $50, was a talk about how wonderful life was in a tenant-owned apartment building called Hawthorne Court, located just across the river in suburban Queens. There were talks on gasoline, greeting cards, cosmetics, automobiles, department stores, but there was no aggressive selling or price mentioning, since just about everyone, including AT&T, felt such tactics would be unacceptable in the American home.

Despite the fact that clients were signing on to broadcast over WEAF, there simply weren't enough of them to make the operation profitable, nor did the little commercial speeches stir up much excitement. At the beginning of 1923 the station's management decided to reach for a broader-based audience by broadcasting popular forms of entertainment. Backed by the enormous resources of AT&T the station began a series of expensive programs (including live vaudeville acts broadcast from a Broadway theater) designed to win audience recognition. The station consciously began to play more contemporary music in order to appeal to the younger generation. Other large stations had been avoiding this kind of music because ASCAP (American Society of Composers, Authors, and Publishers) was demanding that radio reimburse the

composers' anytime a copyrighted song was played over the air. But WEAF, eager to increase the size of its audience and determined to show the economic power of commercial broadcasting, announced that it would reach an agreement with ASCAP and gladly pay the fee. This decision caused bitterness and consternation among the other stations, especially the RCA-owned WJZ which had led the resistance to ASCAP because of Sarnoff's view of radio as a public service. But it also brought a great deal of business to WEAF as the commercial possibilities of popular music were quickly recognized.

The public's enthusiastic reaction to the popular music it heard over WEAF enabled the station's sales staff to convince a few clients to become sponsors, that is, to pay for both time and talent as a means of securing the "good will" of the listening audience. The first to sign up for a regularly scheduled program was the Browning King men's store which agreed to sponsor Anna Byrnes's Orchestra on a weekly basis. The name was changed to *The Browning King Orchestra,* and so began the practice of sponsor identification with its program. For WEAF the implications were clear. If it could convince other firms to do the same the station would have both a series of popular programs and a steadily increasing income as well.

Over the next six months the sales staff concentrated their efforts in this direction. Soon WEAF's listeners were hearing the bouncy sounds of *The Lucky Strike Orchestra, The A&P Gypsies, The Ipana Troubadours,* and *The Cliquot Club Eskimos.* * Typical of WEAF's strategy during 1923 was the case of Billy Jones and Ernie Hare, a popular vaudeville team who specialized in "songs and patter." The station put them on the air as a regular sustaining program and simply waited for the fan mail. Within a few months their appeal to the radio audience was indisputable and they were soon being sponsored by the Happiness Candy Company. They would eventually become nationally famous as *The Happiness Boys.*

Although WEAF lost $100,000 in 1923,

---

*Ipana was a toothpaste; Cliquot Club, a ginger ale.

the discovery of the sponsorship formula would soon make the investment worthwhile. Over the next year more clients were found and some older ones like Eveready Batteries, which presented drama on the *Eveready Hour,* expanded their commitment. By 1925 the station showed a net profit of $150,000, and the future looked even better since four clients were spending over $60,000 a year just for air time. (A radio manufacturer, Atwater Kent, who sponsored symphonic music spent a total of $120,000 that year for both time and talent.)

What lay behind this sudden period of growth and the optimistic mood was the success of so-called "chain broadcasting." From the very beginning AT&T had said it desired to establish a national radio service that would resemble its telephone system. RCA and others thought the same, but since AT&T controlled the wires necessary for long distance broadcasting, its position was obviously the strongest. Between 1922–1924 it developed special telephone wires which dramatically improved long distance reception, and by 1925 thirteen stations around the country could be linked together. The potential size of the audience for WEAF's sponsored programs had grown to include 42 percent of the country's entire population. Radio was well on its way to becoming an effective national advertising medium.

In 1926, as a result of a complicated legal decision, AT&T was forced to abandon its direct involvement in broadcasting. At the urging of David Sarnoff, RCA, already the most powerful force in radio manufacturing and technology, bought WEAF for $200,000 and agreed to lease long-distance wires from AT&T for $800,000 a year. It is not an overstatement to say that from this merger came the basic structure of American broadcasting. Since WEAF had proven conclusively that sponsors made broadcasting very profitable (while at the same time sponsors learned that popular programs drew enormous audiences whose appreciation could be instantly felt at the cash register), RCA believed its stockholders wanted to follow the same route. The result was the formation in November, 1926 of the National Broadcasting Company, our

first and most important network. Two chains were set up, one with WEAF as the chief station (Red Network) and the other WJZ heading the list (Blue Network). Both were to be financed by the acceptance of sponsored broadcasts, especially in the hours between 7 PM and 11 PM.

Since American business is based on the spirit of competition, no one was surprised when a rival network, the Columbia Broadcasting System, began operating less than a year later. Very few thought it would survive, however, and ownership of the new network passed successively from a manager of concert orchestras and his cement-salesman partner to the Columbia Phonograph Co. (who gave it the name Columbia Broadcasting System), a subway builder, a dentist, a lawyer, and, finally, in September 1928 to the family of wealthy Philadelphia cigar manufacturer Sam Paley. Paley's twenty-seven-year-old son, William, took charge of CBS, overseeing financial and programming matters alike, two functions he would perform with great skill for almost fifty consecutive years.

Between 1927 and 1930 radio made gigantic strides on its way to becoming a medium for the masses. Receiving sets were constantly improving and some even worked on regular household current. In 1927 the newly-established Federal Radio Commission (FRC) was finally able to sort out the air waves and establish clear channels for regular programming. And in that short period radio advertising expenditures soared from an estimated $4 million in 1927 to $19 million just two years later. The number of network sponsors increased from 160 in 1928 to 237 in 1929 and familiar brand names were inserted into the titles of America's favorite radio shows: *The Camel Pleasure Hour, The Voice of Firestone, The Kodak Front Porch, The General Motors Party, The Coca-Cola Hour* are only a few.

Music accounted for more than 75 percent of all sponsored broadcasts during this period, but the most famous program and the most popular was *Amos 'n' Andy,* a fifteen minute comedy skit based on a combination of vaudeville and minstrel humor. In 1929 the program doubled the sales of its sponsor,

Pepsodent toothpaste. Together, the networks and the advertisers were creating the most entertaining selling medium yet devised. Even the worst economic disaster in our history couldn't deter it.

A National Entertainment Factory, 1930–1940

During the Depression years radio completely enmeshed itself in the patterns of everyday American life. While almost every other form of business reeled under the impact of international economic stagnation, radio continued to grow in every conceivable way. Indeed, as "hard times" encouraged more and more people to spend their leisure time at home, the nation's preoccupation with radio reached staggering proportions: between 1930–1936 the number of homes with receiving sets literally doubled (12 million to 24.5 million); by 1940, 29 million homes or 90 percent of the total had at least one set, but 22 million of those had two or more; between 1930–1940 the total number of sets in the United States grew from 13 million to 51 million. Advertising expenditures had grown to $112 million by 1935 and then increased to $215 million in 1940. At the same time the network systems of NBC and CBS took a firm hold on the economic aspects of broadcasting and a national radio service was established. The total number of stations affiliated to the principal networks rose from 133 in 1930 to 331 at the end of the decade. Moreover, a group of 4 independent stations which had joined together in 1935 to form the Mutual Broadcasting System had grown to 160 members by 1940.

Generally speaking, the movement toward affiliation had its roots in the old advertising maxim that the cost of selling decreases in direct proportion to the number of people receiving the message. In 1940 the networks received almost one-half of all radio advertising dollars. But since the networks charged about $10,000 an hour for a coast-to-coast hook-up of 30 stations, only the large manufacturers with the potential for national distribution would find network radio an effective selling medium. Moreover, because sponsors

also had to pay for high-priced talent, they demanded and received final control over all aspects of programming. And what programs emerged from this commercial system! Night after night, day in and day out for nearly two decades, sponsors, advertising agencies, writers, talent bureaus, and network programming departments all joined together to produce several hundred thousand hours of entertainment which today are known collectively as the "Golden Age of Radio." For good or ill, it constitutes one of the most significant manifestations of American popular culture.

Throughout the thirties, popular music and star performers remained the most important elements in programming. But in a nation trying hard to forget its economic woes, comedy became an essential ingredient. Out of the audience's desire to have all three came the so-called "variety show" which ruled radio's prime-time hours. The star of the program usually served as the MC, introduced special guests, and took the lead in comedy skits or sang most of the songs, depending on his or her specialty. Still, it should be noted that no matter how popular these stars were, they almost all took second billing after the sponsor. So it was *The Kraft Music Hall* (starring Bing Crosby), *The Jell-O Program* (starring Jack Benny), *The Texaco Star Theater* (Ed Wynn), *The Chase and Sanborn Hour* (Edgar Bergen and Charlie McCarthy), and *The Pepsodent Program* (Bob Hope).

The development of the variety format did not drive out popular programs devoted exclusively to music. Although the number of sponsored broadcasts of classical music declined rapidly (*The Ford Sunday Evening Hour* was one survivor), different kinds of popular music were successfully introduced to network audiences. First came country and western *(The Grand Ole Opry* and *The National Barn Dance),* followed later in the decade by the Big Band sounds of Glenn Miller, Tommy Dorsey, Benny Goodman, and many others. Interestingly enough, virtually all of these bands were sponsored by brand-name cigarettes (*The Chesterfield Program; The Raleigh-Kool Program,* etc.) as the advertising people continued their tradition of associating smoking with the contemporary social scene. Another example, *The Lucky Strike Hit Parade,* which ranked and then performed the country's ten most popular songs, was the prototype for a musical format still very appealing today.

Between 1930 and America's entry into World War II almost all of the major forms of dramatic, nonmusical mass entertainment were developed and broadcast for the first time. These included what we would call "situation comedies" such as *The Aldrich Family* and *Fibber McGee and Molly,* family-oriented drama like *One Man's Family,* detective stories *(The Shadow; Mr. Keen, Tracer of Lost Persons),* police stories *(Gangbusters),* even programs about lawyers *(Mr. District Attorney)* and newspapermen *(Front Page Farrell).* Since about 75% of all Americans lived in urban areas it should not be surprising that many of the themes and settings of radio drama centered on city life. A concern for the interests of the audience has always been the secret to success in popular programming. As the glamour and glory of Hollywood and its stars became a national preoccupation during the Depression, especially among women, radio programs eventually began to reflect this obsession. *The Lux Radio Theater, The Silver Theater,* and *Hollywood Hotel* all presented important movie stars in dramatic renderings of famous novels, plays, and even forthcoming films.*

During the morning and afternoon hours radio serials were presented in fifteen-minute episodes. Designed to reach "the lady of the house," the earliest dramatic programs were often sponsored by manufacturers of soaps and detergents, hence their most common generic name, "soap operas." All of them dealt with love, marriage, raising children, adultery (the "other woman"), and divorce. Many of the most famous and long-lasting ones—including *Our Gal Sunday, The Romance of Helen Trent,* and *Stella Dallas*—were created by Frank Hummert, an advertising man, and his wife, Anne, who put together

a staff of writers capable of producing 100 scripts a week for twenty different "soaps." Most of the soap operas were sponsored by one of Procter & Gamble's products, including the world-famous "Oxydol's own *Ma Perkins.*" In fact, in 1940 P&G spent over $11 million on broadcasting, making it by far the leading broadcast advertiser. Almost all of its expenditures went to daytime serials for women. Thanks mostly to the Hummerts and to Procter & Gamble, the number of soap operas increased from eight in 1934 to forty-one in 1946.

Children, too, had their own serials. Usually they were aired between five and six in the evening and took the form of adventure stories. Many of them, including *Little Orphan Annie, Dick Tracy,* and *Terry and the Pirates,* were created directly from the comic strips of daily newspapers while others, such as *Jack Armstrong, the All-American Boy* or *The Lone Ranger,* became part of American youth culture directly through radio. Whatever the origin or the setting, be it western or science fiction, almost every adventure serial was sponsored by manufacturers of bread, cereal, or malted-milk mixes, all products which the advertiser, rightly or wrongly, linked to good nutrition for "growing boys and girls." During the thirties the first of many campaigns against advertising to children was launched, but the futility of these efforts can be viewed on television every Saturday and Sunday morning.

By 1940, the entertainment tastes of just about every segment of the radio audience were being attended to. Even the quiz program and amateur talent show had become well-established formats. A relatively small number of Americans argued that a larger percentage of radio content should be devoted to what they believed were programs of a "higher" cultural, spiritual, and intellectual order. However, they had no way of imposing this view on the industry or the radio audience. In 1934 Congress passed a comprehensive broadcasting act which not only established the Federal Communications Commission (FCC) as the government's chief regulatory agency, but also put into law the principles that the air waves belong to the people and

---

*This worked both ways, however, since Hollywood pursued radio's biggest names, like Hope and Crosby, and made them movie stars.

that broadcasting was a public service. But Congress also recognized that radio had to be granted the same First Amendment protection as the print media so, in effect, the bill reinforced the foundation of the broadcasting structure which had grown up since 1927. Program schedules and content were to remain the province of those who owned the stations and the networks. As early as 1930 the first "ratings" service (The Cooperative Analysis of Broadcasting, known as CAB) was telling advertisers which shows were the most popular and also giving hard evidence that the radio audience was receiving the kinds of programs it wanted. These programs would supply the content not only of radio for the next decade, but also of television during the first 15 years of its existence.

Even from such a brief description it should be obvious that network programming, like all commercial art, was designed to appeal to enormous numbers of people. In America this meant cutting through or avoiding troublesome regional differences (such as the racial tone of *Amos 'n' Andy*) and, at the very least, blurring class distinctions so that the poor were never mentioned and the rich only mildly satirized. Since one of the major purposes of radio entertainment was attracting audiences for advertisers, sponsored programs could not contain material which might be offensive to any group within the population. Of course, this was possible only if serious religious and political questions were avoided and all allusions to sexuality restricted to the milder forms of prepubescent humor.

To some critics, this less-than-honest response to the real world is typical of the hypocrisy endemic to American business; to others, it means that radio programs reflected not reality but what many people idealistically wished life could be. To students of the history of broadcasting this attitude should stand as a constant reminder that radio was primarily an entertainment medium which provided advertisers with a powerful tool for stimulating consumption. It remained such even during our most severe national crisis.

World War II and Radio News

Throughout World War II radio played a major role in disseminating the propaganda which would unite the nation against its enemies. Enormous numbers of war bonds were sold over the air on special programs hosted by the medium's biggest stars, and almost every program and commercial contained some allusion to the need to buy bonds, to observe rationing regulations, or to remember "the boys overseas." Many of the writers of popular serials involved their characters directly in the war, some in silly and predictable ways (e.g., Superman saving Lois Lane from the clutches of the "Japs"); others in serious, even moving fashion as when Ma Perkins's son John was killed "somewhere in Germany." But, for all Americans, radio's most vital function was the instantaneous transmission of war news from all over the globe. Thanks mainly to the superb news departments organized by NBC and CBS, the war taught people to turn to radio in time of crisis and to trust the medium as a gatherer and supplier of information. Many of broadcasting's finest journalists started as young war correspondents, and some, like Edward R. Murrow, Walter Cronkite, Charles Collingwood, and Eric Severeid, emerged as prominent and respected public personalities.

The impact of the war on the radio industry's opinion of broadcast news was just as strong. Radio executives had previously paid little attention to news on a daily basis. According to one estimate, less than 3 percent of network program time during the thirties was devoted to news reporting and most of this was in the form of special events such as FDR's "Fireside Chats," Presidential election returns, and bulletins. One reason for this was that news wasn't profitable. Sponsors understandably refused to have their names associated with depressing daily occurrences—gangland murders, unemployment, violent strikes, business failures, etc. Without sponsorship the financial burden of newsgathering, even on a national basis, proved far too expensive for the networks to bear. Moreover, the newspaper industry jealously guarded its access to the prestigious international news services, AP and UPI, and for the first five years of the Depression fought legal battles and threatened to excise all reports about radio from the daily press. Many newspapers were struggling for survival and justifiably feared radio's growing power,* although they wrongfully blamed the new medium for the decline in newspaper advertising revenues.

During the mid- and late thirties a few news "commentators" such as Boake Carter and H. V. Kaltenborn obtained sponsors for their network broadcasts, but since the ideas and opinions expressed were neither radical nor challenging, the programs aroused little controversy. However, when in 1939 Kaltenborn refused to end his attacks on the Nazis or on France, General Mills dropped their support immediately. Kaltenborn's popularity helped him quickly secure another sponsor, but broadcast journalists had quickly learned the coercive power of those who paid the broadcasting bills. The virtual unanimity of national public opinion after America entered the war, however, obscured this problem and the number of sponsored commentaries as well as pure broadcasts rose significantly.

Contrary to what one might expect, the broadcasting system, like so many other American businesses, actually expanded during the war. More important, advertising dollars, the major source of revenue, increased substantially. Even though many manufacturers had nothing to sell to the people, their profits grew through sales to the government. A desire to keep their names before the public and to obtain the good will of the radio audience persuaded sponsors to continue to underwrite broadcasting. In addition, since advertising costs could be deducted from income tax reports, radio sponsorship helped many businesses avoid the war-time excess profits tax.

Television and the Changing Nature of Radio

After the war the American people consciously prepared themselves for a period of extra-ordinary economic expansion. To be sure, temporary setbacks could be expected but the war-time experience had proven conclusively that America's production capabilities were unparalleled in the history of the modern world. In this atmosphere radio emerged as the country's most prestigious medium and the five years following the truce resulted in larger audiences than ever, more stations, more elaborate programs, and, of course, more revenue from advertising.

But in the midst of this exuberant display of strength beamed the soft glow of television, foreshadowing a new era in broadcasting. RCA, the most powerful force in the radio industry, had taken control of television development in the late twenties and early thirties. With the end of the war RCA, together with NBC and CBS, began to prepare the public and the broadcasting community for rapid acceptance of the new medium. FM radio had reached the point where it was ready for commercial broadcasting, but it was shunted aside in favor of television and the famous network radio programs were gradually retooled and shifted to the new visual medium. According to Erik Barnouw in his history of broadcasting, the networks even devised a method for using rising radio profits to finance the final stages of research on commercial television.

The end came quickly and without mercy. Between 1950–1955, over 25 million television sets were sold, and the percentage of homes with television rose from 9 percent to 65 percent. Television advertising revenues increased from $90.6 million to $681 million, from 3 percent to 11 percent of the total advertising expenditures in all media. Radio, on the other hand, declined from 11 percent to 6 percent of that total and network advertising revenues were dramatically cut in half ($131 million to $64 million) as radio desperately began to redefine its role from a national to a local medium.

Although total radio revenues actually declined slightly during these years, the groundwork for future growth—an increase of over $200 million in the last half of the decade—was established. Forever locked into the formula that advertising pays the broadcasting bill, station executives working on reduced

---

*Many publishers took the attitude that if you couldn't beat them, join them, and by 1940 about one-third of all stations were owned or controlled by newspapers.

budgets struggled to attract audiences not mesmerized by the tube. Going after inexpensive content, they came up with a proliferation of news reports, talk shows, and recorded music. The Todd Storz station in Omaha provided the first "Top 40" format in 1954, just about the same time as the rock and roll phenomenon began to furnish radio and advertisers with a new target audience, affluent teenagers and young adults. About the same time a media researcher, Alfred Politz, was able to pinpoint the listening habits of a large percentage of adults and the results revolutionized radio programming. Contrary to received opinion, said Politz, the morning and evening hours were the most popular listening times: men were driving to and from work and women were in the kitchen cleaning up the breakfast dishes or preparing the dinner. Most important, neither had access to a television

and so the concept of "drive-time" radio—news, traffic reports, light chatter, music, became a new way for radio to participate in our daily lives.

Sarnoff made his prophetic remarks about the "Radio Music Box" over sixty years ago, but much of what he said remains true today. We may listen in our cars and not in our "parlors," and we may carry the set to the beach in our shirt pockets and no longer worry about "amplifying tubes," but music, news, and baseball are still among the nation's chief interests. And, of course, it is radio we turn to when we find ourselves in an emergency, be it a blackout in a big city, a hurricane along the Gulf, a flood in Pennsylvania, or a tornado in Kansas. Television may dominate our leisure time, but it is still radio that keeps us in touch with the world when we need it most.

Peter Fornatale & Joshua E. Mills

Although radio now seems like an old medium, commercialized FM stations are actually a relatively recent phenomenon. As Peter Fornatale and Joshua E. Mills observe in the following essay, FM did not become a viable (and profitable) system of broadcasting until the late 1960s and early 1970s, when it was recognized as a significant form of radio entertainment, capable of successfully competing with AM. The ultimate success of FM was due to the exceptional quality of its signal, which attracted millions of high-fidelity music lovers. But FM was more than its signal. "The emerging music," the authors point out, "as important as it was, pales beside the explosive force that made FM socially significant: the political and cultural movements of the 1960's."

Peter Fornatale, the midday host of a popular New York FM station, is coauthor of *The Rock Music Source Book*. Joshua E. Mills, a former popular culture columnist for the *Daily News,* is now an assistant professor of journalism at New York University.

The Federal Communications Commission ordered "the opening of the FM spectrum" in July 1964, which led to a steady climb in both the quantity and quality of FM operations, and eventual parity with the older system of program transmission, AM.

Source: From *Radio in the Television Age,* by Peter Fornatale and Joshua E. Mills, published by The Overlook Press, Lewis Hollow Road, Woodstock, New York 12498. Copyright © 1980 by Peter Fornatale and Joshua E. Mills.

FM stands for *f*requency *m*odulation, AM for *a*mplitude *m*odulation. Modulation means the process of changing some characteristic of the radio wave. (Consider why change is important: if a siren howls constantly, it carries no meaning to those hearing it. It is only when a siren interrupts a silence that its message—to be alert—is clear.) In the earliest form of electric transmission, the telegraph, modulation involved interrupting the signal. In Morse code, the variables were the length of the signal (dots and dashes) and the intervals between the signals. Roughly speaking, amplitude modulation means a change is effected in the volume of the signal: the distance between the height of the radio wave and its trough is increased. Frequency modulation involves a change in the pitch of the signal: the height of the wave is constant, but the distance between each crest changes. In its earliest days, radio had one predominant problem: spotty reception. Static from both atmospheric conditions and other broadcasts made clear, continuous reception of a single signal very much an uncertain situation.

Edwin H. Armstrong, an inventor and the holder of several patents for early AM radio devices, resolved to tackle the static problem. In 1922 he sold RCA a patent for the superheterodyne circuit, which greatly enhanced a receiver's ability to separate signals, and became a millionaire. In a basement at Columbia University in New York City, he sought at his own expense to develop a means of broadcasting without static. RCA, in purchasing the earlier patent, also bought first refusal on Armstrong's subsequent work, and he labored long and hard under the impression that RCA was most interested in his work. But what started out as a partnership ended in years of controversy and legal struggle.

Armstrong's work went well, if slowly. In 1933 he took out four patents and notified RCA that his work was ready for inspection. When David Sarnoff and his aides arrived at Columbia University, Armstrong unveiled "frequency modulation." RCA asked him to install an FM transmitter at the Empire State Building for tests. The receiver was placed 70 miles away, in Westhampton Beach on Long Island's south shore. The tests were a complete success: the range of sound and the clarity

and the freedom from static were a revelation to those familiar with broadcasting problems. Armstrong expected RCA to exercise its option and put the FM system into production. But RCA stalled. After a year with no word from corporate headquarters, Armstrong was asked in April 1935 to remove his equipment from the Empire State Building.

Armstrong, bitter at RCA, decided on a public demonstration of FM. Scheduled to read a paper at the convention of the Institute of Radio Engineers in November 1935, Armstrong presented an FM broadcast as well. He rigged a transmitter in Yonkers, just north of New York City. The surprise demonstration stunned the engineers, who, as their astonishment passed, burst into applause. Gathering strength from their plaudits, Armstrong headed for the FCC, seeking spectrum space for FM broadcasts. In Washington he began Round One in a series of head-to-head confrontations with Sarnoff and RCA.

Armstrong thought he brought the FCC —and thereby the public—a better form of radio. RCA did not contest the merits of FM, a tactic that certainly would have failed, but instead offered the FCC a shinier apple: It applied for spectrum space for television. The issue before the FCC was how much room remained in the spectrum and what to do with it. After due consideration the FCC turned down Armstrong's request for an experimental station. (One of RCA's witnesses at the FCC hearings was C. B. Jolliffe, only weeks before the commission's chief engineer, but now in RCA's employ.) But Armstrong lobbied on, offering as proof his successful field experiments, and the FCC granted him a license. In 1937 he built a 50,000-watt FM station in Alpine, New Jersey. W2XMN went on the air in 1939, and its performance became Armstrong's most convincing argument for FM development. CBS decided to throw its weight behind FM and encouraged manufacturers to produce receivers. The FCC received 150 applications for FM stations. In Round Two before the FCC, Armstrong and his new (and mighty) allies, turned back the RCA challenge. The FCC removed Channel 1 from television and assigned it to FM. The FCC also ruled that all televisions must employ FM sound for broadcasting. Armstrong seemed to have won. Then World War II began. In 1942 the FCC froze all station allocations for the duration of the war, with 30 FM stations on the air. FM was widely used in military radio, but domestically it was virtually in the closet, making little dent in the public consciousness against 909 AM stations.

With the war's end, the tide turned in Washington, and Armstrong lost Round Three. The FCC decided to move FM radio to a different range of frequencies: from 42–50 MHz up to the 88–108 it occupies today. The immediate effect was that the half-million sets sold before the war were rendered obsolete. Fans and set owners were alienated, perceiving FM as an unstable industry.

Embittered, Armstrong turned his attention to legal clashes. At the FCC's direction, television was using FM sound. Westinghouse, Zenith, and General Electric were paying Armstrong royalties for his FM patents. RCA and some smaller companies refused. RCA offered instead a million-dollar settlement, far less than Armstrong would have been entitled to in royalties. Armstrong sued in 1948. The fight dragged on. In 1953, fatigued, frail, and bitter, Armstrong suffered a stroke. He became isolated from his family and friends. On February 1, 1954, Armstrong committed suicide by jumping from the 13th-floor window of his Manhattan apartment. RCA settled with his estate for $1 million. But his widow pressed suits against the smaller companies, and over 13 years she won each case.

Despite the shift of frequencies and the problems it caused, many broadcasters were optimistic about FM immediately after the war. The sound was so superior, they thought, that FM was bound to dominate radio. By 1947 more than 900 licenses had been issued for FM operations. But operators faced a double bind, caught between AM and television. AM had benefited from technical progress during the war and made substantial reductions in static. Most Americans owned only AM radios. Weighing what new products to buy, people looked at FM, about which they did not know much, and television, a heavily-advertised glamour product whose differences from and advantages over AM radio were obvious. To build an FM audience, broadcasters had to convince the public to buy FM sets. Without a substantial audience, FM radio could not attract advertisers. Without advertisers FM license holders did not have the revenue either to mount promotional campaigns or to develop unusual or distinguished programming to attract new audiences. These problems were compounded by the mediocre quality of some of the FM radios on the market—receivers that were not well made enough to demonstrate the superiority of FM sound.

In an effort to promote FM and acquaint a wide radio audience with its potential, the FCC proposed simulcasting—broadcasting identical material simultaneously on AM and FM—to free FM radio from the need for advertisers and the costs of program development. Of course simulcasting was not in the best interests of independent FM stations: They were scratching for survival and could hardly compete for advertising when their competition's rates were subsidized by AM operations. (Years later, in the order that opened the spectrum, the FCC noted, indirectly, the sacrifices these independent stations had had to make; the FCC acknowledged that in 1964 most independents were still not making a profit and suggested that their prospects for profits would be improved when they no longer had to compete with simulcasting competitors.) Despite the independents' problems, the FCC decided that the long-range interest of radio would best be served by simulcasting. FCC critics suggested that the commission was preoccupied with television and not thinking clearly about what radio needed. In any case, a majority of the applicants for FM licenses were AM broadcasters. Some thought an FM license would eventually prove lucrative; others wanted to cover their tracks with an inexpensive backup system.

By 1948 the optimism of the previous year was gone. Only three of the 114 FM-only stations showed a profit. More than 100 applicants who had received licenses and construction permits returned them to the FCC. It grew worse. In 1949 AM and FM reeled under a nationwide recession, and radio revenues had their smallest annual increase since

1938. In all, 212 commercial FM stations went off the air. But amid this stumbling, trial-and-error handling of FM, the FCC set aside a slice of the revised FM band, from 88–92 MHz, for noncommercial educational stations, which in 1947 began to proliferate. Slowly, steadily, they built modest audiences, proving to listeners that FM *was* technically superior, establishing that there was an audience for alternative programming and raising, albeit in small quarters, some public consciousness about FM.

But commercial FM broadcasting stations were still doing poorly and the public wasn't buying:

	FM Stations on Air	FM Receivers Sold
1950	676	2,200,000
1952	626	670,000
1954	554	233,000
1956	534	229,000
1958	577	375,000
1960	813	1,600,000
1962	1,078	2,600,000

The popularity of FM started to grow, in the late 1950s, for precisely the reason for which FM was first hailed: its superior sound. Through the early- and mid-1950s the idea of FM was kept alive by independents willing to take a loss in the expectation of better days to come, by a growing number of college radio stations, and by AM-FM simulcasting. Listeners who switched to the FM band couldn't help but note the clarity. These developments provided the tinder. High fidelity recording equipment, and later, stereophonic sound, provided the spark. Quite simply what happened was that a substantial number of Americans were developing more sophisticated ears for music, and demanding higher standards. Improvements in phonographs, including cartridges, styli, and speaker systems, had demonstrated amply how well music could be reproduced. The market for this high fidelity equipment grew by leaps and bounds in the late 1950s. And many consumers began to seek the same fidelity from their radios that they got from their phonograph systems. As early as 1957 stereo albums were on the market, offering the richest sound yet available for home use. Even before FM offered stereo broadcasting, its clarity and richness did more justice to stereo albums than AM radio could.

Stereo, as a recording process, divides the music being performed into two "tracks," one along each side of the groove on the record. Each track is then fed into a separate speaker, and listeners hear a sound more diverse and complex, as it has two distinct sources rather than one. For instance, with a jazz quartet, the drums and piano might be assigned the left track, the bass and trumpet the right track. The result is a richer, denser sound than one speaker could possibly provide.

In 1961 the FCC authorized stereo broadcasting of FM and 57 stations tried it. The FM signal is broader than AM, and on any assigned frequency—for instance, 98.7 on the dial—a station could broadcast two closely related but different signals. This technique of putting more than one signal into a frequency is known as multiplexing. Stereo broadcasting proved popular: By 1970 668 FM stereo stations were on the air and the number continued to grow. (The narrow AM signal did not lend itself to stereo broadcasting for many years.)

The superior sound of stereo created a ripple effect in the marketplace. Equipment manufacturers began developing increasingly sophisticated stereo equipment, which in turn created a demand for more stereo broadcasting. This "FM sound" had two other facets: fewer commercials and longer periods of uninterrupted music. Noncommercial FM stations accepted no advertising; commercial stations found few sponsors, and they had little money for promotional stunts. Because there were so few interruptions, the medium was ideally suited to run longer compositions.

The modest FM growth from 1957 to 1964 provided a solid foundation and a growing audience (the first FM car radios were introduced in 1963). Then the FCC intervened with an order aimed at AM and FM stations owned by the same company (the dual holding was called duopoly) that were simulcasting. In its historic order, the FCC noted:

Our proposals were based upon the view that the time had come to move significantly toward the day when AM and FM stations should be regarded as component parts of a total "aural" service for assignment purpose . . . eventually, there must be an elimination of FM stations which are no more than adjuncts to AM facilities in the same community.

The FCC ordered AM-FM license holders in cities with a population of more than 100,000 to broadcast original programming on FM at least half the time they were on the air. The FCC estimated that about 100 stations were affected; other observers placed the number nearer to 200.

There were several aspects to the FCC order. On the one hand the commissioners were fulfilling their oft-stated and occasionally followed doctrine of serving the public interest by increasing program diversity. On the other hand, their motivation came from an AM problem: The spectrum was full, especially in major markets. In May 1962 the FCC had ordered a freeze on AM license applications while it pondered what to do with the congestion. There were nearly 4,000 AM stations on the air (and almost 1,000 FM stations). Still the clamor continued for more licenses. With nowhere left to turn on AM, the FCC took a new look at FM, about which it had been unable to make up its mind since World War II. The commissioners decided that the time was right to let FM stand, free from AM, on its own legs.

But even as FM's new day dawned, many people in the radio industry saw clouds. This included some FCC commissioners; the vote for the nonduplicating rule was 5–2. Among the critics was Commissioner Robert T. Bartley, who although he eventually voted *for* the rule, complained: "People should not have to switch to AM to get program material they desire. FM should be all-inclusive. . . ." Some broadcasters complained that their experiments in original FM programming had led to listener complaints: the public asked them to resume simulcasting. Other broadcasters and trade organizations argued that the FCC had no business regulating programming. Decisions on what to put on the air,

they contended, should rest with individual stations. More than 100 of them filed applications for waivers with the FCC, asking exemption from the nonduplication rule. The FCC, while generally unsympathetic, extended the deadline for compliance from July 1, 1965, to January 1, 1967.

As the FCC attempted to lead, many station operators elected not to follow. In addition to filing waiver applications and lobbying in Washington for reconsideration of the rule, some broadcasters turned to fascinating schemes to comply with the nonduplication policies. The FCC had defined simultaneous broadcasting as that being "within 24 hours before or after the identical program is broadcast over the AM station." Some stations decided they could comply by taping AM broadcasts and using them after 25 hours. This is hardly what the FCC had in mind, but some station managers consulted with their legal departments and decided they could get away with it. Other stations cut back the hours of AM programming, reducing the number of FM programs they would need to equal half their AM load. But the majority of those affected complied without deceit, and were dragged screaming and kicking into newfound profits. "I made a mistake," recalled Gordon McLendon, the Texas broadcaster. "AM broadcasters by and large, and I was among them, fought the FCC tooth and nail. Todd Storz made a terrible mistake, terrible: he never did get into FM. None of the Storz stations to this day are FM. I did get into FM, but like many AM operators I had to be dragged in. The FCC wanted the good AM operators, who could best afford to do so, to develop this fine new medium, and we did. But it was largely because of the push of the FCC and some of their very alert staff members. Almost singlehandedly, the FCC forced the development of the FM spectrum. If not for the FCC, FM might not have come along for another 10 or 15 years."

However cantankerous the broadcasters, by the mid-1960s FM radio could no longer be denied. Several social and cultural developments found in FM their perfect medium.

Eventually the availability of FM changed the very face of rock 'n' roll, which until the mid-1960s was consigned to the Top 40 stations alone. From rock's beginnings well into the 1960s, most rock songs were written and recorded in lengths of two and one-half to three minutes—precisely because the writers and artists sought AM radio exposure. These stations emphasized short songs, many breaks, promotional jingles, and so on. One study found a typical AM Top 40 station might in one hour play 22 commercials, 73 weather/time/contest announcements, repeat the station's call letters 58 times, throw in a three-and-one-half minute newscast and play about a dozen songs. But as FM grew (and not so coincidentally, album sales grew), more and more rock musicians turned their hands to more complex and longer compositions. The three-chord simplistic rock of the 1950s remained a staple of AM radio; the more complex popular music found an outlet on FM. Musicians felt free to experiment with longer songs, because they knew albums containing those songs had a chance to get FM air play. So as a genre, popular music (particularly rock 'n' roll) was rejuvenated. Among the early pioneers on this frontier were Bob Dylan, who in 1965 recorded "Desolation Row," eleven minutes long, and the Rolling Stones, whose "Going Home" the following year was also eleven minutes long. In 1967, the Doors had a seven-minute-long hit, "Light My Fire" (although they offered AM radio an edited three-minute version), and Arlo Guthrie achieved prominence with "Alice's Restaurant," which was 18 minutes long.

But the emerging music, as important as it was, pales beside the explosive force that made FM socially significant: the political and cultural movements of the 1960s. The adolescent rebellion of the 1950s, even when it addressed social problems, was essentially inarticulate ("rebels without a cause"). A decade later this discontent ripened into an informed, sophisticated, and highly articulate political activism. It began with the civil rights movement, starting with the Freedom Rides in the early 1960s. It had deeper roots in the labor movement. But it spread through the nation after 1963, honed by the assassinations of John F. Kennedy, and, to a lesser extent, Malcolm X. Its cause became the anti-

war movement. As early as 1963 there were protests against American involvement in Vietnam. By 1965 massive, coordinated demonstrations occurred regularly as the war was escalated by the Johnson administration. What was significant from radio's point of view was that the activists took (as labor organizers and civil rights protesters had before them) certain songs as their anthems. And certain songwriters—Dylan, Phil Ochs, Tom Paxton—and singers—Joan Baez and Judy Collins, most prominently—became willing instruments of the movement.

The strength of the youth market had been ably demonstrated by rock 'n' roll in the 1950s; record companies had learned to cater to young taste. Whatever their corporate investments, regardless of whom their executives might support for office, companies moved to record and market the protest music of the 1960s. This was nothing new; RCA Records was busy signing Elvis Presley even as its corporate president, Robert Sarnoff, was denouncing rock 'n' roll. Columbia Records signed Dylan and Pete Seeger; Elektra Records signed Ochs, Paxton and Collins. But even as record companies signed protest singers and the public bought their albums, these performers had little access to the mass media, including radio.

Television steered clear of controversy, and would not broadcast the protest music. Seeger, a social activist with leftist connections, was blacklisted for 17 years, until a 1967 appearance on the Smothers Brothers television show. Dylan, after a successful New York City concert in April 1963, was invited to appear on the Ed Sullivan Show, provided he agreed not to sing "Talking John Birch Society Blues." Dylan refused. (It wasn't only political controversy that television steered clear of. When the Rolling Stones were invited on the Sullivan show in 1967 to sing their hit "Let's Spend the Night Together," Sullivan insisted they change the lyric to "Let's spend some time together," and the Stones, a good deal more eager than Dylan for exposure, agreed.) Television was not alone in avoiding the protest music of the 1960s. AM radio stuck to its hits-based formats, and thus excluded the protest singers.

An exception was Peter, Paul, and Mary's version of Dylan's "Blowing in the Wind," a low-key antiwar song that they turned into a hit single in 1963. Newspapers, in their music criticism and in news and feature stories, had little to say about the new poets of protest. It was FM radio that gave this music of the 1960s —whether it was rock, folk, or jazz—exposure in the mass media. (The "underground press" discussed the music but never achieved true mass impact.)

From the mid-1960s on, this music and its media arm, FM radio, took on a new dimension. Social protests continued and indeed escalated, and many people opted for what came to be called the counterculture: "alternative lifestyles" that acted out protest on several levels. Widespread dabbling in drugs was commonplace, casual or offbeat attire standard. These lifestyles had their music as well—and that music was played on FM radio. The stations that played the recordings of bands like Big Brother and the Holding Company, Jefferson Airplane, Country Joe and the Fish, and Moby Grape became known as "underground radio." But they weren't underground at all. They were easily accessible with a flip of the FM dial. Significantly, this underground radio became prime-time entertainment for many young Americans. Television had not changed its programming to draw in this substantial audience, and viewership in the young adult market plummeted in the late 1960s. Some films tried to fill the void, notably "Easy Rider" and "The Graduate." But most evenings this audience just "did its thing," whatever it was—even if it were something terribly conventional like studying—in front of FM radios, instead of television.

Underground radio soon came out of the pigeonhole the other media had placed it in, and after a while was dubbed "progressive FM radio." Its influence on culture and society far outweighed its revenue; even in its heyday it did not dominate FM radio programming. But it was an important part of the FM story in the 1960s.

Jack Gould of *The New York Times* offered some easily recognizable characteristics of this new mode of broadcasting in a slightly-after-the-fact acknowledgement of the impact of "progressive radio" on May 20, 1970 (ironically, a month after *Rolling Stone* had analyzed the "death" of progressive radio):

- "The technique of picking 'cuts' or segments from long-playing rock albums, which often do not make the list of the top 40 rock tunes offered on single 45 rpm disks."
- "The lyrics of hard rock virtually constitute an arcane language, difficult to comprehend because of the blurred diction of so many rock artists."
- "Stereophonic FM, which surrounds the listener with sound, is purposely raised in volume by the young so that they can physically sense the vibrations of the audio waves and emphasize what one college graduate characterized as the social schism between generations." (Indeed, some albums contained on the jacket a note to consumers: "We suggest that you play this record at the highest possible volume in order to fully appreciate the sound. . . .")
- "Unlike the rapid-fire delivery of earlier rock disk jockeys, their new FM counterparts talk in low and seductive voices."

Perhaps the most readily identifiable element of the progressive FM sound was its use of "sets" of music, where the disc jockey grouped songs using several criteria: songs on the same theme, several songs by the same performer, different interpretations of the same song or songwriter, or similarity of musical sound.

This progressive FM radio had muddled roots. There are three versions of how and where it began:

- The East Coast, WOR-FM story
- The West Coast, Tom Donahue story
- The "young turks" of college radio story

Any habitual listener to WOR-FM must have been startled at 6:00 AM on July 30, 1966. Instead of the usual simulcast of WOR-AM's talk show "Rambling with Gambling," a particularly raucous rock song, "Wild Thing" by the Troggs, came blaring across the airwaves. Thus WOR-FM chose to herald the end of its simulcasting and to introduce new FM programming. The station, owned by RKO, was getting a five-month jump on the FCC deadline.

The new WOR-FM seemed designed for the counterculture audience. The station commissioned graphic designer Milton Glaser to create posters featuring long-haired musicians and plastered them all over town. The changeover in format at WOR-FM came during (though not because of) a strike by on-the-air personnel: There were no disc jockeys at the station until October. The programming ran song-to-song, interrupted only by pre-taped promotions and occasional advertisements. Word about WOR-FM spread through the tri-state area (New York, New Jersey, and Connecticut) and the station began to build a sizable audience of young adults. By the time the deejays went on the air on October 8, 1966 (they included "Murray the K" Kaufman, Scott Muni, and Rosko [Bill Mercer]), WOR-FM was quite a visible tree in the city's media forest, heralded by *The Village Voice* as "the only place to hear vital new music and hear it well."

WOR-FM's glory was not to last, however. A year later, a clash of personalities, and in-house politics, brought the format down. The struggle—which led to the dismissal or resignation of the deejays—served to obscure WOR-FM's seminal role in radio programming, and perhaps explains why so many chroniclers have found the roots of progressive radio in San Francisco. But the evidence clearly shows that Tom Donahue, the so-called "father of progressive radio," did not take his first steps until March 1967.

Like Murray the K, Donahue was a veteran of the East Coast Top 40 wars of the late 1950s and early 1960s. He worked on the air as "Big Daddy" (he weighed nearly 400 pounds) and was a star at Philadelphia's WIBG-AM. During the 1960 payola probes Donahue (though never charged or implicated) resigned from WIBG and left for San Francisco, where he joined KYA-AM, a Top 40 station that billed itself as "the boss of the bay." He quit in 1965, during a broadcast from a glass booth at a teenage fair, accord-

ing to his widow Rachael. They sat at home and listened to records for more than a year, she said, until one day Tom had a vision. He realized the records they listened to were never on the radio.

"The next day, Tom got on the horn and started calling FM stations until he found one whose phone was disconnected," Rachael told *Radio & Records* magazine in 1978. "That was KMPX . . . the station was in a lot of trouble. Its format was varied foreign languages. It was losing money." Deejay Larry Miller already was doing an all-night show on KMPX of the type Donahue envisioned. Full-time progressive programming was implemented on April 7, 1967, with the Donahues in charge, using their own records. Listener support was rapid and rabid: Fans decorated the studio with bells, tapestries, incense, candles, and a Viet Cong banner. The Donahues set a few simple rules, Rachael said: "No jingles, no talkovers, no time-and-temp (Tom took the clock out of the studio), no pop singles."

Donahue, who died April 28, 1975, at age 46, described the KMPX experiment in a 1967 *Rolling Stone* article as "a format that embraces the best of today's rock 'n' roll, folk, traditional and city blues, raga, electronic music and some jazzy and classical selections. I believe this music should not be treated as a group of objects to be sorted out like eggs with each category kept rigidly apart from the others." At the same time that he was revamping KMPX, Donahue began a similar overhaul of KPPC in Pasadena. Within a year, the Donahues and their staffs were embroiled in a heated labor dispute. They struck in March 1968 and whimsically named their union the Amalgamated Federation of International FM Workers of the World. Many musicians supported the strike and entrepreneur Bill Graham provided food for the pickets. The dispute was never settled, and Donahue moved his operations and staff to KSAN, San Francisco, in May 1968.

Because of his size, his zeal, his links to the Haight-Ashbury community in San Francisco and his alliances with other public figures like Graham, Jefferson Airplane, and the Grateful Dead, the legend began that Donahue fathered progressive radio. But he was months behind WOR-FM.

There was a third, more diffuse source of progressive FM programming. While WOR-FM in the East and Donahue in the West were making waves in the commercial marketplace, a similar movement had begun on many campuses. It attracted less attention because it was spread out, unreported, its stations of low power, and after all, its leaders just kids. But these kids had descended on college radio stations and tried to make a case for playing the new music. The most persistent were permitted to air their material a few hours a week. These shows went on the air, in some cases, before the WOR-FM experiment.

One of the best-known of the college shows was run by Tom Gamache, at WTBS, owned by the Massachusetts Institute of Technology in Cambridge, Massachusetts. The station had a modest 30-watt signal but was capable of reaching Boston's large university population. Gamache started in 1966 with a show called "Tee Time." Now a record company executive, Gamache said he designed the show as "a travesty of commercial radio." He brought in his own records to play and did phony commercials, most of them related to marijuana. Gamache, whose on-the-air name was Uncle Tom, developed a wide following and switched to Boston University's WBUR, which had a 20,000-watt signal. Eventually he joined WBCN, and ran Boston's first commercial progressive rock show.

In New York City, Fordham University's WFUV offered a Saturday show, starting in late 1964, called "Campus Caravan," anchored by one of this book's* authors, Peter Fornatale. He offered album material, thematic groupings of songs, interviews with musicians, and topical comments underscored by appropriate musical selections.

This generation of college broadcasters produced two ripples: they encouraged more people to enter college radio's ranks, which in turn led more college stations to switch to progressive FM. And they graduated or dropped out and went into commercial radio, like

Gamache and Fornatale. These young turks received some due—the critic Richard Goldstein, in his formidable "Pop Eye" commentaries in *The Village Voice,* often took note of them—but they did not attract enough of a mass audience or enough media attention to become a prominent force in American broadcasting. Only commercial success would certify the new programming.

And that became the crux of progressive FM's problem: could it survive commercially? Could it pull in advertising revenue? In 1967, 1968, and 1969 progressive FM was put to the test. And it passed . . . if station owners weren't greedy. Initially the stations drew ads from concert promoters, motorcycle shops, "head shops," and sandal makers; its only national advertising came from record companies. But as the audiences grew, and as sales of FM receivers flourished, more advertisers came on board: manufacturers of musical instruments and stereo equipment. Eventually airlines and beer companies joined. By the 1970s suburban home developers and auto makers had watched the children of the 1960s grow up and become affluent and had followed them through their medium, FM radio.

The late 1960s found strange bedfellows in FM radio: social critics and activists, drug users, and corporate giants. The on-the-air personnel at progressive stations often treated their medium as a personal political platform, a tool in a social movement—and only secondarily as business. The stockholders, of course, did not agree. Eventually the different points of view clashed.

As FM progressive radio demonstrated its commercial potential, the ABC network decided to take the plunge. Its first attempt was called the "LOVE" format: a Lutheran minister, Brother John Rydgren, was the deejay. The music was generally mild counterculture, built around the theme of love. It more or less flopped, and ABC switched to a straightforward progressive format that also was unsuccessful. After a while ABC switched to a more structured format, playing recognizable FM hits—popular songs from popular albums—and grew successful with it.

Progressive radio, for all its impact, was but a small piece of the radio revenue pie. To

---

Radio in the Television Age, from which this chapter is drawn [Eds.].

mix a metaphor, it was a trail-blazing piece of pie. It was left to another format, Beautiful Music, to demonstrate just how profitable FM could be. Jim Schulke's Stereo Radio Productions started racking up impressive ratings performances in 1969 and 1970. Schulke said the turning point was the Arbitron ratings of April/May 1972: 29 FM stations were rated among the top four in their markets. Twenty-eight of them were Beautiful Music stations, and all but three were programmed by Schulke. The MOR* format also did well on FM, though never as well as Beautiful Music. Just as progressive FMs demonstrated that they could deliver the much-

sought-after 18- to 24-year-olds to advertisers, Beautiful Music and MOR delivered—and indeed, with far greater profitability—substantial older audiences.

These early successes paved the way for intensive demographic research into FM audiences. They demonstrated to Madison Avenue that FM could draw. And they helped sell more FM sets, as listeners came to appreciate the original programming. Progressive FM even helped prove that radio could attract listeners away from prime-time television.

As the 1960s ended, as the age of assassinations seemed mercifully to pass, FM radio, rock 'n' roll, and the young adult market were all feeling their oats. They had been vindicated by time. For some they were art, for some big business, to everyone they were successful. But the pendulum already had begun to swing: the tides of conservatism were washing over progressive FM, brushing away some of the sand castles that had been built.

---

*middle-of-the-road. Other radio formats are: Top 40, disco, beautiful music, country, classical, jazz, talk, religious, all-news. For more on how formats are devised and promoted, see Donna L. Halper's, "Radio Programming Consultants: The Power Elite" in this section [Eds.].

32
Striking It Rich in Radio

Business Week Staff

Much of radio's new prosperity comes from the business community's increasing awareness of radio's extraordinary flexibility as a mass medium specializing in local programming and advertising. As one industry executive puts it, radio is becoming "more and more like the magazine industry, where there are specialized publications with their own unique audiences and advertisers." According to the following selection from *Business Week,* the rapid segmentation of radio audiences has spurred the growth of new services and research. As a result, to the surprise of many industry executives, radio stations are among the most attractive media properties today.

In the town of Moberly, Mo. (population 12,000), Jerrell A. Shepherd owns a radio station operation so valuable that he claims "no

one can afford to buy it." He charges advertisers only $5 to $10 for 30 seconds of time on KWIX, his AM station, and $6 to $12 per commercial on KRES-FM, but Shepherd's gross revenues are more than $800,000 a year. "A buyer today normally pays two to two and a half times the annual gross for a station," the broadcaster muses. "But if I wanted to sell, who's going to plunk down $2 million for a station in a town they've never heard of?"

The chances are, however, that if Shepherd put his property on the block, he would have no shortage of prospective purchasers. The business of radio is enjoying a prosperity undreamed of just five years ago, and a steady stream of new investors wants to share in it—at almost any price. When Storer Broadcasting Co. decided in December to take advantage of the seller's market and pick up some cash for cable-TV expansion, it received nearly 100 inquiries about the four radio stations it put up for sale, even though one station, WHN in New York, is priced at a record $17 million. "It's gotten to the point," says Richard A. Shaheen, a Chicago media broker, "where people are calling and saying, 'You've got to find a station for me to buy, right now!'"

In the world of advertising, radio as a viable medium is often ignored by anyone over 45, whose memories go back to the days of daytime soap operas—*Ma Perkins, Our Gal Sunday,* and *The Romance of Helen Trent* —and to nighttime broadcasts of *Fibber McGee and Molly, The Shadow,* and *Lux Radio Theater.* That kind of radio, network radio, last year is estimated by Robert J. Coen, senior vice-president of McCann-Erickson Inc., to have attracted only $160 million in advertising expenditures out of a grand total of some $43 billion for all advertising.

But network radio, which peaked in billings in 1950, is a minor factor in the industry today. All radio this year will near the $3 billion mark in terms of ad expenditures, with local advertisers contributing more than $2 billion of that amount. Radio already takes in more ad dollars than does the magazine industry. And, still only one-third the size of the television industry and one-fourth as large as the newspaper industry, radio could outpace its rivals in growth in 1979 and beyond, say its proponents. Because it is neither capital-intensive nor labor-intensive, radio is relatively free of the pressures that force repeated price increases in TV and in print, and advertisers can readily turn to it to stretch inflated media dollars by spending them where they will buy the most exposure.

Unlike television, it does not take a huge sum of money to buy a radio station. An FM station in Santa Fe, N.M., for instance, changed hands last month for $332,500, and one in Waco, Tex., was offered at $140,000. But as with TV, a radio station license is considered by many as "a license to print money." Says Alan R. Griffith, a vice-president at Bank of New York, whose office in the CBS Inc. headquarters building puts him in close proximity to numerous broadcasting executives: "Almost every day a sales or programming person wants to talk about financing a radio station purchase. 'I've made a fortune for my company,' they say. 'Now I want to do it for me.'" A well-managed station can throw off a lot of cash, he adds.

Fueling the New Interest

The interest in radio as a flourishing industry has been heightened by several recent events. Among them:

■ The Federal Communications Commission at yearend released its figures on 1977 profits, showing that radio's pretax income climbed to $178.6 million, 37.8% over the 1976 figure, while revenues jumped 12.6% to a record $2.8 billion. Estimates from industry sources indicate that revenues climbed a further 12% in 1978, and a gain of 10% to 12% is predicted for this year.

■ In Washington, a movement toward almost total deregulation of radio is gathering momentum at both the FCC and in Congress. Although the nation now has some 4,544 AM stations and 3,993 FM stations on the air, the FCC is firmly in favor of more stations and greater competition. It is considering various plans that could make room for anywhere from 125 to several thousand new stations, many of which might be owned by minorities.

■ Stunning the entire industry, an FM station in New York City—a market with 43 AM outlets and 56 FMs—began playing only disco music and virtually overnight jumped from near obscurity to become the country's No. 1 station. Capturing almost 16% of the total radio audience at times, WKTU supplanted WABC, a more powerful AM station that reigned for 16 years, and proved that the newer FM stations can have parity with the familiar AM ones.

■ On Feb. 5, following an increasing number of tentative forays into radio by such TV-oriented national advertisers as General Foods Corp. (for Maxwell House) and Procter & Gamble Co. (for Ivory Liquid), Sears, Roebuck & Co. begins an initial year of nightly sponsorship of *Sears Radio Theater*. Emulating radio's heyday of the 1930s and 1940s, the one-hour series of drama, mysteries, and comedies will be fed by CBS to more than 200 affiliates. Many of them already carry network radio's only drama series, CBS *Radio Mystery Theater*, that began its sixth year on Jan. 8.

The CBS-Sears effort is only one of numerous new ideas at the radio networks, which recovered in 1977 from four straight years of losses to earn $25 million on $85.5 million in revenues. Some of the money—which flows from four networks owned by American Broadcasting Co., two owned by Mutual Broadcasting System, Inc., and one apiece by CBS and National Broadcasting Co.—is being poured back into new approaches in programming, research, and sales. At CBS, explains Sam Cooke Digges, the silver haired president of the Radio Div., "people thought we were crazy when we bought the radio rights to the NFL's *Monday Night Football*. After all, with 45 million people watching the games on ABC-TV, why would anybody want to tune in radio?" But audience research showed 10 million listeners tuned to the broadcasts each week—frequently TV at the same time, while tuning out TV announcer Howard Cosell.

At National Broadcasting Co., the media focus has been on the frenzied efforts of President and Chief Executive Officer Fred Silverman to shore up the TV network's ratings, but one of his first moves was to reorganize the company's radio operations. He followed the lead of ABC and CBS in appointing different executives to head the NBC network and the AM and FM station groups, and he put the former head of the combined radio division in a special slot to study the acquisition of more stations and the creation of additional radio networks.

Such a move is a radical change for a company which only a few years ago was interested in selling its radio stations and which lost an estimated $20 million with a faltering second network service that offered news around the clock. "We're spending money to make our programming more innovative," notes Richard P. Verne, the 39-year-old executive vice-president of the NBC Radio Div. "We're significantly more contemporary now, with features by Liz Smith, the gossip columnist, Mark Russell, the Washington satirist, and Joyce Brothers talking about kids and sex. During Christmas, we anchored our newscasts out of Bethlehem. For the first time, radio has its own sports unit, and this month we had the first convention of our radio affiliates in four years."

The Needs of Local Stations

Less exuberant but equally bullish on the future of network radio is Harold L. Neal Jr., the thoughtful president of ABC Radio, which pioneered the route to profits in 1968 by establishing four different networks. Each furnishes five minutes of news every hour to a different group of stations. (One group is "fed" at five minutes before the hour, a second on the hour, and so on.) In a single bound, ABC increased the number of affiliates carrying its news by 300% and greatly enlarged the number of advertising prospects on which it could draw a head—offering makers of youth-oriented products a lineup of rock-music stations, for example, or giving the marketer of a high-ticket item a group of FM stations that appeal to upper-income listeners.

The move also let ABC amortize the cost of its radio transmission lines, for which the company pays about $3 million per year, over four separate five-minute periods per hour, rather than one or two.

Neal is convinced that "a network can succeed only by gearing its programming these days to the local station's needs." He sees radio at both the network and local level becoming "more and more like the magazine industry, where there are specialized publications with their own unique audiences and advertisers." To help impress on prospective clients that each of ABC's networks targets a different segment of the total radio audience, Neal announced on Jan. 24 a reorganization of the network sales force. Where previously there was one group of salesmen for all four radio services, there are now separate groups of marketing specialists who determine the goals of advertisers in specific product areas and match them to the most suitable network.

The idea that radio today presents listeners in any large market with a number of specialized "magazines" is one of the industry's strengths, notes Miles David, president of the Radio Advertising Bureau (RAB). "We have research that shows the average listener tunes in regularly to 2.2 stations, no matter how many he can receive. That helps advertisers get a very specific fix on where their customers are."

Radio began to segment its audiences in the 1950s, after television had drawn off the listeners who once tuned in regularly. Some pioneer broadcasters—notably Gordon McLendon of Dallas and Todd Storz of Omaha—sought to cut costs by playing phonograph records all day and night. Perceiving that the typical jukebox of the time contained 40 records, they established a "top 40" format and played the same records in an appeal to music-buying youngsters. When the idea caught on, other stations began looking for variations. Some offered new forms of rock music, "soft" rock or "acid" rock; others offered hits of the past—"golden oldies"—or country-and-western music. A few stations hung onto the familiar blend of middle-of-the-road music, chattering "personalities," and sportscasts that typified the

radio programs of the 1940s, much as *Reader's Digest* and *Parade* still survive for a general magazine audience today. Other formats—all-talk, all-news, and now, with the ascendancy of WKTU in New York, all disco—were devised to lure different listener segments.

New Services for Broadcasters

Segmentation of the radio audience has spurred the growth of new services in the industry. Stations that play nothing but a single kind of music all day can be almost entirely automated, and electronics manufacturers are busily selling computerized equipment to many of them. Consultants who specialize in determining a station's format—down to selecting music, network service, announcers, and how fast the announcers should talk—have flourished since the 1960s, but a new group of specialists has recently come on the scene. These are syndicators who provide taped "programs"—anything from a 90-second interview with *The Home Handyman* who talks about fixing a leaky pipe to a half-hour science-fiction drama, *Alien Worlds,* or a weekend-long history of rock-and-roll music. Their customers are a growing list of stations that want to distinguish their programming—largely music—from that of their competitors, but do not want to spend money to produce their own programs. Providing shows at prices that range from $5 for a 60-second news feature to $15,000 for the 52-hour *History of Rock 'n' Roll,* the syndicators have boosted annual volume from $5 million to $25 million in five years.

"Demand from stations is extremely high for this sort of thing," says Dwight Case, president of RKO Radio Group, which has 13 stations. In the past two years alone, at least two dozen new programs have been put on the market, and several scheduled to debut soon include *Odd Tracks,* a 30-minute weekly program of recordings by major stars that were never released, and *The Other Side,* a daily two-minute series providing alternative viewpoints on current issues. A big hit is a two-hour *Dr. Demento Show,* a wacky potpourri of musical nostalgia distributed by Westwood One in Los Angeles.

Some of the shows have built-in appeal to advertisers. Cliff Barrett and Frank Gorin, two newscasters who were with NBC's failing all-news network, went into the syndication business two years ago as Barrett-Gorin Inc. "When NBC closed down the news service," says Frank Gorin, "they left a lot of stations that were committed to all-news out in the cold." BGI now distributes tapes of features on such subjects as photography, home repair, and personal finance—all of which can be sponsored by local camera shops, hardware stores, banks, and the like.

National advertisers also support the special features. Warner-Lambert now spends about 30% of its radio budget on five syndicated programs. "You're getting national coverge in programs appealing to the audience you're trying to reach on stations they listen to," says Robert A. Friedlander, manager of media planning and coordination for the company. Recently, Anheuser-Busch, Peter Paul, and International Harvester stepped up their syndication budgets. Many programs are given to the stations free in a barter arrangement that guarantees a national sponsor that the show will be aired and that he will get time for a commercial message.

The area of radio research also is prospering. With stations and ad agencies now clamoring for more data, two newcomers have begun issuing reports in a challenge to Arbitron Co., the subsidiary of Control Data Corp. that has held a near-monopoly position since it began radio audience measurement a dozen years ago. Trac-7, the new service of Audits & Surveys, says it uses a larger sample of phone respondents than Arbitron. Burke Broadcast Research Inc., a subisidiary of a company that tests TV commercials for their selling power, thinks that its experience with ad agencies will help attract customers for its radio data.

"The availability of more research means that it's easier to measure radio audiences now," says Dawn Sibley, senior vice-president for media at Compton Advertising Inc. "Couple that with the tremendous cost increases that have taken place in the last few years in television and magazines, and you see why everyone's taking a new look at radio."

David of the RAB notes that while agencies such as Compton, which shifted some Procter & Gamble dollars from TV into a test of radio during the last quarter of 1978, are willing to study the medium, many others shy away from examining the research data of hundreds or even thousands of stations. Aware of this built-in liability, individual stations long have concentrated on selling their value to local advertisers: banks, retailers, restaurants, beauty shops, funeral homes, and the rest. Even the smallest local company could afford to spend a few dollars for a commercial, station salesmen argued, and there are no extra costs for typesetting, photography, plate-making, and the other requirements of print advertising. And even with their low rates, the bulk of the stations have grown solidly profitable, selling 18 commercial minutes per hour, as allowed by the FCC.

"It's the greediness of some AM stations that helped FM grow so dramatically," says J. Robert Cole, vice-president in charge of FM stations at CBS. Not only can FM broadcast stereo music—which, after all, is the kind that people buy when they buy record albums—but it started out with much less advertising volume. People began tuning in because they knew that they would not be bombarded with a commercial every few minutes. We work to convince advertisers that they should pay more for our minutes than they might pay elsewhere simply because they're in a less crowded environment." Adds Peter A. Lund, Cole's rival in charge of AM stations: "But one thing we don't do these days is sell against other radio stations by telling media buyers they made a poor selection. We point out to advertisers how they can add radio to TV and print schedules to increase their reach and frequency of impressions."

FM: 'A Great New Business'

Although the 30-year-old FM broadcasting industry trails far behind the older AM service in total revenues, its profits are growing at a faster pace, and most radio executives think the day is not far off when the two services will be of equal size. The surge of FM radio was caused by government regulation, rather than in spite of it. "To think that we used to force applicants for an AM franchise to take an FM assignment as well!" exclaims Charles D. Ferris, chairman of the FCC. "Now, FM is on top in several markets and growing, simply because it really does provide a better signal." In addition to requiring would-be AM broadcasters to put an FM signal on the air, the FCC in 1968 ordered most owners of AM and FM stations in the same market to put different programming on each station, rather than merely play the same shows on both. The added expense angered some station owners, "but the commission dragged us kicking and screaming into a great new business," says Cole of CBS.

Helped once—albeit unwillingly—by the FCC, radio operators are now puzzling over the commission's latest ideas. One FCC proposal announced at yearend would reduce the power of the nation's 25 50,000-watt "clear channel" stations, which once were the only signals to serve rural areas. This proposal has drawn fire from the operators of the broadcasting giants, although one official privately concedes that his station would not lose much business if its New York signal could no longer be picked up in remote areas of the Midwest at night. Still, the plan—which would allow 125 new stations to be built to serve the rural markets—"will be opposed strongly, as a matter of principle, and because we don't think that there will be a rush of applicants for a license in Appalachia," says the broadcaster. "People in areas like that may end up with no radio at all."

The Costs of Deregulation

The FCC is considering two other proposals that could put more stations on the air, and Chairman Ferris says: "The need for more stations is simply self-evident. It springs from the new environment, particularly the recognition of diversity in communities and the profitability of serving parts of markets or specialized markets with news, popular and classical music, community information—you name it," Commissioner Tyrone Brown, a black who tends to be the magnet at the FCC for minority issues, agrees. "We have great evidence of scarcity," he says. "Radio station prices are exploding. That tells me there is a greater demand than supply."

With the strong probability of more stations on the dial and less burdensome regulatory paperwork, the industry may find itself with some new problems, says Ferris. "A lot of the regulatory detail came from the industry itself," he says, "because owners wanted specific rules they could obey to the letter and protect their license franchises. With less regulation, they may not feel so secure."

Now, however, radio executives feel secure that their medium will grow stronger in 1979 and will prosper even if there is a second-half recession. "No other medium is so flexible," says Robert J. Duffy, president of Christal Co., a sales representative for some 70 stations. "Nothing else lets you reach working women in such great numbers, or zero in on the millions who are light viewers of TV." That kind of optimism is expected to keep station prices climbing: Last month a Denver FM station went to an Ohio buyer for $6.7 million, a record for an FM outlet and $4 million more than an offer made a year earlier.

The FCC's actions to clear the way for new stations will have little impact on escalating prices, notes Ted Hepburn, a Cincinnati-based media broker. "I'll bet the expense of legal work and putting a new station on the air will surpass the cost of buying an existing one, even with prices soaring," he says.

33
Radio Programming Consultants: The Power Elite

Donna L. Halper

At noon, on September 8, 1980, New York City's only around-the-clock commercial jazz radio station, WRVR-FM, suddenly became—to the frustration of many of its die-hard fans—an around-the-clock country music station. In one flick of a turntable switch, Charles Mingus gave way to Waylon Jennings. In the following essay, Donna L. Halper discusses the reasons behind such program changes and describes how both AM and FM station formats have recently come into the control of a powerful new group of specialists—independent programming consultants. Armed with market-research data, ratings history, and programming experience, these influential consultants can now offer an ailing station any number of customized services, from an entirely prepackaged and automated format to advice on an announcer's most suitable tone of voice.

Donna L. Halper is a free-lance journalist who has worked as both a disc jockey and music director for several radio stations.

You wake up one morning and your favorite radio station suddenly has switched from an easy-listening to an all-disco format. The lady deejay you had been brushing your teeth to every morning for the last five years has been retired from what's known as morning drive time and replaced by someone who sounds like a used-car salesman. You're furious. You hastily turn your dial in retaliation.

Well, that's your decision. But that's also progress. What your ex-favorite station is quite literally banking on is gaining lots of new listeners for every old faithful one that it loses. Witness New York's WKTU-FM: It went from easy-listening to all-disco and within three months jumped from a one-share

to a ten-share to become the most listened-to station in the Metropolitan area.

Chances are, the person responsible for your station's and for many another's recent mysterious changes was an independent programming consultant. Kent Burkhart, for instance, not only masterminded WKTU's switch, but is in the process of doing the same for over forty other broadcast outlets across the country. WKTU's runaway success is indicative of just how much power he and a handful of colleagues wield in an industry that affects millions of people and in turn generates billions of dollars in record sales.

As in other businesses, a radio station will often call in a third party when it is losing money—usually due to a decreasing listenership and the resulting low ratings. After studying the station's programming formats, ratings history, competition, and—in some cases—market demographics, the consultant will come up with a plan. Management may accept or reject it, but, since the consultant's services have been paid for up to that point, the station will usually avail itself of his market-research data. If it agrees with his plan, it may then contract him to implement it.

Burkhart, in this case, may go as far as restaffing the station, in addition to selecting the music it will broadcast. He and his associate Lee Abrams, who work out of Atlanta, contact all of their clients weekly to let them know what the up-and-coming hits are. Their predictions are based on a combination of record sales, questionnaires, and "ear tests" —i.e., playing a record for randomly selected listeners and asking them what they think of it. Naturally, Burkhart and Abrams—like all consultants—pride themselves on their ability to accurately predict a record's success.

Nowadays consultants work with both AM and FM outlets, but in the earliest days of consulting, most of their attention was focused on AM Top 40—stations that played only the current hits, with some selected oldies. Bill Drake, now in the radio syndication business with Gene Chenault, was one of the first AM consultants, and his work with the RKO General chain has been widely imitated. It was his research—which indicated listeners wanted to hear their favorite songs more often—that caused so many stations to slash their playlists down to thirty or in some cases even fifteen hit singles and repeat them over and over. Claude Hall, of *Claude Hall's Radio Report,* recalls that "Bill Drake refined Top 40 to its ultimate form."

A few years later, Lee Abrams did something similar for album rock. Actually, he got into consulting quite by accident. "In the mid-'60s," he remembers, "the groups that all my friends and I liked weren't being played on AM at all. Rock artists like the Grateful Dead, the Yardbirds, and Cream had excellent albums but no hit singles, so they didn't get any airplay. The only place you could hear their music back then was in concert."

His first opportunity to meet the needs of what he perceived as a growing album-rock audience came when a friend at WQDR-FM, an ailing station in Raleigh, North Carolina, asked for some programming advice. (At the time, Abrams was working for an ABC-FM outlet in Detroit.) Abrams suggested he try an album-rock orientation that featured the best cuts from major acts' LPs, along with the best of the current, non-teeny-bopper hit singles. In essence, he was telling them to aim for the eighteen- to thirty-four-year-old listeners. WQDR in Raleigh tried Lee's ideas and shot to No. 1. This not only delighted management, but eventually helped Lee land a job with Burkhart, who was consulting mostly for AM outlets at the time.

WQDR was among the first instances of FM's transformation into an alternative rock-music outlet. "As the musical tastes of the American people changed and Top 40 radio did not," says Hall, "more and more FMs started switching to pop music and live announcers. Suddenly there was a need for someone with expertise to hire and train the FM staffs." In some cities, the demand for variety led to the emergence of "free-form" FM, which generally broadcast everything from raggas to rock & roll. Top 40 was considered "unhip" at these stations—airing hit singles was strictly verboten. So popular music radio (not including Muzak) offered two extreme choices: FM's free-form, characterized by unpredictable programming of often obscure music, or AM's rigidly structured, very repetitious programming of Top 40.

Bob Henabery, who currently consults for more than thirty stations, was one of the first to recognize the need for a middle ground. He felt the listener should have the chance to hear the more popular albums as well as the hit singles. At the time (the early '70s), Henabery was director of program development for ABC radio. Some of his automated FM outlets were failing to turn a profit anyway, so he decided to try some of his ideas. He directed his stations to play artists with some degree of free-form's "hip" image, but also to play well-known, mass-appeal acts such as the Beatles or Elton John, and to do so in a controlled rotation—that way listeners would know what to expect and when.

The ABC-FM album-rock format, later

named Rock 'n' Stereo, had its first note-worthy success at KLOS in Los Angeles, under the direction of Tom Yates and Tim Powell. The station's ratings quadrupled almost immediately. Powell was soon asked to consult for all six ABC-FM rock stations, and Henabery's success with the FM group led to a promotion to work the AM group. Powell customized a format for each station, so that they wouldn't sound like carbon copies of one another. He showed the program directors, many of whom had come from free-form and had no real experience working within a structure, how to use local and national sales research and how to execute their particular formats effectively. Many of the people he worked with have gone on to do some important things of their own. Dwight Douglas, who was at WDVE in Pittsburgh, now works with Abrams; Yates also went on to become an independent consultant.

Burkhart, Powell, and Henabery all design formats to fit individual stations. Abrams does not. When he first joined Burkhart and became the FM specialist, he came up with the Superstars format—an improved version of the North Carolina station's album-rock, with strong appeal for young adults. One station this has worked well for is Milwaukee's WLPX. "The owners decided to bring Lee in," says program director Tom Daniels, "because they felt WLPX hadn't yet lived up to its full potential. Since the Superstars format had done well in other cities, they felt it could do equally well in Milwaukee." They were right. WLPX is also used as a test market: not only does Abrams advise Daniels on what is selling nationally, but Daniels reports back on local reaction to new or unfamiliar artists. WQDR in Raleigh is another test market for the Abrams group. Former music director Bill Hard (who now writes *The Hard Report* for the trade) says that some records that have become national hits were first aired in on WQDR. "We were the first station to play *At Seventeen* by Janis Ian and *Fooled Around and Fell in Love* by Elvin Bishop. Lee provided us with helpful research about what artists were popular in other cities, but he also trusted us to break new artists."

By comparison, ABC-FM radio is extremely conservative: Nowdays the stations play only name artists whose albums are in the Top 30. If, however, another station airs a new record and management sees a positive reaction to it, it will add that record to the playlists. In most cases, neither the ABC nor the CBS chain uses outside consultants. Rick Sklar, mastermind of WABC-AM in New York, is ABC's current vice president of programming. He and FM president Allen Shaw do their own market research and base their programming decisions on national sales figures. NBC, on the other hand, has used independent consultants, and one of them is Bob Henabery. Two years ago he became one of the first to produce a successful disco station—WKYS, an NBC station in Washington, D.C.

Since so many stations are using consultants, and since record companies depend largely upon airplay for record sales, it's a safe bet that label promotion representatives put on their Sunday best when they go calling on radio consultants. Convincing Lee Abrams that you've got a hit record can mean exposing that record to up to sixty different major audiences across the country. Bobbie Silver, a regional promotion representative for RSO records, says that since Abrams bases most of his decisions on hard marketing research data, making a case for a new artist can be a real challenge. "I try to get him to see my artist in concert," she explains, "or offer to give away albums; sometimes I even offer the artist for a special concert at one of Lee's stations. Fortunately, Lee has some stations that are willing to take a chance."

Roger Lifeset, an independent promoter who works for several labels, calls hundreds of stations weekly—either to persuade them to add a record or to get feedback on those they are playing. He says some stations are free to add a record if they like it, but others must wait for an okay from their consultant. "Most of the time, consultants don't really hamper me. But it would make things easier if I could just deal on a direct basis with each station without that third party." Like most promoters, Lifeset agrees that consultants can break a disc by adding it to their playlists. They can also stop a record dead by telling their stations to drop it.

Are consultants the answer to every problem? Certainly many respected radio programmers like the overview they provide. Chuck Dunaway has been a successful announcer and program director in many major cities. Though he has never used one, he feels that consultants are "a clearinghouse for all kinds of music information as well as a good source of feedback. They do sell a real service, and they do solve problems."

Dick Oppenheimer, former senior vice president of Starr Broadcasting and now the owner of several Texas stations, agrees: "I would not hesitate to make use of a consultant's expertise. When I was with Starr, our Detroit station was having problems, so we called in Abrams, who had some solid ideas."

On the other hand, Shelly Grafman, executive vice president of Century Broadcasting, feels that consultants are fine for some stations but not for his. After eleven years at KSHE-FM, a successful St. Louis rock station, he says, "I know my market better than any outsider. While I respect consultants for what they do, I feel no need to rely on one. Our ratings are excellent, and we have a feel for what St. Louis wants to hear. We aren't afraid to play new records—we even helped to break Rod Stewart. We are involved with our audience and with our city. And you can't get that kind of involvement long-distance."

Jim Ladd, an announcer at the equally popular KMET in Los Angeles and producer of a syndicated interview show called *Inner View,* echoes Grafman's sentiments. Both KSHE and KMET are free-form and thus avoid the use of a fixed or predictable playlist. "Research is valuable, but you shouldn't be a slave to it. We love rock music here—we go to concerts, keep in constant contact with our audience, and play familiar hit groups like Boston as well as new groups. If a record feels right to us, we play it. If we don't think it's appropriate, we don't play it." KMET doesn't play the Bee Gees, for instance, since it feels the group doesn't have a strong enough rock image for the station. All music is chosen by the program director and her staff at weekly music meetings.

WIOQ in Philadelphia, another successful station, has a philosophy similar to KMET's. It concentrates on playing the best of all types of rock—and only rock—music. "WIOQ wasn't supposed to succeed," recalls assistant program director Helen Leicht. "Our owners even called in some consultants for advice, and they all said the market couldn't support another album station. But the owners gave us a year to turn the station around anyway." And they did.

As Kent Burkhart put it when asked to define consulting, "It's a marriage of science and emotion, experience and expertise. It's having the research but knowing how to use it." There is certainly no question that consultants play a major role in radio today, as stations fiercely compete for the No. 1 spot. Hiring a consultant can be expensive, and few will disclose exactly what they charge for their services—probably between $700 and $3,000 a month, depending on the size of the station. But for those stations who owe their new-found success to a programming consultant, that's a small price to pay.

34

King of the Night: Radio's Larry King

Gay Sands Miller

"Teejays," or talk jockeys, are increasingly sought-after personalities in radio. In the following article, Gay Sands Miller reports on the remarkable success of "The Larry King Show," the only coast-to-coast network radio talk show. Aired from 3:00 to 5:30 A.M., "Open Phone America" is King's call-in show, whose popularity can be judged simply by the astonishing number of people who phone in at *that* time—at *their own expense*. Who are the night owls who call in? Research confirms our expectations: they are usually the lonely, the alienated, the disassociated, the insomniacs, the late-night workers. But whatever the psychological motivation of its listeners, "The Larry King Show" offers its audience an opportunity no other American mass medium can match: an accessible, live, national forum for the ordinary person's opinion.

After midnight, when the owls hoot and the night crawlers slither, the fans of Larry King's radio talk show hurry to their telephones.

They call him at their own expense from around the country, dialing again and again in hopes of getting through to the Mutual radio network and onto Mr. King's show. Here's a sample:

"There really are men on Mars," a Seattle man declares.

"Russian influence is spreading like cancer," a Chicago caller fumes.

Then there's the "Portland Laugher," a regular who never speaks but runs up huge phone bills from Oregon just to cackle away. His laugh is different every time.

Welcome to "The Larry King Show," the only coast-to-coast network radio talk show. Broadcast each week night from midnight to dawn, the interview and call-in program is an often-zany lightning rod for a frustrated and alienated nation. The show also offers listeners at a lonesome time of

night some comic relief from their insomnia and graveyard-shift jobs.

Calls Aren't Screened

Encouraging the zaniness is the 44-year-old Mr. King, who surprises and delights listeners by refusing to screen calls and by launching his own irreverent zingers at the powers that be. He treats the ordinary person with respect but heaps abuse on the self-important, be they puffed-up guests on his show or his own bosses.

Don't ask him why he sings off-key in his raw Brooklyn accent, or babbles away about his beloved sports trivia, or belittles the pretensions of Mutual, an underdog network, by one night inventing the stumblebum "Mutual Orchestra" made up of 92 drunken incompetents. "Things happen spontaneously," Mr. King says. "I never plan."

Mr. King's show, which began in January 1978, has yet to turn a profit. With an audience numbering about two million—tiny by daytime standards—Mutual can charge advertisers only about $200 for a 30-second spot. By contrast, the network's morning "drive time" commands up to $1,700 for 30 seconds. Even with the relatively low advertising rates on Mr. King's show, Mutual hasn't been able to sell all the available time to advertisers.

Still, more and more radio stations have been picking up Mr. King's program, in part to save the costs of producing their own late-night music and talk shows. The number of stations carrying the show has increased to 159 from just 28 since the program was initially broadcast. (Mutual, currently a unit of Amway Corp., is primarily a news and sports network that is best known for having aired such radio classics as "The Shadow" and "The Lone Ranger" from the 1930s to the 1950s.)

Listeners identify with Mr. King's common-man image, in spite of his $90,000-a-year salary. He was mobbed by fans during a visit to Philadelphia, and several Southern mayors recently declared a "Larry King Week."

He isn't always a comedian. He often prods callers for "civilized debate" on such issues as abortion, religion, science and politics. And about half of his 5½-hour show is consumed by guest interviews; visitors have included Sophia Loren, John Ehrlichman and Cornelia Wallace. But Mr. King's freewheeling style prevails even during this segment. He openly brags that he doesn't read the books of authors who appear on the show. "That way, the audience and I discover things together," he explains.

"Open Phone America" starts at around 3 a.m. Eastern time. Callers love to play along with Mr. King's flights of fancy. One night, Mr. King solemnly announced that the imaginary Mutual Orchestra had disappeared. The 16-line switchboard lighted up, with one woman phoning all the way from Michigan to say she spotted the musicians jammed into a canoe, petting a huge rabbit.

Mr. King takes particular delight in making fun of the executive turmoil that hit Mutual after the network was acquired by Amway in 1977. "Executives here are never

fired," Mr. King says. "They're always retired, and they're always laughing." So Mr. King invented a room where these slaphappy retirees are imprisoned. He plays a tape of their giddy laughter whenever the mood strikes him, perhaps when a caller gets unusually boring. (Usually, however, he cuts off bores with a simple "thank you.")

Then there's "Gork," the "public-relations minister" from "Fringus," a planet of Mr. King's invention. Gork, an occasional visitor on the show, is played by a friend of Mr. King. One night, when Gork says that he eats dirt, calls pour in from as far as Texas, with one man proudly offering "my fabulous recipe for dirt-and-rock soup."

Gork, whose eerie-sounding voice is produced by a computer synthesizer, also parodies talk-show psychics, people Mr. King abhors. (Fringus is 31 days ahead of the earth, so Gork can predict the future.) Gork's predictions are laced with the same fuzzy insights and vague generalities that mark the pronouncements of earthbound seers. When a caller asks about the future, Gork replies: "You will either find great happiness next Tuesday or it will be just another ordinary day." Warming up to the theme, Gork adds, "A day later, it may or may not seem important to you."

Callers who break through the barrier of busy signals can expect to let the phone ring an average of about 45 minutes before Gina Gordey, a friendly 24-year-old, answers. She asks only the caller's location and alerts Mr. King by flashing a placard with the city's name. There's a seven-second delay before conversations are aired so that an engineer can cut off obscenities.

Some questions and answers: "What are Ted Kennedy's presidential prospects?" ("He'll run and win.") "If you were a scientist, what would you do?" ("Go to Mars.") "Don't you think doctors are to blame for my drug habit? I'm up to three pills a day. . . ."

"How interesting," Mr. King snaps, hanging up abruptly. He refuses to sympathize, fearing this would limit him to an audience of old women. Advertisers usually look for youthful audiences, since younger people tend to spend more freely.

Sometimes, Mr. King promotes what he calls his "Humphrey-Stevenson Democratic views," but he does so without passion. His voice is unemotional as he rattles off ads for such products as The Wall Street Journal or introduces recorded pitches for clothing-store chains, mail-order writing and accounting schools and, ironically, sleep aids.

Fame is coming slowly to Mr. King, a high-school graduate from Brooklyn, who spent his previous 20-year radio career in Miami. Alas, much of that fame came last January, when he filed a bankruptcy petition listing $352,000 in debts and practically no assets. The filing lists a $14,000 racetrack gambling debt. "I lived above my head," Mr. King explains. "It was part of the life style in Miami."

Like many of his callers, he feels a bit alien in this world. After the show ends at 5:30 a.m. Eastern time, he drives home to McLean, Va., and sleeps until noon. "When I wake up," he sighs, "I'm searching for bacon and eggs, and the world is serving knockwurst."

His workday begins about 10 p.m., when he drives his red, company-owned Buick with matching velveteen upholstery 12 miles to Mutual's headquarters in Arlington, a Washington, D.C. suburb. His tiny studio is kept chilly to please a computer, and his interviewing table is covered with a garish-orange, sound-deadening rug.

There he sits, leafing through magazines or gazing fondly at some of the 300 mostly flattering letters he gets each week. ("I never cease to marvel at your patience with nuts," a preacher writes. "You seem to have virtually unlimited potential," a Cleveland fan writes.)

The guest interviews begin at 12:06 a.m. in the East. (Portions are taped to play later in the West, after the call-in segment.)

Although Mr. King is an independent spirit, he recently dropped one feature of the show after getting criticism from the National Association of Broadcasters. Eliminated was a football-handicapping game, in which Mr. King would bet $1,000 of "mythical money" each week. Mr. King says the industry trade association thought his use of point spreads in the game encouraged illegal gambling.

But he isn't about to stop flouting authority and twitting his bosses. At 4 a.m., a businessman calls to say he is tired; he wants to know how to get to sleep. That's the signal for Mr. King to drop in a tape in which his own deepened voice booms: "Management Never Sleeps."

Recordings

Edison's first experiments in recorded sound a century ago, the introduction of electrical recording in 1925, and the almost simultaneous arrival of long-playing records and tape recordings in the late 1940s mark the main technological turning points in today's $2 billion recording industry. But this medium is unique not in its development, which parallels that of other media, but because records and tapes, like books, are paid for directly by their audiences, rather than through advertising, and because of the relatively low intrinsic cost of producing a single recording. As a result, the industry has supported a diversity of styles and contents to a degree unknown in other forms of electronic entertainment.

Yet the industry has unique difficulties along with its unique advantages. Declining growth rates and profit margins since the boom days of popular music in the sixties have been attributed to changing demographic patterns and the runaway royalties demanded by proven performers whose services remain necessary because of radio-dependent promotion. The resulting attempts by recording companies to control royalties and prices have led to recent government investigations in what was formerly almost an unregulated industry.

The selections in this section present the diverse nature of the medium. In "Gentle Revolution," Robert Metz describes the development and impact of the long-playing record. This change in technology was soon to combine with a less gentle revolution in popular music—the development of rock and roll—to bring the recording industry to its present multibillion dollar level.

With such large amounts of money at stake, the competition in every phase of the business remains rabid. The methods by which records are distributed often determine which records sell and which artists become known. Marc Kirkeby, a freelance writer, describes the latest developments in the recording industry, which has many parallels in the book publishing industry. His article, "The Changing Face of Record Distribution," shows how the very success of a few companies may lead to their own regulation.

What is the place of an artist in such an industry? The lifestyle of the handful of well-paid stars is well-known to the public. But what happens to the thousands of other performers and writers? In "Making Music in the Money Business," Peter Stampfel, a musician, gives an unusual view of where some of the industry's billions of dollars of income go—and where they do not go.

"A Hired Gun," shows a different kind of artist at work and, at the same time, looks at the possibilities provided by recording technology. Geoffrey Stokes, in this reading, tells the story of how the two hands of one piano part came to be played by two men who never met.

The final two selections deal with audience tastes. The need to predict audience reaction to assure record company profits is the subject of Michael Gross's "The Hits Just Keep on Coming," which describes a method of testing listeners' physical reactions to pop songs. James Barszcz, on the other hand, speculates that predictability is just what the audience does not want in popular music. In "It's the Same Old Song," Barszcz claims that the growth of the recording industry is directly related to the continuing evolution of rock 'n' roll music.

35
Gentle Revolution

Robert Metz

In the following selection, Robert Metz, a business writer for the *New York Times* and an author of books on investment and business history, describes the postwar expansion of the record industry from technological and economic viewpoints. The story of still another confrontation between the giant media organizations of CBS and RCA shows how inseparable technology and business organization have been in bringing recordings from their crude beginnings to their current state.

In the movie version of the life of Thomas Edison, a tinkerer employed in the Edison labs in the 1890s was shown playing with a makeshift device consisting of a rotating piece of metal with a pointed piece of metal scratching its surface. The device was full of sound and fury—and signified a great deal. Edison seized upon the idea and labored to construct a better device. Eventually he was seen speaking into a metal diaphragm whose vibrations in turn wiggled a needle pressed against a rotating cylinder of wax. And thus, supposedly through idle play, came the first permanent "record" of ephemeral sound. By any measure, it was an invention of genius.

Public relations people at CBS claim that resident genius Peter Goldmark invented the long-playing record. Goddard Lieberson, who heads Columbia Records, puts it differently.

He says that Edison invented recorded sound; that all subsequent developments of the medium—including the 33⅓-rpm long-playing record—sprang from Edison's invention and thus were merely refinements. He notes that a full decade before Goldmark developed the LP in 1948, a standard-size record that played nearly three times as long as the normal 78-rpm record of the time was presented to CBS when it acquired Columbia Records.

But Goldmark did more than just extend the playing time of a record, enough so that full symphonies could be put on a single disc. He also improved record fidelity from the raspy, scratchy sound familiar to exasperated generations of music lovers to glowing reproduction that captured the full, rich tones of the concert hall. And his discovery didn't come as a sudden insightful "Aha!" but

Source: From *CBS: Reflections in a Bloodshot Eye*, by Robert Metz, first published by Playboy Press. Reprinted by permission of Betty Marks, Literary Agent.

through a less dramatic, plodding approach. Through painstaking investigation of each element of the sound-reproduction system and their complex interrelationships, Goldmark and his team brought forth the long-playing record that revolutionized the music business.

Working at CBS, owner of a major record company, and being a serious amateur musician as well as an inventor, Peter Goldmark quite naturally was drawn to the problem of trying to improve recorded sound. Goldmark is a native of Hungary where his great-uncle, Karl, was considered the nation's greatest composer since Franz Liszt. Music was the dominant theme in his home—so much so that one evening, during civil disturbances in Budapest in the wake of World War I, Peter's mother once ignored an order from the street to "turn out the light" when she and her family were playing a Mozart string quartet. When a warning bullet tore into the ceiling of the fourth-floor apartment, 12-year-old Peter, on the cello, panicked, but his totally absorbed mother, on the violin, would not turn from the score until the last notes were played. She then rose calmly, closed the window and pulled down the blinds.

Shortly after World War II, Peter Goldmark spent a musical evening that was marred by a different kind of interruption. With friends at their home in Westport, Connecticut, he was listening to a recording of Brahms's Second Piano Concerto played by Vladimir Horowitz and conducted by Arturo Toscanini. Peter remembers that though the recording was on new 78-rpm records, there were eight sound defects scattered through the 12 sides, intrusions as jarring to his ear as "having the phone ring at intervals while you are making love." In addition there were the periodic interruptions of the records being changed.

He asked his friends to play the records again; and while they did so, he sat gritting his teeth and racking his brain. Finally, he produced a ruler and started calculating, counting 80 grooves to the inch, and he began pondering the principle of the phonograph—how sound was captured on a record and held

there and how it might be done with greater fidelity to the original sound.

He concluded that he could get more mileage by slowing the turntable speed while crowding significantly more grooves onto a disc. Later he chose a 33⅓-rpm speed to match the radio transcription discs then used in recorded broadcasts.

Changing speed and grooves-per-inch weren't his major problems. The more important challenge was to get higher fidelity; RCA in earlier attempts had slowed the turntable speed, but got worse results, not better.

As a first step, Goldmark was inclined to discard the standard record material, shellac, for Vinylite. This new material cost twice as much but was light and unbreakable, and it would end up being cheaper if an entire symphony could be put on one record.

Next, after discovering that 90 percent of all symphonic works could be played in 45 minutes, he settled on 12-inch discs, also practical because turntables were already designed for that size.

All he needed now was a go-ahead, and he went to Edward Wallerstein, who ran Columbia Records, to get it. Wallerstein had worked for RCA, but Bill Paley hired him away on the strength of Wallerstein's reputation as the best phonograph salesman of his day. Wallerstein listened to Goldmark for "exactly three minutes" before saying he didn't like the idea. Peter recalls that "he put an arm around my shoulders, and suggested in a fatherly manner that I drop the entire project and do something in the television line instead." Wallerstein also told Goldmark that RCA had tried and failed with a 33⅓-rpm record for the consumer; and that clearly if RCA with its superior resources had failed, CBS efforts were doomed as well. Fortunately for CBS, this was a totally inappropriate approach to take with Peter Goldmark. The thin, nearsighted Ph.D. and inventor, who had gotten an Austrian patent on an early television device in 1930, had always been driven to more strenuous efforts by skepticism.

This first confrontation between Wallerstein and Goldmark, both men of high standards and keen musical ears, marked the beginning of a long struggle. Goldmark went to Paul

Kesten who was still running the company. He listened attentively and said that if Peter thought he could do it to go ahead and he would back him with $100,000 of CBS money. Kesten didn't seem to think Wallerstein's "no" was important. Though Wallerstein proved to be a stumbling block all along the road, this negative challenge seems to have provided the impetus that brought better results in the end.

Again and again, as Goldmark and a carefully assembled team made some progress, Wallerstein would find fault. When Goldmark and company cut the grooves finer and finer until they were able to get 15 minutes to a side compared with 4 minutes on a standard 12-inch disc spinning at 78 revolutions per minute, Wallerstein promptly reminded him that a Berlioz movement would take 20 minutes. Peter labored again and stretched the side to 22½ minutes, then to a full 25 minutes, but, predictably enough, the sound went sour. If it had been that easy, RCA would have solved the problem years earlier. Peter noted that the violins sounded like flutes, while small cutting variations changed the pitch of the instruments.

Wallerstein had ears "like a bat" and each unsuccessful cutting brought an "I told you so." The Goldmark team worked harder, cutting on vinyl, hoping to produce an orchestral recording with accurate pitch. At last they thought they were successful. They played the recording with anticipation, only to have Wallerstein shake his head and ask, "Where is the fuzz on the bow? I don't hear it. When you get the fuzz, then come back." Peter argued to no avail that the "fuzz" was the noise of the shellac on the old records. Not so, said Wallerstein—it was the scrape of the resin from the violinist's bow.

The Goldmark team had just about reached the point of absolute frustration. But Peter's Belgian-born recording engineer, René Snepvangers, who had been in charge of NBC transcriptions before Peter lured him away, suggested a new approach: Fire pistols, record the sound and see what resulted. Such a sharp report would certainly be a critical test of delicate equipment. They tried it. The crack of the pistol came across on the recording like the sound of a "baked potato falling on the floor."

Component after component was tested as Peter dashed back and forth between his laboratory and the studio next door where the sound was recorded. Everything checked out fine—until they got to the microphone. Was it possible, as a German research study had suggested, that the ribbon microphone was causing "phase distortion"?

When speaking into a ribbon mike, the standard microphone of the day, the sounds traveling along the ribbon failed to arrive at the end of the ribbon in the same sequence as they left the source. Thus, in theory at least, certain sounds reproduced unnaturally.

Condenser microphones, a new design specifically created to eliminate this distortion, were just beginning to come off the assembly line in a German factory. Goldmark obtained one—and the distortion vanished! Excited, Goldmark and two fellow employees sneaked up to a special secret studio. An engineer had his violin, a secretary sat at the piano and Peter set up his cello. They cut a Bach number on vinyl and called in Wallerstein. *Voila!* The results were brilliant, though Goldmark says they left something to be desired musically. This time even Wallerstein showed enthusiasm.

But there was far more to do if this "invention" was to become part of the CBS product line. Wallerstein pointed out that Goldmark would have to find a way to transfer the existing CBS record library, universally recorded on four-minute master discs, onto long-playing records—a tricky but necessary step for Columbia to avoid competing with its own 78-rpm records. The task was to join the four-minute segments so neatly that the listener would not be aware that there was a shift from one turntable to the other. Goldmark had to develop a "musical computer" capable of timing records electronically to hundredths of a second. A timer was used to start the second turntable, then the third. Sometimes the orchestra had recorded four-minute segments on different days so that the pitch of the instruments was slightly different, due primarily to their weather sensitivity. The sound on the different platters had to be blended so well that the listener wouldn't be able to detect it.

The musical computer was perfect—or so Peter thought. It was tested at Columbia Records with Goldmark and Wallerstein standing by. The first turntable on the first cutting finished and the second was cued in when a yell came from Wallerstein: "Hold it! You lost a bar."

"The man was inhuman," Goldmark recalls. "I permitted myself a minor artistic luxury. I swore politely under my breath in Hungarian."

In time, though, the cuing system was perfected and Paley was called in along with Frank Stanton. Paley was interested but he had to rely on Wallerstein's ears, since in Goldmark's words, he had "no sense of pitch." Paley's chief concern was that if the new records were used only for classical recordings, the audience would be small, the profits perhaps nonexistent, yet the new product could touch off a major battle with RCA which he wasn't eager to finance. While Paley was confident the LP was better than anything the General [Sarnoff] could come up with, Paley was unwilling to announce the development until he knew the probable RCA response.

Goldmark says Paley pondered the question and decided that the thing to do was to invite RCA to join forces with CBS in putting out the 33⅓. Goldmark thought the idea ingenious, and Philco, which had already agreed to manufacture the record players, agreed to go along. Paley, according to Goldmark, telephoned Sarnoff and invited him to a demonstration of CBS's new record. The call from CBS must have jarred the General, in terms of his smug attitude toward CBS as a technically inferior company. But Sarnoff agreed to listen to the CBS records. He arrived at the CBS boardroom with a retinue of eight engineers to be greeted by Paley, the cool Frank Stanton, Wallerstein, Goldmark and Peter's boss, Adrian Murphy. Goldmark tells the story:

> Paley stepped forward and smoothly explained that I would first be playing an ordinary seventy-eight and then I would follow it with the CBS invention. I could see Sarnoff stiffen and become attentive. I played the seventy-eight for about fifteen seconds and then switched over to the new record.

> With the first few bars Sarnoff was out of his chair. I played it for ten seconds and then switched back to the seventy-eight. The effect was electrifying, as we knew it would be. I never saw eight engineers look so much like carbon copies of tight-lipped gloom. Turning to Paley, Sarnoff said loudly and with some emotion: "I want to congratulate you and your people, Bill. It is very good."

> Paley offered to delay the announcement of our long-playing record if RCA would join CBS in a simultaneous move so that both companies could benefit from the growth of the business. Paley offered know-how and a franchise.

> Sarnoff said it was a generous offer that he would discuss with his staff. With that statement, Sarnoff and his entourage rose and left the boardroom.

> I later learned what happened after the group returned to RCA headquarters. Sarnoff, who had been so affable and congratulatory, had gone into what could only be described as an executive tantrum. How could little CBS, with a two-by-four laboratory, beat RCA? he demanded. . . . A few days later, Sarnoff phoned Paley to say that he had decided not to come in with us on the record.

Howard Meighan has a different memory of the event: On the eve of a press conference to be held at the Waldorf to announce the LP, RCA was still in the dark. He called the preparations which involved Philco's production of record players—half to carry the CBS name, half Philco's—"a remarkable job of secrecy."

In Meighan's version, Paley had been sitting with his top staff in the executive offices of CBS on the twentieth floor of 485 Madison Avenue. He asked his staff: "Don't you think as a courtesy I should call Sarnoff and tell him we are going to do it?" After a lively debate, Paley made up his mind and called Sarnoff.

According to Meighan, Sarnoff's reaction to the CBS development was that there was "really nothing new to the idea," since he already had seven different long-playing records. Paley said rather skeptically that he'd like to see those seven records, and Sarnoff replied, belligerently, "How early in the morning?" Paley threw back an "Eight A.M."

and Sarnoff told him to come on out to the RCA labs in Princeton, New Jersey. Paley left the next morning, Meighan says, while his senior staff waited anxiously in New York.

Later, Paley walked into the CBS executive offices and told his staff that RCA did indeed have seven different versions and added that they must have worked all night getting them ready to demonstrate. But, Sarnoff supposedly told Paley, the two companies had a big investment in the 78, and the public was satisfied with it, so what would be the use of introducing something different and getting into that kind of competitive struggle? Says Meighan: "Paley explained this so persuasively to the four or five of us that Frank Stanton turned to him and asked apprehensively, 'Do we go at two P.M., then?' [He was referring to the press conference.] Paley said, 'I thought about that all the way back. The answer is yes.'"

Frank Stanton volunteered still another version in an interview a year after he left CBS. Stanton explained that he had a "good, warm relationship" with Sarnoff though the two had "fought like tigers" in representing their respective networks in Washington. "I asked him to come over to my office for lunch and had an RCA speaker in the office, which he saw immediately. He said, 'What's that over there?' I put the needle down on the record and let it play."

And the record played and played and, says Stanton, Sarnoff kept "looking and looking. I said, 'Don't worry, it is going to run for thirty minutes.' I had given him a cigar and I thought he was going to bite the end off it. . . . His reaction was, 'How could it be that the Great Victor Talking Machine Company didn't know about this?'"

. . . General Sarnoff was foolish to refuse Paley's offer of a license. When Sarnoff decided to fight against Columbia's superior system he was guilty—and not for the first time—of allowing pride to triumph over good sense. Paley believes that Sarnoff refused the offer because he was angry with CBS for having just landed Jack Benny.

RCA, as it turned out, had been ready to go with a seven-inch version of the 78, spinning at 45 rpm, which Goldmark says RCA called "Madame X." Madame X had been kept on the shelf—presumably in case of some unexpected emergency. Several weeks after CBS introduced the LP at the Waldorf —to relatively little fanfare in the press that failed to comprehend the importance of the development—RCA announced that it was coming out with the four-minute 45. RCA claimed virtually "instantaneous" and inaudible changes from one record to the next. But the 45 had a hole in the center bigger than a quarter, requiring a disclike plug that caused confusion and no little annoyance. RCA was compelled to offer new record changers at a loss in order to get Madame X under way, while CBS was busy developing a changer that would play 78s, 45s and 33⅓s.

Peter Goldmark says it was Arturo Toscanini who finally persuaded Sarnoff, a number of years later, to see the light and enter the long-play market. Toscanini had listened to Bruno Walter conducting on a Columbia LP and was infuriated that Walter's performance was uninterrupted, while his own renditions were constantly interrupted by record changes. Through his pressure, Sarnoff finally relented, but not before the record business was cluttered with the 45 that, while useful for pop singles, has always been a stepchild in a world that spins at 33⅓. As for the 78, it has been relegated to collectors' files.

36

The Changing Face
of Record Distribution

Marc Kirkeby

The production of a quality recording, as described in the preceding essay, does not assure the success of a record company. Between the performer and producer, on one hand, and the listener, on the other, a distribution system is required. Free-lance writer Marc Kirkeby describes how high-pressure competition among middle-men affects all aspects of the record business.

Remember a mellow tune called "Love Letters in the Sand," sung by a white-bucks-shod Pat Boone 25 years ago? And the early recordings of Ray Charles, whose rendition of "Georgia on My Mind" was just one of his blues hits that soared to the top of the sales charts? These artists and hundreds more, including Johnny Cash, Diana Ross and the Supremes, Buddy Holly and Chuck Berry, began their careers with small, so-called independent record companies whose fortunes were made by searching out and popularizing both new music styles—from country and western and rock and roll to rhythm and blues—and the fledgling musicians playing them.

But as music trends have changed from rock to disco, so have the economics of the record business. The independents—companies that do not own their own facility for manufacturing records or distribution system for selling them to retailers—have found their perennial cash-flow problems magnified by increasing competition, spiraling production costs and the growing power of the giant entertainment conglomerates.

Thus what began slowly in recent years as a move toward more secure financial agreements, with a few independent labels assigning their distribution work to the "majors"—a handful of record companies with their own distribution and manufacturing branches—has in the past two months threatened to become a stampede.

While some independents appear to be thriving—Arista, for instance, whose roster of stars includes Barry Manilow, one of the nation's largest-selling artists—the growing consolidation has sent more than a few tremors among the ranks of another small industry whose survival is keyed to the small labels, independent record distributors, who wonder if they will have any important independent labels left to distribute by mid-year.

Recent Casualties

With such major artists as Peter Frampton, the Brothers Johnson and Pablo Cruise recording for its label, A&M has enjoyed 16 years of success as an "independent" record company.

But as of last week, giant RCA Records became A&M's sole distributor and record-presser, an arrangement that has become typical of a dramatic restructuring of the way the burgeoning record and tape industry gets its goods into stores.

The deal with A&M came just a week after RCA signed 20th Century-Fox Records, a smaller but still significant independent, to a similar distribution contract. During 1978, independent distributors also lost such consistently hit-producing companies as United Artists, Jet, Salsoul, DJM and Private Stock to the distribution arms of major record companies.

ABC Records, another of the largest independents with 1978 sales of about $56 million, will be absorbed into the majors' ranks later this month if its sale to MCA Records is approved by the Federal Trade Commission. ABC, which has suffered heavy losses for several years and closed its own distribution branches in 1977, had long been rumored negotiating with several companies for acquisition or distribution.

The steady migration of independent labels to distribution by one of the six majors—CBS, EMI/Capitol, MCA, Polygram, RCA and the Warner-Elektra-Atlantic division of Warner Communications, Inc.—represents just one facet of the major companies' snowballing control of the record and the marketplace.

The vast financial resources of the majors has also tended to give them first crack at new labels as they are formed and at artists shopping for higher royalties. The small-label owner who opts for distribution by a major receives less money per album sold than he would from an independent distributor, but in return he obtains a degree of financial security, almost always including a sizable cash advance against future royalties that no independent can offer. As a result, the six majors have achieved a share of the domestic record market that has probably now passed 85 percent. A compilation of the 1978 weekly album-rating charts from Record World, a trade publication, shows that the majors owned and distributed a 74 percent share of the year's largest-selling albums. Counting albums released by A&M, ABC, and the other companies that have shifted to major distribution since January 1978, the total climbs to more than 80 percent. The majors' shares of the singles and specialty record charts are similarly high.

Other independent record companies, in-

cluding Arista, Motown, Fantasy, Chrysalis and Mushroom, reportedly have been negotiating distribution deals with one or more of the major record companies, but each has denied that it will abandon independent distribution.

There is little question that the largest independent record labels will survive one way or another. But for the independent distributors, who are among the music industry's most colorful entrepreneurs, the future is cloudy. They have none of the vertical integration of a major to buttress finances, and their profits are being squeezed on two sides.

Distributors make their money buying records from independent labels and marking them up in price and reselling them to large retailers and to sub-distributors who service the small record stores. Competition has pushed up to $3.55 or $3.60 the price he must pay on the labels for an album which carries a list price of $7.98. A major, by contrast, pays only about $3.47 per album for the labels it distributes or owns. And because a major's distribution system primarily is a means to an end—and need not be necessarily a large profit center in itself—a major's gross markup is about two percent less than an independent's markup of about 19 percent—the crucial leeway with which a major can undercut the independent's price to retailers.

Thus, the album that an independent distributor buys at $3.60 must be resold to retailers at about $4.30 (which the independents insist provides them with a bare minimum profit), compared with a major's purchase at $3.47 and sale to retail outlets at about $4.08.

To convince retail accounts to buy his more-expensive records, the independent distributor must have hit records to offer. As the sales charts show, the hits available to him are becoming fewer as independent labels are bought out by the major record companies with their own distribution networks. Faced with shrinking profit margins and a dwindling number of labels, the independent distributors know they have reached a crisis.

"I've never seen such upheaval in my life," said Joe Simone, owner of Progress Record Distributing in Cleveland, in response to the A&M-RCA announcement. "We're making every cutback necessary due to the loss of volume. But we still have a very viable business and enough companies to represent —assuming they're not sold tomorrow.''

Mr. Simone has shored up his defenses by broadening the Midwestern territories in which he distributes records. He recently opened an office in Detroit.

Other independent distributors insist they too must expand to survive, but because every big city already has at least one independent distributor based in it, any expansion or increased competition among independents would almost surely put some of them out of business.

''I don't have any doubt in my mind that it's going to happen,'' said Harvey Korman, owner of Piks Corporation, one of Mr. Simone's competitors. ''Instead of two or three in each market, there will be one strong distributor. As a result, the marriage between manufacturer and distributor will get even closer.''

Even such expansion moves by the ''super independents'' might not completely offset the advantages of distribution by the major companies: advantages that are convincing enough to make independent labels sacrifice 10 cents or more per album to go with a major.

Principal among those advantages is the majors' reputation for paying quickly. A hit record does an independent record company little good if it hasn't gotten the money for those sales from its distributors.

A&M is a case in point. Last year the company, which reported nearly $100 million in sales, had just begun building its own branch system, opening a distribution point in southern California, A&M Pacific, and had plans for additional branches. But A&M Pacific had problems with its slow-paying retail accounts almost from the start, and those money woes, coupled with the receivables problem A&M already had with its remaining independent distributors, put the company in a serious cash-flow bind.

Significantly, a key feature of the A&M deal with RCA is a large cash advance by RCA against the money A&M is still owed by its independent distributors. Even if the distributors never pay—and the independents are almost always slow to pay departing labels —A&M sources say RCA will cover A&M's losses. RCA, for its part, needed the 50 percent increase in sales volume that A&M will bring to keep the large RCA distribution system profitable.

Another important element of the A&M-RCA pact involves record pressing. A&M will save 3 cents to 4 cents per album by moving its pressing business to RCA from Columbia Records, a division of CBS Inc., which had pressed 80 percent of its discs, and independent Monarch, which had handled the remainder. No independent record distributor could offer such a combined deal; five of the six majors—except for Polygram—could. Indeed, independent record labels often use the pressing facilities of the majors—particularly those of Columbia—even if their albums are independently distributed.

Major record companies, and the labels they distribute, also carry more clout with retailers than do independent distributors. Retailers stock records they believe will sell, but in order to obtain favorable deals on best-selling albums—increasingly the majors' province—they will also agree to carry records by a company's new and unproven artists. Similarly, retailers are more likely to pay quickly a company whose records are selling briskly, because that company might otherwise withhold the hit records on which the retailer depends.

Many retailers, however, are wary of the growing power of the few big companies.

''The independent has a stronger motivation to work with people in the marketplace,'' says Tom Modica, owner of Longhair Music, a record store in Portland, Ore. ''With the majors you are just one of the fish in the pond. I'm fearful that things are consolidating so fast around such a small group of executives that those people might really wield an iron fist.''

How can independent distributors and labels contend with the majors' strength? As the consolidation trend has accelerated, the majors have been watching the ongoing investigation of the industry by the antitrust division of the Justice Department as a sign that the Federal Government might come to the aid of the independents.

Justice lawyers took testimony from dozens of record company executives, distributors and retailers in Los Angeles in late 1977, and the investigation is "still open," according to a Justice spokesman, who would not comment further.

But top executives at the major record companies insist that the investigation poses no threat to their expansion plans.

"RCA Records is getting bigger in a very competitive industry," says Robert Summer, the company's president. "We are frankly very proud of our progress and would be surprised if our growth, or the growth of the industry, were challenged."

The independent distributors, and the labels that have remained loyal to them, insist that their fortunes will reverse, claiming that as the majors grow larger they will be less able to give personal attention to their client labels.

Sal Licata, senior vice president of Chrysalis Records says, "A lot of the labels that are with the [majors] are going to become unhappy. The majors can't please all of them. It's a cycle, a vicious cycle."

Mr. Silverman, of Music Trend, adds, "I think a great many entrepreneurs will be encouraged by the void A&M created." "There's a need for more product. Somebody's going to come along and fill these channels."

37
Making Music in the Money Business

Peter Stampfel

The financial rewards to individual artists in the music business is the subject of this autobiographical account by Peter Stampfel, of the Holy Modal Rounders. For nearly two decades, Stampfel was a recording artist. His experience contrasts sharply with the public's perception that all recording stars are millionaires. Stampfel's story is more typical: a performer who lost money despite the moderate success of his recordings.

Back in those fun '60s, a maniac ripped my apartment apart, punched me in the face, and did a bunch of other things which made me believe in harsh punishment for criminals.

Joe Hyman was one of those speed freak-arsonist-rapist-thief bully boys who made the '60s so much fun.

He was looking for money and dope. Because he had seen my name on a record, he thought I had plenty of both.

Joe was shot while breaking into an apartment in 1969. The '60s weren't completely without justice.

I thought that in these less naive '70s people no longer equated records with riches. Apparently not so.

I was walking down Canal Street recently and a guy stopped me and asked for a cigarette.

"Hey," he said when he saw my face, "are you rich?"

What a weird intro to a mugging, I thought. In the '60s they showed you a gun and said, "It's real."

"No, I said, "I ain't rich."

"But you're famous. I've seen you on an album cover."

Well, maybe I'm known to one out of every 20,000 Americans. A low-level cult figure. I've made a dozen records, but I sure ain't rich. The *Wall Street Journal* said only about two dozen pop musicians are really wealthy. Let me tell you just how rich my records have made me.

The first two records, which I made with Steve Weber, were recorded on a New Jersey label. The two of us were paid a total of $500 per record. I got $10 to $20 royalties for a song I wrote on one. If you write a song on a record, you and the publisher get to split two cents (this is called mechanical royalty). It is usually split down the middle, a penny apiece. The composer and publisher have been receiving this same amount since about 1912. Single records have sold for about the same amount since then. They seem to be the most uninflated consumer item of the 20th century.

A composer who has 12 songs on an album gets 12 cents, and the publisher gets 12 cents.

. . .

In 1979, as a result of legislation the writer/publisher stipend will rise to a princely two and three-quarters cents.

Early in this decade, New Jersey label merged with a larger company and re-released our first two albums as a double album set. Until that point, we never received any additional royalties.

Both these records were recorded in just two sessions. Usually the recording costs are paid by the artist and come out of his/her royalties. Our royalties at this point were 20 cents an album. The recording costs were less than $1000, so we should have gotten royalties after 4000 or 5000 records. They never told us how many they sold.

When you receive accountings concerning record sales, they usually neglect to tell you how many records you sold.

We did get $400 or $500 apiece from the reissue. The accountings were mailed from someplace I never heard of in the Caribbean. The first one claimed they had paid us $600, an amount we had never received. I wrote them saying I had never received their $600. I never got a reply. New Jersey and the Caribbean. Hmm.

Weber and I were on the first Fugs recordings in 1965. As an advance we got airplane tickets to Washington, D.C., where we had a job. Material from those first recordings eventually made their way onto three albums, one of which made the charts. Over a period of four years I received $600 or $700 for my parts in those three albums. I got no mechanical royalties for the song I had written on the Fugs second album. Mechanical royalties are paid as soon as the record returns come in, and have nothing to do with the recording costs. It is illegal not to pay them. The company never paid us any mechanical royalties at all.

Weber, Sam Shepard, and I made a record in 1967. Weber and I got $150 each for that. Sam was supposed to get $150 too but never did. We never found out how many copies were sold, and got no artist or mechanical royalties.

We got no royalties from our next record, *The Moray Eels Eat the Holy Modal Rounders,* but we got an advance of several hundred dollars for publishing. We were also flown to California and lodged in a motel for the session; they bought Weber an electric guitar and me an amplifier.

It sold about 8000 copies. There is no way the expenses—recording, motels, airplanes, equipment, etc.—could be recouped out of that.

A song from that album was used in *Easy Rider,* but because of a legal complication, Antonia, its author, never got any money for it.

Sam Shepard, who was our drummer, wrote a play called *Operation Sidewinder,* for which we did the music. A major company was planning to release the soundtrack on a record, and they gave our manager a $20,000 advance. Most of the money went to buy out our previous manager's contract and publishing rights. The play wasn't a big hit, and the record never came out. The company wanted its money back. It was gone, and I had only seen a couple hundred of it. So our royalties were taken from *Easy Rider*.

In 1970 the Rounders recorded *Good Taste Is Timeless*. Our manager told us we hadn't gotten an advance for the record. We had naively given him power of attorney, which meant he could sign for us or endorse our checks.

The record was a real production number. It was even recorded in Nashville. The final costs on it were close to $30,000. No royalties, naturally. And again, we received no mechanical royalties and have no idea how many copies were sold.

Two years later we made *Alleged In Their Own Time* for a company named after our group. The band got an advance of $500 or $600 dollars.

In their early days, this company was doing an unprecedented thing: They were paying for the recordings themselves. Therefore we got royalties as soon as the advance was recouped. Their royalty rate was 50 cents per record. We also got to do our own publishing.

Four of us eventually divided $300 from this record. Almost 6000 copies were pressed, and it is still in print.

Our next, *Have Moicy!*, was also on this label. By now they had reverted to the "artist pays for recording out of royalties" approach. They had found, among other things, it made for much less time wasted in the studio. At 50 cents per record, it took sales of over 7000 to pay the recording costs and advances. The advances were $600. Ten thousand copies have been pressed so far. They should bring me royalties of close to $500.

The final Holy Modal Rounders record, *Last Round,* will be coming out soon on yet another label. They also pay 50 cents per record, and prefer the artist to handle publishing. It's their policy to pay three-quarters of the total production costs, leaving the remaining quarter to be paid by the artist. *Last Round* cost $3700 to record, and the production costs will come to another $3500. By this formula, our royalties will absorb $1900 instead of the full recording costs, as with any other company. The 50 cent royalty will be split seven ways, after giving 10 per cent to Bill Poten, who arranged for the recording studio to do the job on speculation, and 10 per cent to Dan Doyle, who lined up the record contract.

I just finished an acoustic record with Steve Weber, a belated follow-up to the first two records we did together. The total recording costs less a $200 advance for me and mixing expenses will come to $1200. Since we were recording only two voices and two acoustic instruments, we were able to use a four-track machine. Dan Doyle, our producer, has a genius for cutting record production costs. We will begin to make a profit before the record has sold 3000 copies, and we will get 25 cents each because there are only two of us.

So, in the course of 15 years, I have made $4400 from 13 records. That works out to $300 a year.

If that seems like a low wage, and I will be the last person to deny that it is, consider this: hundreds, perhaps thousands of people have made more records than I have—and less money.

38
A Hired Gun

Geoffrey Stokes

All the economics, audience trends, and interrelations of the sound media begin in the recording studio, where it sometimes takes months to make an album. Moreover, studio time is paid for by the band. In *Star-Making Machinery: The Odyssey of an Album,* Geoffrey Stokes, a writer for *The Village Voice,* follows Commander Cody and His Lost Planet Airmen through the entire process of making a record, which the band hoped would take them from years of struggling, middle-level success to the top of their profession. For the first time, the band hired an independent producer, John Boylan, to supervise and direct the recording, a function previously performed by Commander Cody himself (George Frayne). The following section from Stokes' book describes how Frayne's own playing was partly replaced on one cut by an important but unpublicized element in the music business, the studio musician.

. . . The problem [John Boylan] had scrupulously avoided mentioning to the Airmen was Frayne's piano playing. After countless listenings and relistenings to "House of Blue Lights," he had decided that the piano was irremediable. There were twelve versions recorded straight through, and on each of them the piano's tempo was radically different from that of the rest of the instruments. He had talked with Higginbotham and Kirchen about what could be done, and they had both agreed that there might be nothing left to do but scrap the track. But it turned out that there was another alternative. After the Boarding House stint, Frayne arranged to take three days off to fly to Philadelphia and visit a woman friend. As soon as he was sure Frayne was indeed going to be gone, Boylan checked with Kirchen and Stein. With their reluctant but understanding approval, he called Roger Kellaway.

"About a third of the records in the country are recorded on the West Coast," says an A&M executive. "On about half of those records, Roger Kellaway plays piano." In other words, anyone buying a rock album anywhere in the country has about a 15 per-

cent chance of listening to Roger Kellaway. But only the most devoted of fans have ever heard of him, for unlike performers who make their livings by traveling and recording, Kellaway has chosen anonymity. He is a studio musician, a hired gun who comes into a recording session prepared to play whatever the producer wants him to.

Studio musicians in general are an odd breed; in the midst of an industry where success is measured by sales, they hear a very different drummer. Success for them involves the fine tuning of their craft; the resulting sales of whatever songs they've worked on are irrelevant. Even those who have broken through to the point where their names have become public property maintain the studio ethic; Eric Weissberg, who had a number-one hit with a song called "Dueling Banjos" that he recorded for the film *Deliverance,* once responded to an interviewer's question about his best recording with "I guess it's the double-tracked fiddle I did for a Doctor Pepper commercial."

Weissberg's attitude is in many ways typical. The measure of his craft is keyed to the moment of recording rather than its commercial outcome. The studio musicians exist at the peak of their trade, capable of producing whatever is asked of them in the studio. At worst, they are paid the union-scale minimum per session, and the best of them can command more than that. Some of them eventually tire of their anonymity and go public—as when the ubiquitous New Orleans pianist Mac Rebennack surfaced as the glittering Doctor John—but many of them are content with their anonymous $50,000 a year.

They are not anonymous in the trade, however, and the Airmen, who had spent many studio hours talking about session musicians with Boylan, were excited by the chance to play with Kellaway. "It's a whole new standard," said Kirchen. "If we can play with him, we can play with anybody." Frayne was their leader, and they knew he was a good piano player. "The only reason George doesn't practice," said one, "is so that he can knock everybody out about how good he is without practice." But playing with Kellaway would be something special. So special that it muted any pangs of disloyalty they might have been feeling.

When Kellaway stepped off the Marin helicopter a half-hour before the band was to begin recording, he looked every inch the hired gun. At least, with his fringed buckskin jacket and carefully creased cowboy hat, he looked that way until one got close enough to see his developing potbelly and his standard show-biz T-shirt. On the drive to the studio, during which he and Boylan discussed commercial possibilities for a film score he was working on, the impact of his swaggering helicopter entrance dissipated. But when he arrived at the studio, the hired gun image rapidly returned.

After listening to a playback of the best existing version of "House of Blue Lights" Kellaway asked for some blank scores. Owing to its location, the Sausalito Record Plant is not usually home to studio musicians, and records self-contained bands almost exclusively; Cathy Callon, the Record Plant receptionist, was momentarily stunned by his request. "You mean," she asked, "the kind of paper with the lines on it?"

"Right," he said, as laconically as Gary Cooper.

After a certain amount of rousting about, during which the first few Airmen arrived, she found some and delivered them to him. "Thank you," he said politely, then lapsed into Bogart mode: "Play it again, John." The tape ran again, and as the Airmen watched dumbfounded, he took down Frayne's part by dictation. Andy Stein, the most musically sophisticated member of the band, started out looking over Kellaway's shoulder, but was soon reduced to helpless giggles and escaped from the booth. Lurching around the Pong machine, Stein said when he could speak, "He's kidding. I know the problems with that part. He can't play that without practicing for a month.

"I mean"—he paused—"I'm really impressed by what he's done already, but he can't play it. In fact I'll bet he can't even write it down without . . ." Stein stopped again. "What do I mean can't *even* write it down. If that's all he can do, he's already amazing. But he can't play it. It's *very* hard."

Stein's prediction notwithstanding, Kellaway took only one more replay to double-check what he'd taken down, and then he was ready. Buckskin fringe flapping, he strode toward the piano to exercise his fingers. After a few minutes, while the other Airmen were arranging their instruments, he called Boylan into the corridor. "I don't know if I can play this," said the hired gun. "It's not the way I play boogie-woogie, but even if it was, it's an impossible key."

"Don't worry," said Boylan, "you'll get close enough, and what I'm really looking for is time."

"Well I can do *that,* but it's not going to be easy."

It was difficult primarily because the Airmen were indeed a band rather than a collection of Kellaways. The arrangement they had chosen had not actually been chosen at all. It had grown from the idea that it would be fun to do a rock'n'roll song in Dixieland style, featuring a chorus with Kirchen on trombone and Stein on sax.

Kirchen was not a very good trombonist, and he could play only in the most basic key, which for a trombonist is B♭. "It's like my C," Frayne had explained, "and if he's gonna play trombone at all, that's gotta be the key. The only thing is that it means I have to go from C, which is where the song was written and is really easy, into B♭, which is really hard." Kellaway, the prototypical studio musician, had wandered into the middle of the constraints imposed by a live band. The temporary awe which his dictating skills had instilled in the Airmen was about to disappear. "All right," he said, "let's try it. But I don't know if it's gonna work."

It didn't. After a few takes in which Kellaway was excused because everything was new to him, the Airmen suddenly faced the problem that Frayne's part was unplayable. In addition to the tempo difficulties, Kellaway couldn't keep his left and right hand together.

Kellaway, instead of being the solution, had rapidly become part of the problem. His left-hand lead, which set the pace for the rest of the instruments, was stuttering. His right hand, though all the notes were correlated exactly to what Frayne had earlier played, was awkwardly out of phase with his left. "John," said Kellaway as he raced into the booth, "I just can't do it." Compromise was clearly in order.

One would think it might be hard to work out a compromise with a hired gun, but it was easy, at least partly because Kellaway *was* a hired gun. He had little ego invested in this project; it was, after all, only one of a half-dozen that he might have been doing. He and Boylan were quickly able to work out an alternative approach to the song. To begin with, they temporarily abandoned the right hand, and set about playing it through with Kellaway using only his left. Once he was freed from the complex rhythmic coordinations and could concentrate solely on establishing tempo, Kellaway played with a metronomic solidity that anchored the rest of the Airmen. After a couple of takes, everything except the transition from the opening piano bars to the Airmen's entrance was firmly established. Just before take eight, Stein stumbled on the solution.

He and Kirchen, killing time in the isolation booth to the right of the studio, began a trombone and saxophone duet on "Tin Roof Blues," the old Dixieland standard. The other players joined in and had begun an impromptu jam session when Boylan cut them off. "That's it," he said. "Just do that for twelve bars, until everybody is really comfortable in the tempo, *then* go right into the piano intro. OK? Twelve bars of Commander Dixie, and then right into it. Let's go now, rolling on eight."

It worked. Although they did a few more for safety, take eight was the one they kept. After the playback, Kellaway returned to the studio to add the right-hand piano part on another track. In two takes—the second one required only because of mechanical troubles during the first—he had it down, and was on his way back to the heliport. In less than two hours, Kellaway had earned two hundred dollars and the Airmen had made a perfect take of the song that had eluded them through the previous six weeks. "You know," said Stein after Kellaway had gone, "he's *very* good."

But as good and as necessary as Kellaway had been, Frayne was hurt and angry when he returned and discovered that Boylan had brought in an outsider to do his part. "You guys," he said accusingly to Boylan and Grupp, "didn't give me a chance. You didn't tell me what was going wrong, you just went out and got somebody else. You didn't treat me like a serious musician."

With that, he went out to the studio and played it perfectly. He returned somewhat calmer, and was further mollified to learn that even Kellaway had needed to play the part one hand at a time: "I kept on *telling* you guys it was hard." But even though he had just gone out into the studio and proved that he could play it, Frayne was still angry, and Boylan suggested compromise: they would do a playback of the band and Kellaway's left hand, and Frayne could add a right-hand part that would be used in the final recording. Frayne brightened immediately and went back out to overdub the right-hand part.

Even normally there is something a little eerie about the overdubbing process. Only one musician is visible in the studio, but the music of an entire band pours from the studio monitors. There was something even stranger about this effort, which resulted in a record with a piano part recorded in Sausalito by two different people: the left hand by a man who was in Los Angeles when the right hand was recorded by a man who'd been in Philadelphia when the left hand was recorded. From the sound that was finally put down on the tape, however, there was no way a listener could guess. "I guess it was a good thing,"

said Boylan to Grupp as the highly pleased Frayne added his part, "that Roger didn't do it all on one track." When Frayne had finished—and it took him only one try—they went back to work on their nemesis, "Southbound."

39
The Hits
Just Keep On Coming

Michael Gross

Large-scale investment in the record business is supported by sales, which are dependent on widespread popularity. Since record companies exist in a chicken-and-egg relationship to the radio stations (only popularity allows air play, but only air play allows popularity), various attempts to find "objective" means of prediction have been made. One of these attempts is described by Michael Gross, a free-lance writer and the biographer of *Led Zeppelin*'s lead singer, Robert Plant.

Richardson is a suburb of boomtown, one of the many small towns outside Dallas that in the decades since World War II have filled with the shell-shocked, white-collar survivors of post-industrial America. The town has no sidewalks. Instead it has wide roads, apartment complexes with names like Spanish Trails, Lazy Gardens and New Orleans Acres, and a vast array of fast-food palaces, stretching for miles in every direction. Near each of the office parks that pop up at regular intervals along the highways sit Steak and Egg Kitchens, Alfie's Fish and Chips, Hannah's Pies, Steak and Ales, El Chico Mex Palaces, Waffle Houses, Jack in the Box, Long John Silver's Seafood, Taco Bells, Pizza Inns, Dennys, Sambos, Tijuana Tacos, Bonanzas,

omnipresent McDonald's, Minute Man Burgers, Jim Dandys, Chicken Huts and Kentucky Frieds. . . .

Each has its quota of parking spaces, filled at most hours with families and teens and singles, stuffing down their fave foods, careful not to litter, bopping to the sound of car radios and outdoor speakers.

KFIL-DAL-LAS RRREEECYCLES THE BEATLES!!!

Across the parking lots, Tom Turicchi, one of the pilgrims, walks toward his lab in the Spring Valley Office Park from his office in the Keystone Office Park. He's alone. No one else walks in General Motors dreamland. Only the sound of KFIL intrudes.

THIS IS NUMBER ONE IN KAY-FILL

Source: From *New Times* (February 7, 1975). Reprinted by permission of the author.

COUNTRY . . . PAUL ANKA! The lyrics ("You're a woman I love/And I love what it's doin' to you") follow Turicchi into a small building marked "Psychographic Research." He walks through an inner door and up to a lit console, comprised of three tape decks and a large machine with needles and graph paper, much like a lie detector. The working tape deck is playing a new Paul Anka single, Anka's follow-up to "You're Having My Baby." Through a one-way mirror, Turicchi gazes at six people seated at the table. All of them are holding small boxes in their hands, with buttons marked 1, 2, 3, and BOO, and have electrodes attached to their index fingers and pinkies. As the song pounds out of the speakers in the room, the graph paper in front of Turicchi spews forth, etched with peaks and valleys.

Turicchi smiles, as well he might. The graph line happens to tell him a very valuable secret: why "You're Having My Baby"—or any other song—rises to the top of the charts. It is a secret that record company presidents, radio programming directors and publicists across the country are willing to pay for, and every Monday they anxiously wait for Turicchi to share it in his weekly report from Dallas. For this modishly long-haired ex-teacher from Providence, Rhode Island, has found a way to quantify culture—or at least pop culture. Tom Turicchi, academic researcher, man of science, divorced father of four beautiful kids and owner of a Grand Prix, is onto a good thing.

Pointing to the six subjects through the one-way mirror, Turicchi says, "We divide them up by age and sex. There are four groups: teens, 18- to 24-year-old males and females and oldsters." The electrodes, he continues to explain, transmit the subject's physiological responses to the souped-up lie detector next door. And the boxes allow the subjects to make conscious decisions about the songs they will hear in the next hour.

While the six subjects stare at a blown-up B.C. cartoon lampooning American Bandstand's song ratings "I'll give it an 85—it's got a good beat and you can dance to it"), songs are played over two small speakers and the subjects' internal bodily responses are measured, averaged and reduced to a single graph line on a piece of paper.

If the songs affect them, either positively or negatively, hills and peaks cover the graph. If they're simply bored, the line heads inexorably downward. After each song, the subjects vote on the music, pressing a button that tells what they think—from a high of 1 to "boo," the hate button. But the graph line often belies the button tests. Even if they look bored through the one-way mirror separating the two rooms, the line, based on the body's self-produced electricity (Galvanic Skin Response), and a sophisticated measurement of blood pressure and pulse, gives the meaty data: what they really feel.

Both the equipment and the tests have made Tom Turicchi the wunderkind of the music business, the man who can give a song a rating from 1 to 50 and pick hits with 92 percent accuracy, all under the aegis of science.

The assistant, Paul Gentry, a collegiate-looking ex-construction contractor who got into the psychograph biz when he married Turicchi's sister, turns from the controls and says with a smile, "Tom developed a Coca-Cola formula and he sells it." And like America's favorite soft drink, the results of Turicchi's invention are as close as the nearest radio, as easy to remember as

NUMERO UNO ON KFIL DALLAS— PAUL ANKA WITH "YOU'RE HAVING MY BABY," BABEE. . . .

Subjects for the tests are found in schools, colleges and shopping centers. The average person is what Turicchi wants, and average is universal in the Big D. They aren't told what the tests are, or that they'll be paid. Only after screening, when they've fit neatly into Turicchi's middle-class heavy test sample, do they find out what he does. Average is average, whether it's in Dallas or Duluth, and, according to Gentry, "A stiff in New York is a stiff in Dallas. A hit is a hit."

"The kids enjoy coming in," Gentry says. "It's the best thing since masturbation. The teens and the 25-plus group like the same music, which is why Anka can have a number one song. The record companies feel that the teens and the 18- to 24-year-old girls are the critical buying public." Gentry stops talking to monitor the tests. Over the course of the next 48 hours, the simple procedure will be repeated eight times as each demographic group is tested twice. It's a boring process, and as Gentry and Turicchi explain it, they also joke about their subjects.

One girl in the next room looks like a cheerleader sporting hot pink toenails. "She's a hot one with nice jugs," Gentry says, as he sets up the graph by testing each subject for bodily resistance to electrical shock, a necessary preliminary to every test. The average resistance figure for a teenager is 70,000 ohms. Older folks have less resistance. Miss Hot Pink alone rates 100,000 ohms. Gentry changes the graph settings accordingly, so her "hotness" won't affect the all-important average. The rest of the girls in her 18 to 24 group are average.

When the first song, "Rock Me Tender" by Andy Kim, begins the graph line starts a slow upward climb. "It's the belly button response," Gentry laughs. "Their heads may say they hate it, but their belly buttons tell the tale." As the song continues, the line does a long, slow dive. Gentry shakes his head, almost sadly. "Andy Kim," he muses, "has seen his day."

Then comes a song called "Lola," made famous a few years ago by England's Kinks, and the responses look good. But when the line that contains the meaning of the song blurts through speakers—"boys will be girls and girls will be boys"—the young women get restless and the graph takes a quick downward plunge. According to Gentry, sex, death and money get people off, especially when a lyric promises the first and last, or denies the middle. But these girls obviously don't want to hear about any sexuals except the hetero sort.

Besides "Lola," the tests on the girls are uneventful. They like Anka's hit, a Gordon Lightfoot song and Tony Orlando's follow-up to "Tie a Yellow Ribbon," which by late October was nearing the top of the charts. Paul Anka's follow-up, being tested that week for United Artists Records, is, according to Turicchi's ratings, a "turkey."

When the young women leave, six "oldsters" file in who look more tranquilized than

tranquil. Their resistance ratings are low—no 100,000 ohmers in this group. As they listen to the songs, the graph line rises for good, well-produced songs with no lyrical content and falls on the rockers. There's a dental assistant, a housewife, an auto mechanic, a sheet music salesman and Gentry's wife. "They take it slow and serious," he says. "This group is hard to test." But easy to please. Give them Roberta Flack or Anka and they're happy, cruising the highways of Dallas, but let the radio blare one KFIL BLOWS YOUR MIND WITH THE HEAVY SOUND OF LED ZEPPELIN AND "WHOLE LOTTA LOVE" and they tune out fast. As Gentry explained later, any song that isn't good in the belly button department is seen, without conscious knowledge, as an invasion of personal space, a threat or simply a blaaah. And the 25-plusers are tough, because their age makes them the most easily invaded.

The next group in is the teens. Little girls 9 to 14 years old come pouring in and sit around the table, flapping their legs and chattering. You could easily picture them at home, surrounded with Donny Osmond posters, checking out the DeFranco family's latest exploits in a teen magazine, listening to the Top 40 on KFIL and being pretty damned annoyed when a song they hate comes on.

"It's just like being home when we come here," one of them says. They get to hear the new songs and they enjoy it, according to their belly buttons. They love Paul Anka, not noticing, as the adults apparently did, that the woman in the song, who carries Anka's child, sings Black. Her short chorus was a downward turn for the oldsters. With the kids, things go straight up. The response to the song, Turicchi explains, is a purely emotional one. The lyrics get to people, and Anka has a hit. The teens, for example, couldn't care less who sings a song as long as they "like" it. They've never heard of Bob Dylan. They aren't sure, but think they've heard the name Ringo Starr. They think Donny Osmond and Bobby Sherman are cute, but will not admit to liking their music. One girl, asked if she thinks Mick Jagger is as cute as her idol, little Donny, answers, "Who?"

The only group left is the 18- to 24-year-old males. All of them look like high school seniors. Half are long-haired, but in Dallas, they tell me later, long hair often hides a crimson neck. One wears an Allman Brothers T-shirt and they talk about Deep Purple and Black Sabbath—British "heavy metal" bands. They could easily be sitting in the Academy of Music on New York's 14th Street. There they would be clutching bottles of cheap red wine, sucking joints in the men's room or wandering aimlessly with a head full of bootleg Quaaludes. In Dallas the boys are cleaner cut, although they admit a liking for the "evil weed." Still, they're a fair approximation of 1975's rock audience.

As expected, they look at the Top 40-oriented, pop-dominated list of songs they are to hear and begin complaining. "Play some Emerson, Lake and Palmer next time," one of them drawls to Gentry before the test begins. but even though they hit their "boo" buttons hard and often, laughing at sappy lyrics and complaining vociferously, the graph tells it plain: they like Paul Anka. They like Andy Kim. They like Olivia Newton-John. They like the music they say they hate. Or, at least, their belly buttons do. "They're the toughest group," Turicchi said later. "Very discriminating, but they can get crazy. They're good kids, but the least predictable."

It was that profitable faith in prediction that led Turicchi to the powerful fiefdoms of the music business. From a Mafia-run neighborhood in Rhode Island, he gained degrees in math, musicology and educational psychology during a stint in the infantry. He won contests as a musician and conductor and toured Europe with a symphony orchestra. The strange combination of interests gave him the tools to pursue research into a unique area. As a professor of music theory at Texas Women's University, Turicchi began his intriguing research into the effects of music on behavior.

He found out that music increases basic body rhythms by 25 percent, that it increases strength in controlled grip tests and that during the 1968 riots in Washington, D.C., ghettos, group singing was outlawed by an aware police department: aware of the fact that, according to Turicchi, "people get high by singing together."

Then Turicchi put two and two together. "I decided to try and come up with a Top 25 of classical music so my Intro courses could be based on music that really turned kids on rather than 'good' pieces. If I could turn them on, I had them. The theory was there, but there was no methodology."

Texas Women's did have $13,000 worth of physiograph equipment, and so, for two years, unfunded and unaided, Turicchi began experimenting. "I was using the same method as the lie detector and I had to have a statistical model that meant something." Five years later, he had his model, and it seemed to work. The vultures soon descended, dressed, as it were, in sheep's clothing. A radio programming director from San Francisco, Sebastian Stone, appeared in Dallas and agreed to send Turicchi new records for four months in the summer of 1972. On the initial tests Turicchi was over 90 percent accurate in his predictions. El Exigente smiled.

Stone brought Turicchi to radio tipster Bill Gavin's convention in Frisco that year, and when he left Turicchi was working for five radio stations, including WCFL, a pop radio station in Chicago, which changed its entire format based on Turicchi's tests. WCFL subsequently grew to be the number one with a bullet radio station in Chicago. CFL's program director, Lew Witz, became Turicchi's John the Baptist. Each day, his belief in Turicchi grew as more and more psychograph-approved songs hit the top of the charts. Witz helped form Research Consultants Incorporated to work with record companies. Stone formed Entertainment Research Associates to bring Turicchi to radio programmers across the country. Turicchi remained sole owner of the concept and the secret. RCI and ERA were his marketing arms. In the meantime, he'd gone from full- to part-time teaching and, finally, in May 1974, resigned from the ranks of academe and opened his own lab.

Ever since, the number of believers has grown daily. There are very few record companies in America that have not, at one time or another, sent songs to Turicchi. Dickie Klein, head of promotion for Atlantic Records in New York, is typical of the record executives who use the service but see it as secondary to the "magic" in their companies. "I think it's a good idea," Klein explained one afternoon. "It can confirm your thoughts and those of your creative staff, but it can't do the job for you. I can't put 100 percent belief in it. We have our own magic. It's not a Bible." But then, the Bible never claimed 92 percent accuracy.

In a warm-toned office in New York City, Lew Merenstein, head of Artists and Repertoire at Buddah Records, sat back, lit a little cigar and confided that he doesn't really like that Paul Anka song. Then he explained why he is a customer of Tom Turicchi's.

"I had an initial curiosity about it. I wanted to see how the scores related to the eventual success of records. I thought it was an additional aspect—a person's spontaneous stimulation. No service can be 100 percent. Human energy and belief overcome a lot of things when you're trying to reach a person's emotions. There's a magic to breaking a record. I definitely believe in Turicchi, but no machine can tell you what to do."

So, for the record companies, "magic" is as important as science. But, explaining the value of *his* technique, Turicchi stresses its unique importance. Other services, like television's Nielsen ratings, use attitudinal research. "It's an invalid way of testing," Turicchi points out, "unless you use huge samples, and even then people say what they think you want to hear." In other words, if you ask, people will say they watch the news and not *Lucy Show* reruns, but if you test them, psychographically speaking, the line would go up for Lucy and down for Cronkite. That's the difference between attitudes and behavior.

"The record business," Turicchi says, "is based on flying by the seat of your pants. Most companies have 80 to 90 percent misses on their singles releases. We can eliminate a large part of that." The record companies see Turicchi as either a magician or a liar, until they run some tests. The statistics convince them quickly. Somehow, though, it all seems a bit too much like the Ministry of Culture in *1984:* finding out what the people want and giving it to them in its lowest common denominator form. Ya wanna hit, kid, here's a hit.

"Maybe this is really 1984," Turicchi counters, "but I feel that as far as where it can go, we're only limited by our imagination." And he doesn't intend to start churning out music to calm the proles. "I have a tool," he emphasizes, "that helps me know what turns people on physically. There's no way I can change internal body functions. Only yogis can do that. Muzak, for example, can't change you. Aaron Copeland calls Muzak 'the obsequious.' We're super-saturated with shitty music.

"Behavior modification is another thing. If I found a subliminal on a record, I'd sue the company. Any kind of *Clockwork Orange* stuff really frightens me. All we do is give the service of recommending which songs will give the best impression of an artist to the public."

Turicchi chose to stay in Dallas precisely because the public there, the potential test subjects, were "average." In a country where middle-class, upward mobility is the norm, Dallas is Everytown. And in Dallas people became interested in Turicchi for reasons other than his effect on the Top 40. He began testing advertisements, discovering that key words, phrases and sounds made a bodily impression on his subjects. When a fast-food restaurant's ad promised test subjects a dollar saving, the graph line jumped up like a rocket. When an ad for a head shop was played for the 25-plus group, the line dove like Evel Knievel.

"Advertisers have come to us," Turicchi says. "But advertising is never-never land. The reason I haven't gotten into it is, say some guy gave me a $3,000 commercial. I tell him it's shit. Where can he go? I have synthesized commercials from scratch, though. Then, when you test it, you *know* it will work. But music is different. A Paul Anka song and a Todd Rundgren song are not two products competing with each other."

So, advertising remains a sideline, but it has led Turicchi to another, more complex area: television. "We're building a new lab complex for TV and feel we can add a whole new dimension to broadcast media," he explains. Meanwhile, he's doing TV road tests, working out of the Waldorf-Astoria for CBS News. The possibilities seem endless, and that's what scares a lot of people.

Even though Turicchi seems impressively pure about his ideas for applying his discovery, one feels the need to press him. What would happen, for example, if a politician wants to find out how he could best come across to voters?

"It's simply biofeedback that I offer," Turicchi explains slowly. "I can tell Senator X how he affects people. I can't change those responses. If the guy is a phony, the people will know. They react, perhaps 20 percent to what he says and 80 percent to how he says it. It's neo-psychic. We can, whether we're aware of it or not, spot a phony. Psychological Stress Indicators are sophisticated polygraphs and every person has a built-in one. All we are is a barometer.

"Anything that can be used for great good can be used for great harm. I know what I'll do with this. I'm trying to complete the loop between the artist and the public. I'm not looking for the McDonald's hamburger of culture. What I'm looking for is music that will communicate at the gut level, and to me that's art."

Artists, however, take a dimmer view of the whole thing.

Robert Fripp was the leader of a now defunct arty British rock band called King Crimson. He is an intelligent, concerned, working musician whose purpose is the same as Turicchi's—to reach people. But when psychographic research was explained to him, he saw an immediate dilemma in it. "It sounds quite evil," he said. "If this work is geared toward realizing the rules of objective, artistic creation, then I would have sympathy with it. But if it's geared to producing hits, it reminds me too much of the psycho-testing done at the end of the last war."

Many musicians are annoyed that their record companies will cut a promotional budget if a song tests out badly. One singer said he found the technique intriguing but ultimately compromising, because Turicchi is surrounded by music business businessmen. He mentioned a "payola angle" as a result of Witz and Stone's participation in the enterprise. Such charges can't be avoided when radio stations, record companies and TV networks are paying large sums of money to test their media material.

Turicchi, however, is too busy to worry. . . .

40
It's the Same Old Song: Punk, New Wave, and the Marketing of Rock

James Barszcz

The material that fuels the record business (and perhaps the only element that those outside the business care about) is, of course, music. Yet even within categories, such as rock, country, disco, and so on, the music is always changing, as free-lance writer James Barszcz describes in the final selection. While change usually implies progress, Barszcz makes a convincing argument that recent "developments" in rock music are, in fact, a restatement of basic values.

In February 1978, *Rolling Stone* magazine carried a short news story describing the difficulties the Sex Pistols were having in obtaining visas in order to make their first American tour. The American Embassy had a rationale for its reluctance to grant the visas: English courts had convicted the group's singer, Johnny Rotten, of amphetamine possession and guitarist Steve Jones of autotheft; the two remaining members of the band, bassist Sid Vicious and drummer Paul Cook, had been arraigned on charges of assaulting police, an affair which the Embassy took as evidence of their "moral turpitude." Moreover, in their brief careers as rock stars in England, the band members had become notorious for spitting on audiences (and being spit upon by them), and for performing songs such as "God Save the Queen," in which they accuse Her Majesty of leading a fascist regime and imply that she's something other than human.

As a result of their behavior, the Sex Pistols and the punk "movement" they represented generated a great deal of copy both from journalists eager to cash in on a sensationalistic story and from rock and social critics who, perhaps caught up by the group's own claims for relevance, saw punks as a threat to Western-world order and even as harbingers of a new order to come. These interpretations have proved incorrect, of course, at least so far. And today, some years after the demise of the Sex Pistols, it is easier to see that punk rock was no more—and no less—revolutionary than rock had repeatedly shown itself to be in the past.

In fact, it seems more illuminating to describe punk and so-called "new wave" music as being more fundamentally reactionary than revolutionary. First, these styles reacted against the insipid and sometimes affectedly grand styles of rock that immediately preceded them. But, more important, reaction informs each of the best, most representative punk and new wave songs: the lyrics generally express strong dissatisfaction with various aspects of life—from political systems to lovers. The lyrics are coupled with music that uses the limited resources of rock to do little more than build up and then release tension. The songs offer few pretty melodies, and they offer fewer visions of a possibly more satisfying life in the future.

What no doubt contributed to the sense many people had that punk rock held some new kind of potential was the anomalous nature of the rock music that preceded it. The music critic John Rockwell, writing before punk rock became widely known in this country, claimed that "the seventies have been bland in some central sense." And the same 1978 issue of *Rolling Stone* supports such a claim as it applies to rock music. Its record reviewers discuss albums by Bette Midler, Queen, Leonard Cohen, Gary Wright, Graham Nash and David Crosby, and Duke Ellington and his Orchestra. Only the records of Gary Wright and Queen could reasonably be called "rock," and not very distinguished rock at that.

This list of reviewed performers suggests, actually, the presence of qualities in addition to blandness in the "rock" music of the time. From the early seventies on, virtually every aspect of the rock scene had become—in the view of hard rock fans anyway—overblown, inflated, distended. Performers displayed, or pretended to, great virtuosity in playing and singing, something that has always been largely irrelevant to rock. At the same time, more and more songwriters wrote lyrics on relatively exalted topics, often referring to mystical states of consciousness and cosmic fantasies. Of the performers not covered by these generalizations, a large number did indeed develop bland styles of "pop-rock." This music often lacked even the characteristically driving beat of rock; nevertheless it was promoted as rock music and played on rock radio stations. For a while, these trends in rock proved highly successful with a large number of listeners: the volume of records sold increased yearly (as did record prices). Even groups that had achieved only moderate success gave live performances in the largest concert halls and sports arenas.

Around 1974, however, a handful of New York-based rock bands—the Talking Heads, Blondie, the Ramones, Television—started scaling the music down again. Even though these groups developed highly individual styles, they shared some important common elements. They played simplified, sometimes stark, music. They also performed in the smallest venues, mostly located in lower Manhattan where many group members lived. Certainly, some of the music they produced was pretentious, especially toward a kind of avant-garde "minimalist" form of expression. But pretensions of this kind were refreshing and congenial to many rock fans, who found the more popular, large-scale rock music of the day unsatisfying. The Ramones, for example, gained an ardent following by playing short, fast songs, based on the simplest three-chord rock pattern, and singing appropriately puerile lyrics, on such subjects as asking girls to dance and going to the beach.

Although the Ramones enjoyed limited popularity in America, they toured England in 1976 and proved to be hugely successful and influential. They showed English fans the kind of excitement rock 'n' roll could still produce and, in effect, catalyzed the rock scene there. In the wake of their tour, scores of new British bands formed, who also played a reinvigorated, simple style of rock. But, while these bands played music as basic and exciting as the Ramones' music, they sang lyrics thick with political rhetoric. As a result, they elicited what is, for rock music, unfounded and distracting commentary.

The Sex Pistols were the archetypal English punk rockers. They reacted to the then current styles much as the Ramones had: by writing songs that were fast, simple, and short. However, they added a harsher quality to their sound (sometimes by purposely damaging their equipment), and they played in a sloppier, less tightly synchronized fashion. It was the crudest rock to gain public acceptance in many years, and it sparked many listeners to describe the band as completely incompetent. Moreover, the Sex Pistols' lyrics, delivered in Johnny Rotten's snarling shout, were intended to be highly provoking. In observance of Queen Elizabeth's silver jubilee, for example, they released their version of "God Save the Queen" as a single. Another single, "Anarchy in the U.K.," opens with a kind of statement of purpose by Johnny Rotten wherein he proclaims himself first an anti-Christ, then an anarchist with a desire simply to "destroy." The government banned these songs from the radio and from record stores, but they became best sellers nonetheless.

There is, of course, a strong element of humor in this overtly nihilistic posturing. After all, how seriously can you take music produced by musicians called Johnny Rotten and Sid Vicious? But some people took it seriously indeed. Peter Marsh, writing in the British magazine *New Society,* characterized it, with commiseration and regret in his tone, as "dole-queue rock," an entirely appropriate style of music for England's masses of unemployed, disaffected young people. Others disagreed. Simon Frith, a professor of sociology and noted rock critic, responded to Marsh by pointing out that many of the earliest advocates of punk, including Malcolm McClaren, the Sex Pistols' first manager, and Caroline Coon, one-time manager of the Clash, were actually latter-day "bohemians" with ties to a rather arcane life-as-theater movement from the sixties known as Situationism. "Punk was and is a bohemian culture," Frith wrote. He claimed that, from the outset, it was shaped by "young sophisticates" who had little in common with young people of the working class.

These comments on the Sex Pistols' music, as well as some on the Clash to be discussed further on, demonstrate how punk caused a resurgence of critical attitudes toward rock that had lain dormant for some time. Once again, commentators started giving careful consideration to the particular world views expressed in rock songs. Moreover, because of the political nature of so much punk music, many critics, either hopefully or fearfully, felt that punk might spark (or be symptomatic of) large-scale social change. In reviewing the New York debut of the Clash, a writer for *Rolling Stone* said that seeing their show made one think that rock 'n' roll "really does matter." Similarly, two years earlier, when few people made distinctions between new wave and punk, a reporter, writing in the "Zeitgeist" department of the *National Review,* expressed the opinion that "the New Wave movement could be a healthy development, a purgative for the self-delusions of British life." Meanwhile, the same reporter quotes a member of Parliament from the Labour party who vows to "destroy the New Wave before it destroys the nation." People from all quarters thought that this music might do what no rock music had done before—that it might play a decisive role in fundamentally changing society. And probably no rock band has elicited as many comments about the significance or importance of their music as has the Clash.

The second album the Clash recorded, *Give 'Em Enough Rope,* was the first one to be released in the United States. The album contains ten songs that vary little either in musical arrangement or thematic concerns as expressed by the lyrics. The rhythm guitars have been engineered to sound fuzzy and crude, forming a thick wall of sound pierced occasionally by clear-pitched guitar solos. The bass line, made prominent in the mixture of sounds, usually conforms to the standard rock style of one or two notes per chord, although at moments it does break out to become modestly melodic. And on three of the album's four strongest cuts, the tempo, set by a tinny-sounding snare drum and cymbals, is unremittingly fast. Undoubtedly, this album was meant to be played very loud.

The loud, limited music of the Clash is well suited to the subject matter of their songs, which focuses primarily on violent revolution. Some of the songs, "All the Young Punks" and "Stay Free," for example, suggest why England might be ready for a revolution: its economic and social systems offer so little hope for its young people. Other songs, "Tommy Gun," "English Civil War," "Guns on the Roof," present visions of what fighting a revolution might be like and, implicit in the ecstatic, powerfully satisfying music, what fun it might be. But even though their subjects are limited, the songs invite

rather complicated responses, ones that indicate the potentialities and limitations of rock itself. Joe Strummer, lead singer and lyricist, takes some pains in his writing to avoid any flat endorsements of revolution. In "Guns on the Roof," for example, even though he sings of his desire to take part in a jungle war instigated by the Soviets, the song's refrain itself calls into question how apocalyptically bloodthirsty he really wants to appear. But, in a much more obvious way, Strummer's style of singing also raises the question of how deeply committed he is to conveying a message of revolution. His voice, a more raspy and appealing shout than Johnny Rotten's, is often buried in guitar sounds, and he enunciates in such a slovenly manner that, in some songs, nearly all the words are unintelligible.

The group's first album, *The Clash,* lacks the qualities that obscure the political stance on *Give 'Em Enough Rope.* First, the lyrics are printed on the inner sleeve, along with a picture of the band posing before a poster of Chinese Communists. Moreover, the lyrics speak quite plainly, as perhaps these song titles suggest: "London's Burning," "I'm so Bored with the U.S.A.," "White Riot," "I Fought the Law" "Police and Thieves." Several of the songs contain us–them dichotomies, with "them" signifying, at different times, the British government, CBS Records, America, and bosses of all kinds.

(Here and elsewhere in this essay, quoting lyrics in full would allow me to support my points more substantively, but music publishers demand large sums for permission to quote, and this has effectively prohibited me from doing so. Within the context of an essay like this one, there is of course no danger of plagiarism or indeed of anyone directly making a significant amount of money off of someone else's creative labor. Considering the context, then, the music publisher's restrictive copyright policy protects no one, but it does testify to their excessive greed. Also, such a policy obviously hinders discussion of contemporary culture. Finally—and here the issue happens to become pertinent to my thesis—the prevalence of such a policy stands in ironic contrast to the insistently anticapitalist, antibusiness attitudes expressed in so many of the protected songs.)

The political views expressed on the first Clash album seem to coincide with those of the majority of rock critics, at least in their leftist orientation if not in revolutionary fervor. Perhaps, this explains the most hyperbolic critical comments about the band—the greatest rock band in the world, the only rock band that matters. Robert Christgau, generally one of the most intelligent and perceptive rock critics, put this album at the top of his list of best albums of the seventies and suggested that it might be the best rock album ever recorded. But if, in fact, the political thrust of the songs has enhanced the album's critical reception, this suggests the presence of an unfortunate puritanical streak in rock critics. Rock is exciting, fun music (though not especially "happy" music) whose value should not be pinned to the asserted morality or philosophy of its performers. If the Clash deserve high praise (and I think they do), it's only because they provide the peculiar, visceral excitement that rock at its best has always so generously provided. Just as Clash music demands to be played at high volume, it demands to be danced to. It moves listeners not merely to tap their toes to its rhythm, but to get on their feet and jump around in intensely anarchic forms of rock dancing. No rehearsed steps need to be followed (the fast tempo virtually precludes this), and, in fact, one popular movement, the pogo, simply involves hopping up and down in one spot. The Clash write exciting songs that happen to address political and social discontent. But, clearly, other performers who have moved their listeners in the same way through songs concerning the frustrations of, say, romance or family life, rather than more narrow political topics, succeed as rockers no less than do the Clash.

Although punk music did not signal the advent of any widespread social or political changes, it did help restructure many aspects of the rock scene, at least temporarily. It confirmed, for many fans who had forgotten or never realized, that rock is, in Lester Bangs' phrase, "the ultimate populist art form, democracy in action." It certainly *sounded* as if

any three or four people who could gather up the equipment could write and perform music similar to the music of the Sex Pistols. "There shouldn't be any difference between who's on stage and who's in the audience," said John Lydon, formerly Johnny Rotten, in a recent interview. And, in fact, garage bands playing in the punk style began springing up shortly after the Sex Pistols first gained national attention in Great Britain. To accommodate these bands and their growing numbers of fans, many rock clubs opened up; they were generally small, crowded places where newly formed bands played, and people danced and drank beer. Often, enterprising groups that had gained some local popularity would establish a record label in order to release their own records and those of other local bands, with the groups distributing them to local record stores, and perhaps putting them on sale at their shows.

These circumstances under which punk music was produced and made available to its audience indicate some of the ways in which punk styles differed from earlier forms of youth culture. Punks, it has been suggested, are hippies with inverted values. Rather than go to an arena or an outdoor festival, smoke marijuana, and admire the musicianship of a supergroup, they prefer going to a small club, drinking beer (and perhaps taking pills), and dancing to the harsh sounds of some local players. Instead of favoring peace and gentleness, they seem preoccupied with resentment and violence. Sometimes they display a kind of self-directed violence, as when, to take a notorious example, they wear safety pins pushed through their skin as jewelry, or they cut their hair hapazardly with razor blades. Seen in this way, reaction informs not only punk styles of music, but of life and dress as well.

Fans of punk rock also tend to be fans of new wave music, which suggests that these two forms have similar appeals and provide similar satisfactions. In the nature of these similarities lies, perhaps, the clearest evidence for the reactionary spirit at the heart of both forms of music. Hard and fast distinctions between them are difficult to make and, ultimately, of course, they are not very important. For the purposes of the present discussion, however, we might say that new wave music is punk with some refinement. The work of Elvis Costello, widely considered as the preeminent new wave performer, illustrates the distinctions well.

On the four albums he has issued to date, Costello presents himself as a perennially frustrated lover, usually in songs depicting scenes of humiliating rejection. Sometimes he presents such scenes in a tone of resignation, as in "(The Angels Wanna Wear My) Red Shoes," but more often he is simply bitter as in "Pump It Up," a song about the limited rewards of masturbation, which describes some obsessive and destructive sexual fantasies, or "Lipstick Vogue," in which he entertains a morbid comparison between love and a cancerous tumor, both being virulent internal forces. Costello, then, characteristically chooses to write lyrics focusing on the more painful facets of love—rejection, betrayal, resentment—and this distinguishes him, along with many other new wave performers, from the punks, on one side, and from standard pop performers, on the other. He writes as incessantly and venomously about dissatisfaction as did the Sex Pistols or the Clash. But his dissatisfaction is nearly always on an intimate scale, having less to do with political and social issues than with romantic passion. When on the rare occasion he does record a song with some political element in its lyric, he handles it gingerly, as in his cover version of Nick Lowe's "(What's So Funny About) Peace, Love, and Understanding?" the words of which are only partly ironic, or in "Less Than Zero," with its oblique references to Oswald Mosley, who is perhaps Britain's most notorious fascist.

Analogously, Costello's music is considerably more refined than is typical punk music, making use of more sophisticated chord patterns and filled to the brim with melodic hooks. And no discerning listener would ever accuse his backup band, the Attractions, of incompetence. Perhaps in its relative sophistication, Costello's work is less democratic, in Bangs' use of the term, than is punk rock. Yet, he never comes off as pretentious in his music. He appears to be simply a hard-working

songwriter, not a poet, a social critic, or a virtuoso; and the same holds true for Wreckless Eric, Nick Lowe, Graham Parker, and many other first-rate new wave performers.

The similarities between new wave rock and punk rock, however, allow for more useful observations than do their differences. Both styles depend on energy, simplicity, and, despite differences in the nominal topics of their songs, a strong dissatisfaction with things as they are. The important, if obvious, point is that these shared elements have always been central to rock 'n' roll. This venerable tradition (by rock standards) dates back, at least, to the other Elvis's "You Ain't Nothin' but a Hound Dog," and includes such exemplars as Eddie Cochran's "Summertime Blues," "Pushin' Too Hard" by the Seeds, "Human Being" by the New York Dolls, "Rock and Roll" by the Velvet Underground, as well as a host of songs by the Who and the Rolling Stones. In the mid-seventies, punk was no aberration; rather, it was a clearing of the ground, an attempt to eliminate some of the hypertrophied pop styles dominating the radio stations and record stores, and a return to what many fans hoped rock was really all about all along.

Even though it was spawned by American bands, punk rock died before most of the interested people in this country heard any of the music, or so most rock journalists said. Certainly, few bands today play in the style of the Sex Pistols, and those that do seem to lack credibility. John Lydon himself now sings, in a much more subdued manner, with Public Image, Ltd., a band that plays slow, droning songs with highly repetitive melodies. ("We're not a band, we're a company," Lydon insists, with a jaded cynical attitude.) And although the Clash seem to be flourishing, having released their third album in 1979 and following it up by successful tours of Great Britain and America, their sound has changed. In some of their new material, they have added keyboards and horn arrangements, and they have also experimented with other styles of popular music, like reggae, ska, and blues. None of the songs on the new album displays the kind of violence, in lyrics and production values, so evident on their previous records. And, in fact, one of the most popular cuts on the album, "Train in Vain," is a love song. "I've gone through my Starsky and Hutch phase," Joe Strummer reported in a recent *Melody Maker* interview.

Given the nature of the popular music industry in America, new wave is experiencing a somewhat predictable fate: The music has won over many influential fans, including critics and disc jockeys, as well as people who had simply lost interest in rock during the early seventies. Established rock stars, record company executives, advertising executives, concert promoters, and club owners all have taken notice of this increased interest in tough, danceable rock music, and they have been quite successful in their attempts to turn the style into a "trend" they can cash in on. Linda Ronstadt, a pop star of great magnitude, recently recorded a few enervated cover versions of Elvis Costello songs. Several new bands, with great calculation but not much conviction, have appropriated various elements of the new wave style, landed recording contracts, and released records that usually sound boring and derivative. Bands playing on the regional bar and club circuits now regularly add a song by Costello or the Pretenders into their standard Led Zeppelin–Styx–Allman Brothers sets. In New York, meanwhile, the clubs that hire top-name new wave acts charge patrons $10 for admission, after screening them at the door to make sure they're wearing sufficiently funky, chic attire. And Debbie Harry, lead singer of Blondie, has been hired to endorse Gloria Vanderbilt jeans.

Clearly, the intensity of reaction evident in the earliest punk music could not be maintained for long. The new wave style, with its more palatable expressions of reaction, is steadily being diluted and assimilated by the rock industry, so that what was once exciting, alternative music is now contributing to a perhaps irrevocably bland mainstream. But in five years or so, as many hard rockers will tell you, the rock scene should be very interesting once again.

PART FOUR

The Visual Media

Film

Of the mass media developed in the twentieth century, film easily remains the most glamorous. Historically, film became not only the first medium to capture the modern popular imagination, but also the first to be treated as high art. And no wonder. Like nineteenth-century grand opera, film claims to combine and to transcend all media in itself. Offering the sound of radio, a greater visual presence than television, the writing and factual content of books and newspapers—all this and most nineteenth-century grand opera too!—film continues at least to reign over, if not to rule, the mass media.

In "Flashback," David G. Clark and William B. Blankenburg provide a brief history of film from its earliest technology to its most recent business combinations. Although "Hollywood" still symbolizes the movie industry, as some of the following selections illustrate, the creation, financing, distribution, and promotion of movies is less monolithic today than it was in the heydays of the big studios after World War II.

One nontraditional way to promote a film is detailed in the second selection, "The Selling of Billy Jack," by the staff of *Forbes,* the financial magazine. The article explains how, through a combination of advertising and a special distribution technique called "four-walling," a movie that started as a flop was rereleased with a huge return on investment.

Regardless of how well produced and marketed a film is, all movies are made from scripts, and all scripts have to be written. David Freeman, a screenwriter and journalist, describes the numerous, and often confusing, steps that a screenplay frequently takes. He also analyzes the screening-writing market in which an increasing number of writers compete for scarce but lucrative rewards.

The next article profiles George Lucas, a man who has performed all the functions that go into the creation of a film and whose skills have resulted in one of the most popular movies ever made. Michael Pye and Lynda Miles trace Lucas' life and, in so doing, present a case study of the latest generation of Hollywood giants.

Although most people think of films as entertainment, documentaries (movies with an explicitly educational purpose) have a long history and a definite place in the industry. The issue of how documentaries differ from avowedly "fictional" films is the theme of Jeanne Allen's selection, which traces developments in the genre of documentaries from its beginnings to the present.

Nothing has affected the film industry more than has television. In a final, transitional selection, Robert Lindsey of the *New York Times* shows how changes in video continue to affect its sister industry. Such interactions between the various mass media often play a major role in their evolution, as many earlier selections have shown.

41

Flashback:
A Brief Study of the Movie Business

David G. Clark & William B. Blankenburg

The following brief history of the movies, describing technological and business developments, is excerpted from *You & Media: Mass Communications and Society* by David G. Clark and William B. Blankenburg. Both authors teach at the School of Journalism and Mass Communication of the University of Wisconsin, and each has been a consultant to the U. S. Surgeon General's Scientific Advisory Committee on Television and Social Behavior.

By the end of the nineteenth century, science had contrived a number of inventions—some of them no more than toys—which, when combined, permitted the filming and projection of motion. The collaboration that marks today's movie production was also characteristic of motion-picture invention. As early as the seventeenth century a "magic lantern" could project single images upon a wall, and in 1834 a toy called the "zoetrope" presented a moving image to the child who spun its pasteboard drum and peeped through the slots at moving sketches. About the same time, the Frenchmen Niépce and Daguerre and the Englishman Talbot were experimenting with the light-sensitive properties of silver halides, and by 1850 photographic negatives were made upon glass plates.

Though glass negatives were difficult to handle, Mathew Brady recorded the Civil War on film, and William Henry Jackson photographed the American West. Then, in 1872, ex-California Governor and horse-fancier Leland Stanford wagered that all four of a trotter's hooves were off the ground at one time during its stride. Stanford hired photographer Eadweard Muybridge to prove his case. Muybridge succeeded, and Stanford en-

couraged him to continue his photography of horses in motion. For seven years, with some time off to murder his wife's lover (he was acquitted), Muybridge experimented with cameras in series, their shutters tripped by strings snapped by running horses. In 1880 Muybridge attached his still pictures to the edge of a disk, from which could be projected a brief "moving picture."

Muybridge took his show to the East and to Europe. In Paris the scientist Étienne Marey, in the midst of experiments on motion, was inspired to take up the camera as a tool. His contribution was the invention of a circular, slotted shutter that permitted the use of a single camera. Within a few years he showed Thomas Edison his work with serial images on short strips of film.

In France, England, and America between 1885 and 1895 a number of inventors worked out problems of film, cameras, and projectors. Toward the end of the eighties, Edison encouraged his associate, William Kennedy Laurie Dickson, to build motion-picture devices. Dickson acquired a new, flexible film from George Eastman, and eventually fabricated the Kinetograph, a movie camera, and the Kinetoscope, a peep-show viewer that employed 40 feet of film. In France, the Lumière brothers patented an effective projector, and in December, 1895, showed a series of short films in the basement of the Grande Café. They charged one-franc admission and within a few months were grossing 7,000 francs a week for such features as *Lunch Hour at the Lumière Factory.* In 1896 the Edison Vitascope projected ocean waves and prize fights between the acts of a variety show in Koster & Bial's Music Hall in New York. Vaudeville had clutched the asp.

The burgeoning cities provided eager audiences for films that made no great demands on purse or literacy. Movies were shown in vaudeville houses, penny arcades, storefronts, and eventually in more or less permanent Nickelodeons. Even so, there was not an endless audience for five-minute films of waterfalls, and soon news events, real and recreated, were presented. These too were mere episodes and not intentionally fictional. It remained for the imaginative Georges Méliès to explore trickery on film and to turn to storytelling at length. In 1897 Méliès built a glassed-in studio near Paris. The glass admitted strong light and protected the set from rain. Méliès was a gifted storyteller and animator. Many of today's optical illusions had their origins with him.

About the turn of the century English directors experimented with closeups, cutting from one scene to another, and melodrama. In 1903 the English released *The Robbery of the Mail Coach,* and later that year Edwin S. Porter filmed *The Great Train Robbery* in the wilds of New Jersey. The audience was stunned when a bandit fired his pistol directly into the camera, and was not at all perplexed by intercutting. The American Western, and indeed the American movie, was born.

As the demand for films grew, studios sprouted in New Jersey, Flatbush, the Bronx, and on Manhattan rooftops. The largest filmmakers were the equipment manufacturers, who attempted to control production and distribution through a trust called the Motion Picture Patents Company and a subsidiary, the General Film Company. The trust had an exclusive contract with Eastman for film, and independents were forced to buy film, when possible, from Europe. The Patents Company also used goon squads to disrupt independent production and distribution. But independents such as William Fox, Carl Laemmle, Adolph Zukor, and the Warners staged a successful resistance through litigation and by making increasingly popular longer "features." The independents also discovered that in a place called Hollywood they would be a safe 3,000 miles from the trust and a convenient few hours from the Mexican border. California also offered year-round good weather and a varied terrain.

So the trust, by default, emptied the greenhouses of Fort Lee, populated Hollywood, and gave rise to the feature film and star system. Laemmle, head of IMP, a leading independent, learned the value of publicity during the battle with the trust. He also perceived public affection for anonymous players like the Biograph Girl, whose services he acquired and whose name, Florence Lawrence, he shouted from his advertisements. Another inadvertent gift of the Patents Company was David Wark Griffith, who quit Biograph, a member of the trust, and moved to Hollywood in 1913. There he found the freedom to work on films large in length and scope. His *Birth of a Nation, Intolerance,* and *Broken Blossoms* were artistic and technical achievements of the first order, though variously flawed by bigotry, grandiloquence, and hokum.

Also boarding westbound trains in 1913 were Cecil B. DeMille, Jesse L. Lasky and Samuel Goldfish (later Goldwyn), who were to insure the commercial success of the feature film. As the trust collapsed and taxation on studios grew more oppressive in the East, the exodus became a rout, and Hollywood was soon releasing what are now regarded as the classic films of the silent era—as well as a preponderance of rubbish.

In the 1920s Hollywood grew in opulence and ego, with stars commanding salaries (and sometimes percentages) that are still impressive. *Ben Hur*—the 1925 version—began with a budget of $750,000 and finished at nearly $4 million. MGM ultimately lost about $1 million on it despite a gross of over $9 million. Not that it mattered, because Hollywood, like the rest of the country, was riding the giddy boom of the twenties.

But not all the studios flourished. Warner Brothers, especially, felt a cooling of the audience to recurring cycles of westerns, romances, and melodramas. Some of the larger exhibitors were beginning to reach back into vaudeville for live attractions to supplement films, just as films once augmented variety programs. The Warners began to think seriously about talking pictures.

Sound with pictures was not new. Pit musicians, especially organists, accompanied silent films, and Méliès once had an opera tenor sing from behind the screen. Edison's early interest in film was tied to his wish to provide a visual element for his cylindrical records. The development of recorded sound was loosely parallel to that of film, and in 1923 the radio pioneer Lee De Forest exhibited a series of short talkies in New York. The next year he released a two-reel comedy in sound. Fox regularly distributed talking newsreels in 1927. Then late in 1927 Warner Bros. released the *Jazz Singer,* and Al Jolson put the silent film to death.

The timing, though inadvertent, was fortunate for the industry. All the studios adapted to sound before the stock market crash of October 1929, and many exhibitors had been able to finance sound equipment. As the movie historian Kenneth Macgowan points out, had the industry been a bit slower, sound might not have been widespread for another ten years. It might also be noted that commercial television was feasible by the late 1930s, but was delayed by World War II. Perhaps without Jolson and Hitler, movies might have died with their mouths shut.

But Hollywood wasn't leaving everything to chance. It learned early the economic sense of monopoly. The first producers sold their films outright to exhibitors who, stuck with stale prints, exchanged them among themselves. Exchanges evolved into distributorships and the present practice of renting films evolved. About the time the Patents Company died, Paramount under Zukor devised "block booking"—the practice of requiring an exhibitor to contract in advance for a stated number of films and to contribute money (also in advance) to their production. The exhibitor took all or none. Smarting under this restraint, some leading theatre owners banded together as the First National Exhibitors Circuit and contracted for films—sans block booking—with independent producers. Partially thwarted, Paramount and the other major firms backed down a bit on booking and bought more theatres for themselves. First National, meantime, began to produce films. And in 1923 the Federal Trade Commission began sniffing monopoly.

In the early thirties, thanks to the novelty of sound and the power of monopoly and market-splitting, the movies seemed impervious to depression. Each of the five major companies—Fox, Paramount, Warners, Loew's, and RKO—made, distributed, and exhibited its own films. Where their theatres didn't compete directly, they rented films to each other. The Big Five, plus the smaller Columbia, Universal, and United Artists, practically dominated the industry, from screenwriter to ticket-taker.

Quite understandably, Hollywood and Wall Street were mutually attracted. Financiers found what they thought was a depression-proof industry, and Hollywood sought more capital for further ventures into oligopoly. The struggle in the early thirties between RCA (which owned RKO) and American Telephone and Telegraph for dominance in motion-picture sound equipment further helped return the control of movies, though not the studios, to New York City.

In 1938 the Department of Justice brought antitrust action against the eight giants. The industry responded, as it had in 1922 to the threat of federal censorship, with fervent promises of self-regulation. By 1940 a few of the companies entered into consent agreements with the government and divested themselves of their theatres. After another ten years of waffling, Paramount and RKO agreed to get out of exhibition, and Loew's, Twentieth Century Fox, and Warners followed suit within a few years. This meant an end to exhibition controlled by the producer-distributors, and an end to block booking, which had never completely vanished. It also meant greater competition among producers, who now had more equal access to theatres. However, the consent agreements did not separate the studios from their foreign theatres or prevent them from collaborating with television networks. Nor have exhibitors failed to buy stock in producer-distributors.

If the major studios were prevented from vertical consolidation, they could still diversify, and this they did with a desperate vengeance. Some found oil on their back lots, most rented sound stages, all had real estate and film libraries to sell, and some veered into the record business, broadcasting, and electronics. Stanley Warner Theatres got into the girdle business. Studios merged with other firms as, in the late A. J. Liebling's words, the canary merges with the cat. Warner Bros., for example, after establishing its own record company and acquiring Atlantic and Elektra, in 1969 became a part of Kinney Services, Inc., a conglomerate founded on real estate, janitorial services, parking lots, and funeral parlors. Kinney also picked up National Periodical Publications, home of Superman and Batman, as well as *Coronet* and Paperback Library and the Independent News Company, which distributes twenty-seven magazines, including *Playboy*.

42
The Selling of Billy Jack

Forbes Staff

Developments in marketing films have kept pace with developments in making them, as the following article by the staff of the business magazine *Forbes* shows. With the loss of tax shelter opportunities and a trend toward declining attendance, the movie industry, now more than ever, looks for innovation in financing and marketing. Although no longer new, "four-walling" exemplifies the kind of technique always in demand: one that turns a profit from what seemed a flop.

Tip to moviegoers—If you want to avoid being sucked into seeing a stinker, watch out for these telltale signs: A movie, of which you previously never heard, suddenly blankets movie houses throughout your area and advertisements for it suddenly pour out of your TV screen.

Modern marketing has come to the movies, which means that producers have finally figured out how to bypass the critics and bad word of mouth from the fans.

The basic techniques—"four-walling" and saturation promotion—are as old as the hills. But the scale is something new.

Take *Billy Jack,* a modern-day western whose halfbreed hero uses karate kicks rather than six-guns to crusade against injustice and an evil local "Establishment." When it came out in 1971 the critics panned it, audiences stayed away in droves and the film bombed. But Tom Laughlin, the star and director, wouldn't take a yawn for an answer. The former bit player on TV and in movies like *South Pacific, Gidget* and the forgettable *Battle of the Coral Sea,* sued Warner Bros. for the right to reheat his turkey. He won.

The very fact that so few people had seen the film was an asset. It enabled Laughlin and his backers to pack a great deal of sell into 30-second TV commercials that featured Billy

Source: From *Forbes* Magazine (July 1, 1975). Reprinted by permission of the publisher.

Jack taking on small-town bigots, sometimes 12 at a time, with dazzling displays of kung fu. These scenes struck a responsive note with the 16- to 24-year-old set who make up 50% of the movie-viewing audience.

The commercials packed them in at a few trial reengagements. After a $2-million gross in four weeks, Warners saw the light. Laughlin persuaded them to "four-wall" the picture. This means that instead of getting a percentage of the gross from the theater owner, the producer rents the theater at a flat fee. If his promotion pays off, he, not the theater owner, reaps the reward. Laughlin four-walled *Billy Jack* with saturation TV promotion in 62 Southern California theaters and he broke records.

In three years *Billy Jack,* which cost only $1 million to make, has earned an estimated $65 million. Reissued in 1974, it earned almost as much money as the reissue of *Butch Cassidy & the Sundance Kid* and more than *Airport 1975*. The film has been enormously popular with adolescents of all ages at drive-ins and small town theaters. But it has also been analyzed as a pop-culture phenomenon by such big-city folk as New York critic Rex Reed and the rock bible, *Rolling Stone.*

Back Again

In 1974 Laughlin released a sequel, *The Trial of Billy Jack*. The critics agreed it was even worse than the original. It did not "premier" on Broadway. *The Trial* opened simultaneously in 1,100 movie houses. The film cost $2.5 million. The advertising cost $3 million for a one-week saturation splurge.

This was no ordinary movie hoopla. Laughlin's sidekick was John Ruble, a former Assistant Secretary of Defense under Robert McNamara, and later a senior vice president at Litton Industries. Ruble used computer printouts to monitor attendance at the 1,100 theaters showing *Trial* at any given time, and also to determine how many days the picture could expect to continue showing a profit. He hit TV with as many as ten or 11 *different* 30-second spots; after a while a faithful TV viewer need go to the movie only to see how it all came out.

These techniques mean that the producer puts his money into renting theaters and hiring time on TV rather than into the film itself. But it means that he comes on so strong that he is almost certain to make an impact on potential moviegoers. Then, because he saturates an area with bookings, the film is in and out of town before the unfortunate early viewers can warn their neighbors.

Actually, Ruble and Laughlin were updating a technique developed by movie magnate Joseph E. Levine. In 1959 Levine took a real dog, the Italian made *Hercules,* booked it into over 600 theaters simultaneously and splurged with $1.5 million in advertising. The film, whose U.S. rights Levine bought for a song ($200,000), grossed $9 million.

Levine did not four-wall. But this technique is as old as D. W. Griffith's *Birth of a Nation,* although it was used in the Thirties and Forties chiefly for action films and similar types that required heavy promotion.

But four-walling really caught on in the mid-Sixties when a few small independent companies used it to distribute their G-rated wildlife films. Going into a town, they blitzed the local TV stations and walked away with the family audience, long the sole property of Disney. Since these independents had little money invested in the nature pictures, they could afford big bucks for advertising and theater rentals and still come out way ahead.

It remained for Ruble and Laughlin to make four-walling and saturation booking the tails that wagged the movie dog. "When we talk to a director now, we say, 'Don't forget our 30 seconds,'" says John Freidkin, director of publicity and advertising for Twentieth Century-Fox. He is referring to the now obligatory scene of sex or violence that will make a real grabber of a TV spot. "If the 30 seconds aren't there," Freidkin says, "we know we're in trouble."

Last year Twentieth made a killing with saturation advertising on a dismal little film called *Dirty Mary, Crazy Larry*. The film was distinguished only by the suitability of several scenes for TV commercials. The film cost $1 million. It earned $14 million. As Freidkin sees it, the secret was marketing: "If you had come to us before the picture opened and asked if we would settle for $5 million, we would have been delighted."

Not Infallible

But some of the movie majors, including Warner Bros., with its *Exorcist* four-wall campaign, have been burned. Columbia Pictures took out a four-color four-page ad in *Variety* to announce its promotional blitz for Charles Bronson's *Breakout*. But despite $3.5 million worth of advertising (including 42 prime-time TV spots) the grosses have been disappointing. Nor are the slide-rule moguls at *Billy Jack* infallible. When they reissued *Trial* in Los Angeles last May, powered by a big cash prize contest, the compaign did so badly that even Ruble himself admits that it was a flop.

Some old-timers around Hollywood argue that the picture you are selling still makes the difference. You can't fool all of the people all of the time.

43
The Great American Screenplay Competition

David Freeman

For every movie made, hundreds of others never get beyond a necessary first stage— the screenplay. Despite this melancholy fact, an increasing number of people are still trying for the glittering prizes available to the successful. David Freeman, a screenwriter and journalist, describes his own experience, and that of many others, in the following article from *Esquire*.

In the 1950s (you remember them), everyone was a closet novelist. The folklore of the upper middle class had it that each commuter on the five-forty-four to Cos Cob was working on "my book." Longshoremen and co-eds were dreaming of books. Then in the Sixties, everyone wanted to be a New Journalist. Kids ran after every fire engine and Bowery bum, screaming the pronoun "I" and declaring fiction dead. In the Seventies, we all took a breather, and now that nobody can write any-way, everyone's writing a screenplay. Doctors and dentists are doing it, people who once would have written their memoirs are doing it instead, couples are doing it together as a romantic interlude, even (rumor has it) Clive Barnes is doing it. Don Simpson, who is the head of production at Paramount, says, "In the Eighties, everybody is going to want to be Deborah Harry or a screenwriter."

Clearly the whole damn business is out of control. And it's not just in Hollywood—in

Source: From *Esquire* (June 1980). © 1980 by David Freeman. Reprinted by permission of the author c/o International Creative Management.

big cities and small, everyone, young and old, is dreaming of an artistic and financial killing by writing a movie. The studios are swamped with unsolicited manuscripts (they send them back, unopened, to avoid lawsuits that charge them with stealing ideas). Colleges that used to teach the sonnet now have courses in additional dialogue. Related industries are booming. The typing and binding of scripts itself is an enormous business. Barbara's Place, the largest script service in Los Angeles, does as many as 150 scripts a week, keeping between eighteen and twenty-four typists working around the clock. Many trees fall, many Xerox repairmen are kept in toner, all part of the latest collective American wet dream: the salable screenplay.

If you're one of the two or three people in the country not writing a script and not planning to write one, read no further. Go back into your cave. But if you're among the folks dreaming of a $250,000 sale to a "major" (what you used to call a movie studio such as Columbia Pictures), here's a little inside information. The first thing to know is that although everybody's dreaming of it and a few million seem to be trying it, most of them are failing. After all, if it were easy, everybody could do it, and then writing screenplays wouldn't pay so much. To *do it* in Hollywood these days, you need to be a blend of a shoe salesman and poet. Too much of one and you'll fail, but if you mix these magic ingredients properly and season with a sense of the absurd, the result is a screenwriter, a working one.

There are two kinds of screenwriters in Hollywood: failed English professors and failed cowboys. Now I am not using these terms as metaphors for intellectuals and rugged individualists. I do mean (with a *slight* exaggeration) people who used to wear tweeds professionally and guys who used to ride horses and twirl lassos. Either way, they're all aspiring hustlers. The taste that keeps them all hungry is for action, for Hollywood, for the main chance. But it is also, whether they know it or not, to be *effective* in the wide world. Most of them—tweedy or leathery—are actually slightly introverted, with secret dreams of business glory, of being buccaneers, of beautiful lovers.

There are many contradictions in this life of hustle and art. John Gregory Dunne wrote that "writing scripts . . . is like wanting to be a co-pilot." And like the *numero dos* man in the cockpit, screenwriters want to be something else. Everyone seems to know that you can make a great deal of money in Hollywood if you can put together 110 to 135 coherent, amiable, and yet dangerous pages. You can also fail miserably, but then you can quit, and believe me, nobody will notice. The point is that no one really expects anyone to finish a screenplay, let alone sell it, just because he says he's writing it. Claiming you're writing a screenplay and talking about how far along it is, is sort of like jogging talk, an acceptable lie. If you actually do write one, manage to sell it, and then start getting more jobs and actually seeing your scripts turn into films, and if mirabile dictu the films are good, you will become too famous to quit. Besides, you will be in Hollywood having a great time. The last thing you'll want to do is quit.

You will have become a working sybarite; yes, you, oxymoronic you, will embody the Calvinist paradox that is in the dreams you don't even know you're dreaming. You see, whether cowboy or intellectual, all the writers love to think of themselves as poets as they run after deals and meetings (yes, yes, as in "take a meeting"). Screenwriters are what producer Larry Turman called "closet producers." They all—young, old, smart, dumb, boy, girl, or androgyne—love to scheme and "play the town." Everywhere you look, there are little knots of them. Not fantasizing, mind you, but making hard, practical plans to inflict their private dreams on the world and to get rich simultaneously.

The only thing new about all this is the numbers. Historically, novelists and playwrights of achievement came to Hollywood to cash in. Fitzgerald tried it, Faulkner spent his time being miserable here, though Hemingway made it a point of honor never to work in Hollywood. Instead, he sold his books to Hollywood for a fortune, then pretended to be shocked and appalled at what happened to the books. It made for a lot of press.

Now, of course, as every schoolboy knows, the studios mostly finance and distribute, and they don't keep brigades of miserable novelists locked in offices for thousands of dollars a week. Instead of indentured servants, there are mobs of would-be indentured servants begging to write scripts. And why not? The energy of our culture has gone to the movies. I remember once going to the Los Angeles airport for the late flight to New York. On the way, I passed enormous lines for *The Exorcist*. When I got to New York the next morning, I drove through Times Square and saw, that's right, enormous lines for *The Exorcist* waiting for the early show. Now this might be a testament to the power of horror movies, but I think it's also a clear indication of why so many people want to be in this business. There's always been a draw to drama of one sort or another. It's a powerful pull. Everything else, all of it, flows from those lines: all the money, all the adoration, all the fuss and publicity, all the people with their noses pressed to what they take to be Hollywood's window.

Here in the land of famous car washes and forgotten children, there is a way of business and life called development. Until you understand the rules of this game, you will not understand what it is like to be a screenwriter.

Much has been said about the lowly place of the screenwriter in the pecking order, all of it true, particularly compared to the director and the star. Compared to the rest of the universe, however, "screenwriter" carries a big fee and temporary honor. The "temporary" is the key.

A studio feels obligated to release fifteen to twenty films a year. To do this, it commissions many, many scripts. Some production chiefs believe in what they call "casting a wide net." At a wide-net studio, it is often said that an established writer can get his grocery list into development. The point of the wide-net school is to develop everything you can and hope for the best. Other, more cautious, organizations try to be certain that they want to make the film before they commission the script. More sensible, you say?

Maybe, but there is no discernible difference in the records, financial or aesthetic, between the two schools of thought.

At any given time, your wide-net studio can have over 100 script ideas in various stages of development. This means that a first draft is being written, a set of revisions is being composed, a director or a star is being sought. You get the idea. So you think, fifteen out of 100. Rough but not impossible. Wrong! First, all 100 don't stay in development for a whole year. As many as 180 might pass through development in a year. And a few of the fifteen to twenty films come not from development but as fully assembled packages—a star, a director, and a script. Some are acquired fully shot—financed by others and distributed by the studio. So the chances of a script written through development actually getting into the theaters with the studio's logo on it are in some statistical nether land.

Now what happens to the many, many losing scripts, the ones that died in development and were made into scratch pads and fertilizer? Did the screenwriters have to give back the money they were paid? Did they have to apologize and hang their heads in shame? No, yes, and maybe. What happens to these scripts, these unplucked flowers, is nothing. Nothing happens to them. Oh, there are a lot of phone calls and desperate attempts to revive these projects. But, mostly, nothing happens. Except, of course, the writer doesn't have to give the money back. In fact, he or she can raise the price of the next unproduced script.

Thus it is that a subculture has sprung up in Hollywood, this city of forgotten promises and famous parking lot attendants: people who make a lot of money and who never, or rarely, have their scripts made into films. They are in great demand. Oh, there's an emotional price to be paid, but the bucks just keep going up, from one deserted project to the next. Now the money part (what you've all been waiting for, brutish, vulgar lot that you are): We are not talking David Rockefeller here, but we are speaking of jokers who make between $100,000 and $150,000 a year, and that's conservative, with minimally visible film results. Granted, there are not thousands of such people, but there are, I would guess, over 100. There were over 18,000 scripts and "literary properties" registered with the Writers Guild in 1979 and over 35,000 guild contracts—that is where money, real money, changed hands. Now this includes television, but, then, what doesn't. Studios often spend $10 million a year on development. From 1980 to 1981, one major studio is rumored to be spending $20 million on all phases of development. The vast majority of what is developed will not be filmed.

Every producer and every studio has a director of development, or some such title. Screenwriter Steve Gordon calls these people "developists." Many developists want to be screenwriters so they can later want to be directors or producers. Their job is to get ideas into development. They are, collectively, doing a hell of a job.

As the waitresses at the Polo Lounge regularly remark, "action is character." And indeed it is, in what the waitresses call real life and in film scripts. Mostly in film scripts. In real life, there's a lot of marking time. Hanging around. Doing or saying nothing. It gets boring. Know what I mean? Right. In a script, something interesting better get revealed, right away. A film script is almost all structure. It's the bones of a story coherently laid out. There must be at the center of the story, and going from the start to the finish, a relationship that starts one way and, as a result of the actions of the principals, winds up another way. Change. Obstacles surmounted or not surmounted. The background, or, as the waitresses say, "the arena," should be interesting and exciting. An example of a relationship and an arena and the way they interact might be two musicians who are down on their luck and who just have to get a job. The place is Chicago in the Twenties, and the musicians—Tony and Jack—get mixed up with the Saint Valentine's Day Massacre and an all-girl band. They wear drag for much of the story. The central relationship is Tony and Jack and the girl who comes between them. The arena is mobsters, millionaires, and funny music. The script, one of the great farces of the sound era, is that of *Some Like It Hot*.

Most scripts that succeed are in an observable tradition—a romance, a comedy, a mystery. This means the story will sound like a movie to begin with but not too much so. Alfred Hitchcock always says, "Oh, no, that's how they do it in the movies. Let's do it the way it is in life." Of course, then Sir Alfred does it as in the movies, only better. So your arena and primary relationship should be fresh, funny, touching, or whatever, and original but not so original that it's baffling to someone who controls millions of dollars. Millions-of-dollars controllers tend to be conservative. If you want to write *El Topo*, don't do it in Burbank.

There have been a number of books written about scriptwriting—sort of guidebooks in the do-it-yourself tradition. They all seem to have titles such as *Write That Script!* or *Let's Go!—Hollywood on 200 Thou a Year.* There are even, I'm told, such places as movie colleges, where one can take an advanced degree in it all. One of the script books, *Screenplay,* by Syd Field, a well-known story editor, recently passed through my hands. The volume, written in something purporting to be English, is—surprise, surprise—not bad. It's full of common sense, an uncommon commodity, and you can learn a thing or two from it.

I will tell you how I learned the rudiments of scriptwriting, when I decided to do it myself. I wangled copies of professional screenplays. A lot of them. (Remember, hustling is fun. Shameful, sinful, but fun.) And from them I learned the form. The rest is equal parts common sense (no to a story about cavemen set in the Himalayas, yes to a passionate love story between a boy and girl set in modern San Francisco. Get it?) and mystery (the ability to duplicate speech and create character; to tell a lot, using few words; to create images that at once mystify and explain, that tell a complex story and seem to be simple). You're on your own there, but it's possible to do. It's not a high calling, but it has its rewards.

As for the structure (remember, structure is almost all), please commit the following to memory (tattoo it on your brainpan): Film scripts are divided into three acts. These are not marked by a physical curtain falling but by an emotional change in the situation of the central character or characters. Think of them as: Girl gets deal; girl loses deal; girl and deal are reunited. Or as Moss Hart reportedly said, "Get 'em up a tree, shake a stick at 'em, then get 'em down again," and, I might add, in better shape that they started as a result of being in the damn tree for so long.

Keep the scenes short and sharp. Make each event grow out of the preceding—not necessarily in an obvious, linear way (although that's okay sometimes) but in an emotional way. Event A generates event B. A and B combine to make C. Get it? If you don't, don't quit your job teaching English at the dude ranch and head west yet.

Try not to moralize or philosophize. Select and state. The dramatist's task is to create an arrangement of reality. If it is too clever and is full of quotable quotes, it will bring the dramatist to mind, not the drama.

Jerome Coopersmith, a screenwriter of skill, has written a booklet on screenplay and teleplay form. It tells you all you need to know about spacing, margins, and the like. I think he wrote it because he got tired of people endlessly asking him how a screenplay looks. It's available from the Writers Guild East, 555 West Fifty-seventh Street, New York. It's $2.50, and it's a bargain.

Screenwriting is the only form of writing routinely done on a $1,000 typewriter.
—Roni Weisberg

For the moment, put aside all the gags about the cashmere sunglasses, the pool at The Beverly Hills Hotel, and lunches at Ma Maison. Let me try to tell you what a screenwriter actually does. Well, okay, one gag—then what a screenwriter actually does.

SCREENWRITER JOKE
Did you hear the one about the starlet from the Eastern European country? She came to Hollywood and slept with the writer.

There are four major categories of screenplays: originals, adaptations, assigned mate-

rial, and revisions and rewrites. These categories slide into one another, and each is bound up with politics and money.

An *original* can be done speculatively or on assignment. On spec, it's just you and your idea off somewhere, plugging away. When you're done, you put it on the market hoping for the best. If you sell it, you can make a killing and probably a movie. Scripts acquired complete, even from novices, frequently sell for what the columns like to call "six figures" and for what the rest of us call a pile of money. Of course, most don't sell at all. If possible, make a deal before you write. You'll get less, but you'll be assured of getting something, and often it will still be quite a lot.

Now, to get an assignment to write a script of your choice is no small achievement. You have to persuade a producer or a studio that your idea, your private dream of a movie, is in the producer's or the studio's aesthetic and mercantile interest. This is called pitching. You go to an office or a restaurant and you tell your story the best you can. Mel Brooks is famous for pitching. He's been known to jump on desks, upset furniture, and kiss vice-presidents. When you're Mel Brooks, give it a shot. In the meantime, Paul Schrader, a man who has pitched with some success, says, "Have a strong early scene, preferably the opening, a clear but simple spine to the story, one or two killer scenes, and a clear sense of the evolution of the main character or central relationship. And an ending. Any more gets in the way."

Now, if you've been able to persuade the producer or the studio and strike a deal, you must be ready to give up some rights. You now have a partner, and you're accepting his checks, so compromises are in order. Cooking up a script means endless choices and decisions. No two people will agree on everything, unless one of them isn't listening. Sometimes the ideas are imposed on you, sometimes they are mutually agreed upon. Often they seem petty, and they may come from the producer's maid, mistress, gunsel, or just from malice. You must field everyone. It's a collaborative medium. If you don't have any political or diplomatic instincts and don't feel able to develop them, go into another line of work.

An *adaptation* usually means writing from a literary source of identifiable origin—a novel, a play, a short story. A producer or a studio acquires a worst seller and hires a bandit to write a screenplay. Movies frequently used to be dramatized novels, and many of the films you love best began as something else, as in "It's okay, but the book was much better." An adaptation of this sort makes the screenwriter more of a technician than anything else? Maybe, but the transformation of a book into a film script is often a re-creation of the source with all the attendant agonies of the original creation. In recent years, a prime source of material for the movies has been magazine articles. *Saturday Night Fever* came from a magazine piece. A recent Esquire article by Jean Vallely about Aspen ski bums is being turned into a script by William Goldman, one of the most celebrated of screenwriters.

There are scripts that fall somewhere between an adaptation and *assigned material,* which usually means that the idea and some research have already been started by the producer. A newspaper article, for example, about a political situation such as the immigration problems at the Texas-Mexico border, may have triggered additional research, providing a tantalizing arena. The screenwriter would then add the plot and the characters. Each of the situations (with assigned material) is a little different.

Revisions and *rewrites:* After you've done your script—your first draft (or the collection of pages and indecisions you're calling a first draft)—you're ready to face the battle. If you're being sensible, your script will contain no major surprises for your auditors that are not in the spirit of the plans the two or three of you made. That is, if you agreed upon the Texas-Mexico border, don't bring it back set in Sweden. Your work, and as you see it, your future and your integrity are on the line. His money and, as he sees it, his effectiveness are on the line. Where you draw the line between compromise and cracking under pressure is your business.

A rewrite usually means that the previous writer is no longer available or, in the eyes of the boss, is incapable of further improving the script. Another writer is brought in to straighten it out. Usually the task is first to figure out the script's original intentions (Who are these people? What do they want from one another, from the universe? Where does this all take place, physically and emotionally?) and whether those intentions are worth pursuing. If they are, where do they go wrong, and how might it all be repaired? Sometimes the script is an unreadable mess, sometimes not. Scripts of all sorts tend to be horizontal, that is, they skip from event to event across a horizontal story plane. To deepen the characters, that is, to go vertically, is often the first step in a rewrite. To do it, you have to be part critic, part diplomat, and part shark. When it's done to you, you need a thick skin and a few days in Palm Springs.

Rewriting can be done under relaxed circumstances—in your own study or office, at a studio—or it can be done under great pressure. I've done it in cities where English and stationery were considered exotic and on sound stages where $75,000 a day was being spent. It's less fun than it sounds. I was once locked in a basement room in Madrid with a sign on the door that said *NO MOLESTAR.* A ten-million-dollar film was in preproduction, and the script wasn't ready. After being unmolestared for a considerable amount of time, I took the results to a meeting with the director. He read through at least sixty pages of original typescript (no Xerox or even carbon paper in that place) and then picked up a lethal copper letter opener, the size and shape of a stiletto. He waved the thing around and glowered at me. I thought I was about to be reprimanded severely. But, instead of me, he stabbed the script, piercing every page. "This is shit," he screamed. And maybe it was. All I could think of was, where could we find an English-speaking typist? That's rewriting.

Everyone knows that the studios have story departments. Few people seem to know what the story department does. Story analysts, as their union call them, or readers, as they call themselves, make up the story department. They read scripts, books, magazine articles, matchbook covers—whatever someone thinks will make a film—and they do it all the livelong day. As they read, they write a summary of the story line and give an opinion as to the commercial and aesthetic prospects for whatever it is they are covering.

Like the screenwriter who wants to be something else, most of the readers want to be something else. Fast. Producers or directors or executives or even, yes, screenwriters. The readers tend to be very smart and very unhappy. The studios treat them as if they were opinion machines. Very few failed cowboys or cowgirls here.

There's a persistent rumor that studio executives themselves never read anything. Wrong! They read all the time. They read till their eyes are blurry. It's a point of honor among them. They boast (privately) about how many scripts they plowed through over the weekend. But they don't like to read "cold"—that is, without a summary in front of them (so they can skim if they want to) and without an educated opinion in front of them (so they can *react* rather than *act* in forming their own opinions). So on a typical Hollywood weekend, every studio executive takes a stack of scripts and matchbooks home, along with the accompanying coverage. Now this is not necessarily bad. It is kind of funny but not bad. Funny because all the executives tend to have similar stacks, and the coverage, from studio to studio, tends to be similar. But that's how it works.

Now everyone submitting a script or a matchbook wants to be special. They want to get around coverage and get their matchbooks directly to a vice-president. Avoiding coverage is seen by these dreamers as a worthy goal. But, short of standing over the vice-president from the time he or she is handed the damn thing until it's read and returned, attaining this goal is unlikely. You see, the coverage is the studio's way of tracking material. They assign it a number and log it in so the studio can check to see if they've passed on the thing a week before under a different title. It's a clerical necessity as well as a decision-making aid. You can override disastrous coverage and get another reading— sometimes, if you have some muscle. But usually bad coverage from a trusted reader stops your matchbook cold. No one but insiders is meant ever to see the coverage, so a sort of shorthand develops. The readers can be scath-

ing. I remember the following comments about various scripts:

"This thing is to screenwriting what Oblath's [a restaurant adjacent to the Paramount studio lot] is to La Tour d'Argent."

"The writer of this script has the attention span of an eighteen-year-old speed freak."

"This is trying to be *Tammy and the Bachelor.* It should be so lucky."

Now, the readers are not always right. One reader's coverage of *Jaws,* which now hangs framed on a studio vice-president's wall, says: ". . . by definition is uncommercial. . . . It's bad pulp."

To get a little perspective on this, you should know that a major studio gets as many as 2,400 submissions a year from reputable agents. This makes for a lot of coverage, and since the scripts are frequently semireadable, a lot of sarcasm.

How I Did It: A Cautionary Tale

How does it work? How does a poor lad with mammaries and mammon in his eyes come to this place and make a killing and remain so persistently obscure? How? How? Hmmm.

Suppose our lad is me, and when we meet me, I'm in my late twenties, come to Nueva York after going endlessly to graduate school. Soon, artiste that I am, I'm writing plays for theaters you've never heard of, on streets you've never walked. And I fancy myself a journalist and even, yes, an A*U*T*H*O*R.

I manage to wangle an interview with a Very Famous Producer (VFP) with white, wavy hair. So I cook up an earnest story to sell to the VFP. I outline a movie, make a few notes, and go in to tell it and sell it. This is called, as we now all know, pitching. But back then, I didn't know that. I just thought it was a story. On the day of the appointment with the VFP—oh, callow youth, a meeting, I was taking my first meeting, and I called it an appointment—I bopped into his office, which had no discernible desk, only sofas and chairs. Sort of like the faculty lounge. We sat opposite each other, sofa to sofa, and the

VFP said: "Tell me a story." Some primal, tribal instinct told me to put aside my notes and strut a bit. Give the man a show. And I did. Cranking up my little yarn, a simple story of journalists, radicals with bombs (the Sixties were a fresher memory), and romance, I paced about the room, gesturing and approximating creative heat as if all this were just rolling out of me, apparently inspired by the presence of the VFP and his sofas. The VFP listened and nodded and cheered the young shaman (that's me) on. And when my tale was fully unfolded, the VFP reached out his arms and announced, "You have talent! I . . . I . . . bow down to talent." He fell to his knees and crawled across the floor, collapsing at my feet, clutching my ankles, and dropping his silvery brow to the carpet, muttering and stammering (the VFP was known to stammer in heat), "I bow down to talent."

Now what I didn't know then but will tell you now, saving you several years of confusion, is that this means no deal. If the boss gets excited in front of you, he wants to make *another* deal. Some material of *his* choosing. If he wants to make a deal for the story you're pitching, he won't allow so much excitement, lest you try to raise the price. And sure enough, the next day the VFP called and said no to the journalists and the bomb throwers but offered me the opportunity to rewrite another script. That is, take some dog-eared nonsense and try to make it less so.

And with that, there was no looking back. Just one glorious deal after another. One day small sums, next day lots of zeroes, and the next next day, no sums, only zeroes. An adequate living was gained, and it's a long way from East Fourth Street.

Glossary

Step deal: a situation in which you are paid a certain amount to write a script in stages—a treatment, a first draft, a second draft, and so on. In a step deal, the producer or the studio has the right to end the arrangement unilaterally after each of the steps. It's not an ideal situation, but it does keep you on your toes, and its usually the only thing open to a novice.

Cutoff: When you're fired after one of the steps in a step deal, you are said to be cut off, and indeed you are. It's a miserable feeling, and there's no solace for the cutoffee except another deal.

Arbitration: Years ago, I'm told, when a film was finished, the producer or a studio executive decided who should be credited with writing the script. Sometimes it was done fairly, sometimes the producer's brother-in-law got credit. Now we have a union to prevent such abuses and to create abuses of our own. The Writer's Guild has an elaborate procedure for determining who should have screen credit and in what manner. Philip Dunne, a very fine screenwriter and a smart old bird, points out that it is an imperfect system, but like democracy, it beats the hell out of the other ways.

Separated rights: Films often say "Screenplay by so-and-so and story by such and such." A moviegoer might assume that means such and such wrote a story. And perhaps he or she did. More likely, the script has been rewritten by the writer credited with the screenplay. The original script is said to constitute the story (in the wisdom of the arbitrators). This is important because much money can accrue to the story-credit owner. If someone wishes to make a record album or a T-shirt or a sequel or a TV series from the film, the story rights, not the screenplay rights, must be acquired. It gets even more complicated than that, but no one who doesn't live with it should have to deal with it in any more detail.

Turnaround: When your script is finished and "turned in" to the studio (a lot of school jargon in the movie business), it's either ignored, quickly made into a minor motion picture, or put into turnaround. That means the studio doesn't want it, and the producer and, maybe, the writer are free to take it elsewhere, to turn it around. It's a time of great hope.

Set of revisions: After the script is delivered, most contracts call for a set of revisions. The substance of these revisions is to be agreed upon by all the principals. Revisions are usually the product of a lot of wrangling and the studios shoving the changes they want down your overcrowded throat.

Element: a principal cog in putting the machine together. A star, a director, and a script are usually the principal elements. Since the script is usually what entices the star or the director, for a while the script is the *key* *element*. So for a while the script and its creator are sought after. Until the director or star is around. Then the writer is considered an overpaid nuisance.

44
The Man Who Made Star Wars

Michael Pye & Lynda Miles

Seldom do all the elements necessary to the success of a screenwriter's initial idea come together. Even more seldom does a "success" become measurable in hundreds of millions of dollars. The story of George Lucas's exceptional movie career, a career that serves as a symbol for countless others, is told by writers Michael Pye and Lynda Miles in the following article from *Atlantic.*

Modesto is a small California town that gains its livelihood from its shops and its farms. Beyond its few streets lies the walnut ranch where George Lucas was raised. The town has one cinema on its main street. "Films by Jean-Luc Godard," George Lucas says, "do not play Modesto."

It follows that Lucas grew up away from the sophisticated influence that a major city would have offered. His adolescent passion was drag racing. He was one of the "Super-kids," a member of the developing teenage subculture that separated from its community to form a mobile, affluent group on its own. He cruised Modesto's "strip" at night, chasing girls, listening to the blare of the car radio. He was determined to be an auto mechanic and a racing driver, someone who had

access to the marvelous, sleek machines that sped legally on tracks instead of perilously on country roads. The dream left little time for schoolwork. He dropped out of high school and barely made junior college. There, he took photographs for racers, and thought of becoming a painter; he also studied sociology.

His interest in film came accidentally. He helped build a racing car for Haskell Wexler, the cinematographer; and he narrowly escaped death in a car crash. The meeting and the accident convinced him that he should use his visual talents rather than his mechanical ones. Painting was a gamble, and photography was problematic. The simplest and easiest solution seemed to be film school. Wexler helped Lucas to get into the University of Southern California. "I got there on a fluke," Lucas

Source: From *Atlantic Monthly* (March 1979). Copyright © 1979 by Michael Pye and Lynda Miles. Reprinted by permission of the Authors and their Agent, James Brown Associates, Inc.

says, "and coming from a small town with one little theater, I didn't really have that much background. Producer and director were for me the same general category—the person who made the movies."

His background in painting drew Lucas to the animation department of USC, and the benevolent influence of Herb Kosewer. From there he moved to cinematography, and by the end of his film-school days he had become, by his own admission, "an editing freak." The progression is logical. It left him with a fascination for what he calls, "visual film, the sort of thing the French unit of the National Film Board of Canada was producing." It was film as tone-poem, film as metaphor, film divorced from narrative form; he still feels uneasy with theatrical film and its need to push a story along. That weakness shows in *Star Wars:* Lucas makes a marvelous fireworks display, but finds it difficult to link the explosions and stars and rockets.

In school, he found Truffaut and Godard; he learned to love the sensuality of Fellini. He discovered the underground film-makers of San Francisco, avant-garde directors such as Jordan Belson. "At USC we were a rare generation because we were open-minded. I was influenced by John Milius and his taste for Kurosawa and Japanese cinema. I liked documentaries by the Maysles brothers and Leacock and Pennebaker. But we also had guys there who did nothing but Republic serials and comic books. I was being exposed to a whole lot of movies you don't see every day."

Lucas was a star pupil, but not exactly a model. He dominated student film festivals with movies more sophisticated and accomplished than his peers'. But he constantly broke rules. He bought extra footage to make films longer than class projects allowed. He used his first one-minute allocation of film to produce the animated short which won him first prize in the National Student Film Festival. In all, he made eight films while an undergraduate.

Lucas rushed through his undergraduate work because he expected to be drafted for the war in Vietnam, but when his turn came he was classified 4F and exempted from service. For a time, he worked as a cameraman

for Saul Bass, the designer of movie titles and director of animated films. He made a living cutting documentaries for the United States Information Agency. "That," he says, "was when I decided that I really wanted to be a director." He went back to USC graduate school for a single semester—January to June in 1968. He was a teaching assistant; he trained Navy photographers; and he assembled a formidable crew to make a science fiction short called *Electronic Labyrinth: THX 1138: 4EB*. It was a simple, stark picture of some future authoritarian society. Computers and electronic codes are set against a man running the length of a blind white corridor. Every move is watched; reality is monitored by cameras and screens. It is powerful but simplistic, a metaphor rather than a narrative.

In it, Walter Murch played the voice of God; it was partly his script. But George Lucas was the director. The pair made "a blood pact like Tom Sawyer and Huck Finn," according to Murch. Both were up for a Warner Brothers scholarship to watch films being made in a studio. They had been collaborators throughout their college days, and "we agreed," Murch says, "that whoever got the scholarship would turn around and help the other guy."

The winner was Lucas. He went to observe the making of *Finian's Rainbow,* and from that grew his partnership with Francis Ford Coppola. The new alliance gave him a chance to bring Murch into the crew of *The Rain People,* while Lucas served as "general assistant, assistant art director, production aide, general do-everything." On the side, Lucas worked on a documentary about the making of Coppola's film—"more as therapy than anything else," he says. "I hadn't shot film for a long time." But his main occupation between five and nine-thirty every morning, was work on a new version of the *THX 1138* script, a project originally devised with Murch and Hal Barwood. It was Lucas's first feature script; he thought it was "terrible." Coppola, when shown it, said simply: "It is. You're absolutely right."

"I wanted to hire a writer," Lucas says, "but Francis said, 'No, if you're going to make it in this business you have to learn how to write.' " So, with Walter Murch, he prepared a new script; it became the first, and only, project of Coppola's company, American Zoetrope, as a studio.

The making of *THX 1138* was like a film student's dream. There was enough money to work properly, but the studio chiefs in Los Angeles never saw rushes or dailies. Warner Brothers saw no material until the rough-out was taken down from San Francisco for their inspection. Only Coppola, the friend and patron of Lucas and Murch, had immediate influence on the operation; and he was, in effect, one of its architects. Working with friends allowed unorthodox methods. Murch permitted the intricate sound track to grow along with the images that Lucas was photographing, directing, and editing. The sound montage was an organic part of the film, not a decoration imposed afterward. The tiny crew, with the shaven-headed actors, could travel to locations in a single minibus. George Lucas was on his own.

The day Warner Brothers saw *THX 1138,* they abandoned director, producer, the American Zoetrope studio, and all that went with them. They left Lucas, with Coppola, deeply in debt. Worse, they recut *THX 1138.* "I don't feel they had the right to do it," Lucas says; "not after I had worked on that thing for three years for no money. When a studio hires you, that's different. But when a film-maker develops a project himself, he has rights. The ludicrous thing is that they only cut out five minutes, and it really didn't make that much difference. I think it's just a reflex action they have."

The film was not a commercial success, although it found a steady audience in universities around the campus circuit. In 1978, seven years later, when it was re-released in the form George Lucas had originally intended, it still did not take off. Even the fact that it came "from the makers of *Star Wars*" could not make its cold vision into something popular.

While Lucas was cutting *THX 1138,* the producer Gary Kurtz came to visit him. Kurtz wanted to discuss the problems and virtues of the Techniscope process, but the talk ranged more widely. Together they speculated about a rock'n'roll film set in the late 1950s or the early 1960s, in the days before the Beatles and the killing of President Kennedy and the war in Vietnam. Over the next years, Lucas distilled his own adolescence in Modesto into a script. He worked with Willard Huyck and Gloria Katz, USC graduates, but the project was constantly stalled and shelved. George Lucas and his wife, Marcia, exhausted by the horrors of the Zoetrope collapse, set off for a long vacation in Europe, packs on their backs.

When they returned, Lucas found that United Artists was prepared to put up a little development money for his idea. He decided to hire a writer, but he found, quickly, that he should have stuck to Coppola's advice. The script was professional, but not authentic. With distaste, Lucas says: "The man had put in playing chicken on the road instead of drag racing."

"That was my life," Lucas explains. "I spent four years driving around the main street of Modesto, chasing girls. It was the mating ritual of my times, before it disappeared and everybody got into psychedelia and drugs." He had no intention of allowing the film, which was to bear the title *American Graffiti,* to be inexact. He wanted to recreate the years of transition, before Vietnam, corruption, drugs, and time changed everything.

The tension between our dreams and Lucas's life is what makes *American Graffiti* work for so large an audience. The low-light filming, with its curious, golden radiance, becomes a dream. Time is collapsed. All the central characters are confronted with a turning point in the course of a single night. Yet that night could be placed anywhere within a decade. Cars and music span ten years, an era rather than a date. The slogan for the film—"Where were you in '62?"—makes the setting seem fixed in time, but it is not. The reality, the underpinning, is the music, and that goes from the start of Eisenhower's second term to the end of Kennedy's golden years. "George wrote the script," Walter Murch says, "with his old 45's playing in the background." From the beginning, the group—Kurtz, Huyck, Katz, Murch, and Lucas—discussed which tune best went where. They open the film on a giant amber light; as the camera pulls back, we realize it is the marking on a radio dial. The structure of the film comes from the radio program, the songs that disc jockey Wolfman Jack plays. Characters take cues from the music. And Wolfman Jack is the unseen center of it all, father figure as much as circus master. Like a father, he resolves problems, calms fears, arranges for meetings that would otherwise be only longings.

The one character who comes close to him is Curt, and after confronting him, Curt can escape the town, while the others stay fixed in their past. He is the would-be cynic with a romantic spirit, frightened of catching the plane to go away to college. He spends the night of the film's action, against his will, with a gang of punks. He catches a glimpse of a wonderful blond girl in a white T-bird, sailing past him on Third Street. For him, the Wolfman is his only means of contact with this golden vision. He finds the courage to drive out to the radio station, enter the corridors, face the station manager through a maze of reflecting glass; the sound track, in precise counterpoint, plays "Crying in the Chapel." The manager assures him the Wolfman is not there, the Wolfman is only on tape; but as Curt leaves, the manager puts back his head and lets out a Wolfman howl. In that moment of realization, Curt finds the power to face an outside world.

When the script of *American Graffiti* reached Ned Tannen's desk at Universal Pictures, it had already been rejected by United Artists, after their initial flush of interest, and it had been "turned down by every other company in town." But Tannen liked the idea. "God knows," he says, "I've made enough mistakes so I can say this wasn't one of them."

"I was having a very difficult time," Tannen says, "persuading the company to let me make *American Graffiti*." Partly, it was a project that came to Universal at the wrong time. "Universal was a very conservative company," Gary Kurtz says. "It was making most of its money in TV, and gearing most of its theatrical film to an eventual sale to TV." The unconventional would not, Universal feared, attract a free-spending network.

Then there was the problem of explaining *American Graffiti* to a board of directors. For Tannen, "it was just an idea. Nobody knew what it was. It wasn't based on some book that was a huge best-seller. It wasn't a special-effects movie where you have all sorts of gyrations and people could say, 'Oh, boy! That's terrific!' It was a terribly personal small story." There was no single line on which it could be promoted. "Pictures like *American Graffiti* have to be discovered. There's no way you can hype that kind of a movie. What are you going to sell it on?" Even when the film was complete, Tannen says, "nobody in the company had any concept of what the film was. It's funny thinking of it now. It didn't seem funny then."

Universal made a condition for allowing the project to go ahead: Find a big name. Lucas did not want stars. The only figure who could possibly convince the all-powerful head of the studio, Lew Wasserman, was a producer —Francis Ford Coppola. He was finishing *The Godfather*; he was established and known; he would do very well. Gary Kurtz remembers: "George and I went to Francis and asked him if he'd come into the project with us." The name proved enough for Universal to put $780,000 into making the film.

Evidently, the name was not enough to make Universal believe the project stood a chance of success. Lucas asked for $10,000 to buy the album rights to the songs he was planning to use on the sound track; Universal refused. When the film had been released, and its success was obvious, they had to pay $50,000 for the rights to the same material. While Coppola and Lucas were exiled from the lot by a strike of the Screen Writers Guild, the studio recut the film. They refused to release the film in stereophonic sound, although it had specifically been designed for stereo. And when they first saw a print, some angry studio executives believed the entire film was unfit to be released. Only after a stormy outburst by Coppola, standing at the back of a crowded San Francisco cinema, was the film saved. Universal owes its gigantic earnings to Coppola's temper.

Star Wars began as fourteen pages of story. United Artists, entitled to see each Lucas project because of their interest in

American Graffiti, refused it. "Universal never formally said no," Gary Kurtz says, "but I knew from talking to the people there that they were uneasy about the idea." As Kurtz and Lucas continued to build enthusiasm within the film world for their earlier film, their new project for a space fantasy began to seem more plausible. It is a curious form of Hollywood logic: Back winners, whatever they do. "If it hadn't been for that success," Kurtz says, "we would not have been able to get *Star Wars* made at any studio, because they all had the same apprehensions."

This is how it worked. "We finished *Graffiti* at the end of January, and the answer print was ready in the first week of February," Lucas says. "That was when we had the arguments about the release dates. We made the deal [with Twentieth Century-Fox] on *Star Wars* on the first of May, and *Graffiti* came out in August. But the film was building before release. And it was really in Hollywood that it was beginning to build." All Twentieth Century-Fox promised in the May deal was the money to start developing a script. Like all Hollywood deals, this one moved step by cautious step. It did not guarantee the film would ever be written, let alone made. But by the second and third steps in the contract, *American Graffiti* was on release. "It did well in New York and Los Angeles, but it took a while to grow. We didn't know until well into October and November that it was going to be an enormous hit," Gary Kurtz says. Neither he nor Lucas could control the marketing of the film, or prevent Universal from selling off the rights in various states before exhibitors had a chance to see the film. Kurtz had planned to bide his time. "I thought we could go to theaters across the country after the first week and say, 'Look, the first week's take is good, the second week is good—book this picture!' " In the event, the second and third weeks of the release were what *Variety* calls "socko" and even "boffo." Mr. Wasserman intervened. He ordered his executives to scrap other bookings and make theaters bid again for the film. Mr. Wasserman is not lightly disobeyed.

Star Wars was manufactured. When a competent corporation prepares a new product, it does market research. George Lucas did precisely that. When he says that the film was written for toys ("I love them, I'm really into that"), he also means he had merchandising in mind, all the sideshow goods that go with a really successful film. He thought of T-shirts and transfers, records, models, kits, and dolls. His enthusiasm for the comic strips was real and unforced; he had a gallery selling comic-book art in New York.

From the start, Lucas was determined to control the selling of the film, and of its by-products. "Normally you just sign a standard contract with a studio," he says, "but we wanted merchandising, sequels, all those things. I didn't ask for another $1 million—just the merchandising rights. And Fox thought that was a fair trade." Lucasfilm Ltd., the production company George Lucas set up in July 1971, "already had a merchandising department as big as Twentieth Century-Fox has. And it was better. When I was doing the film deal, I had already hired the guy to handle that stuff."

Lucas could argue, with reason, that he was protecting his own investment of two years' research and writing as well as his share of the $300,000 from *Graffiti* which he and Kurtz used as seed money for developing *Star Wars.* "We found Fox was giving away merchandising rights, just for the publicity," he says. "They gave away tie-in promotions with a big fast-food chain. They were actually paying these people to do this big campaign for them. We told them that was insane. We pushed and we pushed and we got a lot of good deals made." When the film appeared, the numbers became otherworldly: $100,000 worth of T-shirts sold in a month; $260,000 worth of intergalactic bubble gum; a $3 million advertising budget for pre-sweetened Star Wars breakfast cereals. That was before the sales of black digital watches and citizens' band radio sets and personal jet sets.

The idea of *Star Wars* was simply to make a "real gee-whiz movie." It would be a high adventure film for children, a pleasure film which would be a logical end to the road down which Coppola had directed his apparently cold, remote associate. As *Graffiti* went out around the country, Lucas refined his ideas. He toyed with remaking the great Flash Gordon serials, with Dale Arden in peril and the evil Emperor Ming; but the owners of the rights wanted a high price and overstringent controls on how their characters were used. Instead, Lucas began to research. "I researched kids' movies," he says, "and how they work and how myths work; and I looked very carefully at the elements of films within that fairytale genre which made them successful." Some of his conclusions were almost fanciful. "I found that myth always took place over the hill, in some exotic, far-off land. For the Greeks, it was Ulysses going off into the unknown. For Victorian England it was India or North Africa or treasure islands. For America it was Out West. There had to be strange savages and bizarre things in an exotic land. Now the last of that mythology died out in the mid-1950s, with the last of the men who knew the Old West. The last 'over the hill' is space."

Other conclusions were more practical. "The title *Star Wars* was an insurance policy. The studio didn't see it that way; they thought science fiction was a very bad genre, that women didn't like it, although they did no market research on that until after the film was finished. But we calculated that there are something like $8 million worth of science fiction freaks in the USA, and they will go to see absolutely anything with a title like *Star Wars*." Beyond that audience, Lucas was firm that the general public should be encouraged to see the film not as esoteric science fiction but as a space fantasy.

The final plot line was concocted after four drafts, in which different heroes in different ages had soared through space to worlds even wilder than those that finally appeared. It was a calculated blend. "I put in all the elements that said this was going to be a hit," Lucas says. He even put value on them. "With *Star Wars* I reckoned we should do $16 million domestic"—that is, the distributors' share in the United States and Canada would amount to $16 million—"and, if the film caught right, maybe $25 million. The chances were a zillion to one of it going further." Wall Street investment analysts, even

after the film had opened, shared his doubts. They felt it could never match *Jaws*.

Both makers and analysts were wrong. *Star Wars* was a "sleeper," a film whose vast success was in doubt until after it had been open for a while. Meanwhile, Lucas and Kurtz had to do battle over budgets. The original sums were so tight that Kurtz told the board at Fox, "This will only work if everything goes perfectly. And it very rarely does." During shooting, the designer of monsters fell sick, his work for the sequence in a space tavern incomplete. The sequence did not work in its original form, but the studio would allow only $20,000 more to restage and reshoot the scene.

Compared with *2001* (Lucas calls Kubrick's film "the ultimate science fiction movie"), the special effects in *Star Wars* were cheap. Where Kubrick could allow his space stations to circle elegantly for a minute, Lucas had to cut swiftly between individual effects. But that became part of the film's design. Where Kubrick's camera was static, Lucas and Kurtz encouraged their special-effects team to develop ways to present a dogfight in space with the same realism as any documentary about World War II. As usual in animation, they prepared storyboards, precise drawings of how each frame was to look; but, unlike most animation, their drawings were based on meticulous study of real war footage. They looked for the elements that made an audience believe what they were seeing. For Lucas, it was a return to his original interests at USC—the basics of film, recreated with models, superimposition, paintings, and animation. "We used a lot of documentary footage," Kurtz says, "and some feature film footage. We looked at every war movie ever made that had air-to-air combat—from the *The Blue Max* to *The Battle of Britain*. We even looked at film from Vietnam. We were looking for the reason each shot worked, the slight roll of the wings that made it look real."

John Dykstra, assistant to Douglas Trumbull on *2001,* retreated to a warehouse in Van Nuys, California. There he developed a camera which could move through any axis, to match real-life movement of wing tips or fuselage; and linked it with a computer that could remember the movements and duplicate them exactly when a different model was before the camera. That way, two separate models, photographed separately, could seem to do precise battle. The surrounding planets were on a painted background; the laser fire was added by animation. Superimposition brought all the elements together. Developing the technique took most of the year and of the budget allocated to special effects. "The fact is that we didn't have the money," Lucas said later, "and the key to special effects is time and money. I had to cut corners like crazy. I cut scenes left and right. And I cut out over 100 special effects shots. The film is about 25 percent of what I wanted it to be."

Arguably, the technique worked better dramatically than did the spectacle of *2001*. Lucas was invading the territory of Edgar Rice Burroughs, not a laboratory. He was making a series of Tolkein episodes, with dragons, hobbits, wizards like Gandalf and dark forces with storm troopers like Naz-Gul for support. There is no respect for science, no residue of a one-time staple of films—the menace of the atomic age. In this patch of deep space, giant craft can thunder like jet airplanes, and the London Symphony Orchestra can blast its romantic horns and violins. Mere physics says that space is silent. And Lucas contrives his battles well enough to spare us any desire to concentrate on the precise specifications of the craft involved.

But he does not tell a story. This is the basic failing of the film. It lacks true narrative drive and force. It is a void, into which any mystic idea can be projected; entertainment, brilliantly confected, which is quite hollow. Its only idea is individualism—that a man must take responsibility for others, even at great personal cost and peril. Its idea is, in classic form, "A man's gotta do what a man's gotta do."

The iconography is bizarre. Darth Vader, the dastardly villain, is black. That is common in science fiction. In the supposedly liberal *Planet of the Apes* series, the wicked and stupid gorillas are the military, and they are black. The honey-colored chimpanzees are the wise, good scientists. The closer to the color of a California WASP, the better the character: it is a fair rule of thumb. But Darth Vader's forces are storm troopers armored in white. The wicked Grand Moff Tarkin lives in a gray-green world, with gray-green uniforms; he is clearly a wicked Nazi. Yet when our heroes take their just reward at the very end, there are images which parallel the finest documentary of Nazism, Riefenstahl's *Triumph of the Will*. "I can see," Kurtz says, "why people think that. I suppose it is like the moment when Hitler crosses the podium to lay the wreath." Critical confusion is not surprising when there are allusions to Nazism as both good and bad. French leftist critics thought the film was fascist; Italian rightists thought it was clearly communistic.

Nor is the vague, pantheistic deism of the film coherent. *Star Wars* talks much of The Force, a field of energy that permeates the universe and can be used for both good and evil. It is passed on with a sword, just as the sword Excalibur is passed on in the Arthurian romance; the influence of chivalric stories is strong. But when The Force is used by Luke Skywalker to help him destroy the monstrous Death Star, he is urged only to relax, to obey his instincts, to close his eyes and fight by feeling. The Force amounts to building a theology out of staying cool.

Star Wars has been taken with ominous seriousness. It should not be. The single strongest impression it leaves is of another great American tradition which involves lights, bells, obstacles, menace, action, technology, and thrills. It is pinball—on a cosmic scale.

On May 25, 1977, *Star Wars* went out on test release to twenty-five theaters. In nine days, it had grossed $3.5 million. Within two months it had recouped its $9 million costs, and it was in profit before its general release.

In real money terms, *Star Wars* was made for money that would not have bought a moderate drama in the early 1960s, if it involved overseas filming. Its marketing was directed, cleverly, at an audience which was known to exist—the young in summer. It was released carefully, at ordinary ticket prices. Its prospects had been properly researched.

The cynics observed the signs and bought stock in Twentieth Century-Fox as fast as they could. As the share price soared, student audiences justified the rise.

On the profits, Twentieth Century-Fox waxed fat. It kept 60 percent of the film's earnings. Neither Kurtz nor Lucas would talk of how the rest was divided. Alec Guinness was said to be the richest actor in the world because the producers had given him an extra half point in the profits. British tax rates made that claim seem unlikely. But the real point of interest was the attitude of Kurtz and Lucas toward giving away profit to thank their associates. "Some of the profit was obligated by contract to certain people. Some of it wasn't," Kurtz says. "We used the uncom-mitted points to say 'thank you' to people for doing a good job. People tell me that's un-heard of in the movie business, but I really don't think so. It's a private contract. People just don't talk about it."

George Lucas kept a sizable interest in any sequels to *Star Wars*. That was written into his original contract with Twentieth Century-Fox, at his insistence. The money will be the seed of his other projects. He still dreams of making personal films, concentrating on the poetry of cinema. Ned Tannen says, "The fact that *Star Wars* is the biggest hit ever made and that he doesn't think it is very good —that's what fascinates me about George. It's what I really admire about him—and I certainly think he is wrong."

45
Documentary:
The Cinema of Record

Jeanne Allen

While the movie industry in the United States is largely characterized by the fiction films produced by Hollywood, the documentary, or nonfiction film, has had a signifi-cant impact on both audiences and the development of moviemaking. In the following selection, written especially for this book, Jeanne Allen, of the University of Wiscon-sin at Madison, examines the importance of documentaries and the validity of their claim to represent their subjects accurately. Allen traces the development of the doc-umentary in an international context and examines several major political, technical, and esthetic influences.

"Documentaries" argue that they have dis-tinctively closer relationships to reality than do fictional, narrative films. The term "docu-mentary" is not only associated with mechan-ical reproduction, implying the absence of subjective interpretation, but also with other techniques that suggest minimized manipula-tion or interference in the process of recording events. It implies that "Harlan County, U.S.A." is a closer representation of labor struggle in America than is "Norma Rae," that "Hearts and Minds" brings the spectator a better approximation of the Vietnam War than does the "The Deerhunter," or that Frederick Wiseman's "Hospital" represents this public institution more accurately than does George C. Scott's characterization in a Hollywood film of the same title. This is a controversial claim, but all documentaries make it, either in an explicit verbal statement or implicitly through visual style, a series of codes or systematic signals that tell the viewer this representation is less "fictional" than other forms of visual entertainment.

The nature of this term, "documentary," involves two difficulties: first, that documentaries have a kind of negative identity—"we're not this"—and second, that the defining characteristics of documentary are not absolute but relative or comparative, and, hence, that they have to be seen in the historical context of dominant practices of visual representation. Depending on historical context, they may be dramatizations, reconstructions, unstaged, dubbed in voices, or sync sound (sound recorded simultaneously with visuals). Documentaries can be grouped into five major categories in chronological order: silent, topical films that claim to be based on historical events ("The White Slave Traffic," 1916), silent films in which historical persons reenact historical events in their actual settings ("Nanook of the North," 1922), sound films in which historical persons reconstruct events that have occurred ("Fires Were Started," 1943), synchronized sound films in which historical persons behave spontaneously and originally ("Primary," 1960), and docudramas which are acted dramatizations based on historical events ("Missiles of October," 1974). Still, the negative, relative identity of documentaries leads unavoidably to questions about the nature of the "truth" or "reality" they claim to offer, questions that have remained controversial for over half a century.

The earliest documentaries were called "actualités," a French word for the short films first shown publicly on theater screens. The excitement generated by the technical achievement of photographic representations in motion sustained public interest in actual events of everyday life: parents feeding their baby, workers arriving at a factory, a train pulling into a station. Wars and political events influenced film representation in the direction of a visual newspaper; McKinley's inauguration, the Spanish-American War, the Boer War, the Cuban and Philippine insurrections, all attracted spectators into vaudeville theaters, where the first films in the United States were exhibited. But as the film industry mushroomed into an enormously profitable business, the uncertainties surrounding the production of actualités proved undesirable; these films were only as good and as frequent as the events they recorded. The industry headed for studio-controlled comedies and dramas, which grew into feature length films, while actualities were relegated to newsreel shorts, which frequently acquiesced to time and entertainment demands with dramatization, stock footage, and special effects "fakery."

Even before World War I, but increasingly in the years after, as the United States dominated international distribution, the Hollywood feature film became synonymous with the public conception of cinema all over the world. Consequently, experiments with nonfictional filming in the United States and Russia in the early 1920s initiated a counter-cinema, which was not named "documentary" until the 1930s. In the United States, Robert Flaherty, an explorer and fur trader, was engaged by the French fur-trader firm Revillon Frères to make a film that became an international sensation, "Nanook of the North." The story of an Eskimo family who reenacted their daily and seasonal activities before Flaherty's camera, "Nanook" played to huge audiences in New York City, where it was a novel event not so much for its "documentary" representation but for its ability to rival feature films in its length, popularity, and narrative construction. Flaherty was to make several other feature length films of a similar genre, like "Moana," "Tabu," "Louisiana Story" (none of them as popular as "Nanook"), spawning a category of films of foreign cultures with varying degrees of travelogue or ethnographic interest.

In Russia, by comparison, interest in a

type of film that would counter the fictional melodrama was stimulated by concern for revolutionary Russian society, rather than by the lure or romance of exotic places. Lenin saw in film a potentially revolutionary tool of communication that could be instrumental in the reconstruction of Russian society. With a concern not unlike that of American Progressives, who saw the motion picture as a counterattraction to the saloon for the immigrant working class, Russian political leaders heralded film as a substitute for vodka or Russian orthodoxy. The 1920s were an exciting time for Russian artists. Stimulated by the work of American director, D. W. Griffith, whose "Birth of a Nation" and "Intolerance" provoked theoretical experimentation with film editing, and by the cross-fertilization of modernist movements in theater and painting, Kuleshov, Pudovkin, Dovzhenko, and Eisenstein created exciting possibilities for the collective hero: asynchronous sound and a spectrum of visual relationships that could be as flexible as figures of speech.

But despairing of their continued ties to melodramatic narrative forms, Dziga Vertov developed a style of filmmaking at once boldly avant-garde and journalistically representational. Vertov's philosophy of the "Kino-Eye" posited film as the analytical tool of the new society. Claiming the motion picture camera's ability to enhance human powers of observation, Vertov argued that film could both enlighten and bond a new revolutionary society. If not conditioned to the conventions of the aristocratically tainted theater, the Russian peasants and workers would flock to see themselves and their neighbors—the new heroes for a new society. The disparate backgrounds of the Russian workers diffused over a huge country could be overcome with the aesthetic and political power of the cinema, a living visual source of news and understanding. But Vertov's rejection of Socialist Realism in favor of an experimental exploration of temporal, spatial, and formal relationships in the film image fell out of favor with political leadership in the late 1920s. Further, the worldwide depression of the 1930s stimulated a different kind of analysis by the motion picture in Russia; the "Kino-Eye" was replaced by the "cine-train."

The Soviet Union was one of many countries caught up in the need to mount a direct and concerted effort at social change in the face of economic collapse. Setting quota goals of production on a five-year basis, the Soviets faced immense tasks in an only recently industrialized nation. Leading a group of dedicated filmmakers across the broad expanses of the USSR, Alexander Medvedkin offered Russian factory workers the services of the cine-train, a railroad car outfitted with film equipment, cameras, developing materials, and projectors as well as the minimal space necessary to house and feed the crew. The filmmakers of the cine-train could photograph factory processes and workers, develop their film in a day, project it the day following, while the same workers analyzed their performance, substantiated the need for innovation in neighboring factories and farms, and generally shared their expertise and their problems. Their announced goals of self-analysis and social-political change would be shared decades later by "documentarists" as diverse as Chris Marker, whose French filmmakers' cooperative S.L.O.N. dedicated itself in the 1960s to labor and political reform, and family therapists, who in the 1970s used video documentaries for the examination of interpersonal relations between families.

In Great Britain, the documentary movement of the 1930s was aimed at both explaining government programs and institutions to the public and raising morale and faith in the possibility of gradual liberal reform. John Grierson, working first for the Empire Marketing Board and then for the General Post Office, saw film as the tool of communication that could answer American political commentator Walter Lippmann's fears that twentieth-century change outpaced the ability of the electorate to respond knowledgeably and competently. Film could not only communicate information but, because of its dramatic force, it could energize and activate the public to respond.

Grierson had admired this forcefulness in the "Kinofist" of Sergei Eisenstein's "Potemkin," a film that showed the spark of revolution fanned to a flame (the film's soundtrack was censored in the United States and was available to Grierson only through the film clubs of Great Britain). Attracting innovative young filmmakers with his energy and determination, Grierson won government sponsorship of films showing the British working class, for the first time, in a dignified rather than comic manner, performing tasks essential to the life of the nation. "Granton Trawler," "Night Mail," "Song of Ceylon" combined artistic innovation with social and political messages. They demonstrated that Britain's strength and will could remain intact, while they acknowledged that the conditions of poverty and labor abuse must be changed. That spirit of "toughing it out" grew stronger in the Grierson-supported films of World War II, for example, in "Listen to Britain," "Fires Were Started," "Britain Can Take It." Not content to spawn a new school of filmmaking that resisted the competition of the Hollywood fictional narrative, which dominated Britain's commercial film industry after World War I, Grierson went to Canada where he was instrumental in the founding of the Canadian Film Board, one of the most successful and imaginative of the government-sponsored film production units in the world.

Depression in America led to diverse and conflicting film responses as the economic crisis deepened. Hollywood seemed to grow more glamorous as it showcased attractive consumer goods and titillated a disheartened but moviegoing public with views of an impossible standard of living—a fleeting feast for the eye. Occasionally a Populist morale booster from Frank Capra or an acknowledgment of social problems from Warner Brothers interrupted the escapist fare. But figures of authority usually proved paternalistically benevolent, or love, as in the person of golden moppet Shirley Temple, overcame every socially systemic malady. This "whistling in the dark" optimism was countered by grass-roots movements like the Workers Film and Photo League, which produced newsreels of events that the Hollywood-Hearst newsreel companies refused to present, events such as federal troops turning on a peaceful demonstration of jobless veterans, destroying their encampment in the nation's capital. Frontier Films offered motion pictures that reenacted and

dramatized difficult labor struggles during high unemployment. Shown in film clubs and civic halls, documentary as a true counter-cinema burgeoned in the 1930s.

At the same time, the Roosevelt administration, needing popular support for its New Deal programs, which reversed the "laissez faire" image of government, experimented with documentary photography and film. Marshalling the talents of Margaret Bourke-White, Paul Strand, and Walker Evans, Rexford Tugwell of the Rural Resettlement Administration, for example, sought to persuade the public of the strength of the "common people" under duress, their natural dignity and their modest almost pleading rather than angry and demanding look through photographic documentation. Like Grierson, Pare Lorentz, who headed the making of "The Plow That Broke the Plain" and "The River," mediated between more radical film crew and government sponsorship, which sought to assure the public that it was going far enough in its reform. Resisted by Hollywood as a threat to its commercial supremacy, government-made films found exhibition outlets only in independent theaters, particularly in the Midwest, but achieved acclaim nevertheless.

It may have been with this experience in mind that Hollywood proved so cooperative with the federal government when World War II was declared, though there was a precedent. President Wilson's Office of War Information had had extensive ties with the film industry during World War I, and these were remade in the 1940s: additionally, a weekly government newsletter reviewed Hollywood's output for its support of government policy and adherence to government positions. The government cooperated in a series of militarily oriented films with Warner Brothers, which were used to encourage enlistment, and, unlike the experience of the 1930s, directly employed Hollywood personnel in the making of war documentaries. William Wyler, John Ford, and John Huston made combat films. Frank Capra, morale booster of Depression America, made a series of training films, the "Why We Fight" series, that explained to enlistees the U.S. motivations in World War II. Capra's task was to match and counter the power of Leni Riefenstahl's masterpiece, "The Triumph of the Will," a brilliant creation of camera and editing that did for Hitler's Nazi Germany what the last part of Griffith's "The Birth of a Nation" did for the Ku Klux Klan: provide justification with irresistible dramatic beauty. The documentaries of World War II, with their images of British steadfastness, German power, and American moral determination, were deeply engaging. Arising in a time of unequaled national unity, they continue to be reedited and rereleased with every decade.

After the war, a euphoria of contentment left documentary without significant political function in the United States. As after World War I, Hollywood's popularity surged abroad while European film industries recuperated. A significant Supreme Court decision, the Paramount decrees, forced Hollywood studios to divest themselves of their theater chains, while the rapid expansion of television stimulated a different kind of documentary production: the commercial documentary made about American businesses by those businesses. Having started in the teens by nationwide firms like National Harvester and Cash Register, the commercial documentary enjoyed Department of Commerce distribution support in the 1920s, and had Hollywood's limited endorsement in the 1930s. Influenced by the British experience (for example, gas company sponsorship of "Housing Problems," a documentary about the need for urban renovation), business periodicals promoted commercial documentaries as a way of stimulating new markets to prevent overproduction by the war-expanded economy. And television, hungry for programming and already raiding radio, was an eager outlet. Unlike France, whose government awarded a "prime de qualité" and financial inducement for artistic documentary production (for example, George Franju's "Blood of the Beasts" despite its controversial goriness), the United States gave no such encouragement to its documentary filmmakers. The era of corporate sponsors for films more dedicated to reinforcing the status quo than to social change was at hand. Some filmmakers learned to live with

this uneasy patron-artist relationship, occasionally subverting their explicit function, as in Bert Haanstra's "Glass" which struck an aesthetic blow at machine production. But by and large, the 1950s were quiescent for documentary.

In the late 1950s, experiments in France and the United States with portable synchronized sound and camera equipment marked a turning point in the history of documentary. Chris Marker's "Letter from Siberia" (1956) seemed to anticipate this breakthrough by illustrating, poetically and self-reflexively, sound-image relationships that could be manipulated because the two were separately recorded. What cinema verité in France and direct cinema in the United States offered was a new authenticity of synchronized recording and a spontaneity that miniaturization and portability afforded. Light-weight, Bell and Howell wind-up cameras had been used during World War II for combat and reconnaissance photography, and the Germans had developed magnetic tape recording during the war. Putting these elements together broke new ground in photographic reproduction. The addition of sound that matched the image had meant the use of bulky equipment. As a consequence, synchronized sound documentary generally meant reenactment or reconstruction of spontaneous historical events for the camera. With the new equipment, light weight and operating separately while synchronized, the portable camera and sound recorder could function as flexibly as individual human observers. Both the appearance of greater spontaneity and the audience's growing knowledge of the conditions under which film usually occurred bolstered the credibility of this kind of filming as a recording of reality.

Cinema verité in France, practiced by such filmmakers as Jean Rouch, used the filming process to provoke people to respond and included it in the film representation. But in the United States, direct cinema made the process of filming as invisible as possible, assuring audiences that it neither obtruded upon nor constructed the events. As practiced by Ricky Leacock, Robert Drew, Don Pennebaker, and the Maysles brothers, among others, direct cinema presented the camera and synch-sound equipment as synonymous with a human observer. "Primary," "Happy Mother's Day," "Salesman," or "Gimme Shelter" were offered as transparent records of historical events.

Although direct cinema spurred an enhanced conviction in documentary's ability to offer evidence, this appeal did not go long unchallenged. Early in the 1960s, critics focused attention on the selectivity of footage used in direct cinema films, as well as the reconstruction of time sequences and other options for manipulation open to film editors. For example, Canadian director Alan King acknowledged critics' contentions that he had temporally rearranged sequences in his film "A Married Couple," a story about the breaking apart of a relationship. Developing in an era of rapid social change that shook people's conceptions of authority and validity internationally, these new film techniques presented audiences with evidence for questioning long-accepted authority. "Minamata," "Yanqui, No!," and "Hour of the Furnaces," for example, were a few films concerned with the oppression of capitalism and imperialism in an increasingly articulate Third World.

But just as television news in the late 1960s was hit by public resentment at a perceived bias and selectivity, direct cinema or cinema verité was challenged at very basic levels. Cultural systems and ideological positions, it was argued, influenced what was selected for filming, the way film sequences were organized, and, perhaps, the way the equipment itself was constructed as well as why it was constructed. At the beginning of the 1980s, social scientists and humanists in academia found themselves at loggerheads over whether film was a scientifically neutral tool of observation or a culturally constructed form that mediates reality and the spectator.

Elsewhere the issues raised by contemporary documentary are just as urgent, if more pragmatically stated. Why should television risk low audience ratings and court injunctions with a controversial documentary like "The Selling of the Pentagon" when it can win large audiences with star-filled docudramas like "Washington: Behind Closed Doors"? Were the Senate Watergate hearings more definitive for the public than Hollywood's "All the President's Men" with Robert Redford and Dustin Hoffman? Would a sizable number of Americans respond that "The China Syndrome" was the most influential documentary they had seen? Does the technical-scientific authority of the filmmaking process and our knowledge of the conventions of documentary filmmaking give Frederick Wiseman's series of PBS-sponsored documentaries on American institutions a greater "truth quotient" than the Hollywood topical films, whose use of melodrama, narrative resolution, and psychological character motivation have become basic categories of reality in our popular culture?

Faced with these questions, the success of independently produced documentaries, such as "Harlan County," "Word Is Out," and "The War at Home," suggests continued life for the documentary as a countercinema. Cable TV promises new programming space, and public broadcasting funding may give a boost to the independent documentary filmmaker. But regardless of these positive signs and the continued high credibility rating of television news and documentary, the documentary, by virtue of its very claim to authenticity and credibility, will continue to be questioned in its function as trustworthy bearer of evidence. The importance of its historical role suggests that the challenge to its claims is a sign of its vitality.

46
Video Methods
Are Reshaping
the Film Industry

Robert Lindsey

While the advent of television in the 1950s was considered by many to be the death-blow to the old Hollywood establishment, the television industry has become the life-blood that nurtures the Hollywood of today. The interaction between film and TV is a story that has no conclusion, since mutual influences continue to manifest themselves in all areas of content, production, distribution, and promotion. Robert Lindsey, of the *New York Times,* discusses the latest developments in this on-going saga.

New television technologies are altering patterns of power and wealth that have prevailed in the entertainment industry for decades and appear to be leading to fundamental changes in the way film entertainment is delivered to American consumers.

In the past, theatrical motion picture production has been controlled by a handful of studios here that not only financed most films but also owned worldwide sales networks that controlled their distribution. At the same time, most American television programming has been controlled by three commercial networks. Together, they have been virtually the only buyers of film entertainment.

But according to interviews with industry leaders and outside analysts, a growing public acceptance of cable and pay television systems, the expansion of pay-television satellite relay systems that bypass the networks and development of home television recording devices are starting to break these organizations' distribution control.

"Power is being diffused to those who own the new electronic networks," said Harold Vogel, a vice president of Merrill Lynch, Pierce, Fenner & Smith Inc, referring to the three largest national pay-television networks: Home Box Office, Showtime and Warner-Amex. Those three, the entertainment analyst said, along with independent producers, were gradually assuming some of the power long held by the studios and networks.

The perception that the old order is changing has touched off a scramble by outsiders to get into a restructured entertainment industry. And it has also touched off efforts by organizations that now dominate the business to protect their interests.

Among the challengers is Time Inc., which owns Time magazine, The Washington Star and other publications. The company already operates Home Box Office, the nation's largest pay television network, and in the last year it has made a strong entry into motion picture production. A number of other newspaper publishing concerns, including The New York Times Company and the Times-Mirror Company, have acquired major cable television systems.

Within the industry, CBS Inc. is planning to enter the cable television industry, whose expansion it had fought bitterly for more than two decades. And its two broadcasting rivals, ABC and NBC, have indicated that they are also developing plans to exploit the market for pay television, video disks and video cassette recordings.

Meanwhile, expectations about the new video market are galvanizing the industry. An estimated $40 million or more will be spent this year to produce original programming for pay-television systems, video disks and video cassette machines.

In addition, Hollywood studios in 1980 have started almost 30 percent more new films than they did a year ago, partly because of a new optimism that they can recoup losses on a movie that fails at the box office by selling rights to it to pay television, for home video recording and other ancillary markets.

In one response to the new technology, four studios—Columbia, Paramount, 20th Century-Fox and Universal—have formed a consortium with the Getty Oil Company giving them exclusive rights to distribute their theatrical movies via cable television. The move was apparently motivated both by fears that their control over distribution was being threatened and an eagerness to increase their pay-television revenues. The arrangement is being scrutinized by Justice Department antitrust specialists.

And as the revenues from pay television, video disks and cassettes have grown more significant, demands by Hollywood labor unions for a share has become the single most contentious point in negotiations this year. In fact, the issue has led to [the] strike by the Screen Actors Guild and American Federation of Radio and Television Artists. . . .

'Pay TV Revolution'

Talk of a "pay television revolution" has been heard periodically in Hollywood and on Wall Street for years. But until recently, the number of homes served by pay television systems was too small for the studios or networks to take seriously. In the last three years, however, the number of subscribers has jumped almost fourfold, to an estimated six million. The number is small as against the 76 million American homes that have television sets, but Hollywood's income from renting films to pay television operators grew to almost $100 million last year.

Norman Lear, the innovative producer of "All in the Family" and other series, said in an interview that he believed that pay television could "cause the demise" of one of the three major networks within five years or so.

"The networks are doing just what Detroit did 10 years ago," he said, "ignoring reality—the competition of the Japanese—and neglecting to build cars that the public wants."

As audiences for pay television and the home video recording devices grow, he said, it will become increasingly attractive economically to develop movies and other programming for these services. "It's almost economical now to make movies for pay television," he added. Thus, he said, independent producers will no longer be limited to selling their ideas to the traditional studios and networks.

Some See Lesser Impact

Others here, however, argue that the impact of the video technologies will be less extensive. Researchers for Young & Rubicam, the advertising agency, agree with and recently released a study asserting that there was no threat to the networks because they would always have much larger audiences than the pay-television networks.

Moreover, few industry observers are predicting the demise of any of the major studios—Columbia, 20th Century-Fox, Walt Disney, Metro Goldwyn Mayer, Warner Brothers, United Artists or Universal—even if pay television expands explosively. Movies are, and are expected to continue to be, the basic product of these systems.

The studios, seeing a rich vein of additional income, are moving in various ways to tap the market. But some outside analysts—and even some studio executives—are warning the film industry that it may be counting its new revenues prematurely.

'Have Only Served to Hurt Us'

Sidney Sheinberg, the president of MCA Inc., which owns Universal Studios and which has fought a so-far losing court battle to halt the sale of home video recorders, said recently, "The reality is that so far these technologies have served only to hurt us." He argues that they have encouraged increased film production for potential new markets that may not materialize and have made it easier for film "pirates" to duplicate copyrighted material.

Arthur Rockwell, an industry analyst for the Security Pacific Bank here, points out that CBS, ABC and Time-Life and a number of smaller entities all entered the movie-making business recently when most of the old-line studios were sharply increasing production. He predicts that the result will be an oversupply of films that will probably continue at least into 1981.

The major studios, he said, made 98 pictures in 1977, 110 in 1978, 123 in 1979, "and at the rate you're going they'll be up to 200 before it's over." Much of the growth, he added, came about because studios regarded the new home television market as a means of ending the traditional Hollywood "crap shoot"; there is a conviction, he said, that a movie can be made for $6 million or so, and then its television and other ancillary rights can be sold in advance and a profit guaranteed before the film opens.

"I think there have been some serious miscalculations," he declared. "They've taken the growth rate of the past five years in these markets and projected it into the future, and I don't think it will be there."

Mr. Vogel of Merrill Lynch stressed much the same thing. He said that the new video technologies would mean significant sources of new income for Hollywood, but that the studios were making too many expensive movies at a time when ticket sales had fallen appreciably.

Many studio executives say that they are unhappy with the low rates charged consumers by pay television—a monthly charge of $10 for 20 or so movies is not unusual—and it was this concern that led Columbia, Fox, Paramount and Universal to set up with the Getty Oil Company a pay television distribution concern that would have exclusive rights to release of their movies.

The consortium, called Premier, is scheduled to begin operating early next year.

Executives of Home Box Office and Showtime have assailed the move. "It's clearly illegal," said Michael Fuchs, a senior vice president of Home Box Office, who charged that it violated Federal antitrust laws.

Formation of the Premier organization appears to be leading to a legal confrontation that raises an old issue in Hollywood: Should the companies that produce filmed entertainment be allowed to exhibit it?

Television

The most pervasive medium in the daily lives of Americans is now television. The average home in the United States has a television set turned on for well over six hours each day; watching "the tube" is the prime leisure-time entertainment for most Americans. The familiar formats of sports, situation comedies, action drama, cartoons, and soap operas are geared to the common denominator of viewing preferences, and thus they generate a mass audience on a regular basis. As John Leonard points out in this section, few Americans can avoid watching at least thirty hours of television each week; most of those do not own TV sets (less than 5 percent of all Americans).

In addition to entertaining us, television has, in the last ten years, become our most significant and trusted source of news. Americans now feel that television journalism presents the fairest, most immediate, and clearest news, as opposed to newspapers, magazines, or radio. Television's in-depth coverage of special events such as the Olympics, space exploration, and political campaigns has created in the mass audience a commonality of experience never before possible.

The economics of commercial television are such that each station attempts to generate the largest possible audience for each time period, as measured by the ratings system. This allows the station to charge advertisers higher fees for commercial time. The business of television, in reality, is the selling of the audience to the advertisers, with the manufacture and sales of television sets a secondary profit source.

This economic support system is very much patterned after that developed for radio. In fact, the commercial television network system as we know it was substantially in place for commercial radio as far back as 1943, when the Radio Corporation of America (RCA), parent company of the National Broadcasting Company (NBC), was required by the FCC to sell one of its two radio networks, which then became the American Broadcasting Company (ABC). The Columbia Broadcasting System (CBS) had been in operation since 1927.

Business historian Robert Sobel traces the technical and industrial development of television in this section's first selection, from *The Manipulators: America in the Media Age.* Sobel argues that the motion picture industry badly misjudged the potential of television. As a result, the radio networks were allowed to develop the new medium almost unrivaled. After World War II ended, television caught on quickly in an economy flushed with postwar prosperity and hungry for new consumer goods. The new television set pushed the radio out of the living room and into the kitchen, bedroom, and automobile. What TV did to the motion picture industry was equally dramatic, as America's entertainment consumption patterns were drastically altered toward television.

What is the cultural effect of the large amount of daily television viewing on most Americans? Does television programming reflect our social environment, or has TV become that environment? In his essay, "And a Picture Tube Shall Lead Them," John Leonard, of the *New York Times,* claims that television has become our one common psychic experience, with nationally televised events such as the Super Bowl our only way of ". . . participating with ourselves as a nation."

The bulk of televised fare is fiction: comedy, drama, and action programs fill most of prime time. One-time television critic and screenwriter David Handler shows the odyssey taken by an idea for one television program. His article provides the reader with a behind-the-scenes process that is more often compromise than composition. In "From Heroes to Sandwiches: The Selling of a TV Pilot," Handler examines how the networks and program packagers reshaped a concept so many times it finally became formless.

An issue related to program development is the underlying value structure represented in the programs. In "Prime Time Chic: Between Newsbreaks and Commercials, the Values are L.A. Liberal," political scientist Michael J. Robinson examines the social messages implicit in many popular situation comedies and dramas. In contrast to the conservative cast of television series produced in the 1950s, Robinson finds a clear trend toward liberal views in recent programs.

A perennially popular, nonfiction television format is the game show, which usually combines celebrities with studio contestants and adds varying degrees of money, skills, and humor. What motivates ordinary people to participate, and why do so many (mostly daytime viewers) watch? Diana J. Janas, in a selection from *Human Behavior,* analyzes both questions in "The American Dream Game."

The need to combine entertainment and journalism is a vital concern in television news, where news gathering has often taken a back seat to personalities and ratings. Edward Jay Epstein's piece, from *News from Nowhere: Television and the News,* describes the combination of technical, editorial, and financial factors that make up the electronic gatekeeping process for national network television news. The critical need for visually interesting news film and the complex logistics of its path from camera to home screen are explained here as well. Recent technical developments in portable video cameras and signal relay systems (generically called ENG in the trade, for Electronic News Gathering) has made TV news more immediate and even more visual.

The final article in this section looks at the future of television in light of the tremendous technological changes represented by cable TV, satellites, and home video systems. Examining these advances from the perspective of audience use, noted business writer Chris Welles observes that future variety might simply mean more of the same. Nevertheless, the promise of specialized programming controlled by the individual viewer raises the possibility that programming need not appeal to only mass audiences. In the final section of this book, entitled "Personal Media," we will examine some alternatives.

47

Television as Invention and Business

Robert Sobel

The story of how the medium of television originally came under the control of the radio industry is a significant one. Historian Robert Sobel traces the development of television as a technology and as a business in the following selection from his comprehensive study, *The Manipulators: America in the Media Age.* Sobel argues that our media environment would be very different today had the motion picture industry played a more dominant role in television's growth.

Radio had its Marconi and motion pictures its Edison, men who could be singled out as "fathers of the industry," even while recognizing that each had a long series of progenitors. These technicians had been followed by businessmen—Sarnoff and the corporate leaders at AT&T, Westinghouse, General Electric, and RCA in the case of radio, Zukor and the other immigrant tycoons for movies—who helped organize the industry and give it a form. In turn the businessmen had been challenged by and in some cases obliged to share power with the artists. Thus there had been a continual tension between form and content, dictated by the demands of the audience, the nature of technology, and the personalities of key individuals—as well as occasional governmental regulation, and competition with rival media.

This situation did not exist in television. No single individual could be credited with inventing the technology, although two, Vladimir Zworykin and Philo Farnsworth, were more important than the others. But they were more akin to DeForest than to Marconi —they produced inventions and perfected techniques that made the work of others practical; neither man was responsible for the keystone effort. Furthermore, television developed within a pre-existent business structure and did not have to create one of its own. The same was true for the art, at least for the first few years. In effect, television was the child of radio, motion pictures, and the press, and in its early days adapted the forms and contents of these to suit its own technology and requirements.

This was to have been expected; after all, radio had borrowed from the concert hall and vaudeville, motion pictures from the stage, and newspapers had evolved over hundreds of years, continually incorporating new technologies and concepts. It was different with television, even though it became a more powerful medium than its predecessors. To this day it has not produced its own essential structure, either artistically or commercially. There was no early period of trial and error among a group of pioneers, as there had been in the other media. Instead, from the first, television was an arena for giants. Nor was there a period of relatively free enterprise, for the government was there at creation. Each of the other media experienced some measure of this;

there was little in the evolution of the television industry.

The position of the artists (performers, writers, directors) was not as clear in television as in other "idea industries." This was due in large part to the nature of the business and the presence of government, but each might have been overcome had the artists themselves some clear idea of what they wanted. Just as there was no single technological genius for television—no Marconi or Edison—there was no pioneering businessman, such as Zukor or the young David Sarnoff. Instead, television was the product of corporate intelligence, and not even the contribution of Sarnoff, important though it was, was indispensable. The industry lacked a "father," a recognized founder, and this, too, is an indication of the essentially derivative nature of the medium and industry.

European technicians explored the possibility of transmitting pictures over wire and through the air a century ago. In 1862 an Italian priest, Abbé Caselli, devised a crude method of sending images over telegraph wires. Twenty-two years later a German engineer, Paul Nipkow, invented an "electrical telescope," really a crude transmitter and receiver. Lazare Weiller conducted experiments with the "Nipkow disc" in the 1890s, and later on Julius Elster, Hans Geitel, Ferdinand Braun, William Crookes, and Boris Rosing added to the technology. On the eve of World War I a British scientist, A. Campbell Swinton, developed a cathode tube capable of electronic scanning, and his papers on the subject were well known to researchers. J. L. Baird, another Englishman, actually constructed receivers and transmitters, and by 1930 was sending test signals over BBC to individuals who had purchased his sets for $130. But the work was not commercialized. Television remained a laboratory curiosity, and these men are memorialized in a handful of histories of technology and in a few other places.

American inventors had a more commercial view of television. Alexander Graham Bell considered wedding sight and sound in his telephone, and in 1880 he took out patents for television devices. Forty years later Herbert Ives of Bell Laboratories was assigned the task of perfecting "telephoto" transmission, and in 1927 he sent a "pictorialized broadcast" of a Herbert Hoover speech from New York to Washington. By the end of the decade Ives and others at Bell had developed a color receiver, and an experimental system was established in New York, where it was witnessed by several thousand people. Bell Laboratories continued to experiment with the device, considering it the kind of telephone Alexander Graham Bell had dreamed about. In time such a telephone was perfected, but in the meanwhile, others pioneered in commercial television.

In order to finance his television experiments, Boris Rosing took a position at the St. Petersburg Institute of Technology, where among other duties he instructed students in electrical subjects. Zworykin was one of these, and just before World War I he became Rosing's assistant. While working for the Russian Wireless Telegraph and Telephone Company in 1917, Zworykin conducted his own experiments. Two years later, Zworykin immigrated to the United States, and after failing to find backing for his own company, he joined Westinghouse as a radio researcher. Unable to convince that company of the importance of television, he left in 1921 to work for a small electrical manufacturing firm in Kansas, only to return to Westinghouse in 1923, when its leaders had a change of heart. Toward the end of the year, Zworykin had perfected the iconoscope, a practical photoelectric tube for television transmission. Although the Westinghouse leadership was pleased with the result and helped Zworykin obtain his patent, the company did nothing to commercialize it, and for the next five years the scientist worked in his laboratory, developing new television tubes, none of which were given commercial application.

At the time of Zworykin's invention, RCA was still owned by other companies, Westinghouse among them. Radio was becoming popular, and all efforts were geared to the increased production of receivers, the development of new transmission apparatus, and the creation of stations. David Sarnoff, who earlier had spoken of the commercial possibilities of the "radio music box," was charged with developing both the art and the commerce of that invention. Like others, he knew of television, of Ives' experiments at Bell Laboratories, and of Zworykin's work at Westinghouse. In a memorandum to the RCA directors early in 1923, he wrote, "I believe that television, which is the technical name for seeing instead of hearing by radio, will come to pass in due course. . . . I also believe that transmission and reception of motion pictures by radio will be worked out within the next decade." In a speech at the University of Missouri the following year, Sarnoff said, "Let us think of every farmhouse equipped not only with a sound-receiving device but with a screen that would mirror the sights of life."[1] He continued to write and talk of television throughout the rest of the decade, but could do nothing more so long as the radio boom continued, RCA remained under the control of other companies, and he lacked authority within the firm. The situation had changed by 1929. Early that year, Sarnoff and Zworykin held a series of meetings, at the conclusion of which the inventor asked for $100,000 to perfect a system of commercial television. Sarnoff agreed to the request, and with this, the company became the leader of the yet-to-be-born industry.

While Zworykin met with Sarnoff, the second American pioneer, Philo Farnsworth, was seeking backing for his inventions. A farmboy from Rigby, Idaho, who became interested in radio through the reading of popular magazines, Farnsworth attended Brigham Young University in Utah, working his way through by repairing radios. In his spare time, he conducted several crude experiments with television. Shortly before graduating, Farnsworth met George Everson, a San Francisco businessman, who agreed to raise money to back further experiments in the field. From 1926 to 1929, Farnsworth spent some $140,000 of his backers' money, with spotty results. He needed additional funds, and headed East to find them. New York's investment banks weren't interested, but some of the directors of Philco Radio were, and they offered to finance Farnsworth's experiments provided they were geared to the creation of a commercial product. The inventor agreed, and in 1930 he took out his first patent. Others followed, along with a visit by Zworykin to the California laboratory to check them out. For a while it appeared that RCA might offer to purchase his patents, or give the inventor a position, but nothing came of this.

Farnsworth had little interest in business, and almost no talent in the board room. His operation was close to bankruptcy in 1938; to salvage it, he offered to sell patents to RCA and was rebuffed. Then he approached Paramount, and talked of the potential in a marriage of motion pictures and television. Once again, he had no success. Obliged either to give up or continue on his own, he organized Farnsworth Television and Radio Corporation, scraped up enough money to purchase the manufacturing facilities of the Capehart Corporation, and began turning out radio receivers. The World War II boom enabled the company to prosper, and Farnsworth became fairly wealthy, but he remained far from the board rooms, in his laboratory, working on television. Due to his efforts, the company owned many key patents, which it licensed to others, RCA in particular.

The same situation existed at Hazeltine Electronics and Allen B. DuMont Laboratories, each headed by a television pioneer. Neither of these had the financial power or the managerial experience to challenge RCA, and so they left the field to others. Columbia Broadcasting, while not as large as RCA, had become its leading competitor in programming, and was interested in entering television. In 1936 it acquired the services of Peter Goldmark, a young Hungarian engineer who led the CBS technological efforts, and three years later the company erected a television transmitter on top of the Chrysler Building at a cost of $650,000. Still, it lacked the funds and the will to make a major drive in the early 1940s, so that RCA continued to lead the others when the war ended.

Need television have become the child of radio? There were other possibilities. The leading newspapers might have taken an interest in the medium, as they had in radio, so that by the early 1950s, several key stations, even networks, might have been owned and managed by newspaper publishers. Under such a system the news function could have taken on primary importance, resulting in a radically different relationship between the stations and the Federal Communications Commission. With the exception of the Hearst organization, however, no publisher had the funds and depth for such an undertaking, and the elderly, ailing William Randolph Hearst showed no interest in the medium. Later on some newspapers did purchase stations, usually unaffiliated ones serving local markets, but few were significant factors by the mid-1950s.

Had the motion picture companies entered television, the development of both industries might also have been quite different. In 1938, when Farnsworth held his conversations with Paramount, the affinity between the two was quite evident, at least as much as that between radio and television. The exhibition of television at the 1939–40 New York World's Fair was geared to such a marriage, as guides told visitors that one day, through the use of the tube, they would be able to see movies at home. During World War II there had been some talk of mass television, with large-screen projectors, piping new movies into hundreds of theaters simultaneously, thus saving fortunes on print costs. Technology militated against this plan, and in any case, home television offered even more interesting possibilities.

Before these could be acted upon, however, one had to consider the anatomy of the new medium. Was television radio with pictures? Or could it be considered as a motion picture set for the home? These were key questions, for the industry might have gone either way. The motion-picture link would have required the development of some system of collecting admissions, either through subscriptions or coin-activated screens. In the 1950s several companies, Zenith and Skiatron among them, experimented with such systems, and although nothing came of it, the idea would have been developed had the motion-picture companies entered a relationship with Farnsworth. For while RCA and other radio-oriented firms possessed capital, management, and even talent, they lacked experience in programming visual shows; in the early days, they tended to point their cameras at radio programs performed on sets. The radio networks had the electronic structure for home television—the form—while the motion picture companies possessed ready-made programs, their films—the content. Either the radio networks would have to develop programs, or the motion-picture firms would have to acquire stations. These appeared to be the prime alternatives in the immediate postwar period.

Some motion-picture firms recognized the situation and began to explore the potential of television. Paramount established an experimental studio, while Columbia had a study group look into the matter. But the other major studios, led by MGM, were not interested in the "small screen," even after the postwar boom began. Most Hollywood executives could not believe the public would reject their superior products for the inferior programming then available on television. Paid admissions had been high during the war, and with the return of the old stars, might soon be better. The motion-picture industry leaders hoped that television would prove a fad, and a high-priced one at that. After a while, audiences would return to the theaters, tired of puppet shows, wrestling, and antique educational films. Even if television persisted, the networks would have to knock on Hollywood's door in the end, and television might become a good dumping ground for old B movies, a source of additional profits for the studios.

There was some talk of network films, low-priced shows produced for television. The threat was more apparent than real in the mid-1940s; the studios had the major stars under contract, as well as the best directors and cameramen, and any who dared offer their services to television would suffer Hollywood's retribution. In addition, new talent was informed that too close an identity with television would mean an end to hopes for a Hollywood career.

Hollywood was in no position to destroy the new medium, but the stations did need programs, especially after the initial novelty began to pall. The leading shows in 1947 were in the area of sports (especially the roller derby and wrestling), some live drama ("Kraft Theater"), and childrens' shows (led by "Howdy Doody"). In most parts of the country, programming was limited to a few hours a day, usually in the late afternoon and evening. Radio was still booming, offering superior dramas, expanded sports programs, rapid and complete news, and many variety and situation comedies. Why should the consumer pay some $350 for a miniscule television set, when for a tenth of that figure he could obtain a fine radio? Sarnoff understood this, for more than any other firm RCA had committed itself to television. The company was busily constructing the NBC television network, manufacturing receivers, and trying to organize presentations. The last problem was the most difficult to overcome, for without content, financial and technological expertise would lead nowhere. The motion-picture companies appreciated the situation, and in 1947 rejected feelers from the networks for old movies.

This changed quickly in 1948, when the combination of anti-Communist sentiment and the U. S. Supreme Court's decision in *United States v. Paramount et al.* frightened all the executives. The red scare could lead to a decline in paid admissions; the Court decision meant that the long-awaited breakup of studios and distribution facilities was about to take place. Shortly thereafter, Twentieth Century-Fox made an offer to purchase the American Broadcasting Company (formed from the old NBC Blue Network in 1943), which was rejected, and in any case was not very serious. The production company's strategy was obvious; it would have entered television through ABC and played its old films on the air. Some Paramount executives, acting even before the divestiture was completed, held conversations with ABC. These continued from 1948 into 1950, when Paramount Pictures was separated from United Paramount Theaters. Industry journals predicted a merger between Paramount Pictures and the television company. But Paramount was unwilling to enter into such a combination. Instead, in 1951, the theater chain joined with ABC to form ABC-Paramount. This combination was surprising, for the new company

still lacked films. Still, United Paramount was able to contribute cash and managerial talent to the industry, and it was an important step in the formation of a television–motion-picture nexus.

Meanwhile, several small motion-picture studios, emboldened by the divestiture, began producing half-hour dramatic and Western films for television, and some of the majors sold a few old movies for viewing. Clearly the new medium was no mere fad, and Hollywood needed a new approach in order to retain audiences. This came in 1949. The studios stopped turning out B movies, and instead began making "blockbusters," spectacles that cost a great deal of money, had many stars, and were filmed in color—the kind of picture one could not adequately see on television's small tube. Big films were booked into many theaters at once, and this saturation policy was supposed to help recoup costs rapidly while drawing the public to the neighborhood movie houses.

The gamble failed. Theater receipts, which were $1.6 billion in 1947, fell to $1.2 billion in 1953 before leveling off and rising somewhat. By then, too, Hollywood had all but capitulated to the new industry, and film sales to television rose rapidly. The surrender was highlighted when in 1955 Mutual Broadcasting (owned by General Tire and Rubber) purchased RKO Pictures. Mutual was not interested in RKO's studios, but rather its film library of 740 features and over 1,000 shorts. These were shown over WOR-TV in New York and stations in other cities under the program title of "Million Dollar Movie" and attracted large enough audiences to repay the purchase price in the first year. The RKO sale opened the floodgates. By mid-1956, more than 1,500 old features had been sold to the networks, while MGM announced it intended to sell an additional 770 movies produced prior to 1949.

Part of the money obtained from film sales went into the conversion of motion-picture sound stages to television operations. Either directly or through affiliates, the large studios became important factors in the production of television films, on occasion producing "packages" of them for the major networks. Columbia Broadcasting took over the old Republic Studios in Hollywood for its productions, while the Music Corporation of America (MCA) purchased Universal Studios, relinquished its talent agency business under government edict, and concentrated upon television programs and low-cost features for theaters (to be sold to television after completing their runs). At the same time television production firms went to Hollywood, either to purchase their own studios or to erect new ones. Mergers, buy-outs, and transformations followed. Within a decade the old Hollywood was gone, its back lots closed down or geared to the needs of television. Theater films continued to be made, but the theaters themselves were closing or converting to other uses, as television became the central American amusement medium. The studio system was rapidly becoming an institution of the past.

The network executives, however, could not await the resolution of their struggle with Hollywood. In the late 1940s they tried to develop their own shows. Given their backgrounds and experience, their early attempts were based on radio models. They utilized radio artists and technical personnel, drew upon the theater and old vaudeville talent, and searched for new ideas and people. As had been the case with radio, the shows were broadcast live, usually from New York, and sent out to affiliates. The radio structure persisted in sponsorship, too. Just as the radio practice had been to have sponsors take or even create their own shows, so it was in early television. The first to do this was "Kraft Theater," in 1947, but the best known was "Texaco Star Theater," starring Milton Berle, which appeared the following year. There were also the "Philco Television Theater," the "General Electric Theater," and the "Ford Theater," as well as the "Colgate Comedy Hour" and the "Camel News Caravan." Almost all such sponsor-identified shows were short-lived, the victims of changing tastes, new film technologies, and just as important, the economics of a new philosophy of advertising.

Simply stated, television shows cost more to produce than did their radio counterparts; in this respect, they were more akin to films than to radio. Talent costs were not high, even though artists in television dramas had to memorize most of their lines, a labor not required for radio dramas. But cameras and sets had to be amortized, costumes rented, makeup artists hired, and many other problems dealt with. Even the electricity bills were higher, the result of the many lights used on the sets. In 1948, "Texaco Star Theater" cost $15,000 a show, and this included Milton Berle's fee. Ten years later, network specials could run well over $100,000 for an hour; by the 1970s, weekly dramatic programs were being budgeted at well over twice that figure. Major advertisers increased their expenditures during the period, but most of them saw little to be gained in placing most of it in one show. Instead, they would purchase "spots" on popular programs, whose prices were geared to their rating in the polls. In the great days of radio, the person who put together the package for the sponsor was a key individual; in television, he was replaced by the time buyer, the executive capable of judging the merits of new shows before they appeared on the tube, paying low rates on the gamble the programs would be a hit.

This structure enabled small production companies to obtain a great deal of power in the late 1950s and early 1960s. Backed by risk capital and often centered around a single artist or businessman, they would rent equipment and studios, hire actors and actresses, and make a pilot film for a series. This would then be presented to the networks, in the hope that it would find approval. Should the network see merit in the show, it would take an option and try to interest advertisers. If all went well, the sponsored programs would appear on the tube, and further success resulted in new and better contracts. Some production companies expanded and became major forces within the industry—Desilu, organized by Lucille Ball and Desi Arnaz, was one of the first. Failure could result in the company's dissolution, after which its members would join other units.[2]

Such production units, the logical response to the omnivorous demands of television, were also products of a technological development that affected the medium as profoundly as sound had the motion picture.

The sensible way to prepare a pilot was through the use of films, which would be sent to the networks and agencies. The alternative was a separate live performance for each interested party, and this was not only unbearable financially but also unrealistic in that the purchasers were interested in the show on the tube, not live. Films had other advantages. Unlike live shows, they could be edited, replayed several times on the network, or rented to local stations, thus spreading the costs over several performances.[3] But there were drawbacks, too. They were expensive to produce, while those who knew best how to make them were still bound to the motion-picture industry. Some pilot films were made, but most were technically unsatisfactory; unlike the Hollywood products, they appeared on the screen like amateur performances. The matter of replays also presented a problem. Television engineers developed "kinescoping," a simple process by which a motion-picture camera was aimed at the televised image to make the film. These tended to be harsh, grainy, and lacking in contrast; kinescopes could be no better than the televised image, and in the early days they left much to be desired.

At the time most companies involved with tape were interested in sound rather than sight; they predicted that within a decade, the tape recorder would replace the phonograph. Zworykin and others at RCA began experimenting with videotape shortly after the war, and demonstrated a camera in 1953. Several new firms pioneered in this field, and one of them, Ampex Corporation, entered videotape research as well. In 1956 one of its scientists, Charles Ginsburg, perfected a videotape camera and recorder, and Ampex won several basic patents. Within less than a year the first Ampex recorders and cameras, selling for over $50,000, were being installed at the studios, and by the end of the 1960s, the videotape revolution had been completed. Unlike motion pictures and radio, this was not a case of a technology seeking utilization but rather the development of technology to fill recognized requirements.

Videotape had almost all the advantages of film and none of the drawbacks. The tape itself was inexpensive and compact. Unlike film, the completed videotape did not have to be processed, but instead could be played back immediately. With film, the director would shoot his scene but not be able to see it for a day or so. With tape, he could have an instantaneous view of what had been produced. The quality of tape was superior to that of film, especially when the latter was used by newcomers. Tape could be reused many times, and this added to its economies. In fact, the technology had only one drawback, in that tape was difficult to edit, since there were none of the familiar "frames" of film. Rather videotape was opaque, not unlike recording tape, and it could be edited only through the use of special viewing machines. These were expensive and, in the early days, difficult to obtain. More often than not the directors would not edit, but instead tape the program live and play it back over the air, hoping for the best. In this way, videotape preserved the illusion of live performances but combined it with the advantages of the canned ones.

Videotape was the bridge between films and live performances; in effect, it enabled producers to combine the best features of both.[4] By the mid-1960s, almost all network drama, variety, comedy, and late-night programs were either taped before live audiences, or in a studio with audience reactions dubbed in afterward. Tape was particularly well suited to sports events. Given the "instant replay," the director was able to show the audience dramatic moments in a contest—umpire or referee calls included, complete with close-ups and in slow motion. Thus the viewer of a dull game might ignore the action, knowing that the truly important plays would be reshown and analyzed. In effect, this afforded the viewer an advantage over those in the stadium or arena. Sports contests became shows, stadiums were stages, and those in the stands were akin to the crowds of extras in motion pictures, in that they provided a touch of reality for the home viewer. But audiences at sports events were not required for any other purpose, since television receipts were becoming more important each year. Owners of baseball and football teams feared poor attendance, since it might indicate to viewers that the contest was somehow not worth watching, and television receipts were becoming increasingly important. Given the higher rates charged the networks with each new contract, baseball team owners could afford to keep the prices of their tickets low, in the hope of luring the "audience" to the "show."

Until the development of videotape, television had developed along lines that were familiar to old radio hands. Just as in the early 1920s, radio stations had relied upon a pre-existing medium, the phonograph, for its programs, so the television networks tried to utilize films. They turned to live programming only after failing to crack the studio film libraries. Then, as films became available, they were used to complement existing programs. The old movies could be replayed many times, and the audiences for them hardly declined. Given the choice between such a movie whose cost had been amortized, and two hours of comedy and variety programs, which might require over $150,000 to produce, station and network executives naturally preferred films. This situation did not change drastically with the advent of videotape, but at least this new

technology encouraged the showing of "live on tape shows," which could be edited for content, and syndicated later on. In some cases the reruns were almost as popular as the original shows, and even attracted larger audiences than well-considered fresh programs.[5] Radio had progressed from a recorded content to a live one, but television, given videotape, went in the opposite direction. Those involved in producing and directing shows welcomed tape, though some actors and actresses professed to prefer the live performance. As for the audiences, after a short time they too accepted videotape and gave the matter little thought. One picture was not that different from the other. By the early 1970s, Americans were being shown news shows in the early evening that appeared up-to-date and live, but in reality had been taped an hour or so earlier so as to take advantage of the medium in programming for different time zones. To further complicate matters, most of the news shows utilized films and other tape to illustrate stories, and so the home viewer really witnessed tape on tape on tube, or film on tape on tube. This, too, he took in his stride.

Notes

1. David Sarnoff, *Looking Ahead* (New York: McGraw-Hill, 1968), p. 88. Eugene Lyons, *David Sarnoff* (New York: Harper & Bros., 1956), pp. 207–10.
2. Muriel Cantor, *The Hollywood TV Producer* (New York: Basic Books, 1971), pp. 71–116ff.
3. Live dramas were considered artistically pleasing in the early years, when miscues and other errors in performance could not be masked. The situation caused much anguish at the time, but later on was remembered fondly. This was the "golden age of television," and the title may have been merited, as young, fresh talent entered television. But the gold was in the writers, directors, and performers, not the technology.
4. Tape also gave a new life to the Hollywood studios. By the end of the 1960s, almost all weekly shows were produced there, often in the same locations as were the motion-picture epics of the 1930s and 1940s. Thus, although Hollywood might no longer be the motion-picture capital of the nation, it remained the entertainment center. Without tape, New York might have retained many shows. Too, special made-for-television movies assisted the motion-picture industry in its new incarnation.
5. "In Washington, which lives on news as Milwaukee lives on beer, the nightly national news shows were staggered in fall 1970—Howard K. Smith at 6, David Brinkley at 6:30, Walter Cronkite at 7. At 6 in the Washington market, according to the November 1970 ratings sweep by the American Research Bureau, the most widely watched program in Washington was reruns of *I Love Lucy*; at 6:30, reruns of *Petticoat Junction*; at 7, reruns of *Dick van Dyke*." Martin Mayer, *About Television* (New York: Harper & Row, 1972), p. 49.

48
And a Picture Tube Shall Lead Them

John Leonard

That the impact of television programming on our culture has been enormous is a truism with which few would argue. John Leonard, chief cultural critic of the *New York Times,* goes one step further in his essay "And a Picture Tube Shall Lead Them." Leonard claims that television now *is* our primary cultural medium.

Leonard adds up the large amount of time most Americans spend in front of the TV screen and comes to the conclusion that we have become what we watch.

Unwittingly, then, had I discovered an invisible Empire of the air.
—Lee De Forest, *who invented the Audion tube*

The relationship between consumer and advertiser is the last demonstration of *necessary* love in the West, and its principal form of expression is the television commercial.
—Gore Vidal, *Myra Breckinridge*

Television is chewing gum for the eyes.
—Fred Allen

It was a dinner party in a handsome apartment in Brooklyn Heights. The view was handsome, and so was the food, and so were the people, with the sort of faces usually to be found stamped on Roman coins. Even the sullen surreal smear of art on the wall above the lowboy in the living room—a Technicolored artichoke, a test pattern—seemed handsome. I was among professors of literature and sociology. I, who professed nothing more compelling than myself, had just been unmasked as a reviewer of TV programs for a local newspaper. The professors wanted to know how anyone could watch 20 to 30 hours of television a week and stay serious, much less sane. They nodded so sympathetically I thought their heads would fall off and scare the cat.

Well, how many hours of TV did *they* watch each week? I took up pen and paper. News? Five and one half hours, if one counted *60 Minutes* on CBS and *Close-Up* on ABC. Documentaries? They all claimed to watch lots of documentaries on hunger, crime, inflation, farm workers, pensions, prisons and the Middle East. I didn't believe them. Nobody watches documentaries. Say one half hour, being generous. Dramatic specials? It was the same. Everybody claimed to have watched Shakespeare, Ibsen, O'Neill, Arthur Miller, Tennessee Williams. I doubt it. Say an hour. Variety shows? Never, they said. Not even Carol Burnett, or Liza Minnelli, or Cher with Bette Midler and Elton John? No. Still, I gave them an hour. Situation comedies? Not really, except, perhaps, for *M*A*S*H* and *The*

Mary Tyler Moore Show and, occasionally, *Rhoda* or *The Bob Newhart Show,* and once in a while *All in the Family,* just to glance at a fever chart on the cultural distemper. No one admitted to watching *Maude,* and yet everyone had a different reason for disliking it. An hour and a half. Talk shows? Hardly ever. Oh, maybe Johnny Carson's opening monolog, which is always interesting because it tells us what can be safely reviled in the nation this week; and then, if the guest is Joan Rivers or Jonathan Winters or Woody Allen or David Steinberg or Flip Wilson, another 15 minutes; and then, of course, if Norman Mailer is visiting Merv Griffin. . . . Two hours. Public television? For Remedial Seriousness—Bill Moyers, Kenneth Clark, Jacob Bronowski, The *Robert MacNeil Report*—an hour and a half; for *Upstairs, Downstairs,* an hour; for William F. Buckley, Jr., 15 minutes. Sports? Ah, that's different. Five shameful hours or so, especially professional football and basketball, or if Catfish Hunter is pitching; more in Olympic years; and much more if a local team looks as if it might make the play-offs. Movies? Professors don't count watching movies as watching television. I do, either in prime time or after the late news. They will watch reruns of the B movies of their youth— *Andy Hardy Meets Frankenstein's Sister-in-Law, Sydney Greenstreet Goes to a Beach Party,* inferior in quality to an average episode of, say, *Columbo*—until the cows come home and the cartoons come on. Ten hours.

That amounts to about 30 hours of TV a week. And the total takes no account of Barbara Walters, game shows, soap operas, political conventions and campaigns, assassinations, moon shots, moratoria, Saturday-night "massacres" (as distinguished from My Lai "incidents"), impeachment proceedings and Presidential pre-emptions. The pre-emptions are particularly time-consuming because, like jet lag, it takes a day or two to recover from them. We had one President on TV impersonating Ed Sullivan, arms aloft in the famous V, operating as a slingshot, flinging our heads through the screen and into incredulity: Government by jack-in-the-box! Surprise! Freeze the wages; go to China! Look what Daddy brought home from the office—an invasion

of Cambodia! Now we have a President [Ford] who impersonates Joe Palooka: Eat your parsnips and the economy will grow strong. This is known as children's programing.

These calculations should not have rained so much on the professors' picnic. Every survey suggests that intellectuals watch almost as much television as the rest of us, even if their sets—instead of being on display prominently in the living room, like a moonstone or a prayer mat—are hidden away in the study, behind Da Vinci's notebooks, under a Ceropegia woodii through whose tendrils their children must hack a path to *Gilligan's Island.* Moreover, intellectuals tend to look at approximately the same programs the *lumpen* do. The evening in Brooklyn Heights ended with everybody talking about *Kojak.* Did you know that the late Lionel Trilling watched *Kojak?*

Morley Safer, who was a superb correspondent covering the war in Vietnam, co-anchors *60 Minutes* with Mike Wallace and Dan Rather. He also takes his Jewishness seriously. Every year he has to explain to his outraged young daughter why there will be no Christmas tree in their house.

Safer used to live in Sneden's Landing, a postage stamp of God's country across the Hudson River from Manhattan. Perhaps the only disadvantage of living in Sneden's Landing is the vagary of television reception. The set in Safer's house couldn't pick up the Channel 13 (public TV) signal.

One afternoon, Safer was ferrying his daughter and several of her friends to the circus or the Metropolitan Museum of Art, it doesn't matter which. His daughter's friends were discussing Big Bird, the Cookie Monster, Bert, Ernie, Oscar the Grouch and the Muppets. Safer's daughter announced: "We don't have *Sesame Street* at our house—because *we're Jewish*."

At a series of seminars at Duke University in the winter and spring of 1975, journalists variously electronic and otherwise met to meditate on their profession. Each was esteemed by his colleagues, which is why he had been chosen to be a Duke fellow in communications. Among them was Russell Baker, nonpareil columnist for *The New York Times,* and Bill Greider of *The Washington Post,* Alan Otten of *The Wall Street Journal,* John Seigenthaler of *The Nashville Tennessean* and Ed Yoder, then of *The Greensboro Daily News.* Sander Vanocur, who has done time with almost every network there is, presided. And Daniel Schorr, the CBS reporter who makes as much news as he reports, was the star.

The president of Duke is Terry Sanford, who used to be governor of North Carolina. Terry Sanford runs for the Presidency of the United States the way other people run for the bathroom; he needs to. At a reception in his executive digs in Durham, there was a receiving line for the Duke fellows. On passing through it, each fellow perfunctorily shook hands with local dignitaries, including the gracious Mrs. Sanford. Just once in the course of these introductions did the eyes of Mr. and Mrs. Sanford light up, like the dial of a radio. That was in their gasp of recognition on meeting Russell Baker. Their taste was impeccable, but their sense of what constitutes glamor in journalism was at least a decade behind the times—which may be one of the reasons Terry Sanford is known as the Harold Stassen of the Piedmont. Real glamor resides elsewhere.

It resides, as the students at Duke knew immediately, in Schorr and Vanocur. Among the students, they were celebrities, in a class with sports heroes, movie actors, rock musicians, only *serious.* Like a Cronkite, a Chancellor, a Howard K. Smith, in the synopsizing of the quotidian on our TV screens, their faces have become front pages, mirrors of events. They are heavy: They have taken on the gravity of all they have reported. *Physically,* they embody the news. History has thickened, substantiated them. And yet they are edited down to essentials: There isn't time, there isn't room for anything that isn't important. This density exerts a mighty pull on our attention. Through their images, we are accustomed to trafficking with momentous occasions. It is altogether natural, then, that when they come personally among us, we should think it an occasion. Otherwise, why would they be here?

Even the print journalists at Duke deferred

to the TV density. The problems of electronic news dominated the seminar discussions. It was clear from film clips that the unblinking camera could record the lump in the throat, the trembling of the hand, the bead of perspiration that may, or may not, signify a lie, whereas the typewriter had to resort to adjectives and adverbs. Nobody believes adjectives and adverbs. The newspaper people were defensive and depressed. What's more, with the exception of Baker, the clothes they wore were not nearly so stylish as those on the backs of the TV people. Newspapermen don't expect to be looked at.

Something similar was apparent at the [*MORE*] "counterconvention" in New York last year. [*MORE*] is a monthly magazine specializing in gossip about, and criticism of, the way journalists do their jobs. For four years now, invoking the name of the late A. J. Liebling, who wrote press criticism for *The New Yorker,* [*MORE*] has sponsored a convention supposedly "counter" to the establishmentarian meetings of the American Newspaper Publishers Association. Last year, all manner of media honchos, mostly male and mostly pale, gathered at the Hotel Commodore to complain about the imperfections of the trade they slum in and to compare book contracts.

Wallace and Rather had to beat off the groupies with a stick. It was not that they were, necessarily, better reporters than David Halberstam or Nora Ephron or Bryce Nelson or Charlayne Hunter. But they were themselves occasions, events—importance made corporeal. So much of our consciousness consists of television images that to meet the embodiment of one of these images is somewhat like meeting what it is you think you know, the contents of your own head. You tingle. At the same time, you are aware of the fact that you are not in their stock of images. They have that advantage over you: an inviolate consciousness . . . pure beings of the ether.

A letter to the July issue of [*MORE*] informs us that two women reporters at the convention

> sat down to await the start of a panel. A young man wearing staff insignia told them to get up. The seats, he said, were reserved for

the panelists. After some discussion, the two intruders vacated the seats. Then Mike Wallace sat down. He was not a panelist and this was pointed out to the apparatchik.

The apparatchik replied: "I'm in awe of power. I don't tell Mike Wallace what to do. There are two kinds of people in this world: people you can push around and people you don't. It's as simple as that."

On the Fourth of July in San Francisco, there was something called a Media Burn. It was organized by the Ant Farm, a local collective of "conceptual artists." They piled 44 old TV sets on top of one another in the parking lot of the Cow Palace, soaked them with kerosene and applied a torch. An actor pretending to be John F. Kennedy made a speech. Then someone climbed behind the wheel of a rebuilt 1959 Biarritz Cadillac, revved up and rammed the car into and through the wall of smoldering electrical detritus. Zowie. According to programs distributed before the event, onlookers were supposed to experience a "cathartic explosion" that would liberate them from the cultural tyranny of television. The conceptual artists—along with the network film crews they had invited to the Happening —recorded it all on video tape and then rushed home to see if their denunciation of TV would make the six-o'clock news. It is a nice existential point: We seem incapable of believing that we have actually done something until we see ourselves do it on television. Then it is "real." "Daddy," asked the little girl in the cartoon, "are we live or on tape?" Only Jack Ruby knows for sure.

> Lionel Barrymore was . . . a great fan of *Time for Beany*. When Louis B. Mayer decided that television was a threat to the motion-picture industry and forbade sets on his Metro-Goldwyn-Mayer studio lot, Barrymore sent his chauffeur to a local bar to watch the show and report on the plot developments.
> —*The Great Television Heroes*

I have been writing about television for eight years. Once I compared the medium to Jorge Luis Borges' concept of "the infinite." In *Avatars of the Tortoise,* Borges claims

once upon a time to have longed to compile "a mobile history" of the infinite, which he describes as "the numerous Hydra (the swamp monster which amounts to a prefiguration or emblem of geometric progressions)."

Swamp monster seemed an appropriate simile for television, as mobile history seemed for hundreds of reviews, each no more than 750 words long. Borges gave up on his project because it would require too many years of "metaphysical, theological and mathematical apprenticeship." He settled instead for gnomic riddles, as I have settled here for anecdotes—arbitrarily, if not randomly, strung together.

Borges at least is taken seriously. TV reviewers are not. Learn a trade, says your mother; weave baskets, find God, sell Wacky Packs, eat your Marcusian Rice Krispies. You are unserious because you are powerless to alter events or to cloud men's minds. By the time your comment appears in print, the object of it will have vanished or, if it persists, millions of other people will also already have seen it and made up their own minds. If your reviews are read at all, it is by those who seek a confirmation, either of their own gut reaction to a new program or of their suspicion that you are a jerk. You can no more review TV according to agreed-upon criteria than you can review politics or sports or old girl-friends—or compile a mobile history of the infinite. The lout on the next barstool also considers himself an expert.

But that is precisely the fascination. In writing about television, you are really writing about everything. Swamp monster isn't, after all, appropriate. TV is the sea we swim in. The trouble is that, like fish, we would be the last ones to notice that we were wet or to ask questions about the nature of *wetness*. Concluding his monumental three-volume history of broadcasting, Erik Barnouw remarks, "Five hours a day, 60 hours a week—for millions, television was merging with the environment. Psychically, it *was* the environment. What did all this mean?"

In fact, it's now up to six hours and eight minutes a day. That's how long the average set is on in the American home. Ninety-seven percent of American homes have at least one set. The average 16-year-old has clocked more time watching TV than he has spent in school. *TV Guide* outsells every other magazine on the nation's newsstands. Television is clearly more serious than venereal disease. And yet we go on breaking down this cultural phenomenon into individual components. We study violence, commercials, children's programing, news bias, situation comedy. Of *wetness,* we have only the dimmest of notions.

Theodore H. White, in his recently published book on the fall of Richard Nixon, *Breach of Faith,* at least gets the ball rolling!

One year before the [1952 Republican] convention opened, an event had exploded in American life comparable in impact to the driving of the Golden Spike, which, in 1869, tied America by one railway net from coast to coast. In September of 1951, engineers had succeeded in splicing together by microwave relay and coaxial cable a national television network; and two months later, late on a Sunday afternoon, November 18, 1951, Edward R. Murrow, sitting in a swivel chair in CBS Studio 41, had swung about, back to audience, and invited his handful of viewers (3,000,000 of them) to look. There before him were two television monitors, one showing the Golden Gate Bridge in San Francisco, the other showing the Brooklyn Bridge in New York. The cameras flicked again—there was the Statue of Liberty in New York and Telegraph Hill in San Francisco. Both at the same time. Live. The nation was collected as one, seeing itself in a new mirror, on a 12-inch television tube. Murrow then swiveled back to the audience and lifted his dark eyebrows in amusement, as if he were a magician performing a trick. . . .

And one realized this was no trick. On that tube, orchestrated by producers in New York, the battles of American politics would take place with ever increasing intensity; on its stage the emotions of America would be manipulated.

This is typical White—a fruitcake over which, with a heavy hand, the rum of foreboding has been poured. A disappointed romantic, he lapses into Spenglerianisms, gloomy odes. One of his many theses in *Breach of Faith* is that television, along with public-

relations agencies, changed American politics for the worse. Symbol and slogan were substituted for substantive discussion. Well, yes, indeed, "the emotions of America would be manipulated," as they had on the airwaves ever since Franklin D. Roosevelt's fireside chats on radio in the Thirties. It is unclear to me why this method of engaging political reality, of influencing decisions, is inferior to the back-room deals that gave us as Presidents Pierce, Buchanan, Grant, Hayes, Garfield, Arthur, two Harrisons, the on-again, off-again Cleveland, Taft, McKinley, Harding, Coolidge.

Such an argument is just a somewhat more elegant version of the apocalyptic nonsense advanced by Pat Buchanan, a recently disenfranchised Nixon Administration flunky who has found a home writing the "News Watch" column for *TV Guide.* According to Buchanan, TV news is undermining our democracy. Surveys show that since 1963, when the networks went to half-hour nightly programing, two thirds of the American people have come to rely on these programs as their principal source of information. Other surveys show that, during the past five years, more and more Americans have thought worse and worse of our Government, the business community, the legal profession, the Congress and our military forces. "What television journalism appears to be doing to the American body politic," says Buchanan, "is to undermine the foundation of public confidence in our institutions, and induce a sense of bewilderment in the American electorate."

Gosh. I'd suggest that more and more Americans think worse and worse of our Government because several Presidents have lied systematically to us on television, and one resigned before he could be impeached, and another pardoned *him* before he could be tried, and almost every agency of the Executive branch seems to have been used for partisan political purposes and/or to have participated in a cover-up of demonstrably illegal acts. We think worse of the business community because of its involvement in illegal campaign contributions, bribery of public officials here and abroad, grain deals, assassinations and other ways of overthrowing foreign governments. We think worse of the legal profession because so many lawyers went directly from Watergate to jail. We think worse of Congress because it let the war go on and let the economy fall apart. (Oddly enough, respect for Congress went up during the televised proceedings of the Rodino committee, a survey it was not in Buchanan's interest to mention, and so he didn't.) We think worse of the military because it lost a war and gained a My Lai.

Of course, the networks brought us all this bad news, sometimes belatedly, as in the cases of Vietnam and Watergate. Therefore, the networks are apparently to blame for doing what most American newspapers have shamefully refused to do for years, which is to tell us what we need to know, whether or not we want to know it. As Garry Wills has pointed out, most newspapers in this country are in business to boost the community; publish ads for movies, restaurants, banks, department stores and retail grocers; provide comic strips, recipes, astrology columns and obituaries. Foreign news is buried, if it is printed at all. National news is hinted at in a couple of paragraphs ripped off a wire-service teletype.

The fact of the matter is that broadcasting —originally a child of the military (wireless, radar, etc.), then a creature of a huge economic consortium (A.T.&T., General Electric, Westinghouse, RCA), then a mindless conduit of advertisers and the agencies who packaged all their programs (the food, auto and cosmetics industries, those wonderful folks who gave you the quiz-show scandals)— has almost by accident achieved an independence from commercial and local pressures unknown to much of our free press. It is this independence, this adversary capacity, that has attracted the attention of those in Government who confuse communication with agitprop. "No other nation on earth," says Buchanan, "tolerates the near unrestricted freedom or untrammeled power enjoyed by the national networks in the United States. And the position of these nations is a good deal more easy to appreciate today than ten years ago." Near unrestricted freedom or untrammeled power is presumably the private property only of Presidents, and Presidential

speechwriters who perpetrate phrases like more easy. General Amin of Uganda would appreciate this point of view, depending, of course, on the point in time.

Yes, Teddy White is more elegant, or, as Buchanan might put it, eleganter. White deplores the emphasis on "style" that television has brought to politics. (Why, then, was Richard Nixon, an almost totally styleless man, a fierce lump of Silly Putty, elected to the Presidency by the largest vote ever accorded a candidate for the office? To be sure, there were other factors. There are *always* other factors, which is why the "manipulation" of emotions antedates, coexists with and will outlast television.) He misses the larger point.

During the Sixties, as everybody by now is tired of hearing, our cultural coherence disintegrated. Whatever perceptions we held of ourselves as a people (sons of the Enlightenment, progressive, perfectible), whatever presumptions we indulged of our destiny as a nation (missionary of democracy, cop of the cosmos) took a brutal beating. There were bloody thumbprints of the irrational on every computer print-out. Our leaders couldn't appear in public without getting shouted down or shot down. We couldn't win a war against a bunch of little people in pajamas. Our children despised us and lost themselves in rock music, in the raptures and terrors of drugs, in dreams of blood; high-class, middle-class, working-class, they were all long-hairs—we couldn't see their ears, and if they hadn't any ears, how could they hear the eternal verities? High culture was routed in the academy. Popular culture turned to savage parody. The blacks stopped wanting any part of us. Women got uppity. Gays came loudly out of the closet. Athletes behaved like ingrates. Home-grown monks appeared on street corners peddling the nostrums of the East. Movies were dirty and the theater was abusive and even our astronauts were on the take.

We saw all this on television, and we saw something else, too. With the Presidency imperial in its arrogance, the Congress sluggish and deaf, the courts choked and confused, we saw the disaffected, the powerless, the outraged, the supplicatory and the spat upon petitioning the media, instead of the Government, for redress of grievance. It was, and is, extraordinary—a babel of victimization. See our faces, hear our voices. Even the oil companies, feeling misunderstood and unfairly blamed for the energy crisis, are doing it, sending out junior executives who have been trained before U.H.F. cameras to propagandize on talk shows. Television, these petitioners quite rightly believe, represents access to the consciousness of the nation. The nation may not like what it sees—it certainly didn't care for the McGovern convention, for instance, nor was it much moved by the various invasions of TV studios by militant homosexuals during "live" news programs—but it watches. What the nation *knows* is what is on TV. I submit that television *is* our culture, the only coherence we have going for us, naturally the repository of our symbols, the attic of old histories and hopes, the hinge on the doors of change. We may not believe our President, our Senators, our novelists, the deans of our universities, the ministers in our pulpits, the children sullen or surly in our living rooms, Jane Fonda, Robert Altman, Bill Buckley, Wilt Chamberlain or Melvin Belli. But we are more likely than not to agree with Jack Paar when he said, "I am not a religious man, but I do believe in Walter Cronkite."

Nor is this interpenetration, or consubstantiation, of American culture and television limited to the news programs. The situation comedy is nothing less than a socializing agency, as the family and the public school system are supposed to be: The sitcom, after a lot of thrashing about with events and personalities, instructs the members of its "family" —and the rest of us—on appropriate behavior, helps them internalize the various decencies, define the wayward virtues, modulate peeves, legislate etiquette, compromise the ineffability of self with the clamors of peer groups.

In the Fifties, that flabby decade, the sitcom proposed as a paradigm the incompetent father, the dizzy mother, the innocent child. In the Sixties, it proposed the incompetent father, the dizzy mother, the innocent child, war as a fun thing and young women with supernatural powers (witch, genie, magical nanny, flying nun) who could take care of their men and their children, look cute and never leave the house. In the Seventies, it proposes the incompetent father, the dizzy mother, the innocent child—all sitting around discussing abortion, infidelity, impotence, homosexuality, drug addiction and death—and the career girl (have talent, need sex). The inability of the American father to lace up the shoes of his own mind without falling off his rocker has been constant, perfectly reflecting and perpetuating our cultural expectations.

If the sitcom is a socializing agency, the talk show is a legitimizing agency. Ed Sullivan for 23 years used to be our legitimizing agency. His was the power of sanction. He advised us on what was permissible. He authenticated celebrity, significance. Without his stamp—right here on our stage—the package hadn't really arrived, whether it was a mayor of New York, a heavyweight champion, an all-American football player, a beauty queen or Elvis Presley. When he closed up shop in 1971, it was almost as if he realized that another legitimizing agency had usurped his function: Johnny Carson. Carson now presides over our consciousness. He sits, a toad with a jeweled eye, on our nights as though they were lily pads, croaking ad lib, conferring celebrity, defining the permissible. When Carson started making Watergate jokes, Nixon was done for: It was *all right* to make fun of the President. When he alluded to a toilet-paper shortage, the nation hoarded. When he left New York for Burbank, New York fell apart.

As it dimly perceives our needs as a nation, television tinkers with itself to accommodate and nurture. A nation cannot afford to lose its children and, therefore, television gave us *Mod Squad, The Young Lawyers, Storefront Lawyers,* John-Boy Walton, *Little House on the Prairie.* A nation cannot afford the secession of 25,000,000 citizens, even if their citizenship has been but partially and grudgingly conceded, and so television gave us Diahann Carroll *(Julia),* Bill Cosby *(I Spy)* and Flip Wilson (the first male TV star since Milton Berle regularly to wear a dress), and when they didn't work, it gave us *Sanford and Son, Good Times, The Jeffersons* and a lot of black detectives, private and public. A nation cannot afford offending and alienating women with brains who do real work, and so television gave us, instead of cutie-pie housewife witches, magical nannies, flying nuns and dreamed-of genies, a Mary Tyler Moore, a Diana Rigg, a Valerie Harper, a Karen Valentine, a Cloris Leachman and *Police Woman*. If two Kennedys were killed off, Hal Holbrook as a *Bold One* would be born and then be borrowed later on to suggest that homosexuals can have Meaningful Relationships. If the institution of marriage was in disrepute, *Rhoda* would do the rehabilitating and the nation would weep with joy for the first time since *I Love Lucy* had a baby in prime time.

In addition, television creates style as much as it records it. Crybabyism was perfect for the Fifties, from Nixon with his Checkers speech to Jack Paar and his fat daughter to Charles Van Doren and Dave Garroway sob-ridden at what President Eisenhower called "a terrible thing to do to the American public"; that is, cheating. The Sixties, as Teddy Kennedy found out after he tried to explain Chappaquiddick on television to an unbelieving public, required something more than squeezing your sincerity like a lemon. TV in the Sixties found it in the style of the media brat. The media brat could be political, like Abbie Hoffman, or commercial, like Mason Reese, but was more likely to be sporty, like Muhammad Ali, Mark Spitz and Jimmy Connors. They are, arguably, the best prize fighter, swimmer and tennis bum in the world. Yet there is something inauthentic about their image on the TV screen and they seem to know it— something pinched in the face, something ungenerous in the eyes, a lack of conviction about themselves as actors, for which they try to compensate by antics and strenuous gesturing. It is a quality of seeming not quite to believe the celebrity conferred on you, so young, by the camera; a fidgety smugness takes over; what if, when the red light blinks off, you cease to exist? The media brats are the new heavies: most of the nation roots for them to lose. They are the children of our watching, and our own children imitate them, and they must be punished.

What are we doing when we watch the Super Bowl each January on television, with a half time full of star-spangled leotards, lunar modules, SAC bombers in friendly overflight, prisoners of war, the obligatory black singing the obligatory anthem and the obligatory Vice-President biting the nose of Pete Rozelle? What does it mean when we celebrate the rising of the national sappiness each spring by watching the Academy Awards? Are both of them exhibition games to prepare for the Bicentennial, when we will bestow a championship cup, an Oscar, on ourselves?

What are we doing and what it means are both aspects of the same activity and significance that attaches to our rapt watching of a Kennedy or a Martin Luther King funeral cortege, an Apollo lift-off, the Olympics with or without the murder of Israeli athletes, Armstrong walking on the moon, a President in China or a President resigning, the world series. We are participating with ourselves as a nation. There is really no other way to participate, given the state of the family, the church, the town, the state, the arts. When there is an assassination or a Cuban Missile Crisis, or the Beatles appear on the Sullivan show, or Joe McCarthy takes on the American Army and loses, or Joe Namath takes on the National Football League and wins, or Kennedy plays Nixon in the Great Debates and Billie Jean King plays Bobby Riggs in the Great Hustle, wherever we are, we turn on the set and watch, because that is what we will talk about tomorrow, that is what we know, that is one of the few things of which we will be certain.

Fragmented, mobile, restless, dispersed, we are nomads on an industrial grid. We get in our cars and go. But when we get there, where are we, and what did we leave behind? With our TV sets, we are one big *Mary Hartman, Mary Hartman* wherever we happen to be, hearing the same messages, commercials for the salvation of the soul and floor wax. Television is another kind of car, a windshield on the world. We climb inside it, drive it, and it drives us, and we all go in the same direction, see the same thing. It is more than a mobile home; it is a mobile nation. It has become, then, our common language, our ceremony, our style, our entertainment and anxiety, our sympathetic magic, our way of celebrating, mourning, worshiping. It's flimsy glue, but for the moment it's the only thing holding us together.

49

From Heroes to Sandwiches: The Selling of a TV Pilot

David Handler

The process by which a program idea is translated into on-screen reality in television demands as much negotiation and sales skill as it does creative imagination. As in the film industry (see David Freeman's "The Great American Screenplay Competition," in the previous section), writers compete to tailor their ideas to current conceptions of what producers and the audience will buy. The process of marketing a television series idea, like a movie idea, involves the input of many people, whose concepts often conflict with one another.

In the following section, syndicated TV critic and screenwriter David Handler tells his tale of a comedy-adventure series script that went through so much rewriting the only element that survived was the title. The initial concept of three guys running a detective agency in a two-hour program gradually shifted to a half-hour comedy series about two guys who run a diner. In the end, the network decided to abandon the effort.

Tease

Give me something small,'' said the New York television producer. "Something doable.'' My partner and I had just rewritten a TV-movie for him. He liked it. He liked it so much, he invited us to bring in some ideas of our own. But first he warned us that he didn't want to do a picture about surfers. "I don't want Malibu. Give me New York.''

Now we are back in the producer's office, ready to dazzle him with a small, non-surfing idea.

The producer, a ferretlike fellow in his late 30s, is dressed casually. He wears an inferiority complex in place of a necktie. The first time I met him, he asked me if I had any idea how it felt being second banana to a rich, powerful executive producer. I said I didn't. Today he leans back in his swivel chair, his feet dangling about a foot from the floor. He plays with an ornate cigarette lighter, which leaves nothing on his desk. No papers. No pens. Producing, a producer once told me, is "basically writing without a typewriter.''

We pitch our small idea. Three young college graduates make a pact to kiss the 9-to-5 world goodbye and pursue a dream instead—to open a New York City detective agency. The hook is that each guy's dream is drawn from fiction, not real life. Jonathan Soames, a gangly math wizard, patterns his life after Sherlock Holmes. Mitch Gerard is an overweight bumbler from the suburbs who wishes he'd been born a Dead End Kid and grown up to be Sam Spade. Terry Rimer is a tough, handsome amateur boxer who draws his personal habits from the Steve McQueen characterization in "Bullitt." They rent an office in a seedy downtown building, next door to a pair of poverty-row talent agents, enlist an old rummy cop to front for the license, and they're in business. They stumble onto a case. Complications, danger and, ultimately, justice ensue. The film will be a comedy held together with a straight detective plot.

It is New York. It may even have pilot possibilities. It is nothing if not doable.

The producer loves it. He can't talk now. Lunch next week, definitely. "We only have one problem," he says as he ushers us out. "The networks aren't buying New York movies."

Roll Title, Credits, Theme Music

My scriptwriting partner, Peter Gethers, and I spend most of our time working for the print media. Many in the print media consider TV a shameless sellout. We are not among them. We write scripts for fun and profit. Even for relative unknowns like ourselves, a script for a TV-movie or a series pilot can be worth $30,000 to $40,000—with perhaps 25 percent up front, another 35 percent when you've finished a draft and the rest usually dribbling in during the stages of revision. If the pilot becomes a series, you might see at least $2000 every week the show is on the air—even if you don't write another word. And for an extraordinary hit, you'll reap a royalty harvest from syndication and overseas sales.

So my partner and I were mildly ecstatic when our small TV-movie idea made it to the next rung on the TV-production ladder—a pilot idea, one of 150 the network bought that season. Of those, only 30 were shot. Ours was not one of them. What happened? Television's lunatic creative process is what happened. Briefly put, what we started with was a two-hour movie. What the network bought was a pilot for a one-hour action comedy about three young guys who open a detective agency. What they ended up with before the

project was mercifully scrapped was a half-hour situation comedy about two guys who run a diner. The project was called "Heroes." That was the only thing that didn't change, except in the beginning the title referred to courage and in the end it meant sandwiches.

You think I'm kidding? Then let's go back to our story.

Act One

We take a lunch. The producer is still gushing. He has one suggestion: instead of making the three leads college buddies, what if they're strangers who bump into each other? That way their backgrounds could be more diverse. It seems a reasonable concession, so we make them three guys who work in the same building. Jonathan, the Holmes character, is a computer expert. Mitch, the bumbler, writes ad slogans. Rimer, the man of action, is a maintenance man. Fate brings them together in a stuck elevator.

The producer has a particular network he thinks he can sell the idea to. He'll set up a meeting; we'll do up a treatment. A treatment is like a prospectus for a housing tract. It lists the salient features in glowing terms and promises plenty. You hope someone nibbles.

A week later we sit in a corner office with the producer and six network people. There are three energetic men in three-piece suits and a woman wearing a plaid wool skirt held together by a large safety pin. These are programming associates. There is also a young, mustachioed intern. And last but decidedly not least is the network's head programming executive, whose desk we are fanned around. He is on the phone to the Coast. He is ashen, being devoured by stomach acid. The Nielsen overnight ratings are very bad. He is talking about canning last night's sitcom for a new sitcom. It's not an easy decision—neither he nor the guy on the other end has seen the new show.

He hangs up, then he slumps in his chair and sighs. He can't figure out why the sitcom had such a bad night. His 14-year-old daughter loved the show. She thought it was cute.

"What else does she like?" the producer asks.

"I don't let her watch much," the executive replies. "I was thinking about getting cable and Home Box Office—those guys have all the good stuff—but I'm afraid she'll spend all her time watching television.

The producer nods sympathetically and tells the executive that we're two writers who have just done some fantastic work for another network and that we have an idea for a two-hour movie with great pilot possibilities.

The executive has already heard good things about our previous movie, which won't be on for another month. Good word travels fast. (The only thing that travels faster is bad word.) So we pitch our idea. It's a smooth sales job by now. The network people nod on cue; they laugh on cue. We dangle bait; they gobble it. They want to like it.

Someone worries it might be too much like the late NBC detective series *Richie Brockelman, Private Eye.* We say it won't be. Someone else is bothered by the nostalgia business, and the seediness. We say the movie doesn't depend on nostalgia or seediness, that they're just Tabasco.

The executive asks if we have anything on paper. We hand him the treatment. He puts it on the desk without looking at it, turns to the producer and says, "I think it's cute as hell." The associates nod in agreement. "I think we can go with this one.

"The only problem is we're not doing two-hour pilots any more. I'd be more comfortable with a one-hour." He turns to us. "Would there be any serious problem with that?"

We shake out heads. It's a deal. Then we're in an elevator going down 32 floors to the street below. We were in the building about 15 minutes.

Act Two

We have to get our pilot story approved before we can actually start writing. The producer is in Rome, but we can meet with his boss, the executive producer. Once he approves the story, we go back to the network for an OK. Then we go to work.

The executive producer comes out to the reception desk to greet us. He wears a sports shirt open to the navel, slacks, Gucci loafers, no socks.

"How are you, you lucky SOBs?" he exclaims as we go into his office and sit down. On the credenza behind his desk are framed photographs of him shaking hands with three former Presidents of the United States.

We go over the setup. We wrap up by saying it's a detective show with the emphasis on comedy.

"What kind of comedy?" he asks.

"Character comedy."

"Any of the guys Jewish?"

"Not exactly. The chubby one is from the suburbs—"

"If you write him funny, you're writing him Jewish." He stands and begins to pace around the room. "Listen, all humor is Jewish. You know what I mean? What you have to do for television," he says, "is Gentile it out." He sits down. "They clean-cut guys? I don't want them Woodstocky, with the hair down to here."

"They're just regular guys," we reply. "Guys you'd like. Guys who have a crazy ambition. For once, they're going to realize their ambition. That's what this show is all about."

It is one of our best lines. It always leaves them speechless.

"OK," he continues, "what didn't the network like?"

"The setting. We want a seedy part of town; they want a nicer atmosphere."

He suggests a compromise—an office in a slightly dogeared brownstone that's on a nice block in midtown.

"There wouldn't be a serious problem with that," we agree. This is a key response in the TV writer's repertoire. It means you can incorporate the suggestion without damaging the whole. If it would do damage, then you fight it. Or you trade. We give up Gold & Gould, the talent agents next door, for a 24-hour answering service staffed by struggling, bosomy actresses. In exchange we get to keep Bert, the old security guard who fronts for the neophyte sleuths. The executive producer isn't crazy about him.

"So where do they go when they're not working?" he asks.

"A bar with a dart board, no women and Billie Holiday on the jukebox."

"You can't have three young guys hang around in a bar."

"Quincy goes to a bar."

"He's a doctor, and it's a nice bar. No, the bar's out. Make it young, make it hip, make it . . . a health-food bar. Yeah, with the broads in sweat pants drinking carrot juice—"

"What about a greasy-spoon diner? It might be more natural."

He stands up, starts pacing again. "OK. What about an owner? Maybe an old Jewish guy?"

"You mean something like Feinberg's Eats? Then we may as well go back to Gold & Gould."

"You're right. Stale. How about a Puerto Rican?"

"Maybe he bought the place from Feinberg but hasn't changed the name yet. So people call him Feinberg—"

"Even though his name is Rojas. Which is hysterical because you'll write him Jewish anyway. A Jewish Puerto Rican. That's funny. Has anybody done that lately?"

It's settled. Next comes the story.

"Don't worry about a plot," he advises. "Steal one. From an old mystery or something. We've all been ripping off Shakespeare for years anyway."

We give him our story. A mad scientist invents a domestic robot and then disappears with the plans and prototype. The boys learn he's been kidnaped. They mount a black-tie dinner party at Feinberg's to smoke out the culprit.

The executive producer is tired. He says the story sounds fine. We win that one on endurance.

We make an appointment to pitch it to the network people. The producer, back from Rome, meets us 30 minutes before the meeting. We tell him the story idea. He doesn't like it. He doesn't like it at all. He can't believe the boss approved it.

"You can't use kidnaping on television any more. He knows that. The network will never go for it."

"Should we cancel the meeting?"

That would mean overruling the executive producer.

"No, let's go in with it and hope for the best. I don't know what he was thinking."

The network executive is now in a different office. Two of the programming associates have gone to the Coast in exchange for one new associate, a first-round draft pick and cash. We tell them the story, and they like it. They wonder if maybe the invention could be something a bit more ordinary, what with so many kooky people. The producer offers a tennis ball that never loses its bounce. We settle on a razor blade that doesn't get dull. They say nothing against the kidnaping. They say nothing about the kidnaping at all.

Act Three

The producer loves our first draft. "This is really something special," he tells us over the phone. "It's funny. No, it's more than funny."

He submits it to the network without asking us to make any revisions. We are, of course, pleased.

The network is not.

"It's not what they were expecting," reports the producer. "They think it's weird. It's a comedy."

"An *action* comedy."

"They don't think the action works. Too complicated."

"So we'll simplify it."

"They think it's funny. They loved the bit with the diner. But they can't relate to an hour comedy."

"It's not an hour comedy. It's a detective show—*with* comedy. That's what we told them we would write."

"We have a meeting with them next week."

We aren't invited. By "we" he means the executive producer and himself. They clue us in a week later, in the producer's office.

"They don't want an hour comedy," says the executive producer.

"But—"

"Look, I'm not going to defend them. I'm just going to tell you what the deal is. I salvaged it as a half-hour."

"*Salvaged? Half-hour?* What kind of detective show can we write in 30 minutes?"

"It's not a detective show any more. It's a sitcom. The network can't deal with it any other way."

We're stunned.

"Keep the locations down," cautions the producer. "A little detective stuff. But funny."

"Simple plots," adds the executive producer. "Neighborhood crimes."

"So most of it takes place in the office?"

"They didn't like the office. They thought the diner was cute. The boys are basically amateurs. Give them regular jobs and have them hang around in the diner on their off hours. A booth in the back is their office—that's all they need."

"What about the old guy?"

"Out."

"The answering service?"

"Out."

"Feinberg?"

"Leave him in. But give him a cute daughter to wait on the tables. Get a broad in there."

"Take out the old detective-movie stuff," urges the producer. "Make it real. It wasn't real."

We put on our coats. "Is the network still interested?"

"Absolutely. They think it's funny."

Back to work. We eliminate the hook that based our heroes' personalities on fictional sleuths. Instead, we give them jobs to fit their natural tendencies. Jonathan becomes a violin teacher, Mitch writes jokes for greeting cards and cocktail napkins, and Rimer is a locksmith.

We give Feinberg/Rojas a daughter and come up with a couple of simple plots involving the diner. The producer loves the job changes and thinks our first story idea sounds perfect. The executive producer likes the job ideas. He doesn't like the story. "You're all over the place. Stay in your arena. Forget the detecting."

"But they're amateur detectives."

"That's a real problem," he admits. "It would be much easier if they weren't."

"That's what we've got going for us."

The boss gets up and starts pacing again. "Why do they hang around in the diner?"

"Because we eliminated the office."

"I know that. But why do they hang out there?"

"It's their hangout. They like it there."

"But why? Do you see what I'm getting at? Just because they like the burgers isn't enough. Why don't we make Feinberg the fat kid's father? That way he has to work there part time."

"But Feinberg is a Puerto Rican."

"So make the kid a Puerto Rican."

"That's kind of getting away from what we—"

"Look, I know I sold the network a half-hour detective comedy, but I don't think it's going to work with this setup."

"All we need is a story."

"If you have trouble with the story, it's because the format doesn't work."

The producer nods.

"If you've got a good format," continues the boss, "you should have five, six, seven ideas right off the top of your head. I don't have any ideas for this." He turns to the producer. "Do you?"

The producer shakes his head.

We promise them that if they give us a week we'll come up with five, six, seven good stories. It's a promise we can't keep. We can't develop a natural detective plot out of the diner. It's true—there is no real reason for them to be in the diner. Unless, as the executive producer suggested, one of the guys is related to the owner. Unless, of course, they own the place themselves.

Act Four

It's the only way the pilot will work. So what if the boys run a beanery? They'll still be three good guys who help out folks in the neighborhood. It wasn't our original idea, but who can remember the original idea?

We come up with a diner-comedy format and call the producer. He's out and won't return our calls. His secretary is no longer authorized to set up appointments on his behalf.

We're not hot any more.

After two weeks of rejection we call our agent. He calls the producer just to say we haven't lost any enthusiasm for the project and hope that he, the producer, hasn't either. Tell them to call me, says the producer. We do. He's not in, but his secretary will be glad to set up a story conference.

He's 45 minutes late for the meeting.

We pitch the new format: our heroes grew up together reading comic books in Feinberg's. Feinberg/Rojas wants to retire, so they buy him out. They want to preserve the old neighborhood, provide a wholesome hangout for kids and prevent mean Moe Sharkey from getting 100 percent of the street's food trade. Sharkey runs the slick, jumbo coffee shop across the street, and has been trying to put Feinberg out of business for 15 years.

Our lead characters plug neatly into the new format. Jonathan is now a temperamental chef, Mitch a clumsy waiter, Rimer the counterman to whom the customers tell their troubles. The diner will be the ultimate teen hangout, with pinball machines, jukebox, etc. A lot of old people eat there, too, because there's no minimum like at Sharkey's. A hangout for the have-nots. It seems like a natural.

"This is tight and good," agrees the producer." "We can do this. How about a story?"

We've got a dandy. Rimer befriends a homely 13-year-old girl who is new to the neighborhood. He asks her why she isn't friends with the rest of the kids. She says nobody ever likes her, that she'd much rather run away to the woods and live there. Rimer says it sounds great. She falls in love with him. As the boys are closing up that night, she shows up. She's running away from home and is fetching Rimer for their journey together—

The producer's phone rings. It's a very big film star. He needs her for a feature he's trying to get off the ground. We offer to step outside. He jovially says not to bother.

"Hi, sweetheart," he says to the big star. "Can we count on you? You've had us on hold for six months and if you don't want the part there are several other actresses in town we can go with."

A loud shriek comes out of the phone. He has made a serious error. "No . . . no . . .

I'm not trying to pressure you," he protests. "No . . . I'm so sorry . . . I didn't mean it." He says he's sorry 10 more times and hangs up. She has reduced him to an apologetic errand boy. It's not the best medicine for his inferiority complex, especially because we've witnessed the entire thing.

We suggest we can resume on another day. He insists we finish the story.

So we finish. Rimer persuades the girl to confront the folks she wants to be friends with. She's a nice person, a good person, and once they get to know her they'll appreciate that.

"Who's going to believe that stuff?" the producer suddenly snarls. "You think you can just earn respect by being nice to people? By being honest? It's like with me and that bitch. You think honesty pays? You have to lie! That's the only way people will like you."

The phone interrupts him. It's the big star's agent. This time we step outside for coffee. The story conference resumes 15 minutes later. The producer is calmer, but his outburst has left its mark on the story. "What I mean," he explains, "is that she has to *prove* herself. You need a contest or something. What about the pinball machines? Make her a wizard. She's better than all the guys. You know, like the girls with the boys' Little League teams."

We agree to toy with the idea.

Act Five

Our third trip to the network. It's the same programming executive but he's in yet another office. One of the associates who had been traded to the Coast is now back.

"We're going to throw a curve ball at you," announces the producer. "We realize that this is a big transish [that's show-biz lingo for transition]. But these guys came back with 10 different stories and we realized that the format we settled on just wouldn't work."

They say fine and sit back to listen. We pitch the diner comedy. They like it. They aren't as enthusiastic as they were about the original idea, but they agree it has possibilities.

Next comes the pinball story. Our homely 13-year-old girl is now a pinball fanatic. So is Moe Sharkey, their arch rival. He often comes into the diner to hustle the kids for quarters.

"Your pilot plot can't come in through the door," interjects an associate. "It has to come from your principals."

"Why don't you make her Feinberg's daughter?" suggests the executive.

"Feinberg is no longer in the show," we reply.

"You could leave him in," he suggests, gently but firmly. "Make him the cook. He's funny."

"Jonathan's the cook."

"Write him as the little girl. She can be the stable one, keeps the books."

"Another thing," pipes up a different associate. "You can't have Sharkey, an adult, competing with little kids. Why don't you give him a son?"

"He can be the neighborhood bully," agrees the executive.

No serious problem. Back to the story. The girl is probably a better pinball player than Sharkey's son, but she's afraid to play him. Rimer persuades her to take him on. She does, betting him the amount of money our heroes owe the butcher for their last three months' worth of meat. They have a showdown—

"Wait," interrupts the executive. "You can't hang a comedy pilot plot on a gambling proposition. I'm sorry. You'll have to come up with another story."

"But we just redesigned the show to accommodate this story," we protest.

"I like the changes," he replies. "Stay with them. Come back to us when you have another story. No rush. You've still got a good shot as a summer replacement." He turns to the producer. "Curve accepted."

Downstairs we agree to call the producer the following week to set up a story confer-ence. He tells us he has a really good feeling about us again.

We come up with two new stories incor-porating the changes that arose out of the de-funct pinball story. We call the producer to set up a meeting, but he is in Mexico scouting locations for a feature. He has left word that we should meet with the executive producer instead. We are transferred to the boss's sec-retary. The next couple of weeks look really bad for him, she tells us. She suggests we call back in two weeks. When we do, he's now on location at the Astoria Studios in Queens. But the producer is back in town. We're trans-ferred to the producer's secretary. Yes, she says, he's back. But he's in preproduction for the feature he was scouting in Mexico. He won't be able to see us until he's finished with that.

"When should we call back?"

"Why don't you try in about two months?" she replies.

Tag

A few weeks later we sell an idea for a film script to one of the studios. Our agent calls the producer's agent to tell him that we'd like to get out of the pilot. The producer has the option to continue it with different writers. The producer's agent says he will pass the word along. He thinks the producer will just let it die.

It occurs to us that we could salvage our "Heroes" experience by turning it into a TV-movie itself. It's got pilot possibilities, but we abandon the idea. It's doable, all right, but we can't figure out whether it's a comedy, a disaster film, a comedy film with disaster or a disaster film with comedy.

Roll Closing Credits, Coming Attractions

50
Prime Time Chic:
Between Newsbreaks
and Commercials,
the Values Are L.A. Liberal

Michael J. Robinson

The themes of television drama and situation comedy have changed over the years to include the most controversial issues of our time, such as abortion, drugs, and religion. In the following article from *Public Opinion,* Michael J. Robinson, who specializes in the relationship between television and politics at Catholic University, examines the values presented on network television series and finds an almost consistent liberal bias. Borrowing from Ben Stein's book, *The View from Sunset Boulevard,* Robinson explains how the political and social values prevalent among television writers and producers find their way into our living rooms.

With few exceptions, prime time has become a plug for sexual openness and freedom. But the plug doesn't stop there. Entertainment television serves as a soft-core, progressive statement about love, marriage, drugs, blacks, women, and gays. Between the news breaks and the commercials, the values on prime-time television are consistently liberal chic.

Programs like "Laverne and Shirley" can dilute but can't neutralize what has developed into a schedule of socially hedonistic, superficially liberal shows.

This season's top twenty contains both kinds of liberal chic—the political and the social. We still watch "M.A.S.H.," a show that satirizes war, the military, U.S. foreign policy, and "All in the Family," the Norman Lear production that made liberal chic legitimate on TV, even in its most blatant political theme.

A good percentage of the newer shows in the top twenty this season are less political, but are every bit as socially liberal as the last generation of programming—shows like "One Day at a Time" that paint life as a socio-sexual odyssey in which mothers and daughters discuss their intimate lives as if they were the weather. Or shows like "Soap" that treat WASP values and behavior as if they were diseases. Shows like "What's Happening" in which blacks act like whites, only better. Or shows like "Three's Company"—last fall's highest rated show—which regards multiple cohabitation as the preferred living arrange-

Source: From *Public Opinion* (March/May 1979). © American Enterprise Institute, 1979. Reprinted by permission of the publisher.

ment and implies that group sex isn't so much immoral as confusing.

Political liberal prime time started with the "Smothers Brothers" and ended, more or less, with "Maude." But the social liberalism of "Laugh-In" remains very much alive. The only programs that are willing (dare?) to offer traditional social values are the *nostalgia* shows like "The Waltons," "Happy Days" or "Little House on the Prairie." Contemporary settings almost always mean liberal chic on network television.

While the era of "All in the Family" may be fading, the Lear revolution has been preserved by painting hookers, housewives, and homosexuals as heroes, junkies as misunderstood kids, and blacks, Indians, and Puerto Ricans as the noblest of all Americans. In the new TV world, bad guys are white, suburban, thirtyish, and straight.

But what can we expect to be the implications of all this? After ten years of prime-time chic, we may finally be seeing some results "out there"—not just in the corporate board rooms and suburban bedrooms, where women, blacks, and gays are asserting themselves in all manner of ways—but in the polls, where more and more Americans are accepting the unconventional, progressive or liberal social behavior that people in prime time either practice or condone. So, although my own values *support* gay rights, feminism, integration, and sexual freedom, I think it's time for admission and recognition by liberals like me, and everybody else, that prime-time chic exists—and that it matters.

A Shift to the Right . . . And the Left?

People don't admit to being liberal anymore. Between 1963 and 1976, the portion of the public labeling itself "liberal" fell from 49 percent to 26 percent. Between 1964 and 1974, the percentage of people who preferred membership in a conservative party jumped from 49 to 57. In November's elections, the Republicans picked up seats in *both* the House and the Senate—the first time they've done that since 1966. Liberals like Udall run as progres-

sive and Jerry Brown is preaching the political economy of Calvin Coolidge.

But the same public which began shifting to the right *politically* in the late sixties has been shifting to the left *socially* since about the same time and at about the same rate. The Gallup poll and Harris poll find that between 1969 and 1977—

- The portion of the public regarding premarital sex as "not at all wrong" increased 16 percent.
- The portion believing that an abortion decision should be left up to a woman and her doctor increased by 13 percent. By 1978 less than 20 percent of the population believed abortions should be illegal in all circumstances.
- The portion regarding marijuana as "a serious problem" decreased by 19 percent.
- The portion admitting to having tried marijuana increased by a factor of six!

The country has even mellowed about gay rights over the last five years. According to last June's Gallup poll, a clear majority— 56 percent—now thinks that homosexuals deserve equality in job opportunities. Anita Bryant has not spoken for a silent majority.

Race relations follow the same pattern. The percentage approving of interracial marriage—in theory at least—has almost doubled since 1968. The percentage willing to vote for a qualified black as president has more than doubled in the last twenty years. As of summer 1978, 77 percent of the white population said that they would support a qualified black.

TV Is Divided into Two Parts

One thing that could help explain why the country has been moving in two directions at once is television. At the networks, television comes in two basic styles—news and entertainment. Although news and entertainment often look alike, they make for different kinds of effects.

Despite the brouhaha about elitist, liberal commentators controlling the airwaves, a good case can be made for believing that over the past decade and a half network news has been helping to move national opinion toward political conservatism.

With its unique audience and with a unique penchant for the sensational, the bizarre, and the negative—especially when it comes to scandals and snafus in Washington—network journalism has played a role in undermining public confidence in national governments, New Deal-style or otherwise.

Tying forty million nightly viewers to the day's most "newsworthy" film clips—as networks define newsworthy—would produce public frustration with almost any imaginable administration or set of policies, and has since 1963. My own research shows that people who depend upon TV news for following current events are more hostile toward the national government and more alienated from politics than people who don't. In addition, people who were most hooked on network news back in the late sixties were also more committed to George Wallace, psychologically and at the polls, than anybody else in the electorate.

Of course, Watts, Vietnam, Watergate, and stagflation were real events as well as media events. None of them made big government look like the bargain that the Roosevelt generation had led us to expect. The about-face of the political right can thus be seen as part medium, part message—and not very surprising.

What is surprising has been the continuing drift in the other direction—toward social liberalism.

Fingering entertainment television as the cause of any social phenomenon—good or bad—has developed into a new form of national pastime. But in this instance, a little fingering is probably deserved. One can make at least as strong a case for arguing that prime time has helped to shift the public toward the "social left" as for arguing that news time has moved us the other way. In fact, the case for prime-time liberalism is easier. Arguing that TV news causes conservative opinion requires subtlety, if not a little intellectual sleight of hand. Arguing that prime time causes social liberalism is very direct.

What's on TV?

We can start with the content. Prime time has been pushing liberal social themes since just after the free speech movement began at Berkeley. Some prime-time critics feel that entertainment television still lacks any sort of solid, liberal credentials. Muriel Cantor, Professor of Communications at American University and long-time analyst of television production, says that despite the new image of prime time, "TV is one of the most conservative of media—an instrument of social control . . . themes which appear to be liberal are really cover-ups." And Cantor is hardly alone in painting prime time as a lesson in corporate state values.

But a growing number of critics think that prime time *is* socially liberal—especially compared with its former shadow self.

Much of the griping about prime-time television comes from the fundamentalist, Christian right wing—groups that send out packets on how to monitor TV programs for indecency or how to get the FCC to stop licensing licentious broadcasters. But social scientists also find that television has plenty of "progressive" social values built into it and that the trend may be getting stronger. The clearest example, as any fundamentalist will tell you, is sex.

Nobody in his right mind could argue that television is hard-core. Sex never happens on serial TV. It has *just* happened or is *about* to happen. But prime time is heavily sex-oriented and getting more so, as producers challenge the censors and, more importantly, as the networks themselves try to compensate viewers for recent cutbacks in violence.

Television loves sex—especially sex between consenting adults who happen *not* to be married to each other. The Summer, 1978 edition of the *Journal of Communication,* perhaps the most distinguished of the scholarly journals that trace popular culture and the media, contains an article that analyzes fifty-eight hours of entertainment TV—one episode from each prime time and Saturday morning dramatic series from the 1976–77 season. In their research, the four authors (Collado, Greenberg, Korzenny, and Atkin) counted and found (actual or implied) "five instances of homosexual or heterosexual rape, seven instances of homosexual acts, twenty-eight instances of prostitution, forty-one instances of sexual intercourse ('unmarried'), and only six instances of sexual intercourse between 'marriage partners.'" Unmarried triumphed over married sex almost seven to one! A second study just completed by Eli Rubinstein at Stony Brook indicates that the level of sexual innuendo in prime time increased by a factor of five between 1975 and 1977.

Neither study makes clear whether all this sex is pictured positively or negatively. But with unmarried sex outdistancing married sex seven-to-one in prime time, network TV can hardly be criticized for reflecting traditional sexual values, although it might be attacked for reflecting contemporary reality.

Of course, prime time rarely takes a dim view of sexuality in any of its hybrid forms. The pilot for ABC's new crime show, "Vega$," turns a teenage hooker into a heroine. In the pilot for "Flying High," CBS's less than adequate answer to "Charlie's Angels," all three female leads, playing stewardesses, try to have sex with the same man—the very unlikely Jim Hutton. As the plot developed, Hutton would have had them all (and they him) except he fell asleep with bachelorette number one and got too sunburned to be touched by bachelorette number two. The end of the show was vintage prime-time chic. The one stewardess (Kathryn Witt) who made the Hutton connection gets applause—not chastisement—from her roommates along with all the flight passengers after they finally figure out what Witt and Hutton have been up to.

Even the straightest of shows practices the same permissive sex. "Love Boat," television's version of Noah's Ark, in which ABC brings on board one of every stereotypic species known to situation comedy, moves back and forth between old-fashioned and new-style permissiveness. "Love Boat's" captain, Gavin MacLeod—the same guy who played hopelessly straight Murray on the old "Mary Tyler Moore Show''—now supports mature, open sexuality among consenting, passenger adults, including himself.

On one show last season MacLeod welcomed aboard a divorced high school crush of thirty years earlier, played by Jessica Walter. MacLeod wooed her until she seduced him. As "Love Boat" reaches its destination, Walter tells the captain that it's been great, but now it's over. In a classic, made-for-modern-TV, sex-role reversal, woman tells man that she's going back to her career and that captains aren't supposed to abandon ship after every affair. It's prime time's vapid version of Bergman telling Bogart what to do—to wise up and get on the plane.

Women of Prime Time

Prime time isn't just sexually progressive—some programs work almost harder at being socially liberal than being libertine. For instance, feminism has been doing much better on prime time than feminist-oriented critics ever admit.

The "Mary Tyler Moore Show" became an ironic target for organized feminist criticism two years ago when the U.S. Civil Rights Commission published its first edition of *Window Dressing on the Set: Women and Minorities in Television*. The Commission report criticized Mary Tyler Moore for calling her boss "Mr. Grant" even though everyone else calls him "Lou," an egregious act that the Commission considered a sign that women on TV "still tend to be subordinate to men in their lives."

But most critics saw Mary Richards—Moore's *nomme de tube*—as a proto-feminist, at the very least. As a single, sexually interested TV producer, Richards was more independent and professional than most mid-thirties American women—and so was Rhoda—and so were all the MTM female leads that spun off from Mary Tyler Moore.

In fact, between 1969 and 1974, 15 percent of the prime-time white females played roles as professional women, according to the very same Rights Commission study that tried to crucify the networks for their continuous sexist programming. That figure of 15 percent not only overstated the percent of professional women "out there," it was greater than the figure for professional black males on TV and wasn't all that far behind the percent for white males.

Judging from the newest edition of *Window Dressing,* published this January, one has to wonder as much about the objectivity of the Commission as the alleged insensitivity of the networks to women. The Commission's own "Update" shows that women are not only doing better on TV but have caught up with men in some important dimensions. Comparing the 1975–1977 performances to 1969–1974, Commission records show that the number of white women depicted in prime time as "professional" had risen to 18 percent, while for white men, the number had fallen to 19 percent. Seven of this season's Top Twenty shows have female leads, and in the new genre of prime time, most of the female leads are smarter and more independent than many of the males. Charlie's "angels"—favorite targets of both Christian and feminist critics—forsake their own dates, à la James Bond, week by week to solve crimes committed by men that the angels always manage to outsmart. Even Laverne and Shirley, who get hung in effigy by critics of all shapes and descriptions, depend on each other, not on their men. Their two male friends, Lenny and Squiggy, play Lucy and Ethel, while Shirley and Laverne really play Ricky and Fred—dumb, but less dumb.

It's hard to make a case for liberated commercials. Ads are the last real frontier for TV's once unrelenting sexist values. Between 1970 and 1976, according to William and Karen O'Donnell, the percentage of women in commercials pictured in the home stayed about the same—80 percent! It's almost as if the industry is willing to gamble with feminism in entertainment but less willing to take a gamble on the really important stuff—the ads.

Blacks Are Oreos

Pseudo progressive values and images extend to race issues, too.

Television treats race relations "liberally," not only by producing more black-oriented programs year by year, but also by removing blacks from criminal roles or unflattering roles of any type.

Joe Dominick, Professor of Journalism at the University of Georgia, identified this tendency for prime time to pour bleach on all the bad guys and have them turn out whiter than white in an article he wrote for *Public Opinion Quarterly* in 1973. Dominick's analysis showed that only 7 percent of the prime-time criminals were black. FBI statistics from that year indicate that blacks accounted for 30 percent of the criminal arrests.

As early as 1970, communications research was discovering that on network television about half of all blacks were portrayed upper middle class and that trend hasn't really abated. The new routine, however, is to put blacks in black settings and have them behave like the better part of the bourgeoisie.

Perhaps the most telling development in black prime time is Norman Lear's recent attempt to do a new series this spring about a black male who serves as a member of the House of Representatives. The plot was built, in part, around the congressman's foolish antics with his staff. The point was apparently to poke fun at a less than competent congressman who *happened* to be black. At first, it seemed like another breakthrough for Lear, but it wasn't to be. As of last month, the word was that under pressure from black members of Congress, who allegedly threatened to sponsor legislation to control some phases of broadcasting, CBS and Lear dropped the show. Prime-time chic and politics mean that, for some time to come, only white males will play frivolous politicians.

Gays Are Victims

Last season's favorite prime-time sop was clearly the misunderstood, harassed homosexual—always white (black gayness is still a bit too much for TV), always professional, and always the innocent victim.

On "Family," last year's theme homosexual was Buddy's teacher, who in the course of the show loses Buddy's respect, since the community bigots have maliciously publicized the fact that she, the teacher, is a lesbian. In the end, the community and Buddy accept the teacher for what she is—a great teacher—and beat down the red-neck styled element who try to have her fired.

On "Starsky and Hutch," the obligatory pro-gay program involved a police detective who gets murdered and is then discovered to have been a closet homosexual. He was, however, also a great cop and a close friend of both Starsky and Hutch, who, by show's end, find the killer (not gay) and express their new-found empathy for the plight of homosexuals. Gay is not beautiful on prime time—but since the early seventies it has never been ugly or sinister, let alone evil.

Networks aren't (can't be) as liberal as other media and progressive themes in prime time usually do fade out by the end of the show when traditional values make a minor comeback. On CBS's "One Day at a Time," last summer's number one rated series, Julie, an eighteen-year-old daughter of Ann Romano, moves in with her boyfriend. Mom loses the fight to bring Julie home—but only for the first half of the episode. Julie eventually comes home intact—and before consummating her lease or her relationship. But traditional? Mom and Julie treat the whole thing as a casual lesson learned—no remorse, no recrimination, no "I told you so." To national audiences that may well come across more as, "living with my boyfriend isn't for me, but it's okay for somebody else"—the essence of TV's social liberalism and what the polls show as a continuing acceptance of other people's lifestyles.

The real criticism that applies from both left and right is that prime-time programming is underdeveloped, vapid and plastic—not that it's traditional. Pseudo-liberal, yes; traditional, no. Radical, never.

Sit Com's the Thing

Things weren't always so liberal on prime time; just think back to Desi and Lucy and Ralph and Alice. The evolution began with the "Smothers Brothers Comedy Hour," continued through "Laugh In," and came of age with "All in the Family." All comedies.

There's no accident to the fact that comedy has led the way toward liberal chic. Comedy has always been important to the networks, not only because comedy excuses so much but because it also sells. CBS used comedy to replace NBC as the number one network back in the fifties. Three seasons back, ABC used comedy, especially situation comedy, to strip CBS of its leadership.

But sit-com may be as important to sociology as it is to the networks. Next to soap opera, sit-com is the most value-packed kind of programming there is. Sit-coms sell values because they don't have much else to sell—no variety, no action, no violence, no suspense. Programs are based on a situation that day-to-day social values have somehow made comic.

A second reason that sit-coms have led the way toward liberal chic is that they have become the very heart of prime time. The Nielsen "Top Ten" list for the last twenty-five years makes the growing importance of situation comedy perfectly clear. In 1956 only two of the top ten shows were situation comedies—"I Love Lucy" and "December Bride." In 1966 there were six sit-coms in the top ten—"Andy Griffith," "The Lucy Show," "Green Acres," "Bewitched," "The Beverly Hillbillies," and "Gomer Pyle USMC." Last season produced a record-tying eight: "Laverne and Shirley," "Happy Days," "Three's Company," "M.A.S.H.," "One Day at a Time," "All in the Family," "Soap," and "Alice." The qualitative differences aren't as great as the quantitative. But compare "One Day at a Time" with "December Bride," or "Three's Company" with "Andy Griffith," or "Soap" with anything.

The only type of programming that even approaches sit-com as a purveyor of social values is soap opera. But soaps are "serious" —they have to meet tougher standards of censorship. On soaps, people who break any of the commandments have to pay—either in guilt, divorce, miscarriage, or impotence. By comparison, sit-com characters get away with murder—or at least promiscuity.

Besides an ability to slip past the censor, sit-coms have other characteristics that make them especially important to anybody trying to explain TV's effects. Popular sit-com characters, who appear every week, who rarely threaten anybody's ego, who lay their own values down gently and humorously on the coffee table and walk away, have a unique potential for affecting their audiences.

If the viewer doesn't like the values being

offered he or she can dismiss them as merely satirical or humorous (as liberals do with Archie Bunker). If the viewer agrees with the values, everything is fine.

As for the bulk of viewers in the middle, or the viewers not-too-sensitive about social issues generally, the values of situation comedy may eventually become part of their own. More likely, the program's values will lead those viewers to think that if decent people like Mary Richards . . . act that way, that's probably a legitimate way to behave. Either way—whether the viewer actually adopts liberal chic values or just accepts their legitimacy—that attitude looks like liberalism in the polls.

Why Liberal Chic?

Nobody denies that television production people are socially liberal. Although Muriel Cantor challenges the premise that programs are really liberal, she is convinced that the writers, actors, and producers are.

Cantor, whose 1969 Ph.D. thesis at UCLA was a sociological analysis of television producers, says that producers and writers are not only Democratic and liberal, they are also Jewish, urban, and from one coast or the other. (Spiro Agnew, where are you?)

Ben Stein, author of a new and controsial book, *The View from Sunset Boulevard* . . . , thinks that TV production, based almost totally in Los Angeles, reflects Hollywood more than personal, deep-seated liberal philosophy. While Stein acknowledges that the values of these people are socially progressive, he sees their liberalism only going so far. "Their values are permissive," says Stein, "but their own personal lives are clean cut." "There was more sex in the White House than out here in Norman Lear's company," a charge made even more remarkable by the fact that Stein worked in Richard Nixon's White House. (Stein is the only man in history who will have worked for both Richard Nixon and Norman Lear.)

But the real fight is not over just how liberal the producers and writers are—everyone agrees they are more liberal than their average viewers; the debate is whether they stick their own values into their programs. As expected, critics on the left say no; critics on the right say definitely.

Cantor, who labels herself "pretty radical," thinks that the TV people "clearly are not espousing their own values" when they produce their shows and that the liberals who worked in television during the early seventies couldn't take it any more and have since left. But Stein, a thinking man's conservative, ridicules what he considers a ludicrous theory—that television people don't bring their own social values to their work with them. And there are some leftist critics who agree with him. Jerry Mander, whose new book, *Four Arguments for the Elimination of Television,* takes a position almost as radical as its title, writes that the "Movement people of the 1960s who were not willing to go to terrorism began dropping out, moving to farms in Vermont or Oregon. Or, and I know many who have done this, they got jobs writing television serials. They justified this with the explanation that they were still reaching people with an occasional revolutionary message, fitted ingeniously into the dialogue."

All serious analysts of television realize that prime time doesn't merely reflect the social values of L.A. producers, or New York executives, or even advertisers. Ratings, affiliates, the FCC, the NAM—all help shape the content. Values are just part of programming.

But some TV analysts see programming as much a case study in social engineering as anything else—a sort of values conspiracy theory. One network executive, a liberal working in audience research in New York, told me that he thinks L.A. production houses, as well as the corporate executives back in New York, figure out how far they can go by using the Midwest—the nation's most traditional region outside the South—as their least common denominator. According to his theory, programs present themes that are acceptable to television production people until the networks or the producers decide that the show won't play in Peoria—a new role for Richard Nixon's favorite barometer.

Is Anybody Out There Listening?

Nobody is certain about the effects of prime time, and some social scientists argue that entertainment television has no impact at all on social values. Some research even makes a case for prime-time television as a _conservatizing_ influence. Russell Weigel and Richard Jessor, two behavioral psychologists from the University of Colorado, claim to have found a link between TV watching and conventional attitudes about religion, drugs, politics, and personal freedom. But most of their work was done in 1970, before the industry turned around. George Gerbner, Director of the Annenberg School of Communications in Philadelphia, also finds that watching television and worrying about crime go very much in hand—that "crime-time" television has made Americans more suspicious of each other and more neurotic about the society they share. The end product of all that is, as Gerbner sees it, more support for governmental crackdowns—in short, more conservatism.

But the fact is there isn't much conclusive evidence one way or the other about prime time. Most of the academic studies have been anything but exciting—discovering, for example, that people who consider "All in the Family" to be funny are more likely to watch it. Part of the analytical problem involves finding an acceptable technique for proving that TV per se, actually _causes_ something. But beyond that, the problem too has been a lack of real interest. The best talent in the academy has been out studying the impact of prime time on violent behavior, not on attitudes toward sex, drugs, or women's issues. While violence research has been getting funding, values research has been getting the crumbs.

Most of the work done on violence, especially the mammoth _Surgeon General's Report,_ argues that TV causes aggression, especially among young people. It seems apparent that if violent programming can cause violence, liberal programming should be able to "cause" liberalism. In fact, because many social scientists think that it is easier to influence attitudes than behavior, the impact of TV on attitudes should be greater than on aggression.

Critics who doubt the impact of entertainment television stress the chicken-and-the-egg problem, arguing that it's impossible to tell what's causing what. Or, alternatively, they argue that television always follows social change and never leads it. While the first argument is hard to dismiss, the second one isn't. Themes on prime time do follow a leader, but the leader in expressed or implied values isn't the public as much as most critics think. Dominant values in much prime-time television, and changes in those dominant values, don't come from the heartland. From civil rights to disco, social movements start in places like New York and L.A., and the media move them out to the boonies. Television gets much of its values and themes from other, classier media (books, and especially magazines), and, to a lesser degree, from an urban-based intelligentsia. Television edits those messages, obviously, before it passes them along as TV chic. But by touching millions, instead of thousands, prime time becomes a highly visible, national, and immediate cause of changing social norms. TV may not be a first cause, but it is a highly apparent one.

Prime time helps to make the social values of the coastline elites the social values of the nation. For decades, prime-time social values have been making us less regional and less heterogeneous. But until the late sixties, that meant national taste in clothes, music, dancing, or accent. With television moving into more serious social themes, the effect is on values, not just tastes. Thus, we find the nation moving into the Global Village that Marshall McLuhan named and predicted—with television in the role of a tribal medicine man who takes his cues from the higher circles but makes the messages palatable, acceptable and enjoyable to the rest of the villagers.

This is not to argue that prime time has singlehandedly transformed social values in America. Television reflects and magnifies change as well as produces it. Moreover, there are at least two alternative interpretations that help to explain the growth of social liberalism, both of which are based in demography. One interpretation stems from the accepted fact that the "young" have socially progressive opinions, the other from the more recent view that the "educated" also have such views. Thus, so the theories go, as the country has grown younger and better educated, it has also grown more socially liberal.

But ignoring television as a factor in social liberalism seems foolish. Prime time has so many qualities that make for effective social learning—vast audiences, close involvement between actors and viewers, programs that center around relevant social relationships and social issues. Theoretically, prime time has more going for it as a teaching device than most college classes, which often go without audience, involvement, or relevance. All that the shows lack is a grading system. As long as prime time continues to be progressive—compared to Cincinnati, not to Sausalito—the lessons should continue to stick.

What Next?

Progressive prime time isn't inevitable. In the fifties television was anything but progressive—and it was much more likely to reflect than mold national folkways or attitudes.

It's doubtful that anything could return television to that wretched state, but it is conceivable that prime time could find a different set of social values to build into its programs. One way would be through pressure.

The newest thing in television is the growth of increasingly powerful organizations that try to change something about network programming that the organizations find offensive. (The PTA is at the top of the list when it comes to pressuring networks these days.)

The toughest assaults against prime time have come from the anti-violence people. And they have been successful in reducing the amount and the intensity of violence, but at an ironic cost. Networks tend to substitute sitcom and social relevance for violence. So, the conservative and religious groups that have pushed the networks out of action-adventure have moved programming even more in the direction of liberal chic.

The irony doesn't stop there. Liberal critics who have organized to end sexist commercials and sexist stereotyping sometimes help the groups and causes that they most want to inhibit—the fundamentalist Christian world. Richard Levinson, who wrote "Columbo" and *The Execution of Private Slovic*, says that the "primary bias of prime-time TV in the last several years has been liberal," but that the liberal trend may generate conservative counterpressures that could one day move the industry out of serious drama and back into cutesy, inoffensive programming. So far, however, that day is nowhere in sight.

The "new" season which started in February and the "new, new" season which started in March show that we've reached a near equilibrium. Gratuitous violence is down, sexy sit-com is up, and liberal chic is pretty much everywhere.

51
The American Dream Game

Diana J. Janas

Originally a radio format, the game show has always been a staple of television programming. In the 1950s, the young television industry was rocked to its foundations
by a scandal, which disclosed that many popular quiz shows were rigged, with some
contestants given the answers in advance. Still, the shows remained popular, with
more variations filling the daytime hours than ever before. In the 1970s, celebrity
game shows and the bizarre creations of Chuck Barris ("The Dating Game," "The
Newlywed Game," "The Gong Show") captured large audiences. In the following selection, from *Human Behavior,* California freelance writer Diana Janas examines the
appeal of these programs to both participants and audience.

The producer was having a bad day. Rehearsal was behind schedule, there was only
one show in the can and the "millennium
board" wasn't working. To top it off, he
couldn't decide whether to use a chime or a
buzz as his primary sound effect.

While engineers fussed over their $50,000
clueboard and its problems (a similar board,
incidentally, to the one that's used as a score-
board in the Houston Astrodome and the Los
Angeles Memorial Coliseum), the production
staff in the booth was using the time for a
high-level meeting on the audience's response
to a particular sound. Cerebral debates took
place over the subliminal effects of a honk, a
buzz or a chime, and the topic of "losing"
music was much discussed. Every "spontaneous" sound was planned with the precision of
a military campaign and the care of a psychological experiment.

Across town at another studio, the producer was chugalugging water directly from a
pitcher and wandering cheerfully amid the
chaos of his set. The audience laughed duti-

fully at the predictably cute routines of the
warmup-man/announcer, while floor directors ran around like participants from *Alice
in Wonderland*'s caucus-race. Guest celebrities sauntered in unnoticed as the audience
strained to hear who had won the door prize.

The set, like most in television, was
smaller and shabbier than one would expect,
waiting for the cosmetic help of lights and
translation to the small screen to transform it
into a thing of tawdry beauty.

At both places, and in several other studios across Hollywood, groups of people hud-
dled in separate holding areas, expectant
Christians waiting for a crack at the lions.
Their appearance in the televised arena could
mean money, prizes, trips and gifts. The people have come to this place after months of
waiting and after a progression of visits to
production offices where they sat in square
rooms, made small talk and hoped that they
were just ordinary enough to make it.

If they are and do, they become part of
the game show, a television staple that domi-

nates our daytime viewing, has seeped into our mass consciousness and may already be a part of our folk culture.

Millions of us watch game shows—enough of us to ensure them a secure position on daytime and prime-time TV. There are currently 12 shows on daily, and another eight on evenings and weekends both on networks and in syndication. The hit "Hollywood Squares" appears on the tube seven times a week. Uniformly, games pull in a 30 to 34 percent share of the market, some as high as a 38 to 40 percent share.

In the TV world, anything over a 30 percent share is considered a solid hit. That means money. And game show revenues are estimated in the hundreds of millions of dollars annually. In fact, from the network standpoint, game shows are far and away the most profitable form of programming available. Their profit-cost ratio may be as high as four to one. In other words, an average game may cost a network $4 million to put on the air, but that $4 million turns into a $16 million profit. Most game shows have one set, one host and few elements that change, so production costs are thus relatively low. Only contestants are needed in quantity—and they're free. In addition, the primary audience for game shows, the 18- to 49-year-old housewife, is a very attractive market for sponsors.

Since daytime programming makes over half a network's profits and is what actually pays the bills for the prime-time programming, games are an obvious and continuing hit with the networks.

Critics and media scholars may find games trash for the masses and appalling examples of our intellectual decay, but one producer has dubbed games the "last real payoff on the American Dream." Anyone who thinks that dream is dead should look at it being relived daily on "The Price Is Right," "Let's Make a Deal," "Match Game" and their companions. It's being perpetuated by stereotypes of our own invention, contestants who "have long hair and answer like Miss America." One starry-eyed contestant said of her experiences on a show: "It was like chasing a lifetime dream, so I did it."

Let's face it, game shows work because we want them to work. All of us—producers, contestants, viewers and studio audience—are willing participants in a scenario that manipulates our emotions and reactions in the most basic way. Flashing lights and catchy music are just part of it. The real reason behind game show popularity is that viewers identify with what they see. Those people competing on the small screen aren't entertainers or athletes or actors. They're ourselves, and their fate somehow becomes our fate.

Peter Clecak, professor of social thought at the University of California at Irvine, dubs game shows a kind of "morality play" in which the myth of the gamble and the myth of winning are continually reenacted for the audience. Yet the spectators can participate without psychological risk. We are not moved, in the classic sense, to pity and fear. We are simply titillated.

The emotions are quick and shallow, Clecak notes, and one can watch the shows with relatively little attentiveness while receiving instant gratification. He sees games as providing a "surrogate success myth," a myth important to us now because of the economic uncertainty we face.

Jay Wolpert, producer of the highly popular "The Price Is Right," agrees: "The worse the economy, the bigger the interest in games. Where else can you stand in line for an hour and come home with $15,000?"

Games fill other needs for us as well. Take the need to be significant. A woman who won big on "Let's Make a Deal" described the scene after her victory: "People were hugging me, kissing me, coming out of the audience saying, 'there she is, the big winner.' Talk about being a celebrity; I wasn't the same for months!"

"Game shows are easy to fantasize about; people identify with winning or losing," says Jonathan Brower, associate professor of sociology at California State University at Fullerton. "Most people lead much of their lives in a neutral feeling zone," he observes. "These shows give them transient and easy ups and downs, not based on big emotional stakes. The feelings are very temporary and quite manageable."

That observation may encapsule the reason why millions of us watch and participate in game shows. They have a uniform scenario that is at once comforting in its stability and exciting in its unpredictability. We know everyone will win something, but we're not sure who will name the $100,000 tune or get to the top of the $20,000 Pyramid."

Like the *Ancient Mariner,* these shows tell their tale again and again. A show may be canceled, but its time slot remains to be filled by another flashy, lucrative variation of a contestant's quest for the big win. When the contestant's long-awaited chance at the big reward comes, it's usually over within 60 seconds. There's near instantaneous victory or oblivion. The risk—blowing it in front of the whole nation; the payoff—money and momentary stardom.

The contestant is crucial to all this. Howard Felsher, veteran producer of games such as "Password," "Concentration" and "Family Feud," puts it directly: "Contestants are our bread and butter; without them we wouldn't be in this business."

Because of this, game show producers could teach the behavior modification folks a few tricks about repeatedly getting desired actions from an individual—in a very short time. Selection methods are not scientific, and, in fact, seem almost random. But they are virtually never wrong when it comes to gauging a person's contestant potential.

It begins innocently enough. You've heard the announcement on each show that invites viewers to be contestants. Additionally, producers run ads in local papers, give out invitations at other network tapings and search out organizations from as far afield as Mensa, Kiwanis, fraternities and sororities. Some even go to supermarkets. It isn't that people aren't willing to be contestants. Quite the contrary. But the "right" players aren't all that easy to find, and some shows need as many as 40 or 50 players a week. Each show looks for a slightly different quality, but in all cases the contestant has to create an immediate bond of empathy with the audience.

Lila Michaels, an 18-year veteran of choosing game show contestants, calls the magical ingredient a "good energy level." That's a combination of enthusiasm, person-

ality and positive vibes. There's definitely no room for anyone who projects a "loser" quality. The contestants must be stereotypes that we recognize as the woman next door, our grandmother, a friend or ourselves, but they must be anonymous enough to dissolve their images after the show.

Producer Wolpert contends that the contestants must establish an instant intimacy. "I look for people who are charming and somehow quickly fill in the blanks about themselves for the viewer," he says.

Contestants are chosen in basically two ways, in each case by the producer of the show. In one method, they are pretested; in another, they are simply interviewed, just before air time. Producers function as psychologists on the hoof, quickly sizing up a potential player. They do have help, because contestants have an idea of what's expected of them so they tend to sort themselves out in advance by selecting certain shows.

The extroverted, try-anything-once types tend to go to highly spontaneous shows that feature gimmicks. At "Let's Make a Deal," for example, contestants are expected to dress up in outrageous costumes for their shot at the Big Deal.

"When they come out, you have to get their attention somehow," said one contestant. "I learned from the people around me that making a noise was a good thing. You stand in line and act like a nut," she laughed. "I got so caught up in it I couldn't sleep. I had gimmicks going through my head, I had costumes coming out of my ears!" It took her six tries to get on the show. But the effort paid off and she won a trip around the world.

The quieter types go to more placid shows such as "Hollywood Squares" or "Wheel of Fortune."

Still others adapt to the style of whatever show interests them. One couple who had been contestants on several different programs were as calculating as producers, and quite successful. They summed up their formula with a shrug, "You say what they want you to say. You do what they want you to do."

"What they want you to do" varies, but the expectations at a "Match Game" contestant screening are typical: 24 potential contestants sit nervously in a small room. They are wearing bright yellow name tags bearing their first name and holding big blue cards with their picture, full name, address and occupation. All have come there by choice after making an appointment for an interview. Some have waited months for the privilege. All are joined in a strained camaraderie.

The contestant coordinator, Diane Janaver, enters. She's a combination cheerleader and coach whose job is to rev up the people for the producer. She begins her spiel in a rapid-fire delivery that demands attention. First, the disclaimers: your being here doesn't mean you'll get on the show. Wait for a letter to tell you the next step, don't call us and so on.

Then she outlines what's expected. "We're looking for outgoing, enthusiastic people who like to play games and show it. I wish we could pick you all, but we need that spark, so the people at home can identify with you." The contestants murmur understanding. They know what identifying means, they do it all the time, that's why they're there.

Next, the test. The producer of the show arrives. He is calm, cordial, tells the hopefuls he wants to hear a little bit about their lives, but speak up, we have to be able to hear you, we'd hate to disqualify you for not hearing you.

The life vignettes begin. Predictable. A certain amount of "Gee, I like your show and hope I make it." An earnest young woman says her hobbies are watching television and collecting pictures of movie stars. You get the feeling she won't make it. She obviously wants it too much and thus projects great vulnerability. That won't do. Vulnerability means pain, and these shows are supposed to be painless.

(Earlier, a man had stood outside the contestant room arguing with a receptionist. He insisted he'd received a letter telling him to come West. He had waited for his tax refund, then spent it on the trip to Hollywood from Nashville. He was not very articulate, but he was determined to get on the show. He probably didn't make it, either—he was too real and too much a figure of pathos.)

After talking with the contestants, the producer plays the game with them. How well they do is important. If they get on the show, they must have a realistic chance at winning. After this, the producer and coordinator leave the room. They go through the contestant cards quickly, separating sheep from goats. They return, ask some people to stay, release others. Even though contestants are eliminated from this first cut, they are all left with the impression that no decision has yet been made.

There are 10 people left. They play the game some more with these 10 and then send everyone away with a variation of the "Don't call us" line. The final selection begins. Each remaining contestant card is marked with two letter grades (the way we received them on term papers: A/A—), one for personality and one for game ability. Those finally chosen as contestants include: an elderly lady who was typically everybody's favorite aunt; a charming character from Mississippi who could have stepped from the pages of Mark Twain (he played the game badly but was such an interesting fellow that the producer decided to risk it); and two blonde women from California who looked exactly like contestants always look. The result, four chosen out of 24. The whole process has taken just one hour.

Wolpert uses an even quicker, though riskier, method of garnering contestants. He does his own selecting from "the line"; that is, those people waiting in line to get into the show as audience. On taping days, Wolpert surveys a line of 300 people before each of three taping sessions. He's not just looking for contestants; he's also making contact with his audience of that day, warming them up so that even those who don't make the show— and that's most of them—won't feel rejected and thus be a bad audience. It's a good trick, really, to keep people cheering even as they don't win anything.

"There's no skill to picking someone who just jumps up and down," Wolpert explains. "You can tell by looking into their eyes who's really into the show, and who's just a schlep. I look for people who are attractive, not necessarily physically, but who the audience can get behind. I want people who in some way externalize, 'Hey, I'd like to have that,' but not necessarily by jumping up and down.''

Wolpert says he knows intuitively what will work on his show. He goes by people's eyes and his own gut reactions, maintaining that he can tell almost without error who will make a good contestant. He avoids men: "Men are treacherous. They tend to be less emotionally honest than women. They're fine in the line; then on camera they turn into pillars of society, philistines. They're perfidious. I'm very careful with my men."

One of Wolpert's favorite stories is that of the elderly gentleman he picked for his twinkling charm. The man was fine until he won a houseboat. For the rest of the taping he kept muttering about what in creation he was supposed to do with a houseboat. The camera caught it all.

Once contestants are chosen, the main challenge is to keep them hyped until air time. On those shows where the players' names are called out right on the air, contestant reaction and hysteria are assured. But on those shows where contestants have been pretested and hauled to the studio as many as six or seven times in expectation of appearing on the air, added manipulation is necessary.

Here, contestant coordinators function as director and coach. One contestant described a typical pep talk: "You will smile, there may be only one show left but you will all be out there and you will all smile. You do want to get on the show, don't you? You do want to win, don't you? Now, don't let us down. Even though you've been here for nine hours, you will all smile till those jaws hurt!"

Another contestant said that every time the group seemed to be losing enthusiasm, a "rookie" was brought in and put on the show without waiting. That made everybody start smiling again. She said, "They play tricky little games with you. I'm sure they do it just to keep you guessing."

Even once a contestant is on the air, the pressure continues. One woman said: "They do suggest that if you're happy, let the audience know. Even if you're not happy, let the audience think you're happy. They prompt the audience a lot, and the producer and assistant producer stand back there and yell, 'Come on! Come on!'"

Another contestant reacted after her appearance: "When you're actually there, it's all so different. You don't think you'll do things and you do. Really, your whole personality changes; you're there, the lights are on, the music is playing. I see them making you a kind of fool. But, on the other hand, I think you can laugh at yourself."

The audience is manipulated as well. Wolpert created a short-lived show called "Double Dare" in which the contestants competed against one another, and then, for the big money, against a panel of Spoilers. The latter were PhDs whose sole task was to wreck the contestant's chances at the grand prize. This Archie Bunker-like tension between player and intellectuals was created for its dramatic effect. "There had never been a show with people serving as obstacles whose sole job was to destroy," explained Wolpert, "so we encouraged our Spoilers to be Vincent Price nasty, but in a campy way."

In true game show tradition, the drama had to be real, but not too real. "Originally, we had college students as the Spoilers. But it turned out that a college student is a rather sympathetic figure. So we went to PhDs, because they're already established in a profession and there would be no worry on the part of the audience."

"Double Dare" had all the right ingredients, but the recipe ultimately didn't work. Its cancellation illustrates how game shows have evolved. Games actually began as quiz shows, with many moving over directly from radio. As such, they had class—Walter Cronkite was even host of one in the '50s. Then the now-infamous quiz show scandals scorched the airwaves and ended quizzes. But the format rose phoenixlike out of its own ashes to become the game show. Today, they're flashier, more complex, with bigger prizes and less stature than their ancestors.

"The audience today is turned off from any intellectual challenge," laments Wolpert, attributing the failure of "Double Dare" to this latter-day distaste for eggheads on TV games shows. While cultural arbiters bemoan the lowbrow status of this TV genre, the rewards must be abundant for those who participate. People who've been on games usually say they'd do it all again. Why? "The appeal is that of attention paid to self," explains Wolpert. "People are looking for something out of the blue to raise them up, godlike. When you have 60 million people cheering for you and caring about you—jeez, you can't buy that kind of attention.

"To say greed is the main motivation is a huge oversimplification," Wolpert continues. "No game show succeeds because of stakes. Shows live or die on the strength of the game itself."

There has never been a year in the history of television that some form of game show hasn't been on the air somewhere. Like Westerns and soap operas, they are always with us. They may change, but they remain.

It makes sense, too. Given the chance, how many of us would turn down a relatively riskfree gamble to win money, adulation and a moment in the spotlight all at once? We once dreamed of being movie stars. Now, in a more jaded era of lowered expectations, we dream of making it to "The Gong Show." After all, if that woman who looks like my neighbor can do it, why can't I?

52
The Selection of Reality

Edward Jay Epstein

Network television news is at the same time journalistic enterprise and entertainment programming. In this excerpt from *News from Nowhere: Television and the News,* media critic Edward Jay Epstein describes the operational and technical factors that determine the ultimate content of network news.

Since this selection was written, technical advances—the reliance on videotape instead of film—have significantly changed the state of television news. Because stories can be replayed without having to develop film, the time to produce TV news has been radically cut. Most stations now have roving vans equipped with ENG (Electronic News Gathering) gear capable of relaying live or taped signals via microwave links directly to the studio. Aside from this time element, the TV news selection process is still as Epstein describes it.

Each weekday evening, the three major television networks—the American Broadcasting Company, the Columbia Broadcasting System, and the National Broadcasting Company—feed filmed news stories over lines leased from the American Telephone & Telegraph Co. to the more than six hundred local stations affiliated with them, which, in turn, broadcast the stories over the public airwaves to a nationwide audience. The CBS Evening News, which is broadcast by two hundred local stations, reaches some nineteen million viewers; the NBC Nightly News, broadcast by two hundred and nine stations, some eighteen million viewers; and the ABC Evening News, broadcast by a hundred and ninety-one stations, some fourteen million. News stories from these programs are recorded on videotape by most affiliates and used again, usually in truncated form, on local news programs late in the evening. Except for the news on the few unaffiliated stations and on the noncommercial stations, virtually all the filmed reports of national and world news seen on television are the product of the three network news organizations.

The process by which news is gathered, edited, and presented the public is more or less similar at the three networks. A limited number of subjects—usually somewhere between twenty and thirty—are selected each day as possible film stories by news executives, producers, anchor men, and assignment editors, who base their choices principally on wire-service and newspaper reports. Camera crews are dispatched to capture these events on 16-mm. color film. The filming is supervised by either a field producer or a correspondent—or, in some cases, the cameraman himself. The film is then shipped to the network's headquarters in New York, or to one of its major news bureaus—in Chicago, Los Angeles, or Washington—or, if time is an important consideration, processed and edited at the nearest available facilities and transmitted electronically to New York. Through editing and rearranging of the filmed scenes, a small fraction of the exposed film—usually less than ten per cent—is reconstructed into a story whose form is to some extent predetermined. Reuven Frank, until two months ago the president of NBC News, has written:

> Every news story should, without any sacrifice of probity or responsibility, display the attributes of fiction, of drama. It should have structure and conflict, problem and denouement, rising action and falling action, a beginning, a middle and an end.

After the addition of a sound track, recorded at the event, the story is explained and pulled together by a narration, written by the correspondent who covered the event or by a writer in the network news offices. Finally, the story is integrated into the news program by the anchor man.

Network news organizations select not only the events that will be shown as national and world news on television but the way in which those events will be depicted. This necessarily involves choosing symbols that will have general meaning for a national audience. "The picture is not a fact but a symbol," Reuven Frank once wrote. "The real child and its real crying become symbols of all children." In the same way, a particular black may be used to symbolize the aspirations of his race, a particular student may be used to symbolize the claims of his generation, and a particular policeman may be used to symbolize the concept of authority. Whether the black chosen is a Black Panther or an integrationist, whether the student is a militant activist or a Young Republican, whether the policeman is engaged in a brutal or a benevolent act obviously affects the impression of the event received by the audience. When the same symbols are consistently used on television to depict the behavior and aspirations of groups, they become stable images—what Walter Lippmann, in his classic study "Public Opinion," has called a "repertory of stereotypes." These images obviously have great power; public-opinion polls show that television is the most believed source of news for most of the population. The director of CBS News in Washington, William Small, has written about television news:

> When television covered its "first war" in Vietnam, it showed a terrible truth of war in a manner new to mass audiences. A case can be made, and certainly should be examined, that this was cardinal to the disillusionment of Americans with this war, the cynicism of many young people toward America, and the destruction of Lyndon Johnson's tenure of office. . . . When television examined a different kind of revolution, it was singularly effective in helping bring about the Black revolution.

And it would be difficult to dispute the claim of Reuven Frank that "there are events which exist in the American mind and recollection primarily because they were reported on regular television news programs."

How were those events selected to be shown on television, and who or what determined the way in which they were depicted? [Former] Vice-President Spiro Agnew believes the answer is that network news is shaped "by a handful of men responsible only to their corporate employers," who have broad "powers of choice" and "yield a free hand in selecting, presenting, and interpreting the great issues in our nation." Television executives and newsmen, on the other hand, often argue that television news is shaped not by men but by events—that news is news. Both of these analyses overlook the economic realities of network television, the effects of government regulation on broadcasting, and the organizational requirements of the network news operations, whose established routines and procedures tend to impose certain forms on television news stories.

David Brinkley, in an NBC News special entitled "From Here to the Seventies," reiterated a description of television news that is frequently offered by television newsmen:

> What television did in the sixties was to show the American people to the American people. . . . It did show the people, places and things they had not seen before. Some they liked, and some they did not. It was not that television produced or created any of it.

In this view, television news does no more than mirror reality. Thus, Leonard Goldenson, the chairman of the board of ABC, testified before the National Commission on the Causes and Prevention of Violence that complaints of news distortion were brought about by the fact that "Americans are reluctant to accept the images reflected by the mirror we have held up to our society." Robert D. Kasmire, a vice-president of NBC, told the commission, "There is no doubt that television is, to a large degree, a mirror of our society. It is also a mirror of public attitudes and preferences." The president of NBC, Julian Goodman, told the commission, "In short, the medium is blamed for the message." Dr. Frank Stanton, vice-chairman and former president of CBS, testifying before a House committee, said, "What the media do is to hold a mirror up to society and try to report it as faithfully as possible." Elmer Lower, the president of ABC News, has described television news as "the television mirror that reflects . . . across oceans and mountains,"

and added, "Let us open the doors of the parliaments everywhere to the electronic mirrors." The imagery has been picked up by critics of television, too. Jack Gould, formerly of the *Times,* wrote of television's coverage of racial riots, "Congress, one would hope, would not conduct an examination of a mirror because of the disquieting images that it beholds."

The mirror analogy has considerable descriptive power, but it also leads to a number of serious misconceptions about the medium. The notion of a "mirror of society" implies that everything of significance that happens will be reflected on television news. Network news organizations, however, far from being ubiquitous and all-seeing, are limited news-gathering operations, which depend on camera crews based in only a few major cities for most of their national stories. Some network executives have advanced the idea that network news is the product of coverage by hundreds of affiliated stations, but the affiliates' contribution to the network news program actually is very small. Most network news stories are assigned in advance to network news crews and correspondents, and in many cases whether or not an event is covered depends on where it occurs and the availability of network crews.

The mirror analogy also suggests immediacy: events are reflected instantaneously, as in a mirror. This notion of immediate reporting is reinforced by the way people in television news depict the process to the public. News executives sometimes say that, given the immediacy of television, the network organization has little opportunity to intervene in news decisions. Reuven Frank once declared, on a television program about television, "News coverage generally happens too fast for anything like that to take place." But does it? Though it is true that elements of certain events, such as space exploration and political conventions, are broadcast live, virtually all of the regular newscasts, except for the commentator's "lead-ins" and "tags" to the news stories, are prerecorded on videotape or else on film, which must be transported, processed, edited, and projected before it can be seen. Some film stories are delayed from one day to two weeks, because of certain organizational needs and policies. Reuven Frank more or less outlined these policies on "prepared," or delayed, news in . . . [an internal] memorandum he wrote when he was executive producer of NBC's Nightly News program. "Except for those rare days when other material becomes available," he wrote, "the gap will be filled by planned and prepared film stories, and we are assuming the availability of two each night." These "longer pieces," he continued, were to be "planned, executed over a longer period of time than spot news, usable and relevant any time within, say, two weeks, rather than that day, receptive to the more sophisticated techniques of production and editing, but journalism withal." The reason for delaying filmed stories, a network vice-president has explained, is that "it gives the producer more control over his program." First, it gives the producer control of the budget, since shipping the film by plane, though it might mean a delay of a day or two, is considerably less expensive than transmitting the film electronically by satellite or A.T.&T. lines. Second, and perhaps more important, it gives the producer control over the content of the individual stories, since it affords him an opportunity to screen the film and, if necessary, reedit it. Eliminating the delay, the same vice-president suggested, could have the effect of reducing network news to a mere "chronicler of events" and forcing it "out of the business of making meaningful comment." Moreover, the delay provides a reserve of stories that can be used to give the program "variety" and "pacing."

In filming delayed stories, newsmen are expected to eliminate any elements of the unexpected, so as not to destroy the illusion of immediacy. This becomes especially important when it is likely that the unusual developments will be reported in other media and thus date the story. A case in point is an NBC News story about the inauguration of a high-speed train service between Montreal and Toronto. While the NBC crew was filming the turbotrain during its inaugural run to Toronto, it collided with—and "sliced in half," as one newspaper put it—a meat trailer-truck, and then suffered a complete mechanical breakdown on the return trip. Persistent "performance flaws" and subsequent breakdowns

eventually led to a temporary suspension of the service. None of these accidents and aberrations were included in the filmed story broadcast two weeks later on the NBC evening news. David Brinkley, keeping to the original story, written before the event, introduced the film by saying, "The only high-speed train now running in North America has just begun in Canada." Four and a half minutes of shots of the streamlined train followed, and the narration suggested that this foreshadowed the future of transportation, since Canada's "new turbo just might shake [American] lethargy" in developing such trains. (The announcement of the suspension of the service, almost two weeks later, was not carried on the program.) This practice of "preparing" stories also has affected the coverage of more serious subjects—for instance, many of the filmed stories about the Vietnam war were delayed for several days. It was possible to transmit war films to the United States in one day by using the satellite relay, but the cost was considerable at the height of the war—more than three thousand dollars for a ten-minute transmission, as opposed to twenty or thirty dollars for shipping the film by plane. And, with the exception of momentous battles, such as the Tet offensive, virtually all of the network film was sent by plane. To avoid the possibility of having the delayed footage dated by newspaper accounts, network correspondents were instructed to report on the routine and continuous aspect of the war rather than unexpected developments, according to a former NBC Saigon bureau manager.

The mirror analogy, in addition, obscures the component of "will"—of initiative in producing feature stories and of decisions made in advance to cover or not to cover certain types of events. A mirror makes no decisions; it simply reflects what takes place in front of it. . . .

The search for news requires a reliable flow of information not only about events in the immediate past but about those scheduled for the near future. Advance information, though necessary to any news operation, is of critical importance to the networks. For, unlike newspapers and radio stations, which can put a news story together within minutes by means of telephone interviews or wire-service dispatches, a television network usually needs hours, if not days, of "lead time" to shoot, process, and edit a film story of even a minute's duration. The types of news stories best suited for television coverage are those specially planned, or induced, for the conveniences of the news media—press conferences, briefings, interviews, and the like—which the historian Daniel J. Boorstin has called "pseudo-events," and which by definition are scheduled well in advance and are certain to be, if only in a self-fulfilling sense, "newsworthy." There are also other news events, such as congressional hearings, trials, and speeches, that, although they may not be induced for the sole purpose of creating news, can still be predicted far in advance. The networks have various procedures for gathering, screening, and evaluating information about future events, and these procedures to some degree systematically *influence* their coverage of news.

Most network news stories, rather than resulting from the initiative of reporters in the field, are located and assigned by an assignment editor in New York (or an editor under his supervision in Washington, Chicago, or Los Angeles). The assignment desk provides material not only for the evening news program but for documentaries, morning and afternoon programs, and a syndicated service for local stations. Instead of maintaining—as newspapers do—regular "beats," where reporters have contact with the same set of newsmakers over an extended period of time, network news organizations rely on ad-hoc coverage. In this system, correspondents are shunted from one story to another—on the basis of availability, logistical convenience, and producers' preferences—after the assignment editor has selected the events to be covered. A correspondent may easily be assigned to three subjects in three different cities in a single week, each assignment lasting only as long as it takes to film the story. To be sure, there are a number of conventional beats in Washington, such as the White House, but these are the exception rather than the rule. Most of the correspondents are "generalists," expected to cover all subjects with equal facil-

ity. And even in fields for which networks do employ special correspondents, such as sports or space exploration, better-known correspondents who are not experts in those fields may be called on to report major stories. The generalist is expected not to be a Jack-of-all-trades but simply to be capable of applying rules of fair inquiry to any subject. One reason network executives tend to prefer generalists is that they are less likely to "become involved in a story to the point of advocacy," as one network vice-president has put it. It is feared that specialists, through their intimate knowledge of a situation, would be prone to champion what they believed was the correct side of a controversy. But perhaps the chief reason that generalists are preferred to specialists is that, being able to cover whatever story develops, they lend themselves to an efficient use of manpower. The use of ad-hoc coverage leads to the constant appearance "on camera" of a relatively small number of correspondents. One network assignment editor has suggested that it is "more for reasons of audience identification than economy" that a few correspondents are relied on for most of the stories. The result, he continued, is a "star system," in which producers request that certain leading correspondents cover major stories, whatever the subject might be. Another consequence of having small, generalist reporting staffs is that the networks are able to do relatively little investigative reporting. . . .

What is seen on network news is not, except in rare instances, the event itself, unfolding live before the camera, or even a filmed record of the event in its entirety, but a story about the event which has been constructed on film from selected fragments of it. Presenting news events exactly as they occur does not meet the requirements of network news. For one thing, the camera often is not in a position to capture events while they are happening. Some news events are completely unexpected and occur before a camera crew can be dispatched to the scene. Others cannot be filmed either because of unfavorable weather or lighting conditions (especially if artificial lighting is unavailable or restricted) or because news crews are not permitted access to them. And when institutions, such as political conventions, do permit television to record their formal proceedings, the significant decisions may still take place outside the purview of the camera. But even if coverage presents no insurmountable problems, it is not sufficient in most cases simply to record events in their natural sequence, with all the digressions, confusions, and inconsistencies that are an inescapable part of any reality, for a network news story is required to have a definite order, time span, and logic.

In producing most news stories, the first necessity is generating sufficient film about an event, so that the editor and the writer can be assured of finding the material they need for the final story. Perhaps the most commonly used device for producing this flow of film is the interview. The interview serves several important purposes for television news. First, it enables a news crew to obtain film footage about an event that it did not attend or was not permitted to film. By finding and interviewing people who either participated in the event or have at least an apparent connection with it, the correspondent can re-create it through their eyes.

Second, the interview assures that the subject will be filmed under favorable circumstances—an important technical consideration. In a memorandum to his news staff, Reuven Frank once gave this advice about interviewing:

> By definition, an interview is at least somewhat controllable. It must be arranged; it must be agreed to. . . . Try not to interview in harsh sunlight. Try not to interview in so noisy a setting that words cannot be heard. Let subjects be lit. If lights bother your subject, talk to him, discuss the weather, gentle him, involve his interest and his emotions so that he forgets or ignores the lights. It takes longer, but speed is poor justification for a piece of scrapped film.

To make the subjects appear even more dignified and articulate, it is the customary practice to repeat the same question a number of times, allowing the respondent to "sharpen his answer," as one correspondent has put it. At times, the person interviewed is permitted to compose his own questions for the interviewer or, at least, to rephrase them. Rehearsals are also quite common.

Third, interviews provide an easy means of presenting an abstract or difficult-to-film concept in human terms, as Reuven Frank has explained:

> The best interviews are of people reacting—or people expounding. . . . No important story is without them. They can be recorded and transmitted tastefully . . . nuclear disarmament, unemployment, flood, automation, name me a recent major story without its human involvement.

Although the networks have instituted strict policies against misleading "reenactments" and "staging," film footage is sometimes generated by having someone demonstrate or enact aspects of a story for the camera. Bruce Cohn, a producer for ABC News at the time, explained the practice to the House Special Subcommittee on Investigations during hearings on "news staging." Describing the difference between hard news and feature stories, Cohn said, "Generally speaking, a feature story is only brought to the public's attention because the journalist who conceived of doing such a report thinks it would be of interest or of importance. Therefore, a feature story must be 'set up' by a journalist if it is to be transformed into usable information. There is no reason why this 'setting up' cannot be done in an honest and responsible manner . . . people involved in feature stories are often asked to demonstrate how they do something . . . in fact, by its very nature, a feature story may be nothing but what the subcommittee negatively refers to as 'staging.' But it can, and should, be honest staging—not altering any facts or circumstances."

The ABC feature stories in question involved the hiring of stand-ins to serve as "customers" in a story about how the recession was affecting Las Vegas gambling casinos (because the casinos would not permit real customers to be filmed) and the simulation of an emergency run by a police car in a film sequence about the Seattle Police Department.

Another basic technique of creating film for editing purposes involves shooting additional silent footage, from various angles, of the principal participants and the background settings of a news event. The silent footage can then be intercut with the sound film according to the demands of the story line. One type of such silent footage that is required by all three networks is the "cutaway shot." Often, the cutaway is a view of an audience's reaction while the news subject is speaking. Most stories involving press conferences, hearings, speeches, and interviews need cutaway shots to facilitate smooth editing. This is because they afford the editor a good deal of flexibility in matching the film to the story line. A CBS manual explains:

> Because of time limits and in order to heighten impact, television must shorten speeches. . . . This is difficult to do unless the cameraman furnishes a visual "meanwhile," or cutaway. For example, in shooting a speech, be sure to make several shots of audience reaction. If there's no audience, shoot other newsmen, or your own sound camera. These clips will furnish the second-and-a-half cutaways which the film editor can insert to avoid a "jump cut" if he wants to clip a sentence from the middle of one lens "take." Otherwise, the speaker's head would seem to jump. . . . In this connection, it often helps to shoot a roll or two of stock cutaways for editing use— various shots of the film crew, close-ups of a hand writing on a pad, reporters' faces, etc.

Though the majority of network news stories involve people talking, there is also a category of stories concerned mainly with visual action, such as riots, demonstrations, and disasters, in which the pictures need not be synchronized with words spoken at the time but can be shown with a "voice-over" narration. In these action stories, cameramen are usually given free rein, with the understanding that they will seek out the most dramatic or exciting moments of the event. One NBC cameraman has explained, "What the producers want on the film is as much blood and violence as we can find. That's the name of the game, and every cameraman knows it."

The producers' fondness for action film is based to some extent on their assumption that the audience is more likely to be engrossed by visual excitement than by "talking heads"— that is, a film of people talking about issues. This assumption, in turn, may be based on network research showing that the audience for network news tends to be older and to have less income and education than the general television audience. (Such research probably indicates not that news is inherently more interesting to older, less educated viewers but only that such viewers usually are in the majority in the early evening, when network news is broadcast.) . . .

Since network television is in the business of attracting and maintaining large audiences, the news operation, which is, after all, part of the networks' programming schedule, is also expected to maintain, if not attract, as large an audience as possible. But a network news program, unlike other news media, apparently can't depend entirely on its content to attract and maintain an audience. To a great extent, the size of its audience is determined by three outside factors. The first is affiliate acceptance. If a program is not carried, or "cleared," by the affiliates, then it simply is not available to the public. (ABC has significantly increased the audience for its evening news program since 1969 by increasing the number of stations that clear it from a hundred and twenty to a hundred and ninety-one.) The second is scheduling. A program that is broadcast at 7 P.M., say, stands a good chance of drawing a larger audience than it would at six-thirty, since more people are usually watching television at the later hour. (The television audience increases all day and reaches a peak at about 9 P.M.) The third factor is what is called "audience flow." Network executives and advertisers believe that a significant portion of the audience for any program is inherited, as they put it, from the preceding program. According to the theory of audience flow, an audience is like a river that continues in the same direction until it is somehow diverted. "The viewing habits of a large portion of the audience—at least, the audience that Nielsen measures—are governed more by the laws of inertia than by free choice,'' a network vice-president responsible for audience studies has remarked. "Unless they have a very definite reason to switch, like a ballgame, they continue to watch the programs on the channel they are tuned in to."

Many network executives believe that network news is even more dependent on audience flow than are entertainment programs, or even local newscasts featuring reports on local sports and weather conditions. Richard Salant, the president of CBS News, has said that "you'll find a general correlation between the ratings of the network news broadcast and the local news broadcast—and probably the local news is the decisive thing." But what of the selective viewer, who changes channels for network news? Network executives, relying on both audience studies and personal intuition, assume, first, that there is not a significant number of such viewers, and, second, that most of them choose particular news programs on the basis of the personalities of the commentators rather than the extent of the news coverage. Acting on these assumptions about audience behavior, the networks attempted to improve the ratings of their news shows by hiring "star" commentators and by investing in the programs that precede the network news. For example, in a memo to the president of NBC several years ago, a vice-president responsible for audience analysis made this suggestion for increasing the ratings in Los Angeles of the network's evening news program:

> It seems to me the only surefire way to increase our audience at 3:30 P.M. (and actually win the time period) is with Mike Douglas [a syndicated talk show, which NBC would have had to buy from Group W Productions, a subsidiary of the Westinghouse Broadcasting Company]. At 5–6 P.M. our news then should get at least what KABC is getting (let's say a 7 rating).
>
> Coming out of this increased lead-in—and a *news* lead-in, at that—I believe that [the evening news] at 6 P.M. will get a couple of rating points more. . . .

Similarly, a network can invest in the local news programs that precede or follow

the network news on the five stations it owns. NBC concluded from a detailed study that it commissioned of the Chicago audience that local news programs, unlike network news, which builds its audience through coverage of special events, can increase their ratings through improved coverage of weather, sports, and local events. The study recommended, for example, that the network-owned station in Chicago hire a more popular local weathercaster, since "almost as many viewers look forward to seeing the weather as the news itself." The networks also assist the affiliated stations with their local news programs, by providing a news syndication service. This supplies subscribing stations with sports and news stories through a half-hour feed, from which the stations can record stories for use on their own news programs.

Implicit in this approach to seeking higher ratings for network news programs is the idea that it doesn't make economic sense to spend large amounts on improving the editorial product. Hiring additional camera crews, reporters, and researchers presumably would not increase a news program's audience, and it definitely would be expensive. For instance, not only does each camera crew cost about a hundred thousand dollars a year to maintain, in equipment, salaries, and overtime, but it generates a prodigious amount of film—about twenty times as much as is used in the final stories—which has to be transported, processed, and edited. NBC accountants use a rule-of-thumb gauge of more than twenty dollars in service cost for every foot of film in the final story, which comes to more than seven hundred and twenty dollars a minute. And it is the number of camera crews a network maintains that defines, in some ways, the scope of its news-gathering operation. "The news you present is actually the news you cover," a network news vice-president has said. "The question is: How wide do you fling your net?"

In 1968, when I had access to staff meetings and assignment sheets at the three networks, NBC covered the nation each day with an average of ten camera crews, in New York, Chicago, Los Angeles, Washington, and Cleveland, plus two staff crews in Texas and one staff cameraman (who could assemble camera crews) in Boston. (In comparison, CBS's local news operation in Los Angeles, according to its news director, uses nine camera crews to cover the news of that one city.) Today, NBC says it has fifty domestic camera crews, but this figure includes sports, special events, and documentary crews, as well as local crews at the network's five stations. CBS says it has twenty full-time network news crews, in New York, Chicago, Los Angeles, Atlanta, and Washington, and ABC says it has sixteen, in New York, Chicago, Los Angeles, Washington, Atlanta, and Miami. Each of the networks also has camera crews in nine cities overseas. To be sure, when there is a momentous news event the networks can quickly mobilize additional crews—those regularly assigned to news documentaries, sports, and local news at network stations, or those of affiliated stations—but the net that is cast for national news on a day-to-day basis is essentially defined by the crews that are routinely available for network assignment, and their number is set by the economic logic of network television.

Another element in the economics of network news is the fact that it costs a good deal more to transmit stories from some places than it does from other places. The lines that connect the networks and their affiliates across the country can normally be used to transmit programs in only one direction—from the network's headquarters in New York to the affiliates. Therefore, to transmit news reports electronically from any "remote" location—that is, anywhere except network facilities in a few cities—to the network for rebroadcast, a news program must order special "long lines" between the two points from the American Telephone & Telegraph Co. The charges for the "long line" are now fifty-five cents a mile for up to an hour's use and seven hundred and fifty dollars for a "loop," which is the package of electronic equipment that connects the transmission point (usually an affiliated station) with the telephone company's "long lines." It is even more expensive to order stories sent electronically by means of the satellite-relay system—eighteen hundred

and fifty dollars for the first ten minutes of a story from London to New York and about twenty-four hundred dollars for the first ten minutes of a story from Tokyo to New York —and these costs are charged against the program's budget. The weekly budget for the NBC Nightly News is in excess of two hundred thousand dollars, and that of the CBS Evening News is almost a hundred thousand dollars, but more than half of each is committed in advance for the salaries and expenses of the producers, editors, writers, and other members of the "unit," and for the studio and other overhead costs that are automatically charged against the program's budget. (Differences in the billing of these charges account for most of the difference in the budgets of the NBC and CBS programs.) At CBS, about forty-nine thousand dollars a week, or eight thousand dollars a program, is left for "remotes." Since a news program needs from six to eight film stories a night, and some satellite charges can be as high as three thousand dollars apiece, the budget, in effect, limits the number of "remote" stories that can be transmitted in an average week.

Because of differences in transmission costs, producers have a strong incentive to take news stories from some areas rather than others, especially when their budgets are strained. The fact that networks base most of their camera crews and correspondents in New York, Washington, Chicago, and Los Angeles reinforces the advantage of using news stories from these areas, since they involve less overtime and travel expense. It is not surprising, then, that so many of the film stories shown on the national news programs originate in these areas. Although the geographical distribution of film stories varies greatly from day to day, over any sustained period it is skewed in the direction of these few large cities. It is economically more efficient to consign news of small-town America and of remote cities to timeless features such as Charles Kuralt's "On the Road" segments on the CBS Evening News. This suggests that if network news programs tend to focus on problems of a few large urban centers, it is less because, as former Vice-President Agnew argued, an "enclosed fraternity" of "commentators and producers live and work in geographical and intellectual confines of Washington, D.C., or New York City . . . [and] draw their political and social views from the same sources" than because the networks' basic economic structure compels producers, willy-nilly, to select a large share of their filmed stories from a few locations. . . .

The Fairness Doctrine requires broadcasters to provide a reasonable opportunity for the presentation of "contrasting viewpoints on controversial issues of public importance" in the course of their news and public-affairs programming. Unlike the "equal time" provisions of Section 315 of the Communications Act—which applies only to candidates running for a public office and requires that if a station grants time to one candidate it must grant equal time to other candidates, except on news programs—the Fairness Doctrine does not require that opposing arguments be given an equal number of minutes, be presented on the same program, or be presented within any specific period. It is left up to the licensee to decide what constitutes a "controversial issue of public importance," a "fair" reply, and a "reasonable time" in which the reply should be made. Moreover, broadcasters are apparently not expected to be equally "fair" on all issues of public importance; for example, the Commission states in its "Fairness Primer" that it is not "the Commission's intention to make time available to Communists or to the Communist viewpoints."

Although no television station has ever lost its license because of a violation of the Fairness Doctrine, the doctrine has affected the form and content of network news in a number of ways. Most notably, the Fairness Doctrine puts an obligation on affiliates to "balance" any network program that advances only one side of an issue by themselves providing, in the course of their own programming, the other side, and the affiliates, rather than risk having to fulfill such an obligation, which could be both costly and bothersome, insist, virtually as a condition of taking network news, that the networks incorporate the obligatory "contrasting viewpoints" in their own news report. The networks, in turn,

make it a policy to present opposing views on any issue that could conceivably be construed as controversial.

This pro-and-con reporting is perfectly consistent with the usual notion of objectivity, if objectivity is defined, as it is by many correspondents, as "telling both sides of a story." It can, however, seriously conflict with the value that journalists place on what is now called investigative reporting, or simply any reporting the purpose of which is "getting to the bottom" of an issue, or "finding the truth," as correspondents often put it. A correspondent is required to present "contrasting points of view" even if he finds the views of one side to be valid and those of the other side to be false and misleading (in the Fairness Doctrine, truth is no defense), and therefore any attempt to resolve a controversial issue and "find the truth" is likely to be self-defeating. . . .

A frequent criticism of television news is that it is superficial—that it affords only scant coverage of news events, lacks depth or sufficient analysis of events, and engages in only a minimum of investigative reporting. The assumption of such criticism is that television newsmen lack journalistic credentials, that producers and executives are lax or indifferent toward their responsibilities, and that changing or educating the broadcasters would improve the news product. But the level of journalism in network news is more or less fixed by the time, money, and manpower that can be allocated to it, and these are determined by the structure of network television. Any substantial improvement in the level of network journalism, such as expanding coverage of events to a truly nationwide scale, would therefore require a structural change in network television that would effectively reorder its economic and political incentives, rather than merely a change of personnel.

Another common criticism is, again, that network news is politically biased in favor of liberal or left-wing causes and leaders, because a small clique of newsmen in New York and Washington shape the news to fit their own political beliefs. In this critique, network news is presumed to be highly politicized by the men who select and report it, and the remedy most often suggested is to employ conservative newsmen to balance the liberal viewpoints. Since, for economic reasons, much of the domestic news on the network programs does in fact come from a few big cities, and since in recent years many of the efforts to change the distribution of political values and services have been concentrated in the big cities, the networks perhaps have reported a disproportionately large share of these activities. The requirement that network news be "nationalized" further adds to the impression that networks are advancing radical causes, for in elevating local disputes to national proportions newscasters appear to be granting them uncalled-for importance.

Left-wing critics complain that network news neglects the inherent contradictions in the American system. Their critique runs as follows: Network news focuses not on substantive problems but on symbolic protests. By overstating the importance of protest actions, television news invites the audience to judge the conduct of the protesters rather than the content of the problem. This creates false issues. Popular support is generated against causes that, on television, appear to rely on violent protests, while underlying economic and social problems are systematically masked or ignored. Broadcasters can be expected to help perpetuate "the system," because they are an important part of it. Thus, one critic writes, "The media owners will do anything to maintain these myths. . . . They will do anything to keep the public from realizing that the Establishment dominates society through its direct and indirect control of the nation's communication system." In fact, however, the tendency to depict symbolic protests rather than substantive problems is closely related to the problem of audience maintenance. Protests can be universally comprehended, it is presumed, if they are presented in purely symbolic terms: one group standing for one cause, challenging another group and cause. The sort of detail that would be necessary to clarify economic and social issues is not easily translated into visual terms, whereas the sort of dramatic images that can be found in violent protests have an immediate impact on an audience. Newsmen

therefore avoid liberal or radical arguments not because they are politically committed to supporting "the system" but because such arguments do not satisfy the requisites of network news.

Finally, in what might best be called the social-science critique, network news is faulted for presenting a picture of society that does not accurately correspond to the empirical data. Spokesmen selected by television to represent groups in society tend to be statistically atypical of the groups for which they are supposedly speaking; for example, militant students may have appeared to be in the majority on college campuses in America during the nineteen-sixties because of the frequency with which they were selected to represent student views, when in fact data collected by social scientists showed that they constituted a small minority. It is generally argued that such discrepancies stem from a lack of readily usable data rather than any intent on the part of journalists to misrepresent situations. The implication in this critique is that if network news organizations had the techniques of social scientists, or employed social scientists as consultants, they would produce a more realistic version of the claims and aspirations of different segments of society. However, the selection of spokesmen to appear on television is determined less by a lack of data than by the organizational needs of network news. In order to hold the attention of viewers to whom the subject of the controversy may be of no interest, television newsmen select spokesmen who are articulate, easily identifiable, and dramatic, and the "average" person in a group cannot be depended on to manifest these qualities. Moreover, the nationalization of news requires that spokesmen represent the major themes of society rather than what is statistically typical. Given the organizational need to illustrate news stories with spokesmen who are both dramatic and thematic, network news cannot be expected to present a picture that conforms to the views of social scientists, no matter how much data or how many technical skills the social scientists might supply.

As long as the requisites remain essentially the same, network news can be expected to define American society by the problems of a few urban areas rather than of the entire nation, by action rather than ideas, by dramatic protests rather than substantive contradictions, by "newsmakers" rather than economic and social structures, by atypical rather than typical views, and by synthetic national themes rather than disparate local events.

53
We Have Seen the Future of Video and It Sure Looks A Lot Like the Same Old Wasteland

Chris Welles

For several years, analysts have been predicting that cable television would significantly diversify available TV programming. As a result, the dominance of the three major networks would be sharply reduced. The recent growth of satellite-delivered programming designed for distribution via cable and the consumer acceptance of home video devices, such as videocassette recorders and videodisc players, have also provided viewing alternatives. Confronted with a far wider range of programs, the futurists predicted that viewers would opt for higher quality, specialized offerings.

Chris Welles, who writes about media industries, examines television's future and comes to the opposite conclusion. Pointing out that the heavy television viewer is essentially insatiable when it comes to the standard comedy, sports, and drama, Welles argues that such programs will continue to dominate television in the future. Further, he sees the use of television as essentially escapist, and, therefore, the tendency to tune in to the "lowest common denominator" programs will also continue. Nevertheless, there still remains the possibility that national audiences for more specialized programming could be assembled via these new technologies.

Nicholas Johnson is smiling, for at last there is hope. As network television's most vociferous critic, he has railed for years against the abominations of the tube, especially the "tyranny of banal mass-audience programming." But the tyranny persisted. Now, however,

Source: From *Esquire* (June 1980). © by Chris Welles. Reprinted by permission of the author c/o International Creative Management.

what is being hailed as the "video revolution" has arrived. "It will be a long time dying," says Johnson, "but the television industry as it's presently known is obsolete." It is only a matter of time, many TV critics predict, before we will witness an electronic unplugging of cataclysmic moment: the demise of the three networks and, even more important, the extinguishment of the "vast wasteland" of images inflicted on our eyeballs for a quarter century.

The instruments of this historic dissolution, as the critics see it, are the three new video technologies that underlie the video revolution:

1. Cable television systems that now transmit over wire to more than fifteen million homes, 20 percent of those with TV sets. For an average of $7 per month, subscribers receive as many as thirty-five channels of programming. About five million homes pay an additional fee for pay-television channels of special programs.
2. Communications satellites that permit low-cost national video transmission to cable systems.
3. Consumer videotape recorders and videodisc players that allow viewers to replace regular network schedules with an extensive variety of home videotape and disc programs.

These technologies, in which such major corporations as IBM, General Electric, Time Inc., American Express, and the New York Times Company have invested millions of dollars, permit viewers and program producers to bypass the heretofore impregnable oligopoly of the airwaves maintained by the three commercial networks. That oligopoly originated mainly from the scarcity of broadcast space on the VHF spectrum, which restricted most communities to no more than three usable channels. Gradually, local stations were linked into three national networks that came to pursue the same business strategy: to maximize profits by attracting the largest possible audiences with what critics term "lowest common denominator" programs. The audiences are then sold, in effect, to advertisers of mass-market consumer products. Network domination of the broadcast airwaves—the only means of electronic visual access to national audiences—always foreclosed serious rivals.

Cable, satellites, and home video devices change all this: They are essentially new distribution systems with virtually unlimited channel capacity. It is as if OPEC were confronted with an inexhaustible new source of petroleum. Numerous video doomsayers predict that the proliferation of new channels will fragment and siphon away the bulk of the networks' audience and their advertising revenues.

As the network oligopoly collapses, we will progress, it is said, toward a glorious age of video programming. It will be a bountiful refoliation of the wasteland, a realization of the promise displayed briefly by television during the golden age of the early 1950s, the era of such widely praised shows as *Playhouse 90, Studio One,* and *See It Now.*

The most salient feature of the new video's golden age, according to predictions, will be what futurist Alvin Toffler calls in his new book, *The Third Wave,* the "demassification" of television. Says Toffler, "We're going to move from a few images distributed widely to many images distributed narrowly." The new narrowcasting will consist of dozens, perhaps hundreds, of sharply focused channels serving the television audience's vastly diverse affinities and tastes. Instead of docilely submitting to mindless, mass-taste network schedules, the viewer will become his own programmer and create his own schedule from the abundance of much more civilized, intelligent, and imaginative fare delivered by the new technologies. With these technologies as weapons, *Chicago Tribune* TV critic Gary Deeb wrote recently, angry viewers "are striking back at the networks that have trampled them and treated them like slobs for so long."

This possesses the irresistible melodramatic appeal of a prime-time mini-series: After years of horrible subjugation, hapless and disgruntled viewers now have the means to dispatch their oppressors into oblivion, seize control of their television sets, and watch what *they* want to watch, not what somebody else wants them to watch.

Close scrutiny of this melodrama, though, reveals some unfortunate plot flaws. The networks, it turns out, are much less vulnerable than they appear. The new weapons being used against them are not very effective and may not be weapons at all. And the viewers don't seem very interested in a revolution.

Michael Fuchs, head of programming for Home Box Office, the largest pay-TV service and a subsidiary of Time Inc., is sitting on a couch in his office in the Time & Life Building. The new videocasters, just like the old broadcasters, are, for the most part, scattered along a short stretch of Manhattan's Sixth Avenue, and from his couch Fuchs has a clear view of the headquarters of CBS, NBC, and ABC.

They also have a clear view of him, which is appropriate, since HBO has emerged as the fourth network. With over four million subscribers, two thirds of the pay-TV market, HBO is by far the most successful new videocaster. With the possible exception of Showtime, its much smaller rival, it is the only one to produce a large volume of original programming, to attract a substantial audience, and to present a serious threat to the three older networks.

HBO's new-video images, however, bear a surprisingly close resemblance to those of its old-video competitors. Its basic fare is popular entertainment: recently released movies, which it can transmit without commercials or cuts (due to its exemption from FCC program regulations); sports events; and original specials, typically nightclub-style shows with stars like Diana Ross and Robin Williams. Among other recent HBO shows was *National Lampoon Presents Disco Beaver from Outer Space,* which included a segment called "The Breast Game," a bare-breasted parody of TV game shows.

"We're trying to make HBO special," says Fuchs, a young, fast-talking lawyer who previously packaged TV properties for the William Morris Agency. "It's not commercial TV. We have tremendous built-in advantages over the networks—language, nudity. But we're still appealing to a mass audience. Our

people are not freaks. They're the same people who watch the networks. They're TV watchers." To build viewer loyalty, HBO is currently developing network-style series. "We're not looking to reinvent the wheel," Fuchs says. "Everything in this business is derivative."

HBO arrived at its present programming mix after disappointing experiences with special-interest cultural programs—just the sort of shows, in fact, that critics have been counting on the video revolution to deliver.

"We learned with a lot of hard knocks," Fuchs says. "We tried culture. We had *The Pallisers* [a BBC series based on the Anthony Trollope novels] on the air. I think it would be wonderful if the American public had a cultural channel. But I don't know anybody in the business who believes the country is ready for that. We decided the only way we could make money was entertainment. If tomorrow we said to people: no movies, all culture . . . well, then, goodbye business. In a way, the process is very democratic. The subscribers vote every month. You've got to keep your eye on that box office."

Old video is the chief stock-in-trade of most of the other new videocasters as well. Showtime also features movies and entertainment specials, including a reunion of *Playboy* Playmates and a Miss Nude California contest. Showtime has taped *The Ed McMahon Show* as a possible pilot for a weekly series. Most nonpay cable channels are merely signals from existing broadcast stations. The other channels carry various satellite-transmitted cable services consisting of such derivative and traditional programming as old movies, network reruns, and sports events. Beyond automated time and weather channels, local cable operators do relatively little serious origination of their own. As CBS Broadcast Group president Gene F. Jankowski put it in a discussion of cable television, "It is a case of new technology clothing itself in the timeworn hand-me-downs and tattered castoffs of established and accepted broadcasting."

Home video, so far, is no different. Virtually all of the available "software," as videocasters call programming, for videotape recorders and disc players consists of movies.

(As much as 60 percent of prerecorded video-tape sales are pornographic films.) Most videotape recorder owners use their machines mainly to "time shift," to record regular television broadcasts for later viewing.

Predictions that the video revolution will vanquish established broadcast programming misconstrue what the revolution is all about. The revolution is basically one of technology —the way signals get to your TV set. Cable, satellite, and home video may eventually supplant most over-the-air transmission. But the signals distributed by the new technologies are not a revolutionary new medium that will necessarily make existing television shows obsolete the way the telegraph replaced the pony express. What people call the new video is not a new medium at all. It is television.

As they become more broadly applied, the new technologies will spur wider experimentation with new forms of television. The new video will not be a precise replica of the old video, but it is unlikely to be very different. As television, the new video is subject to the same inescapable economic exigencies that have always dictated the content of the old video. Whether it is dominated by CBS or Time Inc., television is economics first, art and everything else second. Those economics require that television essentially remain a mass medium catering to mass tastes. "The new technology," says Benton & Bowles senior vice-president George Simko, "will be driven by software that appeals to the largest number of people."

Most television programs are extraordinarily expensive to produce: $600,000 or more for a typical prime-time hour. A broadcaster must deliver a very large audience to advertisers just to cover his costs. Moreover, the cost of a program, unlike that of a magazine, is fixed and independent of the size of its audience. This means that a larger audience generates not only greater revenues for the broadcaster but also larger profits and profit margins. The broadcaster has no incentive to aim for a small audience when for the same cost he can aim for a larger audience and make a bigger profit.

Though it obtains its revenues from subscribers, pay television is ruled by the same economic incentives. Most pay-TV subscribers pay a flat monthly fee for the entire service instead of separate per-program assessments. Thus it is in the economic interest of a pay service to spend its program budget on shows that please the largest number of subscribers. "The dynamics of video are that you can't satisfy little disparate tastes," says Fuchs. "We can't do a show on stamp collecting for one percent of the audience."

Some new-video entrepreneurs, nevertheless, are actively pursuing narrowcasting. Narrowcast networks appealing to such special interests as blacks, children, Spanish Americans, and sports buffs are transmitting programs by satellite to thousands of cable systems.

The narrowcasters' financial success has been marginal, though, because they too are ruled by television economics. Since the channels are provided free to cable subscribers, the narrowcasters are dependent on advertising. And as national services, they have had to seek business from the same mass-consumer-goods companies that advertise on the broadcast networks. Those companies buy narrowcast time the way they buy broadcast time—on a cost-per-thousand-viewers basis. As special-interest services, though, the narrowcasts predictably obtain very low ratings—usually a fraction of a percent of the cable audience—and thus very low ad revenues. Total ad income for the cable industry in 1978, according to the FCC, was just $4.9 million, versus $8 billion for commercial TV broadcasting. A channel of USA Network sports events, perhaps the most popular of the narrowcast services, collected $2 million in ad income in 1979. That is about the cost of four minutes of commercials during a Super Bowl broadcast.

Meager ad revenues have forced the narrowcasters to rely mostly on dated and derivative programming from other media, especially movies. SIN National Spanish Television Network, a Spanish-language station, offers soap operas produced for South American television. Rather than risk developing new forms, most of the handful of narrowcasters producing original programs merely adapt traditional network formats to special audiences. Discussing the time when Black Entertainment Television network, which now airs black movies two hours a week, will have the funds for its own programs, president Robert Johnson remarked that "the black talk shows, sitcoms, and game shows are only a few years away."

Other narrowcasters are trying low-cost production schemes. Cable News Network, an all-news station scheduled to begin operating June 1, intends to produce twenty-four hours of news daily with a staff of 250 and an annual budget of $25 million.* By contrast, each of the broadcast network news divisions, which produce far fewer hours of programming, has a staff of over a thousand and an annual budget of $150 million and is expanding the resources and time devoted to news. "Dollars always force compromises," concedes CNN president Reese Schonfeld. "But people who like news would rather watch news, even plain pipe-rack news, than *Charlie's Angels.*" Instead of tightly edited "high gloss" newscasts, he says, CNN will stress more informally produced live, on-the-scene reports.

Most low-budget narrowcast ventures, though, have fared badly. "The public is spoiled," says Fuchs. "They're used to the lushest video." Robert Rosencrans, president of UA-Columbia Cablevision, which produces the USA Network sports service, says he must use the same slow-motion, instant-replay, multiangle camera techniques the commercial networks use. "It's very expensive," he says, "but you can't get away with cutting corners." The less money a narrowcaster spends on programs, the fewer viewers are likely to be lured away from more attractively produced network and pay-TV shows. Fewer viewers, in turn, means an even lower program budget.

"We try to be supportive of these efforts," says Charles Dolan, founder of HBO and now operator of a cable system in the New York suburbs that is one of the country's largest. "But that doesn't prevent me from being skeptical. I don't think any of them have shown they are viable."

As new-video entrepreneurs continue to look for ways to circumvent television's mass-market economics and develop imaginative alternatives to the old video, some are certain to achieve viability if not prosperity. Though television economics will require most videotape and disc software to have mass appeal, for instance, many experts foresee a respectable market for high-priced, low-budget instructional tapes and discs on such subjects as cooking and golfing.

Rather than develop custom programming or attempt to outbid the networks for programs and talent, as is often predicted, most videocasters will simply continue to plug themselves into existing mass-market video distribution systems. High production costs, the dearth of top-quality talent and product, and the substantial risks of market failure have always required what the trade calls "sequential" distribution. Movies, for instance, are routed from theaters to network television to independent stations. Pay TV, tape, and discs have been forcing themselves into the front end of the movie distribution cycle, ahead of network television. Pay TV will probably sell original shows to the tape and disc market and perhaps even to commercial television.

The major software packagers and suppliers, though, will likely continue to be the three networks. No mere electromagnetic OPEC, the networks have become enormously powerful, wealthy, and efficient. They completely dominate television's production, distribution, and promotion mechanisms. They are creatures less of electronics than of economics, especially economies of scale. They are less dependent on sophisticated technologies than on sophisticated corporate management and strategy.

Compared to cable's $50 million, the networks spend $2.5 billion a year on programming. They produce a rising number of movies, have recently established divisions to create software and hardware for the home video market, and plan to supply programs to pay-TV and even narrowcast services. Not coincidentally, broadcasters own over 30 percent of the nation's cable systems. Says former CBS News president Fred Friendly: "In the end, the networks will dominate [the new video].

---

*CNN began operating in June 1980 [Eds.].

They have the money, the know-how, and the savvy.''

The new video, in sum, will continue to be more of the same old mass-appeal wasteland software that we have all come to know and to loathe. But do we really loathe it?

At the Sixth Avenue offices of A. C. Nielsen Company, the television industry's scorekeeper, researchers traffic not in dreams, hopes, and fears but in statistical measures of observable behavior.

"If you ask people whether they want to see something like Shakespeare on television, half of them will say they do," says David Harkness, a [vice-president] for Nielsen. "They want the interviewer to think well of them. But when you put Shakespeare on TV, nobody watches. You have to be very suspicious when people tell you what their intentions are. That can be a lot different from what they really do.

"I think people are somewhat dissatisfied with TV. But when you offer them something different they don't take it, because they aren't really all that dissatisfied. The American public has a great love affair with the TV set. Consumers today complain about a lot of things. But you don't see mass protests to make TV better."

Some data from Nielsen surveys:

1. Viewing hours per person in 1979 reached an all-time high of 3.9 hours a day, up 11 percent over the past five years.
2. Largely due to cable television expansion, the percentage of TV homes able to receive many channels has been increasing sharply. Between 1970 and 1980, for instance, the percentage receiving eight or more stations rose from 37 to 57.
3. The growth in viewing and viewing options has so far had a negligible impact on the networks' long-standing 90-percent share of the prime-time audience. Of the new video services, only pay TV has displayed any erosion capability. A Nielsen study of a sample month, November 1979, found that in the 7 percent of homes that are pay

subscribers, pay channels had an average prime-time share of 15 percent, versus the networks' 79 percent. Nearly all the remaining viewing by the pay families was of other commercial stations. The audience share of all non-pay programs produced specially for cable systems, including the narrowcasts, was about one percent. Only 6 percent of the pay-TV homes viewed *any* cable programming during the sample month.

4. Instead of replacing network shows, most of the new video seems to be viewed in addition to commercial television. Pay-TV homes, for instance, watch four more hours a week of television than families without pay TV. Says David Harkness, "They're not watching HBO to avoid the trash on the networks. When they're not watching HBO, they're watching *Laverne and Shirley* in heavy quantities. They enjoy TV so much that they're willing to pay for more."

Nielsen does not forecast. But the overwhelming consensus of new and old videocasters is that during the current decade the three networks will suffer an erosion in audience share, mainly due to pay-TV, of no more than 10 percent. Even that figure presumes rapid growth in cable and home video penetration. In the past, that growth has lagged behind most estimates.

As someone with a very low opinion of most network television, I would dearly love to believe, as so many critics do, that the industry is grossly underestimating public taste. I would love to believe that armed with the new video, viewers will soon shout they're mad as hell and will resolve not to take it anymore. But if one searches for even a few traces of yearnings for better programs and inclinations toward revolution, next to nothing is found. For years, public television has striven valiantly to present a cultured, civilized alternative to network television. But despite increased emphasis on entertainment programming, no more than 2 percent of the prime-time audience regularly tunes in. Meanwhile, during any given minute in prime time, close to a hundred million faithful Americans have their sets hooked up to the wasteland. The real enemy, as has often been observed in other contexts, is us.

Those who regard the networks as tyrants fail to appreciate the function most of us assign to television. The millions who watch regularly are not necessarily cultural ignoramuses, intellectual dwarfs, indiscriminate clones of some prototypical Mass Viewer. Many read good books, go to museums, and pursue sophisticated special interests. But when they sit down in front of the TV set, usually at the end of a day of work, they are generally not looking for cultural uplift or particularized information. Says Harlan Kleiman, a former avant-garde Off Broadway producer who now makes programs for various pay-TV services: "People just want to be diverted. TV is chewing gum for the eyes."

Viewers' tastes in television diversion are sufficiently homogeneous and unsophisticated that most are satisfied, if not excited, by such standard entertainment formats as sitcoms and adventure shows. Studies show that better-educated viewers watch the same programs as less-educated viewers.

The tube may offer more than mere diversion. Regular viewers tend to turn on the set less to watch a specific program than simply to watch *something*. Studies suggest that the swift flow of flickering images can have an anesthetizing, almost stupefying, effect on the brain. Some researchers have termed the set an "electronic fireplace." Television seems effective in obliterating rumination on the often unpleasant outside world, though what, if anything, it instills remains unclear.

While the broadcasters effectively serve the needs of the great mass of the television audience, critics are correct in charging that the broadcasters, for economic reasons, have ignored fringe tastes and interests. If the video revolution is not materially affecting the mass, it is at least presenting more options for those on the fringes. "What we've done is democratize television," says Kleiman, "so that many marginal and peripheral markets can exist. They're only going to get a tiny fragment of the audience, but they're going to have the opportunity to reach that fragment. That's what the revolution is." Pornographic films, local basketball games, bawdy nightclub acts, black sitcoms—the current content of these peripheral markets—may not be much to cheer about. But Michael Rice, who before becoming head of the Aspen Institute program on communications and society was general manager of Boston's WGBH, perhaps the most adventurous public television station, does not despair. "Critics who have bemoaned commercial television have typically shared the view that what we need is more demanding drama, more controversy, more serious music," he says. "Basically, their complaint is that TV has not been geared to *their* interests and tastes. But there is a lot more to diversity. The Spanish-language network isn't a rival of *Studio One,* but it does serve a special interest. The new video may be more effective in satisfying that kind of diversity than the long-cherished hope that television could raise the level of civilization."

This is not the end of the story. Recall what Michael Fuchs of HBO said about subscribers' voting every month. Network viewers vote every time they turn the dial. Now consider two groups of voters. Though millions loyally tune in *Laverne and Shirley,* there are probably as many who almost never watch TV. Charles Dolan, the cable operator, says that beyond a certain point it becomes almost impossible to increase cable's penetration of a community. Signing up the holdouts, he claims, "is like selling Bibles to people who don't believe in God." These people could start voting.

Then there are the millions who do watch *Laverne and Shirley.* Fred Friendly accuses the networks of a "self-fulfilling prophecy of defeat. They have been degrading American taste, hour after hour." Degrading, perhaps, but not destroying. These people could change their votes.

More options are now available to us as voters. More people are soliciting our votes. More people are watching the ballot box. If enough of us want something different, we have the power to get it.

PART FIVE

Personal Media

Personal Media

Just where do the masses themselves fit into "mass media"? Most articles in earlier sections have operated on the assumption that while the mass media in America basically exist "for" the people, they are neither "of" nor "by" the people in the senses of direct ownership and created content. The articles that follow focus on means of communication that challenge the basic assumption. What we are calling "personal" media (though our inclusions are representative rather than exclusive) takes Richard Maisel's earlier claims for the contemporary fragmentation of media audiences to their furthest logical extension.

The first selection describes an innovation in which the line between the "person" and the "medium" cannot be drawn at all. The "Bone Fone," written by James Litke of the Associated Press, takes technology inside the individual and makes the human being part of the equipment.

What is possible through technology is similarly possible through distribution. Marshall Cook tells how each writer can become his or her own publisher, thus avoiding some of the pitfalls and disappointments that make up the common fate of all but a few would-be writers.

Not only can people produce and distribute their own books, they can also have their own TV shows. Though unknown to most people, the opportunities for appearing before a cable television audience are surprisingly plentiful—and they may be increasing. Terry Clifford, in "Vanity Video," gives some case histories and explanations for the existence of this interface between "personal" and "mass" media.

Less glamorous and more familiar, the telephone is one of the oldest forms of modern communication, and surely the most widely used medium. In "The Colossus of Talk," John Brooks describes the present status of and future possibilities for the huge network controlled by AT&T. Both the recent ruling that frees the giant corporation to compete in hitherto restricted areas and the already-expanding function of telephone links in computer-data transmission make the telephone's story far from old-fashioned.

Partly because of phone lines, computers for home use are coming of age, as Richard Mikita describes in the next article. Hope and fear of the snowballing technology of computer science will, no doubt, dominate the immediate future of personal communications.

A large part of that future is already here in embryonic form, as John Wicklein shows in "Wired City, U. S. A." The combination of computers, two-way, interactive cable television, and the expanding capacity of satellite transmission are all factors that may make it increasingly unnecessary for the citizen of the future to leave his electronic cave.

54
Wrap Yourself in Music

James Litke

The expression "to feel it in one's bones" has always been a figurative description of ultimate identification with an external experience. James Litke describes the literalization of this metaphor in the following article, originally written for the Associated Press.

If you get annoyed by people carrying loud-playing tape decks and radios in public, you can always recommend the "Bone Fone," a sound system that's more like a scarf than a radio.

"It's like wearing a concert hall around your neck," says Bill Hass, the 32-year-old inventor who was inspired by a skier wearing headphones.

With the Bone Fone, only the listener shakes, rattles and rolls; other folks hear hardly a murmur. The wearer's bones provide the amplification.

The compact, 15-ounce miniaturized AM-FM stereo radio is available only through the mail at present, but Hass, president of Bone Fone Corp., said he expects it to be on store shelves by April.

"Three factors make it better than anyone expected," Hass explained. "The first is close placement of the speaker to the ear, so that a low level of volume creates high sound pressure.

"The second factor—where the name comes from—is that the unit actually pulsates because of the way the speaker is mounted and the vibrations are transmitted through your body."

Because bone acts as an amplifier, he said, "the sound resonates to the inner ear."

Thirdly, the unit delivers quality stereo separation because of the proximity of the right ear to the right channel and conversely, left to left. Further, the proximity of the unit to both ears takes advantage of an acoustic effect called cross-feed—the right channel being picked up by the left ear and vice versa—creating a spatial effect similar to how the music was originally recorded.

"You can understand the idea by relating it to headphones, which seem to center the music inside your head," Hass said. "With the Bone Fone, music tends to surround you."

Hass, an avid skier, designed the unit with the musically inclined sportsman in mind.

The genesis for the "Bone Fone" came to Hass about five years ago while he watched another skier make his way down the slopes wearing headphones.

"I tried it myself, with a $15 dollar tape player on my back and headphones," he said. "It sounded really neat, if you can imagine a Strauss waltz playing while you sail down the mountain. But it looked funny and the headphones kept falling off. I figured there must be an easier way."

Then a director of planning with the accounting firm of Peat, Martwick, Mitchell & Co., Hass developed some prototypes, patented the unit and developed a strategy to market it. But he found several large companies unwilling to promote a product not developed from within their ranks.

"I was faced with the decision every inventor faces trying to realize his idea," Hass said. "Eventually, I decided to leave my job and form my own company, have it made and market it.

Source: From *The Associated Press* (February 27, 1980). Reprinted by permission of the publisher.

"I asked people carrying those 10-pound units which they'd prefer, and about 50 percent went with the Bone Fone," Hass said. "Some people will keep the boxes because they want status. But if we get 50 percent, think what a great thing it would be for society."

55
Personal Publishing

Marshall Cook

Marshall Cook, a writer and teacher at the University of Wisconsin-Extension, has published poems, short stories, and articles, primarily in literary magazines and Sunday supplements. His hobbies include writing novels and collecting rejection slips. In the following article on alternative methods of publishing, he gives pointers on how to separate those hobbies.

Consider the plight of the writer.

Forget the writing. That's the easy part.

After the writing is finished, you bundle that piece of yourself disguised as a manuscript, cart it to the post office, and shell out for first-class postage. You couldn't very well send your baby bulk rate.

You pay, also, to have the manuscript shipped back, in anywhere from a week to two years, augmented by a single printed sheet that invariably begins, "Thank you for submitting your manuscript to Hostile House. We have given it careful consideration. Unfortunately . . . "

"Submit" is the right word.

Your friends accuse you of selling out, but you know better. You can't even find a buyer.

The large publishing houses, many now owned by huge corporate conglomerates, yearly winnow some 350,000 book-length manuscripts to select approximately 40,000 titles for publication. No one keeps count of the unsolicited manuscripts returned unread.

Of the lucky 40,000 survivors, only two in ten stand much chance of achieving commercial success. These 8,000 titles receive most of the promotional energy and money. They are likely to be the proven profit makers: ghosted autobiographies of fading screen stars and sports has-beens; the latest fad diets, political exposés, and get-rich-quick schemes; the annual offerings from Harold Robbins and other fiction factories.

For the other 32,000, it's a short, unhappy tenure on the remaindering tables and then out-of-print oblivion.

With a primary interest in profit, with a huge overhead, with 4–1 odds against them at best, little wonder the corporate publishers won't take a chance on that unsolicited manuscript from the creative writing major in Kadoka, South Dakota.

What's the writer to do?

A great deal.

The writer can apply the same dedication, desire, skill, and perseverance needed to write that manuscript toward publishing it.

I've collected my share of rejection slips. Reams of them. I have been insulted, talked down to, ignored. One magazine publisher regularly steals my paper clips.

The matter-of-fact manner in which my work is dismissed chills me. "We have read your manuscript. We have decided not to publish it."

Oh.

I've also received warm, caring letters, a few near-misses, enough pay-off from the slot machines to keep me pumping in those silver dollars. Even though my confrontation with the corporate giant has thus far been profitless and largely painful, I continue to let them know I'm out here, writing, struggling, dreaming.

And, at last, I've had some poems, stories, and articles published, primarily in the little magazines and Sunday supplements. Each publication brings new hope, justification for the lonely hours barricaded from wife and son, wrestling words onto paper, satisfaction totally out of proportion to financial return.

With this satisfaction has come the realization that there are alternatives to corporate publishing.

The Subsidy Seduction

The first such alternative, subsidy publishing, tempts the weary writer with praise and promises.

The so-called vanity press resembles corporate publishing in several ways. You still submit your manuscript, wait for publisher's acceptance, sign a contract, receive royalties for books sold.

The critical difference can be summed up in two words.

You pay.

And the best advice for you, however frustrated by rejections, enticed by "manuscript wanted" ads, and impressed by promises of fat royalty payments you may be, needs only one word.

Don't.

Vanity publishing is to publishing as prostitution is to love.

The typical vanity press contract requires that you pay all publication costs, plus, of course, the publisher's profit, and usually calls for one-third of the money up front, another one-third on approval of the galley (not page) proofs, and the final one-third on publication of the book. The vanity publisher has a rather unique definition of publication, as we'll see.

When you make that final payment, what exactly do you own?

Nothing.

You pay, and the publisher owns the books.

That's not the worst of it. The vanity publisher has already made its profit before it sells a single book. There's no incentive for the publisher to promote its wares, especially since it must give a 40 to 50 percent discount to bookstores and libraries and has lured you with the promise of another 30 to 40 percent in royalties.

So the vanity publisher doesn't promote the book—beyond an obligatory, and useless, "tombstone" ad in the *New York Times*.

If you attempt to launch your own promotional campaign, you soon find that few bookstores will handle a book stigmatized by the vanity imprint, and few newspapers will give your book a review—even a bad review.

Small wonder the typical vanity book sells fewer than 100 copies.

That's a rather dismal picture.

Case Study:
Aronson versus Vantage

On the chance that it hasn't been dismal enough to dissuade you from resorting to a vanity publisher, I offer the case of Mr. Charles Aronson versus Vantage Press, largest and best known of the subsidy publishers.

Chuck Aronson is no minister seeking to publish a collection of stale sermons (the largest category of vanity clientele, by the way). He is a highly successful manufacturer-inventor who retired from business in 1972 to devote the rest of his life to writing. His prose is vigorous, his voice clear and unique, his tone earnest and compelling.

When his labor of love, *Sculptured Hyacinths,* text and photographs on the work of Harriet Whitney Frishmuth, failed to ignite the passions of the corporate publishers, Aronson turned to Vantage.

Two years and $28,335 later, *Sculptured Hyacinths* had sold exactly 162 copies, and Aronson and wife Jo had sold well over half of those themselves.

For his first $22,000, Aronson received inept editing of his manuscript and unusable galley proofs. Having corrected and forgiven, Aronson eagerly ripped into the package containing the first three bound volumes of his book. His hands may have trembled as he first held his beautiful book.

Setting aside the invoice for the final $6,335 due, Aronson turned to page one and began reading "about the author," in which he was credited with having studied "matermatics." With gathering dread, Aronson plunged on. His wife's name was misspelled. Vantage had misspelled "J-O." Pictures appeared on the wrong pages, in the wrong sizes. Wandering punctuation marks peppered the pages.

Enraged and sickened, Aronson hammered away until Vantage made the necessary corrections. Nineteen weeks after the contracted publication date, he received his "free" (delicious irony) 100 author's copies.

Many had been mutilated by packing staples.

There's more, much more, a trail of contradictions, broken promises, outright lies. Aronson's worst shock came with the realization that Vantage hadn't even bound the full 5,000 copies he contracted for. To this day, Aronson has not been able to find out how many books Vantage actually did bind, but upon terminating his relationship with them, he received 143 copies of his masterpiece, 14 of which had been ruined by moisture.

With his 129 books he also received the disillusioning knowledge that even friends and relatives wouldn't spend $24.95 for a book about Harriet Whitney Frishmuth. He also gained enough material about vanity publishing to fill a large book.

Destroyed but not defeated, Aronson wrote and self-published that book, *The Writer Publisher,* the "don't do it yourself" manual based upon his experiences with Vantage. He has produced eight other books, including his five-volume, 3,922-page autobiographical "Eagle series," and publishes a monthly newsletter, *Peephole on People.*

Self-publishing: From Paine to Poynter

Aronson has thus become one of the more prolific examples of a rapidly growing phenomenon, the self-publisher.

In self-publishing, as with subsidy publishing, you pay to have your book produced. Unlike vanity publishing, you own what you pay for and are free to merchandise, give away, or just lovingly fondle your books.

As a brief look at the lineage of self-publishing in America suggests, this second alternative to corporate publishing is much more than an ego massage for the rich and illiterate. In fact, self-publishers have helped shape our nation's political and literary history.

For example, although Thomas Paine never made a shilling on his self-published *Common Sense,* the pamphlet eventually sold half a million copies and helped prepare the colonies for revolution.

When Reverend Mason L. Weems literally "self-peddled" his *Life of George Washington,* he introduced the cherry tree and other persistent Washington myths into American folklore.

The roster of American self-publishers includes poets Walt Whitman and Carl Sandburg. Whitman, an aggressive promoter, wrote the best reviews of *Leaves of Grass* himself. Sandburg set the type, printed, and bound his own books.

Such reference shelf staples as John Bartlett's *Familiar Quotations,* General Henry M. Robert's *Rules of Order,* and Will Strunk's "Little Book" (later revised by Strunk's foremost student, E. B. White, and published as *The Elements of Style*) were all self-published.

Commercial houses found his *Maggie: A Girl of the Streets* morally objectionable, so Stephen Crane borrowed $200 and published his first novel himself. It sold 100 copies. When Crane's second effort, *The Red Badge of Courage,* gained considerably greater acceptance, publishers lined up like ardent suitors for *Maggie.*

D. H. Lawrence couldn't even find a typist for *Lady Chatterley's Lover* and finally had to resort to an Italian printer, who was perhaps willing to handle the project only because he couldn't read it.

Lawrence and his Lady met with more than modest commercial success, as did a dentist who dreamed of cowboys and sagebrush, Zane Grey, who self-published his first novel, *Betty Zane,* in 1904. He soon became America's best-selling western writer.

Thus, authors often self-published after battering futilely at the corporate-house door, gaining admittance later, after their efforts had proven themselves.

In other cases the process has been reversed, with successful authors turning to self-publishing in order to gain total editorial control of their work—and a 100 percent share of the profits.

James Fennimore Cooper had already scored a commercial success with *The Spy* when he self-published *Pioneers* in 1823. Mark Twain self-published *Huckleberry Finn* as a sequel to his successful, commercially published *Tom Sawyer* (and enjoyed explosive sales after the Concord, Mass., public library banished Huck from its shelves). Seventeen years after his Tarzan books had found their way into homes and libraries across the country, Edgar Rice Burroughs formed his own publishing company.

Long Odds for the Self-publisher

Lest these success stories delude you, I must note that the odds against gaining financial reward and critical acclaim with your self-published book are not better than, and perhaps considerably worse than, the chances with a commercially published book.

Aronson himself cautions the would-be successor to Twain and Burroughs:

> . . . if their goal is to see their name in the newspaper, they have a slim chance; if their goal is to make a living writing, they better get a job as copy boy on the local rag.

The few who make money in self-publishing these days usually don't do so with poetry, polemics, or plot-lines. The path to riches, narrow and seldom trod, is marked "Do it yourself," as self-publishers join their corporate counterparts in seeking to satisfy the voracious American appetite for how-to-live literature.

Dan Poynter's interest was parachuting, not publishing. Unable to find an adequate parachutists' manual, Poynter spent eight years researching and writing one. No publisher wanted it, so Poynter published it himself. A quarter of a million copies later, Poynter has made, as they say, publishing history.

In his *Self-Publishing Manual,* put out under his own Parachuting Publications logo, Poynter trumpets nonfiction self-publishing as "your shortcut to fame and fortune." Writing is easy, Poynter insists, and writing nonfiction simply a matter of "repackaging information."

Once you've repackaged a little of that information, Poynter advises you to "bypass all the middlemen," publish your own book, and "get it all."

Poynter has indeed gotten it all, following his parachuting success with manuals on hang gliding, manned kiting, even a frisbee players' handbook shaped to fit inside a frisbee.

If you have a winning formula for making money, losing weight, or improving sexual performance, you, too, might find the way to "wealth and prestige," as Poynter suggests.

But I doubt it.

Self-publishing, far from the sure thing Poynter depicts, is a lot like betting the ponies. You are in control of the product in each case, publishing whatever you write and betting on whatever looks good to you. The more you study the field, the better your chances for success.

But you are no more in control of what the public will buy than of how the horses will run. The odds still heavily favor the track. The money you spend to publish your book, especially if that book is fiction or poetry, must be money you are willing—indeed expecting—to lose.

How Big a Gamble?

How much money depends on the nature and scope of your material. In general, photo offset is much cheaper than typeset printing, and the larger the press run, the lower your per unit cost.

Prices vary tremendously from printer to printer. It will pay for you to shop around.

If you can supply camera-ready copy, pages that are ready to be photographed and offset printed, a 5 × 7 inch format might cost around $6.50 per page for 500 copies, but 2,000 copies cost only about twice, not four times, as much per page. An 8½ × 11 inch format is just about twice as expensive.

The cost of having a professional firm prepare your copy for the camera runs about $6.50 per page.

Thus, your basic, no frills little novel, 50,000 words, no photographs, black ink on white stock, might cost around $800 for 120 pages of typesetting. Your press run of 2,000, 5½ × 8½ books, more than enough for a first run and probably for ever, would cost another $1,608. Your antique paperback cover for 1,500 copies would cost around $150, and the hard covers for the remaining 500 copies (libraries generally buy hardcover) another $800.

That comes to $3,358 plus tax and ship-ping, for which you will have 2,000 books sitting in your basement, your garage, and under your bed.

Pastor Weems sold his wares from a push cart, but you'll need more sophisticated —and expensive—methods. You should plan on spending at least as much on promoting your book as you did on printing it.

Thus, your book represents a $7,000 bet to win (make money), place (break even), or show (recover at least a chunk of your investment).

If the prospects for financial reward are marginal at best, other rewards can be quite immediate and tangible. As a self-publisher, you produce your work as you want it, limited only by vision and finances. You gain the immense satisfaction of seeing your work in print and of contributing to mankind's accumulated wisdom and myth.

However small, however ephemeral, the self-publisher leaves a mark on the sands, and, occasionally, as with Whitman or Twain or Anais Nin, that mark enriches and elevates us all.

56
Vanity Video

Terry Clifford

In 1972, the Federal Communications Commission ruled that cable television systems over a certain size must provide channels for "public access" on a first-come, first-served basis and without censorship. Court decisions have since eliminated mandated access channels. But cable systems can voluntarily allow them, and many cities require them as part of their franchise agreements with cable companies. In New York City, where public-access programs range from the boring to the outrageous, one has the opportunity to say or do almost anything imaginable on television. In the following selection from *New York* magazine, free-lance writer Terry Clifford provides a sampler of the more unusual programming on public access, where the producers often take the term "personal media" literally.

In other areas of the country, public-access programming tends to be somewhat tamer, although still extremely diversified in nature and audience. Many educational institutions, libraries, and city governments produce programming for access channels as well, with programs ranging from continuing education courses to book talks to coverage of public meetings. On those channels completely open to the public, programs frequently include interviews, coverage of local events, and specialized series aimed at particular segments of the audience ("narrowcasting"). In a sense, public access serves the important function of guaranteeing free speech on cable television—the electronic equivalent of the soapbox.

She's attractive, she's funny, and she's stoned out of her mind. She's Coca Crystal, the incorrigible queen of cable TV. "Hi," says Coca, rolling a large joint as the red light on the camera flashes on, "the sixties generation had a lot to say and still does."

Live from New York—it's *If I Can't Dance You Can Keep Your Revolution,* public-access television's most popular show.

"This is an anti-authoritarian show", explains a smiling Coca as she puffs resolutely into the camera and onto the television screens of thousands of Manhattan viewers. These include her regular fans as well as first-time watchers, channel switchers who have landed on *If I Can't Dance . . .* in their desperate effort to escape network boredom and who are agape with wonder at what's before them. The show's title comes from Emma Goldman, the American anarchist who's Coca's inspiration. (In the late sixties Coca formed the Emma Goldman Brigade, a guerrilla-street-theater troupe which pulled tricks like releasing a number of white mice at a Republican-women's luncheon where Pat Nixon was speaking.)

"And now a subliminal message from Vincent Titus," says Coca, introducing the 71-year-old poet, a decrepit member of a leading Wasp family and a regular on the show. Formerly an involuntary psychiatric patient, a member of the Abraham Lincoln Brigade in the Spanish civil war, an ordained priest in a Franciscan monastery, and Jean Harlow's lover—in that order—Vincent gives a somewhat garbled reading of the poem he has prepared for the evening:

> There was a young man, Anatole,
> Whom the neighbors considered quite droll
> When asked why he hid
> He said, "I fear my id
> And my ego is out of control."

"Hey," says Coca, reaching for the phones on an upbeat note, "I'm going to answer some calls." First caller: "I just tuned in. What's this show about?" "It's about an hour," she replies and hangs up. "You're an ugly bitch, a douche bag," the next voice spits out before Coca cuts him off. "And you're a sexist, reactionary jackass," says she, lighting another joint. Enough calls; it's time for her guests, old hippies like Tuli Kupferberg and Steve Ben Israel, or distinguished anti-nuke physicist Michio Kaku, or even the Radical Lesbian Terrorist Comedy Group.

Commercial message; Leslie Kandell, dressed as Madge the Beautician, is soaking Coca's fingers in a bowl. "Dear, your hands are so bad they deserve the Ayatollah Khomeini treatment—let's cut them off." Coca: "Oh no, isn't there something less drastic?" Madge: "Yes, there's Oil of Khomeini, made according to strict Iranian tradition from the blood of limbs severed from thieves, masturbators, and wearers of phony beards."

Cut to Pam Lloyd, an adorable girl in large shades and a Yankee cap. "Good evening pot fans," she drawls. "Welcome to *Sinsemilla Street,* America's only weekly video marijuana report [named after the primo seedless grass currently being harvested around the nation]. As part of our continuing survey, we're asking, What's the best pot you ever smoked?" The phones are buzzing with heads who want to cast their votes. Hawaiian gold is in the lead. With two minutes to go, rock music starts to blare and Coca, Vincent, and the rest of the gang get up and dance off the air.

New York City's public-access programming is a phenomenon. Nowhere else in the nation is it so outrageous and lively. In these days of unprecedented disgust with network television, public access offers instant exposure and an opportunity to strike back at the media. And you get to be on TV.

"There is no other way a person of my generation can feel gratified except to be on television," says Cliff Price, a high school student who, with four friends, put together the occasionally hilarious, usually awful, access program *The Vole Show.*

Public-access television means exactly what is says: Anybody who wants to can have a TV show. Unbelievable as it may seem, you too can be a television star. All you have to do is call up either of New York's cable companies, Manhattan Cable TV or Teleprompter Manhattan Cable TV and they are legally bound to offer you free air time on a first-come, first-served basis. And there's plenty of show time still available, probably because most New Yorkers simply do not realize how easy it is for them to break into television.

This amazing situation came about in this way. When, in 1966, the federal government assumed regulatory control of the cable companies (whose primary service was—and is —improved television reception), it suggested that some time be made available to the public. Specifications were vague, leaving the details up to the municipalities which would franchise the companies.

Not until the late sixties, when the demand for better television reception grew, did cable companies become big business. By the time the first cable companies applied for New York franchises, numerous educational, artistic, and community groups had developed very definite ideas about what "public access" should be. These groups banded together to help draft the city's franchise charter into one of the most liberal and well defined in the nation. It was made law in 1970 and served as a model for federal legislation in 1972.

The charter said, in effect, that if cable companies were permitted to go into business, using city streets, then the city and its inhabitants should get something out of the deal. So when the franchise was awarded, the city demanded eight cable channels, A, B, C, D, I, J, K, and L, for public use. When public-access programming went on the air in 1971, only C and D were operating; the other six were set aside to be used as the need arose.

The original idea was, of course, that public access would function for the public good, featuring community-board meetings, earnest discussion groups, and so forth. But what happened was that idiosyncratic individuals and groups began to create their own shows for their own private reasons. Gradually, the other six city channels were opened to specific types of public programming. Channels C and D remain open to the public.

The New York City franchise charter was careful to protect the "freedom of expression" of the public-access shows, stipulating that the cable companies could have absolutely no editorial control over them. The only thing the shows were not allowed to do was advertise. But the charter also indicated that if public-access shows grew popular enough, another channel could be used for public access with advertising; in 1976, Channel J began to operate in this way. (Air time is leased for $25 a half hour; then local advertisers cover costs. There's very little profit involved.)

As any cable viewer knows, public-access channels often display somewhat illegal or risqué activities, yet they are practically immune to censorship. They are supposed to abide by FCC guidelines on obscenity on the one hand, but on the other hand no one is supposed to interfere with their free expression. Since the question of who monitors them is unresolved, they do as they like. There was one censorship skirmish over the original cable sex show, *Midnight Blue,* a few years ago, and it was pulled off the air for a few weeks. Then it was back. Short of actual coitus, pretty much anything can go, as long as it happens after 11 P.M. Occasionally a customer will call a cable company to say, "I just moved in from out of town and saw your disgusting program and hereby cancel my subscription." But that is rare indeed; the heaviest complaints so far have been directed not against blue movies but against a film showing a cockfight in Puerto Rico. There has never been a suit for libel or obscenity filed against the cable companies or the individual show producers, and until there is a problem, things will continue on their merry liberated way. Early this year the Supreme Court threw out the federal law mandating public access, saying that the government had no right to regulate the cable business in this manner, but the *city* franchise is still valid and remains the strong protector of public access.

It costs the cable companies plenty to transmit these shows. Manhattan Cable, which is owned by Time Inc., spends "several hundred thousand a year" on its public-access-programming department. Teleprompter has gone so far as to build a studio where public-access shows can be taped by union technicians (Manhattan Cable offers no such service), though this facility is little-used since most access producers can't be bothered going as far uptown as 219th Street. And, surprisingly enough, the cable companies actually like public access. It gives cable programming a unique character and flavor, they say. And they are right.

Although the air time is free on public access, you as producer (and on public access "producer" usually means "star") have to pay for your own production. Yet that can be amazingly cheap, as little as $15 for a live half hour of black and white (you get minimal technology for that price—one live camera). "An hour of cable costs less than an ounce of good grass," Coca Crystal once remarked on her show. Naturally, the more elaborate color shows cost more. Then again, you can make a show in your own living room. All you need is someone to videotape it for you. You then take the tape to the cable company and demand that they show it. There has never yet been more demand for access air time than supply of time slots. However, should that situation arise, the franchise stipulates that shows which have been on for a year or more have to make way for new talent.

Public-access programming has grown steadily over nine years in New York. And now that cable penetration approaches 30 percent of all American homes (it should reach that mark in 1981) and appears to be a viable medium for advertisers, there is a heady optimism among access producers about the glorious and golden future awaiting them. As the cable industry grows, there are more and more cable companies in America's towns and cities with which to syndicate their shows. *Midnight Blue* is widely syndicated, as are a number of other access programs that have already found sponsors and moved to J. And as satellite transmission for cable opens up vast new possibilities (actually it won't be "cable" anymore), there is a rush to work out lucrative satellite deals. But most producers on public access never see any financial gains from their shows. Public access has broken many a heart and bank account.

"What's great about public access," says Joshua Sapan, an executive at Teleprompter cable, "is that it's experimental, alternative television. It's not restricted by the need to be salable or even popular. Of course, technically it's way below regular TV," he adds, "but that's because of the money.

During Coca's show, for example, the video control board has been known to explode and microphones to go dead. Public access is bottom-of-the-barrel broadcasting, do-it-yourself TV. Coca resorts to taking up a collection to pay for her hour, since *Revolution* has no backer and Coca is completely broke.

Coca is just one of approximately 225 public-access producers in the city, about half of whom are from community, educational, and religious groups (there's an increasing amount of preaching on public access). The others use cable as personal showcases and are an idiosyncratic group: socialites, window washers, editors, switchboard operators, teachers, and bored housewives. In the wild and wacky world of public access, they become little luminaries, media people, celebrities. "I'm a star," laughs Coca. "It's a riot. It turned out I had something I didn't know I had: TV personality. When I look at the playbacks I say, 'That's me?' I don't look fat, old, or wrinkled. It's terrific. I get recognized every time I go to the organic supermarket."

Cable changes their lives. Take Helene Zimmerman—a frumpy, successful New York attorney until she had cable installed in her apartment, became transfixed by the access shows, gave up her law practice, got herself her own talk show, and became the first public-access star to transmit her show to the West Coast via satellite. "Every time I'm on cable," exclaims the newly glamorous Helene, "it's the highlight of my life."

The access producers are all bizarre in

some way or another—"weird and wonderful," as Emily Armstrong puts it. Emily does
a masterful job coordinating public access
shows for Manhattan Cable. She admits that
quite a few of the producers are "completely
crazy." "But," she says, "they all have this
amazing concept of public access as a huge
potential. They put incredible energy into doing their shows, and they don't even get any
money out of it. It's vanity video."

People who've appeared on the shows
say they are surprised by the numbers of people who claim to have seen them, but nobody
really knows how many people in the 170,000
cable-subscription homes in Manhattan actually watch. Nielsen has yet to come to public
access. One available indicator is a recent tele-
phone-company survey which registered 3,800
calls in one hour to Tom Leykis's live show,
Bread and Circuses.

For the most part, access viewers are
channel flickers. And depending on the time
of the night they get itchy fingers, they may
be surprised to find such things as Fran Beck's
yearly salute to S & M in which she appeared
in leather garb and, God help us, gave an on-
air enema; serious discussions of politics, literature, and the state of humanity; self-
defense how-to's; an enraptured description
of a vision of the Blessed Virgin Mary; private
parts in living color; and preacher's advice on
how to bring God back into your life. Also
Don Julio singing in eleven languages, *video
verité* of city disasters, telepsychic Morris
Fonte, Efrom Allen's taped interview with Sid
Vicious, and shows on the handicapped, classical music, finance, conceptual art, sex therapy, weight control, and Irish clog dancing.

Aside from extreme technical deficiencies, these shows suffer from amateurish
style, boring conversations, mumbled delivery, moronic humor, sophomoric obsessions,
and plain old bad taste. On the other hand,
it's interesting to see what people will actually
say and do when freed from the constraints of
censorship, commercialism, and rating games.
Anything can happen on the live shows and
usually does. They often rely on telephone interaction, a cable-hookup version of the old
village meeting, which seems to satisfy New
Yorkers' need to communicate.

Most of the gleeful insanity of live public

access transpires at ETC, on East 23rd Street.
ETC is a nonprofit corporation run by former
ABC executive Jim Chladek, a dedicated ec-
centric who is to a large degree responsible for
keeping public access going, since his is the
only studio with an inexpensive live feed into
the cable systems. ETC is so funky, so free-
form, so lacking in the amenities that it tends
to shock well-known guests who come there.
Joan Fontaine once arrived to do a show, immediately sized up the situation, and got into
the spirit of things by rolling up her sleeves and
moving lights around. Cameras are manned by
unpaid volunteers. (The better shows have
their own crews.) The floor in the black-and-
white studio vibrates from the boiler downstairs, and one broken-down bathroom, complete with toilet, urinal, tiny mirror, and sink,
functions as the dressing room. "I keep it
cheap," says Chladek.

He also caters to the vanity of the access
stars. "I let them play out their fantasies," says
he. "Our society pumps them with illusion,
and everyone believes he'll be the next Dylan."

Cable wars go on (Coca Crystal once hired
a yippie to throw a pie at Alex Bennett of *Midnight Blue*), and most access stars are hard-
pressed to name any other show they consider
as good as their own. There is, however, camaraderie. One time when Irwin T. Starwatcher, a
star who wears a hood over his head, had
finished his show in the black-and-white
studio, *Hot Legs,* a sexy show, was going on in
the color studio and the girl of the hour was
taking phone calls. Starwatcher went in to
shake her hand, but she grabbed his ears and
cried, "Give me some hood!" It couldn't happen on CBS, which is probably just as well.

Since most Manhattanites have no idea
who's on public access and since the cable
companies, the newspapers, and *TV Guide* do
not publish a listing of the shows (you can,
however, find them listed in the lesser-known
TV World, or in the moving listings on Channel I), we have provided this information for
you. What we offer are highlights of public-
access pleasures (subject to slight change and
reruns during the summer), guaranteed to
amuse, offend, amaze, and disgust, and never
to remind you of network TV. For many, that
last guarantee should be sufficient.

57
The Colossus of Talk

John Brooks

John Brooks, novelist and writer of books on business affairs, speculates on the future of the most widely used personal medium, the telephone, now in its second century. The impact on American society of the almost total availability of telephone service, largely taken for granted, has been enormous in every area. As Brooks points out in an earlier section of his book *Telephone,* AT&T has over three million shareholders, employs over 1 percent of the national labor force, and has more contact with citizens than does the federal government. As Brooks points out below, the future of this giant, from the public's point of view, holds both promises and threats.

. . . Consider AT&T's product and purpose. Lifeline of the lonely and lifeblood of the busy, the telephone is taken for granted, and for good reason. It comes as near as any human invention to being an extension of the human body. For all the vast and miraculous technology that supports it—the banks of computers and relays that switch messages, the cables that carry them across ocean floors, the wires, radio beams, and satellite stations that carry them over and above the earth—what is the telephone? Only (to translate its name literally from its Greek roots) "far speaking"—only a way of increasing human earshot. With it, man, instead of being able to make himself heard a few hundred yards away with a shout, can make himself heard and understood around the world with a whisper.

What has the telephone done to us, or for us, in the hundred years of its existence? A few effects suggest themselves at once. It has saved lives by getting rapid word of illness, injury, or famine from remote places. By joining with the elevator to make possible the multistory residence or office building, it has made possible—for better or worse—the modern city. By bringing about a quantum leap in the speed and ease with which information moves from place to place, it has greatly accelerated the rate of scientific and technological change and growth in industry. Beyond doubt it has crippled if not killed the ancient art of letter writing. It has made living alone possible for persons with normal social impulses; by so doing, it has played a role in one of the greatest social changes of this century, the breakup of the multigenerational household. It has made the waging of war chillingly more efficient than formerly. Perhaps (though not provably) it has prevented wars that might have arisen out of international misunderstanding caused by written communication. Or perhaps—again not provably—by magnifying and extending irrational personal conflicts based on voice contact, it has caused wars. Certainly it has extended the scope of human conflicts, since it impartially disseminates the useful knowledge of scientists and the babble of bores, the affection of the affectionate and the malice of the malicious.

But the question remains unanswered. The obvious effects just cited seem inadequate, mechanistic; they only scratch the surface. Perhaps the crucial effects are evanescent and unmeasurable. Use of the telephone involves personal risk because it involves exposure; for some, to be "hung up on" is among the worst of fears; others dream of a ringing telephone and wake up with a pounding heart. The telephone's actual ring—more, perhaps, than any other sound in our daily lives—evokes hope, relief, fear, anxiety, joy, according to our expectations. The telephone is our nerve-end to society.

In some ways it is in itself a thing of paradox. In one sense a metaphor for the times it helped create, in another sense the telephone is their polar opposite. It is small and gentle—relying on low voltages and miniature parts—in times of hugeness and violence. It is basically simple in times of complexity. It is so nearly human, recreating voices so faithfully that friends or lovers need not identify themselves by name even when talking across oceans, that to ask its effects on human life may seem hardly more fruitful than to ask the effect of the hand or the foot. The Canadian philosopher Marshall McLuhan —one of the few who have addressed themselves to these questions—was perhaps not far from the mark when he spoke of the telephone as creating "a kind of extra-sensory perception."

Statistics on the growth of telephone use, both nationwide and worldwide, have long puzzled and continue to puzzle sociologists and mathematicians who have applied themselves to the subject. One would expect rapid and continuous telephone growth as technology advances and affluence spreads—up to a saturation point. But one would also expect that in such a highly developed nation as the United States, where telephone use has for some time been not far from universal, the saturation point had long since been reached. Yet telephone use continues to grow at a rapid rate. The obvious explanation is population growth—but the figures show that telephone use is growing much faster than the population. Attempting to explain this phenomenon, social scientists have postulated that since two new telephone talkers may logically be expected to have four new telephone conversations for every conversation by a preexisting user, telephone use increases not directly with population growth but by the square of population growth. However, the social scientists found that the model does not apply; tele-

phone use, it turns out, increases markedly faster than the square of population growth, with no leveling off in sight. The model will not do; another one, perhaps more metaphysical, must be found. "Not to eat, not for love," Emerson said of some puzzling snakes gliding in a hollow for no discernible purpose; similarly, the rate of telephone growth remains an enigma of human behavior.

How is it to be explained, and how dealt with? The latter question preoccupies research scientists in telephony, and may perhaps preoccupy a layman who wonders whether it will end in a creeping paralysis of the world's work brought about by worldwide, simultaneous, continuous telephone communication. Meanwhile, both AT&T and its state and federal watchdogs, ignoring such dangers, are dedicated to the idea that their job is to make such communication possible if the customers want it.

. . .

As much as the structural future of AT&T, the future of telephony itself is cloudy. New developments now in process, which have already been shown to be feasible theoretically, may never come to be because of nontechnical problems such as uneconomically high cost or lack of customer demand. On the other hand, the unpredictable scientific breakthroughs of the future—the Nobel Prize-winning accomplishments of 1980 or 1990—may bring with them telephonic innovations not yet even conceived.

Bell Labs men, carefully explaining that they are not necessarily offering a preview of the future, provide a list of new devices and processes that *may* come into use in the early years of the telephone's second century. One is a pocket-sized cordless telephone that would make it possible for calls to any number in the world to be made by anyone anywhere—a pedestrian waiting for a bus, a stranded mountain climber in need of rescue, a construction worker who, with both hands occupied, could talk to his boss in an office, or to a cousin in Rangoon, through his hat, in which a cordless telephone would be installed. Another is a watchman telephone that, activated by a fire, flood, or burglary, would automatically give notification by calling the appropriate number. Others are medical retrieval of visual information, whereby a doctor could "dial" X ray pictures stored in another city; a service enabling merchants and banks to handle such functions as check verification and check-cashing authorization by telephone; and a service making it possible for daily newspapers and other printed material from afar to be shown on a home wall screen —the screen itself, according to the suggestion of a leading Bell Labs man, to be made decorative when not in use by being made to show, perhaps, a seashore scene equipped electronically with moving waves and the sound of surf. Students of telecommunications outside Bell Labs have suggested one other innovation—already possible technically —that might have important political implications: a home voting terminal, with buttons marked "Yes" and "No" and an attached cable connected to a telephone jack, that would make it possible for a national plebiscite on a current question to be conducted in about ten minutes.

Such visions of the future will be greeted with mixed feelings by those who, like George Orwell in his *1984,* fear that the additional human convenience brought by future technology will be paid for in lost human privacy, individuality, autonomy, taste, and decency. The matter is an enigma. In any case, the likely telephone innovations of the next quarter century of a sort visible to the telephone user are of minor importance when set beside those that have already taken place. They pale, for example, beside the introduction of local telephone service itself; of first limited and then ever-expanding long-distance service; of dial telephones; of overseas service; of direct distance dialing; of transmission of computer data; of television transmission by coaxial cable and earth satellite. So far as the imagination of 1976 can conceive, the world telephone and television network is largely in place.

AT&T's great technical task of the immediate future appears to be the application of new technology toward two objectives: first,

meeting the continuing growth of telephone traffic, which, if projections of present trends may be trusted, will call for five to ten times the present capacity by 1990; and second, supplying that capacity at reduced rates to the customer. The last such application of the telephone's first century—the No. 4 ESS [Electronic Switching System], first put into service in Chicago early in 1976—dramatically furthers the attainment of both objectives. It is capable of processing 350,000 toll calls per hour, three times as many as the fastest nonelectronic switching system, while requiring only one-fourth the space and one-third the maintenance cost; moreover, present estimates are that by 1985 expense savings of the Bell System attributable to No. 4 ESS installations may approach one billion dollars per year. Beyond that, the plan at Bell Labs is to meet increased demand and reduce costs by a vast expansion of the now-still-emergent revolution in telecommunications technology brought about since 1950 by the transistor and the computer. New transmission, switching, and information-storage devices now under development—with names like "magnetic bubble," "light-emitting diode," "charge-coupled device," and "millimeter wave-guide," and functions not capable of being quickly grasped by a layman—will probably come into play. And so, most likely, will the fulfillment of Alexander Graham Bell's dream of the transmission of speech by light beams—through hair-fine flexible fibers of glass that may eventually connect homes and offices to the nationwide communications network (which may itself consist of such fibers). Because glass fiber is plentiful and cheap, such technology offers further potential of cheaper as well as better telephone service.

Like the future of the world, then, one's view of the character of the future of telecommunications balances on the hairline of individual temperament: optimists think of greater efficiency and convenience at less cost, pessimists of a progressive mechanization of man and concomitant loss of his humanity. . . .

58
Computer Communications – Coming of Age

Richard Mikita

The telephone described in the preceding selection has been around long enough to seem unthreatening. But, for most people, computer technology, which is accelerating rapidly, is still a matter of "us" and "them," as free-lance writer Richard Mikita points out in the selection below. Mikita shows that it is practically impossible today to avoid computers in any form of communication other than "speaking directly to another person or posting a local letter."

Early on they didn't seem like much to worry about, and only occasionally were they something to marvel at. Five thousand years ago, they were little more than beads slipped along rods or knots tied in strings. About forty-five hundred years later, they took the form of oddly marked rulers with sliding center pieces. Within the next two hundred years, the wheels and cogs of the Industrial Revolution would be set to the task but turned to no profitable effect. Fewer than a hundred years ago, the use of electricity and paper punch cards enabled one of them to complete the count for the United States census in record time. But it has only been within the last thirty-five years, following the invention of the transistor, that they have begun to insinuate themselves into our lives in annoying and exciting, threatening and thrilling ways.

They, of course, are computers, and what makes the modern computer as different from earlier calculating devices as Homo Sapiens are from earlier hominids is not so much the increased speed and number of calculations they can perform but their ability to store, retrieve, and reorganize all the information involved in those calculations. Memory and programmability have lifted them above the earlier machines in the way that increased cranial capacity and the acquisition of language lifted humans above apes. But so rapid has been their evolution during the last thirty-five years that their inventors have often been left questioning the nature of the beasts they have begotten.

As foreigners from the realm of advanced science, computers could communicate with us only in their own language at first. The difficulties that this caused seemed to forever separate them from the mainstream of society. But familiarity led to friendships, encouraging the creation of various forms of pidgin English. Lately, computers have become better at responding in English but still can only understand complex instructions in one of the hybrid languages. They are learning fast, learning to read our handwriting and typescript, to recognize our speech and speak in reply, making communication easier and thereby releasing them from the closed circles they formed upon arrival. In fact, the ability to communicate freely will be the key to the computer's complete assimilation within our society. Along with their successful integration will come the development of a new mass communications medium, a medium that will exploit the strengths of computers and supplement the deficiencies of television, radio, magazines, and newspapers.

The two most significant differences between computers and other communications media—memory and manipulative ability—have not been fully exploited—yet. Computers can do far more than send out information from a central source to many people, as do television, radio, and the press. And they can do far more than send and receive information from one individual to another, as does the telephone. Computer communication could allow each of us to store in an almost unimaginably tiny space—100 billion bits of information, roughly equivalent to a library of 3,000 volumes, have already been permanently stored on a thin disk the size of a record album—all the information passed in either direction. It could allow us to examine, alter, and interpret that information to suit our present purposes as well as preserve both the original data and what we made of them for later recall, reorganization, and reinterpretation. Unlike print or other static storage media, computers could vastly increase the amount of information we are able to store *and* allow for a perpetually active use of all that vast storage capacity.

Hired to do the drudgery behind the scenes by the other media, computers are nearly ready to spawn a new communications medium. It is now possible to use a home computer (and over 300,000 households already have one) to tap into nationwide networks like "Micronet" and "The Source." By dialing a local telephone number and cradling the receiver into a telecommunications device called a modem, people can connect their computers to a powerful central processor with an incredibly capacious memory in which is stored information as complex and varied as major news wire services, closing

stock market figures, current commodities prices, sports results, syndicated columns, and a library of computer programs. These programs enable the computer to do everything from calculate income taxes to conduct a simulated lunar landing. Other systems, notably Britain's Prestel, eliminate the need for telephone hook-ups by making the TV set a truly two-way medium. A small control box allows Prestel users to call up whatever they want from the system's central processor. Whether by turning your television set into a remote terminal or by working through your own home computer, this new medium not only serves as a port of entry for information, such as a radio or TV, or as a package of information, such as a magazine, book, or newspaper, it becomes more like an open channel, allowing passage both in and out.

As the new medium grows, we may very well see the history of radio and television networks repeating themselves, with a few giants offering slick versions of essentially the same information. But there will probably be more local stations, special interest networks, and even person-to-person lines of communication. With the cost of transportation already well above that of telecommunications, more and more people are likely to be using computer communications to work from their homes or from small local offices. Bedroom communities may well become satellite offices, as the cost of urban real estate and the huge offices built there become increasingly uneconomical to maintain. With the electronic equipment already in many homes, the added push provided as business decentralizes will drive the cost of computers further down and quicken their spread throughout the country.

As the United States moves more quickly toward becoming an information-based, rather than a manufacturing-based economy, a computer will provide its owner with an entry into new modes of communication. Even now, computer technology plays a vital role behind the scenes in all of today's media. But in each of these instances, the computer acts as a conduit of information and not as a producer and manipulator of information.

The first signs of this modern computer

age were seen in the early nineteenth century. It was then that Charles Babbage envisioned his "Analytical Engine." This device would have been the first programmable computer if its theoretical reach had not so far exceeded the century's technological grasp. Though Babbage's Analytical Engine was a failure, a particularly insightful observer foresaw the threat, which some would later feel, from such a machine and sought to calm those fears by assuring all that the "Analytical Engine has no pretensions whatever to originate anything." That observer, Lady Astor Lovelace (Lord Byron's remarkable daughter), knew that Babbage's device would seem like an affront to people's increasingly embattled sense of superiority. But by denying that the machine had the human ability to originate an idea, she set out the terms of comparison and, inadvertently, opened the debate about artificial intelligence, which has continued ever since. Later, as computers reached past number and into the realm of language, they seemed to the popular imagination to put themselves more and more directly into competition with human beings. Fear and resentment have followed, as they always do when there is an incursion from outside the circle of society. Like other immigrants, the computer has often been looked upon as an unwelcome stranger. But unlike other immigrants, the computer was incapable of feeling the sting of that stigma.

Speaking of man-made machines as if they were human immigrants may seem farfetched. And it is—but just a little. Our response to the waves of successive generations of computers has been like our response to previous waves of immigrants: a certain amount of fear and resentment at first, followed by a gradual acceptance and, finally, assimilation.

Already, many of the descendants of the first generation of computers have moved out of their old neighborhood niches in science and business and into the suburbs and country, into schools and homes. Their quickness and immunity from boredom have gained them entrance into all kinds of jobs, particularly as passive partners within the mass media. In fact, speaking directly to another person and posting a local letter are probably the only available means of communication that do not now involve computers in some way. And even these are not inviolable: electronic mail is already being used by large corporations to send information over ordinary phone lines instantly, and pocket computers increasingly come between strangers as the American traveller taps in "hello" then hold up "Bonjour" to the nonplussed Parisian.

As computers become more obviously and actively involved with every aspect of our lives, they will begin to seem even less out of place in our part of town. Not surprisingly, some people are already beginning to feel pushed aside, as if they were little better than bits of information within the computers, translated into binary numbers, zeroes and ones, stored on magnetic disks, whirling at more than 3,000 revolutions per second. For those people, the computer seems like an ominous threat to privacy, job security, and most of all to their personal sense of importance.

Suddenly there seems to be something out there that knows a lot about us. The messages we get in the mail from the bank, book clubs, and utilities suggest that we are no longer the concern of people at those places, but that a computer somewhere has been hired to correspond with us. Most of what the bank knows about us is not known by the teller we see every Friday or by the officer who approved our loan application but by a central computer that attends to all our transactions. Yet we cannot communicate directly with that computer. The dread so many feel for computers comes, I think, largely from this sense of separation, from the computer's capacity to store information about us without our feeling able to influence what is kept or follow how it is used. The uneasiness comes not from a paranoid need for privacy but from the desire to share in the network of information known about us.

Since their memories and mathematical abilities are so awesome and affecting, it is understandable that we should be more likely to let them in the back door for other reasons than admit them through the front door for these. Among the most important of those other reasons is their intriguing ability to entertain. Very likely, the principal cause of computers spreading beyond the range of the hobbiest, who built or brought them into their homes in the early 1970s, was the increasing sophistication of electronic games and the accompanying decreasing cost of the equipment needed to play those games at home. After burying uncounted quarters into Space Invaders, Galaxian, Asteroids, and a host of other electronic descendants of traditional arcade games, more than a few people have been prompted to think about buying a small computer. But if entertainment is the immediate impetus, economics and education provide the rationalization to skeptical friends and family members. Saving money and stimulating interest in all sorts of subjects quickly become more than mere attempts to quiet the conscience of Calvin and get on with the fun. They are real and good reasons for buying a personal computer, as full-page ads in the *New York Times* for the Texas Instruments home computer have already suggested to thousands of readers.

With technology and services available today, it is possible for a person with a home terminal and telephone hook-up to browse and burrow deep into many sources of information more quickly than would be possible if pages were turned, files pulled, and steps taken from one end of the library to the other. But what is available now is merely a tease compared to what will be possible within the next few years.

A market, a means, and a medium of expression open up with the widespread use of home computers. Individual entrepreneurs will be able to sell their programs directly or receive royalties as they are used over the networks. Artists and entertainers will be able to reach out to a new audience through the networks and through private subscription with poems, stories, novels, graphic designs, animated movies, and whatever new forms the medium inspires. Naturally, publishing houses will have their own "e.b." (electronic book) divisions, advertise on the networks, and coordinate the distribution of "big" books in their hardcover, paperback, and e.b. editions. Television, radio, and the press will likewise accommodate themselves to the new medium while continuing to exist in their own rights.

The effect of the computer's coming of age may well be reflected in its ability to integrate aspects of each of the existing media into a new communication medium flexible enough to serve the individual and powerful enough to reach out to and through the nation and the world. The initial awkwardness of the electronic immigrants and the difficulties caused by their coming will then be over. Computers will be so much a part of our lives that they will seem like some of the most solid citizens of the new information-based society.

59

Wired City, U.S.A.: The Charms and Dangers of Two-Way TV

John Wicklein

Perhaps one of the most significant developments since the last edition of this book has been the tremendous growth of cable television—from a primarily relay service for over-the-air television signals to a complete electronic marketplace in the home. Today's cable systems offer, for additional fees, first-run movies, sports on a continual basis, home security alarms, and the like. Future cable services will include shopping, delivery of newspapers, and interconnection with at-home computers. In this selection from *Atlantic* magazine, public broadcasting executive John Wicklein examines QUBE in Columbus, Ohio, the nation's first two-way ("interactive") cable television system. Wicklein, former Dean of Boston University's School of Public Communication and author of the recent *Electronic Nightmare: The New Communications and Freedom* (Viking, 1981), finds great audience interest in two-way cable services and programs. But he is fearful about protection for the privacy of the individual who "talks back" to the television via this important new personal medium.

   Immediately following Wicklein's analysis of the privacy issues raised by QUBE is a brief report on one of its less controversial uses. *Milwaukee Journal* sports columnist Bob Wolf describes how QUBE has recently brought new meaning to the phrase "armchair quarterback."

"Go in," said my host. I stepped through the door into what appeared to be a carpeted inner office lighted from above by fluorescent panels. "Take three steps." I did as he told me. From across the hall, I heard the clatter of a teleprinter springing into operation. "The room has sensed your presence—it sent the alarm to our computer," my host informed me. "The computer activated our printer across the hall, but it could have activated one at police headquarters as well."

   My host was Miklos Korodi, general manager of QUBE, a two-way interactive cable system that Warner Cable Corporation* has installed in Columbus, Ohio. The motion-sensing burglar alarm is one of several home-security services that QUBE plans to offer its subscribers this spring.

   "Here, watch this." Korodi held a piece of burning rope up to a smoke detector in the

---

*In 1980, The American Express Corporation joined Warner Communications to form Warner-Amex Corporation in order to market QUBE [Eds.].

ceiling. A raucous buzzer alarm sounded in the room, and the computer printer became active again. In a real installation, information on the location of the house, on flammables inside it, and on the position of the nearest fire hydrant would be printed out at the firehouse while the alarm was rousing sleepers in the burning home.

QUBE has announced that it will also offer a "duress" button so that a subscriber may call police when a threatening situation exists, and a medical emergency button for use when an ambulance is needed. A personal security medallion will be an optional extra; an elderly woman, for instance, could wear the medallion around her neck so that she could press it if she should slip and fall on the ice while putting out the garbage. The alarm, relayed by radio through a black box inside the house, activates the computer to provide the ambulance crew with her medical history as well as information about what medication she is taking and any medicines she must avoid.

The black box, designed by QUBE's engineers, is a microprocessor about a foot and a half long, six inches wide, and four inches deep. It is filled with miniaturized circuits encased in small silicon chips that can duplicate the operation of a room-sized computer of the 1960s. The Data General computer at QUBE's "head end" queries the box continually, asking, in effect, "Is everything all right there?" If it isn't, the microprocessor spells out the problem so the city's emergency forces can respond.

The security services, the general manager told me, will be sold in modular units or combined packages. A basic fire-alarm package, including duress and medical emergency buttons, would cost about $100 for installations and $12 a month for monitoring.

Korodi, an outgoing, enthusiastic man in his early forties, seems delighted by the things the new two-way cable system can do. So are members of his staff; the ones I talked to obviously believe that they are inventing the wheel of the new communications. To help them make the invention pay off, they have behind them the megadollar financing of the cable company's parent, Warner Communications Inc. This conglomerate, which grew out of and owns Warner Brothers, also owns, among other things, Panavision, Atlantic Records, Warner Brothers Television, Warner Books, and Atari, Inc., maker of video games.

Both Korodi and the Warner Cable management in New York think that the sale of multiple services will make this cable system, technologically the most advanced in the country, a commercial success. QUBE (a trade name that stands for nothing in particular) is never referred to by its developers as cable television. They speak of two-way cable: one line carries signals from the head end out to the customer, one line relays customer responses back to the head end. Or, better yet, two-way *interactive* cable.

There are reasons for the precise terminology. After all, a burglar is interacting with the system when he takes three steps into a home and sets off an alarm. Most of the television services of QUBE's multiservice offering are built around its two-way interactive capability. This permits subscribers at home to make decisions about what the system is offering them and then, through the adapter on their standard TV sets, to tell the computer what those decisions are. On the interactive channels, it allows them to "talk back" to their televisions.

"They like to play the system," says one Warner executive, and, indeed, they are being programmed to do that by QUBE's promotional campaign. "Touch the button," says the large, four-color, slick paper brochure, "and enter the era of two-way participation in the infinite, unfolding, never-ending worlds of QUBE."

These worlds include thirty channels controlled by touch buttons on a keypad console about the size of a plug-in electronic calculator. Ten channels provide the commercial and public television stations, a public access channel (required by the Federal Communications Commission), and a program guide channel. Another ten supply "premium" selections—primarily movies, such as *Julia* and *Equus,* that have not yet appeared on commercial television. Premium channel 10 supplies something else you don't see on commercial television: for $3.50 a selection, you get soft porno (to use the QUBE staff's reference, "hard-R") films with predictable titles such as *Dr. Feelgood* and *Hot Times*. The softcore channel is fed into the home only if a subscriber orders it. In addition, it and all other premium channels can be locked by removing a key that presumably can be kept out of the hands of the children. Premiums also include entertainment specials produced or purchased by QUBE, such self-help courses as "Shorthand" and "How to Prepare for College Entrance Examinations," and local college sports.

Unlike Home Box Office, which charges subscribers a fixed fee for each month of pay-TV programs, QUBE's computer bills viewers for each selection, at prices that range from 75¢ for "Shorthand" to $9.00 (in football-maniacal Columbus) for a live telecast of an Ohio State football game. This is in addition to the $10.95 monthly charge for basic service. You are not a passive viewer when you push a premium channel button, and since the computer is solicitous about your having to make the decision, it allows a two-minute grace period before it enters your selection into its memory.

Even greater participation is demanded by the system in the third group of ten channels —the community channels, where viewers are solicited to "interact" with their sets. Most of the interaction centers on the "Columbus Alive" channel, which every weekday offers programs produced at QUBE's studio building on the Olentangy River Road. This building, the head end, has been reconstructed from a large-appliance warehouse. It has three television studios equipped with color minicams that double as cameras in mobile units on assignments around Columbus. And here is housed the heart of the interactive system, the "polling" computer, which gathers billing and response data from subscribers. The computer scans all subscribers' homes at six-second intervals, asking: Is the set turned on? What channel has been punched up? What was the last response button touched?

The home console has five "response buttons" in addition to the channel-selection buttons. The first two can be used as "yes"

and "no" buttons; all five can be used to answer multiple-choice questions or to punch up number codes to indicate, for example, a selection of products displayed on the screen.

Each evening the production staff of "Columbus Alive" gathers at the Olentangy studio to begin two-way communication with 29,000 subscribers in QUBE's franchise area, which encompasses 104,000 households. I watched the production one night in the office of Ron Giles, one of the program hosts. Giles is chubby and bald, and he clearly enjoyed what he was doing on the tube: conducting a variation of the original *Today* show. Formerly a network executive and now a TV consultant, Mike Dann, who designed the old *Today,* designed this variation to give subscribers a mix of interviews, reports from remote locations, and good-natured banter between Giles and his co-host, Susan Goldwater. The night I saw the show, Goldwater, an attractive, articulate person (now separated from Representative Barry Goldwater, Jr.), was interviewing a priest and a former nun on the question "What is it like to be a homosexual in Columbus?" Goldwater told the audience that an estimated 80,000 homosexuals live in the Columbus "metro" area, which has more than a million people. "Let's find out how many of you know homosexuals," she said.

A statement, superimposed on the living-room furniture of the set, appeared on the screen: *I have a friend, relative, or acquaintance whom I know is homosexual.*

"If you do know a homosexual," said Goldwater, "push button no. 1 for yes; if you do not, press button no. 2 for no. Touch in now."

Within seconds, the computer supplied a result to the studio's character generator, which printed it out on the screen: *Yes—65%; No—35%.*

Goldwater continued the interview, with interruptions to throw similar questions to the audience and get their responses. When the show got slow, I used the keypad to do some channel switching. I punched up the porn channel to find out if it was really there. It was. On another channel, I found a young, bearded instructor from a local college presenting a three-credit course on basic English composition. He took attendance by asking individual members of the class (who had paid tuition directly to the college) to "touch in." Electronically updating the Socratic method, he salted his lecture with question-and-answer segments, asking students to use the response buttons to answer "true" or "false," or pick the correct answer from five choices flashed on their screens. (In some "QUBE Campus" classes, if an enrolled student gets the answer correct, the red "message light" on his keypad lights up—instant reward.)

Back at "Columbus Alive," I found Giles seated beside a man in a dark gray suit who looked like a bookstore clerk. Indeed, he was a representative of Readmor Bookstores in Columbus, and had come to talk to us about hardcover versus paperback books. After a short exchange with his guest, Giles asked the audience a series of questions about their reading habits. The computer reported back that more people bought paperbacks than hardcovers, and the surprising information that 41 percent said they bought more than ten paperbacks a month. This may reflect the fact that QUBE's franchise area is on the affluent western side of Columbus and its suburbs, and encompasses the Ohio State University campus. (Three other cable companies cover the rest of the city. Columbus, which has complete jurisdiction over franchising provisions, formed four service areas so that they might all be wired for cable in a relatively short time. The practice is fairly common in larger cities.) As the segment was ending, the titles of four books mentioned on the program, numbered 1 through 4, were posted on the screen. "If you would like to order one of these books," said Giles, "touch the corresponding buttons. The computer will gather your name and address, and Readmor will send you the book."

I was surprised to learn that this "book interview" was a commercial, paid for by Readmor Bookstores; at no time was it identified as such to the audience. When I asked one of the show's producers why, she said they wanted the show "to flow into informal commercials so it won't interrupt the rest of

the content." QUBE sells this eight-minute segment as an "Informercial," charging the advertiser about $75.00 in the "Columbus Alive" slot. A two-minute version, called a "Qubit," sells for half that rate.

Informercials and Qubits have also been used for test marketing. Advertisers and market-research firms have long used Columbus, with its 600,000 Middle Americans, as Test City, U.S.A. *Us* magazine asked QUBE viewers to touch in their judgments on five proposed magazine covers and then printed the two that rated top: John Wayne and the Incredible Hulk. Judging by their willingness to respond, subscribers apparently enjoyed being part of the commercial process. Korodi sees advertisers asking viewers to choose between pilot commercials, or to rate their interest level at ten-second intervals as they watch sit-com pilots.

Computerized two-way systems, if they catch on, can make Nielsen and Arbitron ratings obsolete. They involve no sampling guesswork—the QUBE computer knows down to the last household how many sets are tuned to one of its channels. Says Korodi, "We can give the advertiser demographics he never had before—how many people in the $20,000 to $30,000 bracket are watching this commercial, that sort of thing." The computer, he went on, can cross-refer answers to opinion questions with income groups, to tell which economic class wants what.

The computer is capable of charging an order for a book or other merchandise to the subscriber's credit card or to a charge account at a department store, if the subscriber provides the number to be fed into its memory. This is only a step from another service called Electronic Funds Transfer, or EFT, which Korodi expects to test in a year or so. In this, subscribers could select products and pay for them immediately by transferring funds from their bank accounts to the accounts of businesses that advertise goods and services. Each subscriber would have a confidential "personal identification number" that only he could punch into the system, which would tell the computer that he, and not an electronic embezzler, was ordering the money to be transferred.

"This is all possible today," Korodi told me, "but on each service we have to ask, Is it a business? We are addressing ourselves to people's needs, then looking at it to see if it is economically justifiable. Then we will market it."

After more than a year of experience with QUBE (the system went into operation on December 1, 1977), Warner is convinced that some form of two-way cable is economically viable. The company has put at least $20 million into QUBE to find this out. To recoup its investment and begin realizing a profit, Warner wants to expand two-way service to others of its 138 cable systems around the country. It intends to . . . wire all of Pittsburgh for two-way cable, and is drafting a plan to refit its one-way system in Akron. Warner now has eight franchises in the suburbs of Boston and expects to make an application in that city as soon as it opens the bidding for franchises. New York City recently granted a cable franchise for Queens to Knickerbocker Communications Corporation on the promise that the system installed will be two-way. Other companies have experimented with this form of service in a limited way, but so far only Warner has staked a lot of money on the idea that two-way cable may be the wave of the future.

Since Warner hopes to amortize the start-up costs of QUBE by extending two-way cable to its other systems, a logical question is whether the prototype in Columbus can make a profit in its day-to-day operations. When I put that question to Gustave M. Hauser, president and chairman of Warner Cable, he said, "The answer is yes."

In December Warner announced that it had agreed to buy out Coaxial Communications, Inc., a 32,000-subscriber system adjacent to QUBE. The acquisition, Hauser said, will enable the company to offer QUBE services to a new franchise area encompassing 72,000 additional homes. "Obviously, from the fact that we have acquired the system next door, we must think things are going quite well now, or we wouldn't be doing it," he said.

Cable industry leaders say they are watching QUBE closely, on the chance that interactive cable may provide the new element

that will enable the industry to achieve the "critical mass" of 30 percent saturation of American homes—agreed by many to be the magic figure for major economic success—by the early 1980s. Cable now reaches into 19 percent, or about 14 million, of the 72 million homes with TV.*

Growth of cable has been steady, but was slow until pay-TV movies and entertainment programs were offered nationally several years ago to systems by HBO and Showtime. These companies distribute their packages to local cable systems by domestic satellite. Warner Cable offers its own package of films and shows, called Star Channel, via satellite. It has . . . [begun] using the satellite to present thirteen hours of children's programs of a nonviolent nature daily to local systems that pay for the service. The programs are an outgrowth of QUBE's children's shows, and will be produced in QUBE's studios.

The attractiveness to subscribers of nationally distributed pay-TV shows helped cable grow from 3000 systems serving 5400 communities in 1974 to 4000 systems serving 9200 communities today. Gross revenues are estimated at something over $1 billion for 1978, up more than $100 million from the year before. In cable, profitability grows with economies of scale, as exemplified by the multiple system operators (MSOs). In 1977, Warner Cable, whose 600,000 subscribers make it the fourth largest MSO, reported a return of $15.7 million on gross revenues of $55.7 million in its basic cable operations. Teleprompter Corporation, which has 1.15 million subscribers in 110 systems and which is the largest MSO, earned $19.6 million on a gross of $99.6 million.

Financial analysts are looking at cable TV as a growth industry, bearing in mind the forecast by Arthur D. Little Company, the research firm in Cambridge, Massachusetts, that movies seen and paid for in the home will put movie theaters out of business by 1985. Promoting the use of two-way cable TV to

---

*As of 1981, when this book went to press, over 22 percent of homes with TVs used cable, and the rate of increased use was climbing rapidly [Eds.].

charge subscribers only for the specific films and shows they watch may make this form of home entertainment big business. It is two-way cable's capability of selective billing for entertainment and consumer services that intrigues cable executives responsible for profit and loss. As one Teleprompter official put it, "We feel definitely that two-way will be here ultimately; it just has to be economically viable."

Supplying only those services that can produce a profit makes sound business sense, but it leaves something to be desired from the standpoint of giving people the services they need, some of which will never turn a profit. A channel whereby a city clinic could conduct a medical diagnosis, with responses, of a person who is housebound is a sure money-loser. So are channels that could be used during a local disaster for two-way communication between city security forces and people in their homes. Two-way system operators may find that they have to provide some nonprofit services in return for gaining the franchise to make a profit from a community.

QUBE has already acknowledged this obligation by offering channel facilities, at no cost to the community, for participatory town meetings and government hearings. One such meeting was held in Upper Arlington, a prosperous suburb in QUBE's franchise area. Using multiple-choice questions, the Upper Arlington Planning Commission asked QUBE subscribers to comment on a draft plan for renewing an older part of the city. The computer was programmed to "narrowcast" the hearing only to those subscribers who lived within the suburb. Two previous public meetings on the issue drew about 125 citizens each. The meeting held by two-way cable TV, the computer reported, attracted 2000 residents during its two and half hours. "The point of doing this was to involve the people of the community in their own future," said Patricia Ritter, an Upper Arlington administrator who coproduced the event for the city. In that, she said, the televised hearing was a success.

Among its questions, the commission asked, "Should a building maintenance code be adopted?" The computer, knowing where each response was coming from, reported that sentiment in favor of such a code ran about 12 percent higher in the older section, which contains a number of apartment houses, than in the newer areas of town, where single-family homes abound. Residents who touched in their responses knew immediately whether they were among friends or in the minority, because results were displayed seconds after they pressed the buttons. To make subscribers feel free to express their views, the QUBE hosts assured them that the computer was set in a way that would not identify answers as coming from specific homes. If it had been set differently, it could have pinpointed the answers supplied by each household and produced a profile of each subscriber's participation for the evening. The participants apparently had no qualms about feeding their opinions into the system. When asked if they wanted to do it again, 96 percent pressed the "yes" button, and within ten seconds the computer, having worked out that percentage, relayed it to the home screens.

As in other parts of the system, the people of Upper Arlington took part enthusiastically in the interactive programming. They had previously been asked to give preferences on products, opinions on political issues, and suggestions for social issues to be discussed on "Columbus Alive." Some had been hooked on the audience-participation game shows presented by QUBE. In one program that is similar to the national *Gong Show,* viewers can direct the show by pressing the "yes" and "no" buttons to say whether an amateur act should continue. When a majority of those watching press "no," the act is dumped in mid-performance. Now, that kind of power gives a person satisfaction. It is fun. Two-way cable is *fun.* Playing the system, subscribers are only vaguely aware that the preferences they state, the products they select, the personal opinions they express can all be stored in the computer's memory and tallied, analyzed, and cross-referenced with demographic and financial information that is known about them. Several subscribers I interviewed said that they were not concerned by this. One young working woman told me, "I don't feel that I have any reason to be afraid—I may be naive, but I don't care if my opinions are recorded.'' Their attitudes seemed to be, Who would *want* that stuff, anyway? Who could profit by it?

Someone might. Since the QUBE system was installed and its capabilities have become known, reporters, city officials, and others in the community have considered the possibility that two-way cable TV might prove to be a method of invading subscribers' privacy. When I discussed this with QUBE executives, they replied, in effect, ''Yes, it *could* happen, but it won't happen here.''

Dr. Vivian Horner, vice president in charge of educational and children's programming, expressed it this way: ''People don't think of the telephone as an invasion of privacy. Yet each call you make is recorded. When people get as used to two-way cable as to the telephone, they will take it much as a matter of fact. If people feel threatened by it, they will drop it—the economic base will keep it honest.'' A QUBE sales executive echoed this idea: ''We have a time bomb here. We have to be extremely careful and set up very strict rules. If we abuse them, we're fools.''

The Warner Cable management, aware that the issue of privacy would inevitably be raised, drew tight security around the system's polling computer. Access to the computer's records, Warner says, is restricted to three top-level executives; entrance to the master control room, which houses the computer, is restricted to those who work there.

At a recent meeting of the Communication Commission of the National Council of Churches in New York, Dr. Gerry Jordan, QUBE's director of educational development, said that moderators of public-affairs programs always warn viewers whenever the computer is set to retrieve and print out the names and addresses of subscribers who push the response buttons. QUBE does not warn subscribers when they push the buttons to make purchases, on the ground that viewers must realize that their names have to be recorded in order for them to receive the product or service and to be billed.

When commission members pressed Dr. Jordan on what safeguards had been built in to protect the individual's right to privacy, he said, ''I think we at QUBE are more concerned than the subscribers are. We expected it to be much more of an issue with the public than it has turned out to be.'' The New York *Times* asked Hauser the same question. ''People who buy the service will simply have to accept that they give up a bit of their privacy for it,'' he replied. ''Beyond that, we'll try to protect their privacy all we can.''

When I interviewed Hauser at the company's headquarters in New York, he said he felt the issue of privacy was ''a serious one for the whole society.'' The amount of personal information QUBE collects is trivial compared to the total amount that the computers of government and business are amassing, he added. ''For us, it is a question of responsibility and using the system properly.''

Let's assume the good faith—and business sense—of the present Warner management, which I do. Could not some future management see it as good business to make commercial and political use of the information derived from two-way cable? Let's build a scenario on that idea.

THE PLACE: San Serra, a city of 150,000, in Southern California.

THE TIME: 1984, when two-way interactive cable has spread to hundreds of cities across the country.

THE SCENARIO: Colbert Paxton, San Serra's mayor, is running for reelection on a law-and-order platform. In a comfortable home on a hill overlooking the city, Martha Johnson, Mayor Paxton's opponent, has just pushed a response button to order a book—displayed in a department store's information commercial—that advocates abolition of laws restricting sexual activity between consenting adults. She pays for it by punching in the number on her department-store charge card. Next she takes a look at a shopping channel that features personal products for women and punches in an order for an aerosol spray deodorant.

Martha leaves for a nighttime political rally and Arnold, her husband, takes over the controls of the two-way set. Punching up a public-affairs channel, he finds the cable company quizzing its subscribers on their attitudes toward homosexuals:

> *Lesbians should be allowed to teach*
> *in the public schools.*
> *Yes: Button no. 1*
> *No: Button no. 2*

Without hesitation, Arnold touches no. 2. Then, making sure that their two small children are in bed, Arnold settles into a chair and selects a premium film entitled *The Professional Cheerleaders*. Fifteen minutes later, the message light on the keypad flashes on, telling Arnold that the cable company or one of its clients has a message for the subscriber. Arnold dials the message light number, and is switched by the computer directly to the department store. In a recording, the store's credit manager points out that the Johnsons are in arrears on their credit payments and says that the book that Mrs. Johnson has just ordered cannot be sent until the Johnsons transfer $15.95 directly from their bank account to the store's account. Angry, Arnold punches in the necessary funds transfer, using the Johnsons' personal identification number, and goes back to his movie.

At the cable-company headquarters, the information sales department, which works around the clock, is compiling for its confidential clients data the computer has collected concerning subscribers who have been interacting with their sets. Several clients have indicated interest in the Johnsons' interactions and have ordered computer profiles from the system.

Client 1, Mayor Paxton's campaign manager, is delighted to learn that Arnold, whose wife is a feminist and a supporter of legislation to eliminate legal restrictions concerning sex, has expressed an opinion against one of her campaign stands. He chuckles at the use he can make of the fact that Arnold also watched a porno movie while his wife was out. He knows what time Martha left the house because the cable company, at the mayor's request, has installed a motion sensor to monitor the Johnsons' doorway from outside the house. It relays information about comings and goings which are then checked out by a police surveillance car parked unobtrusively down the darkened street.

Client 2, a publisher of skin magazines, also gets notification of the porno-film selection, and sends the Johnsons a sales brochure in a plain manila envelope.

Client 3, a local environmental group trying to decide whether to work for Mrs. Johnson, is disappointed to learn that she would unthinkingly order an aerosol that is dangerous to the ozone layer.

Client 4, a national credit-rating company, finds that the department store has rejected Mrs. Johnson's purchase on credit and puts that datum into her dossier for the next customer who purchases credit-rating information on her. It also enters a correction regarding the Johnsons' bank balance, which the computer obtained when Arnold paid for his wife's book.

Is all this possible? It is entirely possible, today, using a two-way cable system no more sophisticated than the one now operating in Columbus, Ohio. And the information-gathering activity described in the scenario is not illegal.

Will people drop out of a two-way system if they discover that their interactions are being monitored? First of all, they do not have to be told that they are being monitored: no law requires the cable operator to tell them. But beyond that, people will probably get used to it. Once the services provided by two-way cable TV become almost indispensable, people won't worry about them. They won't, that is, unless objections are raised by consumer protection groups and by legislators concerned with two-way cable's implications for civil liberties. Federal, state, and local legislation is nonexistent in this area. Most systems are franchised by local municipalities, using guidelines set by the Federal Communications Commission (FCC). The guidelines say nothing about restrictions on two-way cable.

Bills now [considered by] Congress . . . would in fact abolish the FCC and its guidelines, and end any national regulation of cable. The bills, revisions of the Communications Act of 1934, [were] crafted by the House Subcommittee on Communications, supposedly to bring the act into the modern era. It ignores communication of computer information.

[These bills] would drop the requirement that broadcasters serve "the public interest, convenience, and necessity." It would let the carrier determine what services it will render, according to the dictates of the marketplace. Radio would be deregulated, and ten years after enactment of the bill, television licenses would be granted in perpetuity.

In six months of hearings, the bill ran into tough opposition, even from broadcasters and cable operators. The operators liked the freedom from federal restraints, but wanted some protections against state and local regulation built into the act. The subcommittee is now revising the revision, reportedly to meet the industry's concerns about multiple sets of strictures.

Consumer groups were outraged by the bill's disregard of the public-interest standard, and the language may yet be changed to assuage their feelings. But the mood in Congress seems to favor less regulation, not more. Unless state legislatures act—and they don't seem much concerned—the task of protecting subscribers from invasion of privacy is going to fall on community cable-advisory groups and on council members whose local ordinances set the conditions concerning cable franchises. They have the right to do this because the FCC decided that cable franchising should be the province of local jurisdiction, usually municipalities. Thus, a city government may decide to grant a franchise for its entire territory, or, as in Columbus, may divide the area into several sections and grant exclusive or competitive franchises for each. In most states, the local body can approve rates, determine the number of channels to be provided, and decide what those channels will be used for. Often, for example, a municipal-

ity will require that channels be set aside for use by government bodies, the school system, community groups, or individual citizens. All this is in contrast to the licensing of local television and radio stations, which is handled exclusively by the FCC.

In Columbus, a member of the Public Cable Advisory Commission, a citizens' group appointed by the mayor, said the commission had been considering the problem of privacy, but as yet had made no recommendation for regulation.

Bob Kindred, who publishes *Cable TV Programs,* a guide to what can be found on local cable-television systems in the Midwest, would like to see two-way cable thrive. But he is afraid that sometime in the future people will rebel against two-way cable, unless restraints are placed on how it uses the information that its computer collects. "A number of questions they ask, I don't answer," he said. (A vice president of a Columbus bank had the same thought: "I won't put anything in there I don't want people to know.") People are going to want protection built in by law, Kindred added, "and this will probably help cable."

When I asked Hauser what he thought about that, he said, "This is a national problem that is being looked into now—there is no particular onus on our business. What we don't need is local regulation in the name of privacy that will inhibit the growth of this business totally, but which may be all wrong. If there is to be regulation, it should be part of a comprehensive scheme of regulation."

Clearly, federal law concerning privacy would be preferable to thousands of varying local laws. But just as clearly, some law is needed. Otherwise, the privacy of all two-way cable subscribers is potentially for sale.

60
QUBE Viewers Call the Plays and Lose the Game

Bob Wolf

Watching the gimmicked-up football game on Channel 10 the other night must have been frustrating to followers of the Green Bay Packers.

Packer fans have long wanted to tell Coach Bart Starr how to run his team, and they had to sit by as viewers in Columbus, Ohio, called plays for their coach in a minor league exhibition between the Racine Gladiators and Columbus Meteors.

It was a first in televised football, an idea dreamed up by Warner Amex Cable Communications to showcase its two-way interactive system called QUBE.

QUBE, which stands for nothing in particular, is available only in Columbus, although it will soon spread to Pittsburgh, Cincinnati and Houston. The 40,000 home subscribers have consoles equipped with five response buttons, and by using them they can communicate with people in the studio or at the scene of the action.

The system was first used during QUBE's cable telecasts of Ohio State University football games. The games have been shown the last two seasons, and viewers who come closest to selecting the plays that the Buckeyes run receive prizes.

Last month, QUBE had the only cable telecast of the welterweight championship boxing match between Roberto Duran and Sugar Ray Leonard. The viewer who came closest to the consensus scoring of the three judges won a trip for two to the Rose Bowl.

Next was the so-called interactive football game, which was played in Columbus Saturday night and taped for showing Sunday night.

Fans at home were allowed to call the plays for the Columbus team—on defense as well as offense. They had nothing to do with Racine's strategy, and this may explain why the Gladiators won, 10-7.

On offense, there were five choices for each play. They varied somewhat, but a typical list included a run outside, a run inside, a play-action pass, a medium-range pass and a bomb.

On defense, there were three choices, always the same—standard defense, blitz and team choice. The last meant that the fans gave Coach Hal Dyer the right to call his own defense, which wasn't often.

Prior to each play, one of these lists was flashed on the screen, and at the bottom there was a line that read, "Touch now." This meant that each viewer was to touch the button of his choice as soon as possible.

The results were tallied with amazing speed. The percentage of votes for each choice was shown, and the fans' preference was then relayed to Dyer, who sent in a player to convey the message to his quarterback.

According to Ron Quisin, manager of

Source: From *The Milwaukee Journal* (July 15, 1980). Reprinted by permission of the publisher.

Warner Amex's Milwaukee office, an average of only 15 seconds elapsed between the previous play and the time that Dyer was notified of the viewers' choice. This left 15 seconds more to get the play off.

"It worked very well," Quisin said. "At first it took too long to get the choice of calls on the screen, and we missed the first couple of defensive plays, but after that it was smooth."

It was so smooth at one point in the first quarter that when the fans voted for an outside run, Cornelius Greene, former All-Big Ten quarterback from Ohio State, ran for a touchdown on an end-around play. Greene, who didn't make it in the National Football League, is now a wide receiver. . . .

Only one person expressed dissatisfaction with the gimmick—Coach Dyer. To no one's surprise, the fans leaned heavily on the pass, and Dyer, who was wired with a microphone, finally turned to a camera and pleaded to the viewers, "At this point we've got to establish our running game and go with medium-distance passes."

This worked for a while, but Dyer still wasn't satisfied, and issued a public complaint afterward. He must be a born spoilsport.

The telecast also contained an innovation that wasn't scheduled. A severe thunderstorm during the second quarter knocked out the lights and caused a half-hour delay. The camera then switched to the dressing room and caught an interesting lecture by Dyer to his Columbus players.

Among other things, the irate Dyer said, "The diagrams I drew must have been too small, because you sure have no idea what was on them."

It was a highly entertaining show, one that the NFL might want to copy some time when QUBE becomes more widespread. A league game would be out of the question, of course, but it wouldn't hurt to try it in one of those meaningless exhibitions.

Appendix

Collation with Major Textbooks

While the editors have organized this book to stand alone in an introductory course structured by lectures, we expect that it will often be used as a supplement to one of the standard textbooks in the field. The matrix presented below keys *American Mass Media: Industries and Issues* to a number of prominent textbooks currently in use.

The matrix lists each of the eleven sections of this book across the top, and lists nine texts along the vertical axis. The numbers within the matrix refer to suggested chapters in the keyed texts.

Texts Keyed

1. Warren K. Agee, Phillip H. Ault, and Edwin Emery, *Introduction to Mass Communications,* 6th ed. New York: Harper & Row, 1979.
2. John R. Bittner, *Mass Communications: An Introduction,* 2nd ed. Englewood Cliffs, N.J.: Prentice-Hall, 1980.
3. Melvin L. DeFleur and Everette E. Dennis, *Understanding Mass Communication.* Boston: Houghton Mifflin, 1981.
4. Ray Eldon Hiebert, Donald F. Ungurait, and Thomas W. Bohn, *Mass Media II: An Introduction to Modern Communication,* 2nd ed. New York: Longman, 1979.
5. Robert D. Murphy, *Mass Communication and Human Interaction.* Boston: Houghton Mifflin, 1977.
6. Don R. Pember, *Mass Media in America,* 3rd ed. Chicago: Science Research Associates, 1981.
7. Peter M. Sandman, David M. Rubin, and David B. Sachsman, *Media: An Introductory Analysis of American Mass Communication,* 2nd ed. Englewood Cliffs, N.J.: Prentice-Hall, 1976.
8. Edward Jay Whetmore, *Mediamerica: Form, Content, and Consequence of Mass Communication.* Belmont, Calif.: Wadsworth, 1979.
9. Frederick C. Whitney, *Mass Media and Mass Communications in Society.* Dubuque, Iowa: Wm. C. Brown, 1975.

American Mass Media: Industries and Issues

TEXTS	One The Environments of Media Industries			Two The Print Media		
	Audiences	Advertising	Regulation	Books	Newspapers	Magazines
Agee et al.	1, 2	17	3, 6, 7	4, 11	4, 9, 16	10
Bittner	1, 16	10	14, 15, 17	4	2, 13	3, 7
DeFleur et al.	1, 8, 10	13	3	4	2, 4, 7, 12	2, 4
Hiebert et al.	1, 2, 11, 12, 27, 28	3, 24, 25	2, 3, 4, 9	13	14, 21	15, 22
Murphy	1, 12, 14	6, 7	5, 6, 9	3	4, 8, 10	3, 10
Pember	1, 2, 5, 12	9	11, 13	2	3	4
Sandman et al.	intro., 8	5, 14	7, 15	11	1, 10	11
Whetmore	1, 13	12	14	2	3, 4, 11	5
Whitney	1, 2, 4, 6, 21	17, 20	5, 7	9	10	11

TEXTS	Three The Sound Media		Four The Visual Media		Five Personal Media
	Radio	Recordings	Film	Television	
Agee et al.	5, 12	12, 19	5, 14	5, 13	13, 15
Bittner	5	9	8	6	12
DeFleur et al.	5	5	6	5, 12	8, 9
Hiebert et al.	17	19	16	18, 26	20
Murphy	2, 3, 8, 10		3, 5	12	4, 15
Pember	7	7	9	8	13
Sandman et al.	9, 12	12	13	12	8
Whetmore	6	7	10	8, 9, 11	15
Whitney	13	13	12	14, 15	19, 22

Suggestions for
Further Reading

ONE
The Environments of Media Industries

Audiences

Bower, Robert T. *Television and the Public*. New York: Holt, Rinehart and Winston, 1973.

Brown, Charlene J., Trevor R. Brown, and William L. Rivers. *The Media and the People*. New York: Holt, Rinehart and Winston, 1978.

Chafee, Steven H., and Michael Petrick. *Using the Mass Media: Communication Problems in American Society*. New York: McGraw-Hill, 1975.

Cole, Barry, and Mal Oettinger. *Reluctant Regulators: The FCC and the Broadcast Audience*. Reading, Mass.: Addison-Wesley, 1978.

Davison, W. Phillips, James Boylan, and Frederick T. C. Yu. *Mass Media: Systems and Effects*. New York: Praeger, 1976.

Haight, Timothy R., ed. *Telecommunications Policy and the Citizen*. New York: Praeger, 1979.

Real, Michael R. *Mass-Mediated Culture*. Englewood Cliffs, N.J.: Prentice-Hall, 1977.

Rubin, Bernard. *Media, Politics, and Democracy*. New York: Oxford University Press, 1977.

Wright, Charles R. *Mass Communication: A Sociological Perspective*. New York: Random House, 1975.

Advertising

Atwan, Robert, Donald McQuade, and John W. Wright. *Edsels, Luckies & Frigidaires: Advertising the American Way*. New York: Dell, 1979.

Boorstin, Daniel J. *The Image: A Guide to Pseudo-Events in America*. New York: Atheneum, 1971.

Della Femina, Jerry. *From Those Wonderful Folks Who Gave You Pearl Harbor*. New York: Simon and Schuster, 1970.

Ewen, Stuart. *Captains of Consciousness: Advertising and the Social Roots of the Consumer Culture*. New York: McGraw-Hill, 1976.

Fletcher, Alan D., and Thomas A. Bowers. *Fundamentals of Advertising Research*. Columbus, Ohio: Grid Publishing, 1979.

Groome, Harry C., Jr. *This Is Advertising*. Philadelphia: Ayer Press, 1975.

Wright, John W., ed. *The Commercial Connection: Advertising and the American Mass Media*. New York: Dell, 1979.

Government Regulation: Freedom and Controls

Francois, William E. *Mass Media Law and Regulation*. Columbus, Ohio: Grid Publishing, 1975.

Friendly, Fred W. *The Good Guys, The Bad Guys, and the First Amendment: Free Speech vs. Fairness in Broadcasting*. New York: Vintage, 1975.

Jones, William K. *Cases and Materials on Electronic Mass Media: Radio, Television, & Cable*. 2nd ed. Mineola, N.Y.: Foundation Press, 1979.

Kahn, Frank J., ed. *Documents of American Broadcasting*. 3rd ed. Englewood Cliffs, N.J.: Prentice-Hall, 1978.

Krasnow, Erwin G., and Lawrence D. Longley. *The Politics of Broadcast Regulation.* 2nd ed. New York: St. Martin's, 1978.

Nelson, Harold L., and Dwight L. Teeter. *Law of Mass Communications.* 2nd ed. Mineola, N.Y.: Foundation Press, 1973.

Pember, Don R. *Mass Media Law.* Dubuque, Iowa: Wm. C. Brown, 1977.

Robinson, Glen O., ed. *Communications for Tomorrow: Policy Perspectives for the 1980s.* New York: Praeger, 1978.

Schmidt, Benno C., Jr. *Freedom of the Press vs. Public Access.* New York: Praeger, 1976.

TWO
The Print Media

Books

Anderson, Charles B. *Bookselling in America and the World.* New York: Quadrangle, 1975.

Benjamin, Curtis G. *A Candid Critique of Book Publishing.* New York: Bowker, 1977.

Compaigne, Benjamin M. *The Book Industry in Transition: An Economic Study of Book Distribution and Marketing.* White Plains, N.Y.: Knowledge Industries, 1978.

Grannis, Chandler B. *What Happens in Book Publishing.* New York: Columbia University Press, 1967.

Lowenthal, Leo. *Literature, Popular Culture, and Society.* Palo Alto, Calif.: Pacific Books, 1968.

Madison, Charles Allan. *Book Publishing in America.* New York: McGraw-Hill, 1967.

Whiteside, Thomas. *The Block Buster Complex: Conglomerates, Show Business, and Book Publishing.* Middletown, Conn.: Wesleyan University Press, 1981.

Newspapers

Anderson, David, and Peter Benjaminson. *Investigative Reporting.* Bloomington: Indiana University Press, 1976.

Argyris, Chris. *Behind the Front Page.* San Francisco: Jossey-Bass, 1974.

Berry, Thomas Elliott. *Journalism in America.* New York: Hastings House, 1976.

Highton, Jake. *Reporter.* New York: McGraw-Hill, 1978.

Hohenberg, John. *The Professional Journalist.* New York: Holt, Rinehart and Winston, 1973.

Knightley, Phillip. *The First Casualty: From the Crimea to Vietnam: The War Correspondent as Hero, Propagandist, and Myth Maker.* New York: Harcourt Brace Jovanovich, 1975.

Rivers, William L. *The Mass Media: Reporting, Writing, Editing.* New York: Harper & Row, 1975.

Smith, Anthony. *Goodbye Gutenberg: The Newspaper Revolution of the 1980's.* New York: Oxford University Press, 1980.

Schudson, Michael. *Discovering the News.* New York: Basic Books, 1978.

Talese, Gay. *The Kingdom and the Power.* New York: Bantam, 1970.

Webb, Robert A., ed. *The Washington Post Deskbook on Style.* New York: McGraw-Hill, 1978.

Magazines

Ford, James L. *Magazines for Millions: The Story of Specialized Publications.* Carbondale: Southern Illinois University Press, 1969.

Gans, Herbert J. *Deciding What's News: A Study of CBS Evening News, NBC Nightly News, Newsweek, and Time.* New York: Pantheon, 1979.

Johnson, Michael L. *The New Journalism.* Lawrence: University Press of Kansas, 1971.

Mott, Frank L. *A History of American Magazines.* Cambridge, Mass.: Harvard University Press, 1968.

Peterson, Theodore B. *Magazines in the Twentieth Century.* 2nd ed. Urbana: University of Illinois Press, 1969.

Tebbel, John. *The American Magazine: A Compact History.* New York: Hawthorn, 1969.

Wolfe, Tom, and E. W. Johnson, eds. *The New Journalism in America.* New York: Harper & Row, 1973.

Wolseley, Roland E. *The Changing Magazine.* New York: Hastings House, 1973.

THREE
The Sound Media

Radio

Barnouw, Erik. *A History of Broadcasting in the United States.* 3 vols. New York: Oxford University Press, 1966.

Bittner, John R., and Denise Bittner. *Radio Journalism.* Englewood Cliffs, N.J.: Prentice-Hall, 1977.

Buxton, Frank, and Bill Owen. *The Big Broadcast: 1920–1950.* New York: Viking Press, 1972.

Head, Sydney W. *Broadcasting in America.* 3rd ed. Boston: Houghton Mifflin, 1976.

Hilliard, Robert L. *Radio Broadcasting.* New York: Hastings House, 1967.

Johnson, Joseph S., and Kenneth K. Jones. *Modern Radio Station Practices.* 2nd ed. Belmont, Calif.: Wadsworth, 1978.

Milam, Lorenzo. *Sex and Broadcasting: A Handbook on Starting Community Radio Stations.* 2nd ed. Saratoga, Calif.: Dildo Press, 1972.

Post, Steve. *Playing in the FM Band.* New York: Viking Press, 1974.

Routt, Edd, James B. McGrath, and Frederic A. Weiss. *The Radio Format Conundrum.* New York: Hastings House, 1978.

Settel, Irving. *A Pictorial History of Radio.* New York: Grosset & Dunlap, 1967.

Sterling, Christopher H., and John M. Kittross. *Stay Tuned. A Concise History of American Broadcasting.* Belmont, Calif.: Wadsworth, 1978.

Recordings

Belz, Carl. *The Story of Rock.* 2nd ed. New York: Oxford University Press, 1972.

Brown, Duane. *Toward a Theory of Popular Culture: The Sociology and History of American Music and Dance 1920–1968.* Ann Arbor, Mich.: Ann Arbor Publishers, 1969.

Chapple, Steve, and Reebee Garofalo. *Rock 'n' Roll Is Here to Pay: The History and Politics of the Music Industry.* Chicago: Nelson-Hall, 1977.

Cohn, Nik. *Rock from the Beginning.* New York: Stein and Day, 1969.

Davis, Clive, and James Willwerth. *Clive: Inside the Record Business.* New York: Morrow, 1974.

Denisoff, R. Serge. *Solid Gold: The Popular Record Industry.* New Brunswick, N.J.: Transaction Books, 1975.

Gelatt, Roland. *The Fabulous Phonograph: 1877–1977.* 3rd ed. New York: Macmillan, 1977.

Hemphill, Paul. *The Nashville Sound: Bright Lights and Country Music.* New York: Simon and Schuster, 1970.

Palmer, Tony. *All You Need Is Love: The Story of Popular Music.* New York: Viking Press, 1976.

Shaw, Arnold. *Honkers and Shouters: The Golden Years of Rhythm and Blues.* New York: Macmillan, 1978.

Whetmore, Edward. *The Role of Rock.* Englewood Cliffs, N.J.: Prentice-Hall, 1979.

FOUR
The Visual Media

Film

Arijon, Daniel. *Grammar of the Film Language.* London: Focal Press, 1976.

Barsam, Richard M. *Nonfiction Film: A Critical History.* New York: Dutton, 1973.

Bogle, Donald. *Toms, Coons, Mulattoes, Mammies, & Bucks: An Interpretive History of Blacks in American Films.* New York: Viking, 1973.

Dunne, John Gregory. *The Studio.* New York: Simon and Schuster, 1979.

Ellis, Jack C. *A History of Film.* Englewood Cliffs, N.J.: Prentice-Hall, 1979.

Jarvie, I. C. *Movies and Society.* New York: Basic Books, 1970.

Mast, Gerald, and Marshall Cohen. *Film Theory and Criticism.* 2nd ed. New York: Oxford University Press, 1979.

Monaco, James. *How to Read a Film.* New York: Oxford University Press, 1977.

Patterson, Lindsay, ed. *Black Films and Film-makers.* New York: Dodd, Mead, 1975.

Rosen, Marjorie. *Popcorn Venus: Women, Movies, and the American Dream.* New York: Coward, McCann, and Geoghegan, 1973.

Rosenblum, Ralph, and Robert Karen. *When the Shooting Stops . . . the Cutting Begins.* New York: Viking Press, 1979.

Sitney, P. Adams. *Visionary Film: The American Avant-Garde 1943–1978.* 2nd ed. New York: Oxford University Press, 1979.

Sklar, Robert. *Movie-Made America.* New York: Random House, 1975.

Television

Arlen, Michael J. *The View from Highway 1: Essays on Television.* New York: Ballantine, 1976.

Barnouw, Erik. *The Sponsor: Notes on a Modern Potentate.* New York: Oxford University Press, 1978.

Barnouw, Erik. *Tube of Plenty.* New York: Oxford University Press, 1975.

Brown, Les. *Keeping Your Eye on Television.* New York: Pilgrim Press, 1979.

Carnegie Commission on the Future of Public Broadcasting. *A Public Trust.* New York: Bantam, 1979.

Comstock, George, Steven Chaffee, Nathan Katzman, Maxwell McCombs, and Donald Roberts. *Television and Human Behavior.* New York: Columbia University Press, 1978.

Dessart, George, ed. *Television in the Real World.* New York: Hastings House, 1978.

Fang, Irving E. *Television News.* New York: Hastings House, 1972.

Kaye, Evelyn. *The ACT Guide to Children's Television.* Boston: Beacon Press, 1979.

Mander, Jerry. *Four Arguments for the Elimination of Television.* New York: Morrow, 1978.

Mankiewicz, Frank, and Joel Swerdlow. *Remote Control: Television and the Manipulation of American Life.* New York: Ballantine, 1978.

Newcomb, Horace, ed. *Television: The Critical View.* 2nd ed. New York: Oxford University Press, 1979.

Norback, Craig T., and Peter G. Norback, eds. *TV Guide Almanac.* New York: Ballantine, 1980.

FIVE
Personal Media

Bensinger, Charles. *The Home Video Handbook.* 2nd ed. Santa Barbara, Calif.: Video-Info Publications, 1979.

Bensinger, Charles. *The Video Guide.* Santa Barbara, Calif.: Video-Info Publications, 1977.

Hiltz, Starr Roxanne, and Murray Turoff. *The Network Nation: Human Communication via Computer.* Reading, Mass.: Addison-Wesley, 1978.

Hollowell, Mary Louise, ed. *The Cable/Broadband Communications Book 1980.* Washington, D.C.: Communications Press, 1980.

Mahony, Sheila, Nick DeMartino, and Robert Stengel. *Keeping PACE with the New Television: Public Television and the New Technology.* New York: VNU Books International, 1980.

Price, Jonathan. *Video-Visions: A Medium Discovers Itself.* New York: New American Library, 1977.

Robinson, Richard. *The Video Primer.* 2nd ed. New York: Quick Fox, 1978.

Smith, Ralph Lee. *The Wired Nation: The Electronic Communications Highway.* New York: Harper & Row, 1972.

The Big Dummy's Guide to CB Radio. Summertown, Tenn.: The Book Publishing Co., 1976.

Veith, Richard. *Talk-Back TV: Two-Way Cable Television.* Blue Ridge Summit, Penn.: TAB Books, 1976.

Index

About the Authors

Robert Atwan has taught at Rutgers University and has worked in the humanities division of Educational Testing Service in Princeton. The coeditor of *Popular Writing in America* and *Thinking in Writing,* and coauthor of *Edsels, Luckies, & Frigidaires: Advertising the American Way,* Mr. Atwan has written reviews and essays on both literature and the popular arts. He has been a consultant for educational television and the Ford Foundation's Library of America, and is co-host of a New York City radio show. He is currently at work on a comprehensive history of American advertising.

Barry Orton is Assistant Professor of Telecommunications at the University of Wisconsin-Extension and also teaches urban and regional planning at the University of Wisconsin-Madison. Dr. Orton, who has been a city planner, reporter, and video producer, specializes in telecommunications policy, public opinion research, and the effects of electronic media. He has most recently been involved with the municipal regulation of cable television and with the introduction of advertising in the new electronic media.

William Vesterman is an Associate Professor of English at Rutgers University. Author of *The Stylistic Life of Samuel Johnson,* he has also written essays and reviews in English, American, and Latin American literature. Dr. Vesterman has written on film and taught screenwriting at Rutgers. At Bell Laboratories he recently designed and helped to develop a computer-assisted style monitor for use in word-processing technologies.